D1372459

The Columbia History of
Post–World War II America

COLUMBIA GUIDES TO AMERICAN HISTORY AND CULTURES

The Columbia History of Post–World War II America

Edited by Mark C. Carnes

COLUMBIA UNIVERSITY PRESS

NEW YORK

Columbia University Press
Publishers Since 1893
New York   Chichester, West Sussex
Copyright © 2007 Columbia University Press
All rights reserved

Library of Congress Cataloging-in-Publication Data
The Columbia history of post-World War II America / edited by Mark C. Carnes.
p. cm. — (Columbia guides to American history and cultures)
Includes bibliographical references and index.
ISBN 978–0–231–12126–2 (cloth : alk. paper) — ISBN 978–0–231–51180–3 (e-book)
1. United States—History—1945–   2. United States—Social conditions—1945–
3. United States—Politics and government—1945–1989.   4. United States—
Politics and government—1989–   I. Carnes, Mark C.
(Mark Christopher), 1950–   II. Title.   III. Series.
E741.C54   2007
973.92—dc22
2006034304

Columbia University Press books are printed on permanent
and durable acid-free paper.
This book is printed on paper with recycled content.
Printed in the United States of America
c 10 9 8 7 6 5 4 3 2 1

CONTENTS

*The Columbia History of
Post–World War II America*

1. INTRODUCTION

MARK C. CARNES

This book seeks to explain the history of United States during the time that encompasses our lives. Chronicling these years would be a formidable task, even for a book as big as this one, but our purpose is not so much to recapitulate our times as it is to begin to explain what it all meant.

This is no easy task. The complexity of the past renders it nearly incomprehensible, and its subjectivity mocks all who propose tidy conclusions. People experience events differently, and they interpret those experiences in different ways. No summary suffices. Our task is all the more difficult in that the drumbeat of events seems to have quickened during recent decades; the nightly news, formerly a stately recitation of the day's happenings, has evolved into to a swirling kaleidoscope of images and sounds, with multiple lines of text marching double-time across the lower frame. We bob about in a heaving sea of informational flotsam, trying to discern what really matters but sensing that it is all a muddle. Perhaps every epoch bewilders those who live through it, but for Americans the past half-century was, by most measures, a time of breathtaking change and transition.

Where to begin? Perhaps with that analytical tool best suited to measurement and comparison: statistics.

During the last half of the twentieth century, the nation's population nearly doubled, from 152 million in 1950 to 281 million in 2000. The general drift of the people, as always, has been westward. In 1950 the arithmetical "mean center" of the population was located just west of the Indiana-Illinois border; by 2000, it had shifted to a point several hundred miles southwest of St. Louis, Missouri. Statistics can be deceiving, and this provides a cautionary example: though the geographical center of the U.S. population was located in the Midwest, that region experienced the slowest rate of population growth, and some rural areas of the northern Great Plains lost population. The greatest increases were in the Pacific West, the Southwest, Texas, and Florida.

Population growth has been caused by a convergence of factors: the natural increase of a fundamentally healthy people, a declining death rate, and immigration. The 1950 birthrate of 24 babies per 1,000 women of childbearing age approached that of teeming India, and this high birthrate accounted for much of the nation's population increase during the 1950s and 1960s. By the mid-1970s, the birthrate had declined to about 15 per 1,000, and it remained at that level during the next quarter-century. Rising life expectancy added to the population increase. Someone born in 1950 could expect to live to the age of 68; those born in 2000 were projected to live to 77. In 1950, 8 percent of the population was over 65, in 2000, nearly 13 percent. Conversely, infant mortality, measured in infant deaths per 100,000 live births, declined from 29 in 1950 to 7 in 2000. Diseases such as tuberculosis and polio were serious health threats in the 1950s, but have since become relatively rare. Even the onset of acquired immunodeficiency syndrome (AIDS), which first appeared by that name in the health statistics in 1984 and has since killed hundreds of thousands, failed to stop the improvement in life expectancy. The aggregate suicide rate has declined slightly, although the proportion of people aged 15–24 who commit suicide has more than doubled since 1950.

After 1950, too, some thirty million people immigrated to the United States, more than half of that number since 1980. In 1950, 7 percent of the population was foreign-born; by 2000, that had increased to 11 percent. Partly this was caused by shifts in public policy. The Immigration Act of 1965, which terminated the "national-origins" concept, prompted an influx of immigrants from Asia and Latin America. During the 1980s the nation's Hispanic population increased by 53 percent. This was caused both by immigration and a high birthrate. In June 2005 the Census Bureau reported that during the preceding five years, Hispanics counted for more than half of the nation's population growth.

The statistics also show marked changes in the American family. Men and women now marry later in life and are more likely to divorce. In 1950, more than three-fourths of American households included married parents; fifty years later, nearly half of the nation's households lacked them. The 1950 divorce rate of 2.6 per 1,000 couples had increased to 4.1 fifty years later. More women worked outside the home: in 1950, 34 percent of women over sixteen had paid jobs; by 2000, it was 60 percent. The average family size declined from 3.5 to 3.2. School attendance became more common. In 1950, three-fourths of the nation's children aged 14 through 17 were enrolled in school; by 2000, well over 90 percent were in school. In 1950, 6 percent of the adults had completed four years of college; by 2000, well over a quarter had college degrees.

The economy grew substantially, as did personal consumption. In 1950, slightly over half of adult Americans owned homes; by 2000, over two-thirds did so, and their homes dwarfed those of their grandparents. In 1950, 266 of every 1,000 Americans owned automobiles; by 2000, that proportion had nearly doubled. In 1950, there were fewer than four million televisions in the nation; in 2000, there were 248 million sets. But increased consumption of big-ticket items is merely an indicator of a general expansion of consumption of nearly everything. By some estimates, for example, Americans now consume 600 more calories of food a day than did their forebears a half-century ago, which helps explain a population that has grown in more than one sense.

Americans have come to rely increasingly on government. In unadjusted dollars, federal expenditures increased from $43 billion in 1950 to $2,500 billion in 2006. While the population of the United States nearly doubled from 1950 to 2000, federal employment, excluding defense and the postal service, increased by only 50 percent, from two million to three million. This reflects the federal government's preference for direct payments to benefit recipients (social security, farm subsidies) or for contracting out to private companies and state governments.

If government has played an increasingly prominent role in American life, it has not been matched by an increase in voter participation. In 1952, 63 percent of those eligible to vote did so in the Eisenhower-Stevenson presidential election; voter turnout for all presidential elections during the 1950s and 1960s exceeded 60 percent. Since then, the voting percentage has usually declined. In 1996, when the incumbent president, Bill Clinton, ran against Robert Dole and Ross Perot, fewer than half of those registered went to the polls; only 51 percent voted in the George W. Bush–Al Gore race of 2000. The slackening trend in voting was reversed with the record turnout of 2004, the largest ever, when George W. Bush, the Republican incumbent, handily defeated his Democratic opponent, John Kerry.

The statistics of foreign affairs are generally grim. From 1945 through the 1990s, the United States built scores of thousands of nuclear weapons in its Cold War against the Soviet Union; on the other hand, the collapse of the Soviet Union in the 1980s brought about an unexpectedly peaceful end to the Cold War.

American soldiers intervened abroad several score times—most significantly in Korea (1950–1953), with 36,000 American deaths, Vietnam (1964–1975), with 58,000 deaths, and the Persian Gulf War (1990–1991), with 400 deaths. Following the terrorist attack of September 11, 2001, the United States went to war with the Taliban in Afghanistan, resulting in more than 325 American combat deaths over the next five years. In 2003, the United States invaded Iraq, with over 3,000 U.S. military deaths by midsummer 2007.

Statistics indicate how many of us divorce, but not what we expect of marriage; how many of us own homes, but not the social and cultural implications of home-ownership; how many have perished in battle, but not the full consequences of the war; how long we live, but not whether we live happily or well. The essays that follow contain plenty of statistics, but these are offered to advance interpretations about what it all means.

This book is conceived as an early attempt to pose new and interesting questions about our times; its answers are preliminary and speculative. This volume seeks not to summarize existing knowledge, but to examine the interrelationships that commonly elude scholarly specialists.

To that end, in these pages nearly two dozen scholars offer their judgments on the past half-century. Most have strong credentials in particular disciplines—economics, foreign affairs, political science, and social and cultural history—but their essays differ from the usual categorizations: historical groups (women, minorities, workers), institutions (business, technology, transportation, government), or cultural activities (politics, literature, art, music, philanthropy). Such topics can no longer be regarded as intellectually self-sufficient. To feature women within their "own" category may have made sense in earlier times, when women were consigned, if only imaginatively, to a "separate sphere" of domestic duties; but to confine women to their own topical category during the postwar decades, when women have figured prominently in nearly all avenues of endeavor, cannot be justified intellectually. Harvard historian Oscar Handlin made a similar point about immigrants in 1951. "Once I thought to write a history of the immigrants in America," he observed in his book *The Uprooted* (1951). "Then I discovered that the immigrants WERE American history." Subsequent scholars chastised Handlin for failing to appreciate the variation among immigrant groups. Although all Americans were immigrants, or the descendants of immigrants, not all immigrants were the same. Women's historians have similarly documented the diversity within that "topical" category. Indeed, the past two generations of social historians have indicted earlier scholars for positing an erroneous sense of topical coherence. Whether writing about immigrants, blacks, women, or nearly any other group, social historians have discerned deep fractures along the lines of class, ethnicity, geography, and sexual orientation.

Consigning "women" and "blacks" and "immigrants" to their own categories can easily cause scholars to neglect their role in other categories. The inadequacy of the usual categorization applies with equal force to economic endeavors and cultural activities. In the nineteenth century, politics was often regarded as a intellectual field of its own, with occasional resonances in economics and religion; but during the past few decades, when "the personal" has resolutely become "the political" and the role of government has expanded markedly, such a distinction between "politics" and other topics is absurd. Public debates over social security and health insurance, abortion and gay marriage, artistic expression and medical research—all reveal the extent to which one "category" is bound up with others.

The authors for this project were recruited in part for their ability to conceive of topics in unconventional or imaginative ways. Some of the essays explore transformations in how we have responded to the world around us, such as how we see and hear and interact with our spatial environment. The intersection of psychological states and social patterns is examined in essays on topics such as "memorial culture," "scandal culture," and "consumer culture." A handful of writers consider how technological change has affected society and politics, and a few consider as well how crises in belief systems have helped generate new technologies. Many of the essays consider the intersection of social practices and government policies. Although the essays are for the most part not arranged by topical category, the general trend is from cultural themes to issues weighted toward politics and government.

This volume, for example, does not include an essay entitled "Television and the Media." But television appears in many different essays. In my own essay on "Work," I argue that popular culture steadfastly ignored the true nature of work, and I mention that *The Life of Riley*, a television show that ended during the 1950s, was one of the last major series to show blue-collar workers in their workplace. In a discussion of gender and the realignment of politics, Susan Hartmann finds that television has allowed women candidates to make their appeal directly to voters, thereby weakening the hold of backroom power brokers. Paula Fass spotlights television's role as a full-time babysitter in reshaping contemporary childrearing. Julian Zelizer is struck by the way in which C-Span (1979) and CNN (1980), by creating a continuous demand for news, have stimulated the emergence of a scandal-seeking mentality among journalists. Kenneth Cmiel credits MTV and modern television with shifting the nation's visual style. Thomas Collins contends that the rise of television in the 1950s, by eroding the traditional appeal of radio, forced radio broadcasters to cultivate local artists and thus led to the proliferation of rhythm and blues, country music, and black gospel radio stations. David Courtwright proposes that television promoted an individualist ethos that helped distract Americans from "spiritual tasks." In an article on death and memorial culture, Michael Sherry is struck by television's power to create a "vicarious intimacy with death," as with the coverage following JFK's assassination, the Columbine shootings, or the terrorist attacks on September 11, 2001. Thus, while none of the articles in the book is about television per se, the subject gains considerable depth by being viewed from so many different perspectives.

Nor does the book include an article specifically on technology. Still, the subject surfaces repeatedly. Kenneth Cmiel emphasizes the importance of the Leica camera in the evolution of photojournalism; Tom Collins, of magnetic tape on popular music; Andrew Kirk, of photographs of the earth from the NASA lunar orbiter on environmentalism; Paula Fass, of in vitro fertilization on childrearing and adoption practices; and Tony Freyer, of the costs of high-tech research on the structure of the corporation.

Readers should consult the index to chart the various ways particular subjects are addressed. For example, the GI Bill, which provided financial support for World War II veterans, is discussed in Maris Vinovskis's essay on the expanded role of the government in American education; in Sandra Opdycke's analysis of the rise of the suburbs; in George Cotkin's study of how the flood of students into postwar colleges and universities stimulated interest in art and literature; in Richard Lingemann's argument on the postwar tendency toward careerism instead of political activism; and in Michael Sherry's analysis of a shift from an egalitarian system of death benefits to the complicated system navigated by the families of those killed in the attacks on September 11, 2001.

In the mid-eighteenth century, Denis Diderot, the French philosopher, saw the need to create structures of knowledge that would encourage cross-topical pollination. He thus chose to arrange topics in his *Encyclopédie* by alphabetical order, a quasi-random juxtaposition that would encourage readers of entries on, say, art, to consider the alphabetically adjacent ones on literature or science. His goal, he declared, was "to change how people think." The end result of his *Encyclopédie* was to advance the European enlightenment.

This volume seeks, in a modest way, to promote comprehension. Each essay casts some light into the shadowed world of the past. Collectively, the essays do not converge so as to illuminate it with blinding clarity. Each reader will take something different from this book. But some larger themes emerge, or so it seems to me.

The persistence of individual subjectivity and expressiveness is itself significant and perhaps surprising. The post–World War II period, after all, has witnessed the tremendous expansion and significance of large institutions. Government plays an increasingly prominent role in nearly everyone's life, as do giant financial institutions, healthcare empires, and behemoth media, manufacturing and retail corporations. Complaints about the dangers of big government and nefarious private interests are as old as the nation itself, but since World War II many of the largest institutions have become larger still, or new ones have leaped to the fore. These institutions make fundamental decisions about our lives, taking more of our income and determining how we spend it. Our grandparents were mostly treated by their family doctors and shopped at stores owned by local merchants; nowadays, if we are fortunate, our medical care is provided by huge HMOs, and we shop at Wal-Mart and Home Depot.

But this trend of institutional bigness and standardization has also coexisted with and sometimes given rise to a countervailing pattern of individualized expression and consumption. We are exposed to far more types of pictures and music; we choose from an infinite variety of products; we have more options in terms of social and sexual arrangements. We have, in short, more ways of expressing our individuality and learning about the world around us. The political system has evolved so as to accommodate institutional bigness and simultaneously promote individual choice and freedoms. Many had feared that Orwellian institutions would crush the individual, but a major theme of this book is the persistence of individuality and diversity.

Another recurring theme, related to the preceding, is the government's interrelationship with nearly everything else. Federal funds for highway development and home mortgages accelerated the development of the suburbs. Educational trends, too, have been profoundly influenced by federal guidelines and funding initiatives. Federal antitrust and tax policies have shaped the modern corporation. Government regulation has also had a decisive influence on sports, the media, and the family. Sometimes the government's impact on cultural themes is less obvious, as many of the essays in this book point out. During the 1960s, for example, the space program miniaturized transistors, which also allowed teenagers to inhabit a world of popular music. The Cold War, too, profoundly influenced many aspects of modern life, ranging from the promotion of sports to ensure American success in the Olympics to the endorsement of abstract and pop art as alternatives to Soviet realism. The impact of the nation's foreign wars on popular culture, movies, and literature is inestimable. The interpenetration of government and American life has extended to political processes as well. Formerly private issues, ranging from the sexual behavior of politicians and the fabric of gay relationships to the content of popular music, have become central to political discourse.

To understand a historical period requires that it be defined. What marks its "beginning" and end? What are the factors, people, and events that determine how it is to be contoured? Although some major themes gathered momentum during and after World War II and carried through to the present, suggesting substantial continuities within the past sixty years, most scholars divide the long span into multiple historical periods. Some of these periods are identified by decades—"the fifties" or "the sixties"; some by charismatic presidents—"the Kennedy years" or "the Reagan era"; some by signal events—"the Vietnam War," "McCarthyism," "the Watergate Era," "the End of the Cold War"; some by dominant technology—"the atomic age" or the "age of the computer"; and some by cultural trends. The essays in this book do not concur on the best periodization. Neither do they identify the same causal forces. But most of the essays spotlight the mid-1970s as pivotal: the recession that struck in 1973, for instance, undermined the foundations of the nation's manufacturing economy. For a society in which consumption had become so central, this economic downtown had powerful social and cultural resonances. Moreover, the recession of the 1970s coincided with the political failure signified by the Watergate scandal, the withdrawal of American forces from South Vietnam, and the collapse of that nation before the onslaught of the Communist North Vietnamese two years later. The two decades after the 1970s differed markedly from the two decades before it.

What remains less clear, of course, is the terminal point that historians will place upon "our times." Countless pundits proclaimed that the terrorist attacks on September 11, 2001, "changed everything." Future events may prove this to be so. But much of what has occurred since is consistent with themes developed in this book. A new and different world may be just ahead. When we get there, however, it may look more familiar than we had imagined.

PART I

Culture

2. THE SPACES PEOPLE SHARE

The Changing Social Geography of American Life

SANDRA OPDYCKE

In a corner on the second floor of the Museum of African American History in Richmond, Virginia, stands a bright-red lunch counter, an exhibit installed to commemorate Richmond's first civil rights sit-in, which occurred in 1961. The exhibit celebrates the era when African Americans won the legal right to make equal use of the public spaces in their communities. Yet, seen from today's perspective, it carries another message as well. Where is the five-and-dime store where the lunch counter used to stand? It is closed, as are all five of the other major downtown stores where the sit-ins took place. Richmond's central business district, where black citizens made important strides toward winning equal treatment in the 1960s, is no longer the hub of community life. Today most commercial activity takes place elsewhere—in suburban shopping malls and office parks located well beyond the reach of the inner-city neighborhoods where most people of color live. Jim Crow no longer rules, yet many of these suburban facilities are insulated against diversity as effectively as any "Whites Only" restaurant of the 1950s.

The role that public spaces played in American society changed dramatically during the second half of the twentieth century. On one hand, these spaces were forced to become more inclusive, when groups such as African Americans, women, gays, and the disabled asserted their right to equal access and equal treatment in all the arenas of daily life. On the other hand, social phenomena such as suburbanization, the dominance of the automobile, and the growing importance of television and the home computer tended to diminish the number of truly public spaces available and to give Americans from different social groups less and less reason to share the ones that remained.

Tracing this story of the changes in the nation's social geography since 1945 makes clear that the physical arrangements of people's lives—where they live, where they work, where they shop, where they go for fun, and how they travel between these places—can play a vital role in determining the quality of people's connections to the larger society around them.

OPENING UP PUBLIC SPACES

On a Friday night in December 1955, the driver of a city bus in Montgomery, Alabama, noticed that the front rows, which were reserved for whites, had all filled up. He therefore told four African Americans sitting just behind the white section to get up and move to the back. It was a familiar demand, and three of the four people complied. But the fourth, a woman named Rosa Parks, made a historic decision and refused to move. The driver then got off the bus, found a policeman, and had Parks arrested. As word of the arrest spread through the African American community that weekend, a protest was organized, and on Monday morning hardly a black passenger was to be seen on any city bus. Thus began the eleven-month Montgomery Bus Boycott, and with it, the most dramatic ten years of the modern civil rights movement.

FIGHTING JIM CROW

The requirement that black passengers give up their seats to whites was only one part of an elaborate system of racial separation, nicknamed "Jim Crow," that pervaded daily life in Montgomery. Everything in the city was segregated, from the maternity ward to the cemetery. Nor was Montgomery unusual. In all the states of the former Confederacy, from Virginia to Texas, segregation governed the use of innumerable public spaces, including schools, restaurants, libraries, bars, theaters, churches, funeral parlors, swimming pools, hotels, buses, hospitals, and restrooms. Discriminatory practices were common throughout the United States in 1955, but far more state and local laws in the South actually required such racial separation.

During these years, southern blacks experienced discrimination in many other aspects of their lives as well, including wage levels, job opportunities, and treatment by the police. But when Rosa Parks and her fellow African Americans launched their protest against Montgomery's segregated buses, they were drawing national attention to a form of discrimination that was in many ways the most visible and continually obtrusive element of the whole Jim Crow system: the division of public space into different zones for whites and blacks. After eleven punishing months, the protesters finally won their fight when the Supreme Court refused to reconsider a lower court ruling in their favor. They had certainly not defeated all forms of segregation, even in Montgomery, but their battle gave others hope, and a few years later, black college students in Greensboro, North Carolina, launched a campaign against segregation in another kind of public space: the downtown lunch counter.

In Greensboro, as in many other southern towns, segregationists walked a difficult line. Despite the emphasis on racial separation, African Americans' business was important to the local economy. The result was a compromise: black members of the community were permitted to ride the city buses but not to sit in the front; they were permitted to shop in downtown stores, but not to eat at the stores' lunch counters. (Journalist Harry Golden once pointed out that southern whites seemed willing to stand beside African Americans, but not to sit down beside them. He therefore proposed a system of vertical integration under which the seats would be removed from all buses, theaters, restaurants, and schools. Behind Golden's humor lay a sharp truth about the complications inherent in trying to maintain a rigid color line.)

To protest lunch-counter segregation, the Greensboro students introduced a new kind of civil rights demonstration: the sit-in. One afternoon in 1960, they quietly took their places at a downtown lunch counter and waited to be served—hour after hour, day after day. This was indeed a "demonstration." It took a practice that had been going on quietly for generations—the exclusion of African Americans from a space that was open to everyone else—and made it visible, not only to the people of Greensboro but also to a national audience reached by the press. The idea caught fire, and within a year sit-ins had spread across the South, affecting seventy-eight southern cities and involving seventy thousand young activists.

While sit-ins swept the South, other civil rights protests erupted as well. In public schools and universities, courageous black students gave concrete meaning to the courts' desegregation orders by physically entering the space so long reserved for whites. On interstate buses, young black and white people traveling together—the Freedom Riders—drew national attention to the fact that interstate bus terminals were still segregated, despite federal rulings to the contrary. Thus, again and again during these years, African Americans expressed their claims to social justice in terms of the use of public space. Moreover, because the activists' claims were acted out in public spaces, much (though by no means all) of the violence to which they were subjected also occurred in public view. Shown on national television, the verbal harangues, beatings, police dogs, and firehoses used against the demonstrators helped to win widespread sympathy for their cause.

Looking back, many find it difficult to understand the ferocity with which some white southerners responded to the civil rights demonstrators. How could one cup of coffee at a lunch counter, one chair in a classroom, one drink at a water fountain have seemed so threatening? The answer is that each time African Americans won the right to move freely in another contested public space, they further weakened the idea that black people belonged in a separate and debased sphere. To claim one's place, even in such a mundane setting as a bus station or a drugstore, was to assert one's position as a member of the community, with the rights and privileges that community membership entailed. Somewhere down that road, both the demonstrators and their attackers believed, lay equality.

Town by town, the demonstrators encountered almost as many defeats as victories, but their struggle drew national attention and support. This political climate set the stage for the passage of a legislative milestone: the Civil Rights Act of 1964, which spelled the end of legalized segregation. Racial separation still existed in many forms, but the laws that supported and even required it—giving public sanction to private prejudice—were gone.

The civil rights movement as a biracial crusade for integration lost momentum after 1965, but it changed forever the use of public space in the South. The "whites only" signs disappeared, and for the first time in history, white and black southerners could be seen making common use of libraries, public schools and colleges, bus-station waiting rooms, the front rows of city buses, the downstairs seats at the movies, and lunch counters where just a few years earlier African Americans had been assaulted for ordering a cup of coffee. This shared use of public space represented only one step on the long road toward equality, but the early activists had been right to choose it as their starting point, both because of the daily experiences it made possible and because of the larger message it conveyed about the place of African Americans in community life.

OTHER GROUPS TAKE UP THE FIGHT

The legacy of the civil rights movement extended well beyond the South, and well beyond the specific issue of black-white relations. Energized by what they had seen, many other social groups began asserting their own rights with new militancy, and once again, they often chose to express these rights in terms of the free use of public space. For instance, the confrontation that ignited the gay liberation movement revolved around the right of gay men to socialize freely in a Greenwich Village bar. Unlike the sit-ins in the South, gay patrons were welcome on the premises, and there was no law prohibiting their presence there.

For years, however, the New York City police had used catchall provisions such as the disorderly conduct ordinance as an excuse to raid and harass the city's gay bars, and the terror of public exposure had always been enough to make the customers submit without protest.

The rebellious mood of the 1960s, and particularly the example of the civil rights movement, changed the political climate. When the police raided the Stonewall Inn on a hot summer night in 1969, the customers turned on the police, drove them out of the bar, and then took to the streets in an exuberant melee that sizzled and flared for days. This bottle-throwing, catcalling crowd, including many drag queens and transvestites, hardly resembled the spiritual-singing activists who had marched with Martin Luther King, but one conviction animated both groups: that to be a full member of the community, one must be able to congregate freely in public places.

Unlike most African Americans, gay men had always had the choice of "passing" as members of the majority community. For generations, that had been their most common strategy for avoiding harassment. What changed after Stonewall was the protesters' insistence on living public lives on their own terms, without pretending to be what they were not. For the rest of the century they pursued that goal, using both legal action and street demonstrations to affirm their right to full acceptance—not only in gay bars, but also in the workplace, in politics, in military service, and in all the other arenas of daily life.

Women, too, began to seek a more expansive place in American society during these years. The constrictions they faced were more subtle than those experienced by the other disadvantaged groups who raised their voices in the 1960s. Women endured neither the pervasive legal exclusion that had confronted African Americans in the segregated South nor the ostracism with which homosexuals had to contend. Nevertheless, traditional patterns put powerful constraints on what women were allowed or encouraged to do with their lives, and the effect could be seen in all the spaces where Americans lived and worked. Typically, women were to be found in the secretarial pool but not in the boardroom, at the nurses' station but not in the doctors' lounge, in the polling booth but not in the statehouse. More fundamentally, even though by 1960 at least a third of all women (and a much higher proportion of minority women) held paying jobs, the conviction that "woman's place is in the home" still resonated through American culture, reiterated in advertisements, movies, TV shows, novels, and even children's storybooks.

The limitations that this pattern of expectations put on women's lives were blisteringly delineated in Betty Friedan's book *The Feminine Mystique*, which appeared in 1963. Friedan drew on arguments and insights that had been simmering for years, but she articulated them with a verve and passion that turned a longstanding concern into a national movement. Soon women were promoting the cause of gender equality through dozens of new organizations, exuberant marches and protests, political lobbying and campaigning, and a series of groundbreaking lawsuits. When feminists celebrated the election of one of their number with the slogan "Woman's place is in the House (and in the Senate)," they were following an example that was already well established: staking a claim to full membership in the society, and expressing that claim in terms of place.

Of all the groups that found their political voices during these years, the one that linked the question of rights most explicitly to the question of access was the physically disabled. The obstacles these individuals faced were vividly illustrated when one disabled activist notified a committee of her state legislature that she would not be able to make her scheduled speech about handicapped access because she could not get up the steps of the building where the hearing was to be held.

Although debates over handicapped access often focused on prosaic issues like ramps and elevators and toilets, their subtext was profoundly social. Just as spokespersons for gay rights and women's rights had done, advocates for the disabled were reminding their fellow Americans of the injustices that could result when the right to share equally in community life was limited by too narrow a definition of what was "normal." They made clear that being excluded from commonly used spaces such as buses, meeting halls, offices, and theaters did more than make life individually difficult for them—it consigned them to second-class citizenship. When this idea won legislative endorsement in the Americans with Disabilities Act of 1990, it carried on the work of opening up public space that had begun with the Civil Rights Act thirty-six years earlier.

GAINS AND LOSSES

The social movements described above made important changes in American society. By 2000, the kinds of workplaces that in 1950 had been the sole domain of white males contained growing numbers of women and minorities. So, too, did the U.S. Congress and most state legislatures. More diverse faces also began to appear in another kind of public space—the visual world of television and the movies. Meanwhile, in restaurants, bars, parks, beaches, and theaters, it became more common to see a mixing of races, to see women out on their own, to see people in wheelchairs who could not have been there without handicapped access, and to see gay couples whom earlier customs would have consigned to the shadows. The social movements of the mid-twentieth century had helped to broaden access to the public spaces where America's life is played out, and in so doing, they had enhanced the capacity of all Americans to participate in that life.

These were significant gains, but they represented far less change than the activists of midcentury had hoped for. Consider, for example, the experience of working women. Between 1945 and 2000, the proportion of women in the American workforce rose from about a quarter to nearly half. Simply by taking jobs, these women brought new diversity to a variety of spaces that men had had mostly to themselves in the past—not only their places of employment, but also their professional organizations, the restaurants where they congregated at lunchtime, and the bars where they shared a drink after work. Yet it would be mistake to assume that women had achieved full equality with men in the workplace. Even late in the 1990s, millions of working women were still clustered in some of the economy's lowest-paying occupations, like domestic service, garment-manufacture, and childcare. For these women, going to work did not mean winning access to a territory formerly dominated by men; instead, it often meant entering a world of overburdened underpaid women like themselves. In the 1970s, an advertising campaign for cigarettes courted the female market with the slogan, "You've come a long way, baby." Twenty-five years later, it was clear that women still had a long way to go.

Other groups encountered similar obstacles. The project of refitting buildings for the handicapped moved with painful slowness, and the scourge of AIDS brought new stigma and suffering to the gay community. Meanwhile, improvement in race relations seemed to move slowest of all. In 2000, de facto school segregation—that is, segregation because of residential patterns—was as pervasive as legal segregation had been in 1954. Moreover, people of color still ranked lower than whites on every indicator of social well-being, from median income to infant mortality.

The activists of the 1960s had dreamed big dreams, and perhaps they had hoped for too much. A major factor behind their failure to come closer to their aspirations was the American people's declining faith in those dreams. By the mid-1970s, President Lyndon Johnson had left Washington in disgrace, the civil rights movement had splintered, the Watergate scandal had driven President Richard Nixon from the White House, the Vietnam War had ended in debacle, and no one still believed that America would, as Johnson had promised, "end poverty in this decade." Shaken by these turbulent years, Americans began to look with increasing skepticism at government promises of any kind. The economic slowdown of the 1970s legitimized such feelings, creating a climate in which restrictions on social reform came to be accepted as a necessary response to fiscal constraints. Moreover, this perspective retained its grip even after the economy revived in the 1980s. By century's end, the opportunity to participate in national life, as reflected in the use of public space, was indeed more democratic than it had been in 1945, but there seemed to be little political will to strengthen or extend that democratization. Thus, the patterns of American life at the beginning of the twenty-first century reflected both the progress that had been made toward social equality and the considerable distance that remained to be traveled.

The social geography of American life was profoundly affected by two other far-reaching changes: the increasing privatization of public space and the rising importance of home-based activities. These two trends played their own parts in transforming America's social landscape between 1945 and 2000. Instead of reinforcing the opening up of public space, they made it more difficult to bridge the divisions that the activists had hoped to erase.

PRIVATIZING PUBLIC SPACE

Even as citizen advocacy and government action were combining to make public space more accessible, public space itself was starting to melt away, while privately controlled space was expanding. As a result, despite the social breakthroughs described above, the second half of the twentieth century actually left many Americans with fewer opportunities to see and share space with people of different races, classes, and income groups. The growth of the suburbs, the emergence of the automobile as the dominant mode of daily transportation, and the transfer of many daily activities to private premises all contributed to this change. Reinforcing each other, these trends perpetuated and sharpened the racial and economic divisions within American society.

MOVING TO THE SUBURBS

The effect that the growth of the suburbs had on America's social geography becomes clearer if one thinks about how many different kinds of people on how many different kinds of errands had reason to share a typical Main Street in the 1940s. In those days, whether one lived in a town or a city, downtown was truly the hub of the community. Besides going to shop or see a movie, one might also go to transact business at City Hall, serve on a jury, visit a museum, eat in a restaurant, get a book at the public library, watch a parade, see a lawyer or accountant or dentist, get a haircut, go to church, pay an electric bill, mail a package, or catch a train. And, of course, one might go downtown to work in any of the establishments where these activities took place.

In giving people multiple reasons to come downtown, in appealing to them not only as shoppers but also as workers and citizens, Main Street in its heyday provided at least one place where people from very different segments of the community might encounter each other. Social inequities were hardly absent; in fact, the protest movements of the 1960s emerged in part because of them.

Nevertheless, the physical arrangements of daily life tended to encourage at least casual contact and to give people from different parts of the community a stake in many of the same institutions, the same public spaces. Indeed, the very centrality of downtown to community life gave greater visibility to the activists' protests and helped legitimize their claim to equal access.

If this shared public space was so important to American life at midcentury, why did it not remain so? For thousands of cities large and small, the demise of downtown began with a dramatic shift in residential patterns after World War II. American families had accumulated significant savings during the years of wartime rationing, and once the war was over, many were eager to spend their money on new homes. New homes were hard to find, however, because there had been virtually no residential construction for fifteen years—all during the Depression and the war. In 1946, the federal GI Bill added fuel to the fire by offering low-cost housing loans to millions of veterans. Seeking to make the most of the skyrocketing demand, private builders moved into mass production, constructing hundreds and sometimes thousands of houses within a single suburban development.

Millions of American families individually decided to move to these new suburban homes, but a host of public policy decisions helped influence their choices. First, consider the policies that made it more difficult to find affordable housing in the cities. During the postwar decades, tax dollars funded the demolition of acres of inner-city apartment buildings and row houses in the name of slum clearance; many were replaced by office towers and luxury apartments that had little to offer working-class families. Meanwhile, banks, insurers, and government agencies such as the Federal Housing Administration adopted lending criteria that "redlined"—that is, defined as unacceptably risky—the very kinds of neighborhoods best equipped to provide affordable urban housing: areas with older buildings, with mixed commercial and residential uses, and particularly those that were racially diverse. By making it difficult for modest urban homes to qualify for loans and mortgage insurance, this practice of redlining played a significant role in steering both builders and buyers to the suburbs.

Public policy helped push American families to leave the cities. It also helped pull them to the suburbs. The housing tracts developed in the suburbs—being purely residential, all new, and generally closed to minorities—qualified handily for the vast sums available through the GI Bill and the FHA mortgage insurance program, thus offering a generous subsidy to people who moved there. In addition, the decision to buy a home in the suburbs rather than rent in the city was influenced by federal tax laws, which encouraged home ownership by allowing people to write off the interest on their mortgages—a privilege not available to urban tenants, even though a portion of their rent generally went toward paying the interest on their landlords' mortgages.

While initiatives like the GI Bill and FHA mortgages made the suburbs virtually irresistible to middle-income Americans and people in the upper levels of the working class, other public policies made it more likely that the urban poor would remain where they were. By providing minimal mass transit, welfare, public health services, free medical care, or public housing, suburban towns saved their citizens tax money and at the same time made themselves less attractive to those who depended on such facilities. Meanwhile, suburban housing discrimination helped ensure that African Americans and Latinos would be among the ones who remained in the cities. In fact, during these same years, the lure of better jobs was causing record numbers of southern blacks and Puerto Ricans to migrate to the very cities that whites were leaving. The intensity of the change can be seen, for instance, in New York City, which between 1940 and 1970 added more than 1.3 million African Americans and several hundred thousand Latinos to its population, while losing nearly a million whites.

DRIVING EVERYWHERE

The departure of so many white urban residents to the suburbs could not have happened without a parallel expansion in the use of the automobile. Although cars had been invented half a century earlier, most people used them primarily for recreation until after World War II. Even as late as 1948, half of all American families had no car at all. But during the decades that followed, automobiles became a central feature in American life. Once again, public policy played an important role. Just as government funds were used to subsidize suburban home-ownership, so they also subsidized the transportation arrangements necessary to make suburban living feasible. While public bus and subway systems sank into deterioration and neglect, millions of tax dollars were poured into new highways that opened up thoroughfares to the suburban developments and made it easy to travel from one suburb to the next without ever entering the central city. As further encouragement, the nation's energy policy provided American drivers with the cheapest gasoline in the industrial world.

If the use of automobiles had not been so cheap and highways so available, the suburbs could not have expanded so dramatically. Yet the more they did expand, the more owning a car (or two cars, or three) became a necessity of daily life. By 1970, four out of every five American families owned at least one automobile (many owned more than one), and people were driving three times as many miles per year as they had in 1948. Meanwhile, ridership on public transportation dropped nearly 75 percent.

The growing dominance of the automobile had an important impact on the nation's social geography. As long as trains, trolleys, and buses had played a significant role in people's daily lives, it made sense for jobs, stores, and other services to be centrally located downtown, where transit routes converged. Under these circumstances, even routine trips like going to work or going shopping tended to involve casual encounters with friends and strangers—on the bus, on the train, or on the busy downtown streets. Once the automobile emerged as the principal mode of transportation, stores, offices, and factories scattered across the suburban landscape. Workplaces were not usually located within walking distance of each other, and doing a single round of errands could involve driving a twenty-mile circuit. Each person now followed his or her own individual schedule and route. For millions of Americans, daily travel had become privatized.

PRIVATE SPACE IN THE SUBURBS

Transportation was not the only part of people's lives being privatized. The places they spent their days were changing in much the same way. Take, for example, the process of shopping. With the departure of millions of white middle-class families for the suburbs, downtown stores all over the country closed their doors. Many reestablished themselves in a new type of commercial complex: the suburban shopping mall. In 1946, there were only eight such centers in the whole country; by 1972 there were thirteen thousand. Because these malls often replaced their local downtowns as retail centers, they were sometimes referred to as America's new Main Streets. But the malls represented a very constricted version of Main Street—offering greater comfort and convenience for the shoppers they catered to, but lacking the variety and accessibility that had made the urban downtown of earlier years such a vital community center.

The shopping mall represented privatized public space in the most literal sense: unlike Main Street, each mall was entirely owned by a single corporation. As tenants, the store owners were essentially guests of the mall proprietors, selected by them and bound by any guidelines they wished to impose. Stores whose clientele or type of merchandise did not fit the desired profile (or who could not afford the generally expensive and long-term leases the malls required) were simply excluded, as were nearly all activities that did not generate a profit. As a result, few malls served a true cross-section of their communities, and in terms of activities, few ventured much beyond the standard mix of retail stores, restaurants, and movie theaters.

Customers, too, were guests of the mall owners, subject to eviction if they did not conform to the owners' behavioral guidelines. These guidelines went well beyond the conventional requirements of public decorum. For example, most malls forbade any form of political expression (even one as mild as handing out leaflets). Activists in a few states won court decisions affirming the malls' obligation as quasi-public spaces to permit political activities, but most owners continued to discourage such activities, and few citizens contested the policy. Mall owners also maintained private control over their premises by hiring security guards who were answerable to them rather than to the public, by pressuring customers they perceived as "undesirable" to leave the premises, and by locking their doors every evening. In addition, of course, these malls were protected against the need to serve a broader public by the simple fact that they were difficult to reach except by car.

Retail stores were not the only ones that moved to more privatized space in the suburbs during the decades after World War II. Many other types of businesses left downtown as well, including banks, car washes, restaurants, movie theaters, hotels, and professional offices. Some went to the malls, but many chose a type of space that was even more privately controlled: the stand-alone building surrounded by its own parking lot. As new businesses emerged, they too gravitated to these locations. Soon most local highways were lined by mile after mile of low buildings—too close together to leave any open country between them, too far apart to reach except by car. Meanwhile, some larger firms established themselves in campuslike office parks, each complex situated well back from the highway, approached only by a single discreetly marked road winding off between the trees. By the latter part of the twentieth century, whether one worked in a car wash or an elaborate corporate headquarters, one might easily make the round-trip to and from work every day without ever encountering another person face-to-face, except perhaps in a traffic accident. Thanks to drive-in windows, even customers who went to the same bank or fast-food restaurant at the same time would be unlikely to cross paths.

THE DECLINE OF PUBLIC SPACE IN THE CITIES

As suburbanization transformed the countryside into millions of separate commercial and residential enclaves, the nation's cities necessarily changed as well. Urban newcomers (often people of color) faced particularly hard times, because many of the jobs they had expected to find had moved to the suburbs themselves, or to other parts of the country, or even overseas. Faced with needier populations and declining tax revenues, municipal leaders devoted much of their energies to trying to revive their flagging urban economies.

Smaller towns and cities generally made little headway in this effort. By the 1970s, in the hardest-hit communities, few people were to be seen downtown except the low-income residents who lived nearby. The vista along a typical Main Street in one of these cities—vacant buildings interspersed with tiny family businesses, fast-food places, check-cashing services, social agency offices, and thrift stores—provided a sharp reminder that, in one respect (though only one), these downtown areas had come to resemble the more elaborate suburban malls: they were serving a very narrow segment of the population. Technically, they remained open to all, but they had lost their capacity to function as a meeting ground for the wider community.

Larger cities generally managed to retain at least some position in their regional economies, but they too struggled with a steady loss of residents and jobs. To stem the tide, many invested millions of public dollars in projects designed to revitalize their downtowns. Yet few chose to build on the unique strength of cities—their capacity to provide areas where many different kinds of people on many different errands can cross paths. Instead, they tended to focus almost exclusively on coaxing the middle-class downtown again by constructing individual islands of redevelopment, to and from which suburbanites might travel by car while having little to do with the rest of the city or its residents. Two examples of this approach will suggest the pattern: the rebuilding of central business districts and the construction of in-town shopping malls.

The most typical revitalization strategy undertaken during these years was to fill a city's central business district with upscale office space. With the help of private investment and generous public subsidies, clusters of new high-rise buildings began to rise in many American cities, usually holding banks, insurance agencies, brokerages, legal and accounting firms, and corporate offices. Visit one of these districts at noon on a sunny day, and one might almost think that downtown had regained its old vitality. But most of the people thronging the sidewalks would disappear indoors again as soon as lunchtime was over. Furthermore, nearly all of them now traveled by car, and, thanks to underground parking lots and company cafeterias, they could spend the whole day inside if they chose. Since there were few shops, theaters, public institutions, or services among the office buildings, there was little reason for anyone else to come into the area unless they had business there. As a result, these districts had much less sidewalk activity once lunchtime was over, and every night and every weekend they turned into echoing caverns of darkened buildings and empty streets.

The new-style central business districts often achieved their primary goal, which was to generate at least some additional tax revenue. They failed, though, in the larger purpose of reviving the city as a center of community life, because they rarely created space that different groups in the community could use together and care about. Although the streets and sidewalks remained publicly owned, the district as a whole had undergone a kind of privatization, in the sense that a significant number of downtown blocks were now dedicated to a single type of activity involving only one relatively narrow segment of the population. In effect, millions of public dollars had helped to produce a central business district that was off-limits in the practical sense, if not the legal: for most members of the public, it was no longer a relevant destination.

Another type of privatized space that appeared in many cities during these years was the stand-alone complex of shops and restaurants. Like the elegant suburban malls with which they were competing, these complexes tended to concentrate on those goods and services that would attract prosperous customers. Since such people would arrive by car, the in-town malls were usually designed with little connection to the neighborhood outside. They often had no windows on the street, pedestrian entrances were minimized, street crossings (if any) were constructed as "skywalks" at the second-story level, and ground floors were frequently reserved for utilitarian functions like parking, rather than being arranged to draw customers in from the sidewalk. Thus, the very design of these buildings augmented whatever threat might have lurked on the streets outside, by discouraging the active pedestrian traffic that keeps urban neighborhoods lively and safe. Like the redeveloped central business districts, the in-town malls created discrete islands of privatized space while contributing little to the vitality of the surrounding area.

By the latter part of the century, a countermovement had begun to emerge in some cities, placing new value on urban public space. One effort along these lines was the development of "festival markets," often erected in disused factory buildings (Ghirardelli Square in San Francisco) or along abandoned waterfronts (Harbor Place in Baltimore). The strength of such places was their ability to bring huge cheerful crowds together in long-neglected parts of the city. The limitation was that, because nearly all their space was devoted to shops and restaurants (most of them fairly expensive), they tended to attract more tourists than locals, and more upscale couples than working-class families. In the festival market as in the shopping mall, there was only one significant role to play: consumer. Those who were not financially equipped to play that role had little reason to go there.

Some cities set their sights higher and sought to revivify their entire downtowns, challenging not only the dominance of the automobile but also the isolation of the privatized urban spaces created in recent decades. Portland, Oregon, began redefining its course as early as the 1970s. It refused to accept several planned new expressways, even dismantling an existing highway that cut the city off from its riverfront. In addition, it set new height limits for downtown buildings, forbade the construction of windowless walls along the street or skyways between buildings, put a cap on the number of downtown parking places, invested heavily in public transportation, and demolished one large parking deck to make room for a new public square.

Thanks to efforts like these, Portland and a number of other cities did succeed in stimulating more activity downtown, particularly for specialty shops and restaurants. Nevertheless, few cities actually managed to reverse the outward tide of people and jobs. Suburbanization was still the dominant American trend, and in 1990, the United States became the first nation in history to have more people living in the suburbs than in cities and rural areas combined. Every year, thousands more acres of rural land were swallowed up by new housing developments. With these developments came more roads, more cars, more shopping malls, and more commercial strips along the highway—along with fewer opportunities than ever for people of different backgrounds to come together in the same public space.

PRIVATIZING LIFE AT HOME

The dispersal of so many stores and workplaces to separate suburban locations, combined with the growing dominance of the automobile, had a significant impact on America's social geography, because it tended to segregate people according to their daily destinations (which in turn were often defined by their race, income, and personal interests), rather than drawing them together toward a common center, as the typical downtown had done in earlier years. The social impact of these trends was heightened because, during the same period, Americans' lives at home were also changing.

SUBURBAN HOMES FOR WHOM?

During the decades that followed World War II, while highways and shopping malls were spreading across the countryside, even larger sections of rural land were being transformed into acre upon acre of single-family homes. Because government backing made it possible for banks to offer the most generous home financing in history, people with very modest incomes were able to qualify for mortgages. Nevertheless, the pattern of who lived where in the suburbs reflected and even intensified America's existing social divisions.

Income was the first and most obvious basis of classification. Developments with cheaper homes tended to cluster in certain suburban towns, while other communities (usually located further from the city) catered to more prosperous families by offering more expensive houses, by prohibiting lots smaller than three or four acres, and by excluding larger commercial uses which the poorer towns could not afford to reject. Thus, a family's income level often determined not only what kind of house it could buy and who its neighbors would be, but also which suburban towns it could live in, the quality of the malls nearby, the budget of the schools its children attended, and even the capacity of the community at large to defend itself against encroachments such as factories, new highways, and commercial sprawl.

Race and religion played an even larger role in determining who could participate in suburbanization and on what basis. Although the Supreme Court outlawed restrictive covenants in 1948, less overt discrimination continued for decades, excluding Jews from many suburban communities and virtually closing the door to African Americans. During these years, activists made real strides in democratizing access to more public spaces, such as workplaces, restaurants, stores, and public transportation. Residential segregation proved much harder to eradicate, and its persistence helped sustain racial separation in people's daily lives.

Suburbanization intensified this problem. Segregated neighborhoods were nothing new in American life, but in the suburbs it was possible for whole towns to exclude people by race and income, thus avoiding any responsibility for accommodating the region's more vulnerable citizens. (Indeed, the integration of urban schools and the rising minority population in the cities helped speed the retreat of many middle-class families to such white-only suburbs.) Consider, for example, the pioneer of the new suburban towns, Levittown on Long Island. In 1950, Levittown had 65,000 residents, only .02 percent of them black. Forty years later, black residents still represented less than 1 percent of the town's population. These discriminatory patterns influenced city life as well, since the groups who were not welcome in the suburbs formed a steadily larger share of the urban population.

Besides sorting people out by income, race, and religion, suburbanization introduced still another basis for social segregation: age. The process began simply enough, when the first wave of housing was produced after the war. This was the era of the "baby boom," when million of young couples started the families they had been unable to begin during the years of Depression and war. Since builders found it most efficient to produce a few designs over and over, and since young veterans with their GI Bill mortgages constituted the greatest pool of buyers, suburban developments sprang up all over the country, filled with homes tailored precisely to the needs of these young families. Indeed, a resident of these early suburbs was about as unlikely to have a neighbor over the age of fifty as to have one who was African American or from a very different income group.

Even after the baby boom abated, the structure of the housing market encouraged the sorting out by age that had been established in Levittown and its successors. Since individual developments tended to feature houses of a specific size and cost, they rarely attracted people who were at very different stages of life. The majority of developments, whatever their price level, catered to people in their childbearing years, offering houses with family rooms, three or four bedrooms, roomy garages, and big eat-in kitchens. Young singles, on the other hand, gravitated to condominium complexes that offered swimming pools, health clubs, and apartments with one or two bedrooms. Meanwhile, senior citizens often chose the strictest age-segregation of all, moving to retirement communities that admitted no one under the age of fifty-five.

In all these ways, the old practice of dividing neighborhoods according to race and income was perpetuated and even intensified in American suburbs, with age added as a new basis for categorization. Just as changes in the social geography of commerce and work were reducing people's opportunity to interact with those from different social and economic groups, so the stratified pattern of residential neighborhoods was narrowing even further the social circle of the average American household.

In the past, one form of leisure activity that had helped to diversify people's social experience beyond the limitations of their own neighborhoods was their participation in clubs and organizations. During the second half of the twentieth century, traditional organizations such as political parties, labor unions, and established churches generally lost active members, but newer forms of association, such as self-help groups and the environmental movement, expanded dramatically. From a social perspective, did the two changes balance each other out? Probably not. The newer types of organizations enriched many lives, but they were not quite the social melting pots that their predecessors had been. Most self-help groups, such as Alcoholics Anonymous, had a primarily personal focus, despite their stress on mutual support. As for environmental advocacy, membership in a national organization did not usually involve much participation, while many local environmental groups focused mainly on protecting their own towns, thus reinforcing the divisions between one community and the next. The same geographical split occurred in school-based activities: while parents in a wealthy district might be working to add advanced math courses to the high school curriculum, parents in a poor urban district could be bending all their efforts to getting broken windows repaired. Overall, by the latter part of the century much of the country's associational activity was organized in ways that reflected and sometimes even intensified the social divisions created by residential geography.

Meanwhile, something else was happening that introduced another level of social separation into American life. Not only were towns and neighborhoods divided from each other, but increasingly, each individual household was also operating within its own separate world.

LEVITTOWN AND ITS SUCCESSORS

Sometimes a new style of living becomes so well established that the only way to recognize its distinctive characteristics is to watch the behavior of the people who have not yet fully embraced the change. By going against the norm, these people help us recognize the unspoken arrangements that everyone else has come to treat as natural. Thus, a useful way of exploring how suburbanization affected the social experience of American families is to look at what happened when the new style of living was just emerging.

One observer recalls that during the early years in Levittown, it was common to see groups of eight or ten men standing together in someone's driveway, talking for hours, no matter what the weather. She notes that Levittown's houses lacked many of the spaces, such as dens and workshops and even garages, that would later become male domains; this lack, she suggests, is what drove the men outdoors. It is important to remember, though, that few of these men had ever lived in homes that offered such amenities. What they were really compensating for was the lack of what they had known in the past: nearby public spaces where they could gather informally with friends and neighbors. For some men that had meant their local political club; for others it was their church or synagogue, their ethnic lodge, the corner bar, the bowling alley, the park, or perhaps their union hall. (Though most of these facilities catered primarily to men, a number also offered family activities that played an important part in urban neighborhood life.)

The new suburban housing tracts made no accommodation for such spaces, and in any case, contemporary thinking frowned on combining residential property with other uses. As a result, new suburban homes were almost never built within walking distance of a church, a bar, a bowling alley, or even a park. Nor did suburban communities generally have the kind of political, ethnic, and union traditions that had helped to foster organizational life in the cities. Over time, suburban men would accommodate themselves to the new social geography, spending more and more of their leisure hours at home with their families. Their initial effort to create public space where none existed helps reveal more clearly the change that their later accommodation represented. On one hand, the new pattern of living made fathers more available to their wives and children, closing a gulf that had often caused pain in the past; on the other hand, it weakened the families' connections to the world outside their homes.

The women who moved to Levittown in the late 1940s had generally led less active public lives than their husbands, but they, too, had adjustments to make. For instance, where they had lived before, doing the household shopping had generally involved going on foot to different stores in the neighborhood. Owning no freezers (and often no refrigerators), housewives had to shop nearly every day—a nuisance in bad weather, but also a regular opportunity to encounter friends and neighbors. In the suburbs, virtually every household errand required driving somewhere outside the neighborhood. During Levittown's early years, wives often found themselves marooned at home, either because they had not yet learned to drive or because their husbands regularly took the family's only car to work. Later on, many more families bought two cars, and most women learned to drive. This made their lives more convenient, but from a social point of view, the weekly run to the grocery store provided far less opportunity for interaction with friends and neighbors than had the daily round of neighborhood errands. Many Levittown wives enjoyed joining their neighbors for a cup of coffee or a family barbecue, but there was little about the way the community was laid out that made it necessary or appealing to venture much further on foot.

Within a decade after World War II, the patterns established in Levittown had spread nationwide. As in Levittown, the new suburban homes were generally clustered in developments that contained no places of employment, no stores, no services, and no public institutions. Testifying to the indispensability of the automobile, garages became a standard feature in home construction, and soon they were being built with space for two or even three cars. Indeed, the irrelevance of foot travel to suburban living was exemplified by the fact that most of the new developments had no sidewalks. The pattern was clear: one remained at home or drove somewhere by car. The kind of social interaction that was fostered by nearby stores, restaurants, and social institutions—and by pedestrian traffic to and from those destinations along neighborhood streets—was simply not a feature of life in the new suburbs. Instead of serving as an arena where neighborhood life could be shared and observed, the street was now primarily a place where cars and delivery trucks drove by on their way to someone's house.

The architecture of suburban housing tended to minimize still further the importance of the street and the neighborhood in family life. Single-family homes built before World War II, whether urban or suburban, had generally been oriented to the street. The living room was typically on the front of the house, large windows faced the street, and front porches often provided a kind of social bridge between the private world indoors and the public world outside. The new suburban architecture followed a different design. In these homes, the living room moved to the back of the house, as did the big windows, while the front porch disappeared, to be replaced by the backyard patio. Later developments frequently offered even more privacy, with houses set well back on the property, and dense plantings blocking the view from the road. "Gated communities" took seclusion further still by building their developments with only one entrance, manned by a twenty-four-hour guard. Mansions had often been designed to screen their wealthy occupants from public view, but to have homes at every income level turning their backs so decisively on the outside world was a new departure.

STAYING HOME

The changing balance between public and private in American family life took many forms. The increasingly private design of homes and neighborhoods was most visible in the suburbs, because that is where most new residential construction took place. When it came to changes in the way people actually spent their time, though, urban and rural households were as involved as suburban ones. Given the wide availability of cars, one might have expected that Americans would go out more and more. Instead, a growing number of things that people used to do in the community came to be done at home.

During the early postwar years, many observers attributed the American family's inward bent to the fact that so many wives remained at home with their children, while only the fathers ventured out into the world every day. Yet the insufficiency of this explanation became clear during the years that followed, when women's employment situation changed dramatically. Between 1960 and 1995, the proportion of married women with jobs doubled, while the labor participation rate among mothers of young children climbed from 19 to 64 percent. Going to work broadened women's personal horizons in many ways, but it did not do much to rebuild connections between home life and community. In fact, the demands of women's jobs, combined with the expectation that women would still take primary responsibility for housework and childcare once they got home, left them with less time than ever for the volunteer work and neighborhood socializing that fulltime homemakers used to do. Like their husbands, American women increasingly divided their time between a distant occupational world and an entirely private world inside their homes.

Fear of crime gave many Americans another reason to go out less often. Particularly in the cities, fear kept many elderly people home at night, made low-income families in some neighborhoods prisoners in their own homes, and often discouraged suburbanites from venturing downtown at all. Crime levels did rise between 1945 and 1990, but fear of crime itself aggravated the problem. Since bustling crowds are the best guarantee of public safety, the more people's fear of crime kept them off the streets, the less safe the streets became. Even before the attacks on the World Trade Towers and the Pentagon in 2001, a general sense that the world beyond one's home could be unpredictable and possibly dangerous came to shape the leisure activities of many Americans.

Fear of crime, added to the demands of work and family, may have reduced the appeal of going out. But the postwar years produced another compelling reason for Americans to stay home: television. In 1946, television sets were so rare that crowds would gather in the street to watch one in a store window. A dozen years later, there were forty-six million sets in the country, and the average American was spending five hours a day in front of the screen. With TV, instead of seeking your entertainment in the outside world, the world would come to you, sparing you the expense of admission fees, the inconvenience of driving, and the need to hire a babysitter. Moreover, if a given program proved to be a disappointment, you could switch to another one simply by changing channels. While movie attendance plummeted, television became part of the American way of life.

Over the next several decades, many families began to buy multiple TV sets, so that even members of the same household could sit in different rooms of the house watching different programs. Cable TV provided better reception and more channels to choose from; satellite dishes brought in still more channels from around the world; the remote control allowed one to flick from program to program all evening without even leaving one's chair; and pay-per-view, videotapes, and DVDs gave people the choice of seeing almost any film they wanted, any night of the week. These innovations allowed viewers an unprecedented level of individual choice in terms of what they watched and when, but they also exacted a social cost. The experience of seeing a baseball game or movie on television was now private, not public. What you gained was the comfort and convenience of watching precisely what you wanted when you wanted, secure in your own living room. What you lost was the opportunity to move beyond your own private world, to share the experience with other people, and to participate in the life of the wider community.

TV was not the only activity that allowed Americans to spend more of their leisure time at home. Eating takeout food instead of going to a restaurant had the same effect; so did swimming in a backyard pool instead of going to a park or club; so did shopping by catalog instead of going to a store. By far the most far-reaching change along these lines—one that dramatically expanded the capacity of people's homes to encompass their whole lives—was the computer revolution. Although computers had already become well established in business and government as early as the 1960s, their real impact on Americans' lives at home came with the introduction of inexpensive personal computers in the 1980s and the tremendous expansion of the World Wide Web starting in the early 1990s. By 2001, almost 60 percent of all Americans had home computers, and about 30 percent were logging onto the Internet every day.

Most home Internet users began with email. Now, instead of trying to reach someone by phone or going through the steps of writing and mailing a letter, one could simply dash off a message and hit the send button. Critics decried this new style of correspondence as a chilly substitute for face-to-face contact, phone conversations, and "real" letters. Supporters, on the other hand, maintained that because of its speed and simplicity, email helped to foster connections that otherwise would not have been made at all. Certainly, there was much to be said on both sides, but as Internet use expanded into other areas of daily life, the social ramifications of the computer revolution became more troubling.

Thanks to the Internet, it became possible to buy or sell almost anything without leaving one's house. One could also pay taxes online, check one's bank account, get medical advice, bet on a horserace, buy airplane tickets, play the stock market, examine historical documents, access most major library catalogues, pay a "virtual visit" to a museum, read the latest headlines, take a college course, or order dinner from a restaurant. Television had done a great deal to turn formerly public activities into private ones by bringing sports, music, drama, comedy, and news into the living room. Now the Internet made still more recreational opportunities available, plus allowing people to conduct a sizable portion of their personal business without ever leaving the house.

The Internet experience was made more private still by the fact that users could choose their own paths through the materials available, tailoring the information they received to their own personal inclinations. This narrowing of focus diminished the role that experiences such as reading the paper traditionally played in establishing common ground with others. In effect, each Internet user was now reading his or her own private newspaper. One more bloc of experience had been removed from the public domain.

The computer revolution increased social separation in two other ways as well. First, time spent using the computer was almost always time spent alone; thus, even the sociability of watching TV with friends or family was increasingly replaced by solo hours at the computer. Second, there existed a widely acknowledged "digital divide" between the people who had easy access to computers (notably people who were white, well educated, and at least fairly well off) and those who did not. This differential access to a growing array of goods, services, and information intensified the existing divisions within American society.

Social separation took one step further when the computer revolution began making it possible for people to do their jobs from home. Until late in the twentieth century, no matter how insular their houses and neighborhoods might be, most employed Americans had a regular source of wider social contacts because they had to go to work every day. (As growing numbers of wives entered the workforce, this experience became nearly as characteristic of women's lives as of men's.) Some workplaces were more homogeneous than others, but nearly all offered more social diversity than did the typical American neighborhood. During the 1990s, however, this opportunity for interaction was eroded by the growing prevalence of "telecommuting"—that is, working from one's home via the Internet. Telecommuting represented more than a change of work location. It meant that by 2001, more than four million Americans could spend nearly all their time within their own four walls if they chose to do so. The number of these telecommuters was expanding every day, and the trend they exemplified was growing faster still—the tendency to transfer one daily activity after another from public space to private. What had begun as a retreat from urban problems into suburban communities more subject to private control had culminated in a way of life conducted in the most private terrain of all: one's own home.

CONNECTION AND ISOLATION

The story of America's changing social geography during the second half of the twentieth century is the story of certain doors opening while others swing shut. In 1945, the daily sharing of downtown streets and services gave visible expression to the fact that local residents had a common stake in each other's endeavors, and in their community. The value placed on this shared space is what gave meaning to the crusades of groups like African Americans, women, gays, and the disabled, each of whom scored historic victories by successfully staking their claim to an equal place in territory that belonged to everyone.

Between 1945 and 2000, a succession of changes in the social geography of American life served to diminish the significance of these shared spaces. The migration of many Americans (mostly white) to the suburbs after World War II was followed by the exodus of many of the downtown facilities to which people of color were just winning access. The resulting social divide between city and suburb might have been eased if there had still been public spaces in which residents of the whole region might gather. But the suburbs produced few genuinely public spaces of their own to replace the downtowns that were now in decline. Instead, most Americans became accustomed to driving alone to and from work, shopping in stores that catered to their particular income bracket, living in neighborhoods with a fairly narrow social and economic profile, and spending much of their leisure time at home in front of the television or the computer. Legally, during these years, America's public spaces became more widely accessible than ever before. Yet by 2000, public spaces actually played a far smaller part in people's daily lives than they had fifty years earlier. As a result, compared to 1945, Americans living in the twenty-first century had considerably fewer opportunities to encounter a wide range of their fellow citizens face-to-face, and to be reminded every day of their membership in the community.

Looking to the future, this change has important implications for the strength of American society. A hundred years ago, many observers believed that the greatest threat to social cohesion lay in the fact that people were leaving rural villages to live in towns and cities; what would happen to America's sense of community, they asked, if people were continually forced to share space with strangers so different from themselves? Today, the danger to social cohesion may well lie in the opposite direction. What will happen to our sense of community if people have too few opportunities to encounter a broad variety of fellow Americans face-to-face? National politics, mass communications, and the workings of the economy all force us now to function as part of the same complex society. Yet how can people feel genuinely connected to this larger society, and make choices as citizens that are good for the whole country, if their direct personal experiences are limited to people very like themselves?

Some observers argue that social connections in cyberspace will provide an adequate substitute for the connections people used to make in physical space. The Internet has indeed shown a remarkable capacity for bringing like-minded people together, across the country and even around the world. In a diverse country like the United States, though, we need to feel connected not only to like-minded people but also to those whose interests and priorities are entirely different from our own. This kind of diversity is not what the Internet offers; in fact, the whole appeal of going online is the opportunity to tailor one's experience to one's own precise preferences—not to scan the whole newspaper, but to go straight to the articles one chooses; not to stroll through the aisles of a store, but to click on the precise items one wishes to purchase. In this sense, the computer is only the latest in a long line of innovations—including the car and the television set—that have changed countless daily transactions from shared experience into private experience. With these technological changes reinforcing the social insulation produced by geographical trends, it is hardly surprising that many Americans today feel little sense of connection or obligation beyond their own immediate circle of family and friends.

Sharing public space is not, of course, a magical cure for this kind of social separation. But it can help, by allowing people from different social groups to see each other face-to-face, to grow accustomed to each other's presence, and to share common institutions. Fifty years ago, Americans from diverse backgrounds were constantly reminded of their connection to each other because they walked the same streets, rode the same buses, watched the same parades, and used the same parks and banks and libraries. However casual these daily encounters, they provided a visible expression of the community in all its diversity, reinforcing each person's sense of connection to the larger society. The precise form of this public community life cannot be recaptured, but the contribution it made is as important as ever. The challenge for the century ahead is to consider how the social values of shared public space can be reconceived and revivified to benefit a new generation of Americans.

BIBLIOGRAPHIC NOTE

The importance of public space as an arena for democratic engagement is highlighted in Don Mitchell's *The Right to the City: Social Justice and the Fight for Public Space* (2003), and it is a recognizable subtext in more general accounts of postwar social movements, such as Harvard Sitkoff's *The Struggle for Black Equality* (1981) and Ruth Rosen's *The World Split Open: How the Modern Women's Movement Changed America* (2000).

Kenneth Jackson's *Crabgrass Frontier: The Suburbanization of the United States* (1987) provides an excellent overview of how America's suburbs developed and how they have shaped the country's social geography, while Andres Duany, Elizabeth Plater-Zyberk, and Jeff Speck's *Suburban Nation: The Rise of Sprawl and the Decline of the American Dream* (2000) offers one of the most influential critiques of that process. A more positive view of the same trends is offered by Joel Garreau, *Edge City: Life on the New Frontier* (1991).

Jon C. Teaford's *Rough Road to Renaissance: Urban Revitalization in America, 1940–1985* (1990) describes the efforts of a dozen American cities during the postwar years to reshape their public spaces. Jane Jacobs's classic *The Death and Life of Great American Cities* (1961) and, more recently, Michael Sorkin's collection *Variations on a Theme Park: The New American City and the End of Public Space* (1992) discuss the negative effect of those efforts on the urban social environment. The role of racial discrimination in shaping one city's metropolitan geography during the postwar years is discussed in Arnold Hirsch's *Making the Second Ghetto: Race and Housing in Chicago, 1940–1960*, 2d ed. (1998). Mike Davis, in *City of Quartz: Excavating the Future in Los Angeles* (1992), and Allen J. Scott and Edward W. Soja, in their edited volume *The City: Los Angeles and Urban Theory at the End of the Twentieth Century* (1996), provide a West Coast perspective that integrates urban and suburban history.

Recent trends in social geography are explored in works such as James Kunstler's *Geography of Nowhere: The Rise and Decline of America's Man-Made Landscape* (1994); Robert D. Putnam's *Bowling Alone: The Collapse and Revival of American Community* (2000); and Evan McKenzie's *Privatopia: Homeowner Associations and the Rise of Residential Private Government* (1994). The new kind of public space created by computers is discussed in Manuel Castells, *The Internet Galaxy: Reflections on the Internet, Business, and Society* (2003); William J. Mitchell, *City of Bits: Space, Place, and the Infobahn* (1995); and Anthony G. Wilhelm, *Democracy in the Digital Age: Challenges to Political Life in Cyberspace* (2000).

3. DROWNING IN PICTURES

KENNETH CMIEL

In 1945, the most compelling images made in America were wondrously huge, larger than life, and seen by millions each week. They glided across movie screens at hundreds of local theaters and paraded through the hugely popular weekly newsmagazines *Life, Look,* and the *Saturday Evening Post.* These images caught the life of the country, sometimes with a maddening superficiality, sometimes with great profundity—yet they caught it. The country was in control of its visual culture. The story of the next fifty years was of the gradual erosion of that assurance. By the new millennium, the country's images were far more chaotic. There was more play than before, more freedom. But there was also more nervousness and concern. To cultural conservatives by the 1970s, and even many moderates by the 1990s, the image culture seemed dangerous, even sinister. Internet pornography, movie violence, the erosion of TV censorship, the mind-numbing distraction of video games—it all seemed so crass, so ugly. Technology, style, and the law had all somehow colluded to ruin the midcentury safety. Images had spun out of control.

A DEFINED AMERICA

At midcentury, the single most important purveyor of human-made images in the United States was Hollywood. During World War II, weekly movie attendance was in the tens of millions. Even in the first few years after the war, although attendance was dipping, movies remained the most compelling images there were. Hits of the 1940s and early 1950s, films such as *Casablanca, Singin' in the Rain, High Noon*, and *Stalag 17*, each attest to the importance of Hollywood in producing images for the nation.

Hollywood also produced most of a second sort of image—the newsreel. Newsreels were shorts of two to six minutes' length shown before movies in theaters. They usually combined short snippets of four or five stories. Recent events in Europe or Asia might be one story, the latest dance step another. Made from the 1910s to the early 1970s, newsreels were most important during the years of the famous "March of Time" series (1935–51). Sometimes serious, sometimes fun, the newsreels were always wholesome, and, just as much as features, they did their part to define the life of the nation.[1]

A third defining image was the documentary photograph. The 1930s and 1940s witnessed the emergence of new magazines devoted to giving the news through pictures. *Life* was the first. It began publishing in November 1936 and was an immediate success, quickly becoming the most popular magazine in the nation. Shortly after, *Look* was founded by the Iowa newspaper publisher Gardner Cowles; then the *Saturday Evening Post* adapted itself to the genre. Led by *Life*, these magazines brought the "photo essay" from its European origins and perfected it, stringing together one to two dozen pictures on a single theme that told a story. For the first time in modern journalism, the pictures were the stars and the prose played a supporting role.[2]

Along with the great weekly magazines, government agencies also produced documentary photography. The New Deal's Farm Security Administration (FSA) hired dozens of photographers to scour the country and, as Jack Delano, one of these photographers, said, "search for the heart of the American people." Some eighty thousand photos were taken for FSA between 1935 and 1943. Although the project ended in 1943, the pictures continued to circulate. Some became phenomenally famous, such as Dorothea Lange's "Migrant Mother" and Walker Evans's photos of Alabama sharecroppers.[3]

Hollywood and photojournalistic images, despite their very obvious differences, shared certain features. There was an ease of expression and a gracefulness about them, even when they took on somber subjects. They drew the eye in, held its attention. They were fascinating to stare at. They were *meant* to be stared at.

During the 1920s and 1930s, Hollywood learned how to weave countless bits of film together into seemingly seamless stories. By the 1940s, cameras were mobile and directors and editors had mastered techniques like the "eyeline match," "180° rule," and "shot/reverse shot" to move action along in scenes. The introduction of incandescent lighting in the 1920s helped directors use light to draw viewers' eyes to particular points on the screen or to create mood. Light no longer just lit a set.[4]

An ethos grew in Hollywood, one not as strong among European filmmakers, to create smoothly edited product. By midcentury, it was the conventional wisdom: "The use of pictorial continuity is the secret of *good* movie making."[5]

The results were dazzling. While all the techniques had been developed in the 1910s and early 1920s, it still took some time for them to work into routine practice. But by the 1940s, now-classic Hollywood films such as *Casablanca* or *Citizen Kane* fade in and out; their cameras roll along as actors move, their lighting pulls our eyes to particular figures or objects. Each scene is carefully sutured, linking establishing shots, close-ups, character reactions, and cuts back and forth between speakers. Within each shot, characters are posed with nearly the same care that Caravaggio set subjects in his paintings. There was nothing casual about it.

The elaborate staging and editing was done in a way to make the final product seem utterly effortless, to pull attention away from the moviemaking process and to the characters and story. Directors didn't care that moviegoers didn't know what the "shot/reverse shot" was. They wanted to keep the public staring at the screen, eyes riveted on the unfolding stories. The staging and editing were elaborate devices to keep people fascinated with the images but ignorant of the mechanics. Some of the technology was there before the 1930s, and all of the particular editing techniques had been invented earlier. But by the middle of the 1930s, it had been codified into a system. There was a *way* to do it now. These were movies, not plays on film.

The documentary photographers of the 1930s and 1940s had their own craft and technology. The photojournalistic movement owes its origins in large part to a new sort of camera—the Leica, the first small, handheld camera that could produce high-quality pictures. In the early 1900s, Lewis Hine, the photographer of American slums, had to carry his big, clumsy box camera, set it upon a tripod, and then pose his subjects. The Leica, on the other hand, was light, easy to carry, easy to use. Its shutter speed was phenomenal for the time, allowing it to catch unposed action. Invented in 1911 by Oscar Barnack, a German microscope technician, the Leica was mass-produced for the first time in 1925. Germany's first photomagazine appeared the next year. In the United States during the 1930s and 1940s, every major *Life* photographer except Margaret Bourke-White used a Leica.

Technology might have made photojournalism possible, but its characteristic style was not dictated by the camera. Photojournalism and documentary photography more widely conveyed an attitude about the image. While the Leica allowed swift unposed action to be captured cleanly on film, on other occasions documentary photos could still be as carefully crafted as any Hollywood production. According to Arthur Rothstein, a leading documentary photographer, the picture taker had to be "not only a cameraman but a scenarist, dramatist, and director as well." Roy Stryker, who ran the FSA documentary photography project, argued that there were "times when you simply have to pose your model." The key, for Stryker, was how you did it, "honestly" or "dishonestly." It did not have to be natural. It had to look natural. Henry Luce, the owner and editor of *Life*, put in another way: photographers should use "fakery in allegiance to the truth."[6]

Documentary photography, then, was defined less by its artlessness than by the feel of artlessness. Most important, the image had to be more than just a picture, more than an illustration of an event. Form and content had to merge to say something important. Wilson Hicks, the executive editor of *Life* in the 1940s, recalled that the magazine's photographers had to grasp "the camera's extraordinary capacity for recording more than a mere image." Good photojournalists used pictures to grasp an "essence interpreted." The great and famous pictures of the era—Robert Capa's soldier falling in Spain, Margaret Bourke-White's 1945 Buchenwald photos, Joe Rosenthal's flag raising at Iwo Jima—all echo far beyond the event recorded. There was great faith that great photographs could capture the soul of the nation and that adversity would not destroy the human spirit. These photographs were mythic in stature.

In this they were just like classic Hollywood movies. Hollywood did not express as much pain as the photos did. Yet their images were just as mythic. The stories were fables—of everyman fighting corruption (*Mr. Smith Goes to Washington*), of overcoming class and gender divides (*It Happened One Night*), of confronting the unknown (*The Wizard of Oz*), of learning to stand up for yourself (*The Grapes of Wrath*). The convention of generally uplifting endings not only limited Hollywood's range but also helped shape the films. They defined values to the nation at large. Academics, literary people, and journalists of the time would commonly claim that movies had "the power to create the nation's myths and dreams."[7]

Apart from the desire to guide the eye and the national mythic focus, the images of the 1940s were shaped by the law. Censors finally got firm hold of the movie industry in 1934. The Production Code, in effect until the 1960s, seriously limited what might be shown on screen. There needed to be a generally uplifting ending to most movies. There could be no undress, and only the most chaste contact between the sexes. Even mild profanity was strictly forbidden. Viewers had to fill in all the blanks with their imaginations. World War II only intensified the censorship. The most censored war in U.S. history touched film, newsreels, and magazines. The Office of War Information had to approve movie scripts, and Army censors had to clear pictures. Between 1942 and 1945, the nation monitored its images as at no other time in its history.[8]

Some visual modes existed outside of these confines. "Blue movies" and "dirty pictures" quietly circulated at the margins of the culture. And in the open, the popular tabloid press fed an appetite for the sensational and violent that no censors tried to stop.[9] Pinups also became popular in the 1940s. While they might now be seen as a hint of the future, at the time they had a patriotic feel about them, a healthy diversion for the boys in uniform. The system was not seamless, but it was still powerful. Law, technology, and aesthetics merged to produce pictures that were meant to be great summaries of the nation's soul. The midcentury visual culture of the United States strove to find mythic images and stories to capture the essence of American life.

FADE-OUT

This system slowly crumbled during the 1950s and 1960s. The first sign was shrinking movie attendance. In 1946, the industry pulled in $1.7 billion, the top box-office take in American film history. But by 1953, weekly movie attendance was only 25 percent of what it had been five years before. The decline continued: by 1962, movie box-office receipts were only $900 million. In those same years production costs were rising, putting the pinch on the industry.[10]

Although the decline started before the explosion of television, the competition of the new medium after 1950 intensified the pressure on Hollywood. TVs were in about a million homes in 1949 but in ten million by 1952. Within a few years they were ubiquitous, contributing to the decline in movie attendance and the death of the movie newsreel. TV news provided the same images more immediately. Newsreels now appeared to be old-fashioned, and by 1960 they had no important role in the distribution of the news.

Television, moreover, produced a new sort of image. TV pictures were, at first, grainy and without the clarity of movie images. Even when the quality improved later in the decade, television remained different. The larger than life image of the movie was gone. TV images could not overwhelm you, draw you in to their magic the way movies did. Television did its work differently, by allowing the viewer to watch in a comfortable, private setting. One could stretch out on the couch, lounge on the floor, talk during the show, even watch in underwear. TV's attraction was not its pictures, but the comfort and privacy of the viewing environment.

Other changes in the visual culture were underway at the same time. A stream of darker images about American life began to surface outside the grimy world of tabloid newspapers. The vogue for film noir was one sign. Films such as *Mildred Pierce* (1945) and *Out of the Past* (1947) explored murder, female duplicity, and the general hardness of urban life. Such themes were portrayed as the norm rather that the exception, unleavened by any happy ending. The visual style of noir helped build the mood. Interiors tended to be dark and grim.

Characters often found themselves enveloped in shadows, contributing to the pervasive sense of unease and claustrophobia. Bleak and shadowy streetscapes painted a menacing picture of the modern city. Noir was a black and white medium at the moment when Hollywood was going color.

The same darkness turned up in the increasing creepiness of Alfred Hitchcock's films through the 1950s and early 1960s—*Rear Window, Vertigo, Psycho, The Birds.* Similarly, Robert Frank's 1959 book of photos, *The Americans,* displays a very different United States from that of the great photojournalism of the 1930s and 1940s. Harsh light and grainy texture created a grittier, bleaker mood than the Depression-era pictures of a Dorothea Lange. While Lange portrayed poverty, there was also a dignity to her subjects. They were holding up under adversity. Frank's late 1950s camera, however, was less forgiving. The bleakness was not offset.

The censorship that had kept the system running was also breaking down. The legal regime that had propped up the 1940s image culture came under attack shortly after the war ended. By December 1953 it was possible for *Playboy* to publish without recrimination. The now-famous nude pictures of Marilyn Monroe appeared in that first issue. In the first few days after publication, Hugh Hefner kept waiting for the police to pull the magazine from the newsstands, but they never turned up.

In *Burstyn, Inc. v. Wilson* (1952), the U.S. Supreme Court overturned *Mutual Film Corp. v. Industrial Commission of Ohio* (1915) and gave movies First Amendment protection. The decision, though, did not end censorship immediately. During the early 1930s, the Motion Picture Association of America, Hollywood's trade organization, had established the Production Code Administration (PCA) to review—and censor—scripts and images. The 1952 ruling did not eliminate the PCA, but it did give directors new courage to fight it. In the next few years, various moviemakers locked horns with the PCA: Otto Preminger for his light sex farce *The Moon Is Blue* (1953) and his grim portrayal of heroin addiction, *The Man with the Golden Arm* (1955); László Benedek for his tale of roaming motorcycle hoodlums, *The Wild One* (1953); Elia Kazan for *Baby Doll* (1956), his nasty southern gothic of adolescent female sexuality and the slobbering men in tow.[11]

Censors were on the defensive, but they were not dead. Kazan had to negotiate scene changes in *Baby Doll,* just as he had had to five years earlier in *A Streetcar Named Desire.* Through the 1950s and early 1960s, such negotiations continued. The movie industry was not willing to make a full-front challenge. In the 1950s and the early 1960s, new things were portrayed on film, but there were still limits to what was shown.[12]

The same was true of other visual media. Few in the magazine business wanted to challenge conventions. *Life, Look,* and the *Saturday Evening Post* all fixed limits on what they portrayed. Television was the most conservative. In

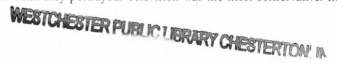

the 1950s, shows such as *The Adventures of Superman*, *Father Knows Best*, and *Gunsmoke* portrayed a strong, self-confident, and benign United States of America. Nuclear families were intact. Leaders cared about the public good. "For truth, justice, and the American way" was how Superman was introduced each week during the show's run from 1952 to 1958. Even into the next decade, family fare like *Bewitched* or *The Dick Van Dyke Show* was the norm. *The Beverly Hillbillies* and *Bonanza* remained among the most popular shows on television. Between October 1967 and April 1968, the most watched television shows in the country were *The Andy Griffith Show*, *The Lucy Show*, *Gomer Pyle*, and *Gunsmoke*, all of them far removed from any counterculture influence.[13] Despite the occasional "daring" show in the late 1960s, TV was a very conservative medium.

Still, the fade-out of the old system continued. Despite a renewed idealism among early 1960s photojournalists, particularly around the civil rights movement, the long-term trend was against striking print pictures. Television news and shifting patterns of advertising revenue would soon kill the great photo-based magazines. *The Saturday Evening Post* died in February 1969, *Look* in October 1971. *Life* hung on until December 1972. The old photojournalism, with the centrality of the photoessay and iconic picture, was dead.

The old censorship system, the movie Production Code, staggered along into the mid-1960s, but then it too died. In the end, a British movie directed by an Italian struck one of the final blows. Michelangelo Antonioni's 1967 film *Blow-Up* broke all the old rules. *Blow-Up* was the story of a hip London fashion photographer who accidentally took pictures of a murder in a London park. Since there was nudity in the film, the producers worried about the censors. After a bout of hand-wringing, they decided simply to ignore the censors and release the film in the United States without any rating. The film did well and there were no repercussions. The old censorship system was now dead.[14]

Blow-Up marked the end of an era in another way. In the film, the photographer only suspects that he has seen the murder being committed. When he returns to the park, the body is gone. He finds no trace of the crime there. He returns to his darkroom, gradually blowing up his photos in larger and larger versions to find proof of the crime in the background. But as the picture gets larger, the resolution gets worse. In the end, the resolution is so poor that that the pictures appear as incomprehensible fields of dots. They can't provide evidence that there ever was a murder.

For over a century, since the invention of the daguerreotype, it was an incessantly invoked truism that the camera helped us see more clearly. It was a window on the world, leaving evidence of what was not immediately viewable. *Blow-Up*, however, suggested that the camera did not necessarily leave us with a better picture of the world. In a few years, the idea that the camera captured reality would be increasingly suspect.

THE NEW REGIME

In the 1970s and 1980s, a new image culture started to take shape. It was far more varied than before. At the same time, however, there were fewer icons. Nothing defined the country the way the great midcentury photojournalism had. Movies did not code national myths with the same confidence. The rise of niche marketing was one factor. Corporate culture in practically every industry marketed to precisely delineated audiences rather than to the whole nation. The rise of cable television was an expression of this marketing. There were now fewer images that everyone saw.[15]

Separating the whole into its parts, however, was not the only force at work. Video and film editing became so quick-cutting that images seemed to blink right by viewers. Similarly, the rise of multicultural sentiment made everyone more suspicious of midcentury presumptions about images. The nation was too diverse to be caught in any single image.

Pictures multiplied. There were more of them, more types of them, and more machines on which to watch them. Video games, cable TV, the Internet, and home video cameras all became popular in the twenty years after 1975. The nation now seemed to be drowning in pictures. TV itself proliferated: in the late 1950s the average home had one TV, but by the late 1990s the norm was 2.9 sets per household, while 65 percent of teenagers had televisions in their bedrooms.[16] In the 1950s, TVs outside the home were generally found only in the local tavern. In the 1980s and 1990s, they spread to sports bars, hotel lobbies, casual restaurants, doctors' waiting rooms, and airports. New channels surfaced for televisions in special places—the Airport Network, the Food Court Entertainment Network, Channel One in the public schools. By 1993, more than twenty-eight million people watched television outside their homes each week.[17]

Americans were increasingly viewing different pictures. In the 1940s, movies, newsreels, and the newsmagazines were generally marketed to the great mass of adult Americans. In the 1970s and 1980s, however, except for the rare movie blockbuster, marketing to segments of the population took over. Magazines were now addressed to targeted age groups. Cable split up the TV audience in the 1980s and 1990s. There were stations for kids, teenagers, adults, and seniors, for men, for women, for African Americans, Hispanics, country music fans, news junkies, sports nuts, old-movie buffs, and more. During these same years, the number of people going to the movies continued to shrink. Hollywood ceased to define the cultural center of the nation. No image really did. To be sure, certain images could still capture the nation's attention—Bill Clinton denying he had sex with "that woman," the *Challenger* space shuttle exploding— but day to day, the country's viewing habits were increasingly fragmented.

The picture itself got smaller, diminishing the power of the image. First there was TV in the 1950s and 1960s. The "small screen" was starting its take-over. Then, in the late 1970s and after, videotape and then DVD allowed people to watch films on television. This changed both the scale and the experience. Movie pictures could now be watched with the same casualness of a TV show. Consuming movies was less of a special event—set off in a distinct social space with the expectation of quiet, sustained attention—than it had been at midcentury. By the new millennium, teens were starting to download whole movies on the Internet, making the images even smaller than TV. 1940s Hollywood had been larger than life. By 2000, moving images were increasingly smaller than life.

One place to see the diminished role of the image was in *People*, Time-Life's replacement for *Life*. *People* was first published in 1974, just over a year after *Life* had folded. Almost immediately, *People* became one of the top-selling magazines in the nation, just as *Life* had been in the 1940s and 1950s. The differences between the two were instructive. The shift in names caught something important—from trying to record modern life to chatting with celebrities. The difference in pictures was just as telling. There were actually more pictures in a typical *People* issue than in *Life*. Yet where *Life* struggled to make the image open out to something large and important, *People*'s photos were smaller and generally inconsequential. Two sorts of shots overwhelmingly dominated the new magazine—the home family snapshot and the paparazzi shot. One tried to reproduce what families did with their home cameras—genial images of friends and family in comfortable surroundings. The other was the voyeuristic ambush of the famous. Both were ephemeral. Unlike its Time-Life forerunner, *People* did not produce memorable pictures. It didn't try to. *People*'s cascade of photos was passing eye candy.

Even when the pictures were not physically smaller, the new image culture was faster-paced, more frenetic. While the 1940s films—"moving pictures"— were meant to flow smoothly, the new image culture of the 1980s and 1990s seemed less coherent, far jumpier. Increasingly, the motion itself—rather than any story or myth—was what fascinated.

There was an explosion in special effects. Spectacle, of course, has always been a part of the movies: the burning of Atlanta in *Gone with the Wind* (1939) or the spectacle of the Emerald City in *The Wizard of Oz* (1939). Yet, beginning with the first James Bond movie (1962), the poetically slow-motion deaths in *Bonnie and Clyde* (1967), and the cavernous portrayal of outer space in *2001: A Space Odyssey* (1968), Hollywood spent more time (and vast sums of money) finding new ways to create stunning images of violence, mayhem, and the extraterrestrial.

The creeping trend turned to a gallop in the 1970s. The mayhem of the popular disaster movies (the *Airport* series from 1970 to 1979 or *The Towering Inferno* in 1974) were done without any new special effects, yet they had great explosions. Two 1977 films, *Star Wars* and *Close Encounters of the Third Kind*, made new and elaborate use of older techniques such as the "blue screen process" to make all sorts of action seem possible in outer space. While these were widely considered the turning point in the history of special effects, there were other, less well-known innovations. Viewers of the first *Godfather* (1972) watched Sonny Corleone (James Caan) being murdered in grisly detail, thanks to both the slow-motion photography and the perfection of "the mole," a small squib put under fake skin that simulated with great realism the effect of flesh and blood bursting after a bullet hit. By the end of the decade, special-effects artists were nearly as important as actors.[18]

In the 1980s and 1990s came the digital revolution. George Lucas's company, Industrial Light and Magic, became a hub for the new technology, although many others were also involved. In movies such as *Terminator 2* (1991), *Jurassic Park* (1993), and *Forrest Gump* (1994), digital moviemaking matured. Whole characters were now created digitally. Digital backdrops were commonplace. There were flashy new techniques like "morphing," the seamless transformation of one shape into another. (Morphing was an important part of *Terminator 2.*) Perhaps most important was the digital editing of film. Once film could be shifted to a computer, edited there, and then put back on film, all without loss of quality, there was practically no end to what stunning things moviemakers could portray. The awesome tilting of the *Titanic* in James Cameron's 1997 epic of the same name is a perfect example; the hundreds of bodies sliding down the deck into the ocean were digital inventions.

By the 1990s, the new technology was changing popular moviemaking. Comparing the top-grossing movies of the 1970s to those of the 1990s made it clear that stunning explosions and digital aliens, freaks, or dinosaurs were now disproportionately part of the nation's most popular films.[19]

The very "wowness" of the effects, moreover, often replaced character development. Spectacle overwhelmed story. Unlike classic Hollywood films that meshed national myths with seamless editing, for these movies the effects were the attraction. The critic Scott Bukatman termed flicks such as *Dick Tracy* (1990) and *Jurassic Park* (1993) "theme park" films. On amusement park rides, we care about the thrills, not any story. These new movies were the same. Critics complained of "rootless, textureless images," of lousy plots and one-dimensional characters. Most of the independent film movement, at least in the 1980s and early 1990s, was devoted to bucking mainstream Hollywood by making smaller movies with interesting characters and no extravagant effects (another sort of niche marketing). But mainstream moviegoers, most importantly young males, loved the new movies. Big, flashy, jumping pictures—computerized dinosaurs galloping toward us, chiseled-bodied tough guys impossibly leaping clear of fantastic explosions, martial arts heroes and heroines running up trees—these were now among the most popular images on the screen.[20]

The new flashiness invaded television as well. Early television, like mid-century cinema, did not call attention to its "made" quality. It preferred what has been called a "zero-degree style," so little emphasis on style as if to seem that it wasn't there at all. In the 1970s and 1980s, however, electronic nonlinear editing machines, new fast film stock, and the ability to warp, move, and bend images in editing rooms were all new. In the 1980s, television production started to shift away from the "zero-degree" aesthetic. Shows like *Miami Vice* used the new technology to create images that called attention to their very stylishness. Other shows, such as the popular *Hill Street Blues* and later *NYPD Blue*, adopted exaggerated cinema verité. Jumpy images made with handheld cameras had the paradoxical effect of at the same time both seeming to be very naturalistic and so unusual that viewers clearly saw them as artfully constructed for a TV show.[21]

The new special effects changed the viewing experience at all levels. Even ads and promos were a part of it. In the 1960s, the famous logo for NBC was the peacock—a single picture, unmoving, on the screen for a few seconds to identify the network. In the middle of the 1980s, however, such logos started to move. Now in network promos, ads of all kinds, and news and sporting events, images, graphics, and logos floated, jumped, bent backward, and sailed on and off the screen. Viewers often did not realize all that had changed, how much of their television experience—prime-time, news, ads, network promos, sports— was different than before, how much of their attention was now being grabbed by jumping pictures and graphics. Insiders, however, knew what was going on. By the early 1980s, many veteran newsmen were indignant. One observed that "bells ring, pictures flip and tumble, and everybody seems to be shouting at me . . . The news is bad enough without added jingle and flash."[22]

One of the most striking new visual genres of the late twentieth century directly attacked Hollywood's continuity editing. The music video premiered in August 1981 during MTV's first broadcast moments. Within a few years, the video network was a huge success, mirroring the growth of cable in general at that time. From the beginning, music videos simply ignored continuity editing. Each video generally mixed three sorts of shots randomly: musicians performing, a fantasy motif or two, and good-looking women for males to look at. Individual shots were extremely short, with an editing cut every two to three seconds. Scenes shifted abruptly. Jump-cuts were de rigueur. Perspective changed with similar abruptness. Unlike classic Hollywood cinema, videos were not sutured to appear as if one shot "naturally" led to another. Quite the contrary, discontinuity was the goal. It was the rare video that created defined narratives with beginnings, middles, and ends. Instead, videomakers created moods. Surrealism was an important visual forebear.[23]

Videotape was remarkably important for the new visual culture. Videotape had been large and unwieldy in the 1950s, principally used for television shows. In the late 1960s and early 1970s, the size, cost, and ease of videotape diminished significantly. In 1974, the first commercial computerized videotape editing machine was put on the market. At the same time, lightweight video cameras became available for news outlets. Now "live from the scene" reporting was possible. News could take on a less-edited, more cinema verité style. The O. J. Simpson car chase (1994) and the beating of Rodney King by the Los Angeles police (1991)—events that captivated the whole nation—were seen only because of the videotape revolution of the 1970s and 1980s.[24]

But when news was edited, there was the same motion, the same artfulness that appeared in ads and sports. Once computerized video editing machines came on the market in the mid-1970s, editors could effortlessly rearrange image and sound. Editing film (as opposed to video) had required the cutting and splicing of the actual tape, a time-consuming, clumsy process that was unsuited to the daily deadline pressures of the evening news. The new equipment, however, allowed video to be edited with the press of a button. Moreover, unlike the splicing of film, which could not be readily undone, digital editing could be modified by a click of the mouse. The ease of electronic editing left ample time for experimentation even in the daily news shows. The result was increasingly slick meshing of image and sound, with far more editing cuts and montage than before, and far less uninterrupted talk. In 1968, the average uninterrupted time a politician spoke on network news was about forty seconds; twenty years later, it was just nine seconds. Politicians themselves altered their speechmaking to develop the one, catchy "sound bite" that would make the news. The new style changed the way reporters worked as well. An executive producer for CBS News observed that because of the new pacing, "the correspondent is not allowed to talk more than twelve or fifteen seconds before there is some intermediate sound." An NBC reporter observed that he was now "making little movies," directing camera crews, writing script to illustrate images, and spending a lot less time than before searching out information.[25]

The technology made these new images possible, but they were not determined by the technology. They were part of a new style, a new aesthetic. "Special effects were no longer just a way of producing difficult or impossible shots—they were becoming the star of the show, and audiences wanted to see more."[26] Newsroom editors looked for flashier, quicker-paced news stories.

Unlike the zero-degree style of earlier television, by the 1990s many directors were committed to "showing off their proficiency at picture making."[27]

Slick editing, fantastic special effects, cinema verité, and direct attacks on continuity editing all contradicted the effortless feel of the midcentury popular visual culture. But one last innovation did as much as anything else to increase the discontinuity and jumpiness of the new image culture. Between the mid-1980s and the mid-1990s, the number of households with television remote controls jumped from 29 percent to 90 percent. This device altered viewing habits dramatically. New slang—"grazing," "zapping," "surfing"—described characteristic uses of the remote, such as running quickly through all channels, following multiple shows simultaneously, and avoiding commercials. Research, in case you needed any convincing, showed that men wanted to control the remotes and flipped far more frequently than women. The result, for the men with the gadgets and the women who loved them (or who just put up with them), was one more way that it now appeared normal that images would quickly leap about without a care for the continuity between them.[28]

THE VANISHING CENSOR

Something else contributed to the new sense of disorder in the visual culture—the erosion of censorship. Images that would have been illegal a generation before—most notably of people having sex—were now so easily accessible that a time traveler from the past would have been astounded. The inability to contain such images contributed mightily to the widespread sense that images were out of control.

Movies and magazines were the first to change. Pressed from the early 1950s, the old film censorship system fell apart completely in the mid-1960s. A string of Supreme Court decisions in the 1950s and 1960s liberalized obscenity law. Shots of frontal female nudity started to appear in movies such as *The Pawnbroker* (1965), *Blow-Up* (1967), and *Five Easy Pieces* (1970). In response, in 1968, the Motion Picture Association of America developed a new system that differentiated between general-audience (G), mature-audience (M), restricted-audience (R), and adults-only (X) movies. (In the 1970s and 1980s, the ratings system was modified: the designation PG, for "parental guidance suggested," replaced M; PG-13 denoted films that might contain material inappropriate for preteen viewers; and NC-17 replaced X.) Unlike under the old Production Code, in the new regime movies were not censored, but rated. One result was that soft-core simulated sex scenes started appearing in movies such as *Last Tango in Paris* (1972) and *Don't Look Back* (1973), the former portraying anal sex. Over the next few decades, slowly, more taboos peeled away. In the early

1990s, Hollywood for the first time portrayed genitalia of both men (*The Sheltering Sky*, 1990) and women (*Basic Instinct*, 1992).[29]

Mainstream Hollywood, however, looked tame when compared to its nastier cousin, the porn industry. The popularity of soft-core porn films such as Russ Meyer's *Vixen* (1968) or the *Emmanuelle* series (1974) was one thing. In 1971, though, hard-core porn, showing real or simulated intercourse, became readily available to large audiences. Between June 1972 and June 1973, the "big three," *Deep Throat*, *Behind the Green Door*, and *The Devil in Miss Jones*, all produced in 1971 and 1972, earned more in theaters than almost every mainstream movie.[30] The porn industry put itself on really firm footing, however, a few years later. In the late 1970s, porn, just like television news, shifted from film to videotape. The porn industry's discreetly but widely marketed tapes meant that viewers could watch it on their VCRs in the privacy of their homes instead of having to venture to some seedy downtown theater. No one had a good handle on who exactly was watching porn, but that was precisely the point. Porn had become a private pleasure. By 1985, it was credibly estimated that sixty-five million X-rated videotapes were played in American homes each year.[31]

Magazines addressed to male voyeurism underwent a parallel shift. *Playboy* found itself being challenged in the United States by a rawer *Penthouse* in 1969. (It was first published in Britain in 1965.) *Penthouse* reached the height of its popularity in the 1970s and 1980s. In August 1971, it showed female genitalia for the first time. *Playboy* followed five months later.[32] In the 1980s, *Penthouse* found itself gradually outflanked by Larry Flynt's even rawer magazine, *Hustler*. In response, in the late 1990s *Penthouse* added pictures of men's penises and oral sex, as well as close-ups of penises entering vaginas. *Playboy*, meanwhile, seemed hopelessly passé.

A variety of factors contributed to the new obscenity. Technology was one. Videotape, as mentioned above, changed the porn industry. The regulatory environment also mattered. HBO and Cinemax, with their doses of nakedness and sex, became commercially viable only when the Federal Communications Commission opened the door to the cable industry in 1972.[33] The Supreme Court simply gave more space to sexual images than it had in the past. Even the outer limits of what the court would tolerate, first announced in *Miller v. California* (1973), did not stem the flow of pornography. Commercial pressures were a third force propelling the new explicitness. The men's magazines had market pressures to keep up with each other, and to not lose audience to the porn-movie trade.

Television held on longer and never went nearly as far as other media, but by the 1990s, the older codes were reeling there as well. Television in the 1950s had adopted the same production code used by the film industry. While there were some tangles with censors in the 1960s, controversy really accelerated in the early 1970s. Beginning with *All in the Family* (first aired in January 1971) and its spin-off, *Maude* (1972), prime-time TV was willing to tackle new, controversial ground. "During the season that began last week," *Time* reported in 1972, "programmers will actually be competing with each other to trace the largest number of touchy—and heretofore forbidden—ethnic, sexual, and psychological themes. Religious quirks, wife swapping, child abuse, venereal disease—all the old taboos will be toppling."[34] A few years later, the new thematic explicitness was joined by new visuals. "Jiggle" or "T & A" shows like *Charlie's Angels* added a dollop of adolescent titillation to prime-time lineups. Between 1950 and 1970, the main pressure groups trying to alter TV content were liberals who pushed for more black faces and integrated programs. At the end of the 1960s, feminists joined this liberal push, looking for better portrayals of women. In the next decade, however, conservatives emerged as the dominant critics of TV. New organizations, mostly led by Christian ministers, organized to complain about the "new era" of TV: "reckless hedonism and hostility toward morals, religion, marriage, free enterprise, family, and country."[35]

This expansion of the possible had limits. TV images were not nearly as explicit as movies or magazines. Still, the 1970s shift created controversy and was one factor in the turn of evangelical Christians to conservative politics at the end of the decade. Certainly, this was one piece of what mobilized evangelical Christians for Ronald Reagan in 1980.

But one paradox of the last decades of the century is that while conservatives have been winning an increasing number of elections, they have not been able to change the visual culture. Ronald Reagan's 1980 victory did not turn TV back to the 1950s. Instead, during the 1980s, images were appearing on the mass media that would have been unthinkable just a few years before. The rise of cable—particularly the channels outside the standard cable package—featured nudity, simulated sex, and foul language. With cable stations winning more viewers, the networks responded in kind. In 1992, the popular comedy *Seinfeld* ran an episode about a contest among friends to see who could avoid masturbating for the longest time. The next year, Donald Wildmon of the American Family Association denounced the popular police drama *NYPD Blue* as "soft core porn" for its signature shots of unclad rear ends and occasional short sex scenes (breasts and genitalia tastefully obscured). In 1994, *Roseanne* aired a lesbian kiss. All this appeared on network television in prime time. (NBC happily sold T-shirts commemorating the *Seinfeld* episode.) By 2003, *TV Guide* was asking, "How much freedom is too much?"[36] The idea of an evening "family time" safe from such material folded under the networks' struggle to prevent the audience from switching to cable.

Far outweighing the erosion of TV censorship in the 1990s was the emergence of Internet porn. With the explosion of the World Wide Web between

1992 and 1996, literally millions of images of every conceivable kind of porn were now entering homes, school computers, and public libraries. Kids had enormously easy access. With both parents now commonly working, afternoons after school were becoming prime-time for porn viewing. Congress tried twice to regulate this in the 1990s, hoping to force filters onto school and public library computers to block this material. Unfortunately, these filters also blocked sites with information about birth control, abortion, and even sites devoted to preaching abstinence. Although laws were eventually enacted to censor the Internet in public places, critics observed that pornography was still widely available.

DROWNING IN PICTURES

By the year 2000, American visual culture differed fundamentally from that of 1950. The image culture seemed more chaotic, more out of control. Visual culture seemed less a force of integration than of fragmentation. While there were always crosscurrents to complicate the story, there were important changes in the way the way that the image—the very nature of the image—was perceived.

There was a growing sense that images did not portray reality. Since the mid-nineteenth century, the photograph had been widely seen as accurately portraying the world. In the 1950s and early 1960s, the dominant position of intellectuals was that both photography and the movies had some intrinsic bias toward realism, thanks to that trace of the real world inevitably captured on a film negative. This connection to "the real," moreover, was something celebrated, not condemned, by these intellectuals.[37] The dominant midcentury popular aesthetics—documentary photography, continuity editing, and zero-degree style television—reinforced these presumptions. Reproduced images were a "window on the world."

But digital culture tore a hole in this perception. Indeed, computers with no link to reality conjured up crowds, explosions, and complete characters. Then, artfully meshed with film, these digital inventions were inserted into movie scenes where reality and invention mixed promiscuously. Digital photographs, at the same time, increasingly smoothed edges, removed blemishes, and made pictures look better while also raising questions about their "realness." As early as 1982, *National Geographic* found itself embroiled in controversy when it was discovered that it had digitally moved two pyramids to create a more attractive cover picture. In August 1989, *TV Guide* scandalized viewers by putting Oprah Winfrey's head on Ann-Margret's body in an effort to create a slimmer Oprah. By that year, the *Wall Street Journal* estimated that a full 10 percent of color pictures published in the United States had been digitally altered.[38]

TV's new stylishness raised its own questions about realism. The cool visual brio of a show like *Miami Vice* called attention to the craft of making pictures instead of hiding it. Music videos were even more dramatic, aggressively parading their antirealism. "Rather than the 'window on the world' concept that was so important in the early years of television," one observer noted, "contemporary televisuality flaunts 'videographic art-objects' of the world."[39]

Intellectuals started attacking the very idea of realism. In 1968, the French literary critic Roland Barthes wrote an influential essay suggesting that there was no such thing as "realism." There were, instead, "reality effects," assorted techniques that successfully created the illusion that the artifice was real. Translated into English, this essay proved to be a seminal contribution for contemporary discussion of visual culture. Within a decade, countless Americans academics were writing books on "the social construction of realism." Nor was this the position only of academics. By the early 1990s, variations could be easily found in the *New York Times* and other mainstream media.[40]

Visual culture also now seemed to be disruptive. Since the middle of the nineteenth century, photographs were thought to stop time, to interrupt the flow of experience. A photo forever captured the fleeting moment. Even the new "moving pictures" of the twentieth century did not dramatically change that perception. Especially once the censorship system was in place, movies tended to reinforce myth.

In the closing years of the century, however, production methods and new technology made the visual culture less soothing, far jerkier. Music videos ignored continuity editing. Pictures now jumped, warped, and faded in and out of our screens. The aggressive violence of the contemporary action film portrayed worlds out of control. The kids were watching porn at the local library— or in their own homes when the adults weren't around. Pictures were increasingly spoken of as something that upset the culture instead of stabilizing it.

Finally, the new visual culture was one where images were not intensely watched but glanced at casually. Grasping the difference between *Life* and *People* made this point: there were just as many pictures now, but none as iconic. So many of our images had become so random and fleeting that we look less carefully. The new visual culture was a culture of distraction.

In his famous 1936 essay, "The Work of Art in the Age of Mechanical Reproduction," Walter Benjamin argued that in the modern industrial world we looked at movies distractedly.[41] Benjamin—who was thinking of avant-garde Soviet film, with its heavy use of montage—had it entirely wrong. At the very moment he was writing, Hollywood cinematographers had perfected the narrative, editing, and lighting techniques that drew the audience's eyes to the screen and kept them raptly staring. Beautiful sets, beautiful stars, and a story nicely packaged in a beginning, middle, and end—it was all designed not to distract us but to hold our attention. Psychologists of the day contrasted the intensity of movie viewing with casual radio listening at home.[42] Classic Hollywood movies, in other words, wanted to draw us in to their worlds. They were part of ongoing efforts, reaching back to the late nineteenth century, of not only entertainers but also industrialists, psychologists, artists, and moralists to make us pay attention.[43]

But if Benjamin was wrong in 1936, he is correct today. Increasingly, we view our images distractedly. We glance at televisions in sports bars or at the airport. In our homes, we watch and chat at the same time. We flip casually through Internet images. When we watch a music video, the disjointed images catch the eye as the ear finds the music. While some early critics, such as Marshall McLuhan, thought that television demanded more attention, others saw it differently. The movie critic Pauline Kael spoke for many when she claimed that TV viewing, with "all its breaks and cuts, and the inattention, except for action" was contributing to the "destruction of the narrative sense." People didn't want to follow detailed stories anymore.[44] By the end of the century, the spread of moving images to all sorts of public venues, the manic pace of digital editing, and the quick flip of the remote control and computer mouse had made such distracted viewing commonplace. The one grand exception was the video game, where intense concentration made virtuosos. But apart from that, there was far more skipping through images and far less gawking at them.

The drift from reality, the sense of disruptiveness, and the increasing distractedness of viewers all made critics nervous. Stark images of violence and sex were dehumanizing, or so the critics claimed. In the early 1990s, the crassness of music videos and video games became part of what was called the "culture wars," a series of clashes between cultural conservatives and cultural liberals about the shape and future of American art and entertainment.

In the next few years, the opposition grew. By the mid-1990s, opposition to the visual culture was not, as it had been in the late 1970s, coming overwhelmingly from the right of the political spectrum. The widespread support for efforts to keep Internet porn from kids was one sign. Nervous discussions about how hard it was to raise a child, and how the mass media did not help, were another. Recent polls showed solid support for the idea that mass media imagery had gotten out of control.[45]

Yet despite the politicians, and despite the polls, nothing really changed. *House of the Living Dead II* was still at the local video arcade. Kids continued to log onto porn websites when parents were at work. Various music videos gave lessons in lap dancing. Parents continued to struggle to keep young teens (even preteens) from seeing the simulated sex scenes now so common in popular movies.

The widespread concern did not lead to a cultural rollback. The inability to craft law able to satisfy even a conservative Supreme Court was one reason. The suspicion that government censorship was not a good thing, no matter what, was another. The quiet and private enjoyment of porn by many adults was still a third. Finally, the sheer dazzle of the music video, Internet, Hollywood explosions, TV flash, and video games was also undeniable. Their energy was enormous, their creativity inescapable. They could be wildly entertaining, whatever their flaws. American media, with all its vulgarity and crassness, was loved by millions.

NOTES

1. Raymond Fielding, *The American Newsreel, 1911–1967* (Norman: University of Oklahoma Press, 1972).

2. For the best discussion of *Life*, see Erika Doss, *Looking at Life Magazine* (Washington, D.C.: Smithsonian Institution Press, 2001), particularly the essays by Doss, Terry Smith, and James Baughman.

3. For the Delano and Stryker quotes, see "Masters of Photography" Web page, www.mastersofphotography.com/Directory/fsa/fsa_background.html (viewed on 18 July 2003).

4. On incandescent lighting and the increasing sophistication about lighting on movie sets, see "Art of Lighting Film Sets," *New York Times*, 22 February 1925; "Art-Director Explains Intricate Task of Side-Lighting of Settings," *New York Times*, 15 August 1926; "New Lighting for Movies," *New York Times*, 12 February 1928.

5. Arthur L. Gaskill and David A. Englander, *Pictorial Continuity: How to Shoot a Movie Story* (New York: Duell, Sloan and Pearce, 1947), 146.

6. Edwin Rothstein, "Direction in the Picture Story," in *The Encyclopedia of Photography*, ed. Willard Morgan, 20 vols. (New York: National Educational Alliance, 1949), 4:1,356–1,357; Roy Stryker, "Documentary Photography," in ibid., 4:1,372. Luce is quoted in Richard Whelan, *Robert Capa: A Biography* (New York: Knopf, 1985), 119.

7. Robert Sklar, *Movie-Made America*, rev. ed. (New York: Vintage Books, 1994), 195.

8. Gregory Black, *Hollywood Censored: Morality Codes, Catholics, and the Movies* (Cambridge: Cambridge University Press, 1994); George Roeder Jr., *The Censored War: American Visual Experience During World War II* (New Haven: Yale University Press, 1995).

9. On porn and the efforts to suppress it, see Jay Gertzman, *Bootleggers and Smuthounds: The Trade in Erotica, 1920–1940* (Philadelphia: University of Pennsylvania Press, 1999); on Weegee, see Miles Barth, *Weegee's World* (New York: Bulfinch Press, 2000), and Weegee, *Weegee's New York, 1935–1960* (New York: Te Neues, 2000).

10. Gerald Mast, *A Short History of the Movies*, 5th ed. (New York: Macmillan, 1992), 275.

11. Jon Lewis, *Hollywood v. Hard Core: How the Struggle Over Censorship Saved the Modern Film Industry* (New York: New York University Press, 2000).

12. Ibid.

13. See the Web site "TV Ratings," http://www.fiftiesweb.com/tv-ratings-60s.htm# 67–68 (viewed July 2003).

14. Lewis, *Hollywood v. Hard Core*, 146–148.

15. On the rise of niche marketing, see Joseph Turow, *Breaking Up America: Advertisers and the New Media World* (Chicago: University of Chicago Press, 1998); Lizabeth Cohen, *A Consumer's Republic: The Politics of Mass Consumption in Postwar America* (New York: Knopf, 2003), 292–344.

16. Todd Gitlin, *Media Unlimited: How the Torrent of Images and Sound Overwhelms Our Lives* (New York: Metropolitan Books, 2001), 17–18.

17. "Morning Report: Where They're Watching," *Los Angeles Times*, 11 March 1993; Frazier Moore, "From Schools to Truck Stops: 'Place-Based' Media Flourish," *TV Guide*, 6–13 March 1993, 7. See also Anna McCarthy, *Ambient Television: Visual Culture and Public Space* (Durham, N.C.: Duke University Press, 2001).

18. "Hollywood's Secret Star Is the Special-Effects Man," *New York Times*, 1 May 1977; "The Black Hole Casts the Computer as Movie Maker," *New York Times*, 16 December 1979.

19. On the shift from the 1970s to the 1990s, see José Arroyo, "Introduction," in *Action/Spectacle Cinema*, ed. José Arroyo (London: British Film Institute, 2000), x–xi.

20. On "theme park" films, see Scott Bukatman, "The End of Offscreen Space," in *The New American Cinema*, ed. Jon Lewis (Durham, N.C.: Duke University Press, 1998), 266; on "rootless, violent images," see Warren Buckland, "Between Science Fact and Science Fiction," *Screen* 40 (Summer 1999): 178. For the best overview of new special effects technology, see Richard Rickitt, *Special Effects: The History and Technique* (New York: Billboard Books, 2000). Other useful literature includes Stephen Keane, *Disaster Movies: The Cinema of Catastrophe* (London: Wallflower, 2001); Yvonne Tasker, *Spectacular Bodies: Gender, Genre and the Action Cinema* (London: Routledge, 1993); Michelle Person, *Special Effects: Still in Search of Wonder* (New York: Columbia University Press, 2002); Brooks Landon, *The Aesthetics of Ambivalence: Rethinking Science Fiction Film in the Age of Electronic Reproduction* (Westport, Conn.: Greenwood Press, 1992).

21. In general, see John Thornton Caldwell, *Televisuality: Style, Crisis, and Authority in American Television* (New Brunswick, N.J.: Rutgers University Press, 1995).

22. Charles Kuralt, "The New Enemies of Journalism," in *Fast Forward: The New Television and American Society*, ed. Les Brown and Savannah Waring Walker (Kansas City, Mo.: Andrews and McMeel, 1983), 95; Av Westin, *Newswatch: How TV Decides the News* (New York: Simon & Schuster, 1982), 51.

23. On the background to MTV, see R. Serge Denisoff, *Inside MTV* (New Brunswick, N.J.: Transaction Publishers, 1988); for analysis of the videos, see P. Aufderheide, "Music Videos: The Look of the Sound," *Journal of Communication* 36 (1986): 57–78; M. Kinder, "Music Video and the Spectator: Television, Ideology, and Dream," *Film Quarterly* 34 (1984): 2–15; E. Ann Kaplan, *Rocking Around the Clock: Music Television, Postmodernism, and Consumer Culture* (New York: Methuen, 1987), 33–88.

24. Frank Davidoff, "Digital Recording for Television Broadcasting," *Journal of the SMPTE* 84 (July 1975): 552; Thomas Battista and Joseph Flaherty, "The All-Electronic Newsgathering Station," *Journal of the SMPTE* 84 (December 1975): 958–962.

25. Kiku Adatto, *Picture Perfect: The Art and Artifice of Public Image Making* (New York: Basic Books, 1993), 25, 63; Lawrence Lichty, "Video versus Print," *The Wilson Quarterly* 6 (1982): 52.

26. Rickitt, *Special Effects*, 33.

27. Caldwell, *Televisuality*, 152.

28. For statistics on household ownership of remotes, see Robert Bellamy Jr. and James Walker, *Television and the Remote Control: Grazing on a Vast Wasteland* (New York: Guildford Press, 1996), 1–2.

29. See Jon Lewis, *Hollywood v. Hard Core: How the Struggle over Censorship Saved the Modern Film Industry* (New York: New York University Press, 2000).

30. Ibid., 192.

31. Edward de Grazia, *Girls Lean Back Everywhere: The Law of Obscenity and the Assault on Genius* (New York: Random House, 1992), 583.

32. Ibid.

33. William Donnelly, *The Confetti Generation: How the New Communications Technology Is Fragmenting America* (New York: Henry Holt, 1986), 80.

34. "The Team Behind Archie Bunker & Co.," *Time*, 25 September 1972.

35. Mary Leis Coakley, *Rated X: The Moral Case Against TV* (New Rochelle, N.Y.: Arlington House, 1977), 13. For a discussion of the emergence of conservative critics of TV, see Kathryn Montgomery, *Target: Prime Time: Advocacy Groups and the Struggle Over Entertainment Television* (New York: Oxford University Press, 1989), 27–50, 154–173.

36. Steven Daly, "Blue Streak," *TV Guide*, 2–8 August 2003, 28.

37. See, for example, Siegfried Kracauer, *Theory of Film: The Redemption of Physical Reality* (New York: Oxford University Press, 1960).

38. On *National Geographic, TV Guide*, and the *Wall Street Journal*, see Vicki Goldberg and Robert Silberman, *American Photography: A Century of Images* (San Francisco: Chronicle Books, 1999), 224.

39. Caldwell, *Televisuality*, 152.

40. Roland Barthes, "L'Effect de reel," *Communications* 11 (1968): 84–89; for examples from the *Times*, see "New Picture Technologies Push Seeing Still Further from Believing," *New York* Times, 3 July 1989; and Andy Grunberg, "Ask It No Questions: The Camera Can Lie," *New York Times*, 12 August 1990; Jonathan Alter, "When Photographs Lie," *Newsweek*, 30 July 1990, 44–48; Robert Mathews, "When Seeing Is Not Believing," *New Scientist* (16 October 1993): 99–104.

41. Walter Benjamin, "The Work of Art in the Age of Mechanical Reproduction," in *Illuminations: Essays and Reflections* (New York: Schocken Books, 1969), 217–251.

42. Hadley Cantril and Gordon Allport, *The Psychology of Radio* (New York: Harper, 1934).

43. Jonathan Crary, *Suspensions of Perception: Attention, Spectacle, and Modern Culture* (Cambridge, Mass.: MIT Press, 2000).

44. See Marshall McLuhan, *Understanding Media* (London: Routledge and Kegan Paul, 1964); Pauline Kael, *I Lost It at the Movies* (Boston: Little, Brown, 1965), 9.

45. For some polling data, see Daly, "Blue Streak," 34.

4. POPULAR MUSIC AND TECHNOLOGY

TOM COLLINS

During the 1970s and 1980s, conglomerates bought out major companies in the American popular music industry, only to be bought out in turn by even larger conglomerates. For example, in 1988 the Sony Corporation purchased the CBS Records Group, which had recently acquired United Artists Music. The following year Warner Communications, which had already gobbled up influential independent music labels such as Atlantic Records and Elektra, was merged with the Time Inc. media empire. By 1991 six conglomerates were responsible for 91 percent of music sales in the United States. Music became one product alongside many others—cable television programs and movies, videogames and magazines—in the conglomerate's entertainment stable; to create synergies, each was used to pitch the others. The emphasis was on a hugeness of scale, with megastars going on megatours with well-known corporate sponsors, tied in to movies and television specials, in the hopes of reaping megaprofits.[1] Such an atmosphere did not foster musical experimentation and risk-taking.

But in this atmosphere—or, more precisely, on the fringes of the industry—a new genre of American popular music was created. In the late 1970s, in ghetto neighborhoods of the South Bronx, African American musicians used whatever musical equipment was available—portable boom boxes, turntables and speakers, inexpensive tape recorders and microphones—setting them up in community centers and on street corners to throw hip-hop parties. Hip-hop DJs rapped over samples of previously recorded music, taking bits and pieces from black and white music traditions and making them their own. For example, the backing music for a rap might be constructed from a Led Zeppelin drum part, a saxophone solo by jazz musician Lou Donaldson, a Joni Mitchell guitar riff, and a vocal snippet by Crosby, Stills & Nash.[2] DJs played their equipment like instruments, "shrinking" or "stretching" the rhythms of classic funk records by slowing or speeding up turntables and manipulating the stylus in the record groove to produce scratching and stuttering effects. Although hip-hop was rarely heard on black radio stations, the style was transmitted through word of mouth and amateur-produced cassette tapes. By 1983, prominent newspapers and magazines were discussing the "rap phenomenon." In 1986, when the group Run-D.M.C. had a major hit with a rap remake of the rock song "Walk This Way" by Aerosmith, the form was introduced to mainstream audiences.

That newfound creativity can coexist with corporate control in American popular music is not easily accounted for by a mode of analysis often used in cultural studies on the subject. This approach follows the lead of German social theorist Theodor Adorno, who was associated with a group of intellectuals known as the "Frankfurt School" during the 1930s. The view holds that popular music, turned into a commodity through technological reproduction, is inevitably debased. Record companies, seeking to minimize risks and maximize profits, create formulaic products gauged to appeal to the broadest possible market. The consumer is driven by false needs created by the culture industry, which uses advertising to persuade; what becomes important is not the music itself but rather that the need to consume be fulfilled.

An opposing approach is based on the work of another German social theorist, Walter Benjamin. He argued that technological reproduction shattered the "aura" of art—its uniqueness and its traditional cultural meaning—and placed it in a democratic context. This perspective suggests that art has become commonplace: anyone can create art, and anyone can find his or her own meaning in art. Consumption is seen as a creative act. For example, consumers do not passively receive but instead use popular music for their own ends, picking and choosing from the performers and genres available in the marketplace as a way to construct a sense of self.

While Adorno's critique is certainly relevant to an industry that has always been dominated by a handful of companies, it describes only one aspect of the story of popular music. In general, innovations in music making have occurred on the periphery of the industry and have become homogenized when absorbed into the mainstream. It is true that popular music history is littered with examples of artists and genres that lost their vitality when they were marketed for a mass audience. Elvis Presley joined a major company, RCA, in 1958 and was soon singing mediocre pop songs for B movies; CBS Records turned the rock counterculture of the 1960s into a marketing ploy with the slogan "The Man can't bust our music"; the first rap hit to reach number one on the *Billboard* charts was achieved not by a black artist, but by an MTV-friendly white singer, Vanilla Ice. But when the mainstream has co-opted artists and genres, it too has been transformed. The general experience of the average listener has been enriched as music has crossed over from the margins. In particular, popular music has drawn from the taproot of assimilated African American forms, with their emphasis on rhythm and repetition.

Adorno was correct that technology makes music into an object that can be exploited for profit, but Benjamin was equally correct that technology situates music making and music listening in new, potentially creative contexts. Many of the significant developments in popular music since 1945 have been spurred by technological innovations, particularly the introduction of magnetic tape in the late 1940s and digital sound in the early 1980s. Both revolutionized production and consumption, pushing a conservative, centralized industry in new directions.

Although magnetic tape recording was not widely used in the United States until 1949, the idea for the technology is almost as old as Thomas Edison's phonograph. In 1878, one year after Edison's first successful experiments in acoustic phonography, Oberlin Smith, an American mechanical engineer, devised the notion of using cotton or silk threads coated with magnetized steel dust to record sound waves that had been converted into electrical currents. Smith believed that this recording medium was a significant advance over Edison's apparatus, which used a steel stylus to cut the pattern of sound waves onto soft tin foil. The drawback of Edison's "talking tin foil" was that the stylus created friction as it cut the grooves and at playback, which caused considerable distortion and surface noise, nearly drowning out the recorded sounds. Smith reasoned that by using electrical currents to alter magnetized steel, the signal of sound waves could be recorded cleanly and clearly. Although he published his idea in the journal *Electrical World* in 1888, he was never able to prove his theory or to invent a recording machine.

A Danish engineer who may have been familiar with Smith's article, Valdemar Poulsen, carried out early experiments in magnetic sound recording during the 1890s. Poulsen invented a device consisting of a length of steel wire, strung in a slant between two parallel walls, with a small electromagnet attached to the wire; a battery connected to a rudimentary microphone charged the electromagnet. He found that when the electromagnet slid down the wire as he spoke into the microphone, a magnetic pattern was impressed on the wire that exactly replicated the electrical currents generated by the microphone. To "play" his recording, he used a telephone earpiece and simply placed the electromagnet at the top of the wire and let it slide. Based on this experiment, Poulsen developed a more sophisticated device, the Telegraphone, that he patented in Denmark in 1898 and Great Britain in 1899—the first magnetic sound recorder. Although the Telegraphone used steel wire, in his patent he also envisioned the use of tape, "a sheet or strip of some insulating material such as paper . . . cover[ed] with a magnetisable metallic dust and . . . used as the magnetisable surface."[3] Poulsen brought his Telegraphone to the United States in 1903, hoping to establish it as a commercial machine for recording telephone messages. That year the American Telegraphone Company was founded in Washington, D.C. But the company was plagued by management scandals and production problems, sold only a few hundred machines, and eventually entered into receivership.

For the next four decades, the technology of magnetic recording was largely forgotten in the United States. During these years, the phonograph was established as the standard device for both recording and reproducing sound, and developmental work focused on fine-tuning phonographic design and on improving the quality of recorded sound through the use of electrical microphones and vacuum-tube amplifiers. Meanwhile, innovative research in magnetic recording was carried out in Germany, where the first magnetic tape, coated with a layer of brown iron oxide, was developed during the late 1920s. In 1935 the German cartel AEG/Telefunken introduced a commercial recording-playback tape machine called the Magnetophone. This device was demonstrated for a group of General Electric engineers in America in 1937, but they dismissed it as an unmarketable technical novelty: although the Magnetophone could record up to thirty minutes of continuous sound—a considerable improvement over the 78 rpm shellac disc, which was typically four minutes long—it also had a very poor frequency response, only slightly better than that of a telephone. During World War II, American intelligence officers responsible for monitoring Nazi radio broadcasts were surprised to hear large symphony orchestras playing long after midnight, with an excellent "live" sound, few breaks in continuity, and none of the crackles and clicks of disc recordings. The orchestras had obviously been recorded somehow, but the quality and duration of the recordings surpassed that of all known technologies. The riddle persisted until the closing months of the war in 1944, when a few improved Magnetophones were found at captured radio stations. This model was the same as the older Magnetophone, except German engineers had added alternating current (a/c) bias in the recording circuit. The machine was now able to reproduce sounds up to 10,000 cycles per second with impressive fidelity, a range matching the finest disc recordings.

The story of how magnetic tape recording was introduced in the United States after the war is a curious one. This landmark technology was first used

because of the obstinacy of recording star Bing Crosby, who disliked performing live radio shows and wanted more free time to play golf. In 1944 the singer
became embroiled in a dispute with the NBC radio network. Rather than perform his weekly, thirty-minute show first for the East Coast and then a few
hours later for the West Coast, Crosby wanted to record on long-playing tran-
scription discs for subsequent broadcast. But putting together a show on disc
was a tortuous, expensive process. Editing was impossible when using a phonographic disc recorder; if a performer made a mistake or the cutting stylus
jumped its groove during recording, the disc became useless, and recording
had to start from the beginning. To minimize the opportunity for errors, show
transcriptions were typically made by cutting short segments on discs, which
were then assembled together in re-recordings on other discs, with the sound
quality deteriorating with each new disc generation. The final "air disc" sometimes represented five or more disc generations. The sound quality of transcriptions was so poor that NBC refused to broadcast them. At loggerheads with
NBC, Crosby sat out the 1945–46 radio season and in the fall of 1946 jumped to
the fledgling ABC network, which permitted him to use transcriptions as long
as his ratings stayed high. His ABC program, *Philco Radio Time*, debuted to a
large listenership, but its ratings began to drop almost immediately because of
the "canned" sound quality.

Casting about for a better-sounding recording technology, Crosby and his
producers learned about the Magnetophone. Although the United States Signal Corps had sequestrated most of the captured machines for military research,
an American engineer, John T. Mullin, had been permitted to disassemble two
Magnetophones and ship them home, piece by piece, as war souvenirs; he had
also managed to procure fifty reels of blank magnetic tape. Mullin rebuilt the
machines in his garage and began to demonstrate them for groups of Hollywood technicians and engineers, including people connected to Crosby's program. In August 1947 Crosby hired Mullin to tape-record all his shows for the
upcoming radio season. With a limited amount of tape at his disposal, Mullin
demonstrated one of the medium's advantages: magnetic tape was remarkably
durable. It could be erased and recorded over, was easily stored and transported,
and could be replayed with only a small amount of surface noise, unlike the
phonographic disc, which inevitably became scratched through contact with
the stylus. Mullin also began to experiment with simple tape-editing techniques, by which he used a scissors and Scotch mending tape to make splices.
If Crosby flubbed a song, Mullin could create a "perfect" version by splicing together the best parts from two or three takes. He later recalled that he also used
splicing to create the first laugh soundtrack. A hillbilly comedian, Bob Burns,
was on the show one day and told several off-color farm stories. "They got
enormous laughs, which just went on and on. We couldn't use the jokes, but

[scriptwriter Bill Morrow] asked us to save the laughs. A couple of weeks later he had a show that wasn't very funny, and he insisted that we put in the salvaged laughs . . . . It brought letters, because those big guffaws sounded ridiculous after the corny jokes."[4]

With its improved sound, Crosby's show quickly regained its ratings eminence. The singer became an influential advocate of magnetic tape recording, investing $50,000 in the Ampex Corporation, a small company in Redwood City, California, that was building an improved version of the Magnetophone. In 1947 the Minnesota Mining and Manufacturing Company developed an improved magnetic tape, which featured a red oxide coating on a plastic base; this tape could record sounds up to 15,000 cycles per second. In 1948 Ampex brought out the first American professional high-fidelity tape recorder, the model 200. The ABC network promptly bought twenty-four machines and 2.5 million feet of tape. That year the other major networks, noting the advantages of broadcasting tape-delayed shows in the different time zones, also began to implement the new technology.

Magnetic tape recording was introduced into a stagnant American popular music industry. Six major recording companies, four of them headquartered in New York City and two in Los Angeles, prevailed in the marketplace, accounting for more than eighty percent of record releases during the 1940s. Each of the majors controlled its own extensive distribution network of pressing plants, warehouses, and record jobbers. Through their connections to the other dominant entertainment companies, the majors turned songs into hits by exposing them in Broadway musicals and Hollywood movies and on the national radio networks. All but five of the 163 million-selling records released between 1946 and 1952 were the products of the majors. The Tin Pan Alley song with its "moon/June" lyrics was ubiquitous, just as it had been in the 1920s; among the most popular performers were crooners such as Crosby, Frank Sinatra, and Perry Como. The majors largely ignored other styles of music. Although they had released budget "race" and "hillbilly" records intermittently during the 1920s and 1930s, they stopped doing so when, faced by a shortage of shellac during the war, they were forced to concentrate on their primary markets. On the few occasions when an independent label threatened to have a nationwide hit, the majors usually co-opted the song, releasing competing "cover" versions that benefited from superior marketing and distribution. For example, in 1946 the small National label released the comical song "Open the Door, Richard," a staple of black-only vaudeville theaters, in a version by its cowriter, Dusty Fletcher. When the song began to sell well, five competing versions on major labels quickly appeared, including a version by the Pied Pipers, a white vocal group. The song eventually became a number-one pop hit for two major labels, RCA Victor and Columbia.

But changes were afoot that would undermine the industry's cohesion. Throughout the 1940s, two powerful industry trade organizations—the American Society of Composers, Authors and Publishers (ASCAP) and Broadcast Music Incorporated (BMI)—skirmished over lucrative music broadcast rights and royalties. ASCAP, representing the interests of the Tin Pan Alley music publishers, insisted that radio stations pay expensive licensing fees in order to use ASCAP songs; in response, the owners of radio stations formed BMI to secure the broadcast rights to other, cheaper sources of music. Impelled to look beyond New York City, BMI gained access to the catalogs of publishers that specialized in regional forms of music—black gospel, white southern gospel, folk, and especially country and rhythm and blues. Although the continued demand for Tin Pan Alley songs forced the station owners to capitulate to many of ASCAP's demands, by the end of the decade radio was beginning to shift the public's listening habits. Between 1947 and 1951 BMI music constituted about 20 percent of all radio musical performances.

At the same time, the radio industry was becoming rapidly decentralized. In 1946 the Federal Communications Commission decided to loosen broadcast standards so that more radio stations could be located in individual markets. A period of explosive growth ensued, as the number of AM stations jumped from 943 in 1945 to 2,127 in 1949. Dozens of stations were shoehorned into urban markets, while the powerful clear-channel stations that had dominated rural markets gave way to hundreds of small-town stations. During these years, television was established as a new force in the entertainment field, raiding the national radio networks for popular performers such as Jack Benny, Bob Hope, and Edgar Bergen; the revenue generated by national advertising campaigns followed the stars. The typical programming fare of network radio—comedy shows, soap operas, and adventure serials—found a new home on television. The radio networks declined precipitously: at the end of the war, 95 percent of all radio stations were affiliated with one of the national networks, while barely 50 percent were affiliated in 1952. Radio became a local business, dependent on local programming and local advertising dollars.

Thus, by the early 1950s, the radio industry's traditional audience was slipping away to television, and the dispute with ASCAP was causing radio to shun the traditional Tin Pan Alley pop song. The industry needed fresh broadcasting material to appeal to its new local markets. The technology of magnetic tape recording met this need. In 1950 Ampex introduced a low-priced, professional-quality tape recorder, intended specifically for small businesses. It became possible to enter the record business for about a thousand dollars, the cost to buy a tape recorder and to press a batch of five hundred discs. Small entrepreneurs joked that the only other overhead necessary was a desk, a telephone, and an attorney, and many of them operated out of basements or spare rooms, with distribution taking place from a car trunk. Hundreds of new record labels were formed, and the handful of older independent labels became more profitable. These labels tapped into fertile musical markets that had been ignored by the majors. In Houston, a nightclub owner with reputed underworld ties, Don Robey, ran one of the first record labels to be owned by African Americans, Peacock Records; the company recorded black gospel groups from across the nation, including the Dixie Hummingbirds and the Five Blind Boys of Mississippi. In Chicago, two brothers, Leonard and Philip Chess, set up the studio of Chess Records in the rear of a store, hanging a microphone in a small bathroom to create acoustical effects; the label recorded blues artists from the city's South Side, including Muddy Waters and Howlin' Wolf. In Cincinnati, Syd Nathan operated King Records in a former icehouse. During the war, the city's industries had drawn tens of thousands of black workers from the South and white workers from Appalachia. Nathan decided to appeal to both consumer groups, developing a roster of artists that featured rhythm and blues stars Wynonie Harris and Bull Moose Jackson alongside country performers Grandpa Jones and Cowboy Copas. When the label had a hit in one musical style, Nathan often promptly recorded the same song in the other. According to King producer Henry Glover, Nathan had a "notion of American music as not being segregated into different styles, but one big cross-ethnic whole. He did that because it was a way to make money." [5]

Local radio stations, more attuned to the tastes of local audiences than the national radio networks, began to program the musical output of the independent labels heavily. By the mid-1950s, more than six hundred stations had switched their programming to include rhythm and blues and black gospel music; at the same time, these programs increasingly attracted young white listeners. For example, Alan Freed, an influential disc jockey in Cleveland, drew a large, racially mixed audience with his program that featured risqué rhythm and blues songs such as the Moonlighters' "Work with Me, Annie" and the Dominoes' "Sixty Minute Man." When the press hounded him out of Cleveland, Freed moved his show to New York City, where his promotional skills were such that new records sold thousands of copies the day after he played them. As young white audiences came to embrace black music, white performers such as Bill Haley and Elvis Presley began to copy it, adding a black rhythmic drive to country music forms, and rock 'n' roll was born. The major labels at first combated the popularity of rock 'n' roll through their practice of offering homogenized "cover" versions of hit songs, but these ultimately succeeded only in propelling black musical forms into the mainstream. Audiences quickly grew to prefer the original versions of rock 'n' roll songs; in 1956 records by Fats Domino, Little Richard, and Chuck Berry outsold versions by white performers. By 1958, the four largest record companies—Columbia, RCA Victor, Decca, and

Capitol—could claim only 36 percent of the records on the *Billboard* hit charts.

Many musicologists have commented on how the content of rock 'n' roll music—with its fast beat, casual lyrics, and emphasis on transitory excitement—was complemented by the means through which it was received by listeners. Handheld transistor radios and car radios became widely available by the early 1960s, a by-product of research conducted by American space agencies, with their imperative for miniaturized electronics. The lightweight 45 rpm vinyl disc, initially introduced by RCA in 1948, became popular during the mid-1950s; the rock 'n' roll audience listened to 45s on small plastic record players, which were sold at the low price of $12.95. Teenagers used these products so that they could have their music with them everywhere—in their bedrooms, in their cars, in their shirt pockets, bulging with radios. They took their 45s to the homes of friends, rifling through them, throwing them onto the turntable, taking them off at a whim; this behavior was perhaps reinforced by the widespread "Top 40" radio programs, with their one-hit wonders and rapid-fire disc jockeys. As the rock historian Carl Belz has pointed out, the 45 record encouraged an offhanded familiarity and an immediacy in the listener's experience of rock 'n' roll that reflected the music itself.[6] Indeed, for teenagers the objects of rock 'n' roll were part of the meaning of the music.

During the 1950s, popular music underwent several fundamental changes that were catalyzed by technological innovations. The means of musical production became more decentralized, and this yielded a popular music that was more democratic, in which previously marginalized idioms were accepted, in their original styles or in the mongrel style of rock 'n' roll, by mainstream audiences. In addition, musical consumption became increasingly democratized: any teenager with pocket money could take part in the world of rock 'n' roll, and the music was bound to commonplace objects—a cheap radio, a stack of 45s. In the words of musicologist Peter Wicke, for these listeners popular music became "an experience of art embedded in everyday life."[7]

In 1950, music critic Edward Tatnall Canby wrote in the *Saturday Review of Literature* of his "astonishment" at the process used to create popular songs: "First, the instrumentalists record their parts on tape. Then, perhaps weeks later, the vocalist comes along, listens to the recorded accompaniment (via earphones, I suppose) and records a separate vocal sound track. Finally the engineers re-record both into a blend . . . . Vocalist and instrumentalist may never meet in the flesh, and there is never an 'original.' . . . How far ought we to go?"[8] Canby's remarks reflected the common wisdom of the American recorded music industry prior to the introduction of magnetic tape: records were based on an "original"—a composed score or song—and the goal of recording was fidelity to an organic musical performance. Musicologists have suggested that this approach to recording reflected the biases of high culture.[9] In classical and operatic forms of music, the performance of the composition was considered sacrosanct, not to be tampered with. For example, *Saturday Review* attacked the "tastelessness" of recordings that used engineering techniques to make familiar symphonies sound more exciting, claiming that this played to the "esthetically infantile segments of the musical public—enormous though those segments may be."[10] High-culture aesthetics demanded sonic realism. For much of the first half of the twentieth century, this standard was also applied to popular music. Advertisements fetishized "high fidelity," boasting that phonographic equipment would bring "the living artist" into the listener's home. The Tin Pan Alley song, with its well-constructed melody and lyrics, was privileged; the record merely served as the medium that faithfully presented the performance of the song.

The use of magnetic tape technology led to a radical departure from these notions. As rock 'n' roll composers Jerry Leiber and Mike Stoller insisted, "We didn't write songs, we wrote records."[11] During the 1950s and 1960s, popular music was increasingly made with sounds—human voices, musical instruments, palpable rhythms—that were manipulated on tape. The sounds on a record became as important and expressive as the song. As the technology developed, many records were constructed with sounds that were impossible for musicians to perform, incapable of creation outside the recording studio.

The preeminent figure in the development of tape-recording techniques was Les Paul, a virtuoso guitarist with jazz and country bands and an inveterate tinkerer in the studio. In 1949, Bing Crosby, for whom the guitarist had worked on radio shows, gave Paul an Ampex tape machine. Paul immediately set about experimenting with the machine, modifying it to see if he could produce different effects. One that he hoped to achieve was an echo. "I didn't want an echo chamber," he later recalled. "If that was the case, I'd record in the bathroom. I didn't want reverb. It was just a clean, repeat echo I was looking for."[12] He found that by reconfiguring the machine with the playback head directly behind the record head, sounds could be recorded and then, milliseconds later, played and fed back to the tape, creating what came to be known as "slapback"; this gave the sounds added resonance. Slapback became one of the trademarks of rock 'n' roll, featured most famously on Elvis Presley's early recordings. Presley's producer, Sam Phillips at Sun Records in Memphis, used slapback liberally to emphasize the beat; the result was records on which all the performers—including Presley, as vocalist—sounded like a rhythm section. An even more significant technique developed by Paul was what he called "sound on sound" recording. Using two tape machines, he first recorded a track—for instance, a drum part, by tapping on the strings of his guitar—and then played this back on tape while playing another part on his guitar, such as the bass line, simultaneously recording both the initial track and his own additional playing. He then continued this process, adding countermelodies and intricate guitar lines, ultimately assembling as many as a dozen overdubs. Using only magnetic tape and his guitar, Paul was able to create a complex, layered sound. With his wife, singer Mary Ford, he released several records that were hailed for their sonic quality, culminating with the number-one hit "How High the Moon" in 1951.

Paul's "sound on sound" efforts were painstaking and labor intensive, but technology soon developed that made multitrack recording a simpler process. The first stereophonic, two-channel tape recorder was introduced in 1954, and a four-channel machine followed in 1958. Several tracks could now be laid down on an inch-wide strip of magnetic tape; the sounds on each track could be manipulated, then combined and balanced on a single track in a mixing session, which freed up the other tracks to record yet more sounds. Significantly, the great majority of record companies were slow to grasp the potential of multitracking. Engineers used dual-track machines to record basic vocal and instrumental tracks, but little else. In part, this was due to a practical reason: the typical recording session was only three hours long, during which time musicians and engineers were expected to cut four songs. "If you couldn't balance a rhythm section and pull up a good level on the horns within five minutes," producer Phil Ramone later remembered, "you were not considered good enough to work with the pros. So the clock often determined what a record would sound like."[13] Musicologists have offered additional explanations: the inherent conservatism of the record industry, which tended to use new technology "to do old things more efficiently or cheaply rather than to do new things";[14] the continued influence of the realist recording aesthetic; and the attitude that popular music (especially for young listeners) was a disposable, formulaic "product" not worthy of extensive attention. During the late 1950s and early 1960s, at a time when the available technology offered expanded creative possibilities, many companies chose to produce a bland form of rock 'n' roll, promoting teen idols such as Frankie Avalon and Paul Anka.

The most creative work in multitracking was carried on outside the industry's mainstream. In Clovis, New Mexico, Buddy Holly, who had been dropped by the major label Decca, teamed with producer Norman Petty on records that featured a dubbing process known as double-tracking. For songs such as "Words of Love" (1957), similar vocal tracks were recorded and layered on top of each other using brief delays; the result multiplied Holly's single voice into voices singing harmony. The independent label Atlantic Records made innovative use of microphones to isolate individual instruments on tape, which made for a crisp, brilliant sound on records by soul artists such as Ray Charles. The company also mixed and matched musicians from studios in different parts of the country: string sections in New York City provided tracks that were combined on tape with music by horn players in Muscle Shoals, Alabama. In Los Angeles, producer Phil Spector, citing classical composer Richard Wagner as his influence, announced his plan to create "little symphonies for the kids." [15] The first pop music producer to be acclaimed as an artist, he enjoyed a string of hits in the early 1960s. His "wall of sound" approach, exemplified by records such as the "Da Doo Ron Ron" by the Crystals, utilized a small army of instruments—three pianos, five or six guitars, three drum sets, violins, saxophones, and more—all fed into a dozen microphones. "Sometimes there might be an acoustic guitar playing and I wasn't able to have a live mic on it, so he never got heard," recording engineer Larry Levine recalled. "[Spector's] philosophy was that even if we couldn't hear the guitar in the booth, the sound might just change, however subtly, if that musician walked out." [16] Spector gave equal emphasis to the various recorded sounds—the instruments, singly and together, and the ambient sounds of the studio—then augmented them by using echoes and tape loops. The result was an overpowering mix that "would pour out of a transistor radio like cake batter." [17]

Inspired by Spector, the Beatles, under the tutelage of producer George Martin, became the first popular music group to take full advantage of multitracking. Four-track tape machines were installed at the Abbey Road studio in London in 1963, and within a year the group was producing songs such as "A Hard Day's Night," which featured elaborate overdubbing. By the mid-1960s, the Beatles were creating psychedelic bricolage and other artificial soundscapes by varying tape speeds, running tape in reverse, and assembling tape segments at random. Their albums *Rubber Soul* (1965) and *Revolver* (1966) served as a measuring stick for Brian Wilson, who had become interested in studio techniques as a member of the Beach Boys. He later noted that he felt a "burning, overwhelming need" to "make music on a real deep level" that would top the Beatles;[18] in return, Paul McCartney of the Beatles admitted that the group was spurred by a mixture of admiration and envy upon hearing Wilson's work. This creative rivalry was emblematic of the growth of rock 'n' roll into serious, selfconsciously artistic rock music. For the album *Pet Sounds* (1966), Wilson used an eight-track tape machine to concoct unique sound combinations. The album featured spacious, cascading harmonies—the result of complicated multitracking—as well as bowed cellos, tympani, glockenspiels, kazoos, finger cymbals, and bicycle bells. Although Wilson was practically illiterate as a formal songwriter—colleagues observed that he put the stems on the wrong side of notes—he would enter the studio with a vague notion of what he wanted from the musicians, and the songs developed through experimentation. Such a creative process broke all the traditional rules about studio time. For example, to produce the single "Good Vibrations" (1966), he directed seventeen sessions over a period of five months, spending approximately $75,000, more than the cost of the production of the typical full-length album.

The new seriousness of rock music was partly derived from the means through which it was disseminated—the 33 rpm long-play record. From the time of its introduction in 1948 by Columbia Records, the LP had been identified with "good" music, particularly with classical and jazz performances that were showcased for the high-end audiophile market. As rock historian Carl Belz has explained, the LP, which held twenty to twenty-five minutes of music on each side, suggested the purposeful commitment of both the artist who recorded it and the listener who played it.[19] Among the first popular singers to take advantage of the format was Frank Sinatra, who released a series of acclaimed "concept" albums, such as *In the Wee Small Hours* (1955), on Capitol. During the mid-1960s, rock musicians began to create their own "concept" albums, such as *Pet Sounds*, *Freak Out!* (1966) by Frank Zappa, and *Sgt. Pepper's Lonely Hearts Club Band* (1967) by the Beatles. When *Sgt. Pepper* proved to be an overwhelming success, critically and commercially, the LP was legitimated as the proper forum for popular music expression. For performers from all genres, it became increasingly unacceptable to release LPs that included two or three potential hit singles and several cuts of "filler." Country musician Merle Haggard, soul singer Marvin Gaye, even the pop band the Young Rascals—all announced their artistic intentions by crafting thematically coherent albums. The various elements of the album were often used to attest to its worth: while listening to the music, fans could study the song lyrics, printed like poetry on the inner jacket or record sleeve, read liner notes written by distinguished critics, and parse the artwork on the cover for meanings.

The technology of the 1960s recording studio had a complex impact on popular music making. The hierarchy that had previously existed at most record companies—in which company producers and A&R men directed short recording sessions and musicians simply did as they were told—gave way to a paradigm that empowered some musicians. Perceived by the public as important artists, Wilson, Zappa, the Beatles, and others were given a great deal of autonomy in the studio. These multitalented, "hyphenated" performers—"the singer-songwriter-producer-engineer-musician-sound designer"[20]—wielded real power at all stages of the recording process. Other musicians, less technologically astute, had little say. For example, while Wilson produced *Pet Sounds*, the other members of the Beach Boys contributed vocals but were otherwise silenced at the studio, not even allowed to play their instruments. A new hierarchy developed around technological production—whether accomplished by a musician, a producer, or an engineer—which was seen as the central creative activity. Technology also turned music making into a fragmentary process. Musicians rarely played together in the studio, but instead were isolated by baffles so that sounds would not leak during recording. Because songs were explored in piece-meal fashion rather than composed, musicians were often required to play end-less retakes of bits of music, with little sense of how their work would ultimately fit on a record. Every note they played was analyzed separately and then manip-ulated by an arsenal of devices—pitch shifters, delay lines, equalizers, limiters, compressors, and reverb units. The result was the objectification and disem-bodiment of what had once been a spontaneous, collective process.[21]

During the 1970s, some critics, musicians, and fans began to question the authenticity of popular music. Some sounds were dismissed as formularized, "perfected" in the studio until they had become glossy and banal, while others were championed as raw and true. Important new musical movements and genres developed that were based, in part, on a rejection of prevalent studio techniques. In Austin, Texas, country musicians such as Willie Nelson and Waylon Jennings became disenchanted with the commercial "Nashville sound," a style that tried to appeal to both pop and country audiences by eliminating traditional instruments such as the fiddle and steel guitar, replacing them with horn sections, soothing backup vocal choruses, and relentless use of echo. Their "Outlaw" movement, a rebellion against the Nashville establishment, sought to replicate the uncomplicated sounds of older forms of country music. In New York City, the Ramones, who were part of an avant-garde punk scene, mocked the artistic pretensions of rock performers by creating brief, crude songs about subjects such as sniffing glue. Rejecting as "bourgeois" the sixteen- and twenty-four-track tape recorders that were commonplace in studios, punk groups in London and Los Angeles proclaimed that their records were "lo-fi" and in "mono-enhanced stereo."[22] One of the ironies of the punk movement was that it cited as authentic the energetic rock 'n' roll of the 1950s—music that had often been the product of the advanced studio techniques of its day. As mu-sicologist Steve Jones has pointed out, another irony is that technology allowed punks and purists to "cook" sounds in the studio until they sounded raw.[23]

In 1982, American consumers purchased approximately 273 million LPs. Four years later, LP sales had plummeted to around 110 million, and by the mid-1990s, the record and the record player—the staples of the recorded music in-dustry since its early days—had become insignificant in the marketplace. They were supplanted by two new devices, the compact disc and the compact disc player, that utilized a new technology, digital recording. In 1982 two corpora-tions, Philips and Sony, collaborated on the introduction of the compact disc. Twelve centimeters wide and about the thickness of a dime, the compact disc was a piece of clear polycarbonate plastic, coated with a layer of aluminum and a layer of lacquer, that stored up to seventy-four minutes of essentially perfect sound. Actually, the disc did not carry sound at all; unlike analog recording mediums such as the record and magnetic tape, which captured the actual pattern of sound waves, the compact disc functioned through the use of binary digits—strings of ones and zeroes—that represented sound. As the writer Frederick Turner has suggested, "It is as if . . . you could write the names of foods so that if you ate the paper on which they were written it would be more tasty and nourishing than the foods themselves." [24] Impressed on the disc was a track of microscopic pits and flat spaces, each signifying a one or a zero, that began at the center of the disc and spiraled outward to the edge; if the track were to be laid out in a straight line, it would extend for more than three miles. The compact disc player utilized a laser beam to reflect light off the track, and a microprocessor interpreted the variations in reflectivity as the digital information, which was then converted into analog sound signals. This laser "reading" method created no surface noise at playback, solving a common problem of previous recording technologies.

The idea for the digitalization of sound originated in the telephone industry, where engineers worked to develop a transmission method that would squeeze more conversations onto phone lines. They hoped to implement a theorem proved in 1929 by physicist and inventor Harry Nyquist, which held that a continuous sound signal could be accurately reconstructed from isolated samples if there were twice as many samples taken per second as the highest frequency of the sound. By transmitting samples instead of a continuous signal, the companies could save space. In 1937 an engineer in France, Alec H. Reeves, devised a process called pulse-code modulation, by which the sound signal was sliced into sample pulses, at a rate of thousands of pulses per second, that were then coded with binary values. The amount of data involved, however, made this nothing more than an intriguing possibility. For example, during World War II, a telephone "hot line" between British prime minister Winston Churchill and American president Franklin Roosevelt utilized a related method of sending coded signals; the equipment required for this single line was so large that it filled the basement of a London department store. Not until 1959, with the invention of the integrated circuit, could pulse-code modulation be practically realized. In 1962 the first pulse-coded telephone conversation was transmitted. The rapid evolution of computer microchips during the 1960s and 1970s, which enabled the storage of enormous amounts of data, made the process a viable method for the recorded music industry.

There were several advantages to digitalization. An analog audio signal replicated the waveform of a sound, the fluctuations of the pattern recorded on magnetic tape or in a record groove matching the variations in air pressure caused by the sound. While analog information eventually deteriorated as records and tapes underwent wear and tear, digital data remained pristine, the same each time it was retrieved and converted into sound. Likewise, it could be copied with no generation loss. As digital audio expert John Watkinson aptly puts it, the copy was a "clone," not a "dub":[25] the strings of numbers represented on a compact disc were the same as the ones recorded by a musician in a studio. Digitalization also allowed for the easy editing of music. Rather than splice tape and rewind and fast forward to search for edit points, musicians called up waveforms on a computer screen, analyzing and tweaking them with programs that functioned like word processors. Hundreds of edits could be performed on a few seconds of sound. While a tape cut was permanent, a digital edit was merely stored on a computer, where it could be retrieved and changed again.

Along with the compact disc, an array of digital music devices was introduced during the late 1970s and early 1980s—drum machines, samplers, sequencers, and synthesizers. One of the significant aspects of these innovations was their affordability, which reflected the ever-decreasing costs of microprocessors. This put powerful music-making capabilities into the hands of average consumers. For example, the analog synthesizer had been a favorite instrument of progressive rock fans in the 1970s, but it was costly and difficult to program. The Minimoog, perhaps the most popular analog synthesizer, sold 12,000 units during the decade. In 1983 Yamaha brought out an inexpensive, user-friendly digital synthesizer, the DX7, which promptly sold 200,000 units in its first three years of release. The musicologist Paul Théberge has pointed out the importance of Casio, a company that sold more than ten million digital keyboards and samplers at department stores and shopping malls during the 1980s. Although scorned by professionals, these devices made a generation of aspiring amateurs comfortable with digital processes.[26] In 1983, the various digital instruments on the market were linked together when manufacturers adopted a common specification for digital signals, the Music Instrument Digital Interface (MIDI). Developed by Yamaha, which offered the patent for free, MIDI allowed all equipment to "speak the same language." The affordability and compatibility of digital machines, which could be controlled through a home computer, had a profound impact on music production, blurring the line between professional and amateur, musician and nonmusician.

Nowhere was this more evident than in the use of samplers and sequencers. In a traditional recording studio, every aspect of a song was performed at some point, even if it was then manipulated into unperformable music on tape; but by using samplers and sequencers it became possible to make music without playing a single note. Samplers stored digital audio information from any number of sources—rhythm tracks and melodic "hooks" from old records, bits of dialogue from films or commercials, real-life "found" sounds such as glass breaking and industrial machines in operation. Samplers also featured built-in libraries with thousands of sound patches; the influence of world music on American pop songs during the 1980s and 1990s can be attributed in part to the patches of Japanese bamboo flutes, Australian Aboriginal didgeridoo, and the like that were programmed into samplers. Sequencers analyzed, manipulated, and stored digital information about the parameters of sound, such as pitches, note durations, and tone colors. For example, a user unable to play the drums could program on a sequencer not only the complex rhythms but also the feel of an actual drum performance, including randomizing the beats by tiny increments so that the rhythm would be slightly off, thus replicating a human, imperfect drummer. Using this digital equipment, a new kind of virtuoso popular musician emerged, one who created complex audio collages. The British group M/A/R/R/S had a major pop hit in America in 1989 with the song "Pump Up the Volume," which sampled from more than thirty sources. In 1996 the American musician DJ Shadow produced the influential compact disc *Introducing,* utilizing no "instruments" other than a sampler, sequencer, and turntable. His recordings, which have been called masterpieces of "used-bin incidentalia," were cut-and-pasted together from a huge record collection.[27]

New popular music genres developed that were characterized by the use—and deliberate misuse—of inexpensive technology, often by economically underprivileged young people in urban areas. The Roland-808 drum machine became a staple of hip-hop recording studios because it could be detuned to produce a heavy, distorted bass sound. Poor-quality engineering boards were prized for the sounds they made. For example, hip-hop producer Eric Sadler of the group Public Enemy described his alternation between two boards: one was "old, . . . disgusting, a lot of stuff doesn't work, there are fuses out," which created a "dirty" sound, while the other made sounds that were "all sweet and crispy clear, it's like the Star Wars room."[28] Machines that failed in the marketplace and became widely available in secondhand stores, such as the Roland TB-303 Bassline, were central to dance-music genres such as house and techno. The limitations of these machines—their robotic, droning sound quality—became the hallmarks of music that relied on minimalism and repetition to create trancelike effects.

As new types of music were made, notions of authenticity and artistry in popular music began to change. Hip-hop was hailed as a significant form of African American vernacular expression, a folk music predicated on the creative and prominent use of technology. Pop music fans may have been outraged in 1990 when it was revealed that members of the group Milli Vanilli, which had won a Grammy Award for best new artist, were in fact models who lip-synched over vocals recorded by studio singers; but there was no outcry the same year when *Rolling Stone* magazine revealed that more than 25 percent of the music heard at arena shows was prerecorded. The lionization of the rock star persona that had been common during the 1960s and 1970s—the musician perceived as an auteur and source of spectacle, communicating to fans through albums and concerts—gave way in some genres to a performer/audience paradigm that was less hierarchical. Musicologists have pointed in particular to the club DJ in electronic dance music as a new kind of performer. Not a musician, he (rarely she) was nevertheless perceived as an artist, using dual turntables, a mixer, and a powerful sound system to create tension and climaxes on the dance floor. Although he was the club's star attraction, he usually remained hidden in a control booth, and his primary role was to react to the crowd, constantly evaluating its energy level and mood and working to produce an appropriate musical atmosphere. Club culture musicologist Sarah Thornton has suggested that in dance clubs, with no star musicians to watch as in a rock concert, the audience—the crowd of dancers—provided spectacle and artistry.[29]

Listeners, too, were involved in creative processes, using technology to make their own meanings out of music. Various playback machines gave them more control over what they heard, in a sense turning the consumption of music into a form of production. A landmark technology in this regard was the cassette tape, introduced in 1963 by Philips. The cassette, which ran for forty-five minutes on each side, enabled consumers to tape music from records, other tapes, or the radio. They could essentially construct their own albums, putting together a mix tape of their favorite songs. In 1980 Sony introduced the Walkman, a miniature tape player/headphone device that allowed users to listen to their cassettes wherever they wished. Recorded music became eminently portable and was often linked to everyday activities such as jogging or riding the subway. Wearing Walkman headphones, listeners could drown out the sounds around them and impose their own. Cultural critics viewed this behavior either as evidence of the "atomization" of modern society or as a new opportunity for creativity in daily life by making soundscapes out of one's surroundings.

The compact disc player gave consumers a great deal of latitude in how they listened to a compact disc. They could skip easily to particular tracks or program tracks in whatever sequence was desired, including leaving off songs they disliked. During the 1990s compact disc changers came on the market, featuring multiple disc trays, which permitted users to program tracks from several discs simultaneously. A five-CD changer gave the listener programming control over 370 minutes of music. Rock listeners during the 1960s had often learned albums by listening to LP sides; artists placed four or five tracks in a deliberate sequence on a side, and listeners came to anticipate this sequence, which became part of the meaning of the album. The compact disc nullified this particular source of meaning: not only were there no sides, but the sequence of songs chosen by the artist could also be easily superseded by the listener's own choice of sequencing.

Increased consumer control proved problematic for the recorded music industry. In 1980 a study concluded that the industry was losing as much as $800 million in revenue annually because of the practice of home taping, by which consumers used cassettes to duplicate albums without purchasing them. A series of congressional hearings ensued over proprietary and copyright issues, with the music industry insisting that a compensatory tax be added to sales of tape recorders and blank tapes, opposed by lobbyist groups representing consumers and recording-equipment manufacturers. Although several European countries imposed similar taxes, in the United States the right of consumers to make recordings was reaffirmed. However, the music industry was successful in the early 1990s in convincing Congress to add a royalty to the sale of digital audio tape (DAT), which hampered the widespread use of a format that enabled the duplication of compact discs with no loss of sound quality. The development in the late 1990s of the MP3 (MPEG-1 Audio Layer 3), a technology that compressed digital music files and allowed them to be easily downloaded from the Internet, caused further serious headaches for the industry. The Internet company Napster made possible MP3 file sharing between peers; the process was widely utilized by college students, who reportedly swapped more than 135,000 copyright-protected songs in 2000. Successful lawsuits by record companies and artists forced Napster into bankruptcy in 2002—but many similar, sometimes clandestine Internet sites emerged to take Napster's place. From their experiences with home taping and file sharing, consumers clearly had expectations about being allowed to duplicate recorded music, and music companies were placed in the difficult position of alienating their customers through their demands for anticopying protections.

During the 1980s and 1990s, the widespread dispersion of the means of music production had a significant impact on the popular music industry. The economics of the business became somewhat less demanding. Because musicians could produce professional-quality work using their home computers, labels assumed less financial risk when they signed new artists. Producer Miles Copeland explained the process: "I've had a lot of music brought into me . . . that's super quality and I'd say, 'You know what? I'm willing to take a shot on this.' 'Cause I'm not being roasted into spending fortunes in a studio and I can hear the thing finished. I can listen and say, 'Wow, this is what I'm paying for.'"[30] At the same time, the role of independent labels was strengthened. Industry observers noted that the structure of the business that had existed in previous decades—major companies and independent labels operating in competition, with the most successful independents eventually being bought out—evolved toward greater flexibility and symbiosis. As musicologist Simon Frith has pointed out, independents served as a kind of "research and development department" with loose links to the conglomerates, finding and nurturing new talent until the artists were ready for crossover stardom.[31] Many successful independents operated with relative autonomy but signed promotion and distribution agreements with larger organizations so that their acts could be widely exposed. The music of thriving regional "scenes"—in large cities such as Seattle and in college towns such as Athens, Georgia—quickly became available to listeners across the country.

The result was a richer musical landscape. Popular music in all its forms, its very history, became ubiquitous. The introduction of the compact disc led music companies to reissue their analog recordings using digital technology; an immense catalog of works, old and new, from all over the world, was readily accessible. Popular music was "sampled" in everyday experience: people heard snippets of Madonna and hip-hop and "Louie Louie" and Al Green and hard rock and Johnny Cash at random in a multitude of places. One might argue that given the democratized circumstances of music making and music listening, Walter Benjamin's predictions about the "aura" of art being broken by reproduction technology came true. Something was surely lost in this stripping of music of its specialness; but at the same time, music in all its diversity became an inevitable part of American life.

BIBLIOGRAPHIC NOTE

An in-depth history of the interrelationship between popular music and technology is André Millard, *America on Record: A History of Recorded Sound* (1995). Michael Chanan's *Repeated Takes: A Short History of Recording and Its Effects on Music* (1995) is a cogent consideration of the same subject. Roland Gelatt, in *The Fabulous Phonograph, 1877–1977* (1977), provides a history of the development of the phonograph. Evan Eisenberg's elegantly written *The Recording Angel: The Experience of Music from Aristotle to Zappa* (1987) considers the effects of recording technology on the experience of listening to music. Simon Frith, a leading pop musicologist, has written several valuable books and articles that deal with music technology, among other topics. Especially relevant are *Performing Rites: On the Value of Popular Music* (1996) and "Art versus Technology: The Strange Case of Popular Music," *Media, Culture and Society* 8 (1986): 263–279.

Among books dealing with popular music and cultural theory, Peter J. Martin's *Sounds and Society: Themes in the Sociology of Music* (1995) is comprehensive and quite readable. Jason Toynbee's *Making Popular Music: Musicians, Creativity and Institutions* (2000) offers a theoretical study of the role of popular musicians, with particular attention to electronic dance music. A useful primer on theorists such as Theodor Adorno and Walter Benjamin is provided by Paul du Gay et al. in *Doing Cultural Studies: The Story of the Sony Walkman* (1997).

One of the best studies of rock 'n' roll, focusing on its institutional context, is Philip H. Ennis's *The Emergence of Rock 'n' Roll in American Popular Music* (1992). Carl Belz's *The Story of Rock* (1969) is dated but insightful. Mark Cunningham's *Good Vibrations: A History of Record Production* (1996) considers the studio creation of rock music, although the focus is on British musicians. German critic Peter Wicke's *Rock Music: Culture, Aesthetics and Sociology* (1987), is an essential musicological study of rock.

Paul Théberge's *Any Sound You Can Imagine: Making Music/Consuming Technology* (1997) analyzes the effects of digital technology on music making. Steve Jones's *Rock Formation: Music, Technology, and Mass Communication* (1992) addresses some of the same issues. Tricia Rose's *Black Noise: Rap Music and Black Culture in Contemporary America* (1994) is one of the most insightful studies on hip-hop. For information on the diverse genres of electronic dance music, see Peter Shapiro, ed., *Modulations: A History of Electronic Music: Throbbing Words on Sound* (2000). See also Sarah Thornton's musicological study *Club Cultures: Music, Media and Subcultural Capital* (1995). For an interesting consideration of sampling, see Andrew Goodwin, "Sample and Hold: Pop Music in the Digital Age of Reproduction," in *On Record: Rock, Pop, and the Written Word*, ed. Simon Frith and Andrew Goodwin, 258–274 (1990).

NOTES

1. André Millard, *America on Record: A History of Recorded Sound* (Cambridge: Cambridge University Press, 1995), 341.

2. Tricia Rose, *Black Noise: Rap Music and Black Culture in Contemporary America* (Hanover, N.H.: Wesleyan University Press, 1994), 52.

3. UK Patent No. 8961 (1899).

4. John T. Mullin, "Creating the Craft of Tape Recording," *High Fidelity*, April 1976, 67.

5. Quoted in Rick Kennedy and Randy McNutt, *Little Labels—Big Sound: Small Record Companies and the Rise of American Music* (Bloomington: Indiana University Press, 1999), 64.

6. Carl Belz, *The Story of Rock* (New York: Oxford University Press, 1969), 54–55.

7. Peter Wicke, *Rock Music: Culture, Aesthetics, and Sociology* (New York: Cambridge University Press, 1990), 25.

8. E. T. Canby, "Sound Editing," *Saturday Review of Literature*, 28 January 1950, 71.

9. See, for example, David Morton, *Off the Record: The Technology and Culture of Sound Recording in America* (New Brunswick, N.J.: Rutgers University Press, 2000), 13–47; and Evan Eisenberg, *The Recording Angel: The Experience of Music from Aristotle to Zappa* (New York: Viking Penguin, 1988), 116–122.

10. R. D. Darrell, "Chromium-Plated Vulgarity," *Saturday Review of Literature*, 25 December 1954, 56.

11. Quoted in Jon Pareles and Patricia Romanowski, *The Rolling Stone Encyclopedia of Rock & Roll* (New York: Rolling Stone Press, 1983), 322.

12. Quoted in Mark Cunningham, *Good Vibrations: A History of Record Production* (Chessington, England: Castle Communications, 1996), 24.

13. Quoted in ibid., 53.

14. Simon Frith, "Art versus Technology: The Strange Case of Popular Music," *Media, Culture and Society* 8 (1986): 272.

15. Quoted in Richard Williams, *Out of His Head: The Sound of Phil Spector* (New York: Outerbridge and Lazard, 1972), 82.

16. Quoted in Cunningham, *Good Vibrations*, 58.

17. Mark Ribowsky, *He's a Rebel* (New York: Dutton, 1989), 119.

18. Quoted in Cunningham, *Good Vibrations*, 67.

19. Belz, *The Story of Rock*, 55.

20. Paul Théberge, *Any Sound You Can Imagine: Making Music/Consuming Technology* (Hanover, N.H.: Wesleyan University Press, 1997), 221–222.

21. Ibid., 221.

22. Jon Savage, *England's Dreaming* (New York: St. Martin's, 1992), 215.

23. Steve Jones, *Rock Formation: Music, Technology, and Mass Communication* (Newbury Park, Calif.: Sage, 1992), 67.

24. Frederick Turner, "Escape from Modernism," *Harper's*, November 1986, 48.

25. John Watkinson, *An Introduction to Digital Audio* (Oxford: Focal Press, 1994), 6.

26. Théberge, *Any Sound You Can Imagine*, 74.

27. *All Music Guide to Electronica* (San Francisco: Backbeat Books, 2001), 145.

28. Quoted in Rose, *Black Noise*, 77.

29. Sarah Thornton, *Club Cultures: Music, Media and Subcultural Capital* (Cambridge: Polity Press, 1995), 65.

30. Quoted in Rick Karr, "Profile: New Technology That Revolutionizes the Sound of Recorded Music," National Public Radio, 25 October 2002.

31. Simon Frith, "Video Pop: Picking Up the Pieces," in *Facing the Music*, ed. Simon Frith (New York: Pantheon Books, 1988), 110.

5. BRINGING IT HOME

Children, Technology, and Family in the Postwar World

PAULA S. FASS

The end of the Second World War came with twinned explosions. The nuclear bomb that destroyed Nagasaki, Japan, ended the costliest foreign war in American history. The baby boom that began at the same time ended one hundred years of steadily declining birthrates. Both of these events would have long-lasting consequences, but unlike the searing fireball that mushroomed in the skies over Japan on August 9, 1945, the explosion in fertility in the United States caused neither havoc nor fear. Instead, it seemed to herald new hope and expectations about a much brighter future. Like its twin, however, it would become intimately linked to the brilliant emergence of American technological and economic superiority. The babies born at the time of the bomb could hardly have known it, but the childhoods that they were about to begin and the lives of the children who would follow them until the end of the century would be defined by this fact. Some of the sources of their experience had begun earlier, of course, some of it half a century before. But it was not until the second half of the twentieth century, after America had become a truly international power, that the dimensions and meanings of these changes became clear.

To name a few of the technological changes that these children were about to inherit and create is to gain some sense of the changed dimensions of the world in which they would grow up: atomic and hydrogen bombs; automatic weapons; television, VCRs, CDs; jet travel, satellites, moonwalks, and manned space stations; wireless telephones, silicon chips, personal computers, the Internet; contact lenses and artificial organs; birth control pills, IUDs, in-vitro fertilization, egg donations, and stem cells; freeze-dried foods and microwaves; antibiotics and the polio vaccine; LSD, methamphetamines, Prozac, and Ritalin. Never in the history of the world would a mere two and a half historical generations experience so many fundamental technological breakthroughs. These technologies would affect how they were conceived and born, and how (and when) they discovered the thrills of sex; what they ate and when; how they spent their time in work and in play; what they studied in school. It also affected what was considered a proper childhood.

Some of these changes came so abruptly that each succeeding group of young people seemed altogether different from its predecessor, so much so that journalists began to denominate them separately, calling them generation X or Y. No child in the 1950s could have anticipated childhood in the 1980s, and looking backward, a child in 1995 would have thought that the childhood of his mother in the early 1960s was quaint.

Nevertheless, in looking back over fifty years, we see some continuous trends. The first is a growing sense of alarm that childhood, as it had been understood for a century, was being endangered by all the changes taking place. By the new millenium, more and more Americans worried that childhood as it had been understood for at least a century was disappearing. The second can best be described as an inexorable move toward the social disengagement with childhood and toward the absorption of children into increasingly private places. These two perceptions, as we will see, were related to each other, and both resulted from a disassembling of the role that the family had played as a mediating social institution. As public supports for childhood and family life declined, parents increasingly came to view their children as a form of personal expression, an extension of the self, rather than as their contribution to a socially approved and highly valued common enterprise.

LET THE GOOD TIMES ROLL

Three and four (even five). These were the strange numbers that demographers began to see as they charted the unusual patterns that dominated the graphs of family size by the mid-1950s. Since the early twentieth century, the middle classes had been steadying their sights on the number two, while the working classes, immigrants, and rural populations had wider fluctuations and tended toward larger size. In the 1930s, even these groups had sharply limited the number of children they bore, some settling for very late marriage as a means to do so, or determining to have no children at all in response to the economic hard times. Even immigrants and farmers who had once clung to large families as a mark of pride or God's gift (and an intergenerational form of old-age insurance) had submitted to the new trend. As a result, the birthrate in 1933 stood at an astonishingly low 76.3 percent. Then starting just before the war ended and accelerating to the middle of the 1950s, the patterns swung conspicuously and unexpectedly, among all groups everywhere in the country, far in the other direction. More children, and children born (quite intentionally) closer together early in the marriage became a sign of the new times. Young Americans married earlier and had their children sooner afterward than at any time in the twentieth century. By 1957, the birthrate stood at 122.9 percent, an enormous increase in just twenty-four years.[1] Children seemed to be a sign of the good times people expected to realize after the war, a sign of the conveniences offered by new kitchen appliances and steadier work, a response to rapidly assembled single-family homes in new suburban tracts (financed by the GI Bill of benefits for veterans). Perhaps above all, they seemed to be the product of a commitment to motherhood and fatherhood as goods in themselves.

Since at least the early twentieth century, the fine art of parenting had been placed on the American public agenda as an aspiration and clothed in the rubrics of science. The middle classes had responded with enthusiasm to childrearing manuals, pediatric advice, and psychological and cognitive measures and standards. Behaviorism and then variants of Freudian psychology had infused beliefs about children's proper development, while new nutritional guidelines about calories, concerns about balancing vitamins, and injunctions to sterilize newly standardized infant formulas made parents aware of how strategically they could influence the well-being of their offspring. This desire to raise the physically healthy, psychologically well-adjusted, effectively socialized child had initially developed in the context of a shrinking household and declining childhood mortality, a trend that was obvious by the 1920s. In this context, maternal attention could be effectively concentrated and expectantly rewarded.

After the war, the craving to raise more perfect children had a much larger terrain for expression. Traditional middle-class families grew in size, and with them increased attention to these matters expanded what it meant to be middle-class as defined by standards of domestic stability, steady work made possible by union membership, old-age insurance, and the widespread secondary education of children. The definition of middle-class had also grown through an acculturated second generation of immigrants and rural migrants recently come into the cities during the boom in war industries. Through newspapers, magazines, school guidance clinics, and hospital births as well as pamphlets and books, more and more children began to be raised according to expert advice. In this atmosphere, the childrearing expert had the potential to become something of a public oracle. Very quickly after the war, Dr. Benjamin Spock, a pediatrician with an ear for psychological nuance and a nose for public anxiety, appropriated this role.

Benjamin Spock dominated the raising of the first postwar generation of children like no other single individual—more than any president, more even than any rock 'n' roll star. His advice came neatly bound between the covers of *Baby and Child Care*, first published in 1946 and then repeatedly reissued, revised, expanded, and updated for the next several decades. *Baby and Child Care* had a reserved seat on the best-seller list and was on the shelves of more homes in America than any book other than the Bible, and it was far more likely to be read and followed. One historian has wittily described Dr. Spock as a confidence man, summarizing both the advice he dispensed and the likely role he played in the home (while hinting at the neat trick he was pulling off).[2] He was trusted by tens of millions of parents as he confidently told them how to distinguish between measles and chicken pox, how to tell the difference between serious developmental delays and ordinary willfulness, and when to call the doctor. Knowing that over the course of the century mothers had grown increasingly anxious about their inadequacies (under the tutelage of other child-care experts), he advised them, above all, to relax and enjoy their babies. Avuncular and assured, but also relaxed and user-friendly, Spock's book was just what the culture needed as Americans set themselves the task of raising the largest, best-fed, and best-housed generation in American history. Spock could speak with new assurance to a generation of mothers who could expect to be protected from childbirth infections by sulfa drugs and whose children's doctors administered antibiotics to protect them from the complications of a variety of childhood ailments. Fueled by the war, American prosperity and technology had provided both the wherewithal and the know-how to overcome the many social deficits that Franklin Delano Roosevelt had made a matter of public concern and policy during the Depression. Now Dr. Spock was going to show the country how to bring it home where it counted.

While his advice would change over time, and each household adapted it to its own inclinations, children raised under Spock's aegis could expect to receive little if any physical correction; neither were parents to bully them emotionally. Instead, a child would be raised to participate in a democratically organized household in which his or her views mattered. Children were encouraged to verbalize their emotions and to understand their misbehavior. A Spock-raised child was likely to have had some role in his or her own toilet training. Spock was also sympathetic to the libidinal theories of the Freudians and to their concern that children's instincts not be repressed. By the 1960s, Dr. Spock would be accused of encouraging a "permissive" form of childrearing, one that put the children in control, and he certainly could be read as someone alert to the dangers of raising children on disciplinary techniques that relied on authoritarian methods. But Spock was eager for children's behavior to be directed and corrected, and for parents to teach them to manage their own emotions, rather than to encourage self-indulgence. However far Spock might be read as leading parents toward a child-centered expressiveness, he certainly never allowed parents much room for their own self-indulgence, though he technically encouraged their enjoyment. And historians have not tired of pointing out that it was almost always the mother, as homebody (homemaker was the preferred 1950s word), and would-be apprentice-childrearing expert, now surrounded by a growing clutch of children closely spaced together, who bore the brunt of reading, interpreting, and applying Spock's advice.

The techniques of childrearing were but one of the growing number of technologies that invaded the home after the war. Communications technologies had begun to nest there earlier in the century in the form of the telephone and radio, which allowed voice connections to and from the neighborhood and beyond. Now, after the war, pictures arrived as well. Where cinematic entertainments required a trip down the street, downtown, or into a neighboring town, the television set delivered entertainment into the private home on several channels, and all times of the day. When the first sets with their fine cabinets began to arrive in the homes of the technologically daring in the late 1940s, no one could have foreseen television's potential as a ubiquitous part of daily life or its constant companionship for children growing up. Even in the 1950s, when a majority of Americans became familiar with its blinking features (and frequent malfunctions), it still stood squarely in the middle of the living room—an embodiment of family entertainment. Early-morning children's television programs, like *Ding-Dong School*, were still carefully monitored and educational, and after-school programming like *The Howdy Doody Show* bore the imprint of adult supervision.

It was only in later decades, when the television was released from its furnishings and became portable, that the TV as a personal companion found its way into the bedroom. Then it rapidly fell into the embrace of marketers who targeted its programming to individual audiences, honed by age, and advertisers keen to prey on the sweet teeth of children and their fascination with gadgety toys. In the 1950s, still dominated by cowboys such as the Lone Ranger, Gene Autry, and Roy Rogers, variety shows such as Ed Sullivan's, movie reruns, and slapstick sitcoms, television was already widely used as a means to entertain. It was hardly yet an all-purpose entertainment medium, full of sports and action-dramas, newsmagazines and reality programs, and no one dreamed that it might become the locale for music videos or pornography. But the children of the 1950s were the first to grow up with the possibility of being amused at almost any time of day in a way that required little active participation, effort, or creativity. Here technology seemed to provide them with a free ticket to ride.

Far less free, it soon became clear, were the demands that technology was about to make on their schooling. Since at least the 1920s, one of the marks of American democracy and economic prosperity had been the vast extension of schooling upward into the teen years, years in which previous generations had been forced to work and help their families provide. Where in 1900, a little over 50 percent of white children, ages 5–19, and just over 13 percent of nonwhite children of this age were enrolled in school, by 1960, almost 90 percent of white children and almost as many nonwhites were enrolled. By the later date, over 90 percent of all 14–17 year olds were in school, registering the extraordinary growth in high school attendance during the first half of the twentieth century.[3] This extension had initially been accompanied by very moderate intellectual demands. Instead, the newly comprehensive high schools and junior highs had evolved multiple programs to meet the needs and aspirations of their increasingly diverse populations. Commercial and vocational programs became as familiar across America as the traditional classical and scientific curricula. And now that everyone could be expected to attend (if not to graduate), more effort was expended to satisfy their needs for citizenship and other kinds of energetic engagements. Sports, musicals, dramatics, debate, school government, and school dances, along with many other diversions, began to fill the school day and year.

Since the early twentieth century, progressive educators had guided this development, urging that the needs of the "whole child" be considered in his or her education. Nowhere was this more important than for adolescents who might otherwise leave school and drift off into delinquencies. As a result, by the late 1940s and early 1950s, American children could all expect to go to school and to proceed to high school without being asked to do too much that was intellectually taxing. Schooling was as much about controlling their behavior away from the streets as it was a way of disciplining their minds. By the mid-1950s this extended development had come to be defined as a necessary part of growing up when psychologist Erik Erikson called for a "moratorium," during adolescence that would facilitate ego integration and strength.[4] America's relaxed attitude toward schooled intellect was in sharp contrast to most of the rest of the world, Europe in particular, where entry into the *lycée* or *gymnasium* was highly competitive and selective and adolescent education was seen to serve the purpose of professional preparation, state advancement, and class prerogative. In contrast, American education encouraged youth as a form of transient leisure class, democratically extended to all. That democratic extension had also assured a good measure of assimilation to the children of the enormous group of European newcomers to the United States who arrived in the early twentieth century. For some members of this immigrant second generation, it provided real opportunities for social mobility and professional prominence.

After the war, however, American technological know-how and its new position on the world stage was poised to make new, invigorated demands on this vast though unintegrated, locally controlled form of schooling. The end of the war had left the United States the one and only nuclear power—but not for long. The technological superiority embodied in that briefly held position soon created challenges of all kinds. The most daunting was that created by the rapid technological advancement of the Soviet Union, against which by the late 1940s the United States was engaged in a Cold War, with potential hotspots all over the world. The friction of that conflict, a war of ideologies and nerves, was usually expressed in competitive machinery—more atomic and then more hydrogen bombs, more and better missiles for long-range delivery, more warships and nuclear submarines, more bases around the world. Finally, the conflict was carried out in space. When in 1956 the Soviet Union successfully orbited the *Sputnik* satellite, and followed with orbiting space satellites that contained first animals and then humans, Americans were put on notice that their educational apparatus could be much more effectively utilized. In the 1960s, the United States would catch up with and surpass the Soviets as it landed a man on the moon, but in the 1950s, its earliest space-directed efforts were more likely to result in collapsed booster rockets than successful space orbits.

The federal government had never been more than marginally involved in American public education, although it had helped to establish the great state universities through land grants in the nineteenth century, and it experimented with a variety of school-based welfare programs during the New Deal. But by the late 1950s, the threat of Soviet technological and scientific advantage forced the federal government to seek out means to enlist the public schools in a quest to educate national manpower and womanpower better. Government and industry scouted various means to find scientific talent and encourage greater academic competence. The general tone and sense of a national emergency was one means; the other was talent selection. All schools began to test children's aptitudes more regularly, and the junior high schools and high schools added enriched science and math curricula as well as a host of foreign languages to their programs. Industry and private foundations began talent searches and science fairs. The states spent more money on schooling in general and scientific schooling in particular, and the colleges and universities especially became places in which the federal expenditures could be used to leverage success in the lower schools.

Going to college became a much more widely shared goal in the 1950s and 1960s. One result of the new importance of higher education was a significant expansion in community and junior colleges, which allowed students to develop their skills, and which helped to democratize college attendance. But for many parents and students, true access to higher learning could be achieved only through the more vigorous traditional college curriculum. And those especially keen to succeed through education placed new pressure on the best and most elite schools, which began to feel the new competitive strain by the early 1960s. The *New York Times* began to register the alarm of those eager to go to the best schools. In 1961, Fred Hechinger, the *Times* education reporter, noted the new gloom about competitive application and the tightening of admissions requirements at the Ivy League and other prominent schools. Hechinger also observed the irony of the greater stringency at selective institutions at a time when places in higher education generally were opening up. "Space May be Plentiful, but Not at the Preferred Colleges," one headline read. The article noted that it was that time of year when "high school seniors in hundreds of thousands of families are again waiting for the mailman to bring the crucial letter from the colleges of their choice." [5] When going to college became more competitive, high school became a more meaningful testing ground for the expression of excellence and academic exertion.

Colleges and universities, which by the 1920s were dominated by research agendas and increasingly devoted to innovation, had been central to American success during the war. By the late 1950s and 1960s, the federal government looked to them as strategic places to fund specialized (and often secret) research necessary to American security during the Cold War. Here federal dollars could be spent with the expectation of effective return. The Defense Department and State Department, the various armed services, the Atomic Energy Commission, and the National Science Foundation supported a wide variety of researches in widely dispersed fields. These dollars also expanded available facilities and made colleges more and more central to the success aspirations of American youth.

Going to college became a mark of middle-class standing for the family and a route to future success for the child. The sifting process that would create a competent citizenry and an educated elite that early in the history of the republic Thomas Jefferson had defined as necessary to democratic success was now put at the direct disposal of the state, whose concerns about national security made it eager to find and to train talent. As the schools became more directly linked to this goal and even the least competitive colleges and universities imposed higher admissions standards, students eager for success worked harder and competed with each other in new ways. Children whose opinions had been sought and treasured at home, found themselves repeatedly tested to comply with new academic demands at school. And the members of the biggest birth cohort in the twentieth century, who had recently become known as the "baby boom generation," once carefully socialized to express themselves, faced each other in a stiffer competition to obtain the more desirable college degrees.

The new college-going aspirations also had other unexpected consequences. Unlike other aspects of American education, higher education was never free, although state-funded colleges were certainly much lower in cost than the private colleges and universities whose many varieties were spread all over the American landscape. But students who went to college had to be supported into ever older ages in ways that incurred a variety of costs beyond tuition. In striving now for new ways to facilitate their children's desire for successful self-definition, many women went to work once their children were out of their dependent childhood years. This was what women had always done to help their families through unexpected expenses or hard times. Now, however, married women's work invaded the precincts of the middle class, no longer just the province of the poor or widowed or deserted wife. New aspirations, rather than need and dire poverty, were beginning to accustom families to dual-earner households, though certainly not when the children were young.

College aspirations in the 1960s were still overwhelmingly white ambitions. Few African American or Latino children were either trained to competition at school or inspired toward the goal at home that now became common for children of native white groups, and among newer immigrants such as Italians, Greeks, and Armenians. But the very expansion of higher education, its newly articulated social role as a site for youth development, and its increasing centrality to mobility aspirations meant that soon this white domination would be challenged as colleges and universities began to figure more and more in national policies. Even in the 1960s, some colleges and universities began to practice early forms of affirmative-action policies as talented African American youth especially were encouraged to attend elite colleges.[6] It was not until the end of the decade that many schools began to debate and to adopt curricular innovations in response to the new constituencies that federal policies began to require colleges actively to recruit.

THE TIMES THEY ARE A-CHANGIN'

Colleges and universities had adjusted throughout the twentieth century to changing student populations and new cultural cues, and college life was always defined as much by the young as by those who were technically in charge and officially *in loco parentis*. By the mid-1960s, these changes had profoundly altered the ancient institution. When Linda LeClair was found to be living off-campus with her boyfriend in 1968, the scandal made the front pages of newspapers across the country and the national news on television. An undergraduate at Barnard College in New York City, one of the esteemed Seven Sister schools that had pioneered in women's higher education a century earlier, LeClair was well aware of the complex parietal rules that were supposed to guide the social lives of college students everywhere. She had knowingly broken them. These rules were meant to protect a woman's reputation (which largely meant sexual honor and its associated behaviors) as colleges guarded their charges' social lives as well as their intellectual adventures through college.[7]

By 1968, however, the peer-mediated rules that governed undergraduate life were being dismantled. The beer binges and risqué panty raids of the late 1950s and early 1960s, in which men stood eagerly outside girls' dorm windows pleading for a favor of underwear, and that had mildly challenged the earlier rules, had been overshadowed. The new student reality was associated with protests against the Vietnam War, new habits including sexual initiations for women as well as men, and various experiments with drugs such as marijuana and LSD. A new youth culture was visible on colleges across the country, a culture recognizable in dress and music tastes, sexual habits and intoxicants, philosophical explorations and radical political ideas. Certainly, not all college students either identified with or participated in this culture, but it was a national phenomenon and had become prominent in the media and the public mind. That culture markedly separated young people (and their older admirers) from most adults on campus as well as from their parents at home. Its manifestations would haunt and challenge the rest of the century.

The culture of the young in general was permeated by music, whether they were part of the visible youth culture of the time or more mainstream, and increasingly helped to define and guide their sensibility. Music, which had begun for many of these young people as a form of entertainment on television's *American Bandstand* and on rock 'n' roll–dominated radio stations in the 1950s, and usually was an accompaniment to sock hops, proms, and Sweet Sixteens, became in the 1960s a measure of mood rather than a form of dance. The sexuality that alarmed 1950s parents in Elvis Presley's voice and moves (and those of his many imitators) became much more subversive as it embraced disenchantment and drugs in the Rolling Stones, the Doors, and Bob Dylan. The Beatles invasion of the United States in 1964 had been a first taste of what was to come—their boyish charm always tinged with riotous neglect of convention in dress, hairstyles, and speech. An anticonventional mood was just what exploded around and through the music of the later 1960s.

Like other historical manifestations of the spirit of revivalism that had been peer-inspired, fueled in outdoor spaces, and wedged in generational irritations, the radical version of 1960s youth culture partook of deep antagonisms to authority and drew heavily on perceptions about the hypocrisy of powerful elders. In the 1960s, the growing threat of the draft for all young people was fueling resentments against an increasingly unpopular war, still publicly defended in the language of a canting liberalism. The war and its defenders were confronted with a generation of young people who were increasingly following Emerson's injunctions to follow their own genius by "doing their own thing" and telling it "like it is." For a sizable portion of the young, the Vietnam War draft, encroaching by the end of the 1960s even on college graduates, government-funded secret research on campus, and the civil rights struggle, which had reignited the language of American idealism and brotherhood, came together to fuel generational (and class) antagonism and to embolden youth's sense that they knew so much more about what was really important than their convention-driven elders. Some of that knowledge came from books written by some of those very elders, who became contemporary gurus, among them Paul Goodman, Herbert Marcuse, and Norman O. Brown. These attacked the structure of capitalism or the sexual repressions of the middle class. Some came from the more direct inspiration of pot smoking or from ingesting the newly available synthetic drug LSD, hyped by onetime Harvard psychologist Timothy Leary. Almost all of it rejected the technological civilization and the science that had made much of it possible. Yearning for new communion with nature, the youth culture of the 1960s condemned the technological civilization that had come to define their lives after the Second World War. They belittled the all-electric kitchens that eased their mothers' lives, excoriated the bomb (and the sham of bomb shelters) that had made their nation powerful, and raged against the government research that allowed napalm to be dropped on Vietnamese villagers. They hated the guardians of that civilization, whether they were college professors, presidential advisors, or street cops. And they did so in language that overthrew the many etiquettes carefully developed over the course of the century as their parents and grandparents had sought respectability. Even if they did not speak for all youth (and they did not even speak for all youth at college), they were certainly extremely vocal and, like most inspired minorities, dominated the public vision of the time.

Most of them attacked the very institutions—the schools—that had made their moratorium possible and their presence both visible and powerful. Few of them thought much about how the sexuality so fundamental to their new sense of the power of nature had been carefully nurtured by the very technologies they now abhorred.

Birth control was nothing new in the 1960s. But 99-percent-effective birth control available for the asking was very new. Since the early twentieth century, first middle-class wives and then gradually others could have birth control prescribed by doctors, while condoms had been commonplace for male use since the First World War. But American pharmaceutical research in the 1950s had developed two powerful new contraceptives, the intrauterine device and the birth control pill (invented by Carl Djerassi in 1960), that transformed sexual behavior in the United States and eventually elsewhere in the world as well. Though still somewhat crude, both means now radically separated sex from conception. The insertion of the IUD by a doctor or the daily morning habit of pill-taking meant that women could now be ready to have sex at any time without expecting any consequences. Unlike the diaphragm, which had a substantial failure rate (it was estimated that this resulted in an often unplanned fourth or fifth child in the 1950s), and which required synchronized insertion, both the pill and the IUD were at once much more effective and required no thought at all. Unlike the condom, these means were wholly within a woman's control. As a result, sex and conception for women were separated effectively for the first time in human history in ways that could make even a respectable undergraduate happy and secure while she challenged her mother's hypocrisies.

The sexual revolution of the 1960s was thus powerfully built on new technological knowledge and, unlike previous revolutions, powerfully affected unmarried as well as married women (because the risks were so much lower). And it brought in its wake other revolutions as well, although, of course, it could not fully account for or fully explain these. First, modern feminism, which spun rapidly out of the anti-authoritarian and anticonventional mood of the 1960s, began seriously to challenge all gendered differences because the most prominent biosocial difference (childbearing) could now be discounted. Then came gay liberation, which took the sexual pleasures articulated by a liberated 1960s to their logical conclusion by proclaiming sexual pleasure as a good in itself regardless of the preferred partner (no longer naturally limited by an implicit goal of conception). These two powerful cultural revolutions necessarily required the effective and permanent divide that opened in the 1960s between sex and conception, sex and childbearing, sex and parenthood.

The destruction of those links would alter the nature of family life and the patterns of childhood in ways that no one, standing at the threshold of the 1950s, could ever have imagined. Instead of parenthood as a central human condition and a proud emblem of American success, the young people who left colleges, universities, and high schools in the 1960s and 1970s opened up a new kind of childless future.

BUST FOLLOWS BOOM

During the first two decades after the war, having a child was a desirable social goal and parenting had a secure place within the culture. This meant that those who could not conceive often sought to adopt children whom they would raise as their own. Taking care of children was an honorable social act, and in adopting a child the personal desire for parenthood meshed with the needs of children for care. Those adoptions were monitored by social service agencies that were usually sectarian and that tried to select among applicants those whose marriages were stable, incomes secure, and future home life promising. This did not mean that all children were perfectly placed, but the placements existed within a context that presumed that this was a social activity and that the adoption was for the good of the child.

Since the early twentieth century, family placements rather than institutions were the preferred choice for children who were unwanted at birth or whose parents could not care for them properly. The family was invested with social purpose and emotional function as the primary caretaker of children, whatever other function it had shed in the process of industrialization. Adoption—the legal incorporation of a child from the family of birth into a family of desire—was one route; the other was family foster care, which grew throughout the century as an alternative to orphanages for children who needed to be placed on a temporary basis or who were unlikely to be adopted. Orphanages were never entirely eclipsed, although they were distinctly viewed as less desirable. In both adoptions and foster care, the community through various welfare agencies oversaw the proper disposition of the children and took an interest in their welfare, even after their placement.

In the 1950s and 1960s, almost all adoptions were both supervised and secret—meaning that the records were sealed and unavailable to all parties concerned. Neither the natural mother (or parents) nor the adoptive parents and child could know the identities of the others, in perpetuity. This corresponded with the presumed desire for privacy of all the parties: the natural mother, usually unmarried, did not want her identity made known, since what society described as her "moral" failure was probably why she surrendered the child in the first place; the adoptive parents wanted to behave like all the spontaneous families around them, unchallenged in their identity as parents; the childhood of the adoptee should blend into the childhoods around her. The child would eventually be told she was adopted because she was loved and wanted by her adoptive parents, but nothing more. This was the bargain struck at the height of the baby boom. All children were wanted; all children should have families; everyone participated in a social compact that protected the identity of the unmarried woman and protected children from being less than fully cared for by "complete" families. There was considerable hypocrisy in this, and, of course, there were always children who were not wanted and not placed. These tended to come from groups whose futures could not be easily blended into the hegemonic, aspiring middle class—African American children; abused or handicapped children; children with developmental problems. But, in general, the social compact was fulfilled through the forms of adoption that prevailed, and in the 1950s and 1960s sometimes even these least-wanted children found homes among parents who took very seriously their sense of being responsible for the welfare of society's children. Interracial adoptions, for example, were never intended to mimic natural families, but revealed the social contract in its most serious and effective form.

By the end of the 1970s, contraception and the accompanying sexual revolution, as well as other value changes associated with feminism, had altered premarital patterns and the views of what a family was and its role in society. Premarital sexual experimentation was the first arena of change. This change was probably earliest signaled by the publication in 1962 of Helen Gurley Brown's *Sex and the Single Girl*, but it was evident as well in the profusion of sex manuals (*The Joy of Sex* being the most aptly named), and the franker discussion of sexuality in magazines and public discourse. Young people who had been restricted at home by parents and in college by parietal rules were freer in their dating behavior and much more likely, once they left home, to live for a while with a boyfriend or girlfriend, or at least to spend nights at each other's places. In fact, these arrangements probably explain the large jump in the average age at marriage during this period and profoundly altered the usual pattern of transition to marriage. Women's new independence also made a difference. Where the expectation in the past had been that girls would move from their parents' house to the home they created with their husbands, with college no more than a carefully guarded transit point, respectable women now lived apart from families. For the first time in the century, the number of people living "alone" in the census ballooned, inflated by young singles living on their own or in makeshift arrangements with other singles of either sex. "Between 1970 and 1975," historian John Modell discovered, "the proportion of young single men living by themselves more than doubled. Among young women, the gains in singles living alone were equally dramatic." [8]

Just as significantly, the number of children born plummeted. In 1978, the birthrate stood at 65.5, the lowest in the century and well below even the sharp Depression-driven dip of the 1930s.[9] The baby boom had collapsed. While children were still being born and conventional households composed of parents and children continued to be formed, these were a shrinking proportion of census households. Side by side with the conventional families were a number of newly experimental patterns: a growing number of childless couples who long delayed childbearing (or decided against bearing children altogether); single people either living alone or with an "unrelated" individual; communal living patterns, some of which had developed out of the idealism of the 1960s; newly dyadic families composed of a mother and her child (or children). American households had always been more diverse than the ideal inscribed in the 1950s, but the proportion of these households had grown significantly. The last configuration of a mother alone with her children was overwhelmingly the result of the enormous growth of divorce. The challenge to conventions and to chastity and the emphasis on self-expression of the previous decades had very specific consequences for families that might have once remained intact in deference to community standards or for the children's sake. It also removed the terrible stigma that still attached to divorced women throughout the first half of the twentieth century, despite decades of familiarity with a growing divorce rate. The family paradigm of the 1950s and early 1960s had tended to enforce this stigma, since divorced women were not only conspicuous in a culture of couples but also carried a whiff of sexual license. In the 1970s, with swinging couples in the news and premarital experimentation all around, the divorced woman became a much safer commonplace.

In this new mixture of family forms, a never-married woman with her children could also now find a place; she was no longer a scandal or a threat but an individual exercising her options. The stigma of illegitimacy, long removed from the law, was also withdrawn now in language as "out-of-wedlock" disappeared from the social-work vocabulary. The result for formal adoptions was catastrophic. Children available for agency adoptions largely disappeared, except, notably, those who came under the auspices of the Catholic Church, whose firm stand against contraception and abortion meant that "unwanted" children were still born. African American children without families to care for them still often went unplaced, as did the handicapped and abused. In the case of African American children, though, the number of children unavailable for adoption actually increased because black social workers began to oppose interracial adoptions, insisting that children needed to be kept within the racial community rather than be viewed as a charge to the whole society.

In the 1980s, the desire for adoptions within a population many of whose older married couples could not easily conceive after their long delay, and marked by a merciless decline in the supply of babies resulted in both panic and creativity. Not everyone wanted to be parents, but those who did and could not have their own children began to seek alternative routes to parenting. One of these was the development of largely unsupervised forms of adoption. These private adoptions were usually facilitated through a lawyer rather than an agency. What had once been a form of underground black market in adoptions, used by those who had been rejected or passed over by agencies, became legal throughout the country. Open adoptions also came into favor. In these cases the birth mother remained involved with the child, who now had two mothers and possibly two sets of parents. So did other strategies. As Americans sought new sources for babies in an increasingly global economy, they turned to Asia (China and Korea), Latin America (Mexico and Peru), and, after the fall of communism, the orphanages of Eastern Europe and the former Soviet Union. Often the laws of these countries had not caught up with the new practice. Sometimes the would-be parents found that the children (abused or inadequately attended as infants) were not what they imagined. Infants were now not exactly sold or traded, but they had become part of a very private world where meeting the needs of the child was distinctly secondary to meeting the desires of the parents. While these children often found a home among good people, there was no one around to make sure that some larger social goal was established. Some of these adopted children were returned because they were not what the parents had expected, thus becoming twice-rejected.[10] Although it had left some disappointed, the delicate bargain of an earlier day had at least assumed that society had a stake in the transaction. The new world of adoptions had become a largely private concern. Whose children these were, which society they belonged to, who oversaw their welfare—all these were matters of chance and luck.

The change in adoption was emblematic of a much wider reality in the world into which children were now, less frequently than ever before, born. The refusal to judge family forms and relationships and the desire not to moralize often led to a failure to supervise children's welfare. This happened in many realms. In the area of television, the government increasingly withdrew from the stringent licensing and supervision of advertising that had once protected children's programming from the full force of commercialism. New educational programs on public television, such as the acclaimed *Sesame Street*, could hardly compensate for the decline of educational programming on the other networks. By the mid-1980s, most programs had been largely freed to float with the market. Children watched programs crammed with ads before, after, and during the show. Some shows were themselves nothing more than ads for toys. In 1990, the Children's Television Act seemed to restore restrictions on commerce, but the loopholes in the law, and the fact that its restrictions on nonviolent or nonsexual programming were irrelevant in a new VCR and cable television age rendered its controls largely meaningless.[11]

In the area of foster case, there was growing uncertainty and ambiguity about the state's role and the standards to apply in supervising families. Was it more important to keep families intact even if it was not clear that their nurture was quite "good enough" (and what, after all was a "good enough" family); was the child better off being adopted even if the parents still wanted her or shunted among foster placements while the mother decided or cleaned up her act; could a filthy, rat-infested home be an effective place to raise children? The crisis in foster care grew throughout the 1980s and into the 1990s as more children found their way into "the system" and as the unstable families that had been long accumulating on their rosters were further devastated by drug addiction (increasingly common among pregnant women) and imprisonments. Gradually, the systems of supervision were cracking under the load they were forced to bear. Those cracks became more and more visible over time. By the 1990s they were exposed in public scandals when a New York City girl, supposedly supervised by state and city welfare agencies, was abused and killed by her parents, and when a child in the Florida system disappeared altogether early in the new century. Most of these children were not white.

Childcare, too, was largely unsupervised and overwhelmingly market-driven. By the early 1980s childcare had become an increasing necessity for the growing number of divorced mothers and households in which mother and father both worked full time, even when the children were young. From the 1970s to the 1990s, the age of children the majority of whose mothers worked declined step by step, from children under six years of age to those under two and then under one. In some ways, these households had fulfilled ideals of the feminist challenge to male power in the marketplace that was launched in the early 1970s. In most other ways, it was the market that had triumphed, by incorporating the skills of millions of women while reducing the wages and salaries of most workers. The decline in real wages that was marked during the long recession of the 1970s and the shorter one of the 1980s was compensated by female work. Most households adapted to this economic reality, accepting women's work—no longer disreputable—as part of the modern bargain where goods rather than time and freedom had become the primary markers of class. The initial feminist agenda had rarely made any provision for children. But this left children at the mercy of private decisions and ad hoc arrangements—family care, young foreign nannies (still mostly illegal before the late 1980s), church childcare, franchised daycare centers, nursery schools that accepted younger and younger children, or temporary babysitters including extended kin. The state exercised some supervision over work conditions and health and safety provisions through licensing requirements in larger establishments, but none at all over quality. For many households where parents worked more than one shift, sometimes children were irregularly cared for by one or the other parent, making fathers now more responsible for the care of children, even if they had not quite adapted to the new reality. Above all, necessary childcare, once assumed to be the work of mothers (who would remain home even if they were poor according to the legislation first established during the New Deal's social security package) had become a matter to be negotiated privately—each parent deciding who took care of the children and what he or she would settle for in terms of quality of care.

This new reality of mother's work ultimately destroyed the pact that had been made between the federal government and the poor, for whom Aid for Families with Dependent Children had provided some means for women to stay home and care for their children. In 1996, that pact came to an end when "welfare as we know it" disappeared during the Clinton administration, and with it the assumption that caring for children was itself a worthy form of social behavior for which the state was willing to pay.

In the case of older children, the schools sometimes filled the breach in childcare. As was so often the case in the past, the education of the "whole" child required that schools attend to more than academic concerns. This time they began to offer various after-school programs for children whose parents came home long past 3:00 p.m. But the schools did this irregularly and unpredictably. Supervision, even after school, was still largely a parental choice and responsibility and in a society where amusements had become cheap and plentiful, this often meant that children came home to fill their time with more numerous and ever more fanciful toys. Some of these toys linked up with the world of television or movies; others were based on the rapidly evolving technologies relying on the silicon chip; still others were lodged in habits of serial acquisition as children collected sets of Ninja Turtles or Care Bears. Almost none of these were related to the toys of previous childhoods, once carefully selected by parents eager to pass on a tradition of play. Most came from television information, rapidly disseminated by school and childcare chums. The supervision of toys, like the supervision of so much else concerning children, declined and gave way to commerce and guilt.

While parents were certain to want their children to benefit from the latest fad so as not to be left out from among their peers, they also increasingly provided their children with goods instead of time. In a new world of working mothers where neither government policies nor social practices developed effectively as expressions of the society's interest in the child, parents found themselves in a time bind. By the mid-1980s, time-strapped parents were more and more told that "quality" in time spent with children was far more important than the quantity that parents (still mostly mothers) devoted to the task. No matter how good the quality of their interactions, few mothers were completely reassured. Somehow the lack of time-intensive attention to children was taking its toll. Increasingly, this was experienced in parental stress and in exaggerated (but not altogether unfounded) fears about their children's safety.

Everywhere childhood itself seemed no longer what it once had been. The perfect childhood was always an illusion, something we want once to have existed rather than something we really had. Since the middle of the nineteenth century, however, Americans had created more than an illusion in the commitment to a childhood protected from the market and given the chance to grow and develop through schooling, public health enforcements of clean water, and safe vaccines and drugs. In the 1950s, the invention of a vaccine against polio (previously a scourge of childhood) had made Jonas Salk into a folk hero. Laws also tried to protect girls from sexual exploitation and all children from abusive parents. The protections had always been firmly lodged in middle-class attitudes and were usually applied variously to the children of others. Still, they had raised childhood to a position of privilege for all, a kind of innocence from the worst kind of abuse that adults readily recognized was an all too human possibility. The middle classes thought they could provide this protection for their own children. By the 1980s, that belief was seriously challenged through the growing publicity about children's dangers. These dangers invaded deep into middle-class homes as parents worried about stranger abductions and discovered that their own spouses could steal their children and hide them away in what became a newly criminalized form of divorce-related behavior. Schools, once the symbol of protected and extended childhood, had become less and less ideal.

In the 1970s, schools became first less community-centered as court-ordered desegregation (an action grounded in a vision of public good) took effect. They became less and less safe as the growing drug problem (and the guns that often went with it) invaded high schools and junior highs, and then eventually even the lower schools. Similarly, the sexualizing of music, popular culture, and advertising was taking its toll on the outward behavior of younger and younger children, whose dress and tastes began to imitate their older siblings, as well as models such as Cindy Crawford and the Calvin Klein billboards that encouraged provocative looks and tight jeans. Many middle-class parents, hoping to protect their own children, fled to suburban enclaves and private schools (whose enrollments began to skyrocket in the 1980s) but found that the trends merely followed their children and their money.

What these parents were beginning to privatize more successfully was the good education that brought college admissions once promised to all children through the public schools, which the race for excellence of the 1950s had delivered more effectively than in the past. By the 1980s, quality schooling tended to be more parceled out than ever since World War II, and more segregated since the end of the segregation era, as the middle class began to protect its educational prerogatives. Public school districts in poorer communities found themselves strangled by lack of funds at a time when going to college had become an imperative for economic success. By the 1980s, the great American system of education for all, great despite its many faults, became more privatized. Wealthy suburbanites raised property taxes or ran successful fundraisers, sent their children to learning centers that taught basic skills such as reading and advanced SAT preparation, while well-off city-dwellers sent their children to selective and academically competitive private schools. Many others went to parochial schools. If these options were not possible, by the 1990s parents began to ask for a new choice, "charter schools," where the public purse paid for schools that emphasized private goals and visions of superior education under parental control and supervision. This disassembling of the public schools into privatized components could not entirely save children from sex and violence, but it did reflect the growing eclipse of the vision of childhood as invested with common public goals.

Even money (maybe especially money) could not protect the children of prosperity from changes that technology and culture had deposited deep within the home. New devices such as microwave ovens and new expensive food purveyors made it possible to split up traditional mealtimes within families as working mothers had less time to shop, cook, and prepare what had once been a family's daily gathering. Parents' hours at work and children's hours at schools and sports meant fewer hours spent together. Expensive vacations were intended to make up the difference. Too often, private family life became at once less private and more dependent on a variety of services performed by others while it also became less public-minded in its concerns and commitments. At the same time, these families could not protect their children against the ultimate exposure that came with divorce, which revealed the family's painful emotional interdependence and its equally painful dependency on judicial intervention and public laws. No-fault divorce laws and new joint-custody decrees made women more autonomous but also less likely to be allowed to determine their children's lives. As parents remarried and blended their offspring into newer units, children often became members of several families—a new family form that joined the innovations of the 1970s. Psychologists debated the costs to children of their parents' divorces and subsequent blendings, but one cost was clearly an older sense of family autonomy.

Happiness seemed much more elusive than sexual satisfaction and freedom from the conventions of an earlier time. By the century's end, however, pharmaceutical innovations were beginning to compensate even for this. A whole range of drugs became available to treat depression in the 1950s and 1960s, with Valium the best known, but these sedatives could never provide a sense of well-being. The 1960s had begun a trend that normalized other kinds of drug-taking, although these remained illegal and were taken surreptitiously and usually in groups. In the 1980s, a whole new category of drugs—serotonin reuptake inhibitors—now provided a legitimate and increasingly widespread way for both baby boomers and their children to feel good. At first given to the really depressed or dysfunctional in tandem with more conventional therapies, Prozac and the drugs that quickly followed in its wake provided relief from mood swings and psychological lows. In fairly short order, these drugs moved into the general society, widely prescribed and dispensed, and used by adults and more and more children and adolescents. In addition, children who were overactive in school were increasingly medicated (often as part of a school requirement) with a potent drug that calmed them down and allowed them to focus. In a short time Ritalin became, in turn, a means to control overactive youngsters, a way for college students to concentrate during exams, and a drug sold on the black market for others to get high. Americans and their children had incorporated drugs into their daily lives.

CLONE AGE

By the late 1980s, biology and electronics had replaced physics as a source of technological wonder. Where once Americans guarded their nuclear secrets, now innovations in microchip technology and the new marketing attached to the Internet (initially a military-sponsored technology) were providing American economic advantage. New fears about the theft of recent developments in this area were raising serious questions about the open nature of university research and its welcome to foreign students, and computers dominated not only the job prospects of America's ever larger college-bound population, now augmented through affirmative action programs and grown to almost 60 percent, but also their school tasks and desk equipment. Knowing how to use a computer became an essential part of growing up and increasingly necessary to the tasks the young were required to perform for homework. The new technologies were linking the children together over Internet-mediated games, while their common culture was being defined by movie characters and special effects in blockbuster movies.

The boldest new research on the frontier between social expectation and ethical dilemmas came in biology. The revolution that Darwin had initiated in the nineteenth century in the understanding of whole species now lodged in the genetic codes of the individual and the technologies of cell division. Between them, these research fields had the potential to transform childhood in fundamental ways that had become genuinely frightening, but also highly desirable in areas of health and medicine. Research in this field promised new cures for cancers and ways to replace vital organs. It also predicted new ways to create babies.

That revolution was already glimpsed when the birth of a "Baby Conceived Outside the Body," was announced in the *New York Times*.[12] Born on July 25, 1978, and delivered by Caesarian section, Louise Brown weighed in at five pounds, twelve ounces. "Baby Louise" was almost immediately labeled the first test tube baby, but, in fact, her first days were spent in a Petri dish where her parents' eggs and sperm had been mixed together, and thereafter she had developed inside her mother's womb like any other child. The original research that led to this potential "cure" for infertility was funded, among others, by the Ford Foundation, to aid in the development of contraception. The contraceptive revolution that had helped to transform sexual behavior and family dynamics had also created a new means to deal with the fertility collapse that had resulted, not all of it intended. Less than three decades later, in 1996, Dolly the cloned sheep was born, also the product of Petri dishes and genetic research, but now much more completely through a different form of conception, since she was wholly the expression of her mother's genetic code. By 2004, copycats, literally, were created and sold at high prices to ease the grief of owners who had lost a pet. Despite widespread rhetoric, nobody really believed that the animal clones would not eventually be followed by a human version.

During those thirty years, fertility research and its associated medical specializations had created new hope for infertile couples, and new possibilities to tailor children to parental desires. What it had not created was an effective area of policy regulation or clear laws to govern a booming new field. Politicians vented their high ethical outrage, but they could control neither the market for the innovations nor the new global parameters of the scientific work being done.

By the mid-1990s, almost any undergraduate in America could pick up her college newspaper and respond to an offer to have her eggs harvested. If she was blonde, tall, pretty, and athletic and had high SAT scores, she might realize as much as $50,000 for this private transaction. Eggs were being bought on the Internet, accompanied by pictures and descriptions of personal features, which presumably were inheritable. The new techniques were making it possible to harvest eggs from a young, fertile girl (made more fertile through hormone treatments), combine them in a Petri dish with the sperm of a couple's male partner, and implant them in the female partner. It was also making it possible for lesbian couples to conceive and for gay partners to father a child. The once imagined "natural" barriers to conception had been broken as sperm, eggs, and wombs became divisible components of a new birthing process. The division between sex and conception heralded by the contraceptive revolution of the 1960s had moved into a new world.

In that world, genetics was king. Genetic technologies that would eventually make the first breakthrough in laying bare the 20,000–25,000 elements of the human genome in 2001 were facilitating the identification of fathers in unprecedented ways. What had once been a social construct became a testable biological fact. Where female chastity and marital fidelity had been the only way to lay claim to fatherhood, now a simple test made social practices irrelevant. This new fact was already transforming paternity suits, altering adoption contracts (as the Baby Jessica case made clear), and transforming the work of state welfare agencies as they pursued absent fathers for child support payments. "Out of wedlock" became truly meaningless in this context. As the genetic components of a child's DNA became the determinant of her social position, she increasingly belonged to or expressed her parents, rather than an identity established through agreed-upon community-established criteria.

Over the course of the second half of the twentieth century, the child's social position and her purchase on the community's commitments had steadily declined as the family, once an honorable social mediator, had been delegitimated. But the desire for children had not therefore declined. It now became a function of personal desire and the emotional need for self-expression. This is what baby-boom women discovered as their "biological clocks" began to tick down in the 1980s. Eager for the personal completion that having a child might offer, rather than the contribution they were making to a community good, or a family identity (historical or contemporary), women sought to become mothers, and the new reproductive technologies grew to meet that need. In this world of children as personal expression, why not tailor the genes to meet the desired image of the self just as the child could be made to wear the right "designer" labels? The desperation of some to create children with their own genetic materials (or at least that of their partner) at almost any cost, while thousands of children (not so well designed) were caught in the despondency of a deteriorating foster-care system, was perhaps as much a mark of ignorance as of selfishness, but it had become difficult to tell the difference.

At the core of the changes had been the eclipse of family as a meaningful social institution and the source of social identity. American families had never had the cultural meaning and weight associated with family in more traditional societies, but their private functions had been invested with social meaning since the middle of the nineteenth century. This was in some ways exaggerated by the social commitment to family life immediately after the Second World War and into the 1950s. By then, however, families had already shrunk in social terms, discarding resident grandparents who had still had a household place earlier in the century. Until the 1960s, this shrinkage of the connections between the intimate family and others that once created a sense of historical meaning had been hidden by the sheer size of baby-boom families. When in the late 1960s and 1970s the numbers of children declined sharply, divorce increased, and alternative residence arrangements blossomed, the family's weakness as a social link was exposed. With no obligation to an older generation whose care could not be paid for, and with fewer children, the part that families had once borne in the social fabric began to seem weightless. Family relations still seemed to matter to individuals, and the rhetoric of family values became ever louder in politics, but the family's real role in the society had shrunk. Despite the political noise around the subject, it found less real support in the political arena, while actual families struggled more than ever to provide the resources of time, money, and knowledge on their own without much social support.

Technology had often been the source of change and a response to change after World War II, but rarely the sole explanation. By the turn of the new century, the many ethical issues that were being aired in relation to the changes in biological knowledge and changes in the family were too often attached to party labels, rather than understood as a measure of a broad social change that had led to a general disengagement from childhood. With some notable variations, liberal Democrats supported abortion, stem-cell research (which used embryonic cells), and contraceptives made available to young people; conservative Republicans, for their part, supported middle-class school vouchers, adult sentencing for juveniles, and an end to welfare. Each side used the image of children to bolster its own position, and both vocally supported "quality schools." Indeed, schools became an important part of America's new competitive strategy in a new global marketplace, a necessary way to assure that Americans would stay ahead of the competition for highly skilled jobs. Neither side took children seriously as part of a fundamental social contract. Few politicians addressed the broad-range disengagement from children's welfare that had already taken place—the increasing privatization of adoptions; the substitution of genetic for family identity; the withdrawal of support from the families of poor children; the targeted marketing of goods to children; the loss of commitment to viewing everyone's child as a charge against the whole; the failure of nerve in making judgments about what was good for children and what was not, apart from the interests of their (voting) parents. Americans and increasingly the populations of Western Europe were haunted by the pedophile—the stranger come to prey on their children and to destroy their innocence.

Few saw that their children had been made strangers to others, and that their innocence, once the potent source of protective legislation, had become little more than a politically convenient catchphrase. We had created a new childhood, but we were still using the images of the past. Understanding this changed childhood and protecting all our children would have to wait for another day.

BIBLIOGRAPHIC NOTE

Excerpts from articles, newspaper clippings and other sources for many of the issues relating to children addressed in this essay can be found in *Childhood in America*, edited by Paula S. Fass and Mary Ann Mason (New York University Press, 2000). The central work for understanding the transformation of childhood in the late nineteenth century and how children were taken out of the calculations of the marketplace is Viviana Zelizer, *Pricing the Priceless Child* (Basic Books, 1985).

On family life during the 1950s and after, Elaine Tyler May's *Homeward Bound* (Basic Books, 1988) and Arlene Skolnick's *Troubled Paradise* (Basic Books, 1991) are good places to start. For Dr. Spock, see Nancy Pottishman Weiss, "Mother the Invention of Necessity: Benjamin Spock's Baby and Child Care," *American Quarterly* 29 (1979): 519–546; and Michael Zuckerman, "Dr. Spock: Confidence Man," in *The Family in History*, ed. Charles E. Rosenberg (University of Pennsylvania Press, 1975). For a longer overview of the history of the American family, see Steven Mintz and Susan Kellogg, *Social History of American Family Life* (Free Press, 1988). A good collection on contemporary family issues is *All Our Families*, edited by Steven Sugarman, Mary Ann Mason, and Arlene Skolnick (Oxford University Press, 1998).

For an excellent introduction to the history of childhood in America that also addresses many contemporary issues, see Steven Mintz, *Huck's Raft: A History of American Childhood* (Oxford University Press, 2004). Childrearing concerns and advice are ably discussed by Peter N. Stearns, *Anxious Parents: Trying to Measure Up in the Twentieth Century* (New York University Press, 2003), and Julia Grant, *Raising Baby by the Book: The Education of American Mothers* (Yale University Press, 1998). A good measure of the growing contemporary revulsion against childrearing advice and the illusion of parental control is Judith Rich Harris, *The Nurture Assumption: Why Children Turn Out the Way They Do* (Free Press, 1998), which rejects the importance of parental influence altogether. Gary Cross, *The Cute and the Cool: Wondrous Innocence and Modern American Children's Culture* (Oxford University Press, 2004), provides important insights into contemporary disengagement and the private dreams fulfilled by children. Adoption has not received the historical attention it deserves, but the place to start is Wayne Carp, *Family Matters: Secrecy and Disclosure in the History of Adoption* (Harvard University Press, 1998). For the globalization of adoption matters, see Agnes Fine, *Adoptions: Ethnologie des Parentes Choisies* (Maison des Sciences de L'Homme, 1998), and Rachel Stryker, "Forging Families, Fixing Families: Adoption and the Cultural Politics of Reactive Attachment Disorder," Ph.D. diss., University of California at Berkeley, 2004.

Ricki Solinger's *Wake Up Little Suzy* (Routledge, 2000) discusses how illegitimacy was treated in the 1950s. A different perspective on modesty can be found in Rochelle Gerstein, *Repeal of Reticence: A History of America's Cultural and Legal Struggles Over Free Speech, Obscenity, Sexual Liberation, and Modern Art* (Hill and Wang, 1996). For changes in sexual behavior in the 1960s, see David Allyn, *Make Love Not War: The Sexual Revolution, an Unfettered History* (Little, Brown, 2000), and Beth Bailey, *Sex in the Heartland* (Harvard University Press, 1999). For the 1960s more generally, see David Farber, *The Age of Great Dreams: America in the 1960s* (Hill and Wang, 1994), and David Farber, ed., *The Sixties: From Memory to History* (University of North Carolina Press, 1994). For college life in the twentieth century more generally, see Helen Lefkowitz Horowitz, *Campus Life: Undergraduate Cultures from the End of the Eighteenth Century to the Present* (Knopf, 1988); Paula S. Fass, *The Damned and the Beautiful: American Youth in the 1920s* (Oxford University Press, 1977); and David O. Levine, *The American College and the Culture of Aspiration, 1915–1940* (Cornell University Press, 1986). For a statistical profile of the population and of the education of that population, see Thomas D. Snyder, "Education Characteristics of the Population," in *120 Years of American Education: A Statistical Portrait* (U.S. Department of Education, Office of Educational Research and Improvement, 1993). For schooling issues more generally, see Diane Ravitch, *Troubled Crusade: American Education, 1945–1980* (Basic Books, 1983), and Paula S. Fass, *Outside In: Minorities and the Transformation of American Education* (Oxford University Press, 1989). The federal government's sponsorship of university research is discussed in Ellen Herman, *The Romance of American Psychology: Political Culture in the Age of Experts* (University of California Press, 1995), and changes in the patterns of growing up in John Modell, *Into One's Own.: From Youth to Adulthood in the United States, 1920–1975* (University of California Press, 1989). For life-course transitions and the changing composition of the American family, see David A. Stevens, "New Evidence on the Timing of Early Life Course Transitions: The United States 1900 to 1980," *Journal of Family History* 15 (1990): 163–178; and Steven Ruggles, "The Transformation of American Family Structure," *American Historical Review* 99 (February 1994): 103–128.

Matters relating to parenting and its relations to time and work and its consequences for children have developed a huge sociological literature and growing attention among historians. Some of this can be glimpsed at the Web site of the Center for Working Families of the University of California at Berkeley, directed by Arlie Hochschild and Barrie Thorne (http://workingfamilies.berkeley.edu). In addition, see Arlie Russell Hochschild's *The Time Bind: When Work Becomes Home and Home Becomes Work* (Metropolitan Books, 1997) and Anne Crittenden's *The Price of Motherhood: Why the Most Important Job in the World Is Still the Least Valued* (Metropolitan Books, 2001). Among historians, Gary Cross has done some of the fundamental work; see *Time and Money: The Making of Consumer Culture* (Routledge, 1993) and *An All-Consuming Century: Why Commercialism Won in Modern America* (Columbia University Press, 2000). In addition, Cross's *Kids' Stuff: Toys and the Changing World of American Childhood* (Harvard University Press, 1997) provides the necessary information on the development of children's toys and its relationships to consumer culture as well as insight into how this reflects on family relations. Also useful is Elizabeth Quinn-Lasch, "Mothers and Markets," *The New Republic*, 6 March 2000.

Issues of divorce and children are discussed in Mary Ann Mason, *The Custody Wars: Why Children Are Losing the Legal Battle, and What We Can Do About It* (Basic Books, 1999), and some of the disagreement over the effects of divorce on children can be seen in Judith Wallerstein and Joan Berlin Kelly, *Surviving the Breakup: How Children and Parents Cope with Divorce* (Basic Books, 1980) and E. Mavis Hetherington and John Kelly, *For Better or Worse: Divorce Reconsidered* (Norton, 2002). The problems of the foster care system and the conflict over policies has unfortunately developed a rich literature. See Nina Bernstein, *The Lost Children of Wilder: The Epic Struggle to Change Foster Care* (Pantheon Books, 2001); Michael Shapiro, *Solomon's Sword: Two Families and the Children the State Took Away* (Times Books, 1999); and Elizabeth Bertolet,

Nobody's Children: Abuse and Neglect, Foster Drift, and the Adoption Alternative (Beacon Press, 2000). Linda Gordon's *Heroes of Their Own Lives: The Politics and History of Family Violence* (Viking, 1988) provides the historical context for agency work. For the politics and consequences of disengaging from welfare, see Jason De Perle, *American Dream: Three Women, Ten Kids, and a Nation's Drive to End Welfare* (Viking, 2004). For the recent fears about child abduction, see Paula S. Fass, *Kidnapped: Child Abduction in America* (Oxford University Press, 1997); Philip Jenkins, *Moral Panic: Changing Conceptions of the Child Molester in Modern America* (Yale University Press, 1998); and James Kincaid, *Erotic Innocence: The Culture of Child Molesting* (Duke University Press, 1998). Lori B. Andrews's *Clone Age: Adventures in the New World of Reproductive Technology* (Henry Holt, 1999) will give readers a sense of the Wild West atmosphere surrounding reproductive technologies. Elaine Tyler May's *Barren in the Promised Land: Childless Americans and the Pursuit of Happiness* (Basic Books, 1995) provides insights into the problem of childlessness and the search for answers.

NOTES

1. The birthrate figures are from Thomas D. Snyder, "Education Characteristics of the Population," in *120 Years of American Education: A Statistical Portrait*, ed. Thomas D. Snyder (Washington, D.C.: U.S. Department of Education, Office of Educational Research and Improvement, 1993), table 1.

2. Michael Zuckerman, "Dr. Spock: Confidence Man," in *The Family in History*, ed. Charles Rosenberg (Philadelphia: University of Pennsylvania Press, 1975), 179–207.

3. Snyder, "Education Characteristics," table 3.

4. Erik H. Erikson, *Identity: Youth and Crisis* (New York: Norton, 1968), 128. This chapter, "The Life Cycle: Epigenesis of Identity," was based on an earlier article published in 1950.

5. "Admissions Dilemma," *New York Times*, 13 May and 16 May 1961.

6. "Admissions Down from Ivy League," *New York Times*, 15 April 1966.

7. Beth Bailey, *Sex in the Heartland* (Cambridge, Mass.: Harvard University Press, 1999), 200–202.

8. John Modell, *Into One's Own: From Youth to Adulthood in the United States, 1920–1975* (Berkeley: University of California Press, 1989).

9. Snyder, "Education Characteristics," table 1.

10. Rachel Stryker, "Forging Families, Fixing Families: Adoption and the Cultural Politics of Reactive Attachment Disorder," Ph.D. diss., University of California at Berkeley, 2004.

11. Gary Cross, *The Cute and the Cool: Wondrous Innocence and Modern American Children's Culture* (New York: Oxford University Press, 2004).

12. *New York Times*, 26 July 1978.

6. THE CULTURE OF WORK

MARK C. CARNES

Work, as God informed the misbehaving Adam and Eve, is humankind's lot in life, and it is a dreary one at that. The subject is off-putting. And apart from its dullness, work—especially work in recent decades—does not call out for scholarly scrutiny. Most of us have an intuitive sense of what work entails and how it has changed. We may recall when repairmen tinkered with automobile engines and vacuums and refrigerators; now they mostly replace parts. Salesmen (and some women) knocked on doors; now automatic dialers and spammers flood us with offers. Retail clerks keyed in numbers at cash registers; now they use scanners.

But if many aspects of work seem numbingly banal, what has attracted considerably less attention and analysis is the great upheaval that has rocked the institutional foundations of work during the past half-century. This is especially true of the large corporations that have become the dominant economic force in the life of the nation. This chapter focuses on the cultural aftershocks of this transformation.

To understand this shifting institutional structure, several overarching factors in the development of the nation's postwar economy must be kept in mind:

1. Employment has shifted from farming and manufacturing to the service sector. In 1940, nearly one in six civilian workers was engaged in agricultural pursuits; by 1960, that had declined to one in twelve, and by 2000, one in

forty. Manufacturing, too, experienced a relative decline in the postwar years, from well over one in three workers in 1940 to one in four in 1960 to less than one in six in 2000. In 1870, one in 160 workers in the United States was employed in clerical work; in 1930, one in twelve; and in 1950, one in eight. In 1947, one-fifth of the employees in manufacturing firms had no direct role in production; by 1975, the ratio of nonproducers had doubled.[1]

2. Jobs have migrated to the South and West, and, in recent decades, to Asia and South America. The Taft-Hartley Act (1947), which allowed states to establish "right-to-work" laws outlawing union shops, played a major role in the shift of labor-intensive jobs to the South: from 1947 through 1953, ten southern states passed right-to-work laws. Hundreds of corporations moved south, bringing with them millions of jobs.

3. Employment has generally been high. From 1949 through 1975, unemployment never climbed over 7 percent. During the mid-1960s it fell well below 4 percent. For people who could recall the Great Depression, when in some years one in four workers went without jobs, the dominant characteristic of the postwar era was not the bomb, Joseph McCarthy, or the Soviet threat to Berlin, but the ready availability of work. When laid off from one job, workers generally found another with little difficulty, often for better pay. If they failed, moreover, they were protected by the rudimentary safety net that had been stitched together during the New Deal and, later, by supplemental union benefits. In 1948, half of the United Auto Workers whom sociologist C. Wright Mills questioned told him that they "hardly ever" worried about losing their jobs.[2] This changed with the recession of the 1970s and 1980s, when the annual civilian unemployment rate nearly always exceeded 7 percent, peaking in 1982 and 1983 at nearly 10 percent. Economic reorganization and recovery came in the mid-1990s, when the unemployment rate fell below 5 percent and remained below that level in the early years of the twenty-first century.

ORGANIZATION MEN AND WOMEN: 1945–1960s

The socialization of young people into the world of adult work is an indispensable component of any social system. One of the oddities of the postwar period was the extent to which young Americans were distanced from the adult world of work. During the nineteenth century, children learned about work by doing it: hoeing fields and harvesting crops, threading bobbins and rolling cigars, washing clothes and fixing meals. Schooling, which only gradually acquired a compulsory character, was fitted into seasons and times when children were not needed to perform essential tasks in the fields and factories and at home. Boys in particular schemed to leave school as soon as possible; most worked full-time at adult tasks by the time they were fifteen or sixteen. Only a tiny (if disproportionately influential) minority delayed entry into the workforce by going to college.

After World War II, however, paid work was increasingly separated from the home. More people lived in suburbs and commuted to work downtown, or to factories and office parks. More children remained in school and for a longer period of time. Parents associated schooling with improved chances of a high-paying adult vocation; a corollary of this type of thinking was a fear that teenagers who took demanding jobs might neglect schooling and thus impair their chances for lucrative adult work.

Some intellectuals in the early postwar years applied this personal calculation for protracted schooling to society as a whole. Harvard's Talcott Parsons, the preeminent sociologist of the era, maintained that industrial societies required well-educated workers with considerable skills to ensure the smooth operation of vast new corporate bureaucracies and high-tech production systems. High levels of education ensured that the United States would surpass other nations in the bureaucratization that generated modernization.

In consequence, children who grew up in postwar America had relatively little knowledge about what took place "at work." Youngsters found some guidance from children's books where anthropomorphic animals and, for boys especially, trucks and trains, delivered pointed messages about work. *Tootle* (1945), reissued in the popular Golden Books series, informed young readers that to become a speedy locomotive, they must first study and work hard and "stay on the rails no matter what." Grade school teachers similarly inculcated basic precepts when they informed students that play was over and they would now go to "work." Away went the toys and crayons and out came the "workbooks." A few years later came that occasionally fatal assault on play—homework. In high school, athletic coaches spurred their charges to "give 120 percent" and emulated Vince Lombardi, the most popular football coach of the postwar years, whose motto was, "Winning isn't everything, it's the only thing." From sources such as these, young people learned that work entailed purposeful diligence and exertion. But the nature of work itself remained something of a mystery.

Popular culture, a many-vaulted repository of the icons of pleasure and consumption, provided even fewer hints about work. "Heigh-ho! Heigh-ho! It's off to work we go," chanted the seven dwarfs in Walt Disney's *Snow White* (1937). Notwithstanding their lusty encomia to work, the dwarfs cavorted in the woods, featherbedders all, leaving Snow White behind to clean house. *The Little Engine That Could*, first published in 1930 and reissued in 1954, chugged up the hill, but for all his grit and determination, he was clueless as to what lay beyond.

Few television shows portrayed blue-collar workers. Chester A. Riley, played by William Bendix, a riveter in an aircraft plant, was the last major television character to be shown in a factory; *The Life of Riley* went off the air in 1958. In the 1960s Archie Bunker (Carroll O'Connor) was the stereotypical blue-collar worker in every respect except that he never could be seen working. In the popular 1950s series *Leave It to Beaver*, young Beaver Cleaver had no idea what his father did "at the office." Nor did viewers learn anything about doctoring from Dr. Huxtable (Bill Cosby), who was shown with a patient only once in eight years on *The Bill Cosby Show* (1984–1992). Donna Reed cooked and cleaned in high heels and lipstick in the popular domestic comedy bearing her name. Wilbur, the architect, mused with "Mr. Ed" in a barn; his drafting table (Wilbur's, of course), though within convenient earshot of his equine friend, was usually off camera. A study of some fifteen thousand TV characters from 1973 to 1985 revealed that only one in ten worked in blue-collar, clerical, or sales jobs, which employed two-thirds of the nation's actual workers; nearly half of the characters had no apparent job whatsoever.[3]

Popular culture indeed spotlighted certain vocations, especially medicine, law, and police work, but usually got it wrong. In 1946, *Occupations* magazine chastised adults for failing to let children know that most work was monotonous. Soap-opera housewives dined in fancy restaurants and lounged on sofas with every pillow in place (at least at the beginning of the scene). In 1954, when a reporter from *TV Guide* asked a veteran cop what he thought of *Dragnet*, the cop noted that he had never unholstered his gun or chased a robber. TV failed to touch on the inescapable fact that his job was a bore: "You never see those lazy TV cops fill out any forms."[4] When Betty Friedan complained of TV's failure in the late 1950s to explore the lives of housewives, a producer explained: "If you showed it honestly, it would be too dull to watch."[5] After returning from the mill, exhausted and catatonic, a steelworker told Studs Terkel that he put on a smile and "faked it": "I got a kid three years old. Sometimes she says, 'Daddy, where've you been?' I say, 'Work.' I could have told her I'd been in Disneyland."[6] Postwar adults enshrined childhood partly because it was untainted by work; but this meant that when children moved into the workplace, they were often in for a shock.

This benign deception did not escape the intellectuals of the era, and the young person's first confrontation with the world of adult work was a major leitmotif of the serious literature and countless movies of the postwar era. John Updike's "Rabbit" quartet, the defining novelistic portrait of the postwar middle-class male, is set in motion in *Rabbit Run* (1961) when Harry Angstrom, a Magipeeler salesman, trounces some ghetto kids in a pickup basketball game, rekindling memories of adolescent triumphs just a few years earlier. He returns home to find his pregnant wife absorbedly watching *The Mickey Mouse Club*. "We must work, boys and girls," says Jimmy, the oldest of the Mouseketeers. "That's the way to be happy." Harry stares at the TV, imagining that Jimmy might help him sell his kitchen gizmos. But then, after Jimmy winks, Harry realizes that Jimmy, like the Magipeeler and work itself, were "all a fraud." Harry's mood changes. He picks a fight with his wife, abandons her and his child, Nelson, and flees from the responsibilities of adulthood. *Rabbit at Rest* (1990), the final novel of the series, resurrects the theme. Harry, now retired, preaches the gospel of work to Nelson, who has succeeded his father in the dealership. When Nelson complains that the Japanese treat him like a robot, Harry puts a sharper spin on Jimmy's words a quarter-century earlier: "Welcome to the real world, kid." In perhaps the most important movie of the 1960s, *The Graduate*, Dustin Hoffman shrinks from both the seductive blandishments of Mrs. Robinson and a balding businessman's key to the future: "Plastics." Hoffman, like Rabbit, decides to make a run for it.

Parents and pundits alike complained of adolescent children whose discontents seemed banal compared to the ordeals experienced by those who came of age during the Great Depression and the Second World War. Adolescents, however, pointed to the irrelevance of protracted schooling and the sterility of adult work. In *Growing Up Absurd* (1960), sociologist Paul Goodman, anticipating a strain of thought that was soon to become commonplace, maintained that adolescents were discontented because the workaday world into which they were to be inducted was by its nature repugnant: segmented, deceitful, and unreal. When he asked young people what they wanted to do as adults, most said, "Nothing." Goodman broke down in tears, dismayed "for the waste of our humanity."[7]

The intellectuals' anguished doubts about the intrinsic benefits of work were a luxury far beyond the means of most people. Work brought in money—a stolid view of life that made sense to postwar Americans who had recently scrambled out of the abyss of the Depression, fear and hunger nipping at their heels. It mattered little whether one wrestled with a lathe or watched over a laser-guided drill press, pounded on a typewriter or clicked away at a computer keyboard, simmered dinner over a stove or stuck it into a microwave. The most important thing about a job was that you had one.

BUREAUCRATIZATION AND THE RISE OF HUMAN RELATIONS

Postwar work was mysterious partly because the trend toward bureaucratization, which had slowed during the Great Depression, greatly accelerated during the Second World War and afterward. The war not only put Americans back to work, but it also greatly extended and strengthened the corporate foundations of the economy. Antitrust prosecutions made little sense when the national defense required immediate and massive levels of production, and the federal government ensured defense industry profits by replacing competitive bidding with cost-plus contracts, by providing the capital for new factories, and by bringing corporate executives into war-planning boards. In 1940, the largest one hundred corporations accounted for 30 percent of the nation's manufacturing output; within three years, that figure had grown to 70 percent.

Although the managerial revolution, by which salaried managers replaced owners in the daily operations of the firm, originated in the mid-nineteenth century, it did not pervade business culture until after World War II. Many postwar managers had themselves received their business education in the armed forces, a tremendous bureaucracy that, despite complaints of excessive paperwork and inefficiency, had driven a voracious war machine all over the globe. The establishment of the American Society for Personnel Administrators in 1948 marked the proliferation of managers in American institutions; by 1972, some twelve million managers ran much of the nation's economic infrastructure, abetted by a vastly larger pool of secretaries, data-entry clerks, and other minions of the vast corporate bureaucracies.

The shift toward the bureaucratized workplace was reflected in the changing fortunes of the salesman. Toward the close of World War II, the salesman retained considerable esteem. The cancellation of war contracts portended a downward slump in demand that might again plunge the nation into a depression. At the time, many observers claimed that the salesman shouldered the heavy "responsibility for preventing another depression" by stimulating demand.[8] The salesman had formerly earned respect precisely because he was on his own, and not "cinched to a desk," in Nathaniel Hawthorne's evocative phrase. Sales remained the last major arena where individual initiative really mattered, where one rose or fell according to his merits. Salesmanship, David R. Osborne explained in *Selling as a Postwar Career* (1945), was the peacetime equivalent of war, and sales managers its commanders-in-chief, charged with making "battle plans," establishing "Officer Training Schools," and fighting "every skirmish as if the whole damned war depended on the outcome."[9]

But the expanding corporate bureaucracies made a mockery of such claims. Power and influence flowed not from individualistic assertion, the corporate managers insisted, but from the collective strength of large bureaucracies. Advertising through the mass media stimulated demand more effectively than salesmen. Thus ambitious men belonged not in sales, pounding the pavement, but upon the corporate ladder, climbing to success. A poll of undergraduates at the University of Minnesota, first taken in 1925 and repeated in 1946, revealed that although the relative status of nearly every occupation had remained unchanged— bankers, physicians, and lawyers headed both lists—salesmen had dropped from eleventh place to sixteenth.[10] At university job conventions, students crowded around recruiters in finance and accounting, while life-insurance recruiters often failed to land a single interview.

The pages of Norman Vincent Peale's religious-tract-as-self-help-manual, *The Power of Positive Thinking* (1952), were littered with the stories of salesmen who were plagued by "fear and defeat thoughts" but who improved their commissions on finding Christ. If even salesmen could rise in life, Peale seemed to suggest, nearly anybody could. The seeming devaluation of sales was reflected by entrance of women into the occupation; indeed, the most visible "salesmen" of the era were the women who sold Tupperware and Mary Kay cosmetics. Arthur Miller's play *Death of a Salesman* (1949) provided both the epitaph for the salesman and the explanation for his demise: Willy Loman (Low-man) had plenty of problems, to be sure, but was fired for being a loner and a loser: a salesman, someone who could not find a place within the protective folds of the corporate bureaucracy.

Quietly interred, the salesman was superseded by a new symbol of the American economy: the "organization man." The phrase came from sociologist William H. Whyte's 1956 book. *The Organization Man* sold 700,000 copies, making it arguably the most popular sociological tract of the twentieth century. He compared the postwar workplace with his experiences as a sales trainee for Vicks many years earlier. He described that training program as "a gladiators' school" where he learned "one simple thing": "The man on the other side of the counter is the ENEMY." But Whyte discerned that by the 1950s the corporate ethos had been transformed. Now the prototypical corporate employee was not a fighter, but someone who had attended college, maintained a B average, joined sporting teams and clubs, and then attached himself to a large corporate bureaucracy and held on tight as it grew larger and richer. This "organization man" was a consummate "yes man" who subsumed his own identity into that of the firm. Upon graduation, Whyte wrote, postwar college students "do not go to a hostile world; they transfer."[11] In Whyte's view, individual initiative had not exactly been killed; indeed, nearly everyone in authority intoned the virtues of ambition and drive. But confined within narrow administrative units, circumscribed by explicit lines of authority, and fettered by precise work rules and job descriptions, individual initiative no longer had much room to maneuver.

The rise of the "organization man" corresponded with the diffusion throughout the corporate world of the principles of Frederick W. Taylor (1856–1915), an efficiency engineer who maintained that "every single act of the workman can be reduced to a science." Workers, Taylor insisted, were "mentally sluggish," hobbled by age-old shop traditions and "rules of thumb" that wasted time, materials, and effort. Taylor-trained consultants, armed with stopwatches and flowcharts, promised to impose order and efficiency upon the chaos of the shop floor. (The applications of his science, Taylor believed, were virtually unlimited, a point he rammed home on the croquet field by calculating his shots with a protractor.)

Ford's assembly line was an early instance of Taylorism, whose concepts had become sufficiently public to be lampooned in Charlie Chaplin's film *Modern Times* (1936). Taylorism gained momentum during World War II, as shop traditions were lost amid the chaotic influx of new workers and the frenzied exigencies of war. The resounding success of the American war machine strengthened the claims of postwar managers who proposed to extend Taylorized regimentation. Before the war, the contract between U.S. Steel and the steelworkers' union took up less than two pages. By contrast, the 1946 contract consisted of over a thousand pages of finely printed text. Every job was pegged to a common denominator of exertion—a "fair day's work"—defined as the effort equal to a normal person walking "without load, on smooth, level ground at the rate of three miles per hour." (The shoveling equivalent was lifting twelve and a half shovelfuls, fifteen pounds each, of 5.5-percent-moisture river sand from a pile to a nearby box, indoors, on a smooth concrete floor.) In subsequent years the contract became even more complex. A quarter-century after the Second World War, *Fortune* reported that the "sternly detailed" work rules of the nation's automobile plants would "make a training sergeant at a Marine boot camp smile with pleasure." [12]

As work became bureaucratized and routinized, its intrinsic meaning faded. Corporate planners and union bargainers who hammered out the job descriptions and applied them to specific projects had little if any contact with workers. Reduced to human terms, the Taylorized workplace was daunting, as Charles R. Walker and Robert H. Guest reported in *The Man on the Assembly Line* (1952). "There is nothing more discouraging," one worker told them, "than having a barrel beside you with 10,000 bolts in it and using them all up. They get you a barrel with another 10,000 bolts, and you know every one has to be picked up and put in exactly the same place as the last 10,000 bolts." "It's like a dogsled," another reported. "As soon as the whistle blows, they yell 'Mush,' and away you go." It was as if, a steelworker mused in the sixties, "da Vinci had to draw his anatomical charts a hundred times a day." [13]

That industrialization was synonymous with deskilled and boring work had long been evident; the bureaucratization of work accelerated rapidly during and after World War II, as did the antidote to Taylorism. In the 1930s, psychologist Elton Mayo turned his attention to the problem of sloppy and inattentive work in large factories. Mayo blamed the Taylorized workplace for depriving workers of their sense of self. Rather than attack the regimentation and differentiation that had become synonymous with the postwar economic machine, however, Mayo sought to "humanize" the workplace by dulling its sharp edges. He believed that just as the large employer kept a physician on staff to handle industrial accidents, it should also have a Mayo-trained psychologist available to salve the psyches of those bruised by the system. It was worth the cost: emotionally healthy employees would work harder and better.

Mayo's doctrine—known as human relations management—became the reigning orthodoxy of the postwar corporation, propounded in business schools and in publications such as *Industrial Medicine, Personnel Psychology, Industrial Psychology*, and *Personnel*. The "organization man" embraced human relations intuitively. "There is no doubt," psychiatrist D. Ewen Cameron wrote in *Industrial Medicine* in 1946, "that every day men and women leave industry in chronic or permanent psychological ill health and that the causation of this is to be found primarily in the nature of their occupation." Staff psychologists could modify the tasks that made employees mentally ill. "The biggest gamble" in modern business, another consulting psychologist explained, was figuring out what workers had on their minds. Who better to ferret out the "hidden factors" behind employee behavior—the elusive "motives, desires, wishes, impulses"— than trained specialists?[14]

Industrial psychiatrists took the notion of treatment literally, boosting the spirits of troubled workers with antidepressant drugs. In 1958, Smith Kline Laboratories advertised in *Industrial Medicine & Surgery* for Compazine, a tranquilizer and antiemetic to promote emotional stability among workers. The following year Pfizer & Co. trumpeted the benefits of Atarax, an antidepressant "for ambulatory neurotics who must work or operate machinery."[15] Psychiatrists were enlisted to assist managers in still other ways. They helped labor mediators by giving deponents shots of sodium amytal (a "truth" drug); sometimes they assisted in the resolution of disputes by treating difficult bosses or workers.[16]

The most pervasive indication of the new clout of human relations was the widespread use of psychological testing. At first, human relations administered skill tests: secretaries, on typing speed and alphabetization; plumbers, on the parts of a faucet. But industrial psychologists persuaded corporate and governmental managers that tests could also discern the mental state of workers, even managers and executives. Was it wise, one psychologist asked, to leave someone "with psychotic tendencies in charge of the Defense Department?" Corporate personnel managers, traditionally scorned by their counterparts in finance and production, leaped at the chance to bring scientific knowledge to bear upon the untidy vagaries of the human spirit. By the mid-1960s, 80 percent of the larger corporations used psychological tests for hiring, placement, and promotion.[17]

The exams, with sly probing questions, induced the types of anxieties Mayo's psychologists were expected to treat. For example, the question—"Do you ever have fears of failure?"—defied a simple "satisfactory" answer. The grading rubric explained that a forthright "Yes" might suggest crippling insecurities and more serious psychological debilities, while a resolute "No" could be taken as a sign of incipient megalomania or downright deceitfulness. Other questions led into the murky depths of Freudian psychology: "Underline the word you think goes best with the word in capitals: RED (hot, color, stain, blood)." The right— that is, "normal"—answer was "color." Those who answered "blood" were suspect, the test designers suggested, for this might betoken incipient psychosis; "stain" hinted at anxiety over female sexuality, perhaps denotative of homosexuality; and "hot" might suggest a tendency toward sadism. As test-takers sought to navigate past such hidden shoals, they wondered what any of it had to do with their potential performance as a mail sorter or vice president of finance.[18]

Mental health professionals were not alone in endorsing Mayo's human relations management. Postwar architects, though enamored of the "clean decency" and "rigid symmetry" of the offices and factories built in the 1920s and 1930s, conceded that employee morale took precedence over aesthetics. *Architectural Record* endorsed freer shapes, emphasizing "fluidity" and "off-center massing," and recommended that interior workplaces be bathed in sunlight. The overall effect would promote "health, wealth and happiness."

Health professionals toured plants to ensure proper lighting and air, while human relations executives attempted to enhance socialization during lunch and coffee breaks. They were especially uncomfortable with the custom of workers bringing lunch in a tin box to work and eating it at the workstation, or grabbing coffee and doughnuts from carts that left the plant floor strewn with litter. Employee cafeterias were hailed as a way to promote nutrition and reduce the worker's isolation and loneliness. A well-designed cafeteria, architects insisted, would cut down on absenteeism and fatigue and improve production. An advertisement for an in-plant feeding service promised to build "an esprit de corps that steps up efficiency." By 1948, *Fortune* reported, ten million workers, 80 percent of the workforce at large factories, were fed in company cafeterias.[19] During the following decade employee cafeterias spread to most of the larger offices and stores.

Music became another anodyne for the ills of the workplace. In 1949, researchers for *Personnel Psychology* reported that six thousand industrial installations piped in music to their workers. To the psychologists' dismay, however, elaborate studies of programming (Lawrence Welk on Mondays, Latin music on Tuesdays, no music on Wednesdays, and so forth) failed to show that music had any influence whatsoever on productivity. But the psychologists were undaunted. Workers themselves believed that the music made them more effective workers, and the psychologists thought this positive outlook itself was salutary. The music stayed.[20]

Soon the larger corporations were lavishing a veritable cornucopia of human relations–style benefits upon employees. By 1950 they reportedly spent $65 million annually to publish four thousand plant newspapers whose purpose was to build a sense of family, complete with birth and marriage announcements and accounts of bowling contests and company picnics. (It was some measure of the triumph of human relations that similarly chatty newsletters became a staple of nearly every branch of the military.) GAF organized "Qunch" contests in the cafeteria, a trivia quiz at lunch, winners to get a free meal. IBM established a country club exclusively for employees. Other companies built bowling alleys, picnic grounds, and dance floors.[21] The Christmas office party evolved into a bacchanalian rite in some ways reminiscent of Halloween: a socially sanctioned safety valve that by celebrating free expression for a single day helped enforce strict discipline for the remainder of the year.

As the business world was becoming increasingly well elaborated and its levels of authority more sharply articulated, some managers muted or eliminated visible badges of status and rank. This trend gained considerable momentum during the 1960s, as many firms closed prestigious executive washrooms and lunchrooms and did away with demeaning time clocks. J. C. Penney and Wal-Mart referred to employees with the egalitarian appellation "associates." In one workplace after another, dress codes were relaxed and uniforms modified or discarded. In 1970, *Time*, noting that many nurses were wearing pantsuits and mailmen shorts, proclaimed that a "Uniform Revolution" had swept the nation.[22]

In the nineteenth century, people seemed to crave uniforms. The self acquired depth and respectability as one layer of identity was piled upon another; the solid citizen characteristically had a closet full of uniforms: work clothes, fraternal costumes, volunteer fire company outfits. But in the twentieth century the self came to be thought of as personal and fragile, something that would crack under the precisely calibrated stresses and constraints of the Taylorized workplace. It was to shelter the self from such pressures that the human relations managers provided workers a pleasing workroom with soothing music, a nice lunch, a thoughtful boss, a secure job, and, at times of psychic peril, a chat with a mental health expert.

By the early 1970s the human relations revolution had transformed many of the nation's workplaces. "Authoritarian direction was on the decline," *Fortune* announced in 1970, replaced by a new "participative order."[23] Even workplaces that had seemingly thrived on rigid hierarchies were affected. Everywhere the domineering boss was in retreat. Few figures were more outmoded than the old-style boss. In cartoons, Sarge kicked the hapless Beetle Bailey, and Mr. Dithers ceaselessly humiliated the napping Dagwood Bumstead, but this anti–human relations management style was funny precisely because it was outmoded. The old-style boss was literally hung from the ceiling in the movie *Nine to Five* (1980); the secretaries played by Dolly Parton, Jane Fonda, and Lily Tomlin, during the boss's suspension, redecorated the office, instituted flex-time, and otherwise "humanized" the workplace.

THE PARADOX OF WOMEN AND WORK

Immediately after the war, many employers laid off women workers and replaced them with returning soldiers. But as the nation abruptly shifted from wartime production to satisfying long-pent-up consumer demand, women were rapidly rehired. Vast new corporate bureaucracies required legions of secretaries and office workers, and the expansion of the retail sector created a demand for sales personnel. Women were deemed ideally suited for such positions; besides, they would work for much lower wages than would men. Thus the postwar corporation, which had previously released women when they got married, reversed such policies. In 1948, Prudential Insurance ended its seventy-seven-year ban on employing married women.[24] This prompted the National Industrial Conference to conduct a survey that found that, only a decade earlier, one-fourth of the large corporations fired women when they married; only 6 percent of employers did so in 1948. The influx of women into the paid workforce was one of the most important aspects of postwar work. In 1940, only one in four civilian employees was female, and only one in three working women was married. By 1970, nearly four in ten paid workers were women, two-thirds of them married. The bureaucratization of the postwar corporation in large part depended on this massive infusion of women workers.

Yet the trend toward working adult women was subverted by a powerful cultural reaction in the opposite direction. Intellectuals and popular entertainments alike enshrined motherhood and insisted that it was a full-time vocation. The social system of the postwar United States succeeded, Talcott Parsons contended, because of its specialization, and that specialization extended to gender: men performed the "instrumental" tasks of society—running institutions, earning money, defending the nation—while women performed its "expressive" tasks—caring for children, guiding the young, and salving the psyches of exhausted husbands. In *Modern Woman: The Lost Sex* (1947), psychoanalysts Marynia Farnham and Ferdinand Lundberg maintained that men were innately suited to fight the battles of the workplace. Women, on the other hand, were biologically conditioned to protect and nurture the young, traits that would be of little use in the business world. Women's "natural" work was housework. Those women who insisted on thrusting themselves into the competitive world of business would find it incompatible with their own desires; they would be forever at war with themselves.

While Farnham and Lundberg's affirmation of feminine domesticity was sending ripples through some academic circles, a blockbuster book was reshaping the nation's cultural landscape. Benjamin Spock's *Common Sense Guide to Baby and Childcare*, first published in 1946, sold more than twenty-five million copies over the next quarter-century; it was arguably the most influential book of its time. Like Farnham and Lundberg, Spock suggested that women were naturally attuned to the tasks of childrearing. Mothers need not rely on the assistance of doctors or counselors; all they really needed was to trust their common sense, love their babies, and consult Spock's book. But if Spock empowered and reassured mothers, he also underscored that theirs was a full-time job. Babies and children required their mothers' love to build up their sense of self. Mothers who took paid work outside the home deprived their children of that nurturance and thus "neglected" them. The child who was "mildly neglected," Spock cautioned, was "apt to be mildly disturbed." "If the mother realized clearly how vital her love and care is to the small child," he concluded, "it may make it easier to decide that the extra money she might earn, or the satisfaction she might receive from an outside job, is not so important after all."

American popular culture concurred, incessantly. One measure of the revival of domesticity was the extent to which postwar Americans rediscovered and enshrined Victorian culture, whose fundamental message was the separation of the male and female spheres of life. Louisa May Alcott's *Little Women* and Charles Dickens's *Christmas Carol* articulated a tight separation of gender spheres—women worked within the home and men outside it—and such books were rediscovered and endlessly republished. Popular culture, especially television, took hold of this neo-Victorian formulation. In the television comedy *I Love Lucy*, Lucille Ball repeatedly attempted to escape from housewifery drudgery and horn in on her husband's career; that such aberrant behavior would be calamitous, and thus amusing, was the presumption of the show. In another popular 1950s sitcom, *Father Knows Best*, Robert Young—the father—was mostly absent and fundamentally clueless as to what was going on at home. *The Waltons*, among the most popular television series of the 1970s, similarly asserted the centrality of a mother who, like Marmee in *Little Women*, zealously attended to her family while her husband (sometimes) brought in the cash.

Women in the paid workforce reconciled the expectation that they remain at home in a variety of ways. In 1947, *Woman's Home Companion* surveyed its readers as to preferable paid occupations and found that the great majority preferred jobs that retained a sense of "femininity": nursing (31 percent), clerical and retailing (26 percent), and teaching (15 percent), because these careers offered the best preparation for women's "prime objective": marriage. Corporations gladly affirmed the stereotypical view that women were inescapably infused with a gender sensibility. In 1950, *Personnel Journal* advised businesses to attend to their female employees' "feminine whims and fancies." It had learned, for example, that women metalworkers took an amusingly maternal interest in their "own" machine and resisted being rotated to a different one. In 1949, when the *Journal of Retailing* reported on a "feminine invasion of executive positions" among 120 leading New York department stores, nearly all of the women executives had been hired as buyers and fashion consultants. A "feeling" for color, fashion and style, the journal explained, were "predominantly feminine traits."[25]

Having preselected women explicitly for the femininity (and their willingness to work for much lower wages than men), employers anticipated that women would to live up (or perhaps down) to expectations. A 1946 industry survey reported that nearly two-thirds of women lost work time due to menstrual cramps. Because women commonly experienced "frank depression" during menstruation, *Industrial Medicine* advised employers to dispense amphetamines and aspirin. In 1948, *Hygeia*, another magazine on health in the workplace, advised employers to attend to women's "unique physical problems" by providing women employees with their own special room, with a nurse in attendance. As late as 1970, *Industry Week* printed an ostensibly humorous piece in which it contrasted different "types" of "office girls." Best was the "low intellect female," because she was "not bored by boring work, and is fun to watch hanging Christmas balls on the tree before the Christmas party." The author repeated a sure-fire rule of thumb for hiring secretaries: estimate the applicant's bust measurement, subtract it from her typing speed, and hire only those with negative numbers.[26]

For much of the postwar decades, millions of American women, after returning home from work, fixing dinner, straightening the house, or doing a load of laundry, collapsed in front of a TV set and watched Livy Walton scurrying about the house, making clothes and cakes from scratch, and soothing the fragile psyches of her husband and children, proving, in essence, what Parsons, Farnham and Lundberg, and Spock had insisted: that women belonged at home, all of the time.

Yet the actual lives of full-time housewives proved to be less idyllic. Although some scholars contend that postwar housewives had it easier than their mothers and grandmothers, largely due to the wider availability of vacuum cleaners, washing machines, dishwashers, and prepared foods, others point out that as more people moved from apartments to houses, and from small houses to larger ones, and as standards of cleanliness and culinary arts became more exacting, housewives had to work harder than before. Moreover, expectations of women's special competence in nurturance required that they assume new duties as psychological counselor and martini mixer: a woman's work, insofar as it entailed emotional sustenance, was never done.

The frustrations of postwar housewives were brought to light by Betty Friedan. A scholar who gave up a life in academia to become a full-time housewife, Friedan felt bored, unfulfilled, and miserable. Then she interviewed scores of other housewives who shared her sentiments. She chronicled their views in *The Feminine Mystique* (1963). She claimed that full-time homemakers devised a set of myths about the delights of being a housewife—the "feminine mystique"—without really believing in the myth. While Farnham and Lundberg claimed that women who worked outside the home would be at war with themselves, Friedan found evidence—subjective, to be sure—that plenty of full-time housewives were profoundly unhappy. And while Spock claimed that full-time mothers were essential to the mental health of their children, Friedan's chronicle of discontented and angry women cast doubt on the mental health and stability of their children. The *Feminist Mystique* became an instant best-seller; Friedan used royalties from the book to found the National Organization for Women (NOW).

The feminist contention that women should be allowed to compete on equal footing with men was partly justified by the transformation of the corporate workplace. Relatively few jobs created during the postwar decades depended on muscle and body mass, where men generally possessed a biological advantage. The large corporations depended, above all else, on teamwork and the smooth flow of information, communications skills for which women were adjudged to be especially well suited. As young women's career expectations rose, so did their test scores and admissions to college. On graduation, women increasingly expected to compete with men for good jobs within the giant corporations that dominated the postwar economy. Thus, married women who worked outside of the home were both overworked and encumbered with guilt at neglecting their children. Housewives, on the other hand, often found their isolation and circumscribed activities to be crushingly boring and unfulfilling.

But the women and men who sought to resolve the stresses and strains of their working lives soon encountered a workplace profoundly different from the one in which they had grown up.

CORPORATIONS IN CRISIS: 1973 TO THE MID-1980s

On October 6, 1973, the eve of Yom Kippur, the Jewish Day of Atonement, Egyptian and Syrian tanks smashed into Israel and threatened to slice it in half. President Richard M. Nixon, though mired in the Watergate scandal, resupplied the battered Israeli army and sent it scores of fighter planes. Israeli defenses stiffened. In a bold counterstroke, the Israeli army crossed the Suez Canal, cut off an entire Egyptian army, and forced it to surrender. The Arab world, furious over American intervention, cut off oil shipments to the West. Skyrocketing oil prices forced up the price of nearly everything else. In 1974, negotiations brought an end to the embargo, but the oil-exporting nations had learned that if they limited production, they could drive up the price of oil.

Their cartel, the Organization of Petroleum Exporting Countries (OPEC), did just that. Gasoline prices doubled almost overnight. Long lines formed at gas pumps.

American automakers who had scoffed at the small European and Japanese imports now winced as foreign competitors claimed the new market for small, fuel-efficient, front-wheel-drive cars. American auto companies were unable to respond to this challenge because their contracts with the United Automobile Workers (UAW) linked wages to consumer prices, which had floated upward with the price of oil. As production costs rose, manufacturers needed to sell more big cars, loaded with expensive options. They could not sell the small cars the public craved. (In 1982, when Ford belatedly entered the front-wheel-drive market, it lost $40 on each car sold.) By the end of the 1970s, Japanese automakers had captured 30 percent of the entire American automobile market. The decline of the automobile industry signaled a broader decline of heavy industry. The nation was plunged in a serious recession.

Recessions are part of the natural business cycle. But for the first time in the nation's history, a business recession and the consequent slackening of demand did not halt inflation. Millions of workers lost their jobs, yet wages and prices continued to rise. The term "stagflation" (a combination of stagnation and inflation) was coined to describe this anomaly. In 1974, when McDonald's employed more people than U.S. Steel, Senator Lloyd Bentsen (D-Tex.) complained, "There is something very wrong with a nation that is long on hamburgers and short on steel." But the two phenomena went hand in hand. Job creation had been built into the dynamics of the post-1973 economy all along. When workers lost relatively high-paying jobs in the automobile factories and steel mills, their wives and teenage children often went to work, usually in restaurants or stores. When the family limped home, benumbed and exhausted, no one doubted that they "deserved a break," as McDonald's put it, and often enough they trudged to the burgeoning malls for cheap meals and window-shopping.

For the millions of young women whose gender consciousness had been shaped by Betty Friedan, Kate Millett, and other feminists, the recession struck at the worst possible time. Those who had anticipated a rapid ascent of the corporate ladder discovered that the lower rungs were the first to collapse during recession. Many abandoned the idea of a career and settled for low-paying, dead-end jobs in the clerical or service sector. A result was that, just when the feminist movement required a united fight to gain legal parity with men, women increasingly were divided into an intellectual and professional elite, eager to prove their merits in fair competition with men, and an underpaid and ill-used underclass, vulnerable to the vagaries of a recessionary economy. Phyllis Schlafly, head of a right-wing antifeminist movement called STOP, played on both economic inequalities and men's fears of being displaced in the workforce in her ultimately successful campaign to defeat the Equal Rights Amendment, which, although approved by Congress in 1972, failed to win ratification.

The recession of the 1970s nearly crippled the labor union movement. Union membership slipped badly from the high point of the mid-1950s, when over one in three nonagricultural workers belonged to unions; by 1978, it was one in four, and by 1990, one in six. During the 1940s and 1950s, most workers had voted to join a union, pay dues, and have it bargain for them. By 1978, however, unions were losing three-fourths of their campaigns to represent workers; worse, workers who belonged to unions were opting to get out. Every year, eight hundred more union shops voted to rescind their affiliation.

During the 1930s and 1940s, organizers fought long and often courageous battles to win union recognition. They established strong ties to workers and won their confidence by articulating and redressing the special grievances of each workplace. But by the early 1970s the unions had become large bureaucracies much like the corporations themselves. Unions responded to internal pressures much as corporate human-resources managers did: union halls became recreational centers; the union newsletter was at first glance indistinguishable from the one put out by the company. To the younger generation, the leadership's tales of a heroic past merely underscored the fact that the present had come to an inglorious dead end. Younger workers grew impatient with a system that linked salary and job security to seniority and that all too often enriched graying union officials. One steelworker, when asked what went through his mind at work, said he fantasized "about a sexy blonde in Miami who's got my union dues."[27] The rift between generations occasionally surfaced over political issues. At the AFL-CIO convention in 1967, a handful of younger leaders proposed a resolution against the Vietnam War that the mostly middle-aged leadership voted down two thousand to six.

By the close of the 1960s, labor leader Walter Reuther was exasperated with young workers, so many of whom "ran away from work" whenever they got the chance.[28] Business concurred; only one in fifty business leaders in 1970 thought the current generation of workers more conscientious than the one that preceded it; 63 percent thought them less so.[29] Simmering generational discontents boiled up two years later at the GM assembly division at Lordstown, Ohio. GM had retooled the plant, installing robotic welding machines, streamlining the workforce, and doubling the speed of the assembly line: one hundred cars passed through each hour, forty more than before. Younger workers, without authorization from the national UAW, refused to work at the faster pace and allowed many chassis to pass untouched. The "almighty dollar," the local UAW leader observed, "is not the only thing in my estimation."[30]

Young workers complained that work itself was boring and meaningless, and they increasingly rejected the postwar accord in which organized labor ceded control of the workplace in return for cost-of-living increases and job security.

Absenteeism at General Motors and Ford doubled during the 1960s; by 1970, 5 percent of GM's workforce was missing without explanation every day, and one in ten workers failed to show up on Mondays and Fridays. At the end of the day workers stampeded toward the parking lots, evidence of their "desperate haste," as one put it, to escape from work. When Chrysler's Sterling Heights stamping plant in 1974 scheduled full shifts at double pay, managers were stunned when only half showed up for work. In some divisions at Ford, 25 percent of the workers quit within a year of being hired.[31] The following year, the U.S. Department of Health, Education and Welfare issued a pessimistic report, *Work in America*. "Significant numbers of American workers," it concluded, had grown profoundly dissatisfied with the "dull, repetitive, seemingly meaningless tasks" of the postwar workplace. Young workers everywhere were rebelling against both the "drudgery of routine jobs" and the unresponsiveness of union leadership.[32] In 1967, a poll indicated that half the respondents nationwide found their jobs personally fulfilling; by 1980, only a quarter felt that way. A decade later, one-fourth of all workers reported that they suffered from anxiety or stress, 13 percent from depression. *Safety and Health* found that poor morale translated into an annual loss of sixteen workdays for each employee.[33]

In 1970, Ford prepared a new type of training film for new workers. In one scene a worker looked up from the moving chassis, his face etched with concern, and he stared at the camera: "I got a good job—but it's pretty bad." An early expression of a type of candor that became increasingly common two decades later, the film laid bare the essential compromise of postwar work. The film was entitled *Don't Paint It Like Disneyland*.[34] In 1976, Gail Sheehy, perceiving a widespread malaise among men in their forties, contended in *Passages*, a best-seller, that a "midlife crisis" was part of their natural life cycle. Sheehy failed to see that the anxieties of many white-collar workers were a well-founded response to the sharp deterioration in the economic climate.

Bad as work was, job tenure had become far more precarious: the layoffs, beginning in the manufacturing sector in the 1970s but spreading into the service sector in the 1980s, proved that the corporations were unable to keep up their end of the postwar bargain with labor.[35]

LEANER AND MEANER: THE MODERN WORKPLACE

The recession of the 1970s rocked the nation's heavy industrial and manufacturing base; it also transformed its political culture. In 1980, Ronald Reagan swept into the presidency with a promise to cut taxes and get government "off people's backs." In terms of economic policy, this meant a relaxation of antitrust rules and government-imposed banking restrictions. This "deregulated" economy gave rise to a frenzy of corporate acquisitions and mergers. In 1982, William Simon, a former secretary of the treasury, led a consortium that bought Gibson Greeting Cards from RCA for $80 million. Of that sum, they borrowed $79 million. The potential of using "junk bonds"—high-yield bonds far in excess of the issuer's assets—for corporate acquisitions became the specialty of Michael Milken, a trader for Drexel Burnham Lambert. With Milken's help, in 1985 Ronald Perelman, head of Pantry Pride, a supermarket chain worth about $145 million, acquired Revlon, a $2 billion conglomerate. This precipitated a wave of similar mergers. During the 1980s, one-fifth of the Fortune 500 companies were taken over, merged, or forced to go private; in all, some twenty-five thousand mergers and acquisitions were undertaken, with a total value of nearly half a trillion dollars. To make their companies less tempting to cash-hungry raiders, many corporations took on whopping debts or acquired unprofitable companies. By the late 1980s, many American corporations were awash in red ink. Debt payments were eating up 50 percent of the nation's corporate pretax earnings.

Corporations coped with the debt either by selling assets, such as factories and warehouses, or by laying off workers. U.S. Steel, whose rusting mills desperately needed capital improvements, instead spent $5 billion to acquire Marathon Oil of Ohio; nearly 100,000 steelworkers lost their jobs. No firm was immune, no worker secure. "A job for life" had long been IBM's unofficial but endlessly repeated slogan. As late as 1985, it ran an advertisement to reassure employees. "Jobs may come and go—But people shouldn't." Yet during the next nine years a crippled IBM eliminated eighty thousand jobs and more than a third of its workforce. During the 1980s, the total number of Fortune 500 employees declined by three million; nearly one-third of all positions in middle management were eliminated. Millions of "organization men" (about one-third of whom were now women) were laid off as the organizations themselves "downsized," the corporate euphemism for wholesale firings. Many jobs went abroad, where labor costs were lower and unions were almost nonexistent. In 1980, Xerox of America, unable to compete with its Japanese subsidiary, laid off tens of thousands of American workers. In 1985, Nike closed its American shoe factory and moved its operations to Indonesia. "Chrysler was supposed to be a big safe cocoon!" bemoaned one employee on learning he had been laid off. Workers' confidence, high in the 1940s and 1950s, evaporated in the parched job market of the 1970s and early 1980s.[36]

During the three decades of prosperity since 1941, the nation's corporations had become big and complacent, more attuned to the demands of the corporate bureaucracy than the needs of consumers. The recession of the 1970s and the merger mania of subsequent decades transformed the corporate ethos. Executives and small businessmen alike listened more carefully to Peter Drucker, who had long railed against the human relations approach to management. "It is not the business of the enterprise to create happiness but to sell and make shoes," he wrote in 1954.[37] Drucker contended that human relations managers had failed to show that their efforts had improved morale, much less raised productivity. It was wiser to subordinate workers "to the claim of economic performance: profitability and productivity." Few managers had much reason to attend to Drucker's words when jobs were plentiful and valuable employees might accept offers from other firms, but Drucker's call for a trim operation suited the more competitive economy of the 1990s. Managers could be especially hard-nosed when they were under pressure to slice hundreds—and sometimes hundreds of thousands—of workers. In 1994, for example, Fleet Bank pioneered the use of "participatory management" to engineer layoffs: teams of workers in one department determined which jobs would be cut elsewhere, rather like having the inmates on death row decide who was be executed first. After AT&T had cut twenty-four thousand workers in a single unit, one employee responded, "It's leaner, meaner, less fun, less playful in the good sense."[38] Employers did not abandon human relations entirely, but they commonly sought to keep it confined to the personnel department, where it touched the lives of workers less frequently.

As profit margins dwindled or disappeared in puddles of red ink, the company cafeterias raised prices and then closed their doors, the newsletters were discontinued, the employee centers were sold outright or leased, and other fringe benefits were sharply curtailed. IBM, once the chief corporate exemplar of enlightened human relations management, sent a strong signal in 1994 when it converted a warehouse in New Jersey into an office space. As workers stared at the spartan cubicles, an executive intoned that there would be "no walls, no boundaries, no compartments, no hierarchies, no epaulets." "I want people to know we're in a warehouse," he added.[39] Some corporations went still further, "outsourcing" much of their activities to companies that achieved economies through no-frills jobs, many of them located overseas.

The leaner and meaner corporations that survived the recession of the 1970s and the merger movement of the 1980s were well positioned to compete in emerging global markets. Productivity increased sharply. Partly this was due to the sharp reductions in the regular workforce of most corporations, many of which hired temporary workers to handle upturns in business or contracted out tasks that were not part of their central mission. Most corporations, too, had sloughed off or sold their least profitable activities; more focused on what they did best. Another major factor was that by the late 1990s the productivity advantages that many had thought would attend the proliferation of computers now generated tangible gains. Computer-monitored coordination of production and delivery resulted in substantial reductions in inventories and labor costs. The maturation of the computer industry gave rise to entirely new industries, especially software. Bill Gates, founder of Microsoft, a pioneer in software, had become the wealthiest man in the world by 1991. The United States became a center for software and computer development and applications.

By the late 1990s, though workers were reeling from layoff announcements, the economy began to rebound. As weeds grew in the parking lots of the factories of the "Rust Belt" of the Northeast and Midwest, new companies and new technology industries sprang up in the "Silicon Valley" of California, along Route 128 outside Boston, and in booming cities such as Seattle and Austin. As globalization created truly worldwide markets and suppliers, moreover, American corporations successfully competed. Fears receded that foreign producers, especially Japan, would dominate American markets. In 1984, the civilian unemployment rate in the United States was 7.5 percent, while Japan's was 2.7 percent. But by 2000, the unemployment rate of the United States had been nearly cut in half (4 percent) and was less than that of Japan (4.7 percent).

Investors worldwide concurred, and the demand for American stocks was truly global. The Dow Jones average, which in 1982 hovered just below 1,000 points, moved past 2,000 in 1987. Then it went wild, exceeding 3,000 in 1991; 5,000 in 1995; 9,000 in 1998; and 11,000 in 1999. The phenomenal success of Microsoft in the 1980s prompted venture capitalists a decade later to pour money into Internet stocks—dot-coms, in the argot of the day—whose values skyrocketed. In 1999, nearly two hundred Internet companies "went public." They raised twenty billion dollars almost immediately. From October 1998 through March 2000, the value of technology-heavy NASDAQ stocks doubled.

Dot-com executives—often software whiz kids in their twenties—promoted a workplace environment that championed creativity and freedom. Bill Gates, who had vanquished corporate America, espoused a flexible work environment that eschewed the trappings of rank and authority. Steve Jobs, founder of Apple Computer, flew a pirate flag over its Silicon Valley headquarters. The founders of the dot-coms exuberantly scoffed at the rigidity of the corporate workplace: time cards, austerely functional offices, bureaucratized work rules and procedures, conformist dress codes—all of these inhibited the creative thinking that were necessary to devise the "next big thing," the application that would transform the Internet, the information superhighway, into a golden bridge to wealth. Dot-com employees, though expected to remain at the office long past dinner, were free to play ping-pong or pinball, to go swimming or work out with weights in company-provided facilities, or to take naps or order pizza. No one punched a time card.

But in March 2000 the dot-com bubble burst. During the next nine months, the value of all NASDAQ stocks fell 50 percent; the Internet stocks did far worse. Most dot-coms folded. The lavish offices were vacated, the leather sofas and pinball machines were sold, and the relaxed worker ethos was discredited.

By the onset of the new millennium, the lean and mean corporations of the 1980s and 1990s had proven their mettle. By 2005, Wal-Mart, the largest of the new giant retail companies, employed nearly 1.5 million workers and had sales approaching $300 billion. Such firms used their massive size to force suppliers to cut costs, including wages. None of Wal-Mart's employees belonged to unions; fewer than half were covered by the company's health plan. Austerity prevailed even at the top. "We do not have limousines," declared H. Lee Scott Jr., the company's chief executive. "I drive a Volkswagen bug."[40] To those managers and investors who sought to emulate Wal-Mart's success, the message could not have been clearer: the human resources revolution of the postwar workplace was over.

A REASSESSMENT OF WORK

In 1992 Juliet Schor, a Harvard economist, published *The Overworked American*, a best-seller whose thesis was contained in its title. Schor contended that postwar Americans had become workaholics. Her data showed that since 1948, the productivity of the United States worker had doubled. If American workers had been willing to live at the fairly comfortable 1948 standard of living, every one of them could have taken off every other year—with pay. Americans instead chose to work more hours to attain a higher standard of living. Schor estimated that since 1969, the average employee worked an additional 163 hours. Some worked overtime; others moonlighted at second and even third jobs. The trend for married women to seek paid work outside the home continued. In 1945, one in five married women had paid jobs; by 1990, nearly 60 percent did. The percentage of teenagers who had jobs increased markedly after 1963. Unlike Europeans, who converted productivity gains into more leisure, Americans—nearly all Americans—worked to consume. Few had much time left for leisure.

Schor's thesis has been challenged by scholars who have conducted time-usage surveys, in which people keep diaries of what they do, each hour, for a particular day. These show that, from 1965 to 1985, the average amount of time spent working had declined by about seven hours a week. This was true in part because more young people were in college, and older Americans, especially men, often retired at an earlier age. Work within the home had declined as parents had fewer children.[41]

What is indisputable, however, is the extent to which people perceive that they are working incessantly, and that leisure time has been nearly squeezed out of their lives. One reason for this is that adults have assumed, as part of their unpaid "leisure" activities, tasks that had formerly been someone else's job. In 1945, filling station attendants pumped gas; deliverymen trucked milk and bread to the home; salesmen (and women) went door-to-door to sell everything from vacuum cleaners to cosmetics; waitresses served meals at fast-food restaurants; travel agents, stockbrokers, accountants, and other experts advised on vacation plans, provided guidance on retirement and filled out tax returns, and provided assistance on countless matters requiring specialized knowledge; clerks rang up sales, packed bags, and carried out the packages; bus drivers and subway conductors took most people to work and back. Nowadays, most people perform these tasks themselves. Leisure time has not been so much squeezed out of people's lives as transformed: nearly everyone has become a service station attendant, a deliveryman, a checkout clerk, a waitress, a travel agent, a stockbroker, an accountant, a bus driver.

Paid work, too, has acquired, for many people, a grim functionality. A half-century ago, most young people first went to work for themselves, cutting grass, babysitting, delivering packages. In recent decades, that has shifted. More work in low-paying service sector jobs and malls and restaurants. According to a 1990 survey, McDonald's was the first employer for one in fifteen American workers. The experience was not successful: three out of four of these workers failed to remain a single year.[42] Popular culture underscored the diminished expectations of young workers. The optimistic renderings provided by Walt Disney and the Golden Books had become relics of another, surprisingly distant age. In 1974, Shel Silverstein, best-selling author of poetry for children, offered a trenchant rebuttal to *The Little Engine That Could*, whose message was that, with enough grit, a young "engine" could surmount any hill (or obstacle). Silverstein's "The Little Blue Engine" falters near the top of the mountain and smashes on the rocks below: "THINKING you can just ain't enough," the poem concludes. Bart Simpson, the enormously popular cartoon character of recent years, learns from his hapless father that work is dull and meaningless; Bart's appalling destiny is to become his father. Little wonder that Bart concludes that life sucks.

If cynicism has become a staple of popular culture, it is partly because of the nature of modern work. The naive expectations of the first two postwar generations were consistent with a culture that evaded the realities of work and sought to soften its sharp edges. The corporations that sustained that culture of work are gone, or they have survived by reconfiguring the workplace. An assuredly more realistic culture of work is now emerging. But perhaps the new realism is not so new: Adam and Eve, on leaving the Garden of Eden, doubtless had forebodings about a life dedicated to ceaseless toil.

NOTES

1. James R. Green, *World of the Worker* (New York: Hill and Wang, 1980), 225.

2. "The Auto Workers' Blues," *Fortune*, September 1948, 213–214.

3. Nancy Signorielli, "Television and Adolescents' Perceptions About Work," *Youth & Society* 24, no. 3 (March 1993): 322.

4. "Monotony in Occupational Life," *Occupations* 24, no. 6 (March 1946); "Real Cop vs. TV Sleuths," *TV Guide*, 16 October 1954.

5. Betty Friedan, "Television and the Feminine Mystique," *TV Guide*, 1 February and 8 February 1964.

6. Studs Terkel, *Working* (New York: Pantheon Books, 1974), 7.

7. Cited in Paul Goodman, *Growing Up Absurd* (New York: Random House, 1960), 35.

8. Kent Sagendorph, "The Salesman: America's Spark Plug," *Coronet*, December 1949, 34.

9. David R. Osborne, *Selling as a Postwar Career* (Chicago: Dartnell Corporation, 1945), 81.

10. Maethel E. Deeg and Donald G. Paterson, "Changes in Social Status of Occupations," *Occupations* 25, no. 4 (January 1947): 205–207.

11. William H. Whyte, *The Organization Man* (New York: Doubleday, 1956), 117, 63.

12. Daniel Bell, "Work and Its Discontents: The Cult of Efficiency in America," *Fortune*, August 1970, 71.

13. Cited in Robert Levering, *Great Places to Work* (New York: Random House, 1988), 228. See also Terkel, *Working*, 9; Ely Chinoy, *Autoworkers and the American Dream* (New York: Doubleday, 1955).

14. D. Ewen Cameron, "Psychologically Hazardous Occupations," *Industrial Medicine* 15, no. 5 (May 1946): 332–335; Donald Laird, "What Do Your Workers Think?" *Personnel Journal* 28, no. 9 (February 1950): 320–324.

15. See the advertisements in *Industrial Medicine & Surgery* 27, no. 12 (December 1958) and 28, no. 2 (February 1959).

16. "Monthly Memo to Stewards and Committeemen," *UAW-CIO Ammunition*, January 1954.

17. Wendell L. French, "Psychological Testing: Some Problems and Solutions," *Personnel Administration* 29, no. 2 (March–April 1966): 19–20.

18. Cited in Martin Gross, *The Brain Watchers* (New York: Random House, 1962), 20; see also French, "Psychological Testing."

19. "The Design of Factories Today," *Architectural Record* 98, no. 5 (November 1945): 120; "In-Plant Feeding," *Architectural Forum* 85, no. 3 (September 1946): 177; "200,000 Meals a Day," *Fortune*, September 1948, 126–131.

20. William McGehee and James E. Gardner, "Music in an Industrial Job," *Personnel Psychology* 2, no. 4 (Winter 1949): 409; and Richard I. Newman Jr., Donald L. Hunt, and Fen Rhodes, "Effects of Music on Employee Attitude and Productivity in a Skateboard Factory," *Journal of Applied Psychology* 50, no. 6 (December 1966): 493–496.

21. Victor Riesel, "The Big Bad Boss Is Vanishing," *Coronet*, February 1950, 81–85.

22. "Uniform Revolution," *Time*, 5 June 1970.

23. Judson Gooding, "It Pays to Wake up the Blue-Collar Worker," *Fortune*, September 1970, 158–160.

24. "Personnel: Prudential and the Ladies," *Newsweek*, 19 April 1948.

25. "The Best Job?" *Woman's Home Companion* (August 1947): 7–8; Francis M. Bogert, "Keeping the Gals Happy," *Personnel Journal* 28, no. 11 (April 1950): 412–413; Karl

Gerstenberg and T. Dart Ellsworth, "Who Wears the Pants in Department and Specialty Stores?" *Journal of Retailing* 25, no. 3 (Fall 1949): 97–102.

26. Cameron, "Psychologically Hazardous Occupations"; Hubert J. Hindes, "Edrisal in the Treatment of Dysmenorrhea," *Industrial Medicine* 15, no. 4 (April 1946): 174; J. V. Sheppard, "Health for the Working Girl," *Hygeia* 26, no. 4 (April 1948): 250–252; "Office Girls—Bless 'Em . . . and Damn 'Em," *Industry Week*, 11 May 1970, 26–30.

27. Cited in Terkel, *Working*, 6.

28. Cited in Judson Gooding, "Blue-Collar Blues on the Assembly Line," *Fortune* July 1970, 71.

29. "What Business Thinks: The Fortune 500-Yankelovich Survey," *Fortune*, July 1970, 73.

30. Terkel, *Working*, 259.

31. Gooding, "Blue-Collar Blues," 117.

32. Cited in Green, *World of the Worker*, 221–222.

33. Jim Castaell, "Work Takes Its Toll on Mental and Emotional Health," *Safety & Health* 141, no. 1 (January 1990): 90.

34. Gooding, "Blue-Collar Blues," 117.

35. Cited in David Halberstam, *The Reckoning* (New York: William Morrow, 1986), 461.

36. Kenneth Root, "The Human Response to Plant Closures," *Annals of the American Academy of Political and Social Sciences* 475 (September 1984): 53.

37. Peter Drucker, *The Practice of Management* (New York: Harper & Row, 1954).

38. Cited in Amanda Bennett, *Death of the Organization Man* (New York: Simon & Schuster, 1990), 47.

39. "In New Jersey, I.B.M. Cuts Space, Frills and Private Desks," *New York Times*, 14 March 1994.

40. Cited in "The Wal-Mart Effect," *Los Angeles Times*, 23 November 2003.

41. John P. Robinson and Geoffrey Godbey, *Time for Life: The Surprising Ways Americans Use Their Time* (University Park: Pennsylvania State University Press, 1997).

42. Bea Wildavsky, "McJobs: Inside America's Largest Youth Training Program," *Policy Review* 49 (Summer 1989): 30–71.

7. THE MILITARY, SPORT, AND WARRIOR CULTURE

DONALD J. MROZEK

The military forces of industrial and postindustrial societies in the twentieth century possessed a divided mind—generally subordinated to the larger political systems they supported, sophisticated in organization and training, and advanced in technology, yet committed to a primal sense of identification as warriors. Anthropologically, they were simultaneously modern and traditional, and these two distinctive sensibilities did not always interact smoothly. In fact, the antimodernist dimensions within military thought expressed both the continued interest in older ways of motivating men for battle and a concerted reaction against the supposedly devitalizing tendencies within a way of life thought to be increasingly controlled and bureaucratized. The individual heroic figure—for the military, the warrior—enjoyed obvious appeal in a culture that celebrated "rugged individualism," yet the more mundane work of the capably trained soldier, sailor, airman, or marine was the real functional base of an effective armed force in the modern age.

Sport was widely thought to compensate for the perceived decline in personal physical risk in an increasingly ordered society. Yet it was susceptible to the same management techniques that were transforming the American workplace—industrial or clerical. Sport thus embodied both primal visceral energy and the impulse to organize it, which accounts for its appeal to the military.

Modes of military identity and ways of pursuing sport have been different in different eras. For the military, for example, a "warrior" focus was typically strongest when the force was a professional one with personnel drawn by voluntary enlistment—but less so when it was augmented by an extensive military draft. Thus, the collective identity of the American military in the twentieth century shifted according to the composition and selectivity of the force as a whole, both enlisted and officer. Those actively seeking their own transformation by voluntary induction into the military were clearly more likely to experience it than those who only complied with a draft notice.

The professional interest of American military officers in sport grew because it was thought to enhance the physical fitness of soldiers, ingrain quick response to orders, instill a "winning spirit," and develop "physical address"—the readiness to put one's body on the line in defense of a position—while habituating them to physical hardship. Sport went from being a personal amusement to a military duty. It was, as William James postulated, "the moral equivalent of war."

During World War I, the armed forces officially sanctioned, managed, and encouraged sport. Some officers used sport to fill time and cut down on idleness, licentiousness, and illness, including sexually transmitted disease. But others thought that sport cultivated rough and aggressive masculinity. Not without precedent was the later description of someone thought to be gay as "sensitive." At the same time, officers de-emphasized sports perceived as European, such as fencing and soccer, and strongly advocated football, boxing, and other sports considered rough and combative—and American.

Career officers who had attended the military academies or who had been in Reserve Officer Training Corps (ROTC) programs at civilian universities before World War II believed that their success in sports had contributed significantly to their success in the military. Physical dominance in sport presumably fostered dominance within formal social organizations such as the military. In essence, athletes were "alpha males." Women experienced gender-based discrimination that restricted their sporting activities, but, especially in the military, men experienced a gender-based obligation to expand them. It was these men who were responsible for the military's use of sport in World War II and in the postwar era.

WORLD WAR II AND ITS AFTERMATH

During World War II, the U.S. military used sport to foster practical effects such as stamina and quick reaction, moral effects such as combativeness, and psychological effects such as manliness and warrior spirit. U.S. forces were larger than ever before—and overwhelmingly male, women's roles being primarily in support and "nurturance" positions. Even so, due to the great personnel needs of industry and agriculture in wartime, a relatively inclusive approach to conscription and enlistment developed. Groups that had been marginalized—racial minorities, women, and gays and lesbians—found some opportunity in the military. The military had to suspend the more elitist, separatist approach to personnel acquisition, training, and other issues that might be possible under sharply different circumstances. The postwar negotiation of "soldier" and "warrior" identity would be affected by wartime service among these marginalized groups.

Some wartime programs contributed in unexpected ways to the postwar sporting culture. Notable was the Navy's V-5 preflight training program, intended to build the bodies of the future aviators while quickening their responses and cultivating aggressiveness. Suitably, the Navy promotional film on V-5 was called *The Winning Spirit*. Simply by its schedule of activities, the V-5 program might not merit special notice. Boxing, football, and other sports identified as "combative" were favored, while others such as basketball were encouraged for imparting quick response and teamwork. Aggressiveness and physical address were esteemed more than finesse and skill. In themselves, though, these were not new ideas.

The V-5 program was the inspiration of longtime Annapolis football coach Thomas Hamilton, but its staff comprised mostly civilian physical educators and coaches, most of them in the early stages of their careers. Among them were Paul "Bear" Bryant, later the football coach at the University of Alabama; Woody Hayes, who would run the football program at Ohio State University and be considered something of a military historian; Darrell Royal, who later coached at the University of Texas at Austin; and Bud Wilkinson, who went on to coach football at the University of Oklahoma and who also served as a special adviser for physical fitness in the Kennedy years. Few programs can claim to have had such impact on a single sport. As football emerged to special importance in the post–World War II era, the tone and manner of exponents such as these had disproportionately great impact on the tone and manner of sport at large.

The postwar years saw nothing less than a partial "militarization" of America's sporting culture. In the first half of the twentieth century, sport was such a thriving institution that its advocates were able to exert substantial influence on other aspects of the culture. But after World War II, it was military culture—as understood especially by its civilian advocates more than by Army and Navy personnel—that exerted a transforming influence on sport and, through it, on the larger society. In the late nineteenth century, Albert Spalding failed to convince Americans that "Baseball is war!" By contrast, after World War II, football quickly became the "60-minute war."

During World War II, the American press—and not just military outlets such as *Stars and Stripes*—used sport analogies and sport-related images to explain international political policy, to generate domestic support for the war, and to outline the basics of military strategy. Sometimes the print media, in cartoons, editorials, and feature stories, depicted business, finance, labor, and agriculture as baseball players or different service branches as members of a football team, presumably united in support of the war. Time and again, sports metaphors were used to help the public grasp elements of the domestic and international scene.

After the war, military metaphors came into broad use, while sports metaphors were exploited to explain public policy. James Forrestal, secretary of the navy from the end of the war up to 1947 and then the first secretary of defense, in advocating military training of all young males, likened preparation for war to training for a boxing match or a "big league" football game. In 1949, General Omar Bradley, chairman of the Joint Chiefs of Staff, chided various officers for undue concern for their particular branches of the armed services, declaring that the military forces were "one team" and that every player, regardless of position, must "be an All-American." In December of that year, Louis Johnson, who had succeeded Forrestal as secretary of defense, characterized the onset of a possible nuclear war as a "first exchange of bombing punts." As the war progressed, each service would hand off the "football" of leading role to another in succession.

The emphasis on combativeness dated back generations, of course, but what is noteworthy is the extent to which civilians took the lead in conflating military and athletic rhetoric. For example, popular writer William Bradford Huie praised the Marines and attributed their combativeness in battle to their background in sports. He insisted that Marine recruiters had combed college football squads looking for men of a suitably "combative type," endorsing the supposed connections among warrior status, aggressive sport, and self-conscious masculinity. On the last point, military officers of higher rank increasingly tended to agree. For example, two Air Force generals, Henry "Hap" Arnold and Ira Eaker, wrote *This Flying Game* (1943) to stimulate interest in military aviation among prospective cadets. The "effeminate or unmanly" were unwelcome, as were the "sullen" and "morose." Tellingly, Arnold became the first chief of staff of the newly independent Air Force in 1947. Pilots were the heroic core of the Air Force—early air advocate Billy Mitchell had compared them to the knights of the medieval era. Their image was not to be challenged by "effeminate" departures from the knightly norm.

Sport, in short, was useful insofar as it instilled the requisite character for military success. Popular culture, too, confirmed the superiority of the military over sport. In the film *Strategic Air Command* (1955), actor James Stewart played a baseball player who gives up his promising career on the diamond for service as a bomber pilot. He tells his long-suffering, ultimately accepting, and soon pregnant wife, played by June Allyson, that although he still loves baseball, his new job is more important. In short, the Air Force—or, more broadly, the military—was as American as baseball and motherhood. Years later, Senate friends successfully advocated Stewart's promotion to brigadier general in the Air Force Reserve on the strength of his performance in *Strategic Air Command*.

The rise of football to special popularity in the 1950s depended in part on the exploitation of its military associations. The annual Army-Navy football game gave the new medium of television an instant tie to one of oldest rivalries in the sport, dating back to the turn of the century, and it did so at a time when the military services enjoyed record-high peacetime budgets and uncommon peacetime popularity. So well known was the Army-Navy gridiron series that it could be identified satisfactorily simply by the term "Army-Navy game"—the football rivalry was the default meaning of the term.

By the 1960s, the military services seemed almost to be serving as national "exercise gurus." For example, an exercise manual based on the Green Berets' regime was widely sold to a civilian market. The Marine Corps, the one service always regarded as a performance-oriented military elite, enjoyed special esteem. In 1968, Major George E. Otott, director of the Marine Corps Physical Fitness Academy, and Dean F. Markham, who had served as executive director of the President's Council on Physical Fitness under President John F. Kennedy, published *The Marine Corps Exercise Book*. Robert F. Kennedy, the murdered president's brother, contributed the preface. National leaders and national institutions were lending their support to the exercise movement. In the case of the *Marine Corps Exercise Book*, the authors paid much attention to exercise for the whole family and to reducing "drudgery." In that respect, they were pointing toward newer tendencies in exercise, fitness programs, and the pursuit of sport within and outside the military. What they were departing from requires mention.

THE CULT OF TOUGHNESS IN THE 1950s AND 1960s

In the midst of Cold War, many Americans harbored renewed (and exaggerated) fears of national weakness and physical "softness." The Kennedy brothers were among them. Sounding very much like predecessors more than half a century earlier, President Kennedy published articles with titles such as "Our Unfit Youth" and "Vigor We Need," the latter in 1962 in *Sports Illustrated*. Without "physical hardihood," the president warned, more ominously than he could have realized, Americans would be unable to meet military demands in Europe and the "jungles of Asia." Such comments were neither rare nor eccentric. Others in the Kennedy administration argued the same line. The previous year,

U.S. News and World Report, citing Secretary of Health, Education, and Welfare Abraham Ribicoff and Bud Wilkinson, special physical fitness adviser and football coach at the University of Oklahoma, warned: "At a time when the world is full of dangers, a number of authorities say American youngsters lack muscle." In 1963, *Time* lionized Marine Corps Commandant David Shoup as "tough to the Corps" for requiring that company-grade officers be able to march fifty miles within twenty hours. President Kennedy expressed his pleasure with Shoup's directive.

College sports training was similarly admired for its growing fixation on a "No Pain, No Gain" psychology. In the especially telling 1964 article entitled "All-Out Agony at Indiana U.," *Life* focused on a swimmer's ascent from hurt through pain to agony as he trained. The caption for this ultimate achievement read "Training by Torture." Meanwhile, Outward Bound programs were praised for resembling Marine training sites, while *Look* had published "Football Is Violence" in 1962, accepting annual high school football deaths as a means of showing the value of sacrifice, courage, and other virtues. "These lessons," the author claimed, "are especially salutary in our modern society with its delinquency problem, lack of discipline and physical softness." In place of softness, Americans needed to be shown "How America Can Get Physically Tough," as *Look* magazine did in featuring the training program at La Sierra High School in Carmichael, California. Bud Wilkinson thought the La Sierra program, designed by a football coach, would make "America's youth as agile and physically tough as any in the world." It was also a sexist program, where girls "admired boys for their achievements and sometimes tried to emulate them in the easier tests." The program was authoritarian, male-centered, and hierarchical—in fact, many of the attributes commonly associated with the military.

This fixation on toughness and on combative sports toughly played exemplified a turn away from the 1950s that had political, social, and cultural dimensions. In his inaugural address in 1961, President Kennedy claimed that the torch of leadership had been passed to "a new generation," and he was keen to cultivate the impression of difference between his administration and that of Dwight Eisenhower. In the Eisenhower years, bowling became the most rapidly expanding recreation, and golf was the sport most associated with the president himself. Eisenhower also liked to fish, especially in the Rocky Mountains. Golf no longer hinted at effeminacy, as it had when Theodore Roosevelt advised William Howard Taft to drop the sport lest he be considered unmanly. But it had no link to aggressive masculinity. Stereotypically, golf was a sport of the social and business elite—indeed, a game more than a sport. This view made all the more sense when Eisenhower suffered a serious heart attack in 1955, while he was on vacation in Colorado. His golfing and his fishing had failed to preserve his basic health, let alone aggressive vigor. Eisenhower's electoral success in 1952 had depended partly on his image as a conquering hero of World War II. But his heart attack had inflicted a lasting wound on his warrior image.

Throughout his presidential campaign in 1960, Kennedy called to "get this country moving again," even when the direction of the movement was not made clear. In the Eisenhower administration itself Kennedy saw reaction and passivity. In the culture—in sport, for example—these traits showed themselvesh in a system that made most people spectators and limited their opportunities to participate directly in sports. What Kennedy was advocating was more than a set of specific policy options. It was a different mentality concerning action and assertiveness.

President Kennedy and other high officials returned often to the theme of "toughness"—which, because it denotes an attitude as well as a condition, different from "fitness" or "health." In 1964, even after the President's death, his brother Robert told *Sports Illustrated*: "Part of a nation's prestige in the cold war is won in the Olympic Games." Winning medals would validate the aggressiveness of Americans and show their ability to project power in the world. These ideas—largely a throwback to a much earlier age—help to explain the peculiar intersection of sport, the military, notions of masculinity, and the exaltation of the aggressive spirit.

Within a decade, there were iconic figures from the Vietnam War embodying what this cult of toughness had inspired. Notable among them was Captain Lance P. Sijan, who would become the first graduate of the Air Force Academy to be awarded the Medal of Honor. After his F-4 aircraft crashed in Laos in 1967, he eluded the enemy for more than forty days despite severe injuries. After capture, he escaped once, was recaptured, and was repeatedly tortured. On January 22, 1968, at the age of twenty-five, he died of malnutrition, untreated wounds, and pneumonia. A popular biography of Sijan, Malcolm McConnell's *Into the Mouth of the Cat* (1985), noticed in Sijan traits much valued in Kennedy's "New Frontier." The senior yearbook at his Milwaukee high school described Sijan's "Promethean amalgamation of dynamism, masculinity, and that certain intangible something which represents everything clean and decent in America." At the Academy, McConnell claimed, Sijan "could absorb pain much better than many of his friends and fellow athletes. His body was tough, stronger than most." He played football, too. But when his schedule of activities forced a choice between continuing at the Academy and continuing with football, he withdrew from the sport—an unintended real-life reprise of the scenario in *Strategic Air Command*. "A self-proclaimed product of the New Frontier," McConnell continued, "[Sijan] had come to equate athletic ability and competitive drive." Even the more austerely written *Honor Bound: American Prisoners of War in Southeast Asia, 1961–1973*, by Stuart Rochester and

Frederick Kiley, described Sijan as having been "a strapping 220-pound football player" at the Air Force Academy. Sport, the military, toughness were woven inseparably into the same fabric—in this case, with the added thread of the warrior's death, the ultimate commitment in circumstances beyond his devising or his wishes. In 1976, a new dormitory at the Air Force Academy was dedicated to Sijan's memory.

SPORTS PROGRAMS IN THE ARMED SERVICES

In the first half of the twentieth century, the Army and Navy never really achieved the goal of creating a comprehensive sport that involved all officers and enlisted men, even though some officers made a good faith effort to do so. For one thing, physical fitness was widely understood as calisthenics, drills, and marches or "hikes." As in civilian institutions, sport was used only partly to develop health and fitness—the less capable players tended to be excluded sooner than those who were more gifted, while lower performance goals were set for females than for males. In short, the effort to use sport comprehensively in pursuit of health as well as for a sense of achievement did not prosper in an age that had yet to develop a sufficiently inclusive ethos or adequate means to embody it. To the extent that a "warrior consciousness" and "winning spirit" were encouraged, moreover, the bias favored elite performance rather than more typical levels of accomplishment.

By contrast, the trajectory of military sport and, more broadly, military recreation in the post–World War II era pointed explicitly toward a policy of "sports for all" and gave gradually increasing attention to related health issues. By the end of the century, morale, welfare, and recreation support services in all the armed forces claimed to offer "Growth," "Peace of Mind," "Renewal," and "Self-Reliance"—not toughness or the warrior spirit. Right after World War II, for example, the Army's Chief of Special Services instituted an unusually diversified program of games and sports to ensure participation by all soldiers regardless of age. Among the sports and games provided were World War I standbys such as "combative" football and boxing as well as track and baseball. But also available were golf, tennis, badminton, bowling, swimming, archery, and horseshoe pitching. Obviously, the cultivation of the combative warrior was not the point. Maintaining morale and welfare meant far more, and this lay beneath the development of recreational programs including sport wherever American forces could be found. Thus, in the Pacific region, the first goal was for every soldier, sailor, marine, and airman to participate in at least one sport, while the second one was to develop teams to engage in theaterwide competition.

In October 1947, one month after the creation of the National Military Establishment (the forerunner of the Department of Defense), the Secretary of the Army authorized an Inter-Service Sports Council for the purpose of encouraging competition among Army, Navy, Marine, and Air Force athletes. The Army Chief of Special Services coordinated with counterparts in the Navy and the Air Force, and the first meeting of the new Council took place in November 1947. A golf tournament was quickly approved, and the Inter-Service Tennis Competition that had been taking place since 1924 was also included. This provided the basis for a much more extensive program in later years.

Although the United States was not a founding member of the Conseil International du Sport Militaire (CISM)—the International Council for Military Sport—which was established in 1949, CISM was actually inspired by an earlier American sports program. Moreover, the United States joined in 1951, and its armed forces participated vigorously. While the broad program of Special Services aimed at all soldiers, and while the Inter-Service Sports Council focused on friendly but spirited interservice rivalry, participation in CISM provided the elite athletes of the armed forces opportunities to compete against some of the best international amateur athletes.

In 1955, Congress passed PL 11, which funded the armed forces to train for and participate in international competitions including the Pan-American Games, the Winter Olympics, and the Summer Olympics. This took place against the context of Cold War rivalry between the West and the East, and the Communist countries' subsidizing their athletes had become a sore spot and, in the West, an explanation for the relative success of East bloc teams. In essence, Congress was, at least to a degree, entering the fray.

The amount authorized in 1955 was small, however—just $800,000 for each four-year cycle on a continuing basis. The figure, once modest but reasonable, remained unchanged for decades. No adjustments had been made for inflation. By October 1984, however, after the Los Angeles Olympic Games, the PL 11 allowance was increased to $3,000,000 per four-year cycle. During the 1988 Summer Olympic Games at Seoul, U.S. Army athletes won three gold medals and one silver.

This government subsidy for athletes put the U.S. military in the business of promoting elite sport and helping elite athletes just as surely as the governments of Communist countries in developing rival teams. The amount that the U.S. government spent for this purpose was smaller, but the principle—providing a source of income to those in training—was similar. Even in the waning years of the Cold War, however, concern for the competitive image of the United States easily trumped worry over the future of "pure" amateur sport. But beyond any contribution to medal counts in the Cold War–era struggle, effective performance by athletes with military affiliations contributed to a positive image of the armed forces among the American public as well as to recruitment.

But aside from what might be done for the most talented competitors, would the armed forces serve their members inclusively? Key facets of inclusiveness involved race and gender, even with respect to elite-level athletes, and opportunity for those below the elite level was a critical test regardless of race and gender. In the area of race, African American soldiers enjoyed at least a modicum of acceptance for their athletic ability even before the desegregation of the armed forces at the end of the 1940s. For example, the 1920 Olympic trials held at Jefferson Barracks, Missouri, focused on identifying the best athletes rather than the best white athletes. Thus, in time, the sports activities of African Americans in the armed forces in the second half of the century had precedent. Even so, opportunity was far from equal, even for the best African American athletes and especially for all others. This changed in 1948 with President Truman's decision to end segregation in the armed forces by executive order. Thus facilities available to any soldier, sailor, airman, or marine were open to all. No special unit was created to further their sporting and recreational programs.

For women in the military, matters were different—just as they were in intramural and, especially, intercollegiate sport. The 1970s witnessed a period of fundamental change in women's place in the military, their opportunities in federally funded educational programs, and in the recruitment basis for the armed forces. The coincidence of these changes was not entirely an accident, and their conjunction in time may have strengthened the force of change within the military on issues affecting women. The most important development was the end of the military draft in the early 1970s and the return to all-volunteer status. Whatever reason there had been in the past to accommodate women and minorities within the military, the need for qualified personnel in a post-draft environment added one of overriding importance. Just as important, suitable accommodation was justifiable on practical grounds—military necessity in the area of recruitment and retention—and not on the basis of "social experimentation."

Simultaneously, as the Army and the other services adjusted to the absence of the draft, Congress was concluding work on legislation to provide girls and women equal opportunity in education including school and college sports programs. This policy, embodied in the Education Amendments of 1972, came to be known by its most hotly contested provision—Title IX. According to this specification, schools receiving federal funds were obliged to provide equal opportunities for male and female students. Precisely what this meant and what the law required precipitated legal battles for decades. Unlike some civilian institutions, which fought over how to define "equality" in funding women's and men's sport, the military identified institutional benefits in developing additional programs to compensate for the earlier exclusion of women from opportunities to participate. In 1973, the Army established an All Army Trial Camp Support Activity (AATCSA) at Fort Indiantown Gap, Pennsylvania. Its mission was to support competition throughout the Army, but to fulfill this mission on a gender-inclusive basis AATCSA in 1975 specifically provided for the All Army Women's Sports Program. Such measures were expected to contribute to retention of women in the Army by providing valued opportunity as well as to enhance their image and credibility as members of the force. Insofar as the U.S. armed forces had long related athletic competition to military success, cultivating women athletes was thus a step in mainstreaming them.

By the mid-1970s, it became clear that the end of the draft jeopardized the highest end of military sports competition—in the Olympic Games, for example. When a draft was in force and inductions were numerous, the services drew on a larger pool of talent to develop their elite competitive corps. (Although the Army was usually the only service depending directly on the draft, the other services gained "voluntary" enlistments from many who wished to avoid service in the Army or, more particularly, wished to ensure that their military service was not performed in the infantry.) In the all-volunteer environment, however, there was considerable pressure to focus on assignments that contributed directly to military strength—not activities on the margins. Increasingly, military personnel were evaluated on the basis of their performance of discretely military duties. The diversion of much time and effort to sports training could thus have a devastating effect, especially on officers, but also on enlisted personnel. In addition, support for Olympic athletes under the aegis of the United States Olympic Committee (USOC) was gradually improving, notably so after 1976 and an extensive reexamination of amateur athletics by a special commission appointed by President Gerald Ford. USOC created a reasonable alternative for funding athletes not interested in military service. In 1978, the Army Sports Office sought to attract elite athletes by establishing the World Class Athlete Program (WCAP). Part of its role was to dedicate funding for the support of athletes, but at least as crucial was its provision of release time for sport training. Under WCAP, qualifying athletes had two years in which to train for their anticipated top-level competitions on a full-time basis. How those athletes reentered the military mainstream and how their careers were affected by their time of peak athletic performance remained a troubling issue at the end of the century. Yet few professions afforded elite athletes greater opportunities than did the armed forces, and few employers could match the fitness and sports facilities available to enlisted personnel and officers, regardless of the degree of their athletic talent.

Changes were also introduced to improve opportunities for the non-elite competitor and for military personnel interested in health and fitness more than competition. Arguably, this was more important than measures to attract, develop, and hold elite athletes. Keeping a force at fighting trim and keeping it happy enough to reenlist at a high rate had become fundamental challenges in the all-volunteer environment. As understanding of this issue evolved during the 1970s, Army leaders moved toward standardization of sports and fitness facilities in order to ensure that a high standard was attained throughout the force. During the Vietnam War the armed forces keenly sought to meet the intramural and unit-level sports needs of the greatly expanded number of enlisted men and officers. To some extent, the effort resulted in some real success as the existing program was expanded to provide for the draft-swollen force. But the details of the expansion of physical plant proved problematic. Sports facilities were being built without centralized guidance and local contractors frequently built gymnasiums according to their own, and sometimes peculiar, criteria. Worse, lacking clear specifications from a central authority, contractors sometimes made big mistakes. For example, some football fields were built ten yards short. The Army's remedy came in 1973, when the Morale Support Directorate and the Adjutant General worked together to prepare standard designs for outdoor playing fields and courts, and the Air Force and Navy adopted the same schemes.

In 1975, the armed forces first developed standardized designs for "fitness centers"—and the term itself suggests the orientation toward health and overall development rather than something overly grand or heroic. It was a term that said what it intended and did not indulge in euphemism (as, say, when ROTC drill was called "leadership laboratory"). The size and scale of sports centers were set according to the size and mission of the post with designs for facilities ranging from 15,000 square feet to 62,000 square feet. The guidelines were reissued a decade later. The use of these designs was optional, however, and mandatory employment of such designs came only after an initiative developed by Army Vice Chief of Staff Maxwell Thurman beginning in 1983. Facing the prospect of tight budgets for the indefinite future, General Thurman standardized facilities to control cost and ensure that sports and fitness facilities were at a uniformly high level of quality across the service. In addition, predictability in facilities made it easy for personnel temporarily or permanently reassigned to new posts to resume their sports and fitness activities with a minimum of time and bother. The designs finally approved incorporated ideas from Army facilities such as at Fort Rucker, Alabama, and from civilian sources such as the University of Florida and St. Louis University—aiming for the best from both worlds—and the facilities built during the 1990s embodied the aspirations of the design team.

General Thurman believed that soccer—in its fluidity and recombination—resembled some of the Army's key ideas about flexible military strategy. Also, he had served at the Army's Training and Doctrine Command (TRADOC), which had the responsibility for instruction throughout the Army except at West Point and the Army War College. When an Army soccer coach retired, he offered to write a program of instruction that could be used to spread soccer coaching knowledge throughout the service. General Thurman retired before the programs could be distributed, and subsequently sports directors at various military bases questioned why soccer would be privileged this way—over basketball, for example. Ironically, however, members of the military and their families had been among the most enthusiastic supporters of soccer even as early as the 1960s, when it was pegged as a "foreign" sport and failed to win wide public acceptance, and their role in its eventual popularization in American schools should not be overlooked.

A CHANGING CULTURE AND
WARRIOR IDENTITY

In the early 1980s, the U.S. Air Force initiated Project Warrior—an effort to focus on the "war-fighting spirit" in an age characterized by ever greater technological sophistication and socio-cultural complexity. The new reality within the Air Force was that the highest leadership could be entrusted to a person who had not been a pilot. In 1978 Lew Allen became chief of staff on the strength of a Ph.D. in nuclear physics, service as director of the National Security Agency, and a tour as commander of the Air Force Systems Command, among other things. Yet he and Charles Gabriel, who succeeded Allen as chief of staff in 1982, did not wish to lose the warrior identity and the warfighting spirit even as they acknowledged the critical impact of new technologies on the military.

But old means of cultivating warrior identity could go only so far in the changing culture. Project Warrior identified outstanding books in military history and encouraged airmen and officers to read them, and they ensured that sports competition went forward—yet it had actually done so for decades. In retrospect, phenomena such as Project Warrior marked not the resurgence of warrior spirit but the emergence of a more complexly textured sense of the modern soldier, sailor, marine, and airman. The warrior tends toward extremes—almost toward the use of conflict as a mode of self-expression and self-identification. Yet this mentality could work against some of the most important functions in modern warfare such as driving trucks and manning computers. The soldier in the end is a worker—in the very best sense. The lingering warrior temperament in the 1980s was often incompatible terms such as "electronic warfare" and "information warfare," yet those were indispensable components of late-twentieth century warfare.

The Air Force had earlier made a contribution to changing America's sporting culture in ways that corresponded to the "information age." Dr. Kenneth Cooper, an Air Force physician, had worked to develop effective fitness programs to maximize the chance of a productive and satisfying life—and, of course, to keep the human assets of the service in the best possible working order. His explanation of the virtues of "aerobic" activity contributed to a major shift in the physical activity and exercise programs of tens of millions of civilians as well as in those of millions of service men and women. (This emphasis on aerobics also provided something of a performance "leveler" for men and women, whose performance was roughly the same.)

All services were affected by Cooper's message. By the 1980s, running was ubiquitous in the armed forces. Service personnel not only participated in large running competitions, but also sponsored some major events, which linked the services with the new definition of fitness and served as positive public relations. Established in 1976 and reflecting the patriotic enthusiasm of the nation's bicentennial, the Marine Corps Marathon in Washington, D.C., became a great favorite among runners throughout the United States. From the beginning, key attractions were its scenic course through Washington and Arlington, Virginia, the association with the Marine Corps (made concrete with marines posted at aid stations), and its dramatic finish line at the Iwo Jima memorial. By the end of the century, the number of entrants in what was billed as "The People's Marathon" was capped at fifteen thousand.

Yet older Marine veterans sometimes derided the fitness vogue in the military. In letters to the *Marine Corps Gazette*, they ridiculed the preference for flimsy sneakers over combat boots. What did it say about marines, some contended, that they were becoming fleet of foot? From the opposite perspective, however, modern warfare was moving—and rapidly so in the 1990s—away from mass and toward agility. The kind of sports and fitness activities that enjoy special favor can reflect shifts in mentality. Massive power used in short bursts describes weightlifting better than distance running, for example, and the military's emerging focus on fitness, endurance, and agility actually did fit remarkably well the parallel movement toward precision weapons, information-based warfare, and the other elements of the late-twentieth-century military revolution. A varied program of sports and fitness activities did more than any "one size fits all" program could to develop the Marine Corps. More than ever before, in the 1980s and 1990s, marines were expected to integrate sports and fitness programs into their regimen. To this end, the service's leaders provided for intramural programs, varsity sports, and an All-Marine Championship Program as well as the "Semper Fit" exercise regime.

The larger truth is that each generation redefines the terms out of which it constructs its identity. The Air Force pressed forward with intensive technological modernization, hoping to preserve some warrior identity, yet contributed to the development of the culture in ways that ultimately gave the military greater texture. The Army, at the same time, prided itself on being about "the basics"—soldiers on the ground—yet it sought to win recruits, hold ROTC cadets, and retain soldiers by touting "adventure training" with activities such as whitewater rafting displacing drill as a symbolic representation of the service. But like some other developments in the 1970s and 1980s, adventure training was one that challenged some of the older stereotypes—about soldiers, men, women, and racial and sexual minorities—that a simplistic sense of warrior identity had allowed and even fostered.

The structures created to manage sports and fitness programs in the last decades of the twentieth century reflected the functional orientation that continued to grow in the services generally. Rather than start with a somatic preconception of what a warrior looked like, the service personnel responsible for sports and fitness programs focused on what needed to be done—the tasks that needed to be performed, the physical skills required, the basic health and fitness standards to be attained. In the Air Force, this meant periodic reorganization of Morale, Welfare, and Recreation, finally merging it with the Air Force Services Agency in 1992. Fitness, recreation, and sports programs were seen holistically, as part of a comprehensive regime of services and, for the participants, as means toward their complete development as airmen and women.

In the most specialized military environments, the most demanding physical standards endured—in a system that mixed coercion and choice. At the end of the century, for example, the Air Force Academy required all cadets to participate in the athletic program including competitive sports as well as physical education courses. In words much like those written a century earlier, cadets were assured that athletic participation developed "courage, initiative, team spirit, and the will to win." Male and female cadets chose among sports such as tennis, soccer, gymnastics, and track—as well as boxing, football, and baseball for men only. Failure to pass the Physical Fitness Test (PFT) or the Aerobic Fitness Test (AFT) resulted in a meeting with a Physical Education Review Committee, which could put a cadet on probation, order corrective action, or recommend dismissal from the academy. Few institutions of any kind, let alone colleges and universities, put such value on physical fitness and accomplishment.

The reality of what was occurring within the military often contrasted sharply with impressions of the military generated in popular culture. In the 1980s and 1990s, the military continued to emphasize lean strength, agility, and teamwork, but Hollywood stressed hypertrophic muscularity and "loner" psychology, most notably in the Rambo series. *First Blood* (1982), also known as *Rambo 1*, stars Sylvester Stallone as ex–Green Beret John Rambo, falsely accused of crimes and resisting arrest in the forests of the Pacific Northwest. He vents his frustration over the U.S. defeat in the Vietnam War and his anger over the purported abandonment of American prisoners of war (POW) and missing in action (MIA) in Southeast. In a sequel and a "prequel" in 1985 and 1988, the heavily muscled Stallone—big and "ripped"—takes on the Vietnamese Communists, ultimately inflicting on them the defeat that the combined U.S. forces could not deliver in the real world.

Rambo was not alone in the cinematic transformation of America's experience in Vietnam. In the series *Braddock: Missing in Action* (1984, 1985, 1988), martial arts expert Chuck Norris plays James Braddock, an Army Special Forces colonel. Braddock fights his way back into Vietnam—and, temporarily, into captivity and torture—to rescue POWs and MIAs left behind after the U.S. withdrawal from Southeast Asia in 1975. Rambo and Braddock both feed the fantasy image of the heroic lone warrior, as did a host of other films playing out essentially the same scenario in Latin America, the Middle East, and elsewhere.

The almost obligatory torture scenes in such films help to explain their attraction, which surely did not depend primarily on dialogue or cinematic artistry. Much like professional wrestling, which emerged as an entertainment powerhouse in the same era, these films appealed to the thinly veiled thirst for bondage and restraint, sadomasochism, and orchestrated violence that have seethed near the surface of American culture since World War II. Rambo's exaggerated musculature reflected a desire for an inflated masculinity—a parody of the real thing to which the real warriors had no need to succumb.

WARRIOR CULTURE AND MINORITY RIGHTS

During the twentieth century, the ability of the U.S. armed forces to function effectively in combat and in military operations other than war resulted far more from skill in exploiting modern and postmodern advantages—such as organization and technology—than from any presumed benefits of self-identification as warriors among enlisted personnel and officers. Indeed, the periodic assertion of warrior culture tended to compromise movements to expand the personnel pool—such as African Americans and other racial minorities, women, and gays—with the resulting risk that individuals whose talents could make them highly useful to the military in practical ways would be excluded and thus lost for essentially psychodynamic reasons.

Racism, for example, drew its strength from a heritage of untested postulates and assumptions—not from sound scientific observation and resultant theory. To the extent that the desirability of the warrior ethos also depended on postulates and suppositions enshrined as an inviolable tradition, the cultivation of warrior identity could also undermine the acceptance of women in the military due to their sex, of African Americans due to their race, and of gays due to their sexual orientation.

Ironically, some of this presumptive tradition was relatively recent in origin. For example, opposition to gays in the military on the basis of identity (as opposed to specifically disapproved activities) seems to have been a mid-twentieth-century development, shaped largely by psychologists working for the armed forces and implemented especially after World War II. During the war, the gay sexual orientation of many servicemen was clearly known to their peers. But their straight comrades evidently cared more about the military support they could provide than about what they did for sex. Among the higher ranks, sentiment was different, especially during the peacetime years of the Cold War, when a moderate force requirement coupled with a draft to meet that need allowed service brass to use sexual orientation to bar gay men from service or to dismiss them if their orientation was discovered.

In 1992, campaigning for the presidency, Bill Clinton promised to end the most severe discrimination against gays in the military—the barrier to entry, if known, and the threat of dismissal, if discovered. After his election, Clinton announced his intention to make good on his campaign promise. Sharp opposition arose immediately—on a bipartisan basis—and critics of his policy claimed that morale and unit cohesion would be badly damaged if the ban on gays and lesbians were lifted. Opponents asked how gays' being allowed to serve openly would affect young straight males' sense of their own masculinity. One of the strongest critics of Clinton's policy was Senator Sam Nunn (D-Ga.), who chaired the Senate Armed Services Committee. His attempt at a solution to the impasse between President Clinton and the Congressional opposition drew on a fact offered by those favoring the president's rule: Gays and lesbians were already in the military, and had always been in it, even though their sexual orientation was not officially acknowledged. Nunn strongly and successfully advocated that the ban not be lifted and, instead, that a policy of "Don't ask, don't tell, don't pursue" be instituted. Superior officers and NCOs especially were not to ask personnel about sexual orientation. Gay and lesbian personnel were under special injunction not to raise the issue and bring attention to their orientation. Nor were individuals suspected of being gay or lesbian to be pursued if they had not themselves "told" about their sexual identity. After "Don't ask, don't tell, don't pursue" became policy, dismissals from the armed forces on grounds of sexual orientation actually increased. A few cases were triggered by gays challenging the policy itself, but the majority evidently resulted from more aggressive investigation in disregard of the policy's "don't pursue" provision.

Among the things at stake in this affair, one of the most important was the image of the American warrior in the minds of the Senate and House leaders most responsible for oversight of the armed forces. For them—and, in fact, commonly—the assertion of a warrior ethos was a deductive, not an inductive, exercise. Most had assumed the superiority and hence the desirability of the warrior character and physical attributes. By the end of the twentieth century, the warrior might more widely be conceived as black or as female and, for a smaller and less public group, as gay as well. Earlier in the century common preconceptions about the warrior precluded all three.

The preconceptions that long prejudiced the warrior image against women, ethnic minorities, and gays showed an eerie symmetry with preconceptions about performance in sports. During World War II, for example, women serving in the Women's Army Corps (WAC), the Air-WAC, the Navy's WAVEs, or elsewhere who proved to be excellent at sports were widely assumed to be lesbians—and, for that matter, lesbians were misunderstood as if they were somehow "partly" male or "manlike." Military thinking that straitjacketed men by artificially limiting the construction of maleness also punished women for something as inherently innocent as athletic talent and the desire to use it. In later years, some observers within the military reported that women service personnel played sports less aggressively when they believed members of the investigative service were in the stands. Of course, there were lesbians in the wartime and postwar military just as there were gays. But athletic achievement was hardly the way to find them. What is particularly telling, then, is that many men and women who attempted to keep lesbians out of the military, motivated by a desire to do the best by their services, imagined that it was.

In the postwar environment, the difficulty in sparking interest in physical fitness and sport among enlisted women was sometimes taken as proof that women lacked sufficient aggressiveness to perform as equals to men within the military. Actually, though, there were some cases where women did their physical training alongside men—and clearly met the challenge. Even more, the assessment failed the test of fairness for ignoring the difficulty that the armed forces had had for generations in trying to promote physical fitness, athletic aggressiveness, and the warrior's attitude among men. Nor, for that matter, did they take into account that the task of motivating the men persisted.

Terms used to describe homosexual males wrote them out of the warrior culture. While the services ceaselessly endorsed the "regular guy," they repudiated those adjudged to be "queer." As a verb, "fag" meant to "tire" or "weaken," neither of which were options for the warrior. "Sissy" and "pansy," used both as nouns and as adjectives, reflected the supposition that gays were "timid"—an attribute, regardless of sexual orientation, inappropriate for a warrior. Any hint of the "effeminate" self-evidently challenged the image of masculine warrior. Even the term "sensitive"—used much later in the age of feminism to describe a quality that women might wish to experience in men—was used to suggest a male whose masculinity was compromised by a homosexual orientation. But these terms also militated against women, at least as they were popularly understood, regardless of their sexual preferences.

For most of the second half of the twentieth century, the military community and the sports community lived in a state of denial as to the sexual orientation of the men—and, increasingly, the women—among their number. Even by the end of the century, for example, the number of football players who had openly acknowledged that they were gay remained minuscule. The mechanisms for exclusion differed—the prospect of ostracism in one and the threat of dishonorable discharge in the other—but the perceived need of both communities to preserve a rigorously stereotypical model of assertive heterosexual masculinity remained the underlying "default" text of the post–World War II era. It was the official mindset against which efforts at change focused.

It is more than coincidence that women's growing success in sports and their pursuit of greater opportunities for military service (including combat roles) developed alongside a growing concern over the question of sexual orientation and military service. The transformation of women's sport was significantly hastened by Title IX—a provision in amendments to key legislation on education—that required equal support of women and men in many areas including intercollegiate athletics. Although the process of shifting the balance of financial resources to meet the requirements of Title IX was contentious, substantial compliance had been achieved by the end of the century. Women's expectations of themselves had changed, and their role models included athletes, astronauts, and other figures—much the same kind as had served as male role models for a longer time. The pursuit of fuller opportunity in the armed forces was a part of this broader transforming process, and it was affected not only by feminist advocates but also by the needs of the armed services themselves. By 1972, the year of Title IX, when they were again committed to operating on an all-volunteer basis, the armed forces faced serious short-term deficits in personnel, and recruitment of women as a permanent—not an emergency—part of the force became routine. The Gates Commission, appointed by President Richard Nixon to outline the key issues in returning to an all-volunteer force, had specifically forecast the need to recruit women more effectively.

Although a direct causal connection is quite unlikely, it is striking that women's calls for greater opportunity in the military—notably, to have access to combat roles—increased and bore fruit as women continued to improve their position in sport. If athletes are perceived as combative "warrior" types and if women become athletes, could women not then be warriors? And if women could be warriors, why not those who had once been considered "womanlike"—gay males?

It was against this context that President Bill Clinton had sought to end the policy of restricting military service to heterosexuals. Some of Clinton's supporters argued that, like resistance to African Americans in the armed forces in 1949, resistance to gays could be overcome in time (as it had been in the armed forces of all other NATO countries except Turkey). Just as the services had worked for decades toward the goal of equality of opportunity regardless of race, why could they not do so toward the goal of equality of opportunity regardless of sexual orientation?

Yet it is not obvious that the beliefs—or biases—of enlisted personnel really account for the insistence on exclusion of gays and lesbians from the military, although differences between a largely conscript armed force and an all-volunteer force complicate final judgment. A study of gay men and women who served in World War II offers much evidence that heterosexual enlisted men often knew which of their company were gay—and, essentially, that most of them did not care. Dependability in combat was key—not sexual orientation—in determining the acceptance of gay soldiers, sailors, and marines. In addition, numerous cases have been recorded showing that many soldiers, sailors, and marines who had been exclusively heterosexual prior to their military service and would become exclusively heterosexual after the war engaged mostly in homosexual sex while the conflict continued. Veteran Greg Aarons recalled, "You were in a strange situation like in the Solomon Islands, your only outlet was each other—a situational type of homosexuality. A lot of these guys would ordinarily never think of doing such a thing in their hometowns, but they would there because it was the only thing to do other than masturbate." Soldiers, sailors, and marines created a "sexual geography" on ships and islands, where, for example, ammunition ready rooms on an aircraft carrier would be default spaces for sexual encounters. In Europe, some otherwise heterosexual soldiers chose to engage in homosexual sexual acts rather than in heterosexual acts with women in bars and "red light" districts. Since all the military training films about venereal disease showed heterosexual acts, some men concluded that they could not contract venereal disease from sexual contact with men.

Perhaps art, too, imitated life. James Jones's novel *The Thin Red Line* (1962), based broadly on his own experiences and those of men he knew before and during World War II, describes a male-to-male sexual encounter between enlisted men as essentially inconsequential to the military unit. The same-sex relationship grows out of combat anxieties, the absence of alternative forms of interpersonal sexual release, and in consequence of the need for intimacy. Jones meted out criticism only to soldiers who were obsessed with advancement in rank, lost in a barely disguised bloodlust, or otherwise prone to behavior that jeopardizes the lives of other men in the unit. Sexual relationships happen, Jones suggests, but they do not undermine the capacity of soldiers to fight.

As in some other circumstances—although the military is curiously among the more benign due to the apparently consensual character of the sex acts—an underlying bisexuality may have been demonstrating itself, and men who faced the prospect of death and wanted a moment of companionship may have been more comfortable with accepting gay men as fellow "warriors" than many of their officers were. During the war, the ground was prepared for a redefinition of the soldier as warrior—aided by the mustering out of the vast number of World War II conscripts. For a period of about two years, until 1948, the draft was allowed to lapse, and the armed services were more able to define themselves as professionals—in essence, an exclusionary process—rather than as "general inductees" or GIs. The wartime move among mid-level and high-level officers to make homosexual identity as opposed to specific acts a basis for discharge from the armed forces reflected the redefinition of masculinity as heterosexual that had emerged early in the twentieth century. It became the basis for policy concerning sexual orientation and military service for the post–World War II era. Yet there is no persuasive evidence that this policy emerged as a response to enlisted personnel's views.

The long-term viability of the policy excluding gays from the military may have been weakened by the gradual change in gay identity in American society as a whole—for example, in the Gay Games and other means of presenting gays as athletes. Similarly, the visibility of some gays discharged from the military for their sexual orientation brought attention to the fact that they had typically been regarded as effective in their military performance until their sexual orientation became known. In any case, the entire process engaged military, athletic, and sexual identities in complex and untidy ways.

Notorious instances of attacks by military personnel on other military men believed to be gay—even to the point of homicide—suggested that enlisted men were dead set against gays being in the military. In 1992, Navy radioman Alan Schindler was beaten to death in a public restroom in Sasebo, Japan, where his ship, USS *Bella Wood*, was in port. The attackers were fellow service members, one of whom was convicted of murder. All conceded that he was killed because he was believed to be gay. In 1999, at Fort Campbell, Kentucky, Army Private Calvin Glover admitted killing fellow soldier Barry Winchell. A third soldier was accused of goading Glover to action by circulating rumors that Winchell was gay. In entering his guilty plea, Glover said that he really did not know why he had hit Winchell several times with a baseball bat: "I wasn't really mad at him, sir. It was just a mistake, sir." Officers, too, engaged in a kind of psychological gay bashing when it was institutionally useful. In April 1989, a large explosion destroyed one gun turret (with three 16-inch guns) aboard USS *Iowa*. Officers were eventually found to have massaged the evidence to suggest that gunner's mate Clayton Hartwig had caused the blast in order to commit suicide (and kill forty-six other sailors in the process), supposedly because of a failing homosexual relationship with fellow sailor Kendall Truitt. Since Truitt was married, Navy investigators had also theorized that there was a "love triangle" and had speculated that Truitt might have caused the blast in order to return to exclusively heterosexual relations. In the end, no evidence of a homosexual relationship was found. Yet it had evidently seemed to Navy investigators to be a plausible and useful alternative—far better than concluding, as proved to be the case, that defects in the World War II–era ammunition itself played the central role. But that was only part of the story. What did military women think of having gays and lesbians in the services? Nor was this the only expression by military men related to the subject of sex.

A highly suggestive—if admittedly self-selecting—group of military men are those who participated, on a part-time paid basis, in making adult videos intended for a gay audience that was sexually interested in military men (much more than in men who merely appeared, for a time, in military uniforms). Made for commercial sale throughout the 1990s and into the new century and advertised on the Web, they were "amateur" in that the featured performers in the solo sex acts and homosexual acts recorded were overwhelmingly active-duty or recently retired military—enlisted men and NCOs. Overwhelmingly, too, they identified themselves as straight men who made such videos out of curiosity rather than from a consuming desire for other men.

More significant than the fetishization of men in uniforms—what behavior cannot be sexualized?—is the evidently tolerant and flexible attitude of the men who participated in such videos toward the gay men who were their "consumers," toward themselves and one another in the midst of a wide-ranging exploration of their sexual identities, and toward their own status as soldiers, sailors, and marines. Most of the participants considered themselves heterosexual, showed little difficulty in engaging in sex with other men, and ended up with their sense of masculinity and their military self-image intact.

The military, sport, and sexuality all assumed exceptional importance in American life in the twentieth century. Especially at the end of the century and into the new one, the interpenetration was perhaps more blatant than ever. Military physical trainer Mark Bender and Bobby Murcer wrote *Train Tough the Army Way: 50 Sports Strategies to Out-Think, Out-Train, and Out-Perform Your Competition* (2002). Bender had overseen the training of ten thousand soldiers for Operation Desert Storm in 1991. Now he and Murcer were bringing a winner-take-all attitude to civilians as well. Promotional text for the book assured readers that they would get the same "proven mental-training techniques developed by the military to prepare warriors for battle." After the main U.S. battles in Afghanistan in 2001, Bowflex developed television advertisements for its home exercise equipment featuring two soldiers who claimed that using the Bowflex machine had helped to keep them combat ready. Magazines devoted to body-building almost routinely featured military personnel, male and female. The October 2003 issue of *Muscle & Fitness*, for example, featured Army First Lieu-tenant Greg Plitt on its cover as well as in an extended article where Marine Corps, Air Force, and Navy personnel were also highlighted. All of them were shown in full or partial uniform, visually suggesting the linkage of bodily strength and military power. Out of uniform, Plitt also served as cover model for the November 2003 *Exercise for Men Only*—a magazine with a readership of mixed sexual orientation—which also included the most recent installment in a series on Air Force workouts under the heading "Military Maneuvers." Even the "cult of toughness" reappeared forcefully. On the eve of war with Iraq, U.S. Marines based in Kuwait engaged in hand-to-hand combat drills described by the *Wall Street Journal* in the March 7, 2003, edition. According to writer Mi-chael Phillips, Marines engaged in "choking, kicking, and gouging each other to get into a killing frame of mind." One 165-pound "trash-talking" lieutenant grew frustrated that one of his platoon sergeants, who weighed in at 206 pounds, was holding back when they were wrestling on the ground. "Bury my face in the sand and smother me," the lieutenant gasped. "I don't want to hurt my lieu-tenant," the staff sergeant explained. But when the action resumed, he grabbed the lieutenant by the throat and fought hard. "There's a difference between be-ing hurt and being injured," explained a gunnery sergeant who was also a mar-tial arts instructor. "Hurting is good."

Civilians could even pay to participate in "recreational" SEAL training pro-grams based on the Navy's own highly rigorous program for developing its spe-cial operations force. In addition, some ex-SEALs—notably in California and along the Gulf of Mexico—capitalized on the appeal of "the most grueling and demanding challenges" and of "enduring a brutal dive training program." They opened scuba diving training companies, their SEAL past not only giving them credibility but also allowing their students a touch of toughness by association. Perhaps some could not decide whether they wanted to be more an athlete or a SEAL—and perhaps a touch of the warrior made them feel like both. The in-terplay of sport, the military, and warrior mentality was not a destination but a continually unfolding process.

BIBLIOGRAPHIC NOTE

The intellectual origins of the twentieth-century linkages between sport and the military are treated in Donald J. Mrozek, *Sport and American Mentality, 1880–1910* (University of Tennessee Press, 1983). See also Mark Dyreson, *Mak-ing the American Team: Sport, Culture, and the Olympic Experience* (University of Illinois Press, 1998). Wanda Ellen Wakefield, *Playing to Win: Sports and the American Military, 1898–1945* (SUNY Press, 1997) provides a valuable account of the military's effort to use sport in training enlisted men and in cultivating their fighting spirit. In addition, *Playing to Win* offers some highly suggestive evaluations of underlying constructions of masculinity and of the prejudicial understanding of women in the military in World War II, thus helping to provide a reference point for the many complexities entailed in women's emergence within the military.

Allan Berube, *Coming Out Under Fire: The History of Gay Men and Women in World War II* (Free Press, 1990) is especially important in helping to understand the complex and often contradictory relationships among the military, concepts of masculinity, warrior identity, and activities then largely coded as male including sport. Studies of the interplay between the military and sport in the second half of the twentieth century are scant. However, see the very helpful essay "History of Army Sports" at the U.S. Army's Web site, www.army.mil. Studies of the military and sport in the latter half of the twentieth century will need to be based on such works as Major General Charles K. Gailey, *The Army Information Digest: A Sports Program for the Army in Europe* (U.S. Army, 1954) and Michael R. Johnson, "SS-156, History of Military Recreation," Norton Air Force Base, Aerospace Audiovisual Service (MAC), 1976.

For a provocative treatment of male "power" and roles in society, including commentary on sport and military service, see Lionel Tiger, *The Decline of Males* (St. Martin's Press, 1999).

8. DEATH, MOURNING, AND MEMORIAL CULTURE

MICHAEL SHERRY

As president, Harry Truman spoke little publicly of death, and more often of pro-spective death in a new war than past death in World War II or the Korean War. As president, Bill Clinton spoke frequently of death—in past wars, in troubled places such as Northern Ireland and the Middle East, after disasters, and among notable figures. Truman issued one brief Memorial Day statement; Clinton never failed to give Memorial Day addresses, usually several. The difference owed to more than Clinton's loquaciousness (Truman was plainspoken but talkative), his skill as mourner-in-chief, or a presidency inclined by the 1990s to comment on al-most any subject. The difference marked the rise of a more expressive, visible, and variegated memorial culture, one also emerging in arenas humbler than the presidency. This essay sketches that development, and it confronts an apparent irony: Americans mourned death less explicitly at midcentury, when death in war so afflicted them, than at century's end, when death in war rarely did. War's dead, once pointers to a dark future, became reminders of a dark past.

More than in most historical writing, arguments on this subject are specula-tive. Like sex or beauty, death has a history so vast and mysterious that the histo-rian's experience—for me, several recent deaths, with more anticipated soon, along with advancing age, previous work on war's history, and so forth—deeply inflects the approach taken. Like most scholars, I emphasize cultural and politi-cal practices regarding war, whose dead are both a public and a private subject since the state usually puts them in harm's way. But scholars have neglected connections between the private and the public, as if the two are either largely unrelated or obviously parallel. I look for correspondences and traffic between the two without assuming they moved in lockstep, examining demographics, attitudes, and practices outside as well as in the arena of war.

PATRIOTIC CULTURE, 1945–65

At midcentury, the prospective death in war of Americans—even of the nation itself—loomed large, and grief over past death was controlled and channeled, especially by the state. For Americans as for any people, death could not be denied. It figured vividly even in a youth-centered culture critics saw as oblivious to death: in the movie *Rebel Without a Cause* (1955), James Dean courts death in a game of automobile "chicken," and Sal Mineo meets it; in the stage and film musical *West Side Story* (1957, 1961), chance, passion, and ethnic violence bring death to young lovers. Polio, which often struck the young, also figured prominently in postwar life. Medical progress encouraged optimism that experts could conquer disease—not death, but at least its premature forms. But optimism regarding war came less easily because evidence of human frailty, evil, capriciousness, and violence abounded: World War II's catastrophic record; the fast lurch of the wartime Soviet-American alliance into postwar enmity; the lethal workings of science, yielding nuclear weapons for America in 1945 and Russia in 1949. In response, national leaders invoked the past dead to deal with threatened death in the future.

World War II had set that pattern. President Franklin Roosevelt spoke eloquently of American losses but above all sought the victory that would halt further destruction. Americans certainly knew those losses, but in this "censored war," political and media authorities suppressed most visual evidence of American dead, until deciding late in the war that more graphic images would counter war-weariness and prepare Americans for the war's costliest phase. (A less obvious development may also have muted attention: while more than 400,000 soldiers, sailors, and marines died, wartime affluence and governmental activism improved the diet, health, and longevity of most Americans.) The visual record became more available after 1945, but as leaders grappled with nuclear weapons and the Cold War, reminders of past carnage served more to sound the alarm about the future than to mourn the fallen. Official memorialization of World War II indicated as much. For one thing, initially there was not much at the national level. Perhaps marble memorials were unnecessary given so many ongoing reminders of the war—millions of veterans; hordes of displaced war victims abroad; a Korean War fought partly with World War II weapons and personnel; a World War II general, Dwight Eisenhower, as president. And in most nations, a focus on the dead of World War I after 1918 yielded to a stress after 1945 on war's veterans, far better treated in part because promises to them of postwar bounty (for Americans through the GI Bill) had been crucial to sustaining the war effort. Besides, Truman maintained in 1945, total victory was the greatest memorial to America's dead, although he added, "No victory can make good [the] loss" for the dead's loved ones.

Memorials that did emerge related to the war against Japan, which aroused among many Americans a greater sense of injury and indignation than the European war (grievance and grieving are closely related). The first major official project, the 1954 Marine Corps War Memorial at the Arlington National Cemetery, depicted the American flag raising on the battle-ravaged Pacific island of Iwo Jima in 1945. The Iwo Jima memorial aggrandized the Marines' political interest, irritated Eisenhower (who declined to speak at its dedication), emphasized triumph more than death, promoted military preparedness, and loomed as mammoth and aloof, inspiring rather than approachable. For years, Karal Ann Marling and John Wetenhall have written, it "betokened military might, the new doctrine of armed deterrence, [and] the global ambitions of American foreign policy in the aftermath of World War II."

Dedicated in 1962, the *Arizona* memorial, built around the sunken battleship that entombed hundreds after Japan attacked Pearl Harbor, did establish "sacred ground" for the dead. But speeches and media comment about it linked the dead to American vulnerability, for which December 7, 1941, was the war's preeminent symbol. The fallen were "celebrated as heroes of the first battle of the war and mourned as victims of an inattentive nation." The motto of the Pearl Harbor Survivors Association was "Remember Pearl Harbor—Keep America Alert." The *Arizona* memorial, like "Pearl Harbor" in its many dimensions, underwrote demands for American military might, lest "a nuclear version of Pearl Harbor" befall all of the United States, and sanctioned "the redemptive function of American strategic bombing" of Japan's cities and the vengeance it unleashed. Memorialization of war's dead always ascribes to them a present meaning, one especially urgent with the *Arizona* memorial.

Militant patriotism and preparedness had no lock on postwar culture, which recognized violence as a trait that Americans, not just their defeated or new enemies, possessed. Popular books about World War II such as John Hersey's *Hiroshima* (1946) and Norman Mailer's *The Naked and the Dead* (1948) suggested that message. Hollywood recounted how harshly American soldiers could treat each other; in *From Here to Eternity* (1953), set in Hawaii before Pearl Harbor, a lumbering, murderous Ernest Borgnine confronts the tough but scrawny Montgomery Clift and Frank Sinatra. Other movies portrayed dangerous impulses among veterans, and film noir, influenced by the war, depicted death's senseless workings in ordinary settings. Such cultural documents expressed mourning, but for the loss of social harmony and national safety as much as individual lives, in a nation taught by the war to think in aggregate more than individual terms. Beyond formal representations lay the private thoughts and utterances about the dead of veterans, friends, and family members. This was not the era of silence about war's dead sometimes later imagined. But in officially sanctioned culture—when official sanction meant more—brevity about the dead, or invocation of them to address looming perils, prevailed.

The dominant vision of death was prospective—death in a nuclear war—and national, because authorities in Washington marshaled it and because the death of the nation, in nuclear fireballs and irradiated landscapes, was imagined. That vision emerged in myriad venues: stern warnings by politicians, generals, scientists, and theologians; cool admonitions in civil defense films; air raid drills at American schools; fallout shelters in cities; "doomsday" movies; and horror or sci-fi films that displaced atomic fears into other arenas. It transcended politics: both friends and foes of a mighty American nuclear arsenal could dip into the same well of fear. Newsreels of postwar nuclear tests and U.S. atomic attacks on Japan, shorn of grisly scenes that might arouse opposition to American policy, shifted focus from past death done by Americans to prospective death done to them. Frequent alarms about Soviet technological and political advances lent immediacy to that prospect. Mourning for the fallen lingered in nuclear fear, but encoded in anxieties about even more dreadful prospects ahead.

How far nuclear fear seeped into Americans' consciousness is debatable. Those "school children ducking under the desks during air raid drills," one historian notes, were also "rushing Good Humor trucks to buy ice-cream sandwiches."[1] National leaders vacillated about sounding the alarm over swelling nuclear arsenals, lest they provoke unreasoning fear, right-wing demands that America bomb Russia, opposing pleas that it disarm, or scary Soviet reactions— possible outcomes of too much talk that worried President Eisenhower. Numbing statistics and jargon about a future war had an abstract, unreal quality. Images of the atomic mushroom cloud obscured the destruction they also symbolized. Despite a culture preoccupied with "seeing" war, Americans rarely saw past or imagined nuclear dead; wartime reticence persisted under new circumstances. But the sheer scale and madness of two world wars and the postwar arms race gave nuclear fear credibility. "The atomic bomb was dropped on Hiroshima and killed everything," one diarist wrote in August 1945. "There are no longer problems of the spirit," William Faulkner observed five years later, "only the question: when will I be blown up?" Prospective death, though indissolubly linked to past death in World War II, outweighed it.[2]

Starting in spring 1945, war's dead also appeared in photographs and newsreels about victims of Nazi genocide. But they were not yet definitively framed as victims of a "holocaust" against the Jews, among whom many survivors focused as much on Israel's creation as on horrors just ended. Often instead rendered as casualties of modern war, totalitarianism, or German evil, genocide's victims were objects of warning more than mourning, reminders of the costs of another world war should the United States not prevent (or win) it. Their corpses consolidated a sense of purpose sometimes uncertain during the war: Americans had fought, it now seemed, to stop such atrocities; and they offset doubts about civilian casualties the United States had inflicted in bombing Germany and Japan, or might inflict in a future nuclear war. In these ways, too, remembrance of the past war's dead justified American power in a frightening postwar world.

People confronted death, as always, in the ordinary venue of private funeral rites. The midcentury marked the apogee of a funeral industry that carefully regulated and sanitized treatment of the dead. As in the nuclear arena, Americans deferred to experts and institutions. Death seemed a thing handled efficiently, coolly, impersonally. Quickly removed from home or hospital and often neighborhood, the deceased was taken to a mortuary, embalmed and cosmetically enhanced, and given a service. The goal, some funeral directors thought, was a beautiful "memory picture" of untroubled death, muted grief, and prompt "closure" (a later generation's term). Variables of class, race, region, and religion produced deviations from standard practice. That observers rarely noticed those deviations indicated how prevailing the standard practice was.

THERAPEUTIC CULTURE, 1965–1985

In the 1960s, as consensus on American war-making and war's dead fell apart, critics identified a "taboo" on death that denied Americans a healthy encounter with it. Increasingly, they regarded death and mourning as processes, not events, that warranted a therapeutic approach, personal control, and vibrant expression. They helped stimulate major shifts in attitude and practice, caused also by changes in death itself. In 1955, Geoffrey Gorer, in an essay called "The Pornography of Death," had claimed that "death had replaced sex as the taboo topic of modern culture." Ensuing complaints about what Jessica Mitford called *The American Way of Death*—her much-noticed 1963 book, its title providing shorthand for others—signaled a new era. So, too, did *The Loved One* (1965), based on Evelyn Waugh's 1948 novel, a wicked cinematic satire of a funeral empire built on exploitative religion and capitalism, with Jonathan Winters the fraudulent funereal genius, Liberace a smarmy casket salesman, and Rod Steiger the cosmetician who confuses sex and death.

Criticism was often angry but intellectually limited. Mitford's assault on the funeral industry's exploitation of customers was an arch version of standard consumer exposés. Critics often suggested that Americans dealt better with death in the past and Europeans still did so, without convincingly exploring how recent and peculiar the "American way of death" was and whether death was everywhere taboo in some ways, if approachable in others. Death critics maintained that funeral homes "minimize the importance of death and grief," James Farrell wrote, by removing the deceased from their homes and prettifying the dead and death itself. Although their key insight was to see death and mourning as extended processes, they often reduced existing practice to the single moment of funeral home control, as if the maternity ward could reveal all about reproduction, birth, and children. By slighting more public efforts to deal with (or avoid) the dead, they replicated the privatization of death they distrusted and neglected how death's "importance" might emerge in conversations, psychiatrists' offices, photo albums, taverns, and other locales difficult to track. Nor did removing the body from a home so obviously distance survivors from death. I remember childhood and adult trips to the funeral "home" (the term itself seemed weird—whose "home"?) as mysterious and terrifying; its very peculiarity highlighted death's finality and strangeness. Would death have been weightier and grief better expressed had I viewed the body in someone's home? As some critics recognized, the determinants of "the importance of grief and death" were too numerous and ineffable for the funeral industry alone to account for them, or for an "American way of death" to consist only of denial and taboo.

Other critics shifted focus and added nuance. Examining the hospital in her sober but popular *On Death and Dying* (1969), Elisabeth Kübler-Ross, unlike Mitford, had the authority of a doctor who faced dying and death, as well as a gentler approach. She described the reluctance of medical personnel, friends, family, and the dying to discuss death, attributing this silence to the vagaries of personality and culture, but also to "rapid technological advancements," "new weapons of mass destruction," and the agonies of the Vietnam War. She offered her soon-famous stages for dealing with death—denial, anger, bargaining, depression, acceptance—as loose categories, not a rigid program to be followed. She wrote in the therapeutic mode but avoided its jargon and talk of crisis, coming across as patient explorer rather than hectoring expert.

Kübler-Ross limned major themes in the changing cultural consciousness of death. No one formula fits all death, she explained; differences in demography, death's causes, families' histories, and patients' wishes impose variety. She thereby opened the door for approaching death in individual, varied ways, even while advocating standard hospital procedures for grappling with it. Disputing doctors' wisdom, she proposed diversifying the death process, so that nurses, therapists, clergy, and above all the dying and their loved ones also had authoritative voices. Formulas set by the state, hospital, mortuary, or church, she suggested, were too rigid, impersonal, and silencing.

Scholars echoed her concern. Philippe Aries's sweeping study *Western Attitudes Toward Death: From the Middle Ages to the Present* (1974 in its English-language edition) found "forbidden death" throughout the modern Western world, not just the United States. Ernest Becker worried that *The Denial of Death* (his prizewinning 1973 book) was "a mainstay of human activity" that could get carried too far. James Farrell's *Inventing the American Way of Death* (1980) traced long-term change, noted "important deviations from the American way of death," and detected limits in Kübler-Ross's challenge (it still "springs from the therapeutic conviction that we can master what we can touch or talk about" and "that death should not be dreadful").

Despite differences, these observers agreed on fundamentals. In Farrell's sympathetic summary, they "charge that, ridden by an unreasoning fear of death, Americans attempt to deny its reality by refusing to discuss the topic even with dying persons, by banishing the old and infirm to institutions isolated from the mainstream of life, by relegating death to hospitals and burial to funeral homes and memorial parks, by glossing the effects of death with embalming and cosmetic treatment, and by compensating for emotional vacuity with expensive, elaborate funeral displays. In short, they claim that 'death is un-American, an affront to every citizen's inalienable right to life, liberty, and the pursuit of happiness.'" It all constituted "the dying of death," Farrell concluded, which "threatens our humanity." The denial of death was peculiarly, though perhaps not solely, American, yielding, Kübler-Ross worried, "a society in which death was taboo."

That notion of a "taboo" constituted the core of criticism of American concepts of death. In offering it, critics deployed a language common in the 1960s and 1970s, when reformers across the ideological spectrum challenged presumed barriers to discussion of homosexuality, gender, reproduction, corporate power, Pentagon machinations, the presidency, and other matters in order to move Americans to a healthier social or political consciousness. Yet asserting that a taboo existed itself challenged the assertion. Challenging the taboo was a way to shift discussion to new voices—to some extent, those of therapists rather than funeral directors—not to initiate it. Death was assuredly a frightening topic before the 1960s, but hardly an unmentioned one.

That the critique struck a responsive chord nonetheless indicated the dissatisfaction among many Americans with prevailing modes of dealing with death. An explosion of popular, expert, and scholarly work after Kübler-Ross's 1969 book signaled a more vigorous and variegated interest in death. So, too, did changing attitudes and practices. Hospice care appealed to those wary of the costs and impersonality of hospitals and willing to regard dying as a process to be lived, not sequestered. Prepaid funeral and burial plans and cremation, an alternative that Mitford championed (and critics saw as another way to erase death), were touted as ways to escape the expensive embrace and prettifying practice of funeral homes and the costly clutch of cemetery operators. Like most services in American life, these proved vulnerable to exploitation, as Mitford later complained, but they did multiply the options for dealing with death. Another option was to look beyond the deceased's body. A service weeks after death separated memorialization from mortuary. Personalized memorial notices, unlike standardized obituaries, expressed a "continued sense of loss and grief," sometimes years after death had occurred, notes historian Robert Wells.

Grieving and memorialization also moved beyond institutional and commercial venues. Adherents of cremation often devised idiosyncratic rituals for scattering the ashes. Along the nation's roadways and at parks and other public places, a vernacular memorialization arose to victims of automobile accident, murder, and disaster, as survivors placed highly decorated crosses or other handcrafted memorial items, often with photographs or other mementoes of the deceased. Costing little, numerous but rarely conspicuous, these shrines expressed powerful impulses to find personal, autonomous, and extended ways to remember death and, in these cases, its tragic circumstances.

New large modes of memorialization also arose. In the 1980s, survivors of those who died of AIDS posted personal tributes in the gay press and memorialized the deceased in an ever-growing AIDS Quilt, each section a personal tribute and the whole thing or huge hunks of it displayed on the Washington Mall, television, and elsewhere. Survivors acted out of disgust at the stigma against mentioning AIDS, the standardized and often homophobic policies of newspapers and funeral homes, the numbers and youth of victims, and the apparent federal and medical inaction against the disease. The slogan of early AIDS activism, "SILENCE=DEATH," was a political denunciation of apathy, and a fitting obituary to a more private, controlled style of mourning. In turn, reactions to AIDS helped inspire political and memorial efforts by and for victims of other afflictions such as cancer, once regarded as a taboo subject in public conversation.

Beyond the spur critics provided, what accounted for new ideas and practices of death and mourning? To some extent they reflected broad changes. Longstanding American distaste for top-down institutional structures and arrogant authority swelled amid challenges to orthodoxy over Vietnam, the Cold War, civil rights, gender roles, and other issues. So too did the quest for self-help means of meeting life's challenges, even if that quest depended on self-help experts. A new informality, variety, and expressiveness in modes of living set in— undoubtedly less new than many thought, often coarse or superficial, but real enough also to reshape modes of dying. That was true not only for the young, too often praised or blamed for all changes coming out of the 1960s, but also for older Americans, now asserting more control for themselves or loved ones over disease and dying.

AIDS activists and assertive senior citizens suggested another broad change: in a more visibly differentiated nation, social groups more readily departed from set norms of the state, church, hospital, or mortuary, both breaking from the mainstream (if there still was one) and pressing harder on it. They also practiced real or invented traditions from their homelands, as did Asian Americans, and as did Hispanic Americans who altered a Catholic Church once dominated by Irish and Italian Americans. Reactions to death thus splintered along the lines of social divisions earlier submerged under the common fear generated by world war and cold war. Blame for death likewise splintered, assigned by pundits or lobbies to a list ever lengthening in the century's last decades: Type A personalities, smokers, abortionists and women who aborted, people with AIDS, fast-food junkies, teenaged school shooters, and so forth. Race and class often shaped differences in how death was perceived and experienced, strikingly in how the death penalty was visited on poorer black men. By observing Martin Luther King Jr. Day after his death in 1968, however, political and institutional authorities wove particular identities back into the fabric of national life.

Change also owed to developments squarely in the arena of dying and death. Given a growing cohort of the old (due to falling birthrates as well as increasing longevity), proportionately more Americans had death on their minds, while the death of younger ones from diseases like AIDS seemed more striking, unjust. The median age of Americans increased from 22.9 years in 1900 to 35.3 in 2000; the over-85 cohort mushroomed 37 percent in the 1990s alone to 4.2 million.[3] New technologies such as life-support systems and organ transplants blurred the line between life and death—when to "pull the plug" became a widespread concern—as did newly noticed pathologies like Alzheimer's, in which functional death preceded biological death.

That is, attitudes toward death also changed because death itself—its modes, duration, causes, and demography—was changing, becoming, as Kübler-Ross suggested, less often a sudden event, more often a prolonged process. Change in death was a long-term development, and the product as well as cause of new attitudes, but reactions to it crystallized in the 1970s and 1980s. Even into the twentieth century, death had often come quickly and to the young—the outcome of infant mortality, illness, war, and industrial, mining, transport, and agricultural accidents in appalling numbers. Some Americans, especially in disadvantaged groups, still die suddenly of illness, accident, crime, war, and disaster. But the share of those dying old and slowly had grown, dramatically by late in the century. In 1992, about half of the 2,183,000 deaths in the United States occurred to those 75 or older, and many more among those only slightly younger.[4]

As dying became a prolonged process, so too did dealing with it. More people could experience those five stages Kübler-Ross imagined, ones impossible to negotiate when dying had taken only seconds or days. Death's stronger association with old age and slow decline made death seem to creep in by increments, a trend explored in literature on AIDS, Alzheimer's, dying parents, and hospice care. The burdens of prolonged dying also aggravated dependence on professional expertise, and opportunities to resent it. And those burdens exposed faultlines of gender: the very aged were mostly women, often earlier the caretakers of male spouses, but feminism and social change also challenged women's primary responsibility for caretaking and grieving. Too, prolonged burdens invited elongated grieving, a staple of nineteenth-century widowhood (at least as remembered). New forms of extended grieving—the delayed memorialization, the therapy group—marked a partial return to earlier practice, before global war and fears of national death imposed urgency and homogeneity.

But these generalized explanations cannot account for the specific timing of change. That is traceable in part to the maelstrom of violence and death for Americans in the Vietnam War era. World War II had featured more violence and death, but mostly far from American shores and contained within sturdy boundaries of wartime purposefulness. Conflict over race and the war, along with violent crime rising toward its peak in the 1970s and 1980s, spread death through 1960s America—the common notion of a "war at home" was a pardonable exaggeration. Neither that "war" nor the one in Vietnam was contained by consensus and purpose. And unlike in World War II, violence by Americans against others and themselves, rather than violence against them by outsiders, seemed to many the defining problem, as they debated the destructive technologies their government used in Southeast Asia. As Howard Brick notes, "it became commonplace to recognize a propensity for violence as nearly a national character trait." New violence also spurred awareness of past violence, like the Nazi and nuclear holocausts of World War II, further underlining an American, Western, or human (to note variants of this position) "propensity" for it. Khmer Rouge genocide in Cambodia in the 1970s suggested to some that mass death knew few boundaries of race and ideology, and that American intervention there had contributed to a tragedy. Blame for American death abroad, as at home, splintered: no longer easily assignable to a unitary communist enemy, it was also attributed by the 1970s to motley other foes like Middle Eastern terrorists, or to Washington for its conduct of the Vietnam War. Death seemed disruptive, hydra-headed, random, troubling, and pervasive.

It did so also because of assassinations in the 1960s of John and Robert Kennedy, Martin Luther King Jr., Malcolm X, and lesser figures. Judged by many Americans' powerful memories of those events (and often violent aftermath), they were jarring encounters with death. FDR died in 1945 of natural causes, with no public lying in state, amid agreement on the goal of victory in war. In contrast, many Americans in the 1960s forged powerful emotive associations between the deaths of leaders and other death—in urban riots, antiwar agitation, and state repression on occasion, and above all the inconclusive war in Vietnam. Leaders' deaths were not isolated events, but the most visible threads in a bloody fabric of violence; not death contained by national purpose, but death run amok.

As understood by many Americans, the Vietnam War wove that fabric. It was a myth that television gave them novel access to war's reality: until late in the war, political, cultural, and technical limits constrained visual coverage, as they had in World War II. If anything, television provided more access to violence *within* America. Yet the myth's endurance suggested that many Americans *thought* they had new access to war's reality, access that showed death's cruel, irrational nature, and the difficulty of reckoning with it. The war also sustained fear that nuclear weapons—and the state that owned them—might unleash Armageddon rather than protect America from it. Every president since 1945, including each in Vietnam's wake, articulated that fear, as did Ronald Reagan in advancing his 1983 "Star Wars" defense against attack (which only intensified his critics' fear).

One clue to connections between public violence and private grieving was the extraordinary effort, examined by historian Michael Allen, to recover the remains of Americans in Vietnam. Since the Civil War, Americans had tried to retrieve the bodies of war dead. After the world wars, Western nations "depended heavily on the symbolism of body recovery in order to make the sacrifices of its citizens meaningful." In scale, contention, duration, and focus on every missing American, this new effort lacked precedent. Pressed by groups such as the National League of Families of American Prisoners and Missing in Southeast Asia, in which women played a prominent role, the recovery effort was initially linked to President Richard Nixon's effort to prolong and prevail in the war. But many activists, alleging government betrayal of the missing, distrusted even conservative administrations. Their agitation to recover the missing and dead prompted extensive congressional investigations during the 1970s and 1980s, herculean efforts by Americans and Vietnamese to recover remains, and activists' anger that little progress was made. Agitation also sparked extraordinary symbolism, as when President Reagan made the POW/MIA flag the first other than the Stars and Stripes ever to adorn the White House, and extravagant promises even about earlier wars, as when President George H. W. Bush pledged that forty years later "no one can rest until all [8,000 American Korean War MIAs] have been accounted for."

Uneasily accommodated by state authorities, the movement to recover Americans from Vietnam sought "to restore America by restoring missing Americans and the virtues they embodied" and to make sure the dead "not serve the interests of the state which sacrificed them." The movement also showed that dealing with death could be an interminable process without "closure" at all. (Maybe not in future wars: the U.S. military now stores genetic material from each service member to identify the dead.) Simultaneously, TV, films, and novels more than ever featured the dead, nearly dead, undead, and nobody-knows-if-they're-dead. With tidy boundaries around death fading in these venues, Americans regarded death in less tidy ways, and the therapeutic industry's goal of "closure" proved more elusive than ever.

Unveiled in 1982, the Vietnam Veterans Memorial, designed by Maya Lin, revealed characteristics of the memorial culture emerging from the Vietnam era. Half-buried and highly accessible, the antithesis of the monumental and aloof 1954 Iwo Jima memorial, it included no verbal text—no official instruction on the meaning of the dead. It emphasized open-ended process over fixed meaning: its chronological arrangement of the names of the 58,000 dead presented the war itself as a (long) process, moved visitors through a process, and continued a long process of controversy over the war's meaning. It invited active participation by visitors who traced and touched names (as had visitors to Europe's World War I memorials), wept or shouted, or left innumerable memorial objects, from poems to beer cans to gay pink triangles, collected daily and later selectively displayed at the National Museum of American History, in another process of memorialization. Responses to the memorial showed that, as in private arenas, extended, expressive, and individualized modes of mourning prevailed, rather than institutional formulas, although the memorial itself was such a formula, albeit implicit and ingenious. The stark listing of all who died evoked individuality as well as mass, loss as well as achievement. The memorial functioned to welcome contention, but not to resolve it. No longer could the state impose one meaning on war's dead. No longer could Americans achieve quick and clear closure on death.

MEMORIAL CULTURE, 1985–2001

Debate over America's Vietnam dead showed that war remained a commanding framework for dealing with death, but also that focus was shifting from prospective to past death and that state efforts to control and deploy the dead were under challenge. A vibrant, contentious, at times tawdry memorial culture was emerging.

Those shifts owed as much to what slid from view as to what moved to the forefront: nuclear terror, intense well into the 1960s and again in the late 1970s and early 1980s, largely disappeared after the Cold War's end in the late 1980s. So, too, did the relentless emphasis on prospective death, the vision of death as uniform and national—the nation's death—and the concerted effort by national leaders to marshal the meanings of death. Visions of apocalyptic death persisted in strains of religious thought, niches of ecological activism, fears of new biomedical terrors, lingering anxieties about nuclear weapons, and new ones about terrorism. The dead still prompted warning—moralists used gay men who died of AIDS to warn against homosexuality; graphic highway billboards depicted bodies ravaged by smoking, drunk driving, and other vices. But the dead's function to warn was shifting from war's arena to others. Through the 1990s, visions of mass death lacked the singularity of nuclear terror and the sustained sanction of national leaders, now less trusted anyway to provide it.

With fear of future mass death diminished, psychic space opened for reckoning with past mass death and other suffering. The major focus was World War II, and its leading edge dealt with the Holocaust, a term consolidated in the 1960s and 1970s. Efforts at its remembrance surged in and after the 1970s through cinematic accounts, scholarly inquiry, and legal action on behalf of survivors or heirs. In the United States, those efforts climaxed with the dedication in 1993 of the United States Holocaust Memorial Museum, which, like the Vietnam Memorial, invited active participation—in the experience of the Holocaust itself—rather than passive observation. More than the American media indicated, World War II remembrance also went beyond the Holocaust to include, for example, the sacrifices of Japanese American, African American, and gay American soldiers, and Japan's crimes against "comfort women," slave laborers, Allied POWs, and Chinese in the 1937–38 Nanjing Massacre (renamed, like some similar moments in war, a "forgotten holocaust").

Remembrance of victims of war, even those of disease and disaster, is never apolitical. It constructs, consolidates, or advances communities and their interests. Regarding World War II, remembrance at times served the cause of Israel and of nonwestern nations, the aspirations of American social groups, and other interests. Remembrance likewise risked exploitation and commercialization ("there's no business like Shoah business," someone quipped during negotiations over the Holocaust Museum). And its tough questions could split the communities it helped constitute, a dilemma faced by Jews, among others. What (if anything) was unique, sacred, instructive, tellable, and showable in war's ghastly record? Remembrance, flowing in some channels, dammed up in others. Protecting the U.S.-Japan alliance, the American government resisted legal efforts at redress against Japan or its corporate entities for crimes in World War II. World War I, and huge Russian and Soviet death tolls in both world wars, received little attention in the United States; American power inhibited reckoning with the costs to others of American war-making; genocide in Yugoslavia got more attention than genocide in Africa. As the establishment of the Holocaust Museum suggested, memorialization was easier for Americans when it did not directly involve American action in war.

Yet contention could generate unwitting attention. In 1995 critics shut down a proposed Smithsonian exhibit on the *Enola Gay*, the B-29 bomber that struck Hiroshima in 1945, accusing its planners of unjustified sympathy for the atomic bomb's victims, inflammatory exhibition of artifacts of their destruction, and offense to World War II veterans, now often deemed the sole legitimate holder of that war's memory despite differences among them. But the controversy also unleashed media and scholarly activity that brought Hiroshima's destruction to the attention of millions unaware or forgetful of it. By the same token, lack of contention might signal forgetfulness: a Korean War memorial, opened in Washington in 1995, risked being as forgotten as the war itself allegedly was. Contention aside, there had been too much carnage in war to commemorate it all evenly. Only a divine power could do that. Commemoration had to find specific focus, or collapse under the weight of the task.

Whatever its limits, remembrance welled up in American consciousness—and flooded into it from outside, for death was less contained geographically as in other ways. Unwittingly, eagerly, or angrily, Americans plunged into international conversations and contests about war's past. Their contributions and controversies—the Vietnam Memorial, the Holocaust Museum, the throttled *Enola Gay* exhibit—had repercussions and rough counterparts throughout much of the globe. But all contestants were not equal. The United States suffered less from war's mass death than most nations, yet possessed unequaled power to inflict it, to protect the world from it, and to shape cultural representations of it. The least harmed and best armed, America could say the most.

Despite that power, a "post-national phase" of memory emerged after the 1960s, historian John Gillis claims, with "the nation no longer the site or frame of memory for most people." "Post-national" captures the proliferation of commemorative sites, actors, and modes. Memory, like the economy and death itself, was seemingly deregulated and globalized. As with the economy, though, such terms exaggerated change. The nation—never the sole "site or frame" anyway—had hardly disappeared, as the Holocaust Museum showed. It recognized one nation's evil (Germany), another's creation (Israel), and still another's work (the United States, by putting the museum on its national space). It did not celebrate the American nation, except implicitly for embracing the museum, but the nation remained part of the story and the storytelling, as the *Enola Gay* uproar also indicated.

Beyond diminishing nuclear fear and diminishing nationalism, what accounted for the outpouring of remembrance about war's dead? Perhaps the costs of the century's wars had been too painful to acknowledge earlier, delaying reactions until late in the century. Evidence exists for such a psychological aversion, just as memories may suddenly erupt later. In *Another World* (1999), novelist Pat Barker captured an eruption of haunting, painful memories of World War I for a centenarian English veteran; she also explored memory's complexity in her *Regeneration* trilogy, set in and immediately after that war.

Asserting a psychological taboo naturalizes an aversion more likely constructed (as Barker recognized) by political and historical forces. The "censored war" had censored death because authorities wanted it censored; nuclear fear and the Cold War had channeled reactions to World War II's carnage. Politics also operated when social groups seemed to compete for status as victims, of war but also of disease and racial oppression. Besides, a large literature suggests, war's combatants and victims have selective and skewed memories from the start. If they do erupt later, they are not the same: memory has played tricks; intervening history has shifted meanings. Popularized therapeutic notions of "repressed" memory, seen as both deeply buried yet remarkably accurate for victims of traumas like child sex abuse, provided a model for war's recovered memories. But those notions—also political constructs, often used unfairly against daycare operators and clients—were largely discredited by the late 1990s, raising more questions about what constituted authentic memory. Controversies in 2001 over alleged American atrocities in the Korean War and revelations that Senator Bob Kerrey's vaunted heroism in the Vietnam War was fraudulent demonstrated how divergent memories, and the politics they are embedded in, could be. In 2004, the "swift-boating" of Democratic presidential candidate John Kerry regarding his service and politics during the Vietnam War demonstrated how vicious the politics of memory could become. And memory, what an individual retains, was not the same as remembrance, what a group shares whose members often had not witnessed the remembered events.

It is difficult to attribute earlier reticence to a pathology of aversion—and difficult to see later remembrance simply as a sign of psychic health, as if therapeutic culture had succeeded in its mission. Some critics detected pathology in efforts to redress wartime injustice, lamenting the "sentimental solidarity of remembered victimhood" and the "morbidity of autistic self-indulgence in victimization"—what a sympathetic interpreter, Laura Hein, saw in 2002 as "a shrewd mobilization of political support for [victims'] claims to be treated as full human beings."[5] War's death, like all death, defeated icy rationality and calm judgment.

Perhaps the new memorial impulse also reflected a fear of losing the past. July 4, 1776, "was not celebrated nationally until the 1820s," as John Gillis summarizes John Bodnar's work, "when Americans had begun to feel that history was accelerating and the heroic past was slipping away from them." By the 1990s, Holocaust survivors, veterans, and others who endured World War II, or those speaking for them, certainly felt that the "heroic [or terrible] past was slipping away from them." Yet the Vietnam Memorial was dedicated only seven years after America's war there ended, in November 1982, long before much "slipping away" occurred, at least in generational terms. Inherently political, remembrance operated on no set, natural timetable.

Gender affected the politics of remembrance, since men mostly fight wars however much women are victimized. Countering the feminist wave of the 1970s, war memorialization shifted cultural and political focus to male sacrifice and achievement. The rituals of memorialization were presided over by men; the conflicts over it by the 1990s were largely among men; trumpeted by news anchor Tom Brokaw and others, the "Greatest Generation" of Americans who won World War II was presumptively male (and often, white and middle class). But here, too, lay submerged complexity: the male focus of memorial culture stood in uneasy relationship to women's greater longevity. If life itself is power, men's achievements and sacrifices could not erase the fact that women hold power longer.

Whatever the activating forces, reactions to the century's wars helped foster a lively memorial culture in the United States and elsewhere. The dead of past wars moved to the center of political and cultural life; the imagined dead of future war dwindled from sight. At times it seemed that memorial culture *was* American culture, so intense were its controversies, so weighty its assigned meanings, and so insistent also the media's stories about murder, disaster, and celebrity death. From the Vietnam Memorial, to Reagan's 1985 visit to a German cemetery holding elite Nazi dead, to the *Enola Gay* exhibit uproar, to the 1990s campaign for a World War II memorial on the Mall, much energy went to these matters.

Remembrance of horrors and achievements also had a quality of reliving war, as if past and present were indistinguishable. When Geordie in *Another World* mutters, "I am in hell," it is unclear whether "hell" is his war experience eighty years earlier or his memory of it eighty years later. When "an electrical storm" erupts in the brain of an aging James Whale, the Hollywood director and war veteran reimagined in the film *Gods and Monsters* (1998), he feels as if he is back in World War I, not merely remembering it. At its darkest, late-century memorial culture evoked the "hell" of current memory beset—individually for Geordie, collectively for surviving peoples—by a century's slaughter. But it also expressed collective relief that war had largely receded into America's past and the threat of nuclear war had diminished.

Elusive closure, chronic contention, and persistent suspicion still characterized much remembrance. The longevity of the Vietnam body recovery story was striking: Bill Clinton's first act as the first president to visit Vietnam since American defeat was to observe—in a highly staged and publicized event—efforts to sift more remains. In 2001, "In Search of the Vanished" in Vietnam still emblazoned the cover of a national Sunday supplement.[6] In 1984, presumably unidentified remains from the war had been placed in the Tomb of the Unknown Soldier, the grave "sealed until the second-coming of Christ," it was intoned at the time. In 1998, aggrieved POW/MIA activists and family members, still distrusting the state, insisted that the bones be exhumed; identified as those of Lt. Michael Blassie, they were transferred to his family.

Complicated reflections on World War II also continued. Unlike work crudely celebrating Americans in that war, Gerald F. Linderman's *The World Within War: America's Combat Experience in World War II* (1997) offered a tribute all the more powerful because it recognized the ugliness and brutality as well as valor that Americans engaged in and witnessed. *Enemy at the Gates* (2001) marked a rare Hollywood foray into the Soviet side of World War II; *The Thin Red Line* (1998) disturbingly portrayed American action in the Pacific War.

Contention and complexity about World War II diminished in the 1990s, especially once the *Enola Gay* fracas faded. The films getting most attention, *Saving Private Ryan* (1998) and *Pearl Harbor* (2001), operated in a new mainstream. Less troubled than earlier blockbusters like *From Here to Eternity*, they captured "the triumphal tone that today's audiences seem to crave more guilelessly than wartime ones did."[7] They focused little on the war's issues, the enemy's nature, the Allies' contributions, the Americans' ambitions, or the military's sordid qualities. Counterbalancing combat sequences of much-ballyhooed "realism," they sentimentalized American fighting men—handsome, innocent, given to heroic acts while the soundtrack gushes—and sacralized them as victims of war who made martyrs' sacrifices (a view most men at the time, usually draftees, did not hold). Few viewers would grasp that most American personnel never entered combat (and more than 100,000 died outside combat). The nostalgic treatment in film and other venues stripped the "Greatest Generation" of its complexity, rarely hinting that many in it went on to attack or defend racial segregation, fight in Korea, beat or love wives, or put Americans into space and Vietnam. These were usually younger voices about that generation, not its voices. "Soldiers never have much to say about why they fight, and even this Good War was no exception," World War II veteran Samuel Hynes observed. Memorial Day in 2001, coinciding with the release of *Pearl Harbor*, was treated as World War II day, with other wars little noted. It was if many Americans wanted World War II—a highly limited view of it at that—to stand for all their wars, the Vietnam War fading away, the Korean War never clearly in focus, the Gulf War too light to have traction on memory.

Yet memorialization of World War II did focus on death, not just heroism. Even more than most war films, *Ryan* did so, vividly portraying the D-Day invasion of France, opening and closing with scenes of a military cemetery. Ceremonies like one in 2001 dedicating a National D-Day Memorial in Virginia emphasized the deaths of those who served. "The order of the day is gratitude," President George W. Bush commented. "We remember what was lost." Death, more than its causes and consequences, was at the center of memory. "Statements of what was lost now eclipse expressions of what was gained," John Bodnar observed. Death figured in another way—quick construction of a World War II memorial, advocates asserted, would also honor veterans now dying, and so the World War II Memorial quickly went up on the National Mall in Washington. Loss and mourning dominated memorial culture, replacing fear of future peril. The shift from warning to mourning was not absolute: mourning occurred in the 1940s; and warning persisted in the 1990s, in efforts to use the Holocaust's dead to spur intervention in the Balkans and to use those dead from disease, vice, and crime to achieve moral and medical uplift. Successive deposits on the American landscape, patriotic, therapeutic, and memorial cultures each added to, rather than obliterating, what preceded. But regarding war, the arc of change was largely complete.

Other evidence of a culture expressively attentive to death was also abundant. Bookstores carried ample sections on "death and dying," a subject parsed in rich ways, as in Sherwin B. Nuland's *How We Die: Reflections on Life's Final Chapter* (1994), Christine Quigley's *The Corpse: A History* (1996), and *The Undertaking: Life Studies from the Dismal Trade* (1997) by Thomas Lynch, who reached many readers writing on his own trade and other subjects. Studs Terkel's oral history *Will the Circle Be Unbroken? Reflections on Death, Rebirth, and Hunger for a Faith* (2001) demonstrated how death had become a series of individual stories, not a master narrative. The HBO cable television channel's respected series *Six Feet Under*, unthinkable a half-century earlier, featured a family funeral home; ironically, creator Alan Ball repeated the hoary claim about "a culture that does everything it can to deny the presence of death."[8] The study of individual and social memory intensified; its context—swelling numbers of older Americans, surging attention to Alzheimer's, Ronald Reagan enduring that disease—linked memory and death closely.

In its preoccupation with violence and disaster, this expressive culture also showed links to concurrent trends in remembrance of war's dead. Aviation crashes were followed by new, collective memorial services prompted by both aggrieved survivors and nervous airline companies. (The steady stream of far greater highway carnage could not compete for attention with an airliner's sudden demise.) A predictable and publicized routine of grief therapy arose at schools (at least affluent ones) visited by murder or other forms of death. Conflict over capital punishment brought attention to another form of death and to issues of class and race, along with rituals for memorializing the condemned.

Some observers saw little change in these developments. Historian Robert Wells disputed earlier critics such as Kübler-Ross on one point: "We are not, in fact, a death-denying society." The media's fascination with the dead merely made Americans "enjoy a vicarious intimacy with death" (a phrase Wells borrowed from Waugh's *The Loved One*). That phrase seems apt given television's frenzied coverage of notable death stories—the shuttle *Challenger*'s explosion in 1986, the Oklahoma City bombing in 1995, Princess Diana's death in 1997, the Columbine High School shootings in 1999—and innumerable local ones. To

Wells, such coverage meant that much had changed on the surface, but little beneath it: "While we are immersed in death . . . at a distance," when "death strikes close to home, we are frequently at a loss to know how to speak of death in any but the most superficial terms." The rush to therapy and self-help groups for the bereaved—finding "strangers with similar afflictions instead of relying on established social contacts"—reveals anew "the reluctance to discuss death in our society."

Yet use of such venues reflected a commonplace therapeutic culture as much as a peculiar "reluctance"—impossible to measure anyway—"to discuss death." The media-driven "vicarious intimacy with death" did entail a cultural focus, however tawdry at times, on death, and arguably it stimulated as much as muffled personal modes of dealing with death. How proximate to death must one be before experience becomes personal rather than "vicarious"? And can vicarious experience—viewing on television a president's assassination or a princess's untimely passing—nonetheless be genuine? Many scholars seem to have replaced the older notion of an American "taboo" on death with its flip side, seeing "a nation preoccupied with death." [9] Whether it was peculiarly preoccupied was doubtful, though perhaps preoccupied in some peculiar ways.

Perhaps this culture attuned to aging and death also reflected a changing sense of the nation's youthfulness. The idea of young America guiding, redeeming, or defeating older, decadent countries and oppressive regimes had long figured in Americans'—and sometimes others'—imagination of their nation. But it diminished as America's world imperial role matured. Leaders positioned the United States as the adult tutor to "young" nations in a "developing" world and to the fledgling democracies and economies of former enemies like Germany, Japan, and Russia. Bicentennial celebrations in 1976 emphasized the longevity of the nation and its institutions. After the space race and the Peace Corps of the 1960s, political leaders defined no youthful adventure for the nation. More than ever in the 1990s, America's unrivaled bigness and power connoted maturity.

Few Americans openly worried that their nation was aging, perhaps only seeing it in a middle-aged prime of power. In middle age, however, intimations of death, though perhaps unheeded, creep in. By the 1990s, most discourse about death in war focused on the past; how to display the *Enola Gay* and build a World War II memorial rivaled for attention with whether to intervene in the Balkans. Indeed, those insistent on memorializing World War II often resisted current uses of American power. While remembering past sacrifices, Americans showed little interest in new ones, nor did their military supremacy seem to risk them, while in action it pushed death far away and rendered it antiseptic. Many Americans looked back to a remembered martial triumph, moral virtue, and national purpose in World War II as the apogee of their nation's experience, so that "Americans now pine for World War II as if it's an Eden from which they have been exiled,"[10] but one to which they hardly wished to return. It was the outlook of a people grown older—especially those older, white, and male—sensing their nation growing older.

9/11 CULTURE

Reactions to the September 11, 2001, attacks on New York's World Trade Center and the Pentagon recapitulated old themes and extended newer ones. Americans, like most peoples, focused on death done to, not by, them. The attacks realized, on lesser scale and in unforeseen ways, midcentury fears of sudden, total destruction. Presumably fearing more attacks on Washington, the Bush administration secretly activated a never-used Cold War plan for a shadow government (only for the executive branch) in hiding. Current and prospective mass death, not death in past wars or slow death for the aged, raced to the fore again, reversing that arc of change traversed between the 1940s and the century's end. Until carted away, ghostly remains of the Trade Center resembled European cathedrals blasted in World War II. Ubiquitous analogies to Pearl Harbor, the renewed prominence of national news anchors, and the destruction of national symbols reinvigorated a national frame for death, mourning, and anxiety. Male "heroes," usually white firefighters and others in uniform at the Trade Center, were assigned the martial, male, and racial qualities remembered for World War II's "Greatest Generation." Their raising of an American flag over the Trade Center's ruins was likened to the Iwo Jima flag raising in 1945. Meanwhile, widows often seemed caught in older gendered roles of grieving.

The response of national leaders also harkened back, awkwardly and partially, to World War II. Their insistence that autumn that Americans restore their economy and self-confidence by shopping at malls and hopping on airliners echoed an older, buttoned-down model of grief: get over it, was the message. President George W. Bush drew on World War II's example without the sustained calls for sacrifice and mourning that Franklin Delano Roosevelt had comfortably offered (and continuing American losses had compelled). Briefly recognizing the nation's grief, he suggested that victory and vengeance, not disabling attention to the dead, would best honor them. On September 14 he promised, in words grandiose even by the standards of American wartime idealism, to "rid the world of evil." In January 2002 he took on the "axis of evil" (Iran, Iraq, and North Korea), a phrase looping back to World War II Axis enemies (Germany, Japan, and Italy). His rhetoric ran the same risk that his father had met in the Gulf War—that he could not secure the total victory that references to World War II implied. But death was again an instrumentality of the state, and few initially resented that it was.

The recent expressive culture was equally in evidence. Americans' transfixed reactions to their TV sets on 9/11 suggested that "a vicarious intimacy with death" still could be heartfelt. Mass death in America further narrowed the gap between public and private mourning. Therapeutic culture, deploying tools from teddy bears to grief counselors to uncounted "heroes," showed anew its multiple capacities to express, trivialize, and depoliticize grief. Efforts to identify the dead employed technologies and attitudes pioneered in post-Vietnam body recovery, again with disappointing results. As if the vernacular roadside memorials scattered about the nation suddenly gathered together, New York's streets and firehouses displayed a profusion of shrines, memorials, flowers, and photographs (resembling "missing child" photos of the 1980s); the somber onlookers were also striking. An expressive culture was already primed for action, in part by the memorial practices of Hispanic Americans, many of whom died at the Trade Center. Social and local identities were manifest, interlaced with the national frame: this story was about New York City—about diverse individuals and groups using diffuse networks of email and cell phones—not about an undifferentiated urban mass or nation. Publicity about fallen Fire Department Chaplain Father Mychal Judge, a gay Catholic priest, further varied the social tapestry of death. National media offered personalized death notices, like the *New York Times* "Portraits of Grief," more than standardized obituaries.

Just as first responses were swift and diversified, so were the first steps toward formal memorialization, not left to languish as it seemingly had after World War II. The National Museum of American History, given to treating events well in the past, moved to open a 9/11 exhibit a year to the day later. As after tragedies like the Holocaust and the Oklahoma City bombing, surviving kin, friends, and others insisted on having voices in memorialization. Neither political nor corporate authority could go it alone, as contests sharpened over whether New York's devastated site was "sacred ground" like American battlefields, and old questions about tourists' deportment and vicarious thrills at battlefields flared anew. Who counted as veterans and kin had been mostly clear-cut after December 7, 1941, when military service defined them (although some facing great peril, such as the merchant marines, were neglected). Who counted was contentious after 9/11, when most dead were civilians who differed greatly in wealth and sometimes lacked U.S. citizenship and left unwed gay or straight partners. Benefits, vigorously sought by many survivors (as they had been by World War II veterans), were calculated by baffling, complex individual formulas, not the standardized ones of the 1944 GI Bill.

Neither midcentury modes of grieving nor later expressive ones enabled Americans to grasp fully the attacks' significance. Such destruction had not visited continental America since the Civil War and by a foreign enemy not since the War of 1812, and never with such suddenness and civilian carnage; yet the death toll of some three thousand was far less than annual mortality on high-ways. Invocations of Pearl Harbor—an attack on military forces, not civilians—were desperate efforts to lodge the unfamiliar in a familiar past. December 7, 1941, and September 11, 2001, had in common mostly the lack of precedent. Pearl Harbor gained significance partly from its context: it climaxed years of ap-prehension among Americans and plunged them officially into a titanic war, but only the specific site of attack was a surprise, not the war. How, and how much, September 11 lodged in remembrance would depend on whether it was a terrible but rogue event or the start of years of violence, amplifying remem-brance as World War II had for Pearl Harbor.

As 9/11 receded, so too did the expressive public culture initially associated with it, and death received the more implicit and indirect treatment notable be-fore the 1960s. Once again, it was harnessed to the prospect of future disaster, this time through more terrorist attacks, and to the political agendas of various parties. Whatever their private grief, survivors of 9/11 victims increasingly gained attention only through their pressure to authorize and empower a public commission to investigate the 9/11 disaster.[11] The Republican national conven-tion, meeting in New York City in September 2004, implicitly used the World Trade Center site as backdrop and leverage for the reelection of George Bush. While the rebuilt site of the Trade Center would memorialize 9/11, its primary focus, it seemed, would be commercial. Shocking photographs and footage of the 9/11 disaster rarely appeared in public, many effectively banned. In the war to overthrow Saddam Hussein and occupy Iraq, the deaths of American mili-tary personnel (more than 2,500 as of July 2006) receded from the front pages of newspapers and the first minutes of news broadcasts, while the far more numer-ous deaths of Iraqis received almost no attention. As usual, a steady stream of deaths, whether by car accidents, war, or disease, did not command the atten-tion that sudden catastrophe, as on 9/11, did, and as in other protracted Ameri-can wars, public attention to death became routinized.

Indeed, death in most societies is—has to be—routinized: perpetual mourn-ing is rarely sustainable. But societies vary in how their culture and politics mute the rawness of death. Bush administration policies—to stir fear of a future attack, to ban photographs of the coffins of returning U.S. soldiers, to "embed" reporters within military units, and in other ways to discourage sharp media at-tention to ongoing losses in Iraq—all further muted attention, while the violence-torn nature of the American occupation of Iraq curbed media efforts to cover the story there. The memory of 9/11 certainly remained powerful, and the deaths of Americans at war certainly got noted, but expressive cultural and political attention to them had diminished. Whether that pattern would con-tinue depended in part on the unpredictable course of the "war on terror" and American foreign policy. The one constant in the history of American death was how much war by and against Americans provided a major prism through which they glimpsed the meanings of death and mourning.

BIBLIOGRAPHIC NOTE

Too large to mention most titles, the scholarship on war, death, and memory includes international perspectives in John R. Gillis, ed., *Commemorations: The Politics of National Identity* (Princeton University Press, 1994), a pioneering work; Jay Winter and Emmanuel Sivan, eds., *War and Remembrance in the Twentieth Century* (Cambridge University Press, 1999); and Laura Hein and Mark Selden, eds., *Censoring History: Citizenship and Memory in Japan, Germany, and the United States* (M. E. Sharpe, 2000). Kenneth E. Foote's *Shadowed Ground: America's Landscapes of Violence and Tragedy* (University of Texas Press, 1997) contains much provocative and fruitful material. Among John Bodnar's studies of commemoration is "*Saving Private Ryan* and Postwar Memory in America," *American Historical Review* 106 (June 2001): 805–817. The foremost historian of American commemorative sites and controversies about war is Edward Tabor Linenthal. See *Sacred Ground: Americans and Their Battlefields* (University of Illinois Press, 1991), especially on Pearl Harbor; *Preserving Memory: The Struggle to Create America's Holocaust Museum* (Viking, 1995); his anthology, coedited by Tom Engelhardt, *History Wars: The Enola Gay and Other Battles for the American Past* (Metropolitan Books, 1996); and "'The Predicament of Aftermath': 19 April 1995 and 11 September 2001," *OAH Newsletter*, November 2001. Samuel Hynes, *The Soldiers' Tale: Bearing Witness to Modern War* (Penguin, 1997) sensitively treats its subject. Karal Ann Marling and John Wetenhall, *Iwo Jima: Monuments, Memories, and the American Hero* (Harvard University Press, 1991) is bracing. For the 1940s, I draw on Robert Lane Fenrich, "Imagining Holocaust: Mass Death and American Consciousness at the End of World War II" (Ph.D. diss., Northwestern University, 1992) and George Roeder, *The Censored War: American Visual Experience During World War II* (Yale University Press, 1993). William S. Graebner, *The Age of Doubt: American Thought and Culture in the 1940s* (Twayne, 1991), and Howard Brick, *The Age of Contradiction: American Thought and Culture in the 1960s* (Cornell University Press, 2000), give valuable background. On post-Vietnam memory and body recovery, I draw on Michael Allen, "'The War's Not Over Until the Last Man Comes Home': Body Recovery and the Vietnam War" (Ph.D. diss., Northwestern University, 2003). Another useful book on the subject is Michael Sledge's *Soldier Dead: How We Recover, Identify, Bury, and Honor Our Military Fallen* (Columbia University Press, 2005). On memorializing Vietnam and other signal events, see Louis Menand, "The Reluctant Memorialist," *New Yorker*, 8 July 2002. Valuable on private death and grieving are James J. Farrell, *Inventing the American Way of Death, 1830–1920* (Temple University Press, 1980); Robert V. Wells, *Facing the "King of Terrors": Death and Society in an American Community, 1750–1990* (Cambridge University Press, 2000); and Stephen Prothero, *Purified by Fire: A History of Cremation in America* (University of California Press, 2001). Among many primary sources— sites, films, speeches, and the like—classic books include Jessica Mitford, *The American Way of Death* (Simon & Schuster, 1963) and *The American Way Death Revisited* (Knopf, 1998); and Elisabeth Kübler-Ross, M.D., *On Death and Dying* (Macmillan, 1969). Laura Hein, Lane Fenrich, Michael Allen, and Mark Carnes provided readings of and ideas for this essay.

NOTES

1. Leo P. Ribuffo, "Will the Sixties Never End? Or Perhaps at Least the Thirties? Or Maybe Even the Progressive Era? Contrarian Thoughts on Change and Continuity in American Political Culture at the Turn of the Millennium," in *Rethinking Cold War Culture*, ed. Peter J. Kuznick and James Gilbert (Washington, D.C.: Smithsonian Press, 2001), 208.

2. William Graebner, *The Age of Doubt: American Thought and Culture in the 1940s* (Boston: Waveland Press, 1991), 21, 103.

3. David Mendell and Evan Osnos, "America Grows Older and Lot Less Traditional," *Chicago Tribune*, 15 May 2001.

4. Figures cited in Christine Quigley, *The Corpse: A History* (Jefferson, N.C.: McFarland, 1996), 3.

5. Quotations from Ian Buruma, Elazar Barkan, and Laura Hein in Hein, "War Compensation: Claims Against the Japanese Government and Japanese Corporations for War Crimes," in *Politics and the Past: On Repairing Historical Injustices*, ed. John Torpey (Lanham, Md.: Rowman & Littlefield, 2003), p. 131.

6. Earl Swift, "In Search of the Vanished," *Parade*, 22 July 2001.

7. Tom Carson, "Groping for Something Inspirational in a Sneak Attack," *New York Times*, 20 May 2001.

8. *TV Guide*, 2–8 March 2002, 12.

9. Gary Laderman, quoted in John Palattella, "Death," *Lingua Franca*, April 2001, 15.

10. Carson, "Groping for Something Inspirational."

11. Officially, the National Commission on Terrorism Attacks on the United States. *The 9/11 Commission Report* was published in 2004.

9. THE COMMERCE OF CULTURE AND CRITICISM

GEORGE COTKIN

Consider two cultural markers. The first is a photograph taken in the late 1950s or early 1960s of poet W. H. Auden, cultural historian Jacques Barzun, and literary critic Lionel Trilling, huddled around a table, pencils in hand. They are meeting to discuss selections for the Readers' Subscription Book Club, a highbrow competitor to the Book of the Month Club. While the Readers' Subscription is a moneymaking enterprise, the connection here between commerce and culture is apparently without tension, largely hidden from view. Guardians of the gates of culture, Auden and company recommend literary works that are appropriate and edifying. Thus, they educate their readers to appreciate Henry James and Virginia Woolf, E. M. Forster and Isaac Babel, Vladimir Nabokov and Saul Bellow, all of whom they see as writing literature marked by moral imagination and stylistic complexity. As critics, the three men seek to make distinctions and to communicate with a wider public that respects their taste and credentials.

The second takes place in 1964, at the Bianchini Gallery "Supermarket" show in New York. Pop artist Andy Warhol displays stacks of real Campbell's soup cans, signed by him, adjacent to his silkscreen of one such can. Against another wall are Warhol's famous Brillo boxes, constructed out of wood upon which he has silkscreened the same insignia and information that appear on real Brillo boxes made out of cardboard, available in most supermarkets. In this gallery world, meant to mimic a supermarket, the distinction between art and everyday consumer object is obliterated. Indeed, with the rise of pop art at this historical moment, even the function of the critic seems to have diminished or disappeared entirely. If everything from Coke bottles to comics is potentially art, then everyone is potentially critic or connoisseur. Warhol and his compatriots in the pop-art movement, many of them with a background in advertising and window designing, enraged leading art critics by shamelessly hawking their artwork as a product, pure and simple, erasing the line between commerce and culture.

Historian Lizabeth Cohen describes America after the Second World War as a "Consumer's Republic," a nation convinced that commerce and consumption would bolster democracy, both at home and abroad.[1] Cohen contends that the ideal of consumption became "almost a national civic religion." In this new world, the suburban mall, for instance, functioned as both a place of commerce and a new public square. The new medium of television promoted middle-class cultural values as normative through commercials and family-oriented shows. But Cohen is silent on how commerce affected American culture, art, and criticism.

Commerce, the movement and interchange of ideas and artifacts across political and cultural boundaries, left few aspects of art and culture untouched in the postwar years. American corporations and cultural institutions grew closer than ever before. By the early 1960s, the advertising industry helped to sweep away much of the staid weight of middle-class restraint through innovative campaigns that sold a new sense of self, freedom, and creativity. Advertisements promoted the notion that consumption of certain items was a mark of nonconformity and daring. While the message might be problematic, to say the least, the slogans and images were creative.

Artists and critics have viewed the rise of commerce and consumption variously. Many regard the rise of mass culture and commercialization as marks of American cultural declension—coarseness and kitsch undermining the high ideals of art and culture. According to the theorists of the Frankfurt School, such as Theodor Adorno and Max Horkheimer, the "culture industry"—the institutions and media that produce and distribute cultural and artistic work—destroys artistic traditions, creates a passive public, and diminishes standards. Moreover, commerce corrupts the aesthetic and literary canon; controls what museums exhibit; determines the production, structure, and distribution of fiction; and influences how artist and artwork are packaged. Art and artist, critic and connoisseur, citizen and consumer: none can escape, in this view, the maw of commerce. In sum, the culture industry co-opts, directs, and infantilizes artist, critic, and the public alike.

However, complaints about postwar commercial intrusions into art have long obscured reality: modernism, from the outset of the twentieth century, connected itself with commerce, marketing, and the creation of a public. The very nature of the argument about commerce's "contaminating" culture is problematic, predicated on the thesis that culture is somehow distinct from commerce and should be kept "pure" from pecuniary considerations. As Karl Marx and Ralph Waldo Emerson understood, capitalist commerce follows a feverish logic, running roughshod over entrenched traditions that stand in its path. Hence the famous line from Marx: "All that is solid melts into air."[2]

In postwar America, however, the searing heat of commerce did not destroy artistic creativity as much as melt artificially rigid categories and preconceptions, thus allowing new currents to flow. Rather than view art and criticism in decline, the postwar era saw a renaissance of immense proportions. A new American culture was being born, marked by erasure of the lines between high and low, by new ways of representing the products of commercial culture, by new self-conceptions of the artist and writer and his or her relationship to commerce, and by the ascendancy of theory. "New" and "more" became the catchwords of this emerging culture. In the midst of all this messy change, as cultural formations and ideals pushed and shoved against one another, the role of the critic remained central. In times of tension and change, when new art forms explode upon the scene, cultural critics arise to help smooth the path, to explicate the shifts, and to make distinctions among cultural products. In the process, as critic Susan Sontag understood, "a new sensibility" in the 1960s emerged, predicated on pleasure, excess, transgression, diversity, and theory.

This new cultural sensibility had to overcome the powerful presence and ideals associated with the New York intellectuals, such as Philip Rahv and William Phillips, clustered around the journal *Partisan Review*. Largely from working-class, Jewish origins, the New York intellectuals emerged in the 1930s as anti-Stalinist activists, upholding as best they could both Marxism and modernism. The New York intellectuals, after their postwar rejection of radicalism, continued to defend the monuments of high modernism and the ideals of an earlier avant-garde; their influence spread as New York emerged as a cultural capital. They approached modernist texts, as well as politics and culture, in sociologist Daniel Bell's words, with "irony, paradox, ambiguity, and complexity."[3] The New York inte llectuals practiced an eclectic form of criticism. Open to structure and form in literature, they also maintained that texts existed at the "dark and bloody crossroads where literature and politics meet."[4]

The New York intellectuals attacked mass culture in a steady stream of analysis and rant. Although few of them, if one is to judge by their writings, regularly attended films, they argued that the products of the culture industry— Hollywood films, popular recordings, comic strips—exuded a kitsch sentimentalism that undermined important analytic and political distinctions. In Dwight Macdonald's words, "There is nothing more vulgar . . . than sophisticated kitsch."[5] The virus of popular culture, in this view, weakened standards, pulling everything down to a debased level. According to Bernard Rosenberg, coeditor of the influential collection *Mass Culture* (1957), "mass culture threatens not merely to cretinize our taste, but to brutalize our senses while paving the way to totalitarianism."[6] Despite their decreasing criticisms of capitalism in the post-war years, the New York intellectuals remained allied with elitist Marxists in maintaining that a commercial culture could not be reconciled with a culture of high art. Commerce sought the lowest common denominator to promote mass sales and to taint serious art.

In effect, the New York intellectuals cordoned themselves off from what was vibrant and interesting in postwar culture. Tone deaf to jazz, the Beats, and John Cage and his compatriots in dance, art, film, and music who were cele-brating a mode of creative spontaneity and rejecting old forms of narrative and musical structure, the New York intellectuals sought to protect their turf of high seriousness and their status as critics. Such an attitude was common in the 1950s. Abstract expressionist and color-field painters such as Jackson Pollock, Mark Rothko, and Barnett Newman established their own cultural integrity upon fanatical core notions of transcendence and attention to the picture plane and to problems internal to the history of art. African American bebop artists, most famously Charlie "Bird" Parker and Miles Davis, revolted against swing music and popular appropriations of jazz by developing a musical style resistant to easy co-optation by commercial and racist forces. But none of these groups would succeed in their quest for purity.

Various forces upended 1950s American cultural conformity, consensus, and stability. The GI Bill changed the face of American education and culture by funneling massive numbers of students and amounts of governmental funds into colleges and universities. By 1947, the number of veterans attending schools of higher education had peaked at over 1.1 million, or close to 50 percent of the student body.[7] Throughout the 1950s, higher education enrollments shot up, with a boost from over 2.3 million attending in 1950 to over 3.5 million students in colleges in 1960, an increase of 57 percent.[8] College attendance created a wider than ever audience for cultural production. Although not necessarily learned in the arts, these college students considered the arts part of the good life, a status symbol, and something worthy of respect. In a culture premised on the notion of achieving some degree of distinction through consumption and with a widening group of individuals possessed with cultural capital and finan-cial means, American culture expanded to meet the demand for its products. Economic growth, although it slowed down in the late 1950s, was remarkable in the postwar years. The gross national product increased 56 percent between 1947 and 1960, while personal consumption in those years increased by over 60 percent. An increasingly educated public now had more money to spend on lei-sure and cultural activities.[9]

This emerging American culture received continuous support from many different sources. The Cold War was, in part, a battle waged on the cultural front, with the U.S. government sending abroad the best, and often most original, works of American art. To be sure, some, such as Rep. George Dondero (R-Mich.), equated modernist art with wanton radicalism. But modernist works of art, despite the repression and conformism of the Red Scare period, also came to represent the openness and creativity of American democratic society. The government, acting through its propaganda and espionage networks, also supported cultural critics and artists opposed to communism. Thus, with funding from the CIA, the Congress for Cultural Freedom, through its magazine *Encounter*, staunchly backed the modernist canon of art and literature as an antidote to narrow and propagandistic Soviet realist art and culture. In response to the challenges of the Cold War, especially in the aftermath of the Soviet Union's launching of the Sputnik satellite in 1957, the American government increased markedly its investment in universities. Although federal spending supported mostly the sciences, such largess spread itself around the entire university system.

Private industry contributed to the boom in the production of culture in America. Corporations became convinced that art collections not only represented a wise financial investment but also bestowed distinction upon their possessors. Public museums and community theaters thrived on public spending and corporate support. After years of tired prose and predictable presentations, the advertising industry transformed itself, adopting new styles that liberated the creative energies of the ad executive.

This flowering of creativity in the advertising agencies affected the society as a whole. The election of John F. Kennedy in 1960 aided this cultural renaissance. As opposed to the proudly lowbrow presidency of Dwight D. Eisenhower, the Kennedy administration created an atmosphere supportive of high art. Thanks in large part to the energy and sophistication of First Lady Jacqueline Kennedy, artists of national stature performed regularly at official government functions, lending an imprimatur to serious art in America.[10]

A cultural revolution, in essence, was afoot in America. By the early 1960s, traditional standards and styles of criticism, as well as the image of the critic, came under attack from individuals already associated with the establishment. Both novelist Norman Mailer and critic Norman Podhoretz undermined the dominant ideal that the intellectual and writer must be distanced from commerce and ambition. With audacity and sly cunning, Mailer's *Advertisements for Myself* (1959) featured his own commentaries on his earlier work. Mailer clearly cherished his literary success and measured himself publicly against other contemporary novelists. His self-professed goal was "to settle for nothing less than making a revolution in the consciousness of our time."[11] He intended to accomplish this end, in part, by marketing himself and his novels. After critics had panned his third novel, *The Deer Park* (1955), Mailer took out an advertisement in New York's alternative newspaper *The Village Voice* that reprinted negative reviews in an attempt to parody the dullness of his reviewers and to generate interest in his book. Podhoretz shared Mailer's ambition, and he made it public in his memoir, *Making It* (1967). There he chronicled his emergence as a literary critic who recognized that success depended on more than literary talent—it required ambition and shrewd marketing skills. To purists in the game of literature and criticism, this was apostasy.

In the 1960s, new forms of cultural apostasy pushed to the fore. In "happenings," artists, often by drawing the audience to participate in the work, performed in a manner that celebrated spontaneity and the ephemeral. A happening could not be reproduced or contained in a museum exhibit. In experimental film, the camera sometimes focused for hours on a single aspect of a person's physiognomy. In rock 'n' roll, the use of synthesizers and poetic expression made the genre more sophisticated and complex. New critics emerged to explain and often to celebrate the changes in these modes of artistic expression. At the same time, these new critics attempted to render judgments, to distinguish between the wheat and the chaff of the new art. The 1960s, then, did not entail the demise of criticism; rather, the decade ushered in a new group of critics and focused their attention on a new set of artistic problems. In addition, the arrival on the scene of pop art, as well as the success of avant-garde experimental films such as Jack Smith's *Flaming Creatures*, blurred the lines between elite and popular culture. At the same time, pop art questioned the very status and function of the trained eye of the critic in determining truth in representation, thus opening the door to a theoretical flowering.

Pop art transformed the commerce of art, culture, and criticism. Beginning in the mid-1950s, artists such as Claes Oldenberg, Robert Rauschenberg, Roy Lichtenstein, Tom Wesselman, and Andy Warhol began to incorporate commercial symbols and effects into their art. Such appropriations went well beyond the occasional inclusion of a ticket stub or trademark in modernist works of collage. Pop art made the world of commerce and its productions the subject of its art, as, for example, in Jasper Johns's painted bronze sculpture of Ballantine Beer cans. The question of whether pop artists were parodying or celebrating commerce remained opaque. However, pop art most certainly obliterated distinctions between commerce and culture, as Oldenberg produced kitsch items that he "exhibited" in a storefront modeled along the lines of a Lower East Side variety store. Lichtenstein's huge paintings presented comic book–type figures with bubbles of dialogue. Pop artists, most of whom came from a commercial art background and had worked in advertising, transformed the subject matter of culture and the very nature of the exhibition space. They also jettisoned the self-perception of the artist as an alienated and tortured individual apart from the mainstream of his or her culture.

Warhol, in particular, rebelled against what he considered the high seriousness—"the anguished, heavy intellects"—of the abstract expressionist artists and the New York intellectuals.[12] Instead, Warhol celebrated the tangential, mass-produced item. He undermined the very notion of originality by having his assistants produce his works at his studio space, appropriately called "The Factory." If the abstract expressionists avoided any taint of the commercial in their art, Warhol turned things on their heads. He announced, gleefully, "I started as a commercial artist, and I want to finish as a business artist. After I did the thing called 'art' or whatever it's called, I went into business art . . . . Being good in business is the most fascinating kind of art . . . . Business art. Art business. The Business Art Business."[13]

The challenge of pop art was immense and, in many ways, liberating for artists and for the public. Pop art often portrayed commodities, and it quickly became a commodity itself. The commercial symbols of an economy of excess drew the attention of pop artists much as the landscape had appealed to nineteenth-century painters such as Thomas Cole or Vincent Van Gogh. Pop artists encountered a new world for the selling and display of their art. In order to survive, galleries increasingly labored to create a public through the clever merchandising and exhibition of pop art.

Pop art arrived at a moment when art criticism was in a state of flux, having achieved an exalted but staid position. The critical method of Clement Greenberg cast an erudite shadow over the production and understanding of art. His formalist criticism promised to settle questions about the particular quality of a work of art through logic and attention to formal problems (value, modeling). Thus, in his typical authoritative manner, Greenberg wrote, "The message of modern art, abstract or not . . . is precisely that means are content."[14] Serious artists, in this view, did not paint representationally or with political programs in mind; they responded only to problems inherent in the medium of art. In practice, intuition and fiat defined much of Greenberg's criticism. While Greenberg's sense of certitude won him many disciples, it also proved incapable of dealing with the seismic shifts then occurring in the art world. Critics, as much as artists, wanted to escape from Greenberg's critical methods and standards. The overweening importance of abstract expressionism as the epitome of artistic development, as indicative of the high seriousness and newfound sophistication of American culture, was about to fall from grace.

Pop art largely triumphed without approval from the arts establishment. Established critics, especially those working in the Greenberg mode, fumed at pop art's affront to their standards and at its celebration of American consumer culture. With pop art, it seemed, commerce proudly exhibited its pretense and power. Especially in the work of Warhol, art appeared as a mechanical act of incessant reproducibility that resembled industrial production. Warhol realized that more was the essence of commercial culture. Thus, in his silk screens of Marilyn Monroe or of art collector Ethel Scull, based on photo-booth snapshots, the very multiplication of images resulted in a dizzy sense of singularity and commonality. Pop art's themes of reproducibility and consumerism challenged the ideal of the artist as creator-figure and questioned the very nature of the exalted objecthood of art. Art critic Peter Selz, writing in *Partisan Review*, found pop art to be empty, a mere reflection of the "banal and chauvinistic" in our culture. Pop, Selz announced, was "art of abject conformity, this extension of Madison Avenue" which had the temerity to parade itself as avant-garde.[15]

Thanks to Warhol, a revolution in the arts had occurred. High modernist art and criticism no longer controlled the field. Irony, clever self-reflexive references, appropriation, and replication all became part of the repertoire of artists and critics. And, as we will see, the Warhol-inspired emphasis on success and celebrity became a mainstay of cultural politics in the 1980s. Warhol, in effect, redefined and reinvigorated the avant-garde in art and theory.

The avant-garde flourished in experimental film and in foreign and mainstream motion pictures. Experimental film, as in the work of Warhol, Maya Deren, Stan Brakhage, Robert Frank, and Jack Smith, was often self-consciously avant-garde. Their films depended upon spontaneity and improvisation, stream of consciousness, disorienting of time and space, intense subjectivity, and outré subject matter. Smith's *Flaming Creatures* lacked a narrative line, but it celebrated homoeroticism and showed genitalia. In films such as Frank's *Pull My Daisy* (1958) the camera work may be crude, but the narration by Jack Kerouac is inspired, and the film's madcap, erratic narrative line attempts to capture the rhythms of Greenwich Village bohemians. But, by the 1960s, an avant-garde imperative was no longer limited to experimental, nonprofit films. Commercial films, both foreign and domestic, became more interesting, more experimental, part of the general explosion in American culture.

The lines between commercial and experimental film were sketchy and sometimes controversial. In 1957, critics lavished praise on John Cassavetes's experimental film *Shadows*, about jazz and interracial love. *Shadows* received the first Independent Film Award, because it managed to "break out of conventional molds and traps and retain original freshness."[16] By 1959, however, Cassavetes had edited his masterpiece, adding more narrative continuity to make it palatable for a wider audience. For some in the avant-garde community, Cassavetes had sold out to commercial culture. Others viewed the revised film as a turning point in American culture, the coming of age of commercial cinema and arrival of an audience willing to appreciate new forms of experimentalism.[17] No longer would a connection between the world of commerce and the world of avant-garde or serious art be considered either an anomaly or an impossibility.

Changes in modes of artistic presentation both constitute and respond to a crisis in epistemology, to what is presumed to be true and secure. Such tensions demand critics armed with new theories of interpretation. Critics cannot protect themselves with a resolute unwillingness to engage the challenges of new art forms—to do so would be to court irrelevancy. The traditional language and assumptions of criticism, employed most famously by the New York intellectuals, could not deal with the new transgressive art, which challenged ideals of high seriousness, political engagement, moral restraint, and transcendence.

A theoretical imperative defined the art criticism of Columbia University philosophy professor Arthur Danto. He began by posing about Warhol's art a particularly striking, ultimately philosophical question: What made Warhol's Brillo boxes art? After all, from a purely ocular perspective, Warhol's boxes were indistinguishable from mass-produced Brillo boxes found in any grocery store. Warhol's challenge to entrenched art ideals—that to see is to believe—was part of a more general epistemological crisis in the sciences, art, and politics in the 1960s. Danto's answer helped to usher in the reign of theory that has come to define much of post-1970s criticism. He argued that Warhol's boxes constituted themselves as art because they entered into an already established "terrain" of theories about art, into debate about problems internal to the practice of art. Significantly, the boxes, by dint of their being shown in established art galleries, gained the imprimatur of art. Thus, to understand avant-garde art, the critic and the viewer needed to grapple with the conceptualization behind an artwork and its place within an established discourse and its institutions.[18]

In many ways, Danto's ideas paralleled the conceptual revolution then building within the history of science, especially in Thomas Kuhn's pathbreaking book *The Structure of Scientific Revolutions* (1962). Kuhn presented science as functioning within a particular paradigm, or theoretical conception, that helped to constitute scientific practice. So, too, in cultural matters: theory made art possible. Without mastery of theory, one could not comprehend art. For Danto, Warhol's art existed within the discourse of art that it, in turn, had revolutionized. Moreover, Warhol's subject matter, the readily recognizable world of commercial, mass-produced items increased, rather than diminished, the power of his art. In Danto's impassioned prose, Warhol's art was "an effort to change people's attitudes toward their world. It might almost be said, paraphrasing Milton, that he sought to reconcile the ways of commerce to those who lived in the world it created. It just happened that in so doing, he made a philosophical breakthrough of almost unparalleled dimension in the history of reflection on the essence of art."[19]

The theory-laden nature of artistic practice elevated the critic into a theoretical guide for viewers through "the rules of the game" and the "discourse of reasons" of a given culture.[20] New critics such as Danto, Susan Sontag, and Andrew Sarris transformed theory itself into an art form while also validating particular artistic expressions and rebelling against earlier ideals of culture.

Both Sarris and Sontag raved about the new wave of French film by directors such as Francois Truffaut, Jean-Luc Godard, Alain Resnais, and Robert Bresson. But Sarris still celebrated American commercial film directors such as John Ford and Orson Welles, and Sontag appreciated American experimental filmmakers such as Jack Smith. All of the exciting waves broke, for them, against a new cultural shore. Above all, Sarris demanded that American scholars and audiences take film seriously. His reviews in *Film Culture* and the *Village Voice* introduced many to European cinema in the mid-1950s and, in the early 1960s, to the seriousness and artistic vision of American films. Borrowing the concept of the auteur from French film theorists, Sarris announced that directors, no less than novelists, impose themselves on their work through technical competence, a recurring personal style, and interior meaning: the director is the author of a film just as the writer is the author of a book. In this manner, commercial films produced in Hollywood became serious works of art demanding attention and respect.[21]

Sontag brought a cultivated and open vision to what was happening throughout American culture. At once cool and passionate in style, she explicated elite texts and authors as well as popular culture expressions in camp, science fiction, and pornography. Although she registered her ambivalent attraction to these genres, the very fact of her exegesis of them granted them a cachet of seriousness. In her collection of essays *Against Interpretation* (1965), Sontag reacted against what she viewed as the narrowness, both of method and sweep, in the critical practice of New York intellectuals. Many critics paid too much attention, she wrote, to content, psychological explanation, and character development. Such interpretive digging made it difficult for a reader to achieve an aesthetic, sensual relationship with texts. Sontag instead marveled at the sensuous surfaces of style; she appreciated the beauty of images and form, in and of themselves. Less emphasis on content as the criterion for appreciation would allow critics, such as Sontag, "to recover our senses . . . to see more, to hear more, to feel more."[22]

"More" became the keynote of Sontag's criticism and of her times. The 1960s, that period of artistic and commercial explosion, Sontag later remarked, saw even the "sluggish art" of fiction open up to the "sophistication" then predominant in film and art. A useful cross-pollination in the arts occurred. Far from compromising the purity of any particular art, this borrowing of style and sensibility enlivened the arts as a whole. But how to discern the truly experimental, to appreciate the complexities of the new European cinema or the rhythms of happenings then populating the Greenwich Village scene? Many of Sontag's writings in this period, like a cultural Baedeker, described an emerging cultural formation. As historians have suggested that the emergence of a consumer culture required advertisers to both sell and explain the etiquette of purchasing, so too did the 1960s bring forth, in Sontag, Sarris, and their peers, critics to guide consumers through the style, meaning, and significance of avant-garde cultural productions.

Sontag appraised films by her favorite directors, almost all European, largely French, in terms of their antinarrative style and their images and surfaces. The greatness of films such as Godard's *Breathless* (1959) or Resnais's *Hiroshima, Mon Amour* (1959) came through their formal aspects, the properties and possibilities of film as an independent medium. Moreover, these films demanded a sense of "postponement" of passion, of understanding that, in Sontag's cool criticism, made paradoxically for a deeper emotional bonding. Immediacy, in her view, became a mode of kitsch enjoyment, something purchased too easily. In a sense, following in the aesthetic tradition of Greenberg's formalism, Sontag offered an aesthetic appreciation of the development of film style. Form, "the desire to prove rather than the desire to analyze," is what constitutes "great art."

In her groundbreaking essay "Notes on 'Camp,'" Sontag opened up a new, critical "space of pleasure" that included pop art, mass-produced objects, artifice, and even bad taste. Extravagance rather than restraint, surface rather than depth, and pleasure over denial became keynotes of a camp sensibility—"The whole point of Camp is to dethrone the serious." [23] Camp style easily flowed from and was made possible, in part, from the rise of mass culture and production. While Sontag acknowledged a gay component to camp style, she refused to limit it to "homosexual taste." [24] Thus, camp addressed the larger problem of "how to be a dandy [an original] in the age of mass culture." By refusing to distinguish "between the unique object and the mass produced object," in the manner of pop art, "Camp taste transcends the nausea of the replica." [25] In the process, camp champions a culture based on enjoyment rather than judgment, on consumption, stylization, and the outrageous. [26]

Commerce and culture now entered into fruitful and fevered communication. Commercial images saturated art, no less than did commercial techniques. Commercial notions—marketing, the blockbuster, reproducibility without end—dominated the arts. At the Metropolitan Museum of Art, director Thomas Hoving engaging in endless wheeling and dealing to secure shows that would attract a mass audience. His marketing techniques brought large numbers of visitors to the museum. The improved museum store, with its glossy reproductions and replicas of art objects, helped augment museum budgets. A new generation of artists, devoted to massive environmental sculptures, thrived with foundation grants. In the go-go years of the 1980s, torrents of money flowed into the arts, with new galleries and collectors vying for the hottest new artists, such as David Salle and Julian Schnabel. Most important, within individual art forms, high and low mingled and genres blended without apparent ill effects. Pop music groups such as Talking Heads mixed pulsating rock style and avant-garde lyrics. The Kronos Quartet comfortably and profitably played avant-garde, traditional classical, and jazz styles. As always, the growth of culture and the confusion of styles demanded new modes of criticism and modes of comprehension.

Theory from the 1970s through the 1990s defined culture and criticism. A babel of theories—poststructuralism, postmodernism, deconstruction, new historicism, and cultural studies—tumbled out, one after another. Some academics welcomed the sweep of theory to pump life into tired debates. Critics became theorists in order to explain trends in art and literature. Despite the often competing and mutually exclusive theories then in circulation, theory brought forth a greater appreciation for the role of discourse in molding ideas and art; postmodernist theory of all sorts dismissed texts as fixed categories, challenged cherished ideals of authorial presence, and questioned established canons.

Theoretical movements sharply contested fixed categories of the text, cherished ideals of the authorial presence, the logic of the literary and aesthetic canon. Artists' works exemplified theoretical developments, questioning the originality of the work of art and accepting the mechanical nature of artistic production and replication. In an age when media-saturated images overwhelmed and broke down any sense of the "original" object, artists sought to exploit this reality. Feminist artist Barbara Kruger appended cartoon captions to pictures of women in order to undermine sexist expectations. Artist Sherrie Levine photographed classic photographs by Edward Weston and signed her "original reproductions" of these canonical works. Of course, one could not discern, except for the signature, the difference between the original and the reproduction. Her work challenged the aura of modernism, the canon of male art heroes, and the commerce-driven nature of art. While she certainly questioned the nature of originality, her own work obtained its own cachet as she became a stellar presence in commercial art galleries.

The industry of theory worked overtime in the 1970s. Before too long, a hyperinflationary currency of theoretical criticism entered into circulation.[27] Everything seemed to gain value, or everything seemed to have lost inherent value. Postmodernist criticism often celebrated the energy and even authenticity of popular, commercial culture. In *Learning from Las Vegas* (1972), a central text of postmodernism, architects Robert Venturi, Denise Scott Brown, and Steven Izenous announced that high modernist, elitist architects had much to learn from the vitality and symbolic kitsch of the Las Vegas Strip or supermarket parking lots. Art galleries and collectors suddenly found authenticity and power, a genuine voice of protest, in graffiti artists such as Jean-Michel Basquiat, young urban kids who covered subway cars and city walls with spray-painted slogans and images. What had begun as a movement far removed from the realm of commerce entered quickly into the inner sanctum of the major galleries and collections.

Defenders of the "theoretical turn" and of the new art forms felt liberated, now able to wage battle against elitism and conservatism. Within a decade or so, by the 1980s, feminism, African American studies, and gay studies shifted from attempting to find forgotten voices and challenging the narrowness of the canon of great works into something quite different. Thanks to the popularity, and marketability, of theory, these imperatives evolved into gender, race, and queer studies, armed with the theoretical premise that all texts, in one manner or another, were implicated in issues of power. Thus, in the work of Columbia University professor Edward Said, the novels of George Eliot became a complex and significant part of a discourse of colonial domination. In the gender-driven analyses of feminist literary critics, the status of modernism rested upon the repression of female authors.

Theory in the 1980s brought forth a new breed of critic, bathed in philosophical sophistication, daring in his or her theoretical turns, and possessed with marketing skills. Harking back to the pugnacity and self-promotion of Mailer and Podhoretz, new critics became figures of notoriety. Universities competed for their services. In the 1990s, the journal *Lingua Franca* charted the careers of these academic superstars, mixing appreciation for their theoretical sophistication with awe at their marketing ability. The critic became part of the celebrity-dominated culture of the 1990s. Literary theorist Stanley Fish—the model for Morris Zapp, a character in David Lodge's popular novels—was a ubiquitous presence at academic convocations around the globe. His works were pointedly controversial, excursions into the cultural wars that seemed only to heighten his own marketability.

Identity politics further sharpened the focus of the critic. Thus, in an attempt to establish her credentials, critic Tricia Rose announced that she had a "polyvocal" approach to the topic of rap music since she was "an African-American woman of biracial parentage with second-generation immigrant parents," who was also a "pro-black, biracial, ex-working-class, New York-based feminist, left cultural critic."[28] Gone, apparently, were the days when the cultural critic presented himself or herself in universal terms, presuming to speak for humanity at large. The new critic existed within specific circumstances. Armed with her inherited and chosen identities, Rose's discourse gained an air of legitimacy and authority no less powerful than that wielded decades earlier by the New York intellectuals.

Few critics loomed larger over the landscape of theory in the 1980s than Fredric Jameson, professor of comparative literature at Duke University. With dense theoretical exposition and polemical flair, Jameson excavated the new cultural formation of the postmodern, most famously in *Postmodernism: Or, The Cultural Logic of Late Capitalism* (1991). He characterized the post-modernist era, beginning largely after the Second World War, as a revolt against high modernist grand narratives and ideals of transcendence. Surface, fashion, nostalgia, historical amnesia, and especially pastiche constituted the essentials of postmodernism. Jameson contended that the postmodern moment was a product of what he termed "late capitalism," characterized by a well-defined and predominant consumer culture.[29] Indeed, postmodernism helped form the very structure of that culture through its emphasis on fashion and newness. Postmodern capitalism superseded the subversiveness of the avant-garde and then consumed "in stride" even the revolting aesthetics of punk rock. Photographer Robert Mapplethorpe's sadomasochistic and transgressive sexual images soon appeared on calendars and coffee mugs, marking something of a culmination of postmodernist themes of appropriation.

But Jameson overstepped himself in many ways. For instance, Mapplethorpe's images did shock many people, proof that the postmodernist triumph was incomplete. In 1990, when Dennis Barrie, curator of the Cincinnati Arts Center, exhibited such images, he was indicted on obscenity charges. A jury trial resulted in a verdict of not guilty, in large part, because the jurors, who were shocked and disgusted by the images, voted to acquit after art experts testified that the works were art and protected under the Constitution. Rather than being a victory for postmodernist relativism, the court case affirmed the continuing relevance of critics and of constitutional guarantees.

The logic of the postmodern system, however, seemed at once pervasive and controlling. Immensely expandable, the new culture of consumption supported inequalities of wealth, undermined a sense of tradition and place, co-opted the avant-garde, and undermined individual agency and responsibility through a media-saturated culture that obliterated historical continuity. Jameson's post-modern commerce of culture cast a dark specter on the American landscape. Resistance and agency, in the work of many postmodernists, appeared as a cul-de-sac, given the presumed ability of postmodern capitalism to transform protest, alienation, and transgression into products for commercial exploitation.

By the end of the century, many analysts bemoaned the reign of postmodernism and especially the connection between commerce and culture. Film critic Richard Schickel argued that business control of films, based upon marketability, commercial tie-ins and lowbrow box-office concoctions, destroyed creativity.[30] Similarly, publisher Andre Schiffrin lamented control of the publishing industry by a few conglomerates that sought to market only blockbuster, formula-driven bestsellers.[31] Artist Hans Haacke depicted the corrosive extent of corporate intrusion into the arts through installations. On a large cigarette pack, mimicking the Philip Morris brand, Haacke painted the face of Jesse Helms in the Morris corporate logo and renamed the brand "Helmsboro." This work condemned the Philip Morris Corporation for backing Jesse Helms, conservative leader of the movement against the National Endowment of the Arts, while also trying to present itself as a supporter of the arts. Ironically, perhaps, some of his interventions have appeared in leading museums and galleries. From a more conservative perspective, Edward Banfield decried the tendency of art museums to equate popularity of exhibits with excellence. In addition, National Endowment of the Arts support, in his view, allowed art to become ever more elitist and irrelevant. Sociologist Robert Nisbet condemned academic entrepreneurs as facile, "jet set" businessmen and contended that the intrusion of "the higher capitalism" into the university undermined standards and traditions without appreciable improvement in thought.[32]

Yet some cultural critics uncover positive aspects to the postmodern age of commerce. In a rather upbeat analysis, French critic Gilles Lipovetsky posited that the reign of fashion, connected with triumphant capitalism, promoted democracy and individualism. While many theorists found that the culture industry, through advertisements and popular media productions, inhibited freedom and expression, Lipovetsky claimed liberation to be possible through participation in the seductive culture of consumption.[33] Through purchases of material goods, the individual expressed individuality. The individual overcame mass-produced conformity by taking objects and employing them in original ways, such as by accessorizing an outfit. A consumer culture generated desires that could be met only in an expansive, democratically driven society.

Lipovetsky's general conclusions received a more concrete expression, within the American context, in the challenging work of economist Tyler Cowan. For Cowan, the postmodern era, despite the rise of cultural conglomerates with vast control over the production and dissemination of culture, had not led to a diminution in creativity or diversity. On the contrary, postmodernist capitalism had given rise to myriad niche cultures, such as markets for classical or ska music. Cowan exulted that technological and marketing innovations resulted in the publication of more books on more subjects than ever before. The Internet and eBay became major sources for a worldwide quickening of communication and commerce. While many analysts condemned chain bookstores such as Barnes & Noble for pushing out independent bookstores and exercising too much control over publishers, Cowan proclaimed that these chains actually stocked a wide array of books in an attractive setting. Moreover, in recent years, according to Cowan, consumption of books has risen; the number of bookstores in America has increased tenfold since the 1940s. In fact, the state of publishing, and the longevity of many midlist titles, might be on the verge of further enhancement with Web-based downloads and publishing on demand.[34]

As a marker of the sometimes blissful romance of culture and commerce, consider the career of Henry Louis Gates Jr., director of the W. E. B. DuBois Institute for Afro-American Studies at Harvard University. He has embraced both commerce and criticism, in the process fulfilling the vaunted ideal of the public intellectual. A cultural entrepreneur of immense energy, Gates has, in addition to the usual scholarly volumes, written and hosted a Public Broadcasting Series on Africa; coedited an interactive CD-ROM encyclopedia, *Encarta Africana*; published essays in the *New Yorker*; produced a memoir; and played a major role in promoting the pursuit of African American studies, both academic and popular.

Art and criticism thrive when there is movement and unfettered exchange. This allows for greater conversation and creativity. The arts flourish most when they are diverse in style and concerns. The explosion of the arts and criticism in the last half-century has been both a motive force and motored by the commerce of America. In a period of expansion, in spite of conglomeration, niches have opened up in which diverse cultural productions thrive. Of course, some would argue that the concept of a niche is problematic, for such niches may be places of retreat, small areas cordoned off from the mainstream of culture. But Cowan contends that niches represent an expanse of options, an ode to how commerce, aided by new forms of technology, is able to accommodate diversity in an age of corporate conglomeration. Entrepreneurs, in this view, produce whatever markets desire. Our culture, at present, is particularly diverse in terms of its art and criticism. The immensely popular artist Thomas Kincade's corporate-kitsch pastoral and nostalgic canvases, alive with light and predictability, coexist along with the more elitist schlock of Jeff Koons's pop-inspired sculptures. Each artist appeals to distinct coteries of consumers. In an age of kitsch and formulaic work, various galleries around the world represent Scottish environmental artist Andy Goldsworthy, despite the rather hermetic nature of his work, some of which he constructs of natural materials that will soon be reclaimed by the environment from which they were produced. In music, classical artists and garage bands find it feasible to produce and distribute their work to specific audiences. The Internet and computer technologies further the creation and distribution of art forms.

The commerce of culture and criticism refuses to bend to any singular perspective or demand. Our culture is all the better for that. Even if the days of the critic speaking with absolute cultural authority are gone, critics remain exalted for their ability to approach texts and artworks with theoretical sophistication and for their ability to explain the expansive niches in our culture, awash in challenging and esoteric works of art.

BIBLIOGRAPHIC NOTE

Harvey Teres's *Renewing the Left: Politics, Imagination, and the New York Intellectuals* (1996), is excellent, as is Neil Jumonville's *Critical Crossings: The New York Intellectuals in Postwar America* (1991). To gain a sense of the terrain of literary criticism in this period, begin with Vincent B. Leitch, *American Literary Criticism from the Thirties to the Eighties* (1988), and Grant Webster, *The Republic of Letters* (1979). For the argument that in the postwar years the intellectual has become a narrow academic, see Russell Jacoby, *The Last Intellectuals: American Intellectuals in the Age of Academe* (1987). Good for an overall view of cultural change in this period is Michael Kammen, *American Culture, American Tastes: Social Change and the 20th Century* (1999). For the antagonism of intellectuals to mass culture, see Paul Gorman, *Left Intellectuals and Popular Culture in Twentieth-Century America* (1996), and Andrew Ross, *No Respect: Intellectuals and Popular Culture* (1989). For a theoretical understanding on the division between elite and popular culture, see Andreas Huyssen, *After the Great Divide: Modernism, Mass Culture, Postmodernism* (1986). For a nuanced view of commercialism in American culture, see Gary Cross, *An All-Consuming Century: Why Commercialism Won in Modern America* (2000).

Indispensable for understanding the rise of theory in the 1970s is Elizabeth W. Bruss, *Beautiful Theories: The Spectacle of Discourse in Contemporary Criticism* (1982). On the introduction of postmodernism and other intellectual currents, see J. David Hoeveler Jr., *The Postmodernist Turn: American Thought and Culture in the 1970s* (1996).

On the growth of the American economy in this period, see Robert M. Collins, *More: The Politics of Economic Growth in Postwar America* (2000). Thomas Frank, *The Conquest of Cool: Business Culture, Counterculture, and the Rise of Hip Consumerism* (1997), is good on the creative aspects of advertising.

The best place to go for an overview of Sontag's criticism is Liam Kennedy, *Susan Sontag: Mind as Passion* (1995). Sohnya Sayres, *Susan Sontag: The Elegiac Modernist* (1990), is good on Sontag's style. On the transgressive in American art, see Anthony Julius, *Transgressions: The Offences of Art* (2002).

On Warhol, read Cecile Whiting, *A Taste for Pop: Pop Art, Gender and Consumer Culture* 1997), and Wayne Koestenbaum, *Andy Warhol* (2001). On pop, see Lucy R. Lippard, *Pop Art* (1966). Excellent for a survey of experimental film is P. Adams Sitney, *Visionary Film and the American Avant-Garde, 1943–1978* (1979). A good introduction to film criticism in American culture is Raymond J. Haberski Jr., *It's Only a Movie: Films and Critics in American Culture* (2001). On the art market, see Diana Crane, *The Transformation of the Avant-Garde: The New York Art World, 1940–1985* (1987). On the penetration of art by commercial interests, see Pierre Bourdieu and Hans Haacke, *Free Exchange* (1995).

The power of business over culture is effectively attacked in Neil Gabler, *Life, The Movie: How Entertainment Conquered Contemporary America* (1998); Herbert I. Schiller, *Culture Inc.: The Corporate Takeover of Public Expression* (1989); and Stuart Ewen, *All Consuming Images: The Politics of Style in Contemporary Culture* (1988). For a counterperspective, consult Gilles Lipovetsky, *The Empire of Fashion: Dressing Modern Democracy* (1994), and Tyler Cowan, *In Praise of Commercial Culture* (1998).

NOTES

1. Lizabeth Cohen, *A Consumer's Republic: The Politics of Mass Consumption in Postwar America* (New York: Knopf, 2003), 127. Cohen makes clear that the consumer republic was an ideal rather than a reality, especially for African Americans and women.

2. Marshall Berman, *All That Is Solid Melts Into Air: The Experience of Modernity* (New York: Simon & Schuster, 1982).

3. Daniel Bell, *The End of Ideology*, rev. ed. (New York: Free Press, 1965), 300.

4. Lionel Trilling, *The Liberal Imagination* (New York: Anchor Books, 1953), 8.

5. Dwight Macdonald, "A Theory of 'Popular Culture,'" *Politics* 1 (February 1944): 20–22.

6. Bernard Rosenberg, "Mass Culture in America," in *Mass Culture: The Popular Arts in America*, ed. Bernard Rosenberg and David Manning White (Glencoe, Ill.: Free Press, 1957), 9.

7. Michael J. Bennett, *When Dreams Came True: The GI Bill and the Making of Modern America* (Washington, D.C.: Brassey's, 1996), 201.

8. Alvin Toffler, *The Culture Consumers: A Controversial Study of Culture and Affluence in America* (New York: St. Martin's Press, 1964), 44.

9. Robert M. Collins, *More: The Politics of Economic Growth in Postwar America* (New York: Oxford University Press, 2000), 41, 53.

10. Alfred Frankfurter, "Editorial," *Art News* 62 (January 1964): 23, 46–48, 60–61.

11. Norman Mailer, *Advertisements for Myself* (Cambridge, Mass.: Harvard University Press, 1992), 17.

12. Andy Warhol and Pat Hackett, *Popism: The Warhol '60s* (New York: Harcourt Brace Jovanovich, 1980), 34.

13. Quoted in Caroline A. Jones, *Machine in the Studio: Constructing the Postwar American Artist* (Chicago: University of Chicago Press, 1996), 203.

14. Clement Greenberg, "Review of an Exhibition of Willem de Kooning," in *Clement Greenberg: The Collected Essays and Criticism*, ed. John O'Brian (Chicago: University of Chicago Press, 1986), 2:228.

15. Peter Selz, "Pop Goes the Artist," *Partisan Review* 20 (Summer 1963): 314, 315.

16. "The Independent Film Award," in *Film Culture Reader*, ed. P. Adams Sitney (New York: Cooper Square Press, 2000), 423.

17. Ray Carney, ed., *Cassavetes on Cassavetes* (London: Faber and Faber, 2001), 82–84; Carney, *Shadows* (London: BFI, 2001), 43. Cassavetes reedited the film according to the recommendations of a British distribution company.

18. Arthur Danto, "The Artworld," *Journal of Philosophy* 61 (15 October 1964): 571–584.

19. Arthur Danto, "The Philosopher as Andy Warhol," in *Philosophizing Art: Selected Essays* (Berkeley: University of California Press, 1999), 74.

20. This theoretical trend in the arts paralleled the more general movement of society toward experts armed with theoretical knowledge that Daniel Bell outlines in *The Coming of Post-Industrial Society* (New York: Basic Books, 1973).

21. Andrew Sarris, "Notes on the Auteur Theory in 1962," in Sitney, *Film Culture Reader*, 121–135; "Toward a Theory of Film History," in Sarris, *The American Cinema: Directors and Direction, 1929–1968* (New York: Dutton, 1968), 19–37.

22. Susan Sontag, *Against Interpretation* (New York: Farrar, Straus and Giroux, 1965), 14.

23. Ibid., 288.

24. Ibid., 290.

25. Ibid., 288.

26. Not all cultural critics approved of this turn toward pleasure and transgression. For an attack on the hedonism of the avant-garde, and increasingly the culture in general, see Daniel Bell, *The Cultural Contradictions of Capitalism* (New York: Basic Books, 1976).

27. Charles Newman, "The Post-Modern Aura: The Act of Fiction in the Age of Inflation," *Salmagundi* 63–64 (Spring–Summer 1984): 190–191.

28. Tricia Rose, *Black Noise: Rap Music and Black Culture in Contemporary America* (Hanover, N.H.: Wesleyan University Press, 1994), xiii.

29. Frederic Jameson, "Postmodernism and Consumer Society" in *The Cultural Turn: Selected Writings on the Postmodern, 1983–1998* (New York: Verso, 1998), 1–20. See also Jameson, *Postmodernism: Or, The Cultural Logic of Late Capitalism* (Durham, N.C.: Duke University Press, 1991).

30. Richard Schickel, "Embracing the Krypton Mensch," *Los Angeles Times Book Review*, 9 March 2003, 2.

31. André Schiffrin, *The Business of Books: How International Conglomerates Took Over Publishing and Changed the Way We Read* (New York: Verso, 2000). However, as Cowan would no doubt point out, Schiffrin, taking advantage of a niche in publishing, formed his own independent publishing house.

32. Edward C. Banfield, *The Democratic Muse: Visual Arts and the Public Interest* (New York: Basic Books, 1984); Robert Nisbet, *The Degradation of the Academic Dogma: The University in America, 1945–1970* (New York: Basic Books, 1971), 82–83, 86.

33. Gilles Lipovetsky, *The Empire of Fashion: Dressing Modern Democracy*, trans. Catherine Porter (Princeton, N.J.: Princeton University Press, 1994).

34. Tyler Cowan, *In Praise of Commercial Culture* (Cambridge, Mass.: Harvard University Press, 1998), 54–55.

PART II

Politics

10. DOMESTIC CONTAINMENT

The Downfall of Postwar Idealism and Left Dissent, 1945–1950

RICHARD LINGEMAN

In the aftermath of the First World War, a widespread mood of supercharged martial patriotism quickly gave way to disillusionment. In 1919, a brushfire of unrest crackled across America—vicious race riots, mob violence, strikes and strikebreaking, mass roundups of radicals and aliens, union busting. Some overenthusiastic veterans belonging to the newly organized American Legion acted as enforcers of "100% Americanism," beating up Socialists and Wobblies and bullying immigrant fruit pickers into working for low wages. Bombs set off in Washington, D.C., by persons unknown, triggered the Palmer Raids, which resulted in the illegal detention and deportation of hundreds of alien radicals, anarchists, and socialists and ushered in the great Red Scare. The returning veterans faced labor unrest, unemployment, and galloping inflation. War novelists of their generation spiked their prose with irony and bitterness, portraying the war as a great patriotic lie. Iconoclasm came into vogue as an antidote to the enforced patriotism of the war years. A college generation of liberated flappers and sad young men kicked up their heels in heedless hedonism, rebelling mainly against Prohibition and the post-Victorian sex code. After a shuddering start, the postwar economy went into overdrive, ultimately overheating.

Compared to 1919, the post–World War II year 1946 seems a time of reunion and hope. Perhaps it was because there had been a greater sense of inevitability about the global conflict just ended. The attack on Pearl Harbor united the

country against a common foe, and no oratory and brass bands were needed—
or wanted. As playwright and FDR speechwriter Robert Sherwood summed up
in *Roosevelt and Hopkins*, World War II was "the first war in American history
in which the general disillusionment preceded the firing of the first shot."

And so, four years later, twelve million men and women came home to hon-
ors, victory parades, and the embraces of loved ones. They had faced war's horrors stoically without a gloss of heroism and glory. Destroying the enemy was
their task, and they had performed it well. Now, the job done, the generation
that had known hard times in the 1930s and austerity in wartime looked forward
to a cornucopia of peacetime abundance.

To be sure, a wave of layoffs from war industries in the throes of reconver-
sion to peacetime production clouded the economic skies, but there was a huge
pent-up demand for civilian goods among consumers holding some $140 bil-
lion in war bonds and savings. The general mood of the country was lingering
grief for the fallen, relief that the war was over, and worrying uncertainty about
the future. (Gallup polls showed over half the respondents variously predicting
a recession well within ten years.) A conservative mood prevailed. The 1946
election swept in a Republican Congress, and the voices of the far right, quiet
during the war, were heard again in the land—with a vengeance.

Labor erupted in paroxysms of strikes, centered on retaining jobs and the
high wages of wartime and catching up with the 45 percent upsurge in the cost
of living. Although probusiness groups and newspapers smeared them as "communistic," these strikes were not crushed like those after the First World War.
The difference was that the New Deal had guaranteed labor's right to organize
and unions had thrived in wartime, their ranks growing from 8.9 million in
1940 to 14.8 million in 1945.

During the war, vicious race riots had tarnished the democratic ideals America proclaimed it was fighting for. Many African American veterans returned to
civilian life vowing to rid their country of the white-superiority doctrines so similar to the master-race theories of Nazi Germany and Imperial Japan. They were
emboldened to step out on the long political march toward equality. This growing campaign would provoke a violent counterreaction in the segregated South.
But the social impact of the great black migration of the 1940s to production centers in the North, coupled with what at the time was a revolutionary demand by
African Americans for equality in hiring for war jobs, a rising postwar militancy
among ex-GIs, and best-selling books on race such as Lillian Smith's *Strange
Fruit*, Sinclair Lewis's *Kingsblood Royal*, and Gunnar Myrdal's *The American
Dilemma*. All sparked an unprecedented, escalating challenge to long-standing
laws and customs predicated on myths of black inferiority.

In 1946, facing a stone wall of segregation in the South, the pacifist Congress
on Racial Equality (CORE) launched sit-ins at Washington restaurants and

"Freedom Rides" testing the enforcement of a Supreme Court decision that overturned state laws segregating interstate travel. Black students and charismatic religious leaders such as Martin Luther King Jr. and their congregations would energize the movement in the late 1950s. But a violent white backlash grew, and the nascent African American protest movement, like the union-organizing drives of the 1930s, lacked crucial protection and support from the federal government, the courts, and Congress.

The political left celebrated the successful outcome of a war against fascism, a "People's War" involving ordinary Americans of all classes, races and creeds. The unity of the Popular Front period in the 1930s, when liberals, labor, and the Communist Party (CPUSA) cooperated to demand expansion of the New Deal, was crumbling. The Communists, who had dutifully supported the Hitler-Stalin pact in 1939, just as obediently swung behind the U.S. war effort after Germany invaded the Soviet Union. In 1945, seeking broader acceptance among Americans, the CPUSA was reborn as the Communist Political Association, guided by General Secretary Earl Browder's "Teheran Doctrine," which called for peaceful coexistence with capitalism. Neither the doctrine nor Browder would outlast the war. The publication of the so-called Duclos letter, allegedly written by a well-connected French Communist in April 1945, signaled Moscow's unhappiness with the coexistence line, and Browder was promptly expelled from the leadership and replaced by the more militant William Z. Foster.

Those identified with the noncommunist liberal left could feel confident that they were still important, if rusty, voices for social justice and economic equity in the Democratic Party. During the war, social reforms had been relegated to the back burner, "Dr. New Deal" being replaced, President Roosevelt said, by "Dr. Win the War." Now there was a pent-up demand for housing, health care, and other public goods that liberals fervently believed it was government's duty to provide.

Most returning vets faced those needs. Many, though, were apolitical, and narrowly focused on their personal readjustment to civilian life—resuming their old jobs if they were still there or finding new ones, readjusting to the homes from which they had long been absent. Pressed by the necessity of supporting wives and the "good-bye" babies conceived before going off to war, they were in a big hurry to make a living. (The so-called baby boom was produced by a rise in the marriage rate during the war—compared with the Depression years—combined with the lowering of the average age of married couples. Among this more fecund group, the birthrate climbed from 19.4 to 25.5 per thousand between 1940 and 1945. The boom continued during the postwar years as young couples, optimistic about the future and family-oriented, all started having more children than had their counterparts during the 1930s.)

Many veterans went off to college or vocational school, living on the GI Bill and determined to improve their lot with careers that were better paid and of higher status than what they anticipated in the Depression years. Their primary focus was on achieving personal satisfactions centered on career, family, job, and home. Government loans helped men become their own bosses, as they had vowed to do while complaining about military bureaucracies, but others sought security in large corporations as hierarchical as the military. These joined the civilian army of stereotypical "organization men," marching daily to their jobs in their gray flannel uniforms.

Another, smaller cadre of veterans, however, was imbued with a vague sense of an obligation to work for a better world. As Harold Russell, a veterans affairs official who lost two hands in the war, put it, "The guys who came out of World War Two were idealistic. They sincerely believed that this time they were coming home to build a new world. Many, many times you'd hear guys say, 'The one thing I want to do when I get out is to make sure that this thing will never happen again.' We felt the day had come when the wars were all over, we were going to break down the bonds that separate people." Russell himself became well known when producer Samuel Goldwyn hired him to play an amputee in *The Best Years of Our Lives*, the Academy Award–winning 1946 movie about returning service members.

Some of those ex-soldiers became active in peace groups. Others had an itch to shake up the political establishments in their hometowns and states. In one Tennessee town, armed veterans engaged in civic-minded vigilantism, ousting a graft-encrusted political machine that miscounted the ballots. Others entered local and national politics, among them John F. Kennedy, Joseph McCarthy, Lyndon Johnson, and Richard M. Nixon, known on Capitol Hill as "the class of '46." They campaigned in uniform and otherwise visibly advertised their wartime service as a prime qualification for office. Sympathetic voters agreed, granting them license to demand a better America in recompense for their sacrifices in war. Other idealistic vets sought to shake up the status quo by founding alternatives to old-line organizations they considered stuck in it.

Yearnings for world peace were particularly potent at the dawn of the postwar era. The euphoria of VJ (Victory Over Japan) Day was compounded partly of relief that the atomic bombings of Hiroshima and Nagasaki had brought about a quick Japanese surrender and rendered unnecessary the widely dreaded invasion of the Japanese homeland, which was predicted to produce as many as half a million American casualties, a figure now considered inflated. But relief gave way to anxiety at the prospect of atomic bombs being used against the United States in the next war. Thoughtful Americans predicted that the next war would be fought with atom bombs and could mean the end of civilization.

Thus in 1945–47 came a burst of idealistic campaigns for banning war and bringing the atom under international control. The groups involved included students, veterans, scientists, intellectuals, and various civic and advocacy groups. For a brief moment, a minority of men and women felt a strong and righteous commitment to ending war as an instrument of national policy by attacking its root causes—political, social, and economic. The driving dream for many was the idea of strengthening the United Nations so that it became a true world government with an international police force that would be used to enforce international law and punish aggressor nations.

At war's end, the Pentagon seemed to be throwing its support behind unilateral disarmament, judging by the speed with which it dismantled the armed forces. Actually, this massive pullout from Europe and the Far East was a response to political pressure to "bring the boys home." The rush to demobilize shrank the U.S. military, which had peaked at thirteen million during the war, to just over a million men and women. In the face of the widespread perception of a growing Soviet threat, most people, relying on the atom bomb to protect them (though as late as 1947 the United States had barely a dozen in its arsenal), supported reduced defense spending until the outbreak of the Korean War in 1950 again caught the U.S. military unready.

On the home front, the female workers who had answered their country's call during an acute wartime labor shortage were rudely forced out of their jobs (as were blacks and other minorities who had broken entrenched color lines). Now their government told them that their patriotic duty was to give up their places to returning GIs. Many of these women were reluctant to stop working, especially those over forty; they liked making good money performing meaningful tasks. A new feminist consciousness was starting to jell, but it lacked leadership and organization. For the time being, the women who had achieved parity with men in job performance, if not paychecks (which averaged one-third less than men's during the war), especially those with returning soldier husbands, retreated into domesticity.

Meanwhile, the former wartime ally was now forcibly installing pro-Soviet regimes in its East European neighbors. Tensions between East and West were rubbed raw at such contact points as Greece (where an indigenous Communist-backed insurgency was defeating the British-propped reactionary monarchy) and Iran (where Soviet probes across the border threatened Western oil companies' concessions). In March 1947 these developments prompted the president to announce the so-called Truman Doctrine, which committed the United States to sending $400 million in economic and military aid to Greece and Turkey, and, in the future, to helping any other Western-allied nation that faced an imminent Soviet-backed threat from without or within.

Economic aid was considered part of the anticommunist arsenal. The U.S. government regarded the resurgent Communist left in war-prostrated Europe as a Trojan horse of Soviet expansionism. To fight it, Washington cobbled together an economic aid package, known as the Marshall Plan, to help reconstruct the war-ravaged democracies of the West. (The offer was open to Eastern Europe as well, but Moscow refused to allow its satellites to participate.) The measure was a model of enlightened foreign policy, as well as a precedent for using economic aid to buttress American influence.

Even before the end of World War II, American elites had begun distrusting their brave Soviet ally. As the big chill between the superpowers set in, the Truman administration adopted a more confrontational stance in various diplomatic venues. These concrete moves, backed up by government and media warnings of a Soviet menace, ushered in a new domestic Red Scare. Unlike the Red Scare of the World War I era, this one came in on cat feet, under cover of law, justified by a proclaimed foreign threat. It was unmarred by mass roundups (although the Internal Security Act of 1950 would authorize "custodial detention" of "subversives" listed by the FBI) or official violence (although there were scattered incidents of vigilante attacks on Communists and radicals). A fog of fear rolled in, obscuring the familiar constitutional and political landmarks, and democracy lost its way.

POSTWAR ANTICOMMUNISM

The domestic containment of the left in the postwar years had its origins even before the advent of Senator Joseph McCarthy, whose name became synonymous with red-baiting. As historian Ellen Schrecker argues, McCarthyism was the recrudescence of a longstanding ideology of anticommunism. A hard core of ultraconservatives, professional red-baiters, and irredentist anti–New Dealers had kept the flame of anticommunism alive during the New Deal years. After the war, with the liberal–Democratic Party coalition falling apart, it flared up into greater prominence than ever before.

It is important to note that the postwar anticommunist mix included voices on the far left as well as on the far right. There were the veteran apostates, the Trotskyists, who had broken with the Communist Party over the issue of Stalin's crimes, and ideological foes such as the Socialist Party, which under Eugene V. Debs had split from the Communist movement in the 1920s and, after Debs's death, continued to oppose it under Norman Thomas's leadership. There were also various splinter groups—radical pacifists and anarchists who believed in socialism but hated the form it had taken in Soviet Russia.

Then there were the relative latecomers, like the American Civil Liberties Union, in which a bitter schism developed over the issue of tolerating

Communists in its ranks. A majority faction considered party members to be by definition pro-Soviet and thus anti–civil liberties, but a vocal minority said that expelling the radicals was contrary to the deepest traditions of the organization, which had been founded, after all, in 1919 when government agents were trampling on civil liberties. When the dust settled, the ACLU adopted a "Commu-Nazi clause" barring Communists and Fascists from its board; it also refused to file a brief in the *Dennis* case, the controversial 1948 prosecution of Communist Party leaders under the Smith Act, an action many ACLU members believed trampled on free speech issues.

The premier political voice for African Americans, the National Association for the Advancement of Colored People (NAACP), remained aloof from the Communist Party's parallel fight for black people's equal rights in the 1930s. To win the Truman administration's support for its domestic agenda, the NAACP emphasized its anticommunist views and shut down its support for black liberation movements in Africa. This cost the group the backing of radicals on the left, including its cofounder, the activist editor of *Crisis*, W. E. B. Du Bois, who resigned in 1948 because of political differences with the leadership.

Another group, Americans for Democratic Action (ADA), was started in 1947, to oppose what it saw as the procommunist liberal left, particularly the Progressive Citizens of America (PCA), which would back Henry Wallace for the presidency in 1948. The ADA attracted liberal intellectuals who wanted to purge the left of all Communist Party influences. Its militant opposition to the PCA delivered the coup de grace to the prewar Popular Front movement, a loose coalition of Communists, labor unions, and progressive youth groups.

During the heyday of anticommunism, between 1945 and 1955, mainstream America experienced something of a quasi-evangelical national revival meeting led by the most vocal anticommunist politicians and professional red-hunters and dedicated to cleansing the nation of political heretics, that is, of Communists and their sympathizers. To administer this political lustration bureaucratic machinery was put in place: federal loyalty review boards; congressional, state, and municipal "Americanism" committees; private employer loyalty boards; law enforcement investigators, from the Justice Department, FBI, State Department, and U.S. military intelligence agencies down through state and local police "Red Squads"; and private vigilante groups that were in the business of exposing Communists and Communist sympathizers and "clearing" them—for a price. The tools of the official agencies included subpoenas, loyalty, and noncommunist oaths; blacklists of alleged subversive individuals and groups, both official (the attorney general's list) and unofficial (compilations for private employers such as *Red Channels*, the directory of supposed Communists that became a de facto blacklist); foreign-agent registration laws; "clearance" requirements for government workers and those in industries with government defense contracts; firings of "security risks"; and organizational bylaws banning Communists from membership.

A purification ritual came into vogue by which persons accused of Communist affiliations could clear their names, purge their guilt, and prove their loyalty. They appeared before an appropriate congressional body such as the House Un-American Activities Committee (HUAC) and submitted to a "degradation ceremony," to borrow Victor Navasky's phrase, which included confession, repentance, and the ultimate test of sincerity: naming names of communistic or left-wing friends or associates.

Aside from ruining the lives of thousands of individuals solely because political views held in an earlier decade had now become unpopular, the main effect of the anticommunist crusade, which caught liberals and progressives in its net, was to constrict the democratic dialogue by hampering the development of a robust, critical, social democratic left in America. This left might have been a natural successor to the aforementioned Popular Front of the 1930s and 1940s. One can only guess, but probably its objectives would have included expansion of the New Deal welfare state, more negotiation and less confrontation with the Soviet Union, and collective security through a strengthened UN.

Contributing to the left's demise were its own fractiousness, tactical mistakes, and political isolation caused by a political paradigm shift to the right driven by anti-Soviet propaganda, media hysteria, justifiable suspicion of the totalitarian Soviet Union, and Americans' long-standing dislike of communism in whatever guise. Postwar espionage cases, such as the Alger Hiss–Whittaker Chambers confrontation in 1948, which led to Hiss's being convicted of perjury for lying about his membership in a Soviet spy ring, and the 1951 conviction of Ethel and Julius Rosenberg as leaders of a ring of Soviet spies who filched America's nuclear plans, convinced many Americans that all Communists and "fellow travelers"—an elastic term that was expanded to include radicals of all stripes—were traitors working for the USSR. (Both Rosenbergs were executed, though later investigations have demonstrated that Ethel was innocent.)

The domestic cold war triggered a national anxiety attack; the nation sheltered behind the circled wagons of anticommunism against an ominously aggressive Soviet Union abroad and a fifth column of Communist spies, saboteurs, and traitors at home. The U.S. response to the former was the doctrine of containment, articulated by the diplomat George Kennan in 1946 and readily adopted by the Truman administration, which called for drawing the line against Soviet expansionism. Although Kennan later said he meant diplomatic rather than military containment, his famous 1946 "long telegram," analyzing a recent bellicose speech by Stalin, galvanized Washington's military, diplomatic, and policy elites, and the doctrine soon dominated U.S. foreign policy. At home, the government responded with a kind of domestic containment, in feminist historian Ellen Tyler May's phrase, a law enforcement effort aimed at stamping out communism and radicalism, which were proclaimed breeding grounds for spies, traitors, and immorality.

The left's response to containment, both domestic and foreign, was spirited but disorganized and ineffectual. It was from the right that the strongest challenge emerged, but the thrust was that it was not anticommunist enough. This ultraconservative doctrine can be called *rollback*, to borrow historian Bruce Cumings's formulation. Its proponents demanded that the United States not merely confine the Soviet Union to hegemony over Eastern Europe but also push it completely out—by launching World War III, if necessary.

Business historian James Burnham, the author of *The Managerial Revolution* (1941), provided the intellectual underpinnings of rollback. In *The Struggle for the World* (1947), Burnham, an ex-Trotskyist and cofounder, with William F. Buckley Jr., of the conservative organ *National Review*, propounded a nationalistic imperialism to challenge the Soviet Union in place of the prewar isolationism on the right. He did not argue for a "preventive war," as did conservative military men such as Air Force General Curtis LeMay and their ultraright civilian supporters, but for liberation of the Soviet bloc nations and of the Soviet people. Burnham, who is credited with coining the term "cold war," preached that the United States must stay committed to continually contesting the spread of communism and must not withdraw into a Fortress America. His second book, *The Coming Defeat of Communism* (1950), was enormously influential among anticommunist liberals such as the historians Samuel Eliot Morison and Arthur Schlesinger Jr.

Only a few left-liberal intellectuals challenged rollback. One of them, Princeton professor Harry Elmer Barnes, dubbed Burnham's doctrine "perpetual war for perpetual peace."

LABOR AND THE RIGHTWARD DRIFT

A new generation of left-identified "revisionist" historians, such as Schrecker, May, historian David Caute, and journalist Godfrey Hodgson, argue that during the Cold War much of the American intelligentsia abdicated its traditional oppositional role and embraced the official ideology of anticommunism with all its authoritarian trappings. The so-called Cold War liberals called for continuation of New Deal reforms but made them subordinate to their main project of purging Communists. In retrospect, the Cold War liberals seem to have expended more energy fighting the radical left than opposing the radical right. As Hodgson put it, it was the victory of the liberals over the left.

Under the pressures of the times, the left split into two main tendencies: the Cold War liberals, centered in Americans for Democratic Action, who worked within the Democratic Party; and the old left, clustered around the PCA, CPUSA, and diehard remnants of the Popular Front of the 1930s. The Cold War liberals moved to occupy the "vital center," in Schlesinger's phrase, and joined the Washington consensus on national security issues.

Labor was a significant force in the rightward shift during the postwar years. All the major unions abandoned the radicalism that had powered the great organizing drives of the 1930s. In no other sector of society—save perhaps among African Americans —had the Communist Party's efforts been so timely and effective. After the war, its historical ties to workers and blacks would be decisively severed.

The United Auto Workers (UAW) provides a case study. During the forty-four-day sit-down strike of 1936–37, the Communists had been the new union's strong left arm. But in 1946, Walter Reuther, himself a former socialist who was now a Cold War liberal, led a center–right coalition that seized power from the Communist faction that was running the union. Reuther steered the UAW on a course of vigorous anticommunism. This story was repeated in other industrial unions. Union leaders put their faith in what Godfrey Hodgson calls the "economy of abundance"—an ever-expanding economic pie, which business and labor would share, though not equally.

Most workers at the time were strongly anticommunist, and those who wavered were pressured by their leaders and by anticommunist groups like the Association of Catholic Trade Unionists (ACTU), which would rush in priests to campaign against incumbent leftists in bargaining elections. The FBI and congressional committees also helped purge the radical unions, interrogating and otherwise harassing their leaders and marginalizing them as "reds."

Much of the unions' energy was expended on internecine battles between communists and anticommunists rather than on organizing drives. Some labor historians argue that the unions were so preoccupied with anticommunism and winning economic benefits at the bargaining table that they devoted inadequate time and money to organizing the unorganized and fighting for a progressive agenda. Rather than work for universal health insurance, unions sought at the bargaining table private health insurance for their members (a fringe benefit that emerged during the war as an alternative to wage increases, which were kept in check). As more prosperous members increasingly identified with middle-class values, they grew more conservative. By the 1960s Big Labor fought the anti–Vietnam War protests mounted by the left.

Wage security was the key demand of the unions that went out in the massive strike wave of 1946. These strikes had a political backlash, however, that ultimately set back labor's cause and contributed to its rightward shift. Exploiting the resentment among the public triggered by the strikes and lingering wartime shortages with the slogan, "Had enough?" the Republicans won control of both houses of Congress in 1946.

Contributing to the GOP sweep were the efforts of propaganda groups financed by big business, which charged that the unions were Moscow pawns. In 1946, the U.S. Chamber of Commerce issued a pamphlet alleging widespread Communist infiltration of the union movement. The American Legion's Americanism Committee loosed antilabor broadsides in various publications, as did the archreactionary National Association of Manufacturers.

The business leaders' real aim was to undo the Wagner Act, which had given the union movement a decisive boost in the 1930s. But they also feared Communist sabotage in the workplace and, in the wake of Labour Party gains in postwar Britain and Canada, the spread of socialist ideas. The business drive bore fruit in the passage in 1947 of the Taft-Hartley Act, over President Truman's veto. The law shrank some of labor's rights under the Wagner Act. Most pernicious was a provision that required union officers to sign a pledge that they did not belong to the Communist Party or any organization that taught the overthrow of the government by violent or unconstitutional means.

Leaders of the leftist unions resisted this requirement, but union bosses allied with the Cold War liberals used it as a tool for purging them. And so the big unions eagerly fell in step with the anticommunist crusade. Emblematic was AFL president George Meany's dispatching of the prominent ex-Communist Jay Lovestone to Europe to help fight Communist-led trade unions.

THE POLITICS OF ANTICOMMUNISM

The Truman White House also joined the anticommunist purge. In response to GOP charges that the administration was "soft on Communism" and riddled with Reds, Truman, who had earlier called such charges a "red herring," instituted a federal loyalty review board in 1947. It vetted government employees and weeded out "disloyal" ones—those whom FBI investigators identified as having Communist sympathies on the evidence of their opinions or affiliations or even those of a friend or wife or second cousin. This evidence was generally hearsay, provided by anonymous informants, whom the accused could not cross-examine.

Like many such concessions, this one failed in its goal of defusing the GOP's heresy hunt, which was less high-minded patriotism than an attempt to discredit the Democratic Party and New Deal legislation. Representative Martin Dies (R-Tex.) and his HUAC spearheaded this effort with a noisy public investigation, grilling government employees who were allegedly dangerous radicals.

Then, in 1950, Senator Joseph McCarthy (R-Wis.) stepped up to a microphone at a rally in Wheeling, West Virginia, holding in his hand what he claimed was a list of 205 Communists in the State Department. The number was later revised downward, and he never revealed the names, if he had them in the first place.

Meanwhile, in a further effort to defang critical Republicans, Truman had fired most of the New Dealers in his cabinet four months after he took office, replacing them with more conservative figures or old cronies. The only two remaining members of the FDR cabinet were curmudgeonly Harold Ickes, the secretary of the interior, and the idealistic Henry Wallace, the former vice president who had become secretary of commerce. Wallace resigned under pressure in 1946 after delivering a speech critical of the administration's hard-line policies toward the Soviet Union, and ran for president in 1948 on the Progressive Party ticket.

Truman was enough of a New Deal politician to stay committed to the welfare state. He was sensitive to the concerns of his liberal base, particularly unions and African Americans. In return, however, he asked for support of his anticommunist policies at home and abroad. Those who opposed the Truman Doctrine turned to Wallace in 1948.

Joining forces under the Wallace banner to challenge Truman's foreign policies were the PCA and CPUSA, who contributed their members' energy and organizational talents. But Wallace, who had begun his criticisms after Winston Churchill delivered his redounding "Iron Curtain" speech in Fulton, Missouri, was hurt by his Communist support. He is supposed to have later said that if the Communists had run their own candidate, it would have cost him 200,000 votes—but gained him three million more among the general populace. His opponents highlighted the CPUSA's support of Wallace and branded his coexistence policy tantamount to treason. His principled stand against segregation stirred up heckling and violence at his racially integrated rallies in the South. Wallace was also personally attacked as a moonbeam chaser who dabbled in the occult and mysticism. The other planks of his platform—expansion of New Deal welfare programs, national health insurance, repeal of the Taft-Hartley Act, and equal rights for Negroes—were co-opted by Truman, helping him to win a come-from-behind victory, with the help of Big Labor's vote-getting muscle.

Labor dealt Wallace's cause a crippling blow by throwing its support behind Truman. Only a few of the far-leftist unions in the CIO, notably the huge United Electrical Workers (UE), worked for Wallace. The UE's leaders would reap the whirlwind for their defection.

Wallace and the armies of the left started out with high hopes of garnering eight million votes; four million would have made the run a successful one, party strategists figured. In the event, Wallace drew only 1.5 million, which was fewer than the number received by Dixiecrat candidate Strom Thurmond, representing segregationist Southern Democrats who had temporarily seceded from the party because of Truman's civil rights stance. The only other credible leftist party, the small-"d" democratic Socialists under the perennial Norman Thomas, who blasted Wallace as a pawn of the CPUSA, reaped a disappointing 140,000 votes.

The 1948 campaign fractured the liberal left into three pieces: ADA types who opted for Truman; socialists and pacifists who chose Thomas; and the PCA and CPUSA, which rallied behind Wallace. The election was the left's last real challenge to the anticommunist consensus. Its failure to attract wider popular support meant, in effect, the ratification of Truman's Cold War policies by default. After that, left dissent was fragmented into scattered guerrilla bands of unreconstructed Wallacites, Communists, and assorted Old Leftists; progressive unionists and traditional liberals in noncommunist publications such as *The Nation* and the *National Guardian*; and pacifists and world government advocates, who in disgust with the mainstream parties sought to form a "Third Camp."

When the Cold War turned hot in Korea in 1950, most Americans (including most of the noncommunist left) supported U.S. intervention under the umbrella of the United Nations, regarding the war as a "police action" meant to punish North Korea for its invasion of the South. The cohort of young men and women whom *Time* had dubbed the "silent generation" marched off to the Korean War with some private trepidation but little public dissent, emulating their World War II big brothers. After two years of mounting causalities and stalemate, Americans signaled to their leaders that they had had enough.

Republicans, save for isolationists like Senator Robert Taft, generally supported the war, though they echoed the criticisms by General Douglas MacArthur, the former Far East commander whom Truman fired for insubordination, that it was not being fought with the objective of victory. Their 1948 presidential designate, Thomas Dewey, had carried out a campaign so vapid and smug that it was hard to tell what he stood for. He was a member in good standing of the internationalist, liberal, Eastern wing of the party. After his defeat, the Republican far right seized the opportunity to try to seize control of the party. Their candidate, Robert Taft, lost the nomination in 1952 to Gen. Dwight D. Eisenhower, the World War II hero who promised to "go to Korea" and who seemed to a majority of war-weary voters the candidate best qualified to end the conflict.

Party conservatives bided their time, strengthened their organizational ties and launched the Barry Goldwater rebellion of '64, which resulted in the ouster of the Easterners from power and a shift in the party's coordinates to the Sunbelt—the booming South and Southwest. Segregationist Southern Democrats who had defected to the Dixiecrats in 1948 had further cause for anger in Lyndon Johnson's Civil Rights Act of 1964. They moved en masse to the GOP, drawn by Richard Nixon's pandering "southern strategy."

THREE CASE STUDIES

For a closer study of the impact of the anticommunist crusade on left dissent, we will now focus on three case histories— three groups that were damaged or eradicated in the immediate postwar years. Each illustrates a different kind of response to the pressures of the times.

THE SCIENTISTS' ANTINUCLEAR MOVEMENT

The Federation of Atomic Scientists (FAS) waged a high-minded campaign to ban the bomb its members had helped create. Their goal was to place nuclear power under international control. As knowledge of the apocalyptic destruction and death the weapon had visited on Hiroshima and Nagasaki in August 1945 percolated through American society, fear and concern welled up. Radio commentators such as Raymond Graham Swing, educators such as University of Chicago president Robert Hutchins, scientists such as Albert Einstein, and editors and writers such as Norman Cousins of the *Saturday Review of Literature* and Freda Kirchwey of *The Nation* sounded the alarm. They warned that that a nuclear war could destroy life on the planet. To avoid that fate, they argued, the nations of the world must give up a measure of their cherished sovereignty and submit to some form of world government that had the power literally to outlaw war.

"We face a choice between one world or none," wrote Kirchwey, coining a phrase that caught on. A book, *One World or None*, prepared by the FAS, was published in March 1946. Hours after the announcement of the Hiroshima bomb, Norman Cousins dashed off an editorial headed "Modern Man Is Obsolete," which he later expanded into a best-selling book with that title. Cousins's impassioned plea stressed that world government was the only hope of saving the planet.

The pro–world government sentiment led to the formation in April 1947 of the United World Federalists, with Cord Meyer Jr., a recent Yale graduate, as its energetic president. Other nonprofit organizations agitating for some form of collective security emerged. The nascent United Nations drew both support and criticism from the one-worlders.

The concerned citizens who wanted to control the atom leaped into the political fray without much discussion of what form a world state might take or how it could be implemented. In the vanguard of the campaign were the scientists who had worked in the wartime Manhattan Project. This achievement, the greatest collective scientific effort in history, a highest-priority, spare-no-expenses effort to make an atomic weapon before the Germans did, encouraged the scientists to believe the peoples of the world, also racing against time, would support a "crash program" to build a world state that could avert a nuclear war.

The atomic scientists' movement had its initial stirrings on September 1, 1945, when several of them gathered for a lunch in Chicago to discuss their feelings of guilt and trepidation over what they had wrought. Out of this nucleus was formed the FAS, dedicated to educating the public and their representatives in government on the hazards of nuclear warfare.

The atomic scientists had great prestige at this time; they were perceived as the high priests of the nuclear mystery. Scientists who had never given much thought to politics became canvassers, publicists, and Washington lobbyists. In addition to their own efforts, they employed a small public relations apparatus that fed data to liberal journals such as *The Nation* and *The New Republic*, as well as to mainstream periodicals such as *Collier's* and *Popular Science* and their own authoritative publication, the *Bulletin of the Atomic Scientists*, famous for its Doomsday Clock, which calculated the current likelihood of a nuclear Armageddon, expressed as minutes before midnight. Throughout much of the 1940s and 1950s, the clock stood at between 11:53 and 11:58.

The FAS's initial goal was to defeat a bill before Congress that placed atomic energy under military control. Their prestige won congressional ears. The result was the Atomic Energy Act of 1946, which adopted their recommendations to some degree. Although the scientists were heartened by this victory in the political arena, the law did not end military control, merely obfuscated it in statutory fine print.

The nuclear scientists agreed on five principles: (1) that the U.S. monopoly of the bomb could not last; (2) that no defense was possible against atomic weapons; (3) that possession of more bombs than a rival had would not guarantee military superiority; (4) that nuclear war would destroy a sizable part of the earth's population; and (5) that international cooperation to control atomic energy was therefore essential to the survival of humankind.

Scientists affiliated with FAS contributed to the report prepared by David E. Lilienthal, who would chair the Atomic Energy Commission, and J. Robert Oppenheimer, the leading physicist of the Manhattan Project. This document sketched the lineaments of an international control body under the United Nations, which would monopolize all atomic weapons, fuel, and atomic energy facilities and enforce a ban on any military use of nuclear energy.

At the start, the plan slammed into resistance from the U.S. government. An appended letter reserved for the United States the right to continue building bombs until the plan was operational, or to go its own way if it disapproved the UN's final document. The old bugaboo of national sovereignty (couched in national security terms) thus reared its head. There was no chance that the Soviets, who were rushing to build their own bomb to nullify the American advantage, would abandon this effort and submit details of it to an international control regime. On June 19, 1946, Soviet UN delegate Andrei Gromyko rejected the U.S. plan, which Wall Street financier Bernard M. Baruch, U.S. delegate to the UN Atomic Energy Committee, had unveiled in a speech the previous day. Soviet rejection effectively killed the idea of international control of atomic energy, but an equal culprit was the United States with its insistence on holding its lead in atomic-bomb development, while demanding that Russia halt its effort.

After that, it was downhill for the FAS. For one thing, polls showed that the American public overwhelmingly wanted to keep the "secret" of the atomic bomb rather than place it under international authority. All that average Americans knew was that the bomb was an awesome weapon, the "secret" of which they did not want to "share" with the Soviet Union. Their government, which was making the bomb the keystone in its security arch, did not seek to dissuade them.

The anticommunist consensus was hardening. Those jolly, hard-fighting Russians in the World War II Hollywood propaganda movies were no longer regarded as our allies. They were transformed into a threat justifying billions for defense and foreign aid. The government, aided by the conservative media, scoffed at all the hysteria about an atomic war's bringing about the end of the world (while conjuring up a comforting vision of prosperity created by the "peaceful atom"). To the contrary, the government preached, we needed these weapons more than ever to deter the huge menacing Red Army from conquering Europe. And the message got through. According to a 1945 Gallup poll, 38 percent of the respondents regarded the Soviet Union as "aggressive"; by 1947, the proportion had risen to 66 percent.

The theologian Reinhold Niebuhr and other "realists" cautioned that the one-worlders, international arms controllers, and pacifists were too idealistic, blind to humankind's incorrigibly sinful nature. Because of their misplaced optimism, the antinuclear faction failed to recognize the growing challenge of Soviet expansionism, which had to be contained by superior force before there could be nuclear disarmament.

The FAS had drawn up a blueprint for controlled atomic disarmament, with inspections and other safeguards, that in retrospect may be seen as a template of later international agreements. But the U.S. national security establishment proved unwilling to make a leap of faith into the uncertain waters of international control. It refused to renounce the most powerful weapon in the national arsenal, the very first use of which President Truman had authorized against Japan in part because he feared what the country would say if it learned he had failed to use the secret superweapon that could have prevented the slaughter of thousands of American boys on Japanese beachheads. In 1948, Truman launched an economy drive to slash the defense budget, which fixed the armed forces at 1.4 million men and women. This decrease was predicated on the buildup of a strategic air force capable of dropping atomic bombs on the Soviet Union as the nation's primary defense against the much larger Soviet army.

Like Truman's 1947 speech on Greece, the scientists' campaign was intended to frighten the American public so that it would accept the radical idea of international control of nuclear weapons. They broadcast the facts about the awful destructiveness of the bomb, with speeches, pamphlets, graphic magazine spreads, and even a Hollywood feature film—MGM's portentously titled *The Beginning or the End* (1946). They succeeded in scaring nearly everybody.

Historian Paul Boyer argues that the FAS succeeded too well: the "rhetoric of fear" used to awaken the people to the atomic threat became an argument for U.S. nuclear superiority, which would keep the country safe behind an atomic shield. Russia's successful test of an atomic weapon in 1949 shook this popular assumption. But the public clung to its faith in security through military strength. By January 1951, a Gallup poll showed that 66 percent of Americans favored first use of atomic weapons in a war with Russia. As Reinhold Niebuhr had foreseen in 1945, when confronted by the relatively remote possibility of atomic vaporization and the immediate menace of Soviet communism, people feared the latter more.

After the Soviet Union detonated its bomb, more and more scientists began to doubt the idea that international control was the best way to protect America from the horrors of war. A majority of them now believed that overwhelming U.S. nuclear superiority was the only answer. In 1952 the U.S. detonated a hydrogen bomb; the Soviets exploded their own hydrogen bomb in 1955 and went on to acquire intercontinental ballistic missiles. Doomsday strategists moved on to the "mad doctrine"—that is, the doctrine of mutually assured destruction—and deterrence theory. The bomb became a necessary component of the superpower's defensive arsenal.

Scientists who continued to work for nuclear disarmament found their loyalty and patriotism increasingly being challenged, especially if they had any present or past leftist associations. As early as June 1947, HUAC chairman J. Parnell Thomas accused all five civilian Atomic Energy Commission (AEC) commissioners of being Communists. Thomas's claim originated in the Pentagon among military men who opposed civilian control of the atom. Later, many scientists in and out of government became objects of disloyalty charges. Investigations within the AEC resulted in firings of several, and the inquisition spread until it reached top scientists such as Edward U. Condon, Linus Pauling, and J. Robert Oppenheimer, whose principled opposition to development of the hydrogen bomb was considered suspicious.

The FAS stepped in to provide legal advice to members whose loyalty had been impugned. But HUAC continued its raids and decimated the AEC's contingent of scientists, ultimately driving out some five hundred of them and scaring many hundreds more into silence. FAS membership fell from 3,000 in 1946 to fewer than 1,500 in 1950.

Edward Teller, who was once an advocate of international control but now supported building the hydrogen bomb, admonished scientists to give up their campaign. Scientists had no business in the political arena, he said; they should confine themselves to understanding natural laws and doing the will of their government, which was now embroiled in a nuclear arms race. Many FAS activists heeded Teller, regarding the building of better bombs to be their patriotic duty.

Of course, Teller's admonition was political in itself. He was an active behind-the-scenes lobbyist for the hydrogen bomb. When he advised his colleagues not to participate in the political debate, he was telling them in effect to trim their sails to the Cold War winds. Scientists such as Leo Szilard, a physicist who had first alerted FDR of the need to build an atomic bomb, continued to campaign for international nuclear control, but they were less and less listened to and more and more became targets for the red-baiters.

As Bruce Cumings writes, the nation had tilted so far to the right that a general could call for preventive war against the Soviet Union and command the U.S. Air Force, while a politician who favored negotiations with Moscow was virtually barred from high office. The rollback doctrine was respected, while the coexistence doctrine was excoriated as appeasement. "World government" was for dwellers in Cloud-Cuckoo Land; real realists aspired to empire. Idealism gave way to realpolitik, collective security to "perpetual war for perpetual peace."

THE AMERICAN VETERANS COMMITTEE

The scientists' movement of 1945–47 was an example of how dissent was swept away by Cold War fears. For a different sort of case history, we next turn to the area of domestic policy, and to the policies affecting fourteen million American veterans. Some veterans came home with dreams of doing their bit to make a more equitable and just society in the nation for which they had fought. These idealists were prominent in the American Veterans Committee, founded in January 1945 by a nucleus formed by Gilbert A. Harrison. Concerned about winning government assistance for their own readjustment to postwar American society, they were also worried about the nature of that society. Some feared a postwar recession leading to social unrest and violence, precipitating a fascist government.

The main veterans' organization, the American Legion, was considered a potential enforcer of such a scenario, reprising its post–World War I role. Its Americanism Committee campaigned to stamp out Communists and radicals. Ideologically, it had not changed much from 1919, except that most of its two million prewar members were getting too old for the hard work of rousting subversives. They shared the organization's values of Americanism and free enterprise, but belonged mainly for camaraderie at the American Legion bar. The Legion and its brother, the Veterans of Foreign Wars (VFW), were dedicated to getting more benefits and perks for vets, and of course anxious to seine new members from the tidal wave of discharged World War II ex-soldiers.

The AVC organizers rejected the idea of vets being another interest group feeding at the Washington trough. Their motto was "Citizens first, veterans second." They pushed for policies they believed would benefit not just veterans but all Americans. For example, the AVC backed a housing bill that would provide cheap homes for low-income folk, veterans or not. So while the Legion supported low-interest loans for vets who wanted to build homes—if any banks would advance them money at such a low rate—the AVC called for the government-subsidized affordable housing. This "socialistic" approach was anathema to the Legion and its conservative friends in Congress. So the AVC members held demonstrations in favor of the Wagner-Ellender-Taft housing bill; some 2,500 members, for example, conducted a sleep-in at MacArthur Park in Los Angeles to publicize the housing shortage. For its part, the Legion denounced the bill as "radical." The AVC accused the Legion of cohabiting with the real estate lobby, a charge that contained much truth.

The AVC favored other liberal social programs. Its bylaws required chapter meetings to be racially integrated, which aroused hostility in the southern states. Representative John Rankin (D-Miss.), a white supremacist who chaired the House Veterans Affairs subcommittee, flew into a high dudgeon and barred the AVC from testifying at its hearings. Since some of the legislation before this body had been drawn up or shaped by the AVC, the ban amounted to no small inconvenience. The AVC's color-blind policies also drew the ire of the secretary of the army, which was still segregated. He banned the committee from meeting on army bases or otherwise using their facilities, a privilege veterans groups traditionally enjoyed.

The AVC never seriously challenged the VFW or the American Legion for primacy among the World War II crop of veterans. By 1947 the Legion's ranks had swelled to 3.2 million members and a million auxiliaries, while the AVC's membership reached only around 100,000 at its peak. Still, it performed a serious policymaking function, generating visionary legislative alternatives to the usual interest-group products, and it acted as a liberal gadfly in challenging establishment policies.

The AVC, though, became embroiled in an internecine battle between pro-communists and anticommunists within its ranks. The CPUSA was eager to make inroads in the large veteran population, but its efforts to infiltrate the Legion and the VFW had failed. It turned to the AVC, some of whose members argued that it should not engage in red-baiting but be open to all. The AVC's liberalism had already drawn charges from conservative columnists that it was a Communist front, which it was not. But in the classic fashion, CPUSA members worked hard to take over. In 1947 they were turned back when they tried to wrest the vice chairmanship away from Harrison.

In 1948, the federal government prosecuted the Communist Party leadership under the Smith Act, which prohibited advocating the forcible overthrow of the government. Among those indicted was AVC member John Gates, who was editor of *The Daily Worker*, the CPUSA paper. This prosecution of individuals for their political ideas and associations raised fundamental free-speech issues; but in the *Dennis* case the Supreme Court would uphold the law, as it would uphold all such antisubversion laws during these years.

The indictment of one of its prominent members as a disloyal American prodded the AVC board into action. Ruling that the CPUSA was a "tight conspiracy" whose followers never acted independently of the party line, it expelled Gates. His allies made an issue of the expulsion at the next national convention, but lost and the members passed a resolution expelling all Communists from their ranks.

After the CPUSA members had departed, the organization lost some of its passion, as though the fight had exhausted its members. Its numbers dwindled, and it ended its days as a Washington think tank, grinding out sober policy papers on veterans issues.

UE: THE PAINS OF LABOR

As we have seen, the major labor unions abandoned the radicalism that had energized the great organizing drives of the thirties. A prominent exception was the UE—the United Electrical, Radio and Machine Workers of America. Representing mainly workers at General Electric (GE), Westinghouse, RCA, Philco, and Delco plants, the UE was the biggest industrial union in the CIO, with 650,000 members in 1946. It contained a large contingent of women radio workers and was ahead of the times in espousing equal pay for them, as well as for its constitution, which declared that it would not discriminate on the basis of race, gender, ethnicity, or political views. It worked for social benefits and opposed Truman's Cold War policies. In 1948 it supported Henry Wallace's presidential candidacy.

The UE's top leaders were, if not party members, believers in much of what Communism stood for. They had taken power in 1941, when Julius Emspak and James B. Matles ousted James B. Carey, a strong anticommunist, and installed Albert Fitzgerald, who talked an anticommunist game but supported the union's leftist policies. Carey fought a running battle against the UE leaders from within and outside the union, in alliances with management and the leadership of the CIO, of which he became secretary.

After winning substantial pay increases in 1946 from General Electric and Westinghouse, the UE became more political; for example, it passed a resolution at its 1947 convention declaring that Wall Street controlled the Truman administration. In 1948, flouting the express wishes of the CIO leadership, it threw its support behind Wallace. The CIO retaliated in 1949 by expelling the UE.

The CIO launched a ferocious campaign against the UE, joined by rival unions, congressional committees, the U.S. Justice Department and the managements of GE (which was virulently antiunion) and other companies. Carey formed a rival union, the International Union of Electrical workers (IUE), and fought the UE in plant elections with open company backing. HUAC held hearings at which Matles, Emspak, and others were grilled about their refusal to sign the noncommunist oath. The Atomic Energy Commission urged GE to expel the UE at one of its laboratories engaging in top-secret work because of its alleged Communist ties.

As U.S. arms production accelerated during the Korean War, companies where UE represented the workers were increasingly involved in defense production under government contracts. There were dire predictions of Communist-instigated strikes disrupting production (in fact, no strikes in defense plants were ever ordered or conducted by the UE). Workers were required to obtain security clearances from loyalty review boards, and those whom the FBI flagged for politically suspect pasts appeared before boards of military officers in order to obtain security clearances. After a hostile hearing at which they had no rights, they were often peremptorily fired or barred from working on classified materials. During bargaining elections, the secretary of labor in the Truman administration might show up to urge employees to opt for the IUE slate. The United Auto Workers also raided UE plants, petitioned a sympathetic National Labor Relations Board for new elections, and evicted the UE local.

Such tactics, combined with workers' fears of losing their jobs if they stayed in the UE and the anticommunist mood of the times, sent the union's membership skidding to 90,000 by 1955. During the same period, the IUE ballooned to 300,000 and another rival, the AFL-affiliated International Brotherhood of Electrical Workers, swelled to 500,000.

Many UE leaders gave in and signed the Taft-Hartley noncommunist affidavits, but some were prosecuted and convicted on other grounds. For example, Emspak was indicted for contempt of Congress after refusing to name names of Communist associates; Matles was deprived of his U.S. citizenship, which was restored on appeal.

The UE was not the only union savaged during the postwar years. Just about any union leader with a leftist past could be entangled in the Kafkaesque anticommunist machinery sooner or later. Of course, plants where people worked on classified defense projects presented legitimate security concerns, but the war against the UE and other radical unions far exceeded in severity the requirements of national security. Perhaps unwisely, unions with left-wing leaderships resisted disclosure requirements or led their memberships into the foreign-policy debates; as one UE member ruefully observed, maybe it was less important for the unions to oppose the Marshall Plan than to win improved benefits for their members.

Yet, in retrospect, the anticommunist chill marked a turning point that started the downward slide of the union movement into the political marginalization and the smaller membership it has today. By making a Faustian bargain with the anticommunist establishment and focusing exclusively on cleaning out the CPUSA members and sympathizers in its ranks, labor was diverted from its main mission, which was resisting corporate dominance and agitating for socially progressive programs. As a result, U.S. workers and the working poor, union or nonunion, lost a voice in the political arena calling for universal health insurance, equal pay for women and minorities and other equities, which now, early in a new century, seem less possible dreams.

THE OLD LEFT AND THE BIRTH OF THE NEW

The United States has a long tradition of liberal-left idealism, a lineage that traces back to the socialist, progressive, populist, and anti-imperialist movements of the late nineteenth and early twentieth centuries. But in the late 1940s, the left idealism of the prewar decade turned sour. The ideology of domestic anticommunism was used successfully to marginalize and render ineffective the social democratic left. As a result, effective opposition to the Cold War consensus, which embraced the domestic and foreign policies of the centrist Truman administration, was feeble and tainted by association—real and concocted—with the Communist Party.

In short, the reformist demands of the American left just after the war were smothered in the cradle. Many of the problems first raised back then—stopping nuclear war, creating full employment, bringing civil rights to minorities, providing universal health insurance—are still on the left's to-do list. In the foreign policy arena there was no real, vigorous debate about the Cold War, as before World War II between the isolationists and the interventionists. The lack of dissent meant that the Truman administration launched a cold war against the

Soviet Union unchecked by popular pressure to consider alternatives such as negotiation and controlled nuclear disarmament.

Out of the ashes of the Old Left, a self-styled New Left would be born in the 1960s. The term was coined by Columbia professor C. Wright Mills, whose book *The Power Elite* (1956) served as a kind of bible for the young students or recent graduates who founded Students for a Democratic Society (SDS), the linchpin of the movement, in 1960. Significantly, SDS started under the wing of an Old Left organization, the League for Industrial Democracy (LID), a socialist student group that had emerged from the fires of the McCarthy era fiercely anticommunist.

Ironically, Cold War anticommunism became anathema to the SDS. Although it had little sympathy for the Soviet Union, the CPUSA, or Marxist thought, the SDS rejected its parents' adjurations to stake out a clear anticommunist position on nuclear disarmament. It considered anticommunism to be a manifestation of right-wing paranoia, a sterile and negativistic ideology. Differences over this issue led to a split with LID.

The SDS was also politically inspired by Martin Luther King Jr. and the young blacks in the Student Nonviolent Coordinating Committee (SNCC) who were then spearheading the sit-in movement in the South. But SDS members were linked to the burgeoning counterculture, which embraced peace, drugs, rock 'n' roll, and sexual freedom as antidotes to the conservative moral consensus of the 1950s. Some of SDS's earliest demonstrations were sparked by hearings on student radicalism conducted by HUAC, and this opposition gave rise to the loosely organized free speech movement that was active on campuses in the early 1960s. Its main tenet was "participatory democracy," an idea central to the teachings of the philosopher John Dewey.

But SDS's program of radical change in the United States was sidetracked, like much else on the left, by the Vietnam War. Its antiwar activism, though it sparked demonstrations against the war, earned it the violent enmity of organized labor and would eventually provide a target for the emergent Republican right under Ronald Reagan. Still, SDS may be credited with mounting one of the first political challenges to the anticommunist Cold War consensus since Wallace's Progressive Party movement in 1948.

In addition to the antiwar movement, the New Left sought to work with the emerging civil rights and feminist movements. But lingering sexism among the New Left males and the black power tendencies among black civil workers hampered coalition building. The New Left also lacked the unity and coherent aims of the other two movements. It degenerated into the mindless nihilistic violence of the Weathermen, which at the end of the decade made a perverse, doomed effort, born of frustration, to foment violent revolution.

The last hurrah of the leftist rebirth in the 1960s was George McGovern's 1972 presidential campaign, which veterans of the ill-starred Wallace campaign of 1948 found similar to theirs in its basic themes and goals. It was also similar in outcome: McGovern's poor showing in the popular vote tallies allowed his enemies to discredit the left wing of the Democratic Party, which had nominally run his campaign, and enabled party centrists to recapture the reins of power. Ironically, left Democrats today refer to themselves as "the Democratic wing of the Democratic Party," unconsciously harking back to the party as it was before the Cold War era.

The anticommunist crusade against left idealism after the war cost greatly in broken lives and diminished free speech. Dissent was quelled; left-progressive groups and individuals were persecuted, marginalized, or demonized. Whether U.S. history would have been different if these people had been able to mount a more robust, outspoken opposition to the reigning Cold War ideology than they did cannot be known, but it is a question worth pondering.

The "revisionist" historians cited throughout this chapter insist that the suppression of free speech and dissent in America was far out of proportion to any threat to national security posed by American Communists or Soviet espionage rings. In constructing their narratives of the Cold War, historians must contemplate the deformation of contemporary policy debates and the muffling of dissident views. What happened in history is important, but so is what did not, what went unsaid or unconsidered or was suppressed. There is new terrain to be discovered by mapping the roads not taken.

BIBLIOGRAPHIC NOTE

The works I have drawn on here have in common a more sympathetic (but not sentimental) view of the left than was displayed in earlier histories of the domestic Cold War. In their interpretations, some could be called revisionist, yet in my view there is an emerging consensus about what is now generally seen as a mean and mendacious period in American life. David Caute's *The Great Fear: The Anti-Communist Purge Under Truman and Eisenhower* (Simon & Schuster, 1978) was a pioneering work of scholarship and is still notable for the volume of facts drawn together from a variety of areas. In *America in Our Time* (Doubleday, 1976) Godfrey Hodgson serves up a njarrative history of United States during the years from John F. Kennedy's assassination to the Watergate scandal and provides a British perspective on the aborted formation of a social-democratic left in the United States. Another narrative history, Joseph C. Goulden's *The Best Years, 1945–1950* (Atheneum, 1976) first started me thinking about the period as it related to my own life and to the idealism of returning veterans. Ellen Schrecker's *Many Are the Crimes* (Princeton University Press, 1998), grounded in extensive data, evinces a lucid grasp of the essentials of the McCarthyite years. Her disdain for the evasions of the CPUSA is matched by her sympathy for the people caught in the fallout from the depredations of over-zealous investigators. In *By the Bomb's Early Light* (Pantheon, 1985), Paul Boyer rewardingly limits himself to a rich analysis of the impact of the atomic bomb on American culture and consciousness between 1945 and 1950; his appraisal of the scientists' movement was particularly valuable to my essay. In the second volume of his magisterial *Origins of the Korean War: The Roaring of the Cataract, 1947–1950* (Princeton University Press, 1990), Bruce Cumings analyzes the causes of the war in the American political context. The social-psychological insights in Elaine Tyler May's *Homeward Bound: American Families in the Cold War Era* (Basic Books, 1988) have informed my thinking. While largely concerned with the Hollywood witch hunts, Victor S. Navasky's *Naming Names* (Hill and Wang, 1980) is essential to understanding the motives of the inquisitors and their victims. Richard Rhodes's Pulitzer Prize–winning *Making of the Atomic Bomb* (Simon & Schuster, 1986) was a valuable guide on nuclear issues. Lawrence S. Wittner's *Rebels Against the War: The American Peace Movement, 1933–1983* (Temple University Press, 1984) is a sympathetic but objective account of what peace groups were up to. *Louis Johnson and the Arming of America* (Indiana University Press, 2005), Keith D. McFarland and David L. Rolf's excellent biography of Truman's defense secretary, describes the thinking of their opposite numbers in the Pentagon.

11. WITHOUT RESTRAINT

Scandal and Politics in America

JULIAN E. ZELIZER

"What began 25 years ago with Watergate as a solemn and necessary process to force a president to adhere to the rule of law, has grown beyond our control so that now we are routinely using criminal accusations and scandal to win the political battles and ideological differences we cannot settle at the ballot box. It has been used with reckless abandon by both parties." So lamented Representative Charles Schumer (D-N.Y.) during the debate over impeaching President William Clinton in 1998. By then, scandal had become a driving force in politics. Many of Schumer's colleagues resembled weary soldiers surveying a bloody battlefield, shocked by what their conflict had wrought. While scandals had been part of American politics since the Revolution, never had they been so pervasive as in the last three decades of the twentieth century. No longer occasional or ancillary events, they had become integral to partisan strategy, political reform, and the public perception of government. While many citizens once viewed Watergate as the climax of scandal politics, it is now clear that President Richard Nixon's downfall in 1974 was only the opening chapter of a much larger story.

During the second half of the twentieth century, scandals became crucial to America's political style. The nation witnessed an unprecedented number of major ones: in Republican and Democratic administrations, in the legislative and executive branches, and in weak and strong economies. The impact was breathtaking. Two presidents were consumed by scandal, with one forced to resign and another impeached. Two more sitting presidents have been subject to intense investigation. Several influential congressmen have been forced out of office because of scandal, including three speakers of the House, two chairmen of the House Ways and Means Committee, and many powerful senators. A nominee for the Supreme Court was rejected because of drug use, while several cabinet members and a vice president have resigned because of conflict-of-interest violations. In 1970, the federal government indicted 45 state, federal, and local politicians and government employees on allegations of corruption. By 1995, that number had reached 824.[1] The types of issues capable of damaging an established politician, moreover, expanded dramatically. A plethora of congressional committees, independent commissions, prosecutors, and ethics codes had been created to fight corruption. Unlike earlier periods, when scandal politics was linked to a particular issue such as communist espionage, scandal had become a usual weapon with which politicians fought their battles.

Of course, scandal politics was not unique to post–World War II America. Democracies have always faced the potential to be consumed by scandal. In state-centered countries, such as China or the Soviet Union, the threat has been insignificant. There was scant opportunity for the revelation of corruption, since in them a unified political elite controlled mass communication, political participation, and the legal system. In democracies, the press tended to be granted significant autonomy, and fewer controls existed on political opposition. Democratic governments usually created internal mechanisms that could be used to expose and punish corruption. Until the 1970s, politicians in the United States relied on "auxiliary precautions" created by the founding fathers that were meant to protect American democracy from excessive power and corrupt politicians, which included the separation of power, freedom of the press, and impeachment.

American history has been replete with scandal. During the Gilded Age, which lasted from roughly 1877 to 1900, for example, upper-class reformers called Mugwumps, Republican supporters of Democratic presidential candidate Grover Cleveland, revealed how big business influenced the decisions of machine politicians. In those years, the Crédit Mobilier scandal exposed government officials who had accepted stock in exchange for political favors. At the turn of the twentieth century, progressive-era reforms were motivated by, and helped to instigate, national revelations of extensive corruption in city and state governments. During Warren Harding's administration in the early 1920s, investigators brought to light evidence of politicians who leased property to oil executives and received payment in return—the Teapot Dome affair.

Like economic corruption, sex scandals also have a long tradition in the United States. Simultaneously reflecting and contradicting the nation's Puritan cultural heritage, politicians have often been willing to wield the weapon of sexual impropriety. In the presidential campaigns of 1824 and 1828, for instance, opponents accused Andrew Jackson of adultery, while in 1884, Republicans lambasted Grover Cleveland for his illegitimate child.

The relationship between politics and scandal thus has deep roots in American history dating back to the Revolution. What changed during the post-1960s period was a gradual erosion of institutional and cultural forces that had temporarily prevented scandal from becoming the dominant partner in that relationship since the end of the progressive era. In contrast to the nineteenth century, moreover, politicians engaged in scandal warfare during a period when Americans retained minimal connection to their civic institutions, thereby creating a situation where there was little to counteract the disenchantment that scandal generated toward government. The centrality of scandal politics cannot be attributed to any single source. Instead, it must be understood as an outgrowth of the 1960s political turmoil that mounted fundamental challenges to American politics, culture, and economics. The transformation of America's political style began with an alliance between liberal northern Democrats and middle-class good-government reform in the 1960s and 1970s. While young liberal Democrats and Republicans were primarily interested in ending the power of southern conservatives—as opposed to good-government reformers whose interest began with preventing corruption—nobody in the coalition believed that politicians would expose or penalize corrupt behavior, nor did they think that the electorate was capable of handling that responsibility. Unlike their predecessors in the progressive era, the reform coalition created a permanent base for themselves in journalism, public-interest organizations, and Congress. The conflicts over Vietnam, civil rights, and Watergate generated widespread public support for their outlook. The institutional infrastructure created by reformers became destabilizing in a new mass media and cultural environment. When politicians turned to scandal after 1980, they encountered few obstacles to prevent them from using it as a partisan weapon. The result was explosive.

THE EARLY POSTWAR ERA, 1945–1964

Right from the end of World War II, scandal played a prominent role in national politics. Numerous charges were brought against President Harry Truman's administration. Televised congressional hearings disclosed intimate connections between local gangsters and the Kansas City Democratic political machine from which Truman had received his initial political support. Several federal agencies were implicated as well. Investigators in 1951, for instance, discovered that hundreds of low-level tax collectors for the Internal Revenue Service (IRS) had accepted bribes from taxpayers.

While these charges of corruption had aided Dwight Eisenhower's presidential bid against Adlai Stevenson in 1952, he was not immune from scandal. During his campaign, *The New York Post* attacked his vice presidential candidate, Richard Nixon, for maintaining a secret slush fund financed by California millionaires. In a televised speech in which he famously insisted that his wife "doesn't have a mink coat, but she does have a respectable Republican cloth coat," while admitting that he had accepted a little cocker spaniel that his six-year-old daughter Tricia had named Checkers, Nixon defended himself as a decent man under attack from overzealous opponents. By speaking directly to the voters, and overcoming the demands that he resign from the ticket, Nixon's so-called Checkers speech indicated the important role of television in scandal warfare. Six years later, Eisenhower forced senior advisor Sherman Adams to resign when it became public that he had helped a businessman receive special treatment from the Federal Trade Commission and the Securities and Exchange Commission. Of course, the most dramatic scandals revolved around anticommunism. Between 1948 and 1954, several prominent members of the national security establishment were brought down by charges of espionage, even if those charges turned out to be false and often of malicious intent. Senator Joseph McCarthy (R-Wis.) led the charge, showing how scandal could enable a politician to move up the ranks rapidly—but also how it could lead to downfall.

Still, during the 1950s and 1960s, scandal politics was limited in scale and scope. In terms of quantity, the number of prominent officials involved in, and seriously harmed by, these incidents remained small. The IRS scandal, for example, did not touch the higher echelons of the agency. The most intense period of the anticommunist crusade that lasted throughout the 1950s was perhaps more noteworthy for its sloppiness than its excesses. Recent information from Soviet archives has proven that espionage in the United States was more extensive than most suspected. Furthermore, the most intense periods of scandal were usually defined by specific issues such as espionage, rather than a usual means of transacting politics. Except in a few cases, scandal failed to dominate news coverage.

Countervailing forces curtailed the importance of scandal within the political system. One force was the power of the senior politicians. Within Congress, for example, senior senators and representatives maintained control over legislative proceedings. Norms of reciprocity, deference to seniority, and institutional patriotism tended to discourage personal attacks on colleagues. Although a few mavericks such as McCarthy were able to elude control, they were outliers. Within the House, those who attempted to outflank senior Democrats were punished by being given inferior committee assignments. "If you want to get along," Speaker Sam Rayburn (D-Tex.) always advised new members, "go along." Such norms promoted professional civility between congressmen even across party lines.

A different type of senior establishment existed in other areas of politics. In presidential elections, urban and southern party leaders retained strong influence over the campaign process. Notwithstanding the introduction of primaries earlier in the century, party operatives selected most delegates to the Democratic and Republican conventions. The media had limited influence in the selection of candidates, and this further inhibited communication with voters.

Scandal was also muted because much of the policymaking process remained hidden from public view. Most legislative deliberations, for instance, were closed to the public. Despite a democratic electoral system, laws requiring disclosure of election contributions were ineffective, and no independent commission tracked campaign data. The national security establishment, which was constructed between 1947 and 1950 as part of the Cold War, entrenched an institutional network that conducted foreign policy in a highly secretive and tightly controlled environment.

Nor did American culture foster a great demand for scandal politics. Amid unprecedented economic prosperity, Americans trusted their political institutions. By the early 1960s, one poll indicated, 75 percent of Americans trusted government to make the right decision. World War II, in which the government defeated fascism, seemed to prove that politicians could be effective. Cold War nationalism intensified loyalty to political leaders by creating a mood favoring politicians rather than discrediting them.

This trust extended to other parts of American society. In 1959, Americans were shocked by news that television executives tampered with a popular quiz show, *Twenty One*, to secure high ratings. They provided answers to contestants, including the handsome young academic Charles Van Doren, whose appearances drew huge ratings. The revelation triggered congressional hearings, while the networks expanded news programming to regain legitimacy. Besides trust, privacy was a cherished cultural value. Americans became more conscious of this right as modern technology and a more intrusive federal government posed a greater threat. Within this early postwar culture, there were strong boundaries to what the public would tolerate. Even with some liberalization in film and television (the men's magazine *Playboy*, for example, first appeared in 1953) open discussion of sexual matters outside a medical context was rare.

The mainstream news media also exhibited restraint. To be sure, some journalists, such as Drew Pearson and I. F. Stone, continued the muckraking tradition by exposing the wrongdoing of public officials. But they were not the norm. Until the mid-1960s, the press was generally respectful of the political establishment. The norm of objectivity, or at least the appearance of objectivity, remained a desired goal. This in itself limited how far reporters would go in attacking politicians. Reporters tried to remove themselves and their opinions from stories by presenting facts without much analysis, along with considerable paraphrasing of the politicians' positions. On television, the image of the reporter did not appear as much as the elected officials they were covering; the average "sound bite" of politicians on television was forty-two seconds in 1968, where it would shrink to ten seconds by 1988.[2] (By several estimates, it was six seconds as of 2006.) McCarthy, for one, knew that reporters would publish what he said without critical commentary. In his case, the passivity of the press, not its investigatory efforts, facilitated scandal warfare.

Many prominent members of the media, moreover, had close ties to government. Like the public, most editors refused to publish on most aspects of a politician's private life. Despite the widespread knowledge of President John F. Kennedy's sexual escapades and Senator Russell Long's alcoholism, reporters refused to write about these stories. As political reporter Jack Germond wrote, "a politician who was a notorious drunk would be described as somebody with a reputation for excessive conviviality. A politician who chased women was known as someone who appreciated a well-turned ankle. And this was the way we went at this. Everyone knew except the reader."[3] Within the media there were boundaries between "news" and "entertainment" shows. The producers of news shows strove to maintain a degree of decorum in their shows that would distinguish them from "cruder" entertainment.

The final force inhibiting scandal politics during the early postwar decades was the salience of other issues: the continued growth of the federal government, the Cold War, the civil rights movement, and the war in Vietnam. During the 1950s and 1960s, civil rights dominated public debates. Other controversial policies, ranging from health care to crime, provided ample material for politicians to battle without resorting to scandal. When scandal emerged in these years, it had to compete for attention with the robust issue agenda of the period.

INSTITUTIONALIZING THE PUBLIC INTEREST, 1958–1973

Democracy and scandal have gone hand in hand, but before 1965, there were countervailing forces working to constrain scandal. Between 1958 and 1973, those countervailing forces started to disintegrate. The change started with liberal Democrats who railed against a political process that, they felt, benefited southern conservatives in the 1950s. Middle-class activists who focused on government corruption joined them in the 1960s. The baby boom generation, as well as older Democrats who were frustrated with their colleagues, lost faith in politicians because of Vietnam, compromises on civil rights, and violent official responses to student protest. As large segments of the population became suspicious of if not downright hostile toward government institutions amidst the political turmoil of the mid-1960s, the time was ripe for those who wanted to reform the political process permanently.

A small group of liberal Democrats attacked the political process that empowered conservative southern Democrats. The 1958 and 1964 elections produced an influx of these liberals in the House and Senate. They argued that legislative conventions such as seniority and the filibuster favored southerners who were stifling the party's agenda by resisting civil rights and prolonging segregation. Younger Democrats such as Senator Joseph Clark of Pennsylvania flagrantly ignored institutional norms in their fight for a new system.

Mainstream journalists became more adversarial in their coverage of politicians in the 1960s. Driven by the same concerns that absorbed students in the universities, many middle-class, well-educated reporters came to regard journalism as political activism. Professionally, scandal provided the media with identifiable characters and dramatic stories full of intrigue. It was a way for them to write in compelling fashion about the problems facing the nation's political institutions. In an age when competition from television news was becoming more pronounced, the print media required stories that would attract readers. Likewise, television newscasters sought dramatic visual images to build their audience. This new journalism was connected to a broader political movement. Its heroes were the reporters who exposed government lies about the war in Vietnam. Colleagues, for example, praised Harrison Salisbury of the *New York Times* for his shocking stories that revealed false claims that President Johnson was issuing about the nature and progress of the Vietnam War. Objectivity was no longer a virtue. Younger journalists regarded themselves as guardians, as key players in politics.

Toward the end of the 1960s, reporters applied this investigative method to the private behavior of politicians. While reporters had refused to write about the sexual escapades of John Kennedy in 1961, his brother Senator Edward Kennedy (D-Mass.) faced a new breed of journalists at the end of the decade. In the early morning of July 18, 1969, after attending a party on Chappaquiddick Island, Massachusetts, Senator Kennedy drove his car off a bridge. His companion, a young staffer named Mary Jo Kopechne, drowned. Kennedy escaped but did not tell the police about the incident until the next morning. Although Kennedy claimed that he immediately went to find help, the print media, which covered the story on front pages, discovered that this was untrue. Reporters openly speculated that Kennedy was afraid the scandal would destroy his career. Kennedy, who was married, insisted that he was not sexually involved with Kopechne. Pulling a page from the Nixon "Checkers" speech, Kennedy went on television to defend himself, claiming that his disorientation after the crash explained his delay in reporting the accident. Although Massachusetts voters repeatedly returned Kennedy to the Senate, the scandal cost him any future presidential aspirations. In May 2006, Kennedy's son Patrick, a congressman, would explain an automobile crash at the Capitol by claiming disorientation as well, but the resulting scandal was short-lived.

Middle-class reformers who operated through interest-group politics became closely allied with the new journalists. The reformers focused on the idea that institutional renewal was needed to protect the democratic process and preserve faith in government. Before sound policymaking could prevail, corruption had to be eliminated. Common Cause became the main proponent of political reform. The organization was founded in 1970 by John Gardner, former secretary of the Department of Health, Education, and Welfare under Lyndon Johnson. Common Cause emphasized the mass media, both print and television, and aspired to create a broad membership base.

Although most Common Cause members did little more than contribute a few dollars, the leadership emerged as a formidable presence in politics by 1971. Its leaders were frequent guests on television talk shows, while its studies, advertisements, and press releases regularly made it into the pages of the nation's leading newspapers. Common Cause spawned imitators, and by 1974 there were eighteen public-interest organizations conducting similar activities. After the elections of 1974 and 1976, such groups obtained strong legislative support from the influx of liberal congressional Democrats representing middle-class, suburban areas who shared their concerns. Focusing primarily on what he called "structure and process issues," Gardner encouraged public-interest organizations to repair institutions to prevent corrupt individuals from gaining power.

The reformers scored several important early victories. In 1971, Democrats instituted a series of party reforms that weakened the power of the political machines in selecting presidential nominees. New party rules opened up the delegate selection process to suburbanites, women, and members of various ethnic and racial minorities whom old party leaders had ignored. This enhanced the power of political activists, who tended to represent the extremes of the spectrum. At the same time, primaries became the principal means for selecting nominees as the party convention became irrelevant and ceremonial. The new rules marked a decisive blow to the traditional party machines, while elevating the role of the television news media to new levels. The results were evident in 1976 when Jimmy Carter became the Democratic nominee, despite having a weak relationship with the party's national leadership. Public-interest organizations were also instrumental in the passage of the campaign finance amendments of 1972 and 1974, which created stringent disclosure requirements and limited campaign contributions.

Working in concert with liberal Democrats, public-interest organizations helped put corruption on the national agenda. Their concerns made sense to the baby boomers, who had participated in an antiwar movement that questioned the legitimacy of government elites. Middle-class reformers distrusted politicians and championed laws that would make leaders more accountable to the public. They articulated the concerns that were driving an entire generation of younger Americans who had lost faith in their leaders as a result of Vietnam and the failures of ending racism across the nation. Although it drew on the ideas that motivated progressive reformers, this generation was able to establish a stronger organizational presence in national politics through the media, interest groups, and legislation.

REFORM POLITICS: 1972–1978

The politics of reform dominated the years between 1972 and 1978, when a series of scandals shook Washington, culminating in extensive reform of the political process and the downfall of powerful politicians. In this period, scandal was the product of liberal Democrats and public-interest reformers who were struggling to open up the democratic process by unseating an entrenched, and in their minds corrupt, political establishment. The biggest scandal of the era started with a burglary at the Democratic National Committee headquarters, housed in Washington's Watergate Complex, in June 1972. Five men were arrested and charged. Two local reporters for the *Washington Post*, Bob Woodward and Carl Bernstein, discovered that the burglars had links to President Nixon's Committee to Re-Elect the President (CREEP), as well as to the anti-Castro Cuban exile community and to the Central Intelligence Agency (CIA). Federal District Judge John Sirica, who handled the trial of the burglars, concluded that the crime somehow related to the presidential campaign. Woodward and Bernstein revealed that high-level officials in the Nixon White House had orchestrated the break-in. One of the burglars, James McCord, chief of security for CREEP, implicated higher-level officials. Under intense pressure, Attorney General Elliot Richardson appointed Archibald Cox to be special prosecutor and investigate the crime. *CBS News* anchor Walter Cronkite hosted a special that wove together all the threads into a broader picture.

The different investigations uncovered broad patterns of executive abuse of power. Whether the president was personally responsible remained in doubt. Then, in July 1973, Alexander Butterfield revealed that Nixon had tape-recorded all Oval Office conversations. The various investigators, along with the media, clamored for release of the tapes. Nixon refused, claiming that a president had the right to withhold documents from the public under certain circumstances.

When special prosecutor Cox persisted in demanding the tapes, Nixon fired him in October 1973 in what critics called the "Saturday Night Massacre." This provoked a fierce backlash from critics and from the media. In July 1974, the Supreme Court ruled that executive privilege did not apply in a criminal matter and that Nixon would have to release the tapes.

Those recordings, which included some suspicious erasures—one of them, famously, eighteen and a half minutes long—revealed that the president had attempted to obstruct the investigation of the burglary. Other charges soon emerged: that Nixon had made policy decisions in exchange for campaign contributions; that he had used federal agencies to intimidate political opponents; and that his operatives had broken into the office of Daniel Ellsberg's psychologist. Ellsberg, a former national security staffer working for the Rand Corporation, had leaked the "Pentagon Papers," secret documents detailing the government's conduct of the Vietnam War, to the *New York Times*. Nixon's travails captivated the public. When the Senate conducted televised hearings in 1973, viewers tuned in high numbers to watch Congress investigate the scandal. Polls revealed public approval of what they saw. Senator Sam Ervin (D-N.C.), a white-haired, folksy eminence once known for his opposition to civil rights, became an overnight celebrity. The investigations confirmed that televised hearings offered one of the few opportunities for legislators to gain media coverage that would propel them to national attention. After the House Judiciary Committee voted to impeach Nixon, the president resigned in August 1974 before the whole membership could vote.

Watergate was a turning point in the politics of scandal. Nixon embodied the corruption that reformers had attacked since the late 1960s, and Watergate was symptomatic of the abuses of those in power. The story marked a major success for the new forces seeking to make politicians accountable to a higher ethical standard. Nixon's activities also provided ample evidence for stronger laws to enforce ethical behavior among public officials. The "auxiliary precautions" that the nation's founders had created in the Constitution were insufficient. Two months after Nixon resigned, Congress enacted campaign finance legislation that created an independent commission to enforce disclosure regulations and imposed new limits on campaign contributions. Congress also passed spending limits, but the Supreme Court overturned them in 1976. The 1978 Ethics in Government Law created the Special Prosecutor's Office to investigate allegations of wrongdoing by high-ranking officials in the executive branch. The law made it extremely difficult for the attorney general to remove the prosecutor. Ethics legislation also strengthened restrictions on lobbying activities and financial disclosure requirements, including the creation of an Office of Government Ethics, to oversee executive branch conflict-of-interest rules. Congress also imposed stringent conflict-of-interest laws on the personal financial transactions of its own members. The power of the new laws became immediately apparent during the administration of President Jimmy Carter, who had campaigned on a platform of integrity. When top members of his staff were accused of activities that ranged from cocaine use to financial improprieties, a special prosecutor was appointed to investigate the charges.

During the 1970s, the executive branch as a whole lost much of its insulation. Congress expanded its oversight power to review the work of federal agencies and bureaus. In 1975, Congress authorized money to support citizen groups such as Common Cause to participate in administrative politics. As more external forces were able to monitor their activities, federal agencies became porous. The national security establishment also came under fire after Vietnam. Senator Frank Church (D-Ida.) chaired committee hearings in the mid-1970s that revealed the types of activities that the CIA had supported, including attempts to assassinate foreign politicians and covert spying on individuals living in the United States. In response to the hearings, Congress imposed numerous regulations and openness requirements on the CIA and other military bodies.

Thanks to the era's reforms, the nation would no longer have to wait until an election to punish government officials, nor would it have to depend on politicians to decide when an investigation was needed. Liberal Democrats and middle-class reformers had institutionalized a concern with corruption so that after the memory of Watergate had faded, the investigatory infrastructure would remain.[4] Those who focused on corruption, including journalists, public-interest organizations, and congressional committees, were given powerful weapons with which to pursue their objectives.

Just as Watergate confirmed distrust of politicians, it elevated journalists who had fought against corruption. Although Woodward and Bernstein were not the first to practice this new style of journalism, they embodied the new adversarial style. Their role in uncovering the scandal legitimated the new outlook. Their popularity soared after they became the subject of a popular film starring Robert Redford and Dustin Hoffman. They were even credited with causing a marked increase in applications to journalism schools across the country.

The Watergate crisis hit as the nation underwent a serious economic decline. High rates of inflation, high unemployment, and an oil crisis crippled the national economy. Whereas unprecedented rates of economic growth in the postwar years had buttressed public trust in government, rapid economic decline in the 1970s fueled general disillusionment. The government appeared incapable of sustaining a strong economy forever, and the era of endless growth came to a dramatic halt. The stagnant economy intensified the impact of Watergate as Americans searched for villains in government to explain the decline.

Although Watergate received more attention than any other political scandal of the time, Congress had its own problems in the 1970s. Partly this was the work of liberal Democrats and public-interest reformers who sought to weaken the committee chairmen who ruled Congress, most of whom were southern Democrats, and to eliminate the secrecy that surrounded the legislative process. Until 1974, the established leadership was able to protect committee leaders from being deposed.

Then, in the early hours of October 7, 1974, the Washington Park Police stopped House Ways and Means Committee Chairman Wilbur Mills's (D-Ark.) speeding car near the Tidal Basin. One of his fellow passengers, Annabel Battistella, a stripper who performed locally as "Fanne Fox, the Argentine Firecracker," jumped out of the car and into the Tidal Basin. A cameraman captured the arrest on film. The media, now attuned to scandal, reported that Battistella was having an affair with Mills and that Mills had been an alcoholic and was also addicted to prescription drugs. Although Mills won reelection in November 1974, he could not control his drinking. In December, before shocked members of the media, Mills staggered onto the stage during Battistella's first public appearance in a Boston strip club. As chairman of the powerful Ways and Means Committee, a stronghold of congressional power, Mills had been able to subvert many reforms in the House. But the day after Mills's Boston debacle, House Democrats divested Ways and Means of its power to assign members to committees and ended rules that helped them control the legislative process. The Democratic leadership forced Mills to step down from the chairmanship.

Emboldened by Mills's downfall and by the success of liberal Democrats in the November election, freshmen moved against other powerful senior chairmen. In 1975, seventy-five freshmen Democrats took over the Democratic Caucus by removing three older congressional leaders from committee chairmanships, including Wright Patman (D-Tex.), chairman of the Banking, Currency and Housing Committee; W. R. Poage (D-Tex.), chairman of the Agriculture Committee; and F. Edward Hebert (D-La.), chairman of the Armed Services Committee. In 1975 and 1976, further reforms decreased the power of committees and opened deliberations to the public. Representatives began to challenge norms of deference by frequently proposing floor amendments, an indication that the tenor of Congress had changed. Scandal brought down other prominent legislators, such as Ohio Democrat Wayne Hays, who was chairman of the House Administration Committee and of the Democratic Congressional Campaign Committee (DCCC), which distributed campaign funds to Democratic candidates.

The concern about the personal behavior of congressman was fueled in part by the feminist movement of the 1970s. Growing out of the argument that the "personal was political," public officials were expected to uphold certain standards of conduct. Feminists argued that men exercised power through all of their personal relationships, from those in the home to those at the workplace.

To empower women, feminists argued, it was essential to eliminate the type of abusive personal behavior by men that denied women equal standing—and this included males who treated female employees and co-workers as sexual objects. Charges were leveled with more frequency than ever before. The charges emerged as these types of issues became prevalent in workplaces across America. The rapid influx of women into journalism during the 1970s heightened awareness of these concerns within the profession. While the interest in the private behavior of politicians was rooted in liberalism, the emerging grassroots conservative movement also made private behavior a major issue. Based on Christian fundamentalism, moral conservatives claimed that morally virtuous conduct should be expected from those who held government office. While the impetus for policing private behavior emerged from the left, the right joined in as well.

These post-Watergate reforms of the mid-1970s made Congress far more volatile. As the infrastructure upon which senior leaders was eroded, young renegade legislators were freer to pursue their own agendas. Moreover, "sunshine laws" opened many congressional hearings to the public. Without norms discouraging younger members from speaking to the media, the Sunday morning talk shows provided ambitious legislators with another national forum.

The conservative movement that flourished in the 1970s thrived in this atmosphere, and the Republican legislators associated with the movement used scandal effectively to advance their political objectives. Given that the central message of conservatism revolved around distrust in the federal government, persistent attacks on politicians as personally and politically corrupt meshed with their broader message. Nowhere was this clearer than with Newt Gingrich (R-Ga.). A young Gingrich, elected in 1978, used the new cable station C-SPAN to gain the attention of voters through special order speeches. Gingrich's combative style, well suited to television, featured the explicit use of scandal as a partisan weapon. While rising to power, Gingrich showed no respect for congressional hierarchies. Speaker Tip O'Neill complained that party discipline had gone "out the window," adding, "New members once were seen and not heard, but now it seemed that even the lowliest freshman could be a power in the House."[5] Conditions became more volatile as centrists disappeared from Congress over the next two decades. Both Democrats and Republicans elected officials who were at the far side of the political spectrum, while moderates retired or were defeated. Government leaders moved farther to the extremes of the political spectrum, while voters remained squarely in the middle.[6] Over the next two decades, moreover, a larger number of elected officials would come from the baby boom generation, which grew up in an era of low trust in government institutions. As a result, they tended to display less reverence for the institutions than their predecessors.

IN SCANDAL WE TRUST, 1978–1992

The 1970s witnessed a sea change in political style that gradually encouraged the latent tendency of democratic politics to veer into scandal. A system that was more porous, more partisan, and subject to more intense oversight combined with a political culture that, by the 1980s, had become obsessed with corruption. There were many reasons that politicians, as they had in the past, turned to scandal warfare in the era of Ronald Reagan. One was that skyrocketing deficits and sacrosanct entitlements, such as social security, resulted in reduced levels of discretionary funds.[7] This, combined with a conservative movement that made it difficult to contemplate starting any programs, meant that the federal government could not really undertake new initiatives. Without as many policy issues on the agenda, especially as the Cold War came to a conclusion, politicians turned to scandal to distinguish themselves.

Another reason behind the renewed interest in scandal was the revitalization of partisanship in the 1980s and 1990s that resulted from two internally homogeneous parties that were eager to tear their opponents apart through these sorts of attacks. As southern conservatives fled the Democratic Party and northeastern liberals abandoned the GOP, both parties moved toward the extremes of the political spectrum and left behind a polarized Washington. There was little room left for anyone seeking a middle ground. Republicans attacked Democrats as the party of bloated bureaucracies, government handouts, cultural hedonism, high taxes, and spineless pacifism. Democrats accused Republicans of favoring tax cuts for the wealthy, privileging puritanical moralism, and recklessly using military power at the expense of international support. Without either party able to maintain complete, long-term control of the federal government, scandal warfare was instrumental in their efforts to gain political ground.

When the politicians made the decision to pursue scandal warfare, there was little to restrain them. Most Americans had grown distrustful of government. According to one Gallup poll, in 1964 80 percent of the American people trusted Washington officials to "do what is right all or most of the time." By 1994, less than 20 percent felt the same. Whereas in the 1970s reformers accepted the need for government but distrusted those elected to lead it, conservatives in the 1980s trusted neither the politicians nor the government. Bureaucrats became the equivalent of the nineteenth-century robber baron.

Even norms of privacy were under strain as more Americans were subjected to monitoring within their own workplace. In the 1980s, for example, more than two million private-sector employees or job applicants were asked to take lie-detector tests or were made subject to drug testing, a consequence of the Reagan administration's vaunted "just say no" policies. In 1989, the Supreme Court legalized drug testing for a large percentage of federal employees. By the 1990s, employer monitoring reached new levels through the surveillance of email correspondence and internet usage.[8] New regulations subjected personal activities between male and female employees to official sanction. As citizens came under greater scrutiny, they became more willing to pry into lives of political figures as well.

Not only had the pressures against scandal diminished, but reformers of the 1970s had actually created institutions to pursue corruption. The clearest example was the independent prosecutor. Each administration after Jimmy Carter's came under nearly constant legal scrutiny. Despite concerted efforts by Republicans to allow the independent prosecutor law to expire, Democrats kept extending the law. The largest investigation directed by Independent Prosecutor Lawrence Walsh took place during the second term of President Ronald Reagan. Walsh launched a multimillion dollar investigation of the National Security Council, learning that senior Reagan administration staffer Lt. Col. Oliver North and National Security Advisor John Poindexter had secretly traded weapons to Iran for hostages and cash. The money was then given to fund anticommunist opponents of Nicaragua's Sandinista government, despite a congressional ban on such activities. Although investigators failed to turn up firm proof that Reagan had knowledge of the most damaging violations, congressional hearings were held on what came to be known as the Iran-Contra affair. The hearings, broadcast on cable television, generated mixed reactions. While some citizens became disenchanted with the Republican administration for these secret activities, others sympathized with the accused or perceived the independent prosecutor as overzealous.

The independent prosecutor was not the only unelected official directing investigations into official corruption. The Federal Bureau of Investigation (FBI) turned away from fighting anticommunism and civil dissent and launched highly publicized investigations of bribery among congressmen. In 1980, the FBI rented a house in Washington, D.C., where FBI officers disguised themselves as Arab employees of a Middle Eastern oil sheik. Six congressmen were convicted of accepting bribes in the so-called Abscam affair.

Politicians were increasingly brought down for actions that once eluded scrutiny. Conflict-of-interest rules adopted in the 1970s criminalized many once-routine activities. House Ways and Means Chairman Dan Rostenkowski (D-Ill.) was the first to face a criminal indictment for violating House rules. He was charged with employing family friends and misusing House mailing privileges. One congressman explained that Rostenkowski, who came to the House in the 1950s, foolishly continued to use the same rules in the 1990s: "The standards changed and he didn't change with them."[9]

Supreme Court nominations also became part of the landscape of scandal warfare. Senate Democrats derailed President Reagan's 1987 nomination of Judge

Robert Bork through an intense interest-group campaign that focused on Bork's ideological biases and character rather than on his record as a jurist. Opponents painted Bork as an unlikable character who was unsympathetic to African Americans, other ethnic minorities, and women. They went so far as to leak to the press records of Bork's video rentals. The Senate voted 42–58 against his confirmation, and the saga gave rise to a new term, "to be borked," meaning to be subject to a confirmation process that fails as a result of character assassination. Reagan's next nominee, Judge Douglas Ginsburg, fell to defeat in November 1987 following revelations that he had occasionally smoked marijuana in the 1960s and 1970s. "Unfortunately," Ginsburg said, "all the attention has been focused on our personal lives, and much of that on events of many years ago. My views on the law and on what kind of Supreme Court justice I would make have been drowned out in the clamor." Democratic presidential contenders Senator Albert Gore Jr. of Tennessee and Arizona governor Bruce Babbitt immediately felt the need to acknowledge that they, too, had smoked marijuana. "I'd much rather be here talking about arms control or the stock market crash," Gore quipped.[10]

Higher standards of sexual behavior undid other politicians. Senator Robert Packwood (R-Ore.), chairman of the Senate Finance Committee, was forced to resign on allegations of sexual harassment, and Senator John Tower (D-Tex.) failed to be confirmed as secretary of defense because of charges of alcoholism and womanizing. In 1991, the military experienced its own scandal. That year, eighty-three women reported being assaulted and harassed at the thirty-fifth annual convention of the Tailhook Association, a private group whose members and activities were associated with the U.S. Navy. More than a hundred officers were implicated, with almost half fined or disciplined. Secretary of the Navy Lawrence H. Garrett III resigned.

It was clear to those whose careers were damaged that scandal politics had been thoroughly institutionalized. When politicians turned to scandal in the 1980s, they discovered an environment highly conducive to these tactics. In fact, the environment often drove politicians into scandal politics rather than vice versa.

TELEVISING SCANDAL: 1980–1996

Another powerful force in this new environment was a communications industry that exploited scandal for its own institutional interests. Television had gradually become the primary medium through which Americans obtained their news. But in the 1980s, television itself changed with cable, where each channel targeted narrow segments of the population. By 1987, more than two-thirds of the population had access to cable television. The advent and widespread distribution of remote controls, which allowed viewers to easily switch channels from their seats, facilitated this proliferation of channels.

From the start, cable television and politics were linked. In 1980, entrepreneur Ted Turner launched the Cable News Network (CNN). CNN broadcast news twenty-four hours a day. By 1985, CNN claimed 2.5 million viewing households. CNN's constant news cycle obliged reporters to search for new material incessantly. Satellite technology enabled networks to broadcast a story immediately from anywhere in the world. The turning point for CNN came in 1991 with its coverage of the Gulf War. Slickly packaged as a show, not just news, that coverage led the cable channels to envision unprecedented strategies for presenting news events as entertainment. With the rapid speed with which stories made it onto the air, network editors and producers had difficulty controlling the release of information, and journalists and politicians alike were often caught off guard by events as they were unfolding.

Cable also brought fierce programming competition between the major firms in the news industry (even as economic competition diminished through corporate consolidation). In the two decades that followed the creation of CNN, news channels and shows proliferated at a brisk pace. NBC, for example, launched two twenty-four-hour cable news stations, CNBC and MSNBC. Specialized channels such as the Christian Broadcast Network devoted time to political news as well. The traditional networks increased the number of news shows. Nighttime programs such as *Nightline* and *Dateline*, as well as live broadcasts of breaking events, allowed the networks to compete with cable. While the original news shows of the 1960s centered on hosts reading dry descriptions of daily events, cable-era news revolved around celebrity hosts openly challenging their guests. NBC pundit Tim Russert warned, "With satellites, everyone now has access to the same pictures and sound bites, and news becomes old with amazing speed, things have changed; networks are feeling the competition. We've become more aggressive. . . . 10 or 15 years ago, the networks acted as if there was a tacit agreement to be 'highbrow' in their definition of news. Now we've got *Geraldo, Inside Edition, Current Affair,* and *Entertainment Tonight.* Will their presence drive us, consciously or unconsciously, to gravitate toward more sex and scandal coverage?"[11]

The line between "highbrow" news and "popular" entertainment shows began to blur. In 1992, Democratic presidential candidate Bill Clinton went on a late-night show to play saxophone while joking with young viewers of the cable music station MTV about his underwear. Independent Ross Perot circumvented the traditional political media by speaking directly to voters through Larry King's CNN talk show.

Computer technology had a similar effect. The spread of the Internet in the 1990s expanded the number of outlets producing the news around the clock.

Networks, magazines, individuals, and political organizations established Web sites through which they published news the moment it happened. By the 1990s, the Internet allowed information to be conveyed directly to computer users without the intermediary institutions of news organizations. The resources required to maintain Web sites were minimal compared to traditional forms of communication. There was almost no control, moreover, over who could establish a site. As the price of personal computers plummeted, more Americans obtained access to the information the Internet provided. In this atmosphere, the speed at which information was disseminated accelerated exponentially as did the media's desperate search to find original material that could attract viewers.

Newspapers struggled to compete. Many city papers closed down, while family-owned publications were bought out by large multimedia conglomerates. The slow production speed of print news constituted a serious structural problem. By the time newspapers hit the stands, their news was often stale. In response, newspapers emulated the style of television. With its premier in 1983, *USA Today*, using color pictures and two-paragraph articles, published sensational stories previously reserved for tabloids or entertainment magazines. Many newspapers followed suit to attract readers. They also upgraded their Web-based operations.

In this hypercompetitive environment, political scandal offered all parties a subject that would attract viewers. Scandals blurred the lines between news and entertainment. Like television drama, scandals were easily understood and dramatic enough to capture viewer attention. Scandals offered heroes and villains in easily understood stories that unfolded in dramatic fashion.

The appeal of scandal was not limited to politics. The 1980s and 1990s were an era where scandal saturated all aspects of American culture. Televangelist Jim Bakker lost his multimillion-dollar empire in 1987 because of his sexual relationship with a young woman. The media could seemingly not get enough of real estate mogul Donald Trump's sexual trysts or the illicit financial schemes of Wall Street financier Michael Milken. Ordinary citizens were caught up in the action as well. Americans became familiar with Lorena Bobbitt, who cut off her husband's penis after he physically abused her. Another citizen celebrity was Mary Jo Buttafuoco, shot in 1992 by a seventeen-year-old with whom her husband had been having an affair. Nothing earned better ratings, of course, than celebrity scandal. Whereas Americans were uncomfortable watching even a modicum of sexuality in 1950s cinema, in 1995 millions tuned to a late-night talk show when the popular British actor Hugh Grant discussed his arrest for soliciting a prostitute. The entire country was mesmerized by the daily coverage of former professional football player O. J. Simpson's 1995 trial for the murder of his ex-wife and a friend of hers. Each scandal pushed the boundaries of what stories were legitimate "news."

Throughout television, film, radio, and print, sex was presented more frequently and more explicitly. While reporting on Lorena Bobbitt, for example, newscasters started to use the word "penis." The news was, at times, equally salacious. One lurid scandal was launched on June 30, 1982, when *CBS Evening News* broadcast a story featuring a young page who claimed that he had organized a homosexual prostitution ring for congressmen and himself had sex with a prominent member; the other said that he had been sexually harassed. As other news outlets flocked to the story, the charges escalated to include widespread cocaine use among congressmen. Although a House Ethics Committee revealed that most of the charges were untrue, it also discovered that two congressmen, Gerry Studds (D-Mass.) and Daniel Crane (R-Ill.), had had sexual relationships with pages. The House censured both.

Sexual behavior was featured during the Supreme Court confirmation of Clarence Thomas in 1991. Anita Hill confidentially told the Senate Judiciary Committee that Thomas had sexually harassed her when she worked for him. Although he never threatened her for spurning his advances, Hill claimed that Thomas's sexual innuendo had created a hostile work environment. One week before the Senate committee was to vote on Thomas's confirmation, Nina Totenberg of National Public Radio and Timothy Phelps of *Newsday* revealed Hill's accusation to the public. Feminist organizations called on the Senate to reject Thomas. Conservatives claimed that Thomas was being persecuted for his conservative beliefs. Hill and Thomas testified during the final hearings, which were broadcast live, and featured frank discussions of Thomas's pornographic tastes and details of his alleged comments to Hill. The Senate confirmed Thomas, but by a narrow vote.

The impact of television was evident in elections. Candidates now communicated directly to voters through television. As they did, the interests of the news media played more of a role in structuring campaigns. This was important, since reporters focused on the competition itself rather than the policies, ideas, or issues in question. By covering campaigns as horse races, reporters were especially drawn to the revelatory scandal that would decide the election. The correlation was simple: because television had a bigger role in campaigns, and scandal was important to television, scandals became more influential in campaigns. Some prominent candidates were destroyed by them. During the 1987 Democratic primaries for president, for example, the *Miami Herald* alleged that Gary Hart, a former senator from Colorado, was having an affair with a young model. Hart challenged the media to prove their allegations. Soon after, the *National Inquirer* obtained pictures of a young model named Donna Rice sitting on Hart's lap on a yacht named *Monkey Business*. Once the pictures were published, Hart dropped out of the race, even though no connection between his private actions and his professional conduct had been demonstrated.

Not all scandals, though, were about sex. Walter Mondale's vice presidential nominee, Geraldine Ferraro, was subject to a ferocious media attack in the 1984 campaign. Reporters accused her husband of unethical business transactions that included Mafia connections. Senator Joseph Biden's (D-Del.) campaign for the Democratic nomination in 1988 failed in part because of evidence that he plagiarized speeches from Neil Kinnock, the leader of Britain's Labour party.

Yet the media often refrained from covering scandals that lacked simplicity or drama. The most notable "missed" scandal involved the savings and loan industry. After Congress deregulated the industry in the early 1980s, savings and loans officials made highly risky investments in order to gain quick profits. Several congressmen had received campaign contributions from industry officials who had profited from deregulation, but who continued to be protected by federal subsidies for investment losses. The financial crisis, which cost the government (and taxpayers) as much as $150 billion, involved top law firms, elected politicians, and two government agencies. Yet it took years for the story to make the news.

The news industry had thus undergone a dramatic transformation between 1980, when Ted Turner founded CNN, and 1996, when NBC launched MSNBC in partnership with the Microsoft Corporation. The reconstructed industry, defined by cable television and the Internet, was sympathetic to scandal politics and offered unlimited airtime to broadcast these stories. While ideological changes in journalism had pushed reporters toward an investigative outlook in the 1970s, it was the structural reconfiguration of the news industry that cemented a decisive shift toward scandal politics.

THE IMPEACHMENT OF BILL CLINTON, 1997–1999

The era of scandal politics culminated with the impeachment of President William Jefferson Clinton in 1999. Since he first ran for the presidency, Clinton had been under investigation. During his 1992 campaign, allegations of an affair with Gennifer Flowers broke right before the crucial New Hampshire primary. Clinton effectively responded by appearing with his wife Hillary on CBS's *60 Minutes*. But during his first term, the investigations continued. The Justice Department appointed independent prosecutors to investigate a questionable real estate transaction that took place while he was governor of Arkansas and to look into the controversial firing of the White House travel office staff. The suicide of Deputy White House Counsel Vincent Foster, a friend of the Clintons, prompted speculation about corruption in high office. When Republicans took over both the House and Senate in 1994, the president's situation deteriorated.

Between 1995 and 1998, the Republican Congress conducted thirty-seven investigations into the White House. Nonetheless, Clinton and his cabinet survived each investigation, partly due to the failure of prosecutors to uncover sufficient evidence and partly because of his staff's skillful use of the media. One notable challenge took place in his 1996 reelection campaign when the tabloids revealed, on the final day of the Democratic convention, that advisor Dick Morris frequently employed the services of a prostitute. The tabloids printed photographs to prove it. Mainstream news organizations picked up the story immediately. But even this incident did not harm the media-savvy president.

Yet Clinton's fortune took a dramatic turn for the worse in 1997. On May 6, 1994, former Arkansas state employee Paula Jones sued Clinton for sexual harassment. She claimed that three years earlier, Clinton, then governor of the state, had made sexual advances on her in a hotel room. On May 27, 1997, in a landmark decision, the Supreme Court allowed the suit to proceed against the sitting president. Jones's lawyers sought to prove the accusations by showing a pattern of such behavior. When prosecutors added the name of former White House intern Monica Lewinsky to the witness list in December, Clinton became concerned. Judge Susan Webber Wright then ruled that prosecutors could investigate other alleged affairs of the president. On December 17, Clinton suggested to Lewinsky that she could avoid being deposed by filing an affidavit denying an affair. On January 7, 1998, Lewinsky signed an affidavit affirming that she had not been sexually involved with the president. Vernon Jordan, a confidant of Clinton's who had met with Lewinsky earlier, helped her secure a job at the Revlon Corporation the day after she signed the affidavit. On January 17, during his deposition, the interrogators surprised the president by asking him a series of pointed questions about his relation with Lewinsky, the former intern. Clinton emphatically denied having any type of sexual relations with her.

An independent prosecutor was simultaneously investigating the Lewinsky affair. Kenneth Starr, a respected solicitor general and federal appellate-court judge, had been appointed in 1994 to investigate the Clintons' allegedly questionable real estate dealings in Arkansas, which became known as the Whitewater affair. Early in January, Linda Tripp, a Pentagon employee and a friend of Lewinsky, provided Starr with audiotapes of phone conversations in which Lewinsky revealed intimate details of her sexual encounters with the president. Tripp also told Starr that Lewinsky had been offered a job in New York in exchange for her silence. FBI prosecutors and staff from Starr's office confronted Lewinsky in a room at the Ritz-Carlton hotel with evidence that Lewinsky's deposition was untruthful.

On January 21, 1998, the *Washington Post* published the first story on Clinton's affair with Lewinsky. The news media swarmed over the story, which was now driven chiefly by cable television and Internet newscasters such as Matt Drudge and Internet magazines such as *Salon*. Lewinsky found herself at the center of a media hurricane. Journalist Jeffrey Toobin noted that she had become "the object of the most intense media surveillance since O. J. Simpson's dash across Southern California."[12]

Clinton, too, was in trouble. Dick Morris advised Clinton that his polls showed that the public would want him out of office if the affair was true. Taking this advice, the president lied. During a television appearance, Clinton wagged his finger at the camera and denied having sexual interactions with Lewinsky. Clinton also told cabinet officials that the story was not true. Meanwhile, Starr continued his investigation. His staff and the courts gradually whittled away the privileges of the president by forcing secret service agents and White House counsel to testify before the grand jury. No longer did anyone in politics seem beyond the reach of investigation.

The scandal evoked fierce reactions. Republican leaders, determined to make sure the president was punished, recalled that many of their colleagues had been destroyed by similar charges. The Republicans also claimed that perjury and obstruction of justice were serious crimes. In response, Clinton and his staff bombarded the media with claims that the investigation was being driven by cabal of right-wing leaders. From the start, congressional Democrats decided to focus on charging that Republicans were mounting a partisan investigation, rather than challenging the charges themselves. On January 27, the day of the State of the Union address, Hillary Clinton appeared on NBC's *Today* show and blamed her husband's problems on a "vast right-wing conspiracy." While Nixon had attempted to end Archibald Cox's bothersome investigation by firing him, Clinton and his allies undermined Starr's credibility through the media.

In the process of the investigation, Republicans sacrificed one of their own, forcing Speaker Newt Gingrich to resign because of his affair with an aide. On the day of the impeachment vote, his successor, Speaker Robert Livingston (R-LA.), announced on the House floor that he too would resign and called on Clinton to do likewise. It soon emerged that men's magazine publisher Larry Flynt, who had offered a reward for evidence of sexual dalliances by Republicans, was about to reveal Livingston's infidelity.

Scandal politics were creating strange bedfellows. Political organizations did the opposite of what was expected. For two decades, feminists had insisted that male politicians be held accountable for their behavior toward women: but now organizations such as the National Organization of Women headed the lobby against Clinton's impeachment. Conservatives, who had attacked the notion of an independent prosecutor as an extraconstitutional institution, stood behind Starr.

On July 28, 1998, Lewinsky agreed to cooperate with the independent prosecutor and admitted that she had an affair with the president. She produced as evidence an unwashed dress stained with what she claimed was Clinton's semen. DNA tests were conducted. On August 17, 1998, Clinton testified on closed-circuit television to Starr's grand jury and admitted to having "improper relationships" with Lewinsky, but insisted that he had not had sexual relations with her as he defined the term. Soon afterward, Starr's office revealed that DNA tests confirmed that the stain was from the president.

On September 9, 1998, Starr sent a report to Congress, which concluded that the president had twice committed perjury and had obstructed justice by coaching witnesses. In the post-sunshine Congress, most of the evidence from the case was made directly available to the public. On September 21, Congress broadcast the president's grand jury testimony on television. Americans saw crucial evidence before Congress deliberated. Congress also posted on the Internet the Starr report, a lurid document filled with sexual details. On October 8, the House Judiciary Committee, chaired by Henry Hyde (R-Ill.), began its investigation. They were interrupted in November by the midterm elections, in which Republicans suffered unexpected losses, indicating to many observers that the public did not favor impeachment. At the end of November, Judiciary Committee Republicans sent Clinton a list of questions. The president responded defiantly, insisting that he had told the truth to the Jones lawyers and grand jurors. In a fiercely partisan atmosphere, committee members from each party were not talking to each other, let alone negotiating a compromise. On strict party lines, the Judiciary Committee approved four articles of impeachment against Clinton for perjury and obstruction of justice.

Throughout the saga, the worlds of entertainment and politics morphed. Earlier in 1997, director Barry Levinson had released the movie *Wag the Dog*, starring Robert De Niro and Dustin Hoffman. That fictional movie, filmed before the Lewinsky affair had become public, portrayed a secret team of presidential advisors seeking to cover up a president's sexual encounter with a young girl in the White House. In the film, the presidential staff works with a Hollywood producer to deflect media attention by orchestrating a fake war with Albania. Reflecting the realities of the 1990s, De Niro and Hoffman's characters calculate every move based on what television broadcasts. At key moments during the impeachment, Clinton initiated two military conflicts. Cabinet members were forced to deny allegations that Clinton had adopted a *Wag the Dog* strategy.

On December 19, 1998, House Republicans voted to impeach the president. The Senate began its trial on January 7, 1999, and broadcast videotaped witness testimony on February 6, 1999. All deliberations, except the final Senate debate, were on television. Enough Republicans defected from the party line so that the president was not convicted.

The impeachment was a product of the developments that had transformed politics since Vietnam. The investigation was driven by the independent prosecutor, framed by the new sexual norms of the 1970s, and judged within a partisan and televised congressional process. Legislators associated with the conservative movement headed the attack, once again claiming that the leaders of the nation's government were corrupt. Cable and Internet organizations dominated the news coverage of the scandal. In the 1950s, McCarthy had furthered his campaign by taking advantage of a press that reported uncritically the charges he made. But in the 1990s, Democrats and Republicans desperately tried to keep up with the media. The saga also uncovered an uneasiness many Americans had with scandal politics. Many thought that Clinton's actions warranted severe punishment, but simultaneously believed that impeachment was excessive. Yet the volatile political world of the 1990s lacked any mechanism or senior establishment that could achieve compromise. The handful of centrists who agreed with public opinion were no longer influential. Information leaked out of Washington at a rapid pace. While the implications of Clinton's crisis remain unclear, Democrats and Republicans agreed on one issue. The independent prosecutor law was allowed to expire quietly. Almost no one called for its renewal.

The 2000 presidential election offered a fitting end to the post–World War II period. Candidates Al Gore Jr. and George W. Bush squared off in a fierce campaign that revealed a country deeply divided ideologically. The election ended in scandal. After an extremely narrow victory, Democrats questioned whether the voting had been fairly conducted in Florida, a state with a decisive twenty-five electoral votes. Democrats and Republicans squared off in the courts—making the electoral process itself fair game in the scandal wars taking place between the parties—while challenging the vote and fighting over recounts. Democrats charged that Republicans were suppressing votes and disenfranchising citizens, while Republicans argued that Democrats were trying to fabricate votes and discounting votes from groups such as the military. On December 12, the Supreme Court (in a split ruling of 5–4) stopped further recounts in Florida. George W. Bush emerged as president. Allegations of election fraud followed his victory in the 2004 race as well.

A NEW CENTURY?

Although some commentators hoped that the elimination of the independent prosecutor would offer a cure, that seems unlikely. Even the trauma of the terrorist attacks of September 11, 2001, did not prevent the parties from engaging in scandal warfare over all sorts of issues ranging from the conduct of war to ethics and campaign finance. Indeed, by 2006 the Republican majority faced a serious political crisis as a result of scandals revolving around lobbying and corruption. The GOP entered into a political freefall going into the final weeks of the election as a result of a sex scandal centered on a legislator who had exhcanged inappropriate e-mails and text messages with underaged pages.

This should not be a surprise. Scandal politics has become deeply imbedded in the structure and culture of our polity. It was the product of a fundamental reorientation in national politics. The first stage involved a shift in what was to be expected from politicians. A reform movement located in Congress, the media, and public-interest organizations raised the standards of behavior for politicians. To remove decisions from untrustworthy politicians or voters, the movement institutionalized investigation. The reform orientation became appealing within a national culture that distrusted government and in a political era that lacked many issues to debate. Members of the conservative movement jumped on scandal as a way to legitimate their claims about the nature of government. When politicians turned to scandal in the 1980s, they found none of the countervailing forces that had prevented them from taking this path earlier. Combined with these reforms was an important transformation in the news industry resulting from the advent of cable television and Internet-based media. As a result of these large-scale changes, scandal became the principal weapon with which political battles were fought.

The impact of a partisan political system where scandal plays such a prominent role is harmful to the body politic. Partisan-based scandal warfare was important in the nineteenth century, but there was a big difference between the two eras. During the 1800s, parties truly connected enfranchised citizens to their government. The parties remained central to social life as well as politics; partisan affiliation crucially defined the identities of American citizens. Party organizations maintained close ties to those Americans who had the right to vote, seducing them during campaigns with parades, picnics, and other events that made politics a form of public entertainment. Parties also used heavy-handed tactics: supplying voters with liquor, intimidating them, even offering outright bribes. The hurly-burly of nineteenth-century democracy led to high voter turnout (among those eligible to vote) and strong party loyalties. Americans identified with the party to which their families belonged and maintained a strong sense of allegiance to these groups. In a nation of joiners, partisan ties overlapped with other associations—church memberships, fraternal organizations, veterans groups, social clubs, ethnic networks, labor unions, and reform societies.

By the end of the twentieth century, however, those affiliations had thinned. Campaigns centered on individual candidates; parties often functioned as fundraising mechanisms rather than sources of political mobilization. Low rates of voter turnout signaled just how many Americans remained alienated from their government and the political process. Party affiliation mattered only on Election Day, if even then. Democracy, according to one expert, had become more like a "kind of consumer good and spectator sport" than an exercise in civic participation.[13]

Today parties are quite strong in influencing politicians and organized interest groups, but they no longer involve Americans in government on a regular basis. The result is a rancorous political system where it is difficult to find compromise and where there is little room for constructive negotiation. Parties devastate each other through scandal warfare, while disaffected citizens watch the ugliest aspects of their system with disgust. Worse yet, the system does not have the beneficial nineteenth-century effect of integrating average people into the political process. We now have intense partisan polarization without durable grassroots connections to political parties; a deeply divided nation watches polarized politicians with whom they feel little identification or trust. In this respect, the dynamics of scandal are very different today from those in previous eras.

The future of scandal politics remains unclear. Some citizens are content with a system that holds politicians accountable and ensures constant surveillance for corruption. Others fear that the prominence of scandal has poisoned relations among political elites to the point that policymaking is impossible. Some of the nation's finest citizens, critics add, refuse to enter into the fray. All of this has become particularly troubling as the nation was thrust into a new dangerous era of warfare after the terrorist attacks against it. What Clinton's impeachment revealed, however, is that eliminating the centrality of scandal would require the nation to reconstruct the processes and culture that have defined national politics since the mid-1960s. Diminishing the role of scandal would likely require bringing back aspects of postwar American politics, such as greater secrecy in the policymaking process and an absence of formal rules governing the behavior of politicians, that were once (and probably remain) unpalatable to a large portion of the American public. Whether citizens have the desire to put the genie back in the bottle will become clear as the new century unfolds.

BIBLIOGRAPHIC NOTE

Despite its importance, few historians have examined the political history of scandal. A handful of political scientists, journalists, and historians have attempted to explain why scandal became so important. The first argument has been that corruption actually increased over time: see Larry L. Berg, Harlan Hahn, and John R. Schidhauser, *Corruption in the American Political System* (1976), and Elizabeth Drew, *The Corruption of American Politics* (1999). Another thesis posits a cyclical process in American history that alternates between periods of corruption and reform; see Abraham S. Eisenstadt, "Political Corruption in American History: Some Further Thoughts," in *Before Watergate*, ed. Abraham S. Eisenstadt, Ari Hoogenboom, and Hans L. Trefousse (1978), 537–556. A third explanation is that politicians were largely responsible because they turned to scandal as an alternative to electoral politics; see Benjamin Ginsberg and Martin Shefter, *Politics by Other Means* (1990). Others claim that specific laws such as the Office of the Independent Prosecutor created a destructive "culture" of distrust; see Suzanne Garment, *Scandal* (1991). One work locates the source of scandal in presidential morality: Charles W. Dunn, *The Scarlet Thread of Scandal* (2000). Finally, John Summers, in an article focusing on why sexual scandal vanished as an issue after the nineteenth century, suggests that the fragmentation of journalism and diminished trust in government produced a return of scandal in politics after its long absence: John H. Summers, "What Happened to Sexual Scandals? Politics and Peccadilloes, Jefferson to Kennedy," *Journal of American History* (2000): 825–854.

None of these arguments is entirely satisfactory. There is scant evidence, for example, that the amount of corruption actually increased over time. A cyclical model fails to explain why scandal has been consistently prevalent over the last twenty-five years. While politicians have turned to scandal warfare as an alternative to electoral competition, this argument does not explain why similar strategies were less effective earlier in the postwar period or were eventually stifled. Finally, scandal intensified before the creation of the independent prosecutor. In fact, the law was reflective of a political culture distrustful of politics, rather than the instigator of change.

Like any synthetic work, this chapter relies on a large body of research conducted by historians, political scientists, and journalists to piece together my story. It also grows out of archival research that I have been undertaking for a new book on the transformation of Congress after World War II. A sizable volume of scholarship has documented declining trust in American political institutions since the 1960s: see Hugh Heclo, "The Sixties' False Dawn: Awakenings, Movements, and Postmodern Policy-making," *Journal of Policy History* (1996): 34–63. *Why People Don't Trust Government*, eds. Joseph S. Nye, Jr., Philip D. Zelikow, and David C. King (1997); and E. J. Dionne Jr., *Why Americans Hate Politics* (1991). Work on scandals during the Truman period tend to be more descriptive than analytical; see Irwin F. Gellman, *The Contender* (1999), 372–390, and Andrew Dunar, *The Truman Scandals and the Politics of Morality* (1984). The best treatment of scandal in this period links anticommunism to partisan politics; see Robert Griffith, *The Politics of Fear: Joseph R. McCarthy and the Senate*, 2nd ed. (1970). There has also been work explaining how ethics laws were institutionalized, particularly the independent prosecutor; see Robert N. Roberts, *White House Ethics* (1988); Terry Eastland, *Ethics, Politics, and the Independent Counsel* (1989); Katy J. Harriger, *Independent Justice* (1992); and

Martin and Susan J. Tolchin, *Glass Houses* (2001). James T. Patterson, *Grand Expectations* (1996), and Michael A. Bernstein and David E. Adler, *Understanding American Economic Decline* (1994), have analyzed the relationship between economic conditions and public attitudes toward government.

Political scientists, sociologists, and journalists have provided excellent accounts of how media practices changed since the advent of television. They have tended to focus on how the commercial structure of the media impacted the type of news presented as well as the emergence of aggressive, watchdog journalism in the 1970s. Moreover, these observers have traced how investigative journalism eventually transformed into news presented as quasi-entertainment. See Larry J. Sabato, *Feeding Frenzy* (1991); Austin Ranney, "Broadcasting, Narrowcasting, and Politics," in *The New American Political System*, ed. Anthony King (1990),175–201; Michael Schudson, *Discovering the News* (1978); Stephen Hess, *Live from Capitol Hill!* (1991); Martin Mayer, *Making News* (1987); Timothy E. Cook, *Governing with the News* (1998); Thomas E. Patterson, *Out of Order* (1993); Howard Kurtz, *Media Circus* (1993) and *Spin Cycle* (1998); Bartholomew H. Sparrow, *Uncertain Guardians* (1999); Nancy E. Bernhard, *U.S. Television News and Cold War Propaganda, 1947–1960* (1999); and John B. Thompson, *Political Scandal* (2000).

Political scientists spent a considerable amount of energy examining the reforms of the 1970s, with particular interest in the breakdown of an older system dominated by economic interest groups and machine-based political parties: Jeffrey M. Berry, *Lobbying for the People* (1977); Andrew S. McFarland, *Common Cause* (1984); Nelson W. Polsby, *Consequences of Party Reform* (1976); Byron E. Shafer, *Quiet Revolution* (1983); Sidney M. Milkis, *Political Parties and Constitutional Government* (1999). Furthermore, political scientists have examined the disintegration of the committee-based congressional system. Among the books that deal with this are Steve Smith, *Call to Order* (1989); Randall Strahan, *New Ways and Means* (1990); Roger H. Davidson and Walter J. Oleszek, *Congress Against Itself* (1979); Leroy N. Rieselbach, *Congressional Reform: The Changing Modern Congress* (1994); and Julian E. Zelizer, *On Capitol Hill: The Struggle to Reform Congress and Its Consequences, 1948–2000* (2004).

The best place to start any examination of scandal during the postwar period would be the two presidential scandals that have received the greatest attention, namely, those surrounding Richard Nixon and Bill Clinton. The books on Nixon debate how much of the scandal was the product of Nixon himself versus the institution of the presidency. The work on Clinton, given its recentness, has tended to be descriptive, although it has tried to situate the drama within the political context of the 1990s. My account relies on Stanley I. Kutler, *The Wars of Watergate* (1990); Fred Emery, *Watergate* (1995); Michael Schudson, *Watergate in American Memory* (1992); Richard Posner, *An Affair of State* (1999); and Peter Baker, *The Breach* (2000).

NOTES

1. Ronald Brownstein, "Life in the Time of Scandal," *U.S. News & World Report*, 27 April 1998, 15.

2. Thomas E. Patterson, "The United States: News in a Free-Market Society," in *Democracy and the Media: A Comparative Perspective*, ed. Richard Gunther and Anthony Mughan (New York: Cambridge University Press, 2000), 250–251.

3. Cited in Larry J. Sabato, *Feeding Frenzy: How Attack Journalism Has Transformed American Politics* (New York: Free Press, 1991), 31.

4. Michael Shudson, *Watergate in American Memory: How We Remember, Forget, and Reconstruct the Past* (New York: Basic Books, 1992), 88–90.

5. Tip O'Neill with William Novak, *Man of the House: The Life and Political Memoirs of Speaker Tip O'Neill* (New York: Random House, 1987), 282–284.

6. David C. King, "The Polarization of American Parties and Mistrust of Government," in *Why People Don't Trust Government*, ed. Joseph S. Nye Jr., Philip D. Zelikow, and David C. King (Cambridge, Mass.: Harvard University Press, 1997), 155–178; Sarah A. Binder, "The Disappearing Political Center: Congress and the Incredible Shrinking Middle," *Brookings Review* 14 (1996): 36–39.

7. C. Eugene Steuerle, "Financing the American State at the Turn of the Century," in *Funding the Modern American State, 1941–1995: The Rise and Fall of the Era of Easy Finance*, ed. W. Elliot Brownlee (New York: Cambridge University Press, 1996), 409–444.

8. Philippa Strum, *Privacy* (New York: Harcourt Brace, 1998), 1–21.

9. Cited in Richard E. Cohen, *Rostenkowski: The Pursuit of Power and the End of the Old Politics* (Chicago: Ivan R. Dee, 1999), 246.

10. Dennis Hevesi, "Drug Use Emerges as Campaign Issue," and "Judge Ginsburg's Statement," *New York Times*, 8 November 1987.

11. Cited in Suzanne Garment, *Scandal: The Culture of Mistrust in American Politics* (New York: Doubleday, 1991), 69–70.

12. Jeffrey Toobin, "The Secret War in Starr's Office," *New Yorker*, 15 November 1999, 72.

13. Todd S. Purdum, "The Year of Passion," *New York Times*, 31 October 2004.

12. TELEVISION, DEMOCRACY, AND
PRESIDENTIAL POLITICS

RICK SHENKMAN

At the opening of the twentieth century, Americans confidently welcomed change. They thrilled at the possibility of taking flight in an airplane or traveling across the country in an automobile. They marveled at the discovery of radio waves and expectantly awaited the day that they could listen to music transmitted wirelessly from concert halls located thousands of miles away. To be sure, not all of the changes of the new century looked promising, communism in Russia being the most obtrusive example. But Americans expected the greatest changes to involve technology, and they viewed these as almost wholly positive. Despite the challenging problems new technologies inevitably wrought, problems as mundane as traffic congestion and as troubling as automobile pollution and radioactive fallout, Americans stubbornly clung to the belief that their country could successfully absorb anything engineers and scientists devised—and not only absorb it, but also become better for it. Technology would even enhance American democracy, giving ordinary people the power only the wealthy formerly had possessed to control both time and space, improving the lot of the masses while reducing the gap between them and the rich. Through technology, average Americans could enjoy elite perquisites: music at dinner, fast rides through the country, vacations in distant places.

Americans' faith in technology was boundless. One is tempted to compare it with the faith their forebears had placed in religion; not dissimilarly, the faith in technology came to be associated with miracles. What was radio—this device that snatched from the air unseen waves of sound—but an awe-inspiring godsend, after all? And radio was just the beginning of an expected revolution in mass media. As early as 1930 the *New York Times* promised that soon one would be able to reproduce facsimiles of pictures, photographs, "or even a complete page in a newspaper, instantaneously, through space." Most astonishing of all, soon it would be possible to transmit moving pictures, too, through a device now known as "television." Some considered the word, a cross between the Greek *tele* and the Latin *visio*, "seen from afar," a boorish monstrosity—a portent? In defense of the neologism, the *New York Times* editorialized that "television" would at least be readily understood by the "man on the street." From its birth, television would be justified by its appeal to the masses.

Television is usually identified with the second half of the twentieth century, when it went into commercial production and became a central factor in American daily life and politics. But it was in the first half that the expectations for the new medium were acquired. Only by examining those expectations, openly and naively expressed, can the gaping chasm that eventually opened between expectation and reality be gauged accurately.

The dream of television had enchanted inventors since the late nineteenth century. As the new century began not one of the many people working on the device in Europe or the United States was close to success. Yet failure was inconceivable. In early 1925, the *Times* observed that while television was as yet only a dream, "such dreams have come true so often in recent years that if this one does nobody will be much surprised." A few months later, the *Times*—publishing the first of many front-page stories about television—disclosed that Washington inventor C. Francis Jenkins had televised pictures of a windmill at a radio station near Anacostia "and broadcast them to his studio 5 miles away on Connecticut Avenue." Two years later came news that Bell Laboratories had demonstrated a device that flashed pictures of human beings on a screen while simultaneously broadcasting their voices via radio. In 1928, amateur inventor Philo T. Farnsworth, the son of a Utah farmer, remembering the straight lines formed by the plowed fields of his youth, produced a television image by scanning a picture line by line in rapid succession.

Television was not yet near commercial development. But in the atmosphere of the still-roaring twenties, people fantasized extravagantly. In 1929 a headline in the *New York Times* even dared ask if television might "be ready for the next inaugural." It would not, but the technology was developing so quickly that by 1930 experimental station W2XAF, operating from Long Island, was able to broadcast a "rectangular design painted in black on a white card" to a receiver in Sydney, Australia. Amazingly, as the papers noted, many times during the five-minute experiment "the lines of the rectangle were distinct enough for observers to distinguish the picture being broadcast."

No invention held out more promise of dramatic and exciting change, none seemed more profoundly emblematic of the future, than television. As science-fiction writer Hugo Gernsback cheered in 1918, television "would revolutionize our present mode of living."[1] Throughout the 1920s, as technical developments brought television closer to reality, people were enthusiastic about the changes it would bring. The inventor who had broadcast pictures of a windmill predicted "that someday audiences would be able to see prize fights and baseball games" on television. Military officials expressed the hope that television would revolutionize warfare, allowing generals to monitor battles from cameras mounted on airplanes flying overhead. The *New York Times* foresaw that one day television would be the "greatest home entertainer ever devised for young and old alike." David Sarnoff, the head of the Radio Corporation of America (RCA), wrote that television would bring culture, such as the treasures of the Louvre, into the homes of the masses.

Excitement at the prospect of television survived even the arrival of the Great Depression. Though the shortage of financial resources hampered the development of television technology, if anything the medium loomed ever more important as a promising symbol of the prosperity people hoped was just around the corner. As the unemployment lines lengthened, leading figures began making predictions about the speed with which television would arrive, stirring even the unemployed with visions of the new America slowly coming into view. "I am confident," Sarnoff wrote in 1930, "that in less than five years you will be able to receive images through space as well as you are able to receive sound through space at the present time." That same year inventor Lee De Forest imagined that within half a century Americans would "see and hear everything of national interest in the home. Man will have plenty of leisure." Accurately foreseeing the development of cable television, he emphasized that "we will eventually go to the theater by television over a wire line. We will be seated at home in easy chairs with our families and see everything that is worth seeing."

Nothing that promised to change society as dramatically as television could long remain outside the purview of American politics. Beginning in the late 1920s, from the president of the United States on down, Americans began to calculate the effect the new medium would have on voters and elections. In 1932 Colonel Theodore Roosevelt Jr., governor general of the Philippines and son of the late president, struck a common theme, emphasizing television's democratic possibilities. Television, he predicted, would "stir the nation to a lively interest in those who are directing its policies and in the policies themselves" by bringing politics into the home. "The result," he foresaw, "will normally be that we may expect more intelligent, more concerted action from an electorate; the people will think more for themselves and less simply at the direction of local members of the political machines."[2]

Decades later, many would come to regard television's effect upon politics as harmful. At this early stage, however, few outside the academy expressed any misgivings. The expectation was that television would change politics for the better, though there might be some missteps along the way, as there had been with radio. In 1916, De Forest, broadcasting the presidential election returns to a handful of ham-radio operators, had falsely announced that Charles Evans Hughes had defeated Woodrow Wilson, but the mishap had barely registered.[3] What was considered significant was not what was said over the radio but that anything was said at all. Just four years later radio redeemed itself by expertly broadcasting the political conventions, allowing Americans, in a startling democratic development, to hear what happened at these once-sequestered events. That November, upon its debut, Pittsburgh station KDKA, the first to receive a federal license, broadcast the returns of the Harding-Cox contest to an audience of thousands. This time the new medium got the election results right. Two years later, radio gave the American people the new thrill of hearing their president via the airwaves, which helped link the voters to their elected leader in a new and presumably deeper way. By the 1928 election, a scant eight years after KDKA's inaugural broadcast, radio had fundamentally transformed American politics. Campaigns, once mainly fought in the open air, now were waged on the radio, politicians no longer screaming their way through their speeches. As the *New York Times* observed, the "tearing of hair or stamping of feet" was now out.

Radio became so powerful that Congress acted quickly to guarantee that the medium remained available to a wide spectrum of political voices. Section 315 of the Communications Act of 1934 stated: "If any licensee shall permit any person who is a legally qualified candidate for any public office to use a broadcasting station, he shall afford equal opportunities to all other such candidates for that office." When a station in 1936 refused to allow Communist presidential candidate Earl Browder to go on the air, the Federal Communications Commission investigated. Franklin Roosevelt, fearful that demagogues like Father Charles Coughlin might use radio to undermine American democracy, warned that the medium "must be maintained for the American people, free of bias, or prejudice, or sinister control."

On Wednesday October 11, 1932, a handful of newspaper reporters and engineers, squeezing into a darkened room on the fifty-seventh floor of the Chrysler Building in New York City, stood at rapt attention in front of a television measuring two feet by two feet. It was tuned to Columbia station W2XAB, which was located a few blocks away on Madison Avenue. At approximately 7:30 p.m., singer Melvina Passmore appeared on the screen, accompanied in succession by other entertainers, including the star of the hit musical *Show Boat*. The press noted the next day that "the reception was clear enough for the observers to detect wisps of hair, a ring on a finger, or the delicate facial characteristics of the female performers." The men, for some reason, "did not come across the air so well." The show, put on by the Democrats and lasting just half an hour, was the first television broadcast sponsored by a political party. It was an ominous beginning, a sign of what was to become the nefarious marriage of politics and entertainment.

Four years later, in the fall of 1936, in another television first, newsreels showing Franklin Roosevelt and Alf Landon campaigning for president were broadcast. The pictures, transmitted from a tower atop the Empire State Building, were picked up by a small number of receivers located as far away as New Jersey and Connecticut. That November, at an exhibit at Radio City, the public first saw a president on television. Significantly, Orrin Dunlap Jr., a reporter for the *New York Times*, reviewed the event as if it were a Broadway play, another ominous portent of the disappointing effect television would have:

> As [the president] nodded and smiled through space there could be no doubt that he will excel as a television "actor," for his magnetic smile and magnificent radio voice make an ideal combination for telecasting. It would seem that the art of smiling is now likely to be cultivated as much as the voice is for broadcasting. But just as there are natural-born voices for radio, so no doubt there will be captivating smiles, and they will count more than the forced smile, which by television seems to speed through space as an affected grin. Naturalness is to be a keynote of success before the "seeing-microphone," as the radio-camera is called. President Roosevelt's telecasts are proof of this.[4]

At the end of the 1930s, delayed by the difficulty of raising capital during the Depression, commercial television remained a thing of the future, but many of the main elements were being put in place. Stations were being licensed, small networks were being established, advertisers were beginning to sponsor shows, shows were being rated (with *Jane Eyre* attracting the biggest audience in 1940), and stations were experimenting with live news. In 1938, using a mobile unit with a fixed camera on top, RCA happened to capture live pictures of a woman falling to her death from the eleventh-floor window of the Time and Life Building at Rockefeller Center. A microphone picked up the sound of her body as it landed. It was a first, a live news event caught by a television camera, and it made headlines, even though only the studio engineers were watching; they actually missed the fall but heard the thud and focused quickly to see the crowds gathering.

These were the days of "firsts" in television. Among those related to politics was the 1940 broadcast of select moments of the Republican National Convention held in Philadelphia, "the first [live] political event ever to be televised," the *New York Times* informed readers. Fifty thousand viewers watched, "some of them 200 miles away." A crowd of one hundred spectators viewed the proceedings on a television displayed at Bloomingdale's in Manhattan. Visitors to the New York World's Fair—aptly dedicated to life in the future—watched the convention on monitors featured at the RCA exhibit, where the year before David Sarnoff had inaugurated regular television programming. Herbert Hoover, appearing on television for the first time, left viewers snoring—just as the former president had left radio audiences when he was in office. Toward the end of his speech, as the papers noted the next day, the cameramen pleaded with him to smile, but it was to no avail. By contrast, Harold Stassen came off well. He smiled. He exuded charisma. He seemed warm and human. Stassen was a "comer," "televiewers" told the New York Times.

More political broadcasts followed. When Roosevelt and Republican presidential candidate Wendell Willkie spoke to large crowds in separate appearances at Madison Square Garden their speeches were broadcast on television. In November NBC's W2XBS became the first television station to broadcast election returns. Leo Rosenberg, a guest commentator who twenty years earlier had broadcast the returns on Pittsburgh radio station KDKA, marveled at the experience: "I am moved to wonder what the next twenty years will bring forth." Newspapers pronounced the experiment a success. As one reporter observed, "television nearly stole the show."

On the eve of World War II, radio reigned virtually unchallenged as America's predominant mass medium. But all across the country it was television that people debated most fervently, television that they seemed most curious about and dreamed about. When would this new medium finally take hold? What would be its impact on daily life? Who would control it? What role would Sarnoff play in its development? And finally, how would it change politics?

About its impact on politics, pundits were sure of one thing. It would transform the relationship that existed between the governed and the governing. As Orrin Dunlap, in an essay in the Times, observed, it would make politics more intimate, placing a premium on naturalness and sincerity: "Just as a voice personality became paramount [with the establishment of radio]," Dunlap wrote, "now a face, a smile, the stature and appearance of a man, add to his living presence on the air." It did not occur to Dunlap—or seemingly anybody else—that a politician could fake sincerity or use commercials to project a false image. To the contrary. With television "trickery has less chance to operate" because cameras now would be focusing on the "lights and shadows of politics." Like the early prognosticators who twenty years earlier had discoursed on the future of television, Dunlap could still see only the positive effects of the medium. And its effects would be astonishingly grand, he contended, nothing less than the elimination of "hokus pokus." "More than ever," he wrote, "as the politician chieftains observe, 'we are approaching the dawn of clear, intelligent politics.'"

With more accuracy, Dunlap foresaw that television would force "candidates to speak for themselves directly to the people, not through party leaders." Observers had already noted that this was an effect of radio. Television would enhance the effect. Candidates would be "nominated in front of the people; not in a smoke-filled hotel room where politicians of the past are said to have bartered and hatched history." He acknowledged that television would draw attention to the way politicians "comb their hair, how they smile and how they loop their necktie," but beholden to an optimistic outlook, he failed to anticipate the often superficial basis upon which voters relying on television would cast a ballot. Just one cautious note crept into his account. Might the day ever come "when a telegenic candidate can conduct a front-porch campaign, never travel, but sit at home, and be elected President of the United States by television?"

At the end of World War II, television finally arrived. As financial credit became available, thousands, and then hundreds of thousands, began buying big-ticket television sets. In 1948 consumers bought more than 65,000 sets a month. In response, broadcasting corporations such as CBS, NBC, and ABC established networks from coast to coast using coaxial cables—thick collections of wires wrapped in a metal jacket allowing the transmission of high frequency transmission signals—to carry their programs. Dr. Allen B. DuMont, head of the small network that bore his name, predicted in 1948 that within five years television would be a nearly $6 billion industry and employ nearly a million people; by then, he wrote, there would be eleven million television sets. Sarnoff, always eager to make the boldest claims, went further, predicting that there would be eighteen million. Openly bragging, he boasted that "before the polls close on the 1948 Presidential election television will reach substantial areas in at least twenty-one states having more than two-thirds of the national total of electoral votes." "Through television more persons would witness the inauguration" of the next president "than attended all previous thirty-one Presidential inaugurations combined." FCC chairman Wayne Coy said flatly that television was "the most powerful medium of mass communication ever conceived by the mind of man."

The first politician to appear on television regularly was Harry Truman. In the first twenty months after the end of World War II, Truman appeared on the small screen eight times, from New York City, the White House, and Capitol Hill, garnering headlines for his performances. Upon the occasion of Truman's speech to Congress in November 1947, the *New York Times*, emphasizing the positive as usual, editorialized that with television "democracy will again be a town meeting."

The year 1948 would come to be remembered for Truman's stirring speeches from the platform of a train car and his surprise come-from-behind victory over Thomas Dewey in November. But it was also notable as the first election in which television played a practical role.

Decades later the networks would conclude that politics—and political conventions in particular—bored people. But in the early years of the medium viewers were believed to be fascinated by politics. Hoping to build the audience for television, TV manufacturers used the political conventions of 1948 as a high-profile platform to generate sales. In the months before the conventions, newspapers were filled with advertisements for new models ranging in price from $150 for a bargain-basement tabletop television to $4,000 for a deluxe console. A running theme of the ads was that television would give viewers a chance to participate in politics as never before. Buy a Stromberg-Carlson, proclaimed one ad, and you "can see and hear more of the Presidential Conventions than the delegates themselves . . . . You're in the scenes and behind the scenes—with history in the making!" An ad for GE's Model 802D proclaimed, "See History Made When They Pick Their Man for the World's Biggest Job." WJZ-TV, the ABC affiliate in New York, boasted, "These are thrilling historic days; and, thanks to the magic of television, the great events of '48 will happen in front of your eyes."

Three years earlier, Americans had helped win a war overseas waged in the name of liberation. With television they could liberate themselves from the old politics. With the help of television they could decide for themselves the great political questions confronting the country. No longer would they need to take their instructions from party bosses like Tom Pendergast, the discredited Missouri kingpin who had helped make Truman a United States senator.

The bosses still ran the parties, but television now would have a hand in key decisions. In 1948, one of those key decisions was where to hold the conventions. For a century and a half, party officials had made such choices by themselves. But in 1948 the networks resolved to avoid a repeat of 1944, when both political parties had held their conventions in Chicago and undeveloped footage of the proceedings had to be shipped by airplane at 2:00 p.m. to New York for processing, delaying the broadcast of the material over the existing East Coast–based network facilities. Four years later, still lacking adequate transmission facilities in the Midwest to accommodate live broadcasts to the rest of the country, the networks pressured the parties to hold their conventions on the East Coast. Significantly, the bosses in both parties decided to accommodate the networks.

It was the beginning of a pattern of accommodations. That summer the politicians appearing on the dais wore makeup. Delegates were formally instructed to "take the toothpick out of your mouth" and to "keep your clothes neat." Whatever they did, they were admonished, "Don't take off your shoes." Television was watching.

The power of television in politics had yet to be demonstrated. But the evidence was ample that the medium, which viewers on average watched three hours a day, had the power to trigger action. When Howdy-Doody of NBC's WNBT in New York offered a giveaway button, the show received 100,000 requests. Television was becoming so important in people's lives that landlords in major cities were discovering that to keep tenants happy they had to install master antennas on the roofs of their buildings. Even Hollywood reacted; fearful of losing customers, the moviemakers hatched a plan to begin releasing films in color to compete with television, which would broadcast in black and white for another few years.

On Monday June 21, 1948, the Republican convention opened in Philadelphia's Municipal Auditorium. The hall seated fifteen thousand. Up to ten million caught some of the proceedings on television. The *New York Times* observed that because politics was now in people's living rooms, politicians would be required to act differently. Sampling the opinions of one group of viewers in New York—perhaps the first television focus group ever—the paper concluded that partisanship did not go over well on television and advised the party to drop rank appeals that might alienate Democrats or independents. In addition, the party was warned that viewers did not approve of the "numerous demonstrations and the carnival-like atmosphere." The voters felt the parades were "not in keeping with the dignity . . . [that] should prevail in the business of selecting a Presidential nominee." What the viewers did like was the drama. The fight between the forces of Harold Stassen, Robert Taft, and Thomas Dewey assured a lively show. "Televiewers" remained glued to their sets.

The Democratic convention, held a few weeks later, proved considerably less interesting, even with the walkout of the southern delegates after the party endorsed a strong civil rights plank. Jack Gould, the acerbic inaugural television critic for the *Times*, pronounced the first few days of the convention dull, "an arduous grind"—a death sentence in the fast-paced medium.

The *Times* had predicted that television would reward naturalness. But because the cameras could catch them randomly at any moment, convention delegates were warned that they had to behave as if they were always on stage in front of a large audience, which was most unnatural. A politician could tell a newspaper that what he was saying was off the record, but no camera could be entrusted with confidences. The camera was ubiquitous and captured everything, as President Truman discovered when he was caught straightening his tie as he mounted the convention platform to deliver his acceptance speech. The incident became the subject of newspaper stories. With television, the insignificant could appear significant simply because it had happened in front of millions of people.

When Truman finally took the stage—at the awkward hour of 2:00 a.m.—the convention came alive. So did the television audience. "Appearing in a white suit and dark tie, which perhaps is the best masculine garb for the video cameras," wrote Jack Gould, "the President's performance was probably his most impressive since assuming office . . . . He was relaxed and supremely confident, swaying on the balls of his feet with almost a methodical rhythm. But of chief interest was his new style of delivery which well could become a widely-copied pattern on video." Instead of reading from a speech, Truman ad-libbed his remarks.

However much the conventions might have to change to accommodate television, the *Times* did not believe that the new medium would alter their fundamental structure or mission. "It is something to participate by sound and sight in a great political event, but conventions seem destined to remain what they always were—demonstrations of the mysterious ways in which democracy works its wonders to perform." A mere four years later there would be abundant evidence that television *would* materially affect what happened at the conventions. Three decades later the conventions would be ghosts of themselves, mainly owing to the effects of television. By then they would become so dull that the networks would choose mainly to ignore them.

On January 20, 1949, Harry Truman was sworn in as the thirty-third president of the United States. A million people stood in the cold to see the proceedings in person. More than ten million watched on television. The vastness of the television audience impressed even Gould, who reported that this was the "largest number ever to witness a single event" in history. Fourteen cameras recorded the day's events. The pictures were so clear that viewers could see that both Truman and Vice President Alben Barkley "had obtained fresh haircuts." But Gould disapproved of the running commentary. Instead of letting the pictures tell the story, the television anchors talked and talked. "In their grasp for words they usually sounded trite and superfluous when what their audience was seeing was sufficiently moving and inspiring in itself." Gould's story made the front page. Television's place in politics had become obvious.

One sign of the medium's new power was that Congress began to investigate whether powerful senators and representatives improperly influenced the FCC's approval of television licenses. Another was the sheer scale of television programming. A survey of television schedules in New York City found that six stations were producing 225 hours of programming a week, old films filling most of the schedule, followed by sports (boxing being the most popular and the cheapest to produce). Most of the fare was drivel. Jack Gould, as usual ahead of others, noted that the questions television raised had changed. "A year ago the big question in television was: What is the future of the new medium? Today the question is: What is the future of those who look at television? How will it change their lives and habits?"[5]

As the new decade opened, critics increasingly lamented the low quality of television programming. TV, said some, would be "the death of culture."

Television executives, abandoning the hope held out by David Sarnoff in the 1930s that television would bring the Louvre to the masses, responded that the networks were simply practicing "what might be called 'cultural democracy' . . . giving the majority of people what they want." "If it is to fulfill its destiny," Dr. Frank Stanton, the president of CBS, insisted to the dismay of elitists, "television will have to program itself—as must all mass media—with features that appeal to everyone."

While the debate about the quality of television raged, the politicians determined how they could turn the device to their advantage. Leading the pack was Thomas Dewey. In 1948 he had largely avoided television. Now, just two years later, running for reelection as governor of New York, Dewey ran a robust television campaign, appearing on fifteen-minute shows in which he answered questions from voters.[6] The campaign, designed by Madison Avenue wizard Bruce Barton, culminated in a spectacular eighteen-hour-long television marathon featuring celebrities and politicians. The program was carried live simultaneously on four channels in New York City. Dewey won in a landslide.

It began to dawn on print journalists that television cameras did not simply record newsmaking events, but television itself could become an event meriting news coverage. Those covering the news had become the news.

While the perspicacious figured out the transformative effects of television on politics, millions of others remained in the dark. But not for long. In 1951 television suddenly sprang to life as a force so powerful that it reshaped the country's national agenda, putting organized crime at the top of the list of Americans' priorities. Before no one had taken gangland bosses seriously. They were cardboard cutouts. But now, at televised Senate Crime Investigating Committee hearings held by Estes Kefauver in cities across the country, they suddenly became real, paradoxically appearing both more dangerous and more vulnerable. Jake Guzik, a Chicago gang leader, refused to answer any questions on the grounds "it might incriminate me." Asked where he had picked up the phrase, which seemed beyond a man of his level of education, he answered, "I heard it on television."

The hearings attracted millions of viewers. Gould, writing in the *Times*, noted that "housewives have left the housework undone and husbands have slipped away from their jobs to watch. The city has been under a hypnotic spell, absorbed, fascinated, angered and amused. It has been a rare community experience." To idealists like Gould, the hearings delivered on the great hopes of television, a medium whose promise was not always visible on nights when the typical fare included bouts between bare-chested wrestlers such as Adrian Baillargeon and Fred von Schacht. "The power to elicit this public participation," commented Gould in a reference to the Cold War, "is a priceless asset at a time when democracy is facing one of its severest tests."

By the time the hearings ended a small number of people had become national celebrities. There was Frank Costello, whose twisting hands had been featured in close-ups after he refused to allow the cameras to focus on his face while he testified. And there was the Senate committee's chief attorney, Rudolph Halley, who used his newfound fame to win a seat as president of the New York City Council. But, most important, there was Estes Kefauver.

In 1948, Kefauver had been elected to the Senate from Tennessee. Though a gifted politician, under ordinary circumstances he would have to wait years before he would be in a position to exercise power in the Senate, where seniority determined committee chairmanships, and years more if he hoped to be considered a viable candidate for president of the United States. Certainly without television he could not have succeeded in making crime a critical issue of concern to voters across the country. But because of television the old rules no longer applied. Television suddenly thrust Kefauver into the national spotlight under favorable circumstances, turning him into an instant celebrity politician—a species with which the public would now become more and more familiar. In 1952 he announced for the presidency, entering eleven primaries and winning ten of them. Going into the convention he was widely considered the most popular of the Democratic candidates. Columnist Arthur Krock wrote that the "degree of popular support for Senator Kefauver of Tennessee in his bid to be the Democratic nominee for President is perhaps the outstanding political development of 1952." In state after state Kefauver had taken on the machine candidate, and in state after state he had won.

Years later, historian Richard Reeves observed that John Kennedy's importance derived not so much from any decision he made as from his own political ambition: "He did not wait his turn."[7] But it was actually Kefauver who showed that a young man with ambition could circumvent tradition and go after the White House without waiting. It was television that made this possible.

Television made Kefauver a viable candidate, but it could not make him the nominee. In 1952 party bosses still ruled, and they did not approve of a television candidate, at least not Kefauver. As always, they wanted to reserve to themselves the right to name the party's candidate. And because most delegates at the time were chosen by the bosses, the bosses could block a candidate if they chose to do so.[8] They chose to do so in this case because Kefauver was a party maverick. (At the convention he was the subject of an NBC show titled *The People Versus the Bosses.*)

President Truman considered himself a man of the people, but he had become a senator with Pendergast's support and had become vice president with the help of other bosses. So he was inclined to take their view when Kefauver challenged the party system. In addition, he had a particular reason for disliking Kefauver. At a hearing the senator had challenged the integrity of former

New York City Mayor William O'Dwyer, whom Truman had appointed ambassador to Mexico. In a statement released to the press, the White House, without naming Kefauver, denounced televising congressional hearings:

The President thinks highly of television. He insists on full use of it in all of his major speeches. The President has real misgivings, however, about the use of television at hearings because of the tendency to make Roman holidays of them. One day he observed that one of the major factors in the weakening of the governments of Athens and of other democratic Greek states was the adoption of trial by mass jury. In that way emotions sway over reason. Socrates was tried in that way and the result was most unfair. On this the President is most seriously concerned. The trouble with television hearings, he said, is that a man is held before cameras and 40,000,000 people more or less hear him charged with so and so, and the public, untrained generally with evaluating the presentation of evidence, is inclined to think him guilty just because he is charged. Then the pressure begins mounting on the committee and the result can be that the witness is pushed around. It is the very negation of judicial process, with the committee acting as prosecutor and defense, and the public acting as the jury.[9]

Many politicians, even those like Truman who used television to advantage, were now beginning to express reservations about the medium. Governor Dewey said that televising congressional hearings "smacks too much of the Russian method to fit in with our institutions." Senators Robert Taft (R-Ohio) and Harry F. Byrd (D-Va.) said that televising the Senate would be distracting. Speaker of the House of Representatives Sam Rayburn (D-Tex.) adamantly opposed televising the House: "Televise sessions of the House? Hell no! Not while I'm around here." "Can I quote you on that, Mr. Speaker?" a reporter asked. "Hell, yes." Decades before, Americans had predicted that television would improve American democracy. Now, just a few years after television had made its debut in politics, leaders had their doubts.

Thus far, ordinary Americans did not concur. That summer events conspired to put television in a positive light. The nomination had become a neck-and-neck fight between Taft and Dwight Eisenhower. Eisenhower, the clear popular favorite, seemed in danger of losing the nomination when Taft's people, who controlled the party machinery, excluded television cameras from a meeting of the national committee, which was faced with two slates from Texas, one pro-Taft, one pro-Eisenhower. The mere exclusion of the cameras struck most Americans as un-American, giving Eisenhower a clear moral victory and undermining Taft's candidacy.

But that fall television was put to a use that gave rise to profound doubts about the medium—and even many voters who loved television found themselves wondering if the doubters did not have a point. On September 23, 1952, Richard Nixon, the Republican vice presidential candidate, took to the air to answer charges raised by the *New York Post* that wealthy Californians had contributed to an $18,000 "slush fund" for his personal benefit. The charges threatened to soil the Republican campaign, which had heaped scorn on the Truman administration's many scandals. In defending himself, Nixon employed emotional arguments that played on the audience's social prejudices. He noted that he had been born poor. He said that he still did not possess much property even as a U.S. senator and noted of his wife that "Pat doesn't own a mink coat." The emotional high point of the speech came when he told a story about a dog: "One other thing I probably should tell you, because if I don't they'll probably be saying this about me, too—we did get something, a gift, after the election. . . . The day before we left on this campaign trip, we got a message from the Union Station in Baltimore, saying they had a package for us. It was a little cocker-spaniel dog . . . and our little girl Tricia, the six-year-old, named it Checkers. And you know the kids, like all kids, love the dog and . . . regardless of what they say about it, we're going to keep it."

Thirty million people tuned in to watch the speech. It saved Nixon's career. Eisenhower, who had declined to defend his running mate, now embraced him. "Dick," Ike told Nixon a few days later, "you're my boy." Partisan Republicans leaped to Nixon's side, but many worried about Nixon's use of television. "There is enough emotionalism in a campaign under the best of circumstances," Jack Gould wrote, "without using it as a premeditated policy and tactic. If either Republicans or Democrats should tread on the edge of demagoguery, in the long run it will be the country that will suffer and television's usefulness will be dangerously impaired."

Compounding these concerns was the Republican Party's decision to feature Eisenhower in thirty-second commercials—known as spots—in the final three weeks of the campaign. The ads were the idea of Rosser Reeves Jr., a leading advertiser with the Ted Bates Agency, responsible for the slogan, "The candy that melts in your mouth, not in your hand." As once he had sold M&M candy, now he would sell Eisenhower. To finance the spots, which cost $2 million to design and broadcast, Reeves leaned on his friends in the oil industry, establishing a pattern that would soon become familiar as politicians turned to special interests to pick up the big tabs needed to pay for television advertising.

America had never seen anything like it. There on the screen was "Ike," General Eisenhower, the hero of World War II, answering questions posed by ordinary voters as if he were an ordinary citizen—as if they were on the same level. In one spot, a voter asks Ike, "Are we going to have to fight another war?" The general answers, "No, not if we have a sound program for peace. And I'll add this, we won't spend hundreds of billions and still not have enough tanks and planes for Korea." Eisenhower had qualms about the spots. He reportedly groused during the filming, "To think that an old soldier should come to this!" But like candidates in subsequent elections, he agreed to take his orders from Madison Avenue TV consultants.

Opponent Adlai Stevenson pounced on the ads. "I don't think the American people want politics and the presidency to become the plaything of the high-pressure men, of the ghostwriters, of the public relations men," he said. "I think they will be shocked by such contempt for the intelligence of the American people. This isn't soap opera, this isn't Ivory Soap versus Palmolive." But four years later, when Stevenson ran for president against Eisenhower a second time, he ran spots, too, even going along with a controversial television ad campaign that harped on the administration's alleged flaws, introducing the negative ad as the latest twist in television politics.

At the dawn of the twentieth century, social scientists had feared that manipulative politicians could use the mass media to control voters. Like FDR later, they had worried about the mass media falling into the hands of a few individuals. But these fears slowly had abated as researchers concluded that the mass media did not seem to posses the power attributed to it. Al Smith, for instance, had run an aggressive radio campaign in the election of 1928 and yet lost in a landslide. FDR and Truman had won their elections despite the overwhelming opposition of newspaper owners. After World War II, as media scholars Kurt Lang and Gladys Lang have observed, social scientists generally felt that "changes in attitudes, beliefs, and behavior directly traceable to the mass media are the exception rather than the rule. This is because exposure is highly self-selective; people pay attention primarily to content that already interests them and that is congenial to their point of view." [10]

But when the Langs began measuring the effect of television on politics, they discovered that the conventional wisdom was misleading. In an innovative and pathbreaking study, they arranged for three groups of viewers to restrict their viewing to a single channel during the Democratic convention of 1952. One group watched NBC, another ABC, and another CBS. Through content analysis, the Langs determined that all three networks presented, with minor exceptions, the same information. But each network approached the convention differently. NBC decided to focus on personalities and left analysis largely up to the newspapers; the network's motto was to "let the pictures speak for themselves." ABC, the weakest of the big three networks and short of viewers, financial resources, and journalists, chose to offer nonstop action as a means of attracting attention, emphasizing inside scoops. CBS, blessed with a strong bench of seasoned and well-known reporters, decided to tell viewers what was happening as it happened and to offer running analysis. If this approach risked boring the viewers, so be it, said CBS. As one senior producer told the Langs, "It's not up to us to make it a good show."

To the Langs' surprise, the way the networks covered the convention decisively shaped the impressions of viewers. NBC viewers, for instance, seized on the seemingly rude manner in which Sam Rayburn presided. They thought he was impolite when he refused to recognize a delegate who wanted to make a motion to adjourn in order to give liberal forces time to rally. ABC viewers came away confused because the network's jumpy coverage made it difficult to follow the action. But they, too, focused on Rayburn, concluding that his rulings were often arbitrary. CBS viewers, informed step by step of the reasons for Rayburn's rulings, had a much more rational understanding of the proceedings. Properly, "they interpreted what they saw . . . as a showdown among several factions with Rayburn trying to mediate."

Television not only shaped how viewers saw the election, but it also shaped the election itself. If 1948 was the first election in which television played a role, 1952 was the first in which it decisively affected the course of events. It made a candidate out of Estes Kefauver, helped eliminate the candidacy of Robert Taft, saved the candidacy of Richard Nixon, and turned Ike into an ordinary pitchman, with himself as the product for sale. From then on television would be a decisive force in American politics.

Television did not alter the outcome of the election of 1952. Eisenhower, the greatest hero to emerge from World War II, no doubt would have defeated Stevenson with or without Rosser Reeves's help. But television changed the way campaigns were won and became associated with four broad undemocratic postwar trends. First, it helped undermine the two-party system, which traditionally had been the vehicle through which voters exercised their control of the selection of political leaders. Second, it shifted power from party bosses who were somewhat responsive to the will of the voters to the unelected Madison Avenue advertisers who designed the television campaigns that now helped win elections. Third, it dramatically increased the cost of campaigns, making both parties dependent on large donors like Reeves's oilmen. And fourth, it expanded the power of the media elite, who increasingly replaced the party bosses in shaping the fortunes of various leaders.

Against these trends were several that seemed to enhance the prospect of participatory democracy. Candidates discovered that they could win by appealing over the heads of the bosses to the people directly. Television also made politics more transparent, pressuring the parties to fling open the doors to meetings that once had been held in secret. And television spotlighted social problems such as poverty and segregation, giving grassroots groups like those active in the civil rights movement the power to shape public opinion and achieve change.

By the mid-1950s, observers no longer championed television with naive enthusiasm. Now it was slowly being regarded as an intoxicating cocktail of both democratic and undemocratic forces. Nothing illustrated better the mixed impact of television than the uses to which it was put by Senator Joseph McCarthy (R-Wis.) and his adversaries. McCarthy used television throughout the early 1950s to ridicule and smear a long line of innocent people as Communist threats to the nation. Emboldened by the public reaction to his wild charges, he continued to up the ante, intimidating opponents and political allies alike, including Eisenhower, who campaigned with McCarthy even after McCarthy had called Ike's mentor George Marshall a traitor. But television also helped lead to McCarthy's undoing. In a celebrated report on CBS, Edward R. Murrow carefully let McCarthy hang himself by a rope made of his own words. Murrow's show concluded, "The actions of the junior Senator from Wisconsin have caused alarm and dismay among our allies abroad and given considerable comfort to our enemies, and whose fault is that? Not really his, he didn't create the situation of fear, he merely exploited it and rather successfully. Cassius was right: 'The fault, dear Brutus, is not in our stars but in ourselves.'" "For TV," observed Jack Gould, "so often plagued by timidity and hesitation, the program was a milestone that reflected enlightened citizenship on the part of the Columbia Broadcasting System and, particularly, the Aluminum Company of America who paid the bill to make it possible. No voice is braver than those who enable it to be heard."[11]

Murrow's broadcast was not solely responsible for bringing McCarthy down. Fred Greenstein has argued persuasively that Eisenhower had a decisive effect. When McCarthy recklessly charged the U.S. Army with harboring Communists, Eisenhower secretly began feeding senators compromising information about McCarthy's repeated attempts to win special favors for former employees of his investigating subcommittee. Not until Eisenhower's papers were opened two decades later, however, was the president's key role in undermining McCarthy disclosed. By then the myth of television's preeminence in the fight had taken hold. As always with television, the truth almost did not matter. In a television world now shaped by imagery, what mattered was what people saw. What they saw was what they believed. And what they believed they saw they believed intently.

Dwight Eisenhower, the last president born in the nineteenth century, never quite adapted to the television revolution. Though he came across well on television—he only had to flash his famous smile, it was said, and people trusted him instantly—he never became comfortable with the medium. Each encounter with television was an ordeal to be endured. Insecure in front of the cameras, he hired the famed actor Robert Montgomery to give him acting lessons. Worried that he might say something at press conferences he would later regret, Ike resisted pressure to let them be televised live. Press secretary James Hagerty reserved the right to edit the film before it was released. That Eisenhower let in the cameras at all was considered noteworthy. As Hagerty later modestly boasted, "Before we came into office, only the reporter's pencil was allowed there." (One reason for the change was technological. In 1954 Eastman Kodak perfected a new type of fast film that allowed press conferences to be televised without the use of high-intensity lights.)[12]

Eisenhower's successor in the White House loved television. While a senator, John Kennedy wangled his way onto NBC's *Meet the Press*. After their high-society wedding, he and his wife Jacqueline appeared on Murrow's CBS show *Person to Person*. In 1959, on the eve of his announcement as a candidate for the presidency, he wrote an article for *TV Guide* describing television as "A Force That Has Changed the Political Scene." Critics of television, thinking of Nixon's Checkers speech, had expressed the concern that the medium would allow superficial or corrupt politicians to bewitch the American people. Kennedy disagreed. "Honesty, vigor, compassion, intelligence—the presence or lack of these and other qualities make up what is called the candidate's 'image'. . . . My own conviction is that these images or impressions are likely to be uncannily correct." After he formally announced his candidacy, he allowed a camera crew to follow him on the campaign trail in Wisconsin and West Virginia. In the West Virginia primary he used his father's fortune to help pay for an expensive television campaign. Historian Mary Ann Watson has concluded that Kennedy's use of television there was a "turning point" in his path to the nomination. After a half-hour broadcast on the Sunday before the election, Kennedy, who had been slightly behind opponent Hubert Humphrey, pulled slightly ahead. Confident that television offered him unique access to the electorate—87 percent of households by 1960 owned at least one television—he appeared as often as he could, even agreeing to be interviewed by entertainer Jack Paar on the *Tonight Show*.[13]

The high point of the 1960 campaign came on the night of the first of four live televised presidential debates with opponent Richard Nixon. Kennedy told his television advisor, "Television may be the most important part of the campaign. It may decide the election." After watching that first debate, most Americans would have agreed that Kennedy was right.

On September 26, 1960, at 9:00 p.m. eastern time, between sixty and seventy million people tuned in to watch the first debate. Nixon, cocky because of his success with the Checkers speech eight years earlier, declined to undertake serious preparations. Kennedy prepared extensively. The producer of the show invited both candidates to visit the set in advance and go over camera angles. Nixon did not, but Kennedy went. The night of the debate Nixon, pale after a recent illness, refused to wear makeup and came across as pallid. Under the hot lights, he perspired. (The Kennedy TV advisor, knowing Nixon's tendency to sweat, made threats to pressure a janitor to increase the temperature inside the studio "as high as we could.") Kennedy, benefiting from a deep tan (partly caused by the effect of the cortisone treatments taken for Addison's disease), did not wear makeup either, but on the advice of the producer he donned a blue shirt and a blue suit. He appeared composed and handsome. During the show Kennedy's advisor importuned the producer to switch to reaction shots of Nixon while Kennedy was talking. Forty minutes into the ninety-minute show, Nixon was caught "mopping his brow." [14]

A Gallup poll found that Kennedy won the debate by a two-to-one margin. Many social scientists found the results surprising. The conventional wisdom was that voters were not blank slates and that they judged candidates appearing on television on the basis of preconceived ideas, which should have led to a more even split. As one researcher put it in 1957, "before [a voter] even sits down to the television set, he is prepared to react in a preset way to whatever comes out of it." The 1960 debate suggested that television might actually decisively shape a viewer's response, a somewhat frightening development, confirming the fears Franklin Roosevelt and others had expressed about the impact of mass media.

How had viewers decided who won the debate? Once again the findings of researchers was confounding. Disturbingly, the studies showed that voters did not decide on the basis of the arguments or the facts the candidates marshaled. Instead, viewers seemed to focus on personality. Anecdotal evidence indicated that voters who heard the debate on the radio believed that Nixon had won, suggesting that television imagery had an important effect on viewer response. If true, the theory upon which American democracy rested—that voters with access to information can be trusted to reach sound conclusions—was profoundly superficial and perhaps dangerously flawed.[15]

Journalists, largely unaware of the scholarly debate about its influence, came to the conclusion that television was having an extraordinary effect. Russell Baker, writing in the *New York Times*, wrote that whether Nixon or Kennedy won, "That night television replaced newspapers as the most important communications medium in American politics."

But a favorable reaction to Kennedy's performance did not necessarily translate into support at the ballot box in November. The University of Michigan Survey Research Center found that voting behavior was in the end determined by a variety of factors: voter identification with a political party, the opinions of friends and family, and what voters read about the candidates. Researchers found this result reassuring. But a study by the Langs offered troublesome evidence that public opinion was malleable. They found that Democrats who had voted for Eisenhower in 1952 and 1956 came home to the Democratic Party in 1960 after the first debate, suggesting that television actually did affect how people voted.

As president, Kennedy experimented constantly with television. One of his first decisions was to allow his press conferences to be carried live; in his three years as president Kennedy held more than sixty televised press conferences. In his first year in office he arranged for the making of several TV documentaries. He allowed filmmaker Bob Drew to follow him around the White House as Kennedy conducted the affairs of state. Subsequently, the president encouraged Jackie to provide a televised tour of the White House.

Kennedy always shone on television. But critics murmured that television was transforming American politics, and not always in ways guaranteed to enhance democracy. Reporters attending news conferences complained that they had become mere props for a White House show. Newspapers expressed astonishment at Bob Drew's documentary, which included a scene showing Kennedy at work during the Congo crisis. "To eavesdrop on executive decisions of serious Government matters while they are in progress," the New York Times objected in an editorial, "is highly inappropriate." The New York Herald Tribune agreed, worrying that the documentary turned the president into an actor: "The President has no business in show business." Others complained that Kennedy was using television to manipulate public opinion.

Newspaper people complained the loudest. As television rose in importance, the influence of newspapers declined. Newspaper reporters discovered that Kennedy's press secretary, Pierre Salinger, was quicker to return the calls of TV reporters and give them more access.

One of the first items on the new president's domestic agenda was revamping the moribund Federal Communications Commission. It was widely agreed among social critics that something had gone wrong with television. Despite David Sarnoff's promises that television would uplift American culture, each night Americans saw, as reformer Newton Minow complained, a mediocre mélange of "game shows, violence, audience participation shows, formula comedies about totally unbelievable families, blood and thunder, mayhem, violence, sadism, murder, western bad men, western good men, private eyes, gangsters, more violence, and cartoons." Social critics famously jibed that television was "chewing gum for the eyes." Even the people at whom these shows were targeted held television in low regard. In 1957 it had been disclosed that the popular quiz shows millions watched were rigged, leading to mass disillusionment with the medium.

To help prod broadcasters to do better, Kennedy appointed Minow as the new head of the FCC. At the annual meeting of broadcasters held in the spring of 1961, Minow bemoaned that television had become a "vast wasteland" and bluntly warned broadcasters that their licenses might be in jeopardy if programming did not improve. "There is nothing permanent or sacred about a broadcast license," he ominously declared.

The broadcasters' response was to begin adding documentaries and news shows. In the 1961–62 season the networks broadcast 254 hours of documentaries, more than ever before or since. By 1963 both CBS and NBC had expanded their showcase evening news shows from fifteen minutes to half an hour.

On November 22, 1963, out of the range of television cameras, John Kennedy was assassinated in Dallas. The networks, demonstrating new seriousness, suspended commercials to provide four days of nonstop news coverage, garnering universal praise for their thoughtful and responsible approach. Some critics claimed that "the broadcasting industry saved democracy in this country that November weekend."

In the decades that followed, 1963 would be regarded as a bellwether year in the history of television. Symbolically, for the first time in the nation's history, more Americans that year relied on television for news than newspapers.[16] By then it was well established that political events would be remembered for the television images they generated almost as much as for the events themselves. As historian Daniel Boorstin observed in *The Image*, "What happens on television will overshadow what happens off television." Thinking back on the second half of the twentieth century, Americans would remember the television images: Martin Luther King's "I Have a Dream" speech; JFK's funeral; looters carrying away TV sets during the race riots of the 1960s; helicopters swooping down on rice paddies during the Vietnam War; Lyndon Johnson's prime-time announcement that he would not run for reelection; Neil Armstrong's walk on the moon; Nixon toasting Mao Zedong in China and boarding a helicopter following his resignation; Jimmy Carter's malaise speech; the taking of American hostages in Iran; Ronald Reagan's demand in Berlin that Soviet leader Mikhail Gorbachev "tear down this wall"; George H. W. Bush's "read my lips"; Bill Clinton's claim that he "did not have sexual relations with that woman"; election night mishaps in the year 2000. And in the new century television conveyed with vivid clarity the horror of the destruction of the twin towers at the World Trade Center on September 11, 2001.

As television became embedded deeply in American culture, a new emphasis was placed on image, prompting profound and gloomy questions about the fate of democracy. One of the first to seize on the dangers inherent in image politics was the writer Norman Mailer. In an essay in *Esquire* about the Democratic convention of 1960, "Superman Comes to the Supermarket," Mailer worried that television reduced political figures to caricatures. Thus Kennedy, though a serious student of politics and history, "was indisputably and willy-nilly going to be seen as a great box-office actor, and the consequences of that were staggering and not at all easy to calculate." Others worried about the way images could be manipulated. The fear that slick operators could forge palpable images to shape public opinion repeatedly surfaced. One thirty-second ad broadcast in the 1964 presidential campaign came to represent the dangers that image manipulation posed. Playing on the fear that Republican candidate Barry Goldwater was unstable, the Johnson campaign aired a spot featuring a little girl removing the petals on a daisy, counting downward. Suddenly, a deep voiced narrator took over as the count reached "three," "two," "one"—and the screen filled with the image of an exploding nuclear bomb, a blunt reminder of the power presidents have to trigger Armageddon. Critics denounced the ad as demagogic. It ran only once. LBJ, insisting that he had nixed it in advance, said that underlings had broadcast it by mistake.

Four years later, it was the Republicans' turn to use television to manipulate the voters. Manipulation was necessary, Ray Price explained in a Nixon campaign memo recounted by Joe McGinniss in *The Selling of the President 1968*, because voters respond to images. "It's not what's there that counts, it's what's projected— and carrying it one step further, it's not what *he* [Nixon] projects but rather what the voter receives." Nixon, astutely assessing the change television wrought, surrounded himself with people from the world of public relations. If he had an image problem, the obvious solution was to hire people expert at image making.

Even student protesters got into the habit of manipulating images. At the 1968 Democratic Convention in Chicago they staged their demonstrations in places where the television cameramen could get good pictures. The cameramen, in turn, reportedly urged the demonstrators to reenact violent confrontations with the police. When Hubert Humphrey gave his acceptance speech, the networks provided a split screen showing a beaming Humphrey opposite pictures filmed earlier of violent student protests. By then it seemed that everybody in politics was using images to manipulate everybody else.

As television became increasingly important, the power the networks wielded came under scrutiny. Southerners had expressed the first sustained public criticism during the civil rights demonstrations that began in the 1950s. Network news crews transmitted to the rest of the world the powerful images of oppression that conservative southerners wanted to conceal. To discredit the networks, southern reactionaries bitterly remarked that the initials of the big three stood for the African Broadcasting Company, the Negro Broadcasting Company, and the Colored Broadcasting System.[17]

In the 1960s the circle of critics grew to include Republican politicians, beginning with Barry Goldwater in 1964. Within a few years it became common for Republicans to charge that a liberal media elite was destroying American democracy. On November 13, 1969, at 7:00 p.m., Spiro Agnew launched a frontal attack, claiming in a speech carried live nationwide that "a small group of men, numbering perhaps no more than a dozen anchormen, commentators, and executive producers, settle upon the twenty minutes or so of film and commentary" that are broadcast each night. He added ominously: "We'd never trust such power as I've described over public opinion in the hands of an elected government. It's time we questioned it in the hands of a small and unelected elite." Polls afterward showed that the public overwhelmingly approved of Agnew's indictment.

The actual power of the networks to shape public opinion was questionable, and certainly less direct than Agnew imagined. At the 1968 Democratic convention the network anchors had clearly expressed sympathy for the student protesters while making harsh statements about the Chicago police, Walter Cronkite referring on the air at one point to a group of officers who jostled Dan Rather as "thugs." Yet studies showed that three out of four viewers sided with the police.

Still, Agnew's attack resonated. For a year, with Nixon's blessing, he hammered at the theme, to the cheers of millions eager to direct at a specific target the deep frustration and anger that had accumulated in the 1960s as the country was rocked by urban riots, discouraged by the lack of progress in Vietnam, and appalled by the steady stream of radical social changes. Despite Agnew's success in drawing attention to the power of the media elite, their power increased in the years afterward, in part as a consequence of the disastrous Democratic Convention of 1968 that ironically had helped bring Nixon and Agnew to power.

Determined to rein in party bosses like Chicago's Mayor Richard Daley, who had delivered the nomination to Humphrey even though Humphrey had not won a single primary, reformers overhauled the rules governing the selection of delegates, dramatically increasing the number picked in open caucuses and primaries. In 1968, fewer than half the delegates in the Democratic Party were chosen in primaries; by 1972, two-thirds were. (Republicans also increased the number of delegates chosen in primaries.) While reformers celebrated this victory, the media elite inadvertently accumulated yet more power. Now it would be up to them to decide who was ahead and deserving of free time on the news and who was inconsequential, a task that required network executives to divine the likely winners and losers in the primaries—and to decide which primaries were worthy of attention and which could safely be ignored.

Going into the primary season in 1972, Edmund Muskie of Maine was widely considered the leading Democratic candidate. On the eve of the first primary, held in New Hampshire, a neighboring state, his campaign manager told journalists, "I'll shoot myself if Muskie doesn't get 50 percent." When Muskie won 47 percent, gathering far more votes than any other candidate, the networks declared his victory a defeat, virtually ending his prospects. George McGovern, who received 37 percent of the votes, was declared the winner because he had confounded the networks' predictions. The networks then debated endlessly what had caused Muskie's "defeat," ultimately attributing it to a moment of human weakness when Muskie had openly cried after the *Manchester Union Leader* cruelly accused his wife of using the ethnic slur "Canuck," meaning Canadian. Significantly, they did not dwell on the role they had played in undermining his candidacy by declaring him a loser even though he had actually won.

In the next quadrennial cycle, the networks, eager to begin the political season early, heavily publicized a heretofore inconsequential straw poll taken in

Ames, Iowa. The winner of this poll was the little-known former governor of Georgia, Jimmy Carter. The networks immediately declared that Carter was a leading contender for the nomination. Crowning him a contender instantly made him one. By the 1980s it became abundantly clear that the democratic reforms of 1972, while increasing the power of the people, had also resulted in the shift of power from the bosses of the party to those of the networks.[18]

The chaos that destroyed the Democratic Party convention of 1968 had horrified the leaders of both parties, persuading them that with television looking on events and images had to be scripted in advance. The Republicans learned how by 1972. That year their convention was made to order for what now was commonly called the "boob tube," as Dan Rather discovered when he got hold of White House staffer David Gergen's television script, which indicated second by second exactly what was going to happen during the four-day meeting. At the time, Rather's report was considered a scoop. Eight years later the conventions had become so scripted—and because of primaries almost unnecessary—that the networks decided to stop providing gavel-to-gavel coverage. By then the parties so carefully choreographed their conventions that officials handed out their scripts in advance so the networks could schedule commercials during lulls in the proceedings.

The decline in the importance of the conventions mirrored a decline in the parties themselves. Was television to blame? Political scientist Thomas Patterson argues in *The Vanishing Voter* that the parties were fated to decline after the 1930s when the creation of a social safety net "greatly reduced the sources of economic resentment and insecurity that had fueled party conflict" in the past. Lacking such conflict, the parties increasingly relied on ever-changing cultural and symbolic issues to provoke partisan support. These appeals crossed class lines, Patterson argues, and weakened the identification of the parties with specific causes. Over time, voters became less and less sure what the parties stood for, undermining party loyalty and contributing to lower voter turnout.

Patterson's fascinating analysis is a useful reminder that other forces besides television shaped politics. But no accounting sheet of the debits political parties racked up in the postwar period can omit television. Whether its role was decisive or merely a factor in the decline of the parties, television transformed the way elections were won and lost. And each change undermined the parties as they originally had been conceived and nurtured. Television broke the power of the bosses, gave candidates the means to appeal directly to voters, made a candidate's personality more important than issues, and transferred power to the media elite. Because television gave the viewers a front-row seat in politics, voters by the millions became persuaded that they no longer needed the parties for political guidance and proudly proclaimed their independence.

Reformers in the 1940s and 1950s had hoped that television would lead to the creation of more independent voters. It did, but with an unintended consequence: it turned out that those registered as independents were far less likely to cast a ballot than those enrolled as Republicans and Democrats. Beginning with the 1960 election turnout at the polls began a slow steady and seemingly inexorable decline. In 1960, 64 percent of eligible voters went to the polls; in 1972, 55 percent; in 2000, 51 percent. Numbers in the off-year elections were even worse; in the midterm election of 2002, only 39 percent voted. Those who failed to vote also failed to show much interest in presidential debates. In 1976 and 1980 just half of the households with television watched the debates. In 1984 only 46 percent of the audience watched; in 1988, 36 percent; in 1996, 29 percent. In 2004 viewership increased, as did voter turnout, but 2004 may well have been an exception owing to the unusual polarization of the electorate. Whether television was mainly responsible for the general downward trends, it had certainly betrayed the hopes of reformers who expected it to invigorate democracy. Perhaps, some suggested, Americans had been wrong to believe that their society could successfully absorb all new technology.

Other signs in the last three decades of the twentieth century contributed to the impression that American democracy was in trouble. All of them were in some way associated with television. Television campaign advertising was increasingly nasty and superficial. Presidents no longer made themselves available for interrogation by the press on a regular basis. Voters displayed more ignorance about the issues than they had when they relied primarily on newspapers as a source of information. Polls showed that voters approved of candidates whose policies they disagreed with merely because they found the candidates' personalities pleasing. Politicians complained that they had to devote tens of hours a week making calls to big donors to raise money for the television kitty. The cost of campaigns skyrocketed. The content of TV news increasingly focused on soft human-interest stories rather than politics even as the overwhelming majority of voters came to rely almost exclusively on television as their chief source of news. While every four years the party nominees subjected themselves to the rigors of staged debates, the debates increasingly came to be defined by catchy sound bites and post-debate spin. And after Democratic presidential candidate Gary Hart's affair with Donna Rice in 1988 received extensive coverage, people complained that TV was exploitive and insensitive, bound to drive good people out of politics.[19]

Perhaps most seriously of all, survey results showed that people had little faith in American institutions, particularly government. In 1964, 76 percent said that they trusted their government to do the right thing "most of the time." By 1994 this number had fallen to 21 percent. Many blamed Vietnam, Watergate, and the Iran-Contra affair for the decline, but a number of critics pointed the finger at television. In their opinion, television magnified social problems and discredited institutions that gave the cameras easy access. It was no coincidence, they concluded, that the Supreme Court, the institution that denied access to TV cameras, ranked far higher in the polls in the 1980s and 1990s than Congress and the presidency, both of which had embraced cameras. Apologists for television noted that the cameras had merely shown the public how these damaged institutions actually operated, and they insisted that TV was neutral. They noted that during Watergate television had given the members of the Senate Select Committee chaired by Sam Ervin (D-N.C.) the opportunity to shine, proof that television could work to the advantage of politicians who acted responsibly. Later, the members of the House Judiciary Committee investigating impeachment charges against Nixon also performed well on television. But more typical were the embarrassing hearings on the nomination of Clarence Thomas to the Supreme Court in 1991. After a former staffer, Anita Hill, accused Thomas of sexual harassment, the hearings devolved into a crass exchange of degrading insults and allegations, culminating in public debate about the significance of a pubic hair allegedly discovered on a can of Coke.

TV journalists themselves became alarmed by the complaints but gave in to defeatism. In a famous case, CBS reporter Lesley Stahl, convinced that President Ronald Reagan's expert White House spin machine was leaving voters with a false impression of his policies through the manipulation of visual symbols, produced a remarkable piece to attempt to set the record straight at least once. "Mr. Reagan," she dutifully explained in a long piece on the evening news, "tries to counter the memory of an unpopular issue with a carefully chosen backdrop that actually contradicts the president's policy. Look at the handicapped Olympics, or the opening ceremony of an old-age home. No hint that he tried to cut the budgets for the disabled and for federally subsidized housing for the elderly." After the story ran she braced herself for criticism from the White House. Instead, she received a phone call from a Reagan official complimenting her for a "great piece." "We loved it," he said. "You what?" she responded. "We loved it!" But "how can you say you loved it—it was tough! Don't you think it was tough?" she asked. "We're in the middle of a campaign," the official explained, "and you gave us four and a half minutes of great pictures of Ronald Reagan. And that's all the American people see. . . . They don't listen to you if you're contradicting great pictures. They don't hear what you are saying if the pictures are saying something different." [20]

What if the public did listen? Some studies showed that network reporters could affect public opinion. Thomas Patterson's study of campaigns from 1960 to 1992 demonstrated a strong link between negative campaign coverage and a candidate's negative image. But would that be any more reassuring? Who wanted network reporters decisively influencing public opinion, particularly since other studies showed that viewers relying on television based their conclusions on their emotional responses?[21]

Some political scientists, taking a hard look at the way people make choices, contended that voters did not actually give in to rank emotionalism. One study in the 1980s indicated that people "deal with the flood of information in their environment by employing cognitive shortcuts." By using inferences to "fill in missing information," voters evaluated candidates in terms of "their own embellished perceptions" based upon real-world experience. These embellished perceptions shaped a voter's sense of a candidate's character, reliability, and competence.

The study seemed to offer a compelling argument in favor of television journalism, which tended to reduce campaigns to tests of political character since the issues at stake in politics were often too abstruse to be analyzed meaningfully in a two-minute news report. But few people outside the political science profession seemed aware of the study, and in any case, it was suggestive without being definitive.[22]

Other political scientists came to the defense of the long-derided spot ads. Kathleen Hall Jamieson, reviewing scores of them over decades, concluded that the ads helped candidates build name recognition, reveal agendas, and provide hard information about opponents. "In part because more voters attend to spot ads than to network news," she wrote, "and in part because reporters are fixated with who's winning and losing instead of what the candidates are proposing, some scholars believe that the ads provide the electorate with more information than network news."[23]

Still others approvingly cited the networks' generally reliable election night forecasts, which produced an astounding array of useful computer-generated data. By the end of election night viewers usually knew not only who won but also which groups supplied the winning margin, providing a wonderfully detailed demographic portrait of American politics. On only a few election nights did the networks stumble: In 1954 CBS wrongly predicted a Democratic landslide, and in 1960 ABC and CBS wrongly predicted that Nixon would defeat Kennedy. In 2000 the networks were utterly flummoxed on election night. Republican George W. Bush and Democrat Al Gore were nearly even, with Florida's electoral votes holding the winning margin. At first the networks claimed that Gore won the state, then they shifted to Bush, and finally, early in the morning, they reported that the state was actually too close to call, bringing to an end the most embarrassing night in broadcast history.

But the voices in support of television were largely drowned out by a loud chorus of criticism. By the 1980s nothing was being said in the public square on behalf of television. Television, in short, had become America's problem. And almost every year somebody published a book pointing out yet another cause for alarm. In a popular 1978 study of the news industry, *The Newscasters*, critic

Ron Powers wrote, "The biggest heist of the 1970s never made it on the five o'clock news. The biggest heist of the 1970s *was* the five o'clock news. The salesmen took it. They took it away from the journalists." In 1985 social critic Neil Postman took a broader swipe in *Amusing Ourselves to Death*: "There is no shortage of critics who have observed and recorded the dissolution of public discourse in America and its conversion into the arts of show business. But most of them, I believe, have barely begun to tell the story of the origin and meaning of this descent into a vast triviality." The cause of this descent was "the ascendancy of the Age of Television."

With the same intensity with which they once had embraced television as a technological cure for democracy's ailments, Americans now eagerly raced to find a fix for television in order to save democracy. By the end of the century no consensus had developed. But a breathtaking array of nostrums was offered. Conservatives, persuaded that the problem was that television tilted left, bankrolled the establishment of the Fox News network to provide putative balance. Liberal reformers, financed by wealthy backers like the Florence and John Schumann Foundation, lobbied for campaign finance reform to break the grip special interests were believed to have on government now that politicians had to beg for millions of dollars to pay for costly television campaigns. Other reformers associated with the Alliance for Better Campaigns contended that the best way to level the playing field would be to give political candidates free access to television.[24]

As the century ended, television was as it always had been, a thing of wonder, putting viewers in touch with events and personalities from around the world. But Americans expressed a profound ambivalence about the medium that their ancestors a hundred years earlier would have found impossible to comprehend. For an invention that once had been defined as an instrument of democratic change and promise, it was a stunning reversal of fortune.

BIBLIOGRAPHIC NOTE

In *Television and Politics* (Transaction Publishers, 2002), Kurt and Gladys Lang provide an excellent introduction to television themes that sociologists and political scientists have explored over three decades. Recent research about the effect of television on American politics is summarized in Thomas Patterson's *The Vanishing Voter* (Knopf, 2002), which is based on the most comprehensive study of voting behavior ever undertaken. The best guide to the importance of television in the Kennedy presidency is Mary Ann Watson's *The Expanding Vista: American Television in the Kennedy Years* (Oxford University Press, 1990). The use of political advertising on TV is explored by Edwin Diamond and Stephen Bates in *The*

Spot: The Rise of Political Advertising on Television (MIT Press, 1984) and Kathleen Hall Jamieson in *Packaging the Presidency: A History and Criticism of Presidential Campaign Advertising* (Oxford University Press, 1996). The history of presidential debates is provided by Alan Schroeder's *Presidential Debates: Forty Years of High-Risk TV* (Columbia University Press, 2000). The differences between journalism practiced by television news and wire services are laid out clearly in *Over the Wire and on TV: CBS and UPI in Campaign '80*, by Michael J. Robinson and Margaret A. Sheehan (Russell Sage Foundation, 1980).

Journalistic accounts of the history of television are provided by Martin Plissner in *The Control Room: How Television Calls the Shots in Presidential Elections* (Free Press, 1999), Robert MacNeil in *The People Machine: The Influence of Television on American Politics* (Harper & Row, 1968), Martin Schram in *The Great American Video Game: Presidential Politics in the Television Age* (William Morrow, 1987) and David Halberstam in *The Powers That Be* (Knopf, 1979).

Criticism of the effect of television on American society can be found in Neil Postman's *Amusing Ourselves to Death: Public Discourse in the Age of Show Business* (Viking, 1985).

NOTES

1. Daniel Stashower, *The Boy Genius and the Mogul* (New York: Broadway Books, 2002), xv.

2. *New York Times*, 20 June 1932.

3. Martin Plissner, *The Control Room: How Television Calls the Shots in Presidential Elections* (New York: Free Press, 1999), 69.

4. *New York Times*, 15 November 1936.

5. Gould, "What Is Television Doing to Us?" *New York Times Magazine*, 12 June 1949.

6. Edwin Diamond and Stephen Bates, *The Spot: The Rise of Political Advertising on Television* (Cambridge, Mass.: MIT Press, 1984), 43.

7. Richard Reeves, *President Kennedy: Profile of Power* (New York: Simon & Schuster, 1993), 14.

8. In 1952, 39 percent of the delegates to the Democratic National Convention were chosen in sixteen primaries. Lyn Ragsdale, *Vital Statistics on the Presidency*, rev. ed. (Washington, D.C.: Congressional Quarterly, 1998), 40.

9. *New York Times*, 25 June 1951.

10. Kurt Lang and Gladys Engel Lang, *Television and Politics* (New Brunswick, N.J.: Transaction, 2002), 11–15; Michael J. Robinson, "Television and American Politics: 1956–1976," *Public Interest* 48 (Summer 1977): 6.

11. Lewis L. Gould, ed., *Watching Television Come of Age* (Austin: University of Texas Press, 2002), 84–86.

12. Glen D. Phillips, "The Use of Radio and Television by Presidents of the United States," Ph.D. diss., University of Michigan, 1968, 25–26.

13. Mary Ann Watson, *The Expanding Vista: American Television in the Kennedy Years* (New York: Oxford University Press, 1990), 6–7.

14. Ibid., 13–14; Robert MacNeil, *The People Machine: The Influence of Television on American Politics* (New York: Harper & Row, 1968), 88.

15. Gene Wyckoff, *The Image Candidates: American Politics in the Age of Television* (New York: Macmillan, 1968), 52–53, 210–212.

16. Bernard Rubin, *Political Television* (San Francisco: Wadsworth, 1967), 3.

17. Michael J. Robinson, "Television and American Politics: 1956–1976," *The Public Interest* 11 (Summer 1977): 12.

18. Plissner, *Control Room*, 11–13. See also Thomas R. Marshall, "The News Verdict and Public Opinion During the Primaries," in *Television Coverage After the 1980 Presidential Campaign*, ed. William C. Adams (Norwood, N.J.: Ablex, 1983), 49–67.

19. One study showed that between 1980 and 1996, 50 percent of television spots were negative. See William L. Benoit, *Seeing Spots: A Functional Analysis of Presidential Television Advertisements, 1952–1996* (Westport, Conn.: Praeger, 1999), 6. During his first term, Franklin Roosevelt averaged seventy news conferences a year; in his first term, Ronald Reagan averaged six. See Ragsdale, *Vital Statistics*, 170–171. Thomas Patterson, *Out of Order* (New York: Knopf, 1993), chapter 4, concerns "pleasing personalities." Bill Bradley once remarked, "Today's political campaigns function as collection agencies for broadcasters. You simply transfer money from contributors to television stations"; quoted by Paul Taylor and Norman Ornstein, *The Case for Free Air Time* (New America Foundation pamphlet, June 1, 2002). Studies showed that the length of sound bites of presidential candidates broadcast on the nightly newscasts gradually declined from forty-three seconds on average in 1968 to nine seconds in 1988; see Benoit, *Spots*, 5. See also Alan Schroeder, *Presidential Debates: Forty Years of High-Risk TV* (New York: Columbia University Press, 2000).

20. Martin Schram, *The Great American Video Game: Presidential Politics in the Television Age* (New York: William Morrow, 1987), 24–26.

21. Patterson, *Out of Order*, chapter 1.

22. Milton Lodge and Ruth Hamill, "A Partisan Schema for Political Information Processing." *American Political Science Review* 80, no. 2 (June 1986): 505–520.

23. Kathleen Hall Jamieson, *Packaging the Presidency* (New York: Oxford University Press, 1996), 517.

24. Taylor and Ornstein, *The Case for Free Air Time*, 4: "The broadcast airwaves are not only the most important communications medium for politics and democracy, they are also a publicly owned asset—like the oceans, the atmosphere and the national forests. Indeed, the airwaves are the most valuable resource of the Information Age, a core ingredient for a variety of emerging, innovative technologies. But broadcasters, who earn huge profits from this public resource, pay the public nothing in return for its use. It is time for the public to reclaim a share of the airwaves we collectively own to strengthen our democracy."

13. GENDER AND THE
TRANSFORMATION OF POLITICS

SUSAN HARTMANN

In 1948, Harry S. Truman stood off the Soviet Union during the Berlin block-
ade, recognized the new state of Israel, aligned his presidency with goals of the
civil rights movement, and ran a reelection campaign that almost no one thought
he could win—all without having to give a thought to women as voters, politicians, or officeholders. This did not mean that gender was absent from politics in
the 1940s. In fact, it was everywhere. Few noticed the deeply gendered nature of
politics, because male control of the public sphere seemed to represent the natural order. No woman sat on the Supreme Court or in the Cabinet; only seven
women served among the 425 members of the House of Representatives. Over
the next half-century, that system crumbled. Large numbers of women were politicized because of gender; gender became an agent of party realignment as
women gained influence in both major parties; women developed distinct voting patterns; and both women and women's issues occupied larger and more visible spaces in electoral politics and government.

When maleness so strictly defined the norm in the 1940s and 1950s, gender
became manifest only when women's traditional roles offered political capital or
when the occasional female politician appeared on stage. At such times of gender transparency, and especially when the press introduced a female candidate
or official for the first time, photographs and text accentuated traditional femininity with references to the subject's appearance, husband, children, kitchen,

and domestic skills. Such emphases also attended the increasingly public roles occupied by First Ladies. Even presidential wives like Bess Truman or Mamie Eisenhower, who pursued no public purposes of their own, became political factors as the growth of mass media and rise of celebrity pulled the president's family out into the limelight.

When political leaders referred to gender, they did so in ways that reinforced the naturalness of a masculine political system. For example, Adlai Stevenson, the moderately liberal presidential candidate in 1952 and 1956, defined women's political responsibilities in strictly domestic terms. In 1955 he told the Smith College graduating class that as women they could sustain the values of "freedom, tolerance, charity and free inquiry . . . in the humble role of housewife . . . in the living-room with a baby in your lap or in the kitchen with a can opener in your hand." [1] Women's domestic roles became assets in the rhetoric of Cold War competition, extolled to demonstrate the superiority of the United States. During the "kitchen debate" with Soviet Premier Nikita Khrushchev at an exhibit of American products in Moscow in 1959, Vice President Richard M. Nixon countered his adversary's boasts about Soviet women factory workers by emphasizing how American productivity allowed women to stay at home and American technology made their housework easier.

Women, of course, had participated in politics even before they had the vote, but usually in ways that were compatible with their domestic roles. Increasingly in the twentieth century, they performed indispensable, if mundane, work for the Democratic and Republican parties at the grassroots level. That labor increased in the post–World War II era, even after both parties eliminated their women's divisions in 1953, paying lip service to "integration." With less patronage to attract men, parties turned to a still substantial pool of married women who did not hold jobs, encouraging them to volunteer as canvassers, office staff, and poll workers, under the direction of male professionals. Women constituted substantial majorities of these grassroots volunteers, and they filled seats on state and national party committees; but they had little voice in key decisions. At a time when party conventions still controlled the nominating process, women constituted less than 15 percent of the delegates.

No woman sat in Truman's inner circle. He appreciated the unwavering support and political skills of India Edwards, who mobilized women for the Democratic Party, complimenting her for acting like a man. In response to her urging, Truman appointed a few more women to federal office than had his predecessor. Yet, he was not comfortable working with women, believing that they inhibited free discussion among men. He explained to an aide his refusal to appoint a woman to his cabinet or the Supreme Court: "The Justices don't want a woman. They say they couldn't sit around with their robes off and their feet up and discuss their problems." [2] Because so few women sat in Congress, and only two chaired important committees—Mary T. Norton (D-N.J.), Labor, and Edith Nourse Rogers (R-Mass.), Veterans Affairs—Truman rarely had to consider a woman's position on legislation.

Nor did Truman feel much pressure from civil society to act on issues of specific concern to women. Tens of thousands belonged to women's organizations that addressed political issues, but most, like the League of Women Voters, were determinedly nonpartisan and defined their civic duty as working for the general good, not their own self-interest. The relatively few women who challenged the normality of women's exclusion from politics did so primarily at the margins. From the 1940s to the 1960s, politically active women—in women's organizations, in labor unions, and at the fringes of party politics—focused on four gender-specific goals: appointment of women to official positions; establishment of a national equal-pay law; creation of a federal commission to investigate the status of women and recommend policy changes; and adoption of an equal rights amendment (ERA) to the Constitution. A handful of states enacted equal-pay laws, and Congress gave some attention to these policy goals during the 1940s and 1950s, but it enacted just two laws affecting women as women: the Women's Armed Services Integration Act of 1948, which made women a permanent, if small and unequal, component of the military; and a provision in the Revenue Act of 1954 allowing lower-income employed mothers to take income tax deductions for childcare expenses.

Activist women were themselves divided over the ERA, which the National Woman's Party had been pushing since 1923. Most women's organizations and key social reformers such as Eleanor Roosevelt opposed it, because it would require men and women to be treated alike under the law and thus nullify state labor laws providing special protections for working women. Truman felt sufficiently insulated to dismiss challenges to the gender status quo. When Emma Guffey Miller, a prominent member of the DNC, pleaded with Truman to support the ERA, the president blew her off with the quip, "It has been my experience that there is no equality—men are just slaves and I suppose they will always continue to be." [3]

Small cracks in the gendered political system appeared in the 1950s, as more extensive polling yielded information about women's voting behavior. Election polls in 1952 indicated that women's support for Eisenhower surpassed that of men by about five percentage points (though he would have won even absent this gender gap), and until 1980 a larger portion of women voted for the Republican national ticket than did men. Meanwhile, women's presence in the electorate grew: although their turnout rate did not exceed that of men until 1980, the fact that larger numbers of women were eligible meant that by 1964 more women than men actually voted.

Before the 1970s, little distinguished Democrats from Republicans in terms of women's place within the parties or their stands on gender-specific policy. In the 1956 campaign, President Dwight D. Eisenhower provided rhetorical support for equal-pay legislation and the ERA, but he was as dismissive as Truman of women's grievances, insisting that "it's hard for a mere man to believe that woman doesn't have equal rights."[4] Like his predecessor, Ike's primary effort was to select more women for federal office, including appointing Oveta Culp Hobby to his cabinet (as secretary of health, education, and welfare) and Clare Booth Luce as ambassador to Italy. Overall, though, women's numbers in high office remained tiny. Neither party yet appealed to women in terms of women's issues, although both parties competed actively for women's votes in the 1960 election. Democrats feared the loss of New Deal supporters who were moving to the rapidly growing suburbs and sought to break women's tendency to vote Republican. John F. Kennedy's campaign featured activities to mobilize women at the grass roots, including tea parties hosted by his female relatives.

AN EMERGING MOVEMENT

Although women activists expressed anger that Kennedy's search for "the best and the brightest" brought a paltry few women into significant government positions, and although women's concerns ranked low among his priorities, two key initiatives against sex discrimination made his administration a minor turning point in the politics of gender. One was passage of the Equal Pay Act of 1963, banning the practice of paying women less for the same work as men. Several factors contributed to the landmark legislation. Championed by union women and other women's groups since World War II, the measure had the support of the AFL-CIO, one of the Democrats' most important constituencies, and it complemented the Kennedy administration's promise of reform and economic revitalization. Women's lives increasingly included paid employment, with twenty-four million women constituting one-third of the labor force by 1960. Enacted before the emergence of a broad-based feminist movement, the Equal Pay Act raised gender consciousness as women filed and won grievances to implement it.

The equal-pay measure also benefited from the expert leadership of Esther Peterson, director of the Women's Bureau and assistant secretary of labor. As a labor lobbyist, she had worked with Kennedy when he was a senator and advised his presidential campaign. She used her political clout and his narrow victory to persuade him to fulfill another decade-old goal of activist women, appointment of a President's Commission on the Status of Women. Headed by Eleanor Roosevelt, composed of leaders from government and the private sector, and involving more than a hundred individuals through its subcommittees, the commission issued a report in 1963 that documented and proposed remedies for widespread discrimination against women while at the same time affirming the primacy of their maternal role. Though far from a radical document, it provided credibility for women's grievances and led to the creation of similar commissions in forty-nine states and a national network of individuals—predominantly women—who shared copious data, concern about gender inequities, and heightened expectations for government action to eliminate sex discrimination. In addition to creating institutions for the gender-based politicization of women, the commissions gave women a sense of collective identity and a sense of their political power.

Two more developments during the early 1960s heightened attention to gender and fostered challenges to male domination of politics. In 1963, Betty Friedan published *The Feminine Mystique*, a national best-seller that raised consciousness about gender inequities. Focusing on the frustrations of white, educated, middle-class women unfulfilled by family life and uninspiring jobs, Friedan analyzed and criticized American society for not permitting women "to accept or gratify their basic need to grow and fulfill their potentialities as human beings." Equally important, the black freedom struggle inadvertently encouraged feminism by creating a moral climate more sensitive to injustice, establishing legal precedents to which sex discrimination could be attached, inventing effective new protest strategies and tactics that other groups soon borrowed, and leading some African American women to consider gender as well as racial injustice. Moreover, civil rights activism disrupted traditional politics, creating conflicts over racial issues within both parties and providing openings for the demands of other groups. Finally, the experiences of some white women in the black freedom struggle and other reform and radical movements of the 1960s led to a growing sense of gender oppression. Though this "women's liberation" wing kept aloof of mainstream politics, it provided a radical critique of heterosexuality, marriage, and other elements of the traditional sex/gender system, introduced into the political arena such new issues as abortion, rape, domestic violence, and sexual harassment, and eventually shared issues and activism with feminism's liberal wing.

A landmark achievement of the black freedom struggle, the Civil Rights Act of 1964, served as another important catalyst to women's politicization. Representative Howard Smith, a Virginia Democrat and civil rights opponent, slyly introduced an amendment to include discrimination "on account of sex" in Title VII of the bill, which banned employment discrimination. But a handful of congresswomen supported by a small group of feminist policy activists pushed it through Congress with the sex-discrimination ban intact. Then, when the agency created to enforce the law, the Equal Employment Opportunity Commission (EEOC), failed to treat claims of sex discrimination seriously, women organized in protest. At a meeting of state commissions on the status of women in Washington in 1966, a group led by Betty Friedan, civil rights activist Pauli Murray, and others from labor and women's groups founded the National Organization for Women (NOW), to realize "the democratic goal of full participation and equal partnership for all citizens."[5] NOW became the first of dozens of new organizations created to advance women's equality in the public arena and remedy their disadvantages in the private sphere. Although its immediate roots were the President's Commission on the Status of Women and Title VII of the Civil Rights Act of 1964, NOW and the resurgence of feminism in general reflected larger trends: women's growing presence in the labor force; their increasing participation in higher education; and their changing patterns of childbearing.

The late 1960s formed a transitional period in gender politics as the fledgling feminist movement increasingly demanded the attention of policymakers, who responded in ways that eventually transformed women's status under the law. In producing these policy initiatives, feminists counted heavily on help from traditional women's organizations, such as the National Federation of Business and Professional Women and the American Association of University Women, as well as from key congresswomen such as Edith Green (D-Ore.) and Martha Griffiths (D-Mich.), who had the seniority and connections to make male colleagues and administration officials listen to them. Although their numbers remained tiny, congresswomen from both parties became more outspoken on issues concerning sex discrimination. Moreover, by 1970, staff in some of these women's congressional offices, including those of Green, Griffiths, Patsy Mink (D-Hawaii), and Margaret Heckler (R-Mass.), were providing the still young and politically inexperienced women's movement invaluable help in mobilizing lobbying campaigns. "Does this interest Martha Griffiths?" Lyndon Johnson scrawled on a report from the EEOC in 1967, indicating both the recent appearance of women's policy concerns on the presidential radar screen and the ability of feminist legislators to claim presidential attention.[6]

Johnson in fact became the first president to appeal to women on the basis of their interests as women. As vice president he had provided strong support for the PCSW and the Equal Pay law, but these initiatives were associated with Kennedy. To claim his own ground, in 1964 he promised to end "stag government," with considerable fanfare about the appointment of women to government positions. Johnson's actual record in this respect represented just modest gains—he did not appoint even a "token" female to his cabinet—and after the election he shifted from appealing to women as women to mobilizing women as citizens in support of his antipoverty program. But some activists had other things in mind. Mobilized and encouraged by the two Democratic presidents of the 1960s, they now began to seek their own agenda, compelling Johnson to approve a number of policy changes: the extension of affirmative action to include women, equality in federal jury service, and more equitable treatment of women in the military.

That was just the beginning. In the late 1960s, feminists began to capture national attention with marches, demonstrations, and sit-ins, including a

NOW-instigated disruption of a Senate subcommittee hearing to demand consideration of the ERA. For the first time since the suffrage movement, women's issues appeared on front pages and op-ed pages of newspapers. Until 1980, both parties responded positively to the women's movement, contributing to a virtual revolution in the status of women under the law. In addition to passing the ERA in 1972 by large margins (84–8 in the Senate and 354–23 in the House), Congress outlawed sex discrimination in all areas and all levels of federally funded education and in the granting of credit; included domestic workers under minimum-wage coverage; banned employment discrimination against pregnant women; and opened the military academies to women. Responding to suits filed by feminist lawyers, the Supreme Court for the first time struck down a state law on the grounds of sex discrimination (*Reed v. Reed*, 1971) and ruled that the Constitution protected women's right to abortion (*Roe v. Wade*, 1973). Using the equal protection clause of the Fourteenth Amendment, it also struck down laws that treated men and women differently in such areas as social security, welfare benefits, workers' compensation, and military benefits programs.

Even though the ERA ultimately fell three states short of the minimum needed for ratification, the combination of legislation and judicial rulings amounted to a sea change in public policy, reversing centuries of law based on women's dependency as daughters, wives, and mothers. Moreover, women's burdens that had been invisible, nameless, or assumed to be private circumstances beyond the reach of government now became matters of public policy. Domestic violence, for example, was a term so novel that some legislators initially thought the topic dealt with terrorists in airports. Yet Congress came close to enacting a domestic violence bill in 1979, and executive agencies provided funds for battered women's shelters and services through broader programs, as was the case with assistance to displaced homemakers. Although rape, as a criminal law issue, received most attention at the state and local levels, Congress established a National Center for the Prevention and Control of Rape and amended federal rules of evidence to ban defendants' use of a victim's sexual history as evidence in trials. Finally, Congress appropriated funds for a National Women's Conference that met in Houston, Texas, in 1977. Conference delegates approved a twenty-five-plank plan of action covering virtually every aspect of women's disadvantage and referring to the needs of such specific groups of women as older women, homemakers, lesbians, and criminal offenders. To be sure, feminists suffered defeats in the public policy arena, notably in Richard Nixon's veto of a comprehensive childcare bill and in the passage of legislation restricting women's access to abortions. Nonetheless, the bipartisan support attending most of the policy reforms reflected not only the growth of feminist groups in the 1970s, but also women's increasing demands on both major parties for inclusion and attention. These policy changes as well signaled a shift in liberalism by extending the economic benefits of the New Deal to hitherto excluded groups and addressing social inequities formerly hidden in the private sphere.

WOMEN ADVANCE IN POLITICS

The shocks to the New Deal order dealt by the black freedom struggle and the Vietnam War opened opportunities for women to gain influence in the parties as well as the policymaking arena. In the aftermath of its conflict-ridden national convention in 1968, the Democrats established a commission to find ways to accommodate disaffected groups. Implemented for the 1972 convention, the commission's reforms diminished the power of traditional party leaders by requiring that a majority of delegates be chosen by voters in the primaries and that each delegation reflect the distribution of women, minorities, young people, and other groups in the population of its state. A door now opened wide for women, who constituted 51 percent of the national population but just 13 percent of the delegates at the 1968 Democratic national convention.

At the same time, feminists developed new instruments of political influence. While NOW and other women's groups exerted pressure in the policy arena, all were nonpartisan and none focused explicitly or exclusively on politics until the founding of the National Women's Political Caucus in 1971. Composed of self-identified feminists, such as Betty Friedan and Gloria Steinem, and women from civil rights, labor, religious, and welfare groups, including Fannie Lou Hamer, Olga Madar, and LaDonna Harris, the broad-based bipartisan organization dedicated itself to electing women to office and increasing their voice in party affairs and to combating sexism, racism, institutional violence, and poverty by supporting feminist candidates of both sexes. Immediately NWPC members from both parties began to mobilize for the 1972 party conventions. In place of the deference that had characterized women's approach to male party leaders since the late nineteenth century, women now confronted them with demands. Influencing their parties' stands on issues became as or more important than their traditional role of helping them to win elections.

In 1972, 40 percent of the Democratic delegates were women, more than one-third of whom reported that they had been active in the women's liberation movement. Although feminists failed to get reproductive freedom into the platform, they did win fifteen women's rights planks and the election of Jean Westwood, the first woman to chair the Democratic National Committee. At the Republican convention, women's share of the delegates went to 30 percent, up from 17 percent in 1968. Although the Republicans paid less attention than the Democrats to feminist issues, the convention endorsed the ERA and federally assisted day care and passed a rule calling for more equal representation of women at the next convention. Two years after the convention, Mary Louise Smith, a longtime party activist and founder of the Iowa Women's Political Caucus, became the first female chair of the Republican National Committee.

A number of external developments combined to create a small pool of politically experienced women who provided a base for these efforts to increase women's political presence. Whereas well over half of women elected to Congress before 1965 filled their dead husbands' seats, women increasingly won election in their own right, often having cut their political teeth discussing issues and exercising leadership in traditional women's organizations. During the 1950s, for example, three hundred officers and board members of the strictly nonpartisan League of Women Voters (LWV) resigned every year so that they could enter partisan politics. One of these, Ella Grasso, moved from the League to the Connecticut General Assembly in 1952 and eventually to the governor's mansion, the first female governor not to follow her husband in office. Civil rights and other highly charged issues in the 1960s also served as magnets drawing more women into politics. In New York, Shirley Chisholm parlayed activism in reform Democratic politics in Bedford-Stuyvesant in New York City to a seat in the state assembly and later in Congress. Harriet Woods honed political skills in the St. Louis LWV, worked to promote integrated neighborhoods in the 1960s, won election to her suburban city council in 1967 and the Missouri Senate in 1976, and lost a race for the U.S. Senate by a hair's breadth in 1982. A founder of Women Strike for Peace and an activist lawyer in the 1960s, Bella Abzug won election to the House from Manhattan in 1970. After defending African Americans arrested during the 1965 Watts riots, Yvonne Braithwaite Burke served three terms representing Los Angeles in the California assembly and gained election to the House in 1972. Burke and Abzug were harbingers of another change that opened political opportunities for women: their increasing possession of law degrees, the most typical pathway to elective office. In 1970 only 3 percent of lawyers were women, but in the last half of the decade, women comprised 24 percent of new admissions to the bar, and the numbers continued to rise.

Two additional factors eased women's way into political office. The distrust of and disillusionment with government that grew out of the Vietnam war and Watergate made voters more likely to support "outsiders," a condition that Mary Anne Krupsak capitalized on to become lieutenant governor of New York with the campaign slogan, "She's Not Just One of the Boys." The concomitant decline of party control over nominations and candidates, furthered by the increasing number of direct primaries and the ability to appeal directly to voters through TV and other instruments of mass communication, similarly proved beneficial to fresh faces. As parties' ability to deliver voters to the polls weakened, opportunities emerged for interest groups, including feminists, to mobilize the electorate. These developments helped elect such women as Patricia Schroeder (D-Colo.), Bella Abzug (D-N.Y.), and Margaret Heckler, even when they lacked support from or were opposed by their party's leadership. This independence, in turn, gave them both the freedom to pursue women's policy issues and an incentive to do so as a means of attracting media attention and building constituency support. Even though the number of women in Congress increased only from fifteen in 1971 to twenty-three in 1981, they made important contributions to the success of the feminist agenda in the 1970s.

POLARIZATION AROUND GENDER ISSUES: THE 1970s

While the upheavals of the 1960s made the parties and holding office more accessible to women and assisted enactment of feminist policy, that turbulence and the rise of feminism itself also produced a counter trend. The politicization of women around gender issues was no one-way street: some women were initiated into politics on behalf of feminist goals, but others joined anti-abortion and antifeminist movements that would have their own dramatic effects on the American political order. In the 1970s feminist policy goals commanded considerable bipartisan support, and both Republicans and Democrats responded positively to women's demands for a larger voice in party deliberations. Yet the beginnings of polarization on gender issues became visible during the Nixon administration, as conservatism gained increasing prominence in the Republican Party.

Traditional conservatism, like New Deal liberalism—and politics in general—was largely impervious to gender. Conservatives were concerned above all with limiting the reach of the federal government within the nation, strengthening the military establishment, and fighting communism everywhere. These issues formed the core of Barry Goldwater's campaign for the presidency in 1964, but his capture of the Republican nomination also reflected a growing hostility to federal intervention to protect civil rights. In addition, a hint of what was to become a fundamental element of conservatism appeared when Goldwater appealed to female voters' concerns about stable family life. Running against the liberal Nelson Rockefeller, Goldwater seized upon his opponent's divorce and remarriage to a much younger woman and ran ads promoting himself as "a responsible family man . . . a fine example of . . . loyalty for the White House." Only temporarily thwarted by the Democrats' overwhelming victory in 1964, conservative ranks grew, feeding on sentiment that government was spending the taxes of hard-working Americans on undeserving populations, going too far to appease African Americans, and tolerating antipatriotism, drugs, disorder in the streets, sexual indulgence, a general loosening of moral standards, and a weakening of the family.

Both Richard Nixon and George Wallace appealed to that sentiment in 1968, while feminist issues remained largely outside of party and electoral politics, overshadowed by the Vietnam War, student demonstrations, and urban violence. As president, however, Nixon could not entirely ignore the feminist movement or women's issues, which by 1970 claimed a national audience. Although generally uninterested in domestic policy, he did not oppose the flood of anti–sex discrimination legislation that came across his desk in the early 1970s, just as he signed a host of other liberal measures such as environmental protection and government support for the arts. Nixon also followed the pattern established by his predecessors, appointing a number of women to high positions in government, especially during the run-up to the 1972 election. The first female Secret Service agents protected the president's family, and the first female FBI agents began training in 1972. In 1971 Nixon considered appointing a woman to the Supreme Court to improve his reelection prospects, even though he considered women more "erratic and emotional" than men. "Thank God we don't have any in the Cabinet," he said to Bob Haldeman. "I'm not for women, frankly, in any job . . . But I must say the Cabinet's so lousy we might just as well have a woman there, too."[7]

Although gender played no large role in Nixon's strategy to pry southerners and urban ethnic voters from the Democratic Party, in two areas he took the first steps toward courting an emerging antifeminist sentiment and realigning the parties on gender issues. In 1971, Congress passed a comprehensive childcare bill, pushed by a broad coalition of labor unions, religious organizations, civil rights, feminist, and child-welfare groups. Because the bill authorized government-subsidized childcare centers, it angered traditional conservatives, who opposed additional federal programs in principle and decried government sponsorship of a practice that had been pioneered by Soviet Communism. At the same time, because childcare clearly spoke to the rapidly increasing presence of mothers in the workforce (affecting nearly 30 percent of all children by 1970), it drew fire from a newer conservative element, closely connected to fundamentalist religions and firmly attached to norms and values centered around conventional gender roles and the patriarchal family. Nixon's veto message combined both the old and new conservatism. He declared that the role of the federal government should be to help parents purchase the childcare services they needed "in the private, open market," not to administer a fiscally irresponsible program with "a new army of bureaucrats." At the same time, he played to concerns of social conservatives by warning about the "family-weakening implications" of the measure that he contended would replace "the family-centered approach [with] communal approaches to child rearing."

While Nixon was compelled to take a stand on the childcare bill, his goal of moving Catholic Democrats into the Republican Party prompted him to seize the initiative on the other issue that proved a powerful mobilizing issue for the new religious right. By 1970, an abortion reform movement had begun making an impact in several states, including California and New York. The Catholic Church responded with a countermovement, and when the church campaigned to repeal the New York law liberalizing abortion, Nixon leapt to its aid, praising the "defenders of the right to life of the unborn." Again, in receiving a report from his Commission on Population Growth and the American Future, Nixon called "abortion an unacceptable form of population control . . . [that] would demean human life," thus foreshadowing the Republican Party's eventual embrace of a key issue of the Christian right.

More than anyone else, however, it was Phyllis Schlafly who wove the new strands of conservatism into the more traditional fabric of the right. A devoted conservative in the Republican Party since the early 1950s, Schlafly performed women's typical voluntary work for her party, but her political ambitions, keen knowledge of issues, and prodigious public speaking set her apart from most party women and led to her election as first vice president of the National Federation of Republican Women (NFRW) in 1964. That year she also gained national prominence as author of A Choice Not an Echo, a small self-published book in which she decried the takeover of the Republican Party by Eastern internationalist liberals and pushed Barry Goldwater for the presidential nomination. Selling more than a million copies, with its title serving as Goldwater's campaign slogan, the book also enhanced Schlafly's reputation as a conservative and, she believed, ended her career in the NFRW. She charged that Republican leaders manipulated the women's organization to prevent her from moving up from first vice president to president. And they did so, she asserted, not just as moderates or liberals trying to redeem the party from Goldwater's disastrous defeat in 1964, but also as men who wanted women to serve the party but not influence its choices. "The Republican party is carried on the shoulders of the women who do . . . the menial work, while the selection of candidates and the policy decisions are taken care of by the men in the smoke-filled rooms," she charged.[8]

Schlafly's gender consciousness, however, did not lead to feminism. She built an independent base among conservative women, politicizing new groups of women around an alternative construction of their interests and making antifeminism an integral part of the conservative agenda. In 1967, shortly after the NFRW convention, she began a monthly newsletter, The Phyllis Schlafly Report. At first she concentrated on issues that had concerned her since the 1950s—the Communist threat, the need for a strong national defense, and the dangers of big government—with only occasional mention of the social or moral issues that would mobilize the Christian right in the 1970s and 1980s, such as abortion and sexual permissiveness. In 1972, however, she began to organize STOP ERA, the movement that ultimately defeated the Equal Rights Amendment, and from that time on, she blended the old laissez-faire conservatism with the new social conservatism.

A devout Catholic who believed that traditional gender roles were God-given and that abortion was a sin, Schlafly faced the dissonance between social conservatives' religion-based aim to control private behavior and the older secular right's attachment to laissez faire. She merged the two conservative streams in a variety of ways. For example, she derogated the Soviet version of equal rights for women, declaring that American women were the most privileged in the world because the free enterprise system had liberated them from drudgery. The ERA, which empowered Congress to enforce sexual equality throughout the nation, she held up as an extreme example of big government overriding state's rights. Like Nixon, she attacked day care and other feminist projects as Communist-inspired and threatening to American institutions. Equality in military service, she warned, "would be destructive of our military defenses and of the morale of our fighting forces."[9] More subtly, by focusing on women, Schlafly and the thousands of women in her camp provided conservatism with a respectable cover for attacking affirmative action and other programs that benefited racial and ethnic minorities as well as women. Schlafly merged race and gender, for example in equating the ERA's enforcement provisions with the Voting Rights Act. As a whole, antifeminism furnished conservatives with another weapon with which to attack liberalism.

The growing ranks of both social conservatism and feminism, along with the 1973 *Roe v. Wade* Supreme Court decision legalizing abortion, thrust gender issues into contention within both major parties. Gerald Ford, with a wife who publicly championed the ERA and other feminist measures, began his presidency as an outspoken champion of sexual equality. When confronted with a challenge for the nomination in 1976 by the conservative Ronald Reagan, however, Ford back-pedaled. He publicly announced his disagreement with *Roe*, and the Republican platform supported a constitutional amendment "to restore protection of the right to life for unborn children." Although both parties supported ratification of the ERA, the Democrats' plank calling "undesirable" a constitutional amendment to reverse *Roe* marked the first partisan division on an issue of central concern to activist women.

As the Republicans edged away from profeminist positions, the Democrats became more explicit in support of women's rights. With political feminists tending overwhelmingly to be Democrats and the women's movement enjoying its peak years, Jimmy Carter broke new ground for presidential candidates in addressing gender-specific issues. He negotiated directly with feminist leaders at the Democratic National Convention and created a "51.3 percent committee" (named for the percentage of women in the population) to advise him on strategy and policy. While Ford declined an invitation to address the National Women's Agenda Conference, attended by a broad spectrum of women's organizations, feminist and nonfeminist, Carter promised that audience a nine-point program to advance women's status. Friedan claimed to be "moved to tears by Carter," while Abzug compared his commitment to improving conditions for women to President Johnson's commitment to African Americans. Yet gender issues, however much they reflected the growing influence of antifeminists and feminists within the parties, figured insignificantly in the presidential campaign. Although Ford narrowly lost the election, exit polls revealed that he maintained the Republican pattern of appealing more strongly to women than to men, winning 51 percent of the female vote and 45 percent of the male vote.

Carter's administration ushered the feminist movement into the Democratic Party coalition. He and his wife Rosalynn went out of their way to promote ratification of the ERA. Moreover, Carter made women's rights a part of his human-rights priority and appointed unparalleled numbers of women, including such visible feminists as Bella Abzug (chair of his National Advisory Committee for Women), Sarah Weddington (White House staff), Eleanor Holmes Norton (head of the EEOC), and Juanita Kreps (secretary of commerce) to government positions. Female officials in turn hired women in lower-level positions, and feminist networks grew within the federal bureaucracy, resulting in policy advances even in the absence of White House attention. Thus, while Carter focused on legal equality for women, feminists in the administration pushed initiatives for displaced homemakers, victims of domestic violence, and female entrepreneurs, breaking entirely new ground for women in the policy area. Despite the feminist policy advances of the Carter administration, however, by 1980 organized feminism stood opposed to his renomination.

The rift between feminists and Carter had numerous sources. For one thing, feminists exaggerated both the power of their movement and the reach of the president's command. The flood of legislation against sex discrimination in the preceding two Republican administrations led them to anticipate even more with a Democrat in the White House. Yet, Carter never committed himself to certain feminist goals. He expressed his personal opposition to abortion except in extreme cases, and he signed the Hyde Amendment, which denied Medicaid funds for abortion. He waited to endorse a domestic violence prevention bill until Schlafly and other conservatives had rallied opposition to what they considered federal intrusion into the family and government-supported battered women's shelters that would serve as feminist "indoctrination centers." In addition, clashes between Carter and Democratic Party feminists occurred over their insistence that "women's issues" included economic and defense policies.

When Abzug, whom Carter had appointed as co-chair of the National Advisory Committee for Women, protested Carter's plans to curb inflation by cutting the domestic budget and safety-net programs that protected poor women, while increasing military spending, he fired her. Even when Carter and feminists agreed on a goal such as the ERA, the president could not necessarily deliver: all of his public endorsements and personal appeals to state legislators could not pry approval out of three state legislatures needed for ratification. Angry at Carter's limited efforts on behalf of their goals and powerless to block his renomination for the presidency in 1980, Democratic feminists still maintained sufficient clout to get into the party platform a plank supporting federal funding of abortion for poor women, despite Carter's opposition.

By contrast, the Republicans went in the opposite direction, resulting in the polarization of the major parties around gender issues. The 1980 national convention was dominated by a broad spectrum of conservatives, with the older free-market advocates and anticommunists now strongly augmented by Schlafly's supporters and like-minded men and women mobilized by evangelical ministers and their allies around issues of Christian morality, family values, and law and order. Although not all subscribed to the doctrine of wifely submission preached by the immensely successful founder of the Moral Majority, Jerry Falwell, this New Right clustered around the slogan "family values," a shorthand code for maintaining women's traditional position in the heterosexual two-parent family organized around a conventional division of labor between men and women. The New Right opposed the social and economic changes that were dramatically altering gender roles as well as the feminist policies that helped women take advantage of and accommodate to these changes. Pro-family advocates did not publicly object to women's employment or equal pay for equal work, but they decried government intervention to promote sexual equality, valorized the primacy of motherhood for women, and preferred that mothers of young children did not work outside the home. In terms of policy, this translated into opposition to abortion, state-sponsored day-care centers, affirmative action, protection of homosexual rights, government programs to help victims of domestic violence, and other measures to promote women's autonomy.

Although political commentators and scholars defined the conflict between pro-family traditionalists and feminists as a "culture war" fought over "social issues," the antagonism hid deep economic frustrations that were also related to changing gender roles. Economic stagnation and a decline in real wages were forcing more women into the labor force; one paycheck was ever less sufficient for families to participate in the consumer economy. Pro-family ideas proved attractive to women who wanted conventional family roles and feared losing economic security if abandoned by their husbands. Such ideas also appealed to men and women who saw husbands' economic prospects constrained by new competition from women entering the labor force (although in reality most new women workers still occupied traditional female occupations). Stating explicitly the economic foundations of antifeminism, Schlafly, for example, charged that banning information about marital status and number of dependents from employment applications was "clear and cruel discrimination (especially in a time of high unemployment) . . . against a man's right and ability to fulfill his role as provider, and against the right of his wife to be a full-time homemaker."[10] According to Schlafly, affirmative action prevented skilled male workers from supporting their families, "because the government has forced the employer to hire an artificial quota of women.[11]

In addition to securing the nomination of Ronald Reagan for president in 1980, the right also captured the party that historically had been the more sympathetic to women's rights. The Republican national convention reaffirmed its support for a right-to-life amendment to the Constitution and called for the appointment of judges who "respect . . . the sanctity of innocent human life." It pledged support for equality for women but abandoned the longstanding commitment to the Equal Rights Amendment, as women in the party's liberal and moderate wings, dressed in the traditional white of the suffragists, joined more than ten thousand women marching in protest outside the convention hall. Most of the feminists were outside the party as well. Schlafly demonstrated the leverage of the female right in the Republican Party by withdrawing the volunteer labor of her followers from campaign offices when party leaders created a women's policy advisory board that she considered too feminist. To retrieve the valuable resources provided by grassroots women, Republican leaders capitulated to some of Schlafly's demands by reconfiguring the board and creating an additional one on family policy for her supporters. Because Reagan had to appeal to a broader, more centrist electorate, once nominated, he soft-pedaled the social issues. Instead, he hammered the Carter administration on its inability to control inflation and unemployment and to secure release of American hostages held by Iran, concerns that delivered Reagan the presidency with a whopping Electoral College victory of 489–49.

GENDER POLITICS IN A CONSERVATIVE ERA

Taking control of the White House and Senate, Republican leaders recognized that Reagan drew much stronger support from male than from female voters and sought to appeal to women voters. Reagan appointed the first woman, Sandra Day O'Connor, to the Supreme Court and ultimately named three women to his cabinet (Margaret Heckler, Elizabeth Dole, and Ann Dore McLaughlin) and another, Jeane Kirkpatrick, as ambassador to the United Nations. Those appointments, along with efforts by party leaders to recruit and support Republican women as candidates for political office and to showcase women at subsequent national conventions, demonstrated that while feminists had lost all influence within the party, feminism had not. Republican leaders downplayed gender issues, trumpeting the control of inflation and the economic recovery after 1982. They endeavored to convince women, especially party feminists, who tended to be on the upper rungs of the economic ladder, that their economic interests were not unique to women and were best served by Reagan. As he told a group of Republican women officeholders, "Today our nation has one big program to help every American man, woman, and child. It's called economic recovery."[12]

In the policy area, the Reagan administration walked a political tightrope to maintain the allegiance of moderates and satisfy the New Right, while concentrating on the economic and defense issues that were most important to him. On one hand, Reagan supported antiabortion measures and other New Right goals primarily with rhetoric and symbolism rather than with concentrated action. Moreover, he signed two measures advanced by the women's movement that were also compatible with women's traditional roles as wives and mothers— a law to assist women in obtaining child-support payments, and one to strengthen the claims of divorced women and widows on their husbands' pensions. On the other hand, the Reagan administration took a number of actions that undermined feminist policies—cutting funds for welfare and other social services, removing Republican feminists from the U.S. Commission on Civil Rights, and securing a Supreme Court decision that temporarily gutted Title IX of the 1972 legislation banning sex-discrimination in education.

The influence of antifeminism in the Republican Party and the party's move toward the right was further manifest in the career of Reagan's successor, George H. W. Bush, who had contested Reagan for the presidential nomination in 1980. A strong advocate of family planning and birth control as a congressman, and married to a longtime supporter of Planned Parenthood, Bush had attacked Reagan's position on abortion as "unwise" and opposition to the ERA as "backward thinking" in the primaries. Offered the vice-presidential nomination, however, Bush trimmed his moderate sails on women's issues as well as on economic and foreign policy. Republican feminists who had supported Bush in hopes that he would exercise a moderating influence on the Reagan administration were disappointed. Succeeding Reagan in the White House in 1988, Bush vetoed four bills passed by the Democratic Congress that would have eased restrictions on access to abortion and mandated unpaid family and medical leave for workers in large companies.

Although the end of the Cold War, the dissolution of the Soviet Union, and the Gulf War overshadowed controversy around women's issues, Bush's nomination of Clarence Thomas, a federal appeals court judge, for the Supreme Court put gender and politics at the center of national attention in November 1991. The selection of Thomas, an African American with a record of opposition to affirmative action and other civil rights measures, galvanized a liberal coalition to oppose his confirmation. When law professor Anita Hill reported that Thomas had sexually harassed her when she worked for him at the EEOC during the Reagan administration, the Senate Judiciary Committee held three days of hearings before a national television audience. Thomas angrily denied the charges, and Hill's testimony failed to sway the Senate, which narrowly confirmed him.

Despite the Senate's dismissal of Hill's charges, the hearings riveted attention on sexual harassment, once more politicizing a previously personal and hidden issue. Public opinion divided over whom to believe. Schlafly and other conservative women discounted Hill's testimony and called feminists inconsistent for implying that women were so weak that they needed government protection from sexual harassment. Other women, however, focused on Hill's shabby treatment by senators who tried to discredit her. That no women sat on the Judiciary Committee was starkly visible in the TV coverage (of the entire Senate, only two were women), and feminists redoubled efforts to get women into political office. The press called 1992 the "Year of the Woman," when twice as many women ran for Congress as had two years earlier, and women increased their presence in the Senate from two to six and in the House from twenty-eight to forty-seven.

These gains built on a movement already under way. Joining a national trend that helped displace political parties as the prime recruiters and supporters of candidates, and building upon initiatives of the NWPC and other women's groups in the 1970s, feminists formed a number of new political action committees (PACs). EMILY's List, founded in 1985 by Democrat and feminist Ellen Malcolm, was the most prominent of these. Supporting only pro-choice Democratic women (the acronym stands for Early Money Is Like Yeast, because it "makes the dough rise"), it carefully screened candidates for electoral viability and collected and distributed funds to such candidates well in advance of their primaries, sometimes providing as much as 25 percent of a candidate's treasury. By its own count EMILY's List contributed $6.2 million to women's campaigns in 1992 and $8.4 million in 1996. In 2000, it raised $9.3 million for candidates in addition to nearly $11 million for a special project to mobilize women voters in key contested states.

After the 1980 election, feminists in the Democratic Party seized upon and publicized a "gender gap" in voting behavior, when exit polls revealed that women favored Reagan by considerably slimmer margins than did men. They contended that the gender gap, which amounted to as much as 8 percentage points depending on the poll, demonstrated that women acted on distinct interests and could exercise serious leverage at the polls. Scholars quickly found that the different voting patterns turned less on women's legal and reproductive rights than they did on issues of peace, the environment, and government's responsibility for social welfare. Moreover, a point that feminists did not emphasize, the gender gap indicated that men were moving toward the Republican Party and conservative values. Nonetheless, as voting differences between men and women persisted throughout the 1980s and 1990s, women not infrequently made the difference for Democratic candidates. In 1986, women's votes altered national politics by providing the margins of victory in several key races and enabled the Democrats to take control of the Senate for the first time since the election of 1980.

The 1984 presidential election demonstrated both the considerable strength of feminists within the Democratic Party as well as the limitations of gender gap strategies. Nearly a year before the election NOW abandoned its nonpartisanship and endorsed Walter Mondale for president. Representatives of NOW, the NWPC, and several other women's organizations, began to press for the nomination of a woman for vice president, and Mondale complied by choosing as running mate Geraldine Ferraro, a third-term member of Congress from Queens, New York. Although the choice electrified the national convention, and Ferraro proved an able campaigner who drew large crowds, questions about her husband's finances clouded the campaign, and Republicans cast her nomination as evidence that "special interests" had bullied Mondale into choosing the first female vice-presidential candidate on a major party ticket. A gender gap in voting persisted, but both women and men testified to Reagan's immense popularity at the polls and sealed the Republican ticket's landslide victory. Feminists faulted the Mondale-Ferraro ticket with failing to focus on women's issues. Despite the crushing defeat, her campaign was a critical breakthrough for women, for, as Ferraro put it, "gender no longer constituted a disqualification for national office."

Her nomination, nonetheless, signaled the peak of feminist influence in the Democratic Party. Already a movement had emerged among party elites, calling themselves "New Democrats," to regain national ascendancy by moving the party to the right. They wanted to silence Republican charges that Democrats were hostage to "special interest groups" by reconstituting the party around an ideology that would appeal to a broad middle class rather than specifically to such constituency groups as labor, minorities, and women. In contrast to party feminists, these New Democrats read in the gender gap the lesson that white men were abandoning the party, and they set about to contain that loss with the creation of the Democratic Leadership Council (DLC) in early 1985. The DLC did not advocate an antifeminist agenda; in fact, it supported female (and often feminist) candidates and counted women among its leaders and members. Yet it also sought variously to downplay social issues, to reduce reliance on the government rather than private institutions to address social problems, and to stress the importance of the two-parent, heterosexual family. These positions aimed to depoliticize gender and worked against feminist goals of defending abortion rights, using government to eliminate sex discrimination and improve the welfare of women, affirming a diverse range of family structures, and advancing gay and lesbian rights.

Bill Clinton's election to the presidency in 1992 encouraged both feminists and the DLC, which had sponsored him in a candidate pool depleted by a general belief that the successful Gulf War virtually assured the incumbent Bush's reelection. The party platform and Clinton's campaign had soft-pedaled feminist issues, and the election was fought on the terrain of the economy, which had slipped into a recession in 1991. Yet feminists saw Clinton as a welcome contrast to the twelve years of Republican rule, and they counted on his support as the first president whose wife was a feminist (though deliberately unacknowledged at critical points during the campaign and presidency) and had practiced her own profession throughout their marriage. Through one of the instruments of the women's political movement, the Coalition for Women's Appointments, feminists pressured Clinton to live up to his promise to appoint a staff and cabinet that "look like America." Although Clinton expressed his annoyance with the coalition by calling its members "bean counters," he did make unprecedented numbers of female appointments, including a second female Supreme Court justice, Ruth Bader Ginsburg, a self-identified feminist, and six women among his twenty-three cabinet-level appointees. More than numbers distinguished his female appointments from those of previous presidents. Clinton set a precedent in appointing women to positions hitherto considered male territory, including Janet Reno as attorney general, Laura Tyson as chair of the President's Council of Economic Advisers, Sheila Widnall as secretary of the Air Force, and, in his second term, Madeleine Albright as secretary of state. Clinton's successor, George W. Bush, continued the movement away from the gendered division of policymaking by appointing Condoleezza Rice as his national security advisor and, in his second term, secretary of state.

Policy also reflected the capture of the White House by the party of feminism. Deviating from the DLC strategy to reduce the visibility of social issues, Clinton issued executive orders to ease restrictions on abortion, and he vetoed a bill that would have made late-term abortions illegal. He attempted to end the ban on gays and lesbians in the military, although he was forced into a compromise that pleased no one. Clinton also signed bills that addressed two important issues. The Family and Medical Leave Act, which Bush had vetoed, took a small step toward easing women's dual family and work responsibilities by requiring larger companies to offer unpaid leave for employees for childbirth, adoption, and family medical emergencies. Clinton also signed the Violence Against

Women Act of 1994, providing significant funding and a host of programs to reduce rape and domestic violence, prosecute offenders, and assist victims.

Moving to the center after the Republicans captured the House of Representatives in 1994, Clinton signed the Personal Responsibility and Work Opportunity Reconciliation Act, ending the safety net of welfare policies that had
provided for poor children since the 1930s. Although Clinton had twice vetoed
more punitive legislation, most feminists were outraged by his assent to a measure that would force mothers of small children to be cut off welfare in two
years whether or not they could find adequate paying jobs and childcare. Clinton bowed to the right again in signing the Defense of Marriage Act, which prohibited the federal government from recognizing state-licensed marriages
between same-sex couples. Still, the largest gender gap to date appeared in
1996, when women gave Clinton 54 percent of their votes while men split their
votes between Clinton and the Republican candidate Robert Dole. If only men
had voted, Dole would have won the election.

Women's ties to the Democratic Party even endured revelations that Clinton
had had sexual relations with a twenty-one-year-old White House intern, Monica Lewinsky, and then had tried to cover it up by lying to a federal grand jury.
Conservatives and many other Americans, outraged at the president's affront to
conventional moral standards and his recklessness with the truth, called for impeachment. In the midst of a booming economy, a majority of the public, including most feminist spokeswomen, continued to support his presidency and
opposed impeachment. While conservatives who had attacked Anita Hill now
cried sexual harassment, feminists like Gloria Steinem, who had insisted that
"the personal is political," deplored Clinton's tawdry behavior but contended
that his private conduct should be kept separate from his public actions, which
they found beneficial to women overall.

Women's preference for the Democratic Party continued in the 2000 election,
though pollsters discovered a twist to the gender gap. While 54 percent of women
voted for Al Gore in contrast to just 42 percent of men, both married women and
married men favored the Republican, George W. Bush. This marriage gap was
no doubt linked in part to economic circumstances: two-parent households
tended to be better off, while single women's overwhelming preference for Gore
testified to their lower incomes and need for a government-sponsored safety net
and action to promote women's economic opportunities. Employed women divided their votes 58 percent for Gore and 39 percent for Bush.

These large differences underscore the economic foundations of women's
and feminists' allegiance to the Democratic Party. Although the parties' realignment over feminism and feminist policies reflected differences over social and
moral issues, that polarization also depended greatly on how women defined
their economic interests. Contrary to what many scholars have argued, in

embracing feminist policy goals the Democratic Party did not so much abandon economic issues as it extended the New Deal principle of activist government to support the economic well-being of large numbers of women.

The Republicans continued to appeal to women but not in terms of their interests as women. Instead, the Bush campaign sought their votes by focusing on education and the blows Clinton's sexual recklessness had dealt to family values. Still under the sway of the right, the Republican Party maintained its antifeminist stand on abortion and other issues, but its implicit acceptance of changes promoted by the women's political movement was manifest in the large number of female delegates at the national convention and in its recruitment and support of female candidates for office.

Both parties sent unprecedented numbers of women to Congress. When the 107th Congress convened in 2001, thirteen women sat in the Senate (ten Democrats and three Republicans) and fifty-nine in the House (forty-one Democrats and eighteen Republicans), numbers that reflected women's greater attachment to the Democratic Party. In 2002, House Democrats elected Nancy Pelosi of California as the first woman to serve as minority leader, the highest party position in the House. Yet, compared to other nations, women in the United States moved more slowly into political power. Comprising just 13 percent of the House, American women fell behind those in the lower houses of parliaments in Canada and all of the European Union nations save Ireland, Italy, and France.

Institutional factors help to account for the differences. In 1998, women had the highest parliamentary representation—as high as 42 percent in Sweden—in nations using a proportional electoral system where multimember districts allow voters to select more than one candidate. Germany, which combined proportional and plurality elements, saw women win 30 percent of parliamentary seats. In contrast, the United Kingdom and France, with electoral systems more like that of the United States where voters may select just one candidate, had parliaments where women held only 18.4 and 10.9, respectively, of the seats. When voters could mark a ballot for more than one candidate, they more frequently chose women than when they could vote for just one.

A second institutional feature that has helped European women is the strong role parties play as gatekeepers to political office and governments' and parties' increasing use of quotas to ensure that women comprise a minimum of parliamentary candidates. Begun in Norway in 1975, by 2000 the practice had spread throughout Europe (and to other parts of the world, including Egypt and India), at least among liberal and left parties. For example, after the British Labour Party guaranteed a female candidate in half of all winnable districts in the 1997 general election, women's representation in the parliamentary party rose from 14 to 24 percent, and their overall presence in Parliament grew from 9 to 18 percent. A comparable result occurred in France after the Socialists reserved

30 percent of its candidacies for women. Especially in the early years of the women's political movement, the relatively weak role of U.S. parties in candidate selection facilitated access for newcomers, but it also left American parties without certain tools used by European parties that could promote women's advance into elective office.

Between 1945 and the turn of the twenty-first century, economic and social changes combined with a mass women's movement to transform American politics. Where once gender powerfully defined the political arena and sharply circumscribed women's place within it (yet remained nearly invisible), in the 1960s large numbers of women transformed how gender operated in the political system, as they themselves were politicized on the basis of gender. If norms of masculinity did not change substantially, what was appropriately feminine did change. The attention political elites paid to women as party members and voters, the familiarity of women in political office, the salience of gender-specific issues in electoral politics and government policies, and the polarization of the major parties around those issues—all were absent from the political landscape in 1945, all a part of it in 2001.

Although the five changes were interrelated, they did not proceed hand in hand. Republicans and Democrats began to look for specific ways to appeal to women voters in the 1950s, and in the 1960s both Kennedy and Johnson took initiatives that addressed women's interests as women. By conferring a measure of visibility and credibility on women's issues and raising expectations, these initiatives, in turn, contributed to the resurgence of feminism in the second half of the 1960s, a movement that was fueled by the black freedom struggle on the foundation of broad demographic changes, notably women's increasing education and employment and their decreasing fertility.

The 1970s proved a watershed decade. Disruptions to the political system arising from the turmoil of the 1960s and Watergate provided openings for female candidates and feminist policies. The women's movement spawned a strong political arm that focused on electing female candidates, gaining power for women in the parties, and achieving legislation and court decisions to promote gender equity and women's well-being. The policy changes of the 1970s reflected a new construction of what constituted political issues, not only outlawing all forms of sex discrimination and transforming women's legal status, but also reflecting the movement of such issues as domestic violence and sexual harassment onto the public agenda and the increased visibility of such issues as abortion and rape.

Women were politicized not just as feminists but also as antifeminists, and the 1970s ended with the realignment of the major parties on an axis of feminism-antifeminism. Before 1973, little differentiated the parties' support for feminist policies either in their platforms or in congressional voting. As the feminist agenda expanded beyond nondiscrimination measures to embrace such issues as childcare, domestic violence, and welfare reform, however, it challenged traditional Republican principles of limited and frugal government. Moreover, as the antifeminist movement gained strength, exemplified by Schlafly's hugely effective STOP ERA movement, and contributed to a rising tide of social conservatism, Republican elites saw opportunities to increase the party's appeal. The 1980 Republican national convention, with its nomination of Ronald Reagan and explicitly antifeminist platform, marked the parties' cleavage over women's issues, a polarization that endured into the twenty-first century.

The steepest change in women's holding office at the national level came in the 1990s, as women's presence in Congress grew to 13 percent and women moved into key cabinet posts, including areas previously monopolized by men. That advance built on the gains women had made in local and state governments, where women in 2001 filled 22 percent of seats in state legislatures, and it reflected the more inclusive appointment approach of the party in the White House. Perhaps, too, women's stronger voice in policymaking resulted from the end of the Cold War and the declining importance of foreign and defense issues. When these issues consumed the nation again in the aftermath of the terrorist attacks on September 11, 2001, the president's female national security advisor stood in the shadows, and women were nearly invisible among the leaders speaking to the public, determining and directing the national response. If that fact reflected the capture of the White House by the party of antifeminism, it also revealed how much gender inequality survived the reshaping of American politics in the second half of the twentieth century.

BIBLIOGRAPHIC NOTE

U.S. political history and women's history in the post–World War II era have tended to comprise two separate narratives. The abundant studies of party politics, presidential administrations, and conservatism and liberalism have paid little attention to women or gender, while studies that focus on women and politics often do not fully contextualize their subjects. One happy exception to this tendency is Helene Norma Silverberg's dissertation, "Political Organization and the Origin of Political Identity: The Emergence and Containment of Gender in American Politics, 1960–1984" (1988), which examines the politicization of feminists and conservative women. Like this study, most of the scholarship on women, gender, and politics lies in the fields of political science or sociology.

For background to the post–World War II period, see Jo Freeman, *A Room at a Time: How Women Entered Party Politics* (2000); Melanie Gustafson et al.,

We Have Come to Stay: American Women and Political Parties, 1880–1960 (1999); Anna L. Harvey, *Votes Without Leverage: Women in American Electoral Politics, 1920–1970* (1998); and Catherine E. Rymph, *Republican Women: Feminism and Conservatism from Suffrage Through the Rise of the New Right* (2006).

Important studies of policy formation include Cynthia Harrison, *On Account of Sex: The Politics of Women's Issues, 1945–1968* (1988); Anne N. Costain, *Inviting Women's Rebellion: A Political Process Interpretation of the Women's Movement* (1992); Joyce Gelb and Marian Lief Palley, *Women and Public Policies* (1982); Nancy MacLean, *Freedom Is Not Enough: The Opening of the American Workplace* (2006); and John D. Skrentny, *The Minority Rights Revolution* (2002). I examine women's issues in three administrations in "Behind the Silences: Challenges to the Gender Status Quo During the Truman Years," in *Harry's Farewell: Interpreting and Teaching the Truman Presidency*, ed. Richard S. Kirkendall (2004), 257–279; "Women's Issues and the Johnson Administration," in *The Johnson Years*, vol. 3, *LBJ at Home and Abroad*, ed. Robert A. Divine (1994), 53–81; and "Feminism, Public Policy, and the Carter Administration," in *The Carter Presidency: Policy Choices in the Post–New Deal Era*, ed. Gary M. Fink and Hugh Davis Graham (1998), 224–243.

For party polarization around feminist issues, see Christina Wolbrecht, *The Politics of Women's Rights: Parties, Positions, and Change* (2000), and Jo Freeman, "Whom You Know Versus Whom You Represent: Feminist Influence in the Democrat and Republican Parties," in *The Women's Movements of the United States and Western Europe*, ed. Mary Fainsod Katzenstein and Carol McClurg Mueller (1987), 215–244. Susan E. Marshall examines conservative women in "Rattle on the Right: Bridge Labor in Antifeminist Organizations," in *No Middle Ground: Women and Radical Protest*, ed. Kathleen M. Blee (1998), 155–179. Kenneth S. Baer's *Reinventing Democrats: The Politics of Liberalism from Reagan to Clinton* (2000) relates the Democrats' response to conservatism.

For studies of the United States in comparative perspective, see Lisa Young, *Feminists and Party Politics* (2000), which compares feminist strategies and influence in the United States and Canada; Sylvia Bashevkin, *Women on the Defensive: Living Through Conservative Times* (1998), which focuses on Britain, Canada, and the United States; and Ruth Henig and Simon Henig, *Women and Political Power: Europe Since 1945* (2001), which examines women's advances into the parties and governments of Western Europe.

NOTES

1. Stevenson speech reprinted in Michael P. Johnson, *Reading the American Past: Selected Historical Documents* (Boston: Bedford Books, 1998), 2:205–208.

2. Truman quoted in Cynthia Harrison, *On Account of Sex: The Politics of Women's Issues, 1945–1968* (Berkeley: University of California Press, 1988), 57.

3. Truman to Miller, August 12, 1950, Truman Papers, Official File 120-A, Harry S. Truman Library, Independence, Mo.

4. Eisenhower quoted in Harrison, *On Account of Sex*, 37.

5. NOW quoted in ibid., 197.

6. Memo from Robert E. Kintner to Henry Wilson, March 27, 1967, FG 655, White House Central Files, Lyndon Baines Johnson Library, Austin, Texas.

7. Nixon quoted in John W. Dean, *The Rehnquist Choice* (New York: Free Press, 2001), 104.

8. Schlafly quoted in Catherine E. Rymph, "Neither Neutral nor Neutralized: Phyllis Schlafly's Battle Against Sexism," in *Women's America*, ed. Linda K. Kerber and Jane Sherron De Hart, 5th ed. (New York: Oxford University Press, 2000), 505; second quote from *The Phyllis Schlafly Report* 1 (November 1967): 2.

9. "E.R.A. and the Military Academies," *Phyllis Schlafly Report* 10 (June 1977): 1.

10. "How E.R.A. Will Hurt Men," *Phyllis Schlafly Report* 8 (May 1975): 3.

11. "Do Women Get Equal Pay for Equal Work?" *Phyllis Schlafly Report* 14 (May 1981): 1.

12. Reagan quoted in Helene Norma Silverberg, "Political Organization and the Origin of Political Identity: The Emergence and Containment of Gender in American Politics, 1960–1984," Ph.D. diss., Cornell University, 1988, 313.

14. WHICH SIDES ARE YOU ON?

Religion, Sexuality, and Culture-War Politics

DAVID T. COURTWRIGHT

Two distinct constellations of issues divided Americans and defined their politics in the late twentieth century. The first involved moral questions like abortion and homosexuality, the second economic questions like taxation and government regulation. Rather than being simply left or right, Americans evolved a complex politics in which it was possible to be morally left but economically right, or vice versa. As with postwar ideology, so with postwar revolutions. Americans experienced two upheavals within the span of a single generation. The pronounced moral shift of "the 1960s" was followed two decades later by the pronounced economic shift of "Reaganism." By the 1990s American voters were more secular and permissive than their counterparts of the 1940s, but also more suspicious of the government's size and interference with market forces.[1] Though seemingly opposed—the 1960s being more congenial to liberals, Reaganism to conservatives—these two revolutions of the self were in fact mutually supportive. The unfettered capitalism and the renewed prosperity of the 1980s and 1990s undermined religious conservatives' efforts to reverse the moral revolution, stalling their counterrevolution.

RELIGIOUS TEMPERAMENTS

Americans' views on moral issues have largely depended on their religious temperaments. "Temperaments" are personal conceptions of God, self, and sin that cut across denominational lines. Until the early nineteenth century, most Americans of European descent manifested one of three Protestant temperaments, which historian Philip Greven called Evangelical, Moderate, and Genteel. The inner experience of the evangelicals was one of self-suppression. They believed that humanity was deeply flawed and that those who thought otherwise, who preoccupied themselves with earthly pleasures, were likely headed for hell. Evangelicals hoped to escape this fate because they had undergone a life-transforming religious experience rooted in the conviction of personal worthlessness and a resolve to subjugate their wills to God's. Moderates thought the self needed to be controlled rather than annihilated. They believed in sin, but not that everything worldly was sinful. Grace might come to an individual gradually, in the course of a restrained and dutiful life. The genteel led a more self-indulgent existence. They took their state of grace for granted, confident that the church and sacraments would suffice for their personal salvation. Raised by affectionate parents inclined to spare the rod, they had relaxed consciences, a benevolent conception of God, and a notion that church was a good place to catch up on gossip.

The three Protestant temperaments formed a continuum of attitudes toward the self, running from genteel self-assertion on the left to moderate self-control in the middle to evangelical self-suppression on the right. These Protestant types persisted through the nineteenth and twentieth centuries, even as immigration made America a more pluralistic nation. The growing non-Protestant segment of the population evolved its own religious temperaments, shown in table 14.1 as Devout, Observant, and Selective for the Catholics, and as Orthodox, Conservative, and Reform for the Jews. Devout Catholics involved themselves in numerous devotional practices, attended Mass daily, and confessed their sins weekly. The observant were less involved in devotional practices, but attended Mass weekly and confessed at least once a year. The selective graced their parish churches at Easter or Christmas and confessed sins rarely, if at all. Among Jews, the Orthodox punctiliously observed the Torah as God's binding law. Conservative Jews minded the law but worried less about pious comportment or avoiding the non-Jewish world. Reform Jews regarded the law as a product of human history, to be selectively obeyed while going about their worldly affairs. "Some of us cover our heads, some don't," said Rabbi Aaron Peller. "That's exactly what I think Reform is all about—individual autonomy."[2]

Then there were Americans who belonged to no church or synagogue and who professed no creed. They comprised a fourth, nonreligious category in which the self had become dominant. The nonreligious did not always think or act selfishly. Some embraced communitarian ideals and lifestyles, and some, such as the

Table 14.1
Late Twentieth-Century Religious Temperaments for the
Three Principal American Historical Groups*

Self-dominant	Self-asserted	Self-controlled	Self-suppressed
X————————————X————————————X————————————X			
Nonreligious	Genteel (Protestant)	Moderate	Evangelical
Nonreligious	Selective (Catholic)	Observant	Devout
Nonreligious	Reform (Jewish)	Conservative	Orthodox
← "Moral Left"		"Moral Right" →	

* American Mormons, Muslims, Buddhists, Hindus, and adherents of other religions evolved their own temperaments, omitted here for the sake of space. The devout Massachusetts woman who said, "How can I send [my daughter] to public school, where they talk about condoms? No way," could have come from the moral right of any faith tradition. She was, in fact, a Muslim.

philosopher Peter Singer, committed themselves to philanthropic sacrifice. But they did so out of a sense that whatever meaning or pleasure life holds was to be realized in this world rather than the next. They identified with no religion and often doubted or denied the existence of God. In 1957 the number of persons willing to admit such beliefs to pollsters was very small, 3 percent of the population. But in 1972 it increased to 5 percent, in 1980 to 7 percent, in 1988 to 10 percent, and in 2001 to 14 percent. Nonbelievers were most likely to be highly educated male baby boomers living in the Northeast or along the Pacific Coast, though this temperament was not confined to one class, sex, age, or region.[3]

Greven thought early upbringing determined religious outlook. Twentieth-century biographies, however, are full of surprising shifts in adolescent and adult life. Sex researcher Alfred C. Kinsey grew up in an intensely Methodist household. *Penthouse* publisher Bob Guccione, activist Michael Harrington, novelist Robert Stone, and musician Frank Zappa were all active, committed Catholics when they were young. So was Madonna, until she discovered boys. Writer Michael Novak, on the other hand, was a liberal Catholic who moved right. In 1935 Thomas Merton was a brilliant, self-centered, vaguely leftist student at Columbia University. In 1941 he entered the Abbey of Our Lady of Gethsemani as a Trappist monk. In 1949 he became a Catholic priest.

Some people completely jumped their tracks. Temple Morgan was a blue-blooded Harvard student (Porcellian Club, captain of the boxing team) who fell under the spell of an archconservative Jesuit homilist named Leonard Feeney. In 1947 Morgan quit Harvard and embraced Rome, scandalizing Boston's Protestant establishment. The novelist Mary Gordon's father was another Harvard man who converted to Catholicism: he was a Jew who came to admire Franco and hate Protestants. Mary Gordon herself became a selective Catholic, though raised in a devout household. The gay artist Andy Warhol, steeped in the Byzantine Catholic piety of Pittsburgh's Carpatho-Rusyn ghetto, kept a crucifix by his bed and frequented Mass—but always sat in the back, keeping well clear of the communion rail and the confessional.

IDEOLOGICAL TENDENCIES OF THE MORAL RIGHT AND LEFT

Though individuals can change their religious beliefs and practices over the course of a lifetime, they manifest a single temperament at any one point in time. Knowing where they are at that moment makes it possible to generalize, or at least make statistical predictions, about their moral attitudes and political behavior. The farther one is to the right of a given faith continuum, the more likely one is to believe in free will, sin, and the appropriateness of punishment. The farther to the moral right, the more likely one is to believe in absolute moral standards grounded in sacred scriptures. To violate these standards is to provoke God and to invite his punishment, as well as that of civil authorities. Moral rightists support state action to suppress gambling, prostitution, obscenity, drunkenness, illicit drug use, sodomy, and abortion. Such legislation is at once symbolic and instrumental. It reiterates conservative moral norms and discourages behavior regarded as reprehensible and destructive of family life. For moral rightists the family is the fundamental unit of society. Hierarchical thinking predominates. Individuals should subordinate personal desires to the wishes of familial, community, state, and other legitimate authorities, provided only that their orders do not countermand God's.

Those on the moral left are inclined to question authority, to reject the concept of absolute, let alone divinely inspired, moral standards. They often oppose the prosecution of victimless crimes. Confronted with a prohibition, they ask, "Why not?" If unconvinced by a secular answer (whether couched in utilitarian, consequentialist, or, more rarely, deontic terms), they assume the prohibition is unjustified and should be repealed. This assumption is based upon another, that human beings are fundamentally good and, if liberated from arbitrary and oppressive authority, will flourish. "We regard men as infinitely precious," proclaimed the 1962 "Port Huron Statement" of the Students for a Democratic Society, "and possessed of unfulfilled capacities for reason, freedom, and love."[4]

And sex. In the second half of the twentieth century, the tendency of the moral leftists to challenge the old rules was nowhere more apparent than with respect to sexuality. They regarded sex as a great and legitimate pleasure, a means of growth and self-fulfillment, and, in some contexts, a vehicle of political expression. They did not regard it as necessarily linked to marriage or procreation, and hence opposed Judeo-Christian sexual ethics. In the 1960s and 1970s, moral leftists fought hard and successfully to push back the frontiers of sexual freedom, and might have advanced even further had it not been for the AIDS epidemic of the 1980s. AIDS proved a serious contretemps, insofar as it permitted their opponents to advance a public health, as well as a theological, argument against permissiveness. The moral left's answer to the AIDS crisis was safer sex and medical research. The moral right's was to condemn promiscuity and drug abuse.

The farther one was to the moral left, the more likely one's thinking was to be influenced by determinism and relativism. If individual beliefs about truth and morality were conditioned by historical, social, and cultural circumstances, there was good reason to be cautious about imposing any particular set of moral standards, or to punish those who violated existing ones. Much energy went into unmasking moral claims, exposing assumptions thought to be natural and universal as so many myths of a dominant, coercive ideology. The denial of transcendent morality was the common rhetorical strand running through feminist and sexual-minority literature, itself the activist edge of social constructionism, the ambitious late-century intellectual movement that sought to replace existing conceptions of knowledge, empirical or religious, and that denied the very possibility of an autonomous individual thinker, let alone an autonomous moral agent.

Why those who believed ideologies to be historically contingent should engage in so much "rights talk" for preferred causes was an apparent inconsistency, often noted by philosophers and intellectual historians.[5] One explanation is that moral leftists, rather than denying the existence of evil, tended to locate it in oppressive systems or privileged groups rather than in individuals. Thus fascism was evil, or Stalinism, or segregation, or the bourgeoisie. Postmodernism notwithstanding, the moral left's dominant pattern of thinking remained progressive: identify a social evil, analyze its causes, and use the knowledge to modify social arrangements to make the evil disappear. The basic political assumption remained that of the Enlightenment. Humans, or at least their educated vanguard, could improve the world. Nor was this a purely secular impulse. The idea of targeting unjust social arrangements became entrenched in twentieth-century liberal religion, such as the Protestant Social Gospel movement, the Jewish Social Justice movement, and liberation theologies.

The corresponding de-emphasis of individual sin, guilt, and repentance drew the fire of religious traditionalists. Changing social and economic structures to create "a new man and a new world" was an illusion, Joseph Cardinal Ratzinger (now Pope Benedict XVI) told an interviewer in 1984. "It is precisely personal sin that is in reality at the root of unjust social structures."[6] John Ashcroft, the attorney general in George W. Bush's first term, agreed, saying the moral condition of a country was simply "an aggregation of the moral choices made by individuals."[7] Individual responsibility remained the moral right's irreducible bottom line—which was why, for example, most white evangelicals supported the death penalty or denied that racial discrimination was systematic. If sinners would repent and embrace Jesus, they believed, people would make friends across racial lines.[8]

Nowhere were the differences between the moral left and right sharper than with respect to the existence, nature, and consequences of lust. "So seriously is sexual sin regarded in evangelical circles," commented the sociologist William Martin, that "when the term 'immorality' is used without elaboration, it almost always refers to sexual relations outside the bonds of one's own marriage."[9] Thus Gary Hart's protest during a 1988 Iowa campaign debate—that "we are all sinners," but that "true immorality" was to be found in the Reagan administration's neglect of childhood poverty—succeeded only in setting evangelical eyes to rolling.[10] The same attitude explained their reluctance to honor Martin Luther King Jr. with a national holiday. King offered a devastating critique of de jure segregation and was more responsible than perhaps any other person for its elimination from American life. Yet King also drank to excess and indulged in casual sexual affairs, up to and including the night before his assassination. For those on the moral left, King's hotel flings were irrelevant peccadilloes, and hardly exceptional. Everyone in the movement, as Michael Harrington put it, "was out getting laid."[11] King's national significance stemmed from his leadership and courage, his willingness to put his life on the line. But the dalliances were anything but irrelevant to Senator Jesse Helms and others who regarded King's sexuality and left-leaning politics as symbols of a society in spiritual crisis. Though the rearguard action against King struck most Americans as petty, it illustrated an important point made by sociologist James Davison Hunter. Culture-war clashes were ugly and protracted precisely because they involved different visions of the sacred.[12] The politics of tax legislation lent themselves to compromise. The politics of sin did not.

The high psychological stakes—for ultimately what was at issue was the propriety of one's own conduct and identity—help explain the intolerant tone of late twentieth-century cultural politics. Episodes such as the 1990 suspension of television commentator Andy Rooney, who made offhand remarks offensive to blacks and homosexuals, reminded everyone that words had become weapons that could discharge even without conscious intent. Academics and clergy enforced their own taboos. In 1985 Howard Moody, senior pastor of Judson Memorial Church in New York City, drew a line in the theological sand, suggesting that vocal opponents of homosexuality should themselves face denial of ordination.[13] This, of course, was a mirror image of the Protestant right's position that active homosexuality would constitute a ground for denial of ordination. Moody's comment was in many ways prescient. Over the next two decades questions of homosexuality, such as gay marriage or openly gay clergy, roiled the Methodist, Presbyterian, and other mainline churches, with the denominational leadership and some ministers taking more progressive positions on these issues than their dwindling congregations. The Reverend J. Robert Williams, a gay Episcopal priest, went so far as to suggest that Mother Teresa would be a better person if she were sexually active.

He succeeded only in stunning his audience. The what-next reaction of disaffected laity offers a final clue to the mentality of religious conservatives in the last third of the twentieth century. They felt besieged by a hostile modernity that everywhere undermined traditional values and coarsened daily life. It was this sense of being attacked, writer Karen Armstrong observes, that provoked such a strong and often distorted response among fundamentalists in different faiths. The relentless push of modernity generated the hard shove of religious reaction, surprising secular elites who supposed that religion was dead and that the future belonged to them.[14]

THE DRIFT FROM THE MORAL CENTER

Despite the political assertiveness of the religious right, and the growth of the Mormons, Southern Baptists, Hasidic Jews, and other conservative groups, the larger story of postwar religion is of a shift from the center toward the self-assertive and self-dominant temperaments. Few would have predicted this trend in the late 1940s through the early 1960s, boom years for most American religions, above all for Catholics. By 1965 Rome could claim 46.6 million American Catholics, some 70 percent of whom attended Mass at least weekly. They supported the world's wealthiest national Catholic church and, with no assistance from the government, the largest private school system, including 112 seminaries. The ratio of seminarians to Catholics stood at a healthy 10 per 10,000. By 1990, however, the rate was just 1 per 10,000. The number of nominal Catholics continued to increase, reaching 62 million by century's end. But only about a quarter of these attended weekly Mass, presided over by silver-haired priests whose average age had reached fifty-nine. (Had participation in the Mass and sacraments not declined so precipitously, the bishops would have been even harder pressed to staff all their parishes.) Selectivism had triumphed. American Catholicism had become another mainline denomination, a religion to which the majority remained sentimentally attached, but to which they paid less attention and obeisance, especially on matters of sexual morality.[15]

Some commentators, citing poll data that more than four-fifths of Americans profess to believe in an afterlife and that overall church attendance has remained stable at around 40 percent, concluded that, despite everything, America remained uniquely religious among Western nations. The problem was that Americans often lied to pollsters about religion, especially church attendance. Actual national weekly attendance in the 1990s, for example, was closer to 20 percent than the reported 40 percent. One group of Catholics polled by phone claimed 51 percent; 24 percent showed up when researchers checked the parishes. Observers such as Andrew Walsh suspected that religious institutions, far from being stable, had weakened under misleadingly stable poll data. Political scientist Robert Putnam agreed. He found that postwar gains in religious activity began to erode during the 1960s, as did participation in community-based organizations generally. The classic institutions of American civic life, religious and secular, had been "hollowed out." [16]

A person can remain religious, theoretically, without benefit of church or clergy. In 1988 four in ten unchurched Americans said that they had made a commitment to Jesus; six in ten that there was life after death; and eight in ten that they sometimes prayed. But what did such avowals amount to? Apparently to an updated form of Pelagianism, the heresy that denies original sin. Three-quarters of Americans polled in 2000 agreed with the statement "all people are inherently good when they are born," repudiating the basic Christian belief in original sin. [17] Biblical illiteracy was another unmistakable sign of the shift toward soft, privatized religion. By the early 1980s a sizable majority of America adults—58 percent—could not identify who delivered the Sermon on the Mount or name even five of the Ten Commandments. [18] These were nominal Christians who had a dusty Bible somewhere in the house, a disinclination to spend too many Sunday mornings in church, and a bland optimism in a benevolent but infrequently consulted God. They had their counterparts among the Jews, 42 percent of whom reported themselves strongly committed to Judaism but only 13 percent of whom regularly attended religious services. [19] While participation in Jewish community life went beyond the synagogue, Reform Jews were nevertheless involved in explicitly religious activities far less often than Orthodox Jews. As far as the Orthodox Jews were concerned, Reform Jews were unbelievers.

Vestigial religious beliefs offered some comfort to adults, but did little for their children. Those raised in genteel families hungered for a deeper religious experience, often becoming converts to evangelical churches. (The equivalent Jewish type, the ba'alei teshuvah, returned to Orthodoxy.) Or they gave up on organized religion altogether. Half of all Presbyterian baby boomers became unchurched adults. [20] Membership in the mainline churches peaked in the 1960s and then began falling, leaving behind aging congregations. Meanwhile their conservative denominational rivals were growing, partly by attracting disaffected young people, partly by their own higher fertility, and partly by making greater demands on—but offering richer emotional rewards to—their adherents.

Moderates also found themselves in a difficult position as American society became morally polarized. Moderates believed that sin inhered both in persons and in unjust social systems and that, while limited good might come from gradual change, moral and liturgical norms should be abandoned with reluctance. Yet they were not obsessed with those norms. Some Conservative Jews, for example, refrained from eating pork or mixing meat and dairy products, but refused to follow all the dietary laws observed by the orthodox. Such balancing acts were psychologically tricky, however, and always subject to challenge from the Orthodox religious right. Who said God had exempted them from any of the 613 commandments of the Torah?

American Catholicism offers a compelling example of tension between moderates and true believers. The aforementioned Leonard Feeney was so intolerant that he ran afoul of Boston's Archbishop Richard Cushing. Like other rising figures in the postwar American hierarchy, Cushing was more pragmatic and tolerant than his predecessors. His experience of Boston politics had made him aware of cultural diversity; the happy marriage of his own sister to a Jew made him a vigorous opponent of anti-Semitism. The crux of the conflict was Feeney's insistence on *extra ecclesiam nulla salus,* the outmoded doctrine that salvation was impossible outside of the Church. Feeney's uncompromising exclusivism, compounded by his habit of Jew-baiting, provoked Cushing's censure in 1949. That same year Feeney was dismissed from the Society of Jesus and, from 1953 to 1972, he was excommunicated from the Church.

None of this deterred Feeney and his lay followers, the Slaves of the Immaculate Heart of Mary. They persisted in vilifying Cushing, liberal Catholics, Protestants, and Jews. They protested the opening of a Catholic chapel at predominantly Jewish Brandeis University. They even interrupted a Notre Dame football game. As had been true since the days of Roger Williams and Anne Hutchinson, the impulse toward purity led to physical separation. In 1958 Feeney and a hundred Slaves hived off to rural Harvard, Massachusetts. There they established a monastery with no newspapers, radios, or televisions, and with separate quarters for women and men. All who lived in the monastery, including married couples, swore vows of chastity. Such children as they had already borne were raised collectively.[21]

Conviction that leads men and women to forsake the comforts of the marital bed (or Catholics to trash Notre Dame football) is a powerful thing. Intensity of faith, more than anything else, determines where individuals fall on the spectrum of religious temperaments. Total self-denial requires total belief. Christianity, as William James observed, is a religion of deliverance. Christians must be willing to die to an unreal life so that they might be born into a real one.[22] What makes worldly death palatable is the release from guilt and the accompanying sense of inner peace, feelings shared by a supportive community of like-minded worshipers. Belief in God and the afterlife acts as a psychological brake on selfish behavior, even more so if one anticipates His justice rather than His mercy. One takes no chances with the God of Calvin, or of Augustine, or of Moses. If one does not believe in God, however, one's behavior is unchecked by fear of divine retribution. Self-assertion thrives on weakened faith, self-dominance on disbelief. Hence religious conservatives felt it necessary to mobilize against secular intellectuals, whom they accused of undermining faith by foisting humanism on the impressionable young, and to snipe at the teaching of evolutionary biology, which subverted the biblical foundations of their faith.

ECONOMIC AND RELIGIOUS TEMPERAMENTS

Given the moral right's emphasis on individual responsibility, it might seem that late-twentieth-century religious conservatives were also economic conservatives. Yet most empirical studies showed that race and class were much better predictors of support for government assistance than religious belief. Wealthy Protestants, for example, may have been theologically liberal, but they attended closely to their pocketbooks.[23] The smaller-than-average incomes or larger-than-average families of black evangelicals and Hasidic Jews, by contrast, disposed them to favor government assistance. Beyond self-interest lay the problem of scriptural ambiguity. The sacred texts contained injunctions about wealth and poverty, but lacked a detailed blueprint for a just political economy. "Render unto Caesar the things that are Caesar's" failed to specify the maximum marginal tax rate. Christians, Jews, Muslims, and others agreed that they should help the poor, yet disagreed over whether it was best to do so through the welfare state or through the unhampered production of wealth and consequent creation of jobs.

The simmering debate over the relationship between government and enterprise, which came to a boil during the 1930s, gave rise to a spectrum of economic temperaments. There were four general positions: those who embraced capitalism and resisted interference with market forces; those who accepted capitalism, provided that corporations behaved themselves and that the government had the power to correct abuses; those who accepted capitalism, but only if the government acted as a continuous watchdog and oversaw an array of welfare programs; and those who rejected capitalism, favoring collective ownership and a comprehensive welfare state. Often individuals shared the same economic temperament yet differed religiously, as in the famous case of William Jennings Bryan and Clarence Darrow, two economic progressives who ended up on opposite sides of the Scopes trial.

Figure 14.1 represents these differences as ideological planes bounded by the moral and economic axes, with one plane for each of the three principal Ameri-

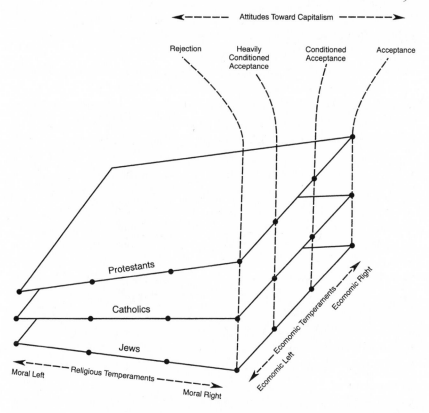

Figure 14.1   Late-twentieth-century religious and economic temperaments combined

can faith traditions in the late twentieth century.[24] (Those for Muslims, Mormons, and other groups are implicit.) The planes are nonparallel, closer together on the moral left than on the moral right, because religious and ethnic differences mattered less to those who were assimilated into the secular culture. Nonreligious Jews were far more likely to marry Gentiles than were Orthodox Jews. Intellectuals of the moral left ignored or discounted the religious backgrounds of their peers, provided they did not take them too seriously. Liberal churches were more ecumenical, less exclusivist. On the moral right, however, theological differences still mattered. When salvation was at stake—when, as G. K. Chesterton said, one was balancing over an abyss—the difference of an inch could mean everything. Interdenominational controversy, as when Southern Baptists attacked Mormon beliefs, was a sign of health and commitment. There are no heresies in a dead religion.

The important point is that the distance separating the planes on the moral right diminished during the last four decades of the century. Religious prejudice was a fact of life in Eisenhower's America. As late as 1958 Jews could not marry in Harvard's Memorial Church unless a Protestant minister performed the ceremony. Though Americans told pollsters that they would not hold John Kennedy's religion against him, this turned out to be another polite evasion. Underground anti-Catholicism made the 1960 popular vote much closer than it would otherwise have been. But Kennedy had campaigned on a promise of rigid church-state separation, and he proved more than good to his word. Kennedy, said Billy Graham, "turned out to be a Baptist president." Actually, he was an ultraselective Catholic who once told Ben Bradlee that he was "all for people solving their problems by abortion." [25] But we know what Graham meant. The scrupulous religious neutrality of the Kennedy administration dissipated traditional Protestant anti-Catholicism, at least in presidential politics. The Kennedy years likewise hastened the assimilation of American Catholics. The children and grandchildren of the immigrants were moving away from the ornate marble churches in the old neighborhoods to the ersatz-modern parishes sprouting in the suburbs. [26]

Graham's own relationship with the Catholic Church changed. In the late 1950s many priests warned parishioners to stay away from his revival meetings. By 1964 Cardinal Cushing was urging Catholic youth to attend, commenting that Graham's message was "one of Christ crucified, and no Catholic can do anything but become a better Catholic from hearing him." In 1977 Graham held a crusade in the Notre Dame stadium. Over the next decade, Graham's organization began routinely courting Catholics. More than 100 parishes promoted participation in his 1991 Madison Square Garden rally. [27]

By then interfaith cooperation was apparent in the campaigns to promote school prayer, secure public funds for religious schools, and outlaw obscenity and abortion. One Operation Rescue protest resulted in the arrests of Orthodox rabbis, evangelical ministers, and Catholic clergy. In war, antagonists take their allies where they find them. In the culture war, moral rightists discovered that their allies lay across traditionally hostile boundaries. While theological tensions remained, religious conservatives discovered they had more in common with one another than with the "amoral" secularists transforming the culture in the name of church-state separation. It mattered less where one stood relative to Jesus, Luther, and Calvin, James Hunter observed in 1991, than where one stood relative to Voltaire, Nietzsche, and Rorty. "The politically relevant world-historical event . . . is now the secular Enlightenment of the eighteenth century and its philosophical aftermath. This is what inspires the divisions of popular culture in the United States today." [28]

Hunter was only half right. The rise of industrial capitalism and its information-intensive successor was another world-historical event that inspired cultural divisions—the economic temperaments. These proved to be independent of the religious temperaments: knowing a person's views on sexual morality would not necessarily predict his or her views on emission standards. Yet Hunter's larger point remains valid. After 1960 the old ethnic politics of interfaith suspicion gave way to a new moral politics of opposing religious temperaments.

THE CRISIS OF THE DEMOCRATIC PARTY

This development had critical implications for national politics, above all for the Democratic Party. Though it had dominated Congress from 1945 to 1960—only during his first two years did Eisenhower enjoy Republican majorities in both houses—the Democratic Party was an unstable coalition, with northern and southern, black and white, urban and rural, and liberal and conservative elements. This too-big tent was the historical legacy of the struggle over slavery, the Civil War and Reconstruction, immigration and the rise of urban political machines, and the political success of the New Deal. Beginning in 1964, however, a series of racially and ideologically charged elections sorted things out. The Democrats emerged from these redefining elections as the party of the moral and economic left.

Barry Goldwater, the 1964 Republican presidential nominee, began the process by winning away disaffected segregationists, carrying five historically Democratic southern states. Racism, Democratic advance man John Bartlow Martin wrote in his campaign journal, was Goldwater's best issue. The telegenic Goldwater had a chance to win, he thought, if he could forge an emotional link between white backlash and the widespread, almost intuitive dislike of Lyndon Johnson.[29] Goldwater also attracted economic conservatives who hated the "socialistic" and pro-union legacy of the New and Fair Deals. His appeal to moral conservatives was more limited, however. A strongly anticommunist libertarian, Goldwater thought the government should not legislate matters of morality—his stated reason for opposing the 1964 Civil Rights Act. Goldwater also proved an inept campaigner, prone to questioning mandatory social security and loose talk about tactical nuclear weapons. Johnson defeated him easily.

Johnson did so by painting Goldwater as a Cold War extremist. Johnson, however, turned out to be the one with the war problem. Like Truman and Kennedy before him, he feared any charges of softness on communism. In 1950 Johnson had seen the political career of his own lover, Helen Gahagan Douglas, destroyed by Richard Nixon's red-baiting. Worse followed. "I knew that Harry Truman and Dean Acheson had lost their effectiveness from the day that the Communists took over in China," Johnson explained to Doris Kearns. "I believed that the loss of China had played a large role in the rise of Joe McCarthy.

And I knew that all these problems, taken together, were chickenshit compared with what might happen if we lost Vietnam."[30] Discounting the hyperbole, the political vulnerability of which Johnson spoke was real. Both economic and moral conservatives hated communism and dreaded its expansion. Any conspicuous failure of containment could be lethal. Johnson's concern for his right flank, already weakened by rising black militancy and new social welfare spending, laid the political foundation for the Vietnam War.

Had the conflict ended quickly, Johnson's judgment would have been vindicated. But the war only escalated, bringing lengthening casualty lists, higher taxes, and inflation. Hawks denounced the war as ineffectual. Doves condemned it as immoral, imperialist, mindlessly anticommunist. The most visible New Left critics were, disproportionately, nonreligious Jews raised by indulgent liberal parents. Their countercultural lifestyles and abrasive tactics alienated Americans of more moderate and conservative temperaments. "As unpopular as the war had become," admitted Todd Gitlin, an SDS activist turned sociologist and historian, "the antiwar movement was detested still more—the most hated political group in America, disliked even by most of the people who supported immediate withdrawal from Vietnam."[31]

Both Richard Nixon and third-party candidate George Wallace capitalized on popular discontent arising from antiwar street protests and racial violence. "They start a riot down here," Wallace told a cheering Madison Square Garden rally, "first one of 'em to pick up a brick gets a bullet in the brain, that's all."[32] Nixon's appeal was more subtle. He understood that, in addition to southern whites angrily opposed to Democratic racial policies, he could pick up ordinary citizens worried by the country's moral turn. Dubbed "the forgotten Americans" and later "the silent majority," Nixon kept these voters in his sights during the campaign and throughout his first term. Though he had shed his childhood Quakerism, Nixon knew that clergy influenced large voting blocs and that he could woo blue-collar Catholics who had come to identify with the Republicans on social issues. He buttered up John Cardinal Krol, invited religious leaders into the Oval Office, held church services in the East Room. No gesture was too small. Nixon ordered the removal of *Portnoy's Complaint*, Philip Roth's comedic novel of sexual obsession, from the White House library and then leaked the news that he had done so.[33]

A cheap trick, but one with undeniable political logic. The reformed Democratic Party, increasingly under the sway of antiwar and moral-left interests, had made itself vulnerable. Michael Novak remembered trying to find out why Slovak factory workers in Joliet, Illinois, turned a cold shoulder to Sargent Shriver, the 1972 Democratic vice-presidential nominee. He found his answer when he met with the party's miniskirted "advance person," who sported a pro-abortion button on the collar of her see-through blouse. "The clash of social classes and cultural politics," he wrote, "could scarcely have been more discordant."[34] In 1964, 27 percent of Americans said they strongly identified with the Democratic Party. In 1972, just 15 percent did so. In 1964, Johnson captured 61.1 percent of the popular vote. In 1972, McGovern got 37.5 percent. Nixon carried every state except Massachusetts.

Jimmy Carter's post-Watergate victory in 1976 offered hope of winning back disaffected Democrats, especially southern evangelicals. The first adult convert to occupy the White House since Woodrow Wilson, Carter was an active Baptist layman of classically moderate temperament. His problem was that, though he talked the Bible talk, he did not walk the policy walk. Moral rightists judged him soft on drugs. Marijuana use was at an all-time high. So was the number of abortions, which had doubled from 744,000 in 1973, the year of legalization, to 1,550,000 in 1980. Carter ducked the issue. He compounded the damage by naming pro-choice advocates to his staff. One of them, Sarah Weddington, had been the winning attorney in *Roe v. Wade*. Joseph J. Reilly, a prominent Catholic layman, called her appointment a "slap in the face" and "an existential repudiation of your own claimed stance in opposition to widespread abortion."[35]

Bob Maddox, a Southern Baptist minister who advised Carter on religious matters, sensed an even bigger storm brewing on the Protestant right. "The coalescing of conservative, evangelical, religious groups for political action," Maddox warned in August 1979, had created a powerful new electoral force. As many as twenty million viewers a week watched televangelists denounce abortion, the Equal Rights Amendment, and the Strategic Arms Limitation Treaty. Carter should meet with their leaders, try to win them over. Policy adviser Anne Wexler agreed. "If the meeting is organized carefully, the President can move some of these folks to his point of view on energy, if not SALT. Also Hospital Cost Containment. Why not?"[36]

The determined ministers who finally assembled at the White House for a breakfast meeting on January 22, 1980, cared not one whit about hospital policy. Jerry Falwell, Tim LaHaye, Oral Roberts, Rex Humbard, Jim Bakker, and several others asked Carter about abortion, homosexuality, the lack of evangelicals in his administration, and his support for the Equal Rights Amendment. Carter gave answers they considered vague, evasive, or just plain wrong. "We had a man in the White House who professed to be a Christian, but didn't understand how un-Christian his administration was," LaHaye recalled. While waiting to leave, "I stood there and I prayed this prayer: 'God, we have got to get this man out of the White House and get someone in here who will be aggressive about bringing back traditional moral values.'" Unbeknownst to LaHaye, several of the other ministers present silently offered the same prayer and swore to work more actively for candidates committed to their values.[37] The 1960s and

1970s may have been the Friday and Saturday nights of American history, but they were going to make the 1980s the Sunday morning when the sins were denounced.

THE REAGAN REVOLUTION

LaHaye's prayer was apparently granted when Carter, beset by economic and foreign-policy problems, lost the 1980 election. Ronald Reagan's victory excited the pro-life movement; the National Right to Life Committee was the first citizens' group to meet with the new president in the White House. But Reagan never went beyond rhetorical support, delivered by telephone hookups to pro-life rallies. The administration failed to back the Helms-Hyde anti-abortion bill and its first Supreme Court nominee, Sandra Day O'Connor, came with unmistakable pro-choice credentials. "Good-bye, we don't need you," was how activist Connie Marshner interpreted the Day nomination. "We can keep our base without diving into the crowd," was the way Senator Robert Dole summed up Reagan's approach to the abortion issue.[38]

Reagan likewise failed to deliver on school prayer, aid to religious schools, and most other issues dear to the moral right. Instead he tossed off one-liners: "We don't need a bunch of sociology majors on the bench."[39] The main exception, and the single most important legal legacy of the moral counterrevolution, was the Drug War. Launched by Reagan in the midst of a cocaine epidemic and expanded further by Reagan's successor, George H. W. Bush, the Drug War ran its course through the 1990s partly because Democrats feared that de-escalation would open them to charges of softness on drugs—just as their Cold War predecessors had feared charges of softness on Communism.

Reagan and his advisers' real agenda lay in the realm of economic and foreign policy. Domestically, they had three primary targets: progressive taxation, federal regulation, and government transfer payments. Though they largely failed to cut spending—well-connected interest groups managed to hang on to their federal assistance, running up the deficit in the process—they did succeed in reducing tax rates to the lowest level since the Coolidge administration and pruning the number of pages in the *Federal Register* by 45 percent. But Reagan's greatest achievement may have been to shift economic attitudes. Thanks to Reagan, notes historian and political philosopher Mark Lilla, the majority of Americans came to doubt the wisdom of regulations, redistribution, and unions while accepting unbridled growth as the one true engine of progress.[40]

In foreign policy Reagan sought to reverse the defeatist "Vietnam syndrome" and counter the Soviet military buildup by expanding and modernizing America's conventional and nuclear forces. These efforts stimulated a pro-life movement of the moral left, the campaign to reduce and eliminate nuclear arsenals. It had strikingly little to do with the pro-life movement of the moral right, the campaign against abortion. Accustomed to finding evil in systems rather than in persons, nuclear-weapons opponents wanted the superpowers to come to grips with the problem and to solve it through a feat of diplomatic engineering. The anti-abortionists thought in terms of individual sin. The fetal life at issue was begun (as a rule) by extramarital intercourse and terminated (as a rule) so that the woman would not have to bear the child to term. One offense, fornication, was compounded by a second offense, the selfish taking of innocent life. Abortion was doubly sinful, and of more immediate concern than nuclear winter. This was why, outside of Catholic theological circles, the two major American pro-life movements of the 1980s failed to converge. They proceeded from and attracted people with opposing religious temperaments. (The same thing happened in the 1990s, when a reinvigorated environmentalist movement kept its distance from abortion protesters, who mocked them by singing, to the tune of the civil rights song, "Be a hero, save a whale / Save a baby, go to jail / Keep your eyes on the prize, hold on.") Eugene McCarthy caught the irony of the situation. "The liberals, being pro-choice and antiwar, don't want anybody to be born but they want everybody who's already alive to live forever," he observed in 1987. "Whereas the conservatives want everyone to be born that can be but they don't care how long they live or under what conditions—you can blow them up or starve them, just get them born. Those are the irreconcilable positions now." [41]

The opponents of Reagan's defense policies at least had somewhere to go, to the Mondale and Dukakis campaigns in 1984 and 1988. At the national level anti-abortionists and other moral rightists were stuck with the professional politicians of the Republican Party. (Televangelist Pat Robertson made an insurgent bid for the presidential nomination, but it collapsed when George H. W. Bush swept the 1988 Super Tuesday primaries.) A pattern emerged. Successful Republican candidates knew that the religious right, though organized and motivated, was likely to prove decisive only during the primaries. They therefore tacked right during primary campaigns, then back to the center during the general election, caricaturing their Democratic opponents as "liberals." No linguistic change was more revealing of the course of American politics after 1980 than the way this word, once a badge of honor for Democratic activists and intellectuals, became an epithet.

All these tactics were on display in the 1988 presidential campaign. Bush and his advisers elbowed through the primary field with the help of attack ads. One went so far as to blame Senate Majority Leader Bob Dole, Bush's chief rival, for the failure to confirm Robert Bork, the controversial conservative nominee to the Supreme Court. During the general election, the Bush team turned on Democratic nominee Michael Dukakis, branding him as a card-carrying member of the ACLU, a releaser of black rapists, a big-spending statist, and a foreign policy naif who could not stand up to the Russians. Or would not stand up to the Russians, his pledge-of-allegiance veto having made his patriotism suspect.

Dukakis fought back. He talked tough on drugs. He deplored the deficit. He had his picture taken in a tank. But by September the South was gone and with it any realistic chance of election. For the anti-abortionists who dogged Dukakis, for the evangelicals who worked for Bush, the campaign assumed the air of a triumphant crusade. "Michael Dukakis is almost the devil for us," explained the Reverend Jerry Provo, pastor of the Anchorage Baptist Temple and chairman of Alaska's Republican delegation. "For us, this is like battling the devil." [42]

As president, Bush did no more to advance the moral right's legislative agenda than had Reagan. As an upper-class Episcopalian, Bush's religious style grated on evangelicals. Operation Rescue's Randall Terry once attempted to meet with Bush about abortion while the president was golfing in Maine. Bush tried to fob off Terry with an appeal to good manners. "Golf days mean an awful lot to a fellow," he said. "I think the president and Sununu and his advisers viewed us as a political liability," Terry recalled. "This is that lukewarm, mealy-mouthed, 'pro-life' Republican position that has no teeth and that is really of very little use to ending this slaughter." [43] The Republican strategy was to feint right, then govern toward the center—a center that was itself shifting toward the moral left and economic right.

THE STRUGGLE FOR THE CENTER

Evangelical disenchantment hurt Bush in 1992, though the most decisive factor, mentioned by 41 percent of voters in exit polls, was the sour economy. The winner, Bill Clinton, also helped his own cause with some astute symbolism. He understood that the Republicans were winning because they had, with help from Democratic romantics, painted his party into a left-left corner, making it seem too liberal morally and economically. The Republicans, he said later, had even persuaded those Americans who disagreed with them on issues of gay rights and abortion to "give them credit for sort of being more stern and more righteous and more moral and all that." [44] The way out was to hold on to the pro-choice majority while signaling moral backbone (support for the death penalty, telling the militant rapper Sister Souljah where to get off) and pushing a pro-growth economic policy. Clinton and his New Democrat allies repositioned the party, as commentator George Will put it, to serve "the comfortable middle class eager for more comforts." [45]

Once in office, though, Clinton got his signals crossed. Two early moves, an executive order to end the ban on gays in the military and a secretive effort to craft national health insurance, lent credence to conservative charges that he was a stealth liberal. "He managed to unite doctors, insurers, gun owners, religious conservatives, country-club Republicans, and blue-collar workers," Republican Congressman Mark Souder remembered. "When I would go to meetings, I would find guys rising with long hair, tattoos, and a cigarette agreeing with me!"[46] Following the debacle of the 1994 elections, in which the Republicans regained control of both houses of Congress for the first time in forty years, Clinton survived by moving right on the budget, trade policy, welfare reform, and such symbolic issues as uniforms for public-school students. Buoyed by a robust economy and declining crime, he also proved lucky in his enemies. House Speaker Newt Gingrich kept pounding the culture-war drums: "We have to say to the counterculture: Nice try, you failed, you're wrong." But Gingrich was the one who was wrong. The majority of Americans, especially the younger ones, had no intention of abandoning sexual freedom and moral self-guidance. Gingrich's brand of techno-reaction—to "methodically reassert American civilization," but keep all the computers—went nowhere.[47] Nor did Americans appreciate the Republicans shutting down the government over a budget dispute with Clinton. Who, Democrats asked, were the extremists now?

Clinton's other big problem was that, as he told pollster Dick Morris, elections no longer seemed to settle anything. Ever since Nixon's fall, determined partisans had devised means of extending political combat indefinitely. These included defunding the opposition; orchestrating campaigns against key judicial nominees; protracted civil rights and environmental litigation; and the "RIP" process of revelation, investigation, and prosecution.[48] Clinton was by no means the first victim of RIP. But he became its most spectacular one when the long-running Whitewater land investigation evolved into a sex-and-perjury scandal. Amplified by talk-radio celebrities and unrelenting Republican hostility, the scandal resulted in his impeachment in late 1998.

Clinton's behavior, said Max Karrer, president of Florida's Christian Coalition, epitomized what conservative Christians were against. "I hate everything about the man," said Harvey Golden, a Houston salesman. "I hate him for dodging the draft, for not inhaling, for treating women the way he does and for just being so damned insufferable. He's a product of the '60s, and he has no sense of morality." But the moral left stood by its man. "You want to know why the left swallows hard and defends Clinton?" asked Sidney Zion, a New York City writer. "It's because they don't want to give a victory to the racist scum, the anti-abortionists and the Christian right." Sexual politics permeated the impeachment battle. Alissa Mitchell, another New Yorker, saw it as a referendum on the 1960s, which had brought personal freedom and abortion rights to her and other women. She didn't like Clinton's behavior, she said, "but people who talk about absolute morals scare me even more." The journalist Nina Burleigh made the political personal, saying that she would "be happy to give the President a blow job just to thank him for keeping abortion legal." [49]

Other Americans shrugged off the affair. "Look, we're the only superpower left on the earth. We've got money in our pockets. Who cares?" said a Massachusetts taxi driver.[50] The core of the "conspiracy" was sexual indiscretion, scoffed Clinton adviser James Carville. "No phone was tapped, no one's office burglarized, no tax return audited." [51] Carville welcomed the Republican attacks. Extreme partisanship worked in Clinton's favor. The president's approval rating took a four-point bounce the day after impeachment and remained in the 60 and 70 percent range for the rest of his term. He finished more popular than Reagan and just as popular as Eisenhower, the other postwar presidents who had served two full terms.

The Lewinksy affair and its outcome, Clinton's acquittal in the Senate and in the court of public opinion, became enduring symbols of the culture war. They were also an unmistakable sign that the moral right's campaign had stalled. Some commentators thought Clinton escaped because the special prosecutor, Kenneth Starr, made tactical errors or that the House managers fumbled the impeachment trial. This misses the deeper social significance of Clinton's survival, captured by the Illinois woman who said, "I don't want people asking questions about the President's sex life because I don't want anyone asking about mine." [52] Paul Weyrich, the conservative activist who coined the phrase "moral majority," conceded the cultural shift. "We lost the culture war," he said. "I no longer believe that there is a moral majority," adding that, if there were, Clinton would have been long gone. Alan Wolfe, a sociologist who studied the beliefs of ordinary Americans, interpreted the post-impeachment situation more broadly. "The right won the economic war," he said, "the left won the cultural war and the center won the political war." [53]

That did not mean that religious conservatives disappeared as a political force. They remained active in school board and state legislative contests, helped Republicans maintain their congressional ascendancy, and played a key role in George W. Bush and political adviser Karl Rove's 2000 campaign strategy—a strategy to hang on to the conservative religious base while saying nothing to arouse fears of moral or economic extremism among centrists. Bush spoke of compassionate conservatism, not righteous impeachment. A bemused Clinton remembered the first time he heard Bush's stump speech: "I thought, this is pretty good; this basically says, okay, I'm a New Democrat, except I'll do more of it with the private sector, . . . and I'll give you a bigger tax cut." [54] In addition to wooing centrists, Bush kept the Republican core, southern and rural white men, NRA members, small-business owners, corporate executives, and the religious right, to whom he had genuflected in the caucuses and primaries. In 2000 white voters who went to church once a week or more favored Bush over Gore by

79 to 20 percent. Those who never attended services favored Gore over Bush, 59 to 33 percent.[55] Gore also drew well from union members, city dwellers, women, the unmarried, minorities, and highly educated professionals. He ran up a half-million popular-vote majority, but lost the Electoral College by four votes. Ralph Nader's third-party appeal to environmental and economic-left voters denied Gore victory in Florida and possibly other close states.[56] Gore might still have won Florida had not civically illiterate or confused voters spoiled thousands of Democratic ballots, giving Bush, with an assist from the United States Supreme Court, the state's twenty-five electoral votes.

Like Carter, George W. Bush was an adult convert. A genteel alcoholic, he took to reading the Bible and quit drinking. He spoke the language of right and wrong, of individual responsibility. Once in office, however, he gave priority to the corporate agenda of tax cuts and deregulation. In the eyes of critics like Paul Krugman, he was a stealth reactionary, pushing the country harder and faster to the economic right than even Reagan had dared to do. Bush was less concerned with moral issues. He marked time on abortion—in fact, he seldom mentioned it—and struck an awkward compromise on embryonic stem cells, permitting federal research financing for existing cell lines. When, in the wake of September 11, Pat Robertson and Jerry Falwell speculated that abortionists, pagans, feminists, gays, lesbians, pornographers, and the ACLU bore some responsibility, an angry God having lifted his protection from America, Bush immediately called their remarks "inappropriate." Such sentiments seemed almost unpatriotic as the administration pledged war in defense of freedom and the American way of life against the threats of terrorism and radical Islam.

Bush's subsequent decision to invade Iraq and overthrow Saddam Hussein in the name of preventing further terrorist attacks proved the most controversial foreign policy decision since Vietnam. Anger over Iraq and anxieties over job losses, health care, and the future of the Supreme Court brought record numbers of Democrats to the polls in 2004. John Kerry finished more than eight million votes ahead of Al Gore in 2000, and lost anyway when Bush bested his own 2000 total by more than eleven million. The majority of Bush voters in electorally critical Ohio told exit pollsters that their main concern, outranking even terrorism, was "moral values." Whatever the exact meaning of that contested phrase, it included concern over homosexual assertiveness. Anti–gay marriage initiatives in eleven states, including Ohio, encouraged white evangelicals to turn out. Three out of four of their votes went to Bush. Orthodox Jews and devout Catholics likewise favored the incumbent.[57]

Though Kerry was himself a Catholic, he found himself in the opposite of John Kennedy's 1960 predicament. Kerry was not Catholic enough for many Protestants, or for the traditionalists of his own faith. The culture war had trumped the old denominational concerns. Kerry's altar-boy past cut no ice with religious conservatives, who saw him as a liberal Hamlet, mired in complex thought and defiant of his own church's teachings on life issues. "The true Catholic," said one Florida parishioner, "would have voted for Bush just on moral reasons alone."[58]

ON THE BUS

Alan Wolfe's remark that the culture war was won by the left is in one respect misleading. "The" culture war that erupted in the United States in the late twentieth century was only one manifestation of the deeper, recurrent conflict among people of opposing religious temperaments. Neither side was about to surrender. Any judgment must be tentative. That said, how did moral conservatives fare after they launched their counterrevolution in the 1970s?

They won notable victories in the criminal justice arena: more punitive drug laws, more rigid sentencing guidelines, and more prisons. Executions, which had come to a standstill in the late 1960s and early 1970s, made a comeback after thirty-eight states and the federal government reenacted death penalty laws to conform to the Supreme Court's new procedural standards. Nearly six hundred condemned prisoners were put to death between 1977 and 1999.[59] Moral rightists claimed credit for Republican electoral gains, especially in the South. Though antiblack and antiunion sentiments also figured in the southern Republican revival, evangelicals became a crucial part of the party's base. Their votes, combined with those of white moderates, made Republican candidates competitive and, after 1994, increasingly dominant in southern congressional races.

Evangelicals did not, however, control the party's agenda. The Republican strategy, as political scientist Earl Black put it, was to have Pat Robertson on the bus, not driving the bus.[60] If so, he and his followers were seated well to the rear. The Republican ascendancy from 1980 to 2004 translated into few gains for moral rightists on key issues. They made little progress on abortion or school prayer, and lost ground on obscenity and legalized vices like gambling. Popular culture grew steadily raunchier, a trend symbolized by Janet Jackson flashing her nipple ring during the 2004 Super Bowl halftime show. Thirty-five years before, in the supposedly revolutionary year of 1969, the entertainment had consisted of the Florida A&M University band and a sideline interview with Bob Hope. Moral conservatives had plainly failed to stem the secular tide.

The puzzle of electoral success but cultural failure provoked an outpouring of commentary, much of it concerned with religion, capitalism, and social class. David Brooks thought the big story of the late twentieth century was the displacement of the old WASP establishment ("dumb good-looking people with great parents") by a more diverse, merit-based upper-class of "bourgeois bohemians." Absorbing the ethos of the selective colleges in which they were educated, the members of this new elite had embraced the self-liberation of the counterculture, but also the capitalist possibilities of a liberated economy. They merged the two into a lifestyle of hard work, refined consumption, energetic (but safe) sex, New Age experimentation, and lots of Starbucks coffee. Having forged a post-Christian version of the genteel temperament, they leavened self-assertion with sensitivity and good taste. As far as they were concerned, the culture war was over.[61]

Mark Lilla thought this true of the whole society as well as its educated class. For all the neoconservative talk of the "cultural contradictions of capitalism"—disharmony between the Protestant ethic and the hedonistic culture to which sustained economic growth inevitably led—late-twentieth-century America showed that it was possible to maintain "a morally lax yet economically successful capitalist society." The cultural revolution of the 1960s and Reaganism were fundamentally harmonious, grounded in the individualism that was America's most enduring legacy. "The revolution *is* over," Lilla wrote, "and the revolution *is* one."[62]

Thomas Frank agreed that entrepreneurs had co-opted the moral revolution, but, unlike Lilla, he thought the culture war too politically useful to be declared over. On the contrary, corporate tycoons and libertarians had cynically nurtured it, using the moral right's political mobilization to achieve the Republican majorities necessary for their economic ends. Moral rightists voted against abortion and political correctness, but got capital gains rollbacks and deregulation in return. Residual anger at the 1960s sustained the economic revolution that had begun in the 1980s, as hapless yahoos riled up over liberal elites voted in opposition to their own class interests.[63]

All tales of false consciousness oversimplify. Frank understated the depth of genuine religious conviction behind single-issue politics and overlooked the trap of the two-party system. Where else were moral conservatives to turn, once the Democratic Party became culturally unavailable to them? But he was right on one count. The single most important source of America's continuous "moral free fall" was the corporate bottom line. Thinkers as diverse as Max Weber, Jürgen Habermas, Christopher Lasch, Garry Wills, Stanley Hauerwas, and Pope John Paul II all reached the same conclusion: sooner or later, capitalism gives rise to an affluent, self-indulgent culture at odds with traditional religious values.

The deregulated, high-tech consumer capitalism created by the Reagan revolution and the new digital technologies in the 1980s and 1990s proved especially abrasive. As Americans became a nation of compulsive "multitaskers," driving between jobs while talking on cell phones and listening to their CD players, they had less time and energy for everything else, even the physiological basics. Americans slept an average of 20 percent more at the beginning of the century than at the end, when some 30 percent of adults got by on six hours or less; college students lived in a chronic state of sleep-deprivation; and wired teenagers disdained sleep as a "waste of time" and "boring."[64]

Religious commitment requires work. That means prayer, contemplation, study of sacred writings, service to others, and communal worship. Quite apart from the self-assertion of its core message, consumer capitalism distracted Americans from these spiritual tasks simply by flooding the world with goods to be located, priced, purchased, assembled, operated, serviced, repaired, guarded, and amortized by unremitting toil. Merchandise turned out to be the opiate of the masses, and television its needle. Cable, to vary the metaphor, was the intravenous drip, plugged in and turned on all the time. Those Americans who admitted to pollsters that they did not go to church cited, as the single most important reason, that they were just too busy. Studies of time diaries, detailed accounts of how much time Americans spent on various activities, confirmed that religious worship and related social activities dropped by a third from 1965 to 1995, with children recording even sharper declines. One Catholic priest said that the most common complaint he heard when counseling people in the confessional (presumably about missing Mass) was that there was not enough time. "Make more time" was his invariable penance.[65]

Consumer capitalism fostered secularization while simultaneously adapting to and profiting from it. At the end of the nineteenth century, Christmas was a religious holiday on which relatives and close friends got together and exchanged token bits of gimcrackery. By the end of the twentieth century, it had become the climax of the retailers' year, a months-long campaign featuring Internet-posted wish lists, layaway plans, big-ticket purchases, and boxes of cards to be inscribed and mailed. The cards themselves reflected the diversity of religious temperaments, depicting secular and erotic themes as well as religious icons, with tidings of Christmas and Noël for Christian believers, Happy Holidays and Seasons Greetings for those who were not. Corporations finessed religious differences by treating them as manifestations of a large, segmented market. The inadvertent effect was to make pluralism and moral relativism more visible and legitimate, undercutting religious conservatives in the process. Every drugstore greeting-card display, every magazine rack, every movie shelf radiated doubt. A few determined religious groups, such as the Amish or the Hasidim, tried to escape its influence by isolating themselves. Most did not, with the result that they had always to fight the leftward drift of consumer capitalism's moral current.

If America's late-twentieth-century capitalism acted as the ultimate cultural (and, for some, environmental) solvent, why didn't moral rightists join with economic leftists against the common enemy? They had done so a hundred years before, during the Populist movement, when Bryan evoked the symbols of crucifixion to defend America's farmers and laborers. Noting Pat Buchanan's protectionist and family-values candidacy as an exception (and, judging from his minuscule 2000 vote total, not much of an exception at that), nothing like a "Tory socialist" coalition emerged after Reagan. Perhaps religious conservatives had been so seduced by mass advertising that they clung to a consumer lifestyle at odds with their convictions: the fat Baptist in the Cadillac. But the political philosopher Jean Bethke Elshtain offered a deeper psychological answer. Going to the heart of the culture war's opposing religious temperaments, she wrote that the "traditional conservatives" and "humane socialists" simply inhabited different moral and political universes. Modern socialist ideals had "emerged in opposition to transcendent moments and beliefs," not in support of them.[66]

But so did modern libertarian ideals, and therein lies the central paradox of politics in late-twentieth-century America. The religious right climbed on board the Republican bus, only the bus was bound for Market Street rather than Church Road. Whatever sins the moral revolution had visited upon America, the Ken Lays and Dick Cheneys of the world were unlikely to purge them. Like the Democrats of the 1940s and 1950s, the Republicans had become an uneasy coalition of half-enemies. The Democrats had finally achieved, at steep political cost, ideological unity as the Party of Enlightenment. This unity made it easier for Republicans to recruit the Enlightenment's religious enemies and to keep their anger on boil against the "liberals" who had wrought such abrasive change. But this tactic could not conceal the cultural abrasiveness of capitalism itself, nor eliminate the gap between the objectives of the moral and economic right, however skillfully Republican operatives papered it over with the rhetoric of personal responsibility. In a two-party system, the four-cornered question about moral and economic temperaments—Which sides are you on?—inevitably translates into another, and more pointed, intraparty question: Who is using whom?

BIBLIOGRAPHIC NOTE

The endnotes, limited to key ideas, quotations, and statistics, include several standard works on postwar religion and politics. Three good places to begin research in this field are James Davison Hunter, *Culture Wars* (1991), Roger Finke and Rodney Stark, *The Churching of America, 1776–1990* (1992), and William Martin, *With God on Our Side* (1996). Karen Armstrong, *The Battle for God* (2000), frames the culture war as a dialectic between *mythos* and *logos* and tells the story on a world-historical scale. My humbler scheme of American religious temperaments draws on William James's *The Varieties of Religious Experience* (1902) and, more explicitly, on Philip Greven's *The Protestant Temperament* (1977). Though neither book focuses on the twentieth century, both offer psychological insights still pertinent to Americans' religious and political views. My essay "Morality, Religion, and Drug Use," in *Morality and Health*, ed. Allan M. Brandt and Paul Rozin (1997), takes this same framework of American religious temperaments and shows, in greater detail, how it explains differing attitudes toward drug policy and personal drug use.

NOTES

1. Mark Lilla, "A Tale of Two Reactions," *New York Review of Books* 45 (14 May 1998): 4–7.

2. Paula Story, "Leaders Urge Return to Traditional Values in Reform Judaism," AP Wire, 26 May 1999.

3. Donald J. Bogue et al., *The Population of the United States: Historical Trends and Future Projections*, rev. ed. (New York: Free Press, 1985), chapter 18; Benton Johnson, "Liberal Protestantism: End of the Road?" and Patrick H. McNamara, "American Catholicism in the Mid-Eighties: Pluralism and Conflict in a Changing Church," both in *Annals of the American Academy of Political and Social Science* 480 (July 1985): 39–52 and 63–74, respectively; "Religion in America," *The Gallup Report* 201–202 (June–July 1982): 20, 41, 44, 45; Williamsburg Charter Foundation, *The Williamsburg Charter Survey on Religion and Public Life* (Washington, D.C.: Williamsburg Charter Foundation, 1988), 34–35; and Egon Mayer and Barry Kosmin, "American Religious Identification Survey," www.gc.cuny.edu/studies/key_findings.htm, accessed 9 November 2001.

4. "*Port Huron Statement*," in *Takin' It to the Streets: A Sixties Reader*, ed. Alexander Bloom and Wini Breines (New York: Oxford University Press, 1995), 65, italics deleted.

5. Thomas L. Haskell, "The Curious Persistence of Rights Talk in the 'Age of Interpretation,'" *Journal of American History* 74 (1987): 984–1012.

6. Joseph Cardinal Ratzinger and Vittorio Messori, *The Ratzinger Report: An Exclusive Interview on the State of the Church* (San Francisco: Ignatius Press, 1985), 51, 146, 149, 173; quotation at 190.

7. Cal Thomas, "Justice Needs Ashcroft," *Denver Post*, 31 December 2000.

8. Michael O. Emerson and Christian Smith, *Divided by Faith: Evangelical Religion and the Problem of Race in America* (New York: Oxford University Press), chapter 4.

9. William Martin, *With God on Our Side: The Rise of the Religious Right in America* (New York: Broadway Books, 1996), 100.

10. Mike Glover, "Democrats Debate," AP Wire, 15 January 1988.

11. David J. Garrow, *Bearing the Cross: Martin Luther King, Jr., and the Southern Christian Leadership Conference* (New York: William Morrow, 1986), 375.

12. James Davison Hunter, *Culture Wars: The Struggle to Define America* (New York: Basic Books, 1991). Garrett Epps, "The Discreet Charms of a Demagogue," *New York Review of Books* 34 (7 May 1987): 30–35, offers an excellent account of Helms's moral and political views.

13. Howard Moody, "Pleasure, Too, Is a Gift from God," *Christianity and Crisis* 45 (10 June 1985): 231.

14. Karen Armstrong, *The Battle for God* (New York: Knopf, 2000). Williams quoted in Ari L. Goldman, "Ouster of Gay Priest: Who Betrayed Whom?" *New York Times*, 12 February 2000.

15. William S. Hudson, *Religion in America* (New York: Scribner's, 1965), 396; Hazel Gaudet Erskine, "The Polls: Church Attendance," *Public Opinion Quarterly* 28 (1964): 672; Roger Schwietz, "Recruiting Vocations," *America* 185 (29 July 2001): 7; D. Paul Sullins, "Empty Pews and Empty Altars: A Reconsideration of the Catholic Priest Shortage," *America* 186 (13 May 2002): 13; Roger Finke and Rodney Stark, *The Churching of America, 1776–1990: Winners and Losers in Our Religious Economy* (New Brunswick, N.J.: Rutgers University Press, 1992), 255–274.

16. Walsh in Karen Owen, "Study Shows Facts Are Fudged in Polls on Attending Church," Knight Ridder/Tribune News Wire, 15 January 1999; Robert Putnam, *Bowling Alone: The Collapse and Revival of American Community* (New York: Simon & Schuster, 2000), esp. 72.

17. *The Unchurched American . . . 10 Years Later* (Princeton, N.J.: Princeton Religion Research Center, 1988), 27, 28, 31; Alan Wolfe, "The Pursuit of Autonomy?" *New York Times Magazine*, 7 May 2000, 54.

18. George Gallup Jr. and Sarah Jones, *100 Questions and Answers: Religion in America* (Princeton, N.J.: Princeton Research Center, 1989), 42.

19. Wade Clark Roof and William McKinney, *American Mainline Religion: Its Changing Shape and Future* (New Brunswick, N.J.: Rutgers University Press, 1987), 97.

20. Kenneth L. Woodward, "Dead End for the Mainline?" *Newsweek*, 9 August 1993, 47.

21. Mark Silk, *Spiritual Politics: Religion and America Since World War II* (New York: Simon & Schuster, 1988), 70–83, 188 note 12; Mark S. Massa, *Catholics and American Culture: Fulton Sheen, Dorothy Day, and the Notre Dame Football Team* (New York: Crossroad, 1999), chapter 1; "Leonard Feeney, Jesuit Priest, 80," *New York Times*, 1 February 1978.

22. William James, *Writings, 1902–1910: The Varieties of Religious Experience* (New York: Library of America, 1987), 154.

23. Ralph E. Pyle, "Faith and Commitment to the Poor: Theological Orientation and Support for Government Assistance Programs," *Sociology of Religion* 54 (1993): 385–401.

24. Political scientists sometimes call these planes "Nolan charts," after David Nolan, who devised a survey instrument to separate and measure attitudes toward moral and economic freedom.

25. Benjamin C. Bradlee, *Conversations with Kennedy* (New York: Norton, 1975), 166.

26. Allen J. Matusow, *The Unraveling of America: A History of Liberalism in the 1960s* (New York: Harper & Row, 1984), chapter 1; Mark A. Noll, "The Eclipse of Old Hostilities *between* and the Potential for New Strife *among* Catholics and Protestants since World War II," in *Uncivil Religion: Interreligious Hostility in America*, ed. Robert N.

Bellah and Frederick E. Greenspahn (New York: Crossroad, 1987), 86–109, Graham quotation at 88.

27. William Martin, *A Prophet with Honor: The Billy Graham Story* (New York: William Morrow, 1991), 310 (Cushing), 460; Bruce Bryant-Friedland, "Graham Rally Courts Catholics," *Florida Times-Union*, 15 December 1999.

28. Hunter, *Culture Wars*, 132.

29. Martin campaign journal, 15 September 1964, and Martin to Bill Moyers, 1 October 1964, both box 78, John Bartlow Martin Papers, Library of Congress.

30. Doris Kearns Goodwin, *Lyndon Johnson and the American Dream* (New York: Harper & Row, 1976), 252–253.

31. Todd Gitlin, *The Sixties: Years of Hope, Days of Rage* (New York: Bantam, 1987), 335.

32. Dan T. Carter, "Legacy of Rage: George Wallace and the Transformation of American Politics," *Journal of Southern History* 62 (1996): 11.

33. H. R. Haldeman, *The Haldeman Diaries: Inside the Nixon White House* (New York: G. P. Putnam's, 1994), 127. See also Martin, *With God on Our Side*, 98.

34. Michael Novak, "Errand into the Wilderness," in *Political Passages: Journeys of Change Through Two Decades, 1968–1988*, ed. John H. Bunzel (New York: Free Press, 1988), 257.

35. Reilly to Carter, 28 September 1978, White House Central Files Subject File: Religious Matters, box RM 2, Carter Library, Atlanta.

36. Maddox to Phil Wise and Anne Wexler, 28 August 1979, and Wexler to Wise, 10 September 1979, White House Central Files Subject File: Religious Matters, box RM 1, Carter Library, Atlanta.

37. Martin, *With God on Our Side*, 189.

38. Ibid., 229; Dole interview with the author, 13 June 2006.

39. "Remarks by the President at Broyhill for U.S. Senate Campaign Rally," Raleigh, North Carolina, 8 October 1986 (photocopy provided by the White House), 4.

40. Lilla, "A Tale of Two Reactions," 6.

41. Quoted in Peter Occhiogrosso, *Once a Catholic: Prominent Catholics and Ex-Catholics Reveal the Influence of the Church on Their Lives and Work* (Boston: Houghton Mifflin, 1987), 288.

42. Don Yaeger, "Evangelicals Riding High in GOP," *Florida Times-Union*, 21 August 1988.

43. Martin, *With God on Our Side*, 189.

44. "An Interview with Bill Clinton," *New York Times on the Web*, 24 December 2000.

45. George F. Will, "Clinton's Mark," *Washington Post*, 11 January 2001.

46. Lars-Erik Nelson, "The Republicans' War," *New York Review of Books* 46 (4 February 1999): 8.

47. Quotations from a speech of 11 November 1994, reprinted in *Left, Right, and Center: Voices from Across the Political Spectrum*, ed. Robert Atwan and Jon Roberts (Boston: Bedford Books, 1996), 555.

48. Bob Woodward, *Shadow: Five Presidents and the Legacy of Watergate* (New York: Simon & Schuster, 1999), 336 (Morris); Benjamin Ginsberg and Martin Shefter,

Politics by Other Means: Politicians, Prosecutors, and the Press from Watergate to Whitewater, rev. ed. (New York: Norton, 1999), 39–41.

49. Bruce Bryant-Friedland, "Evangelicals See Issue as Moral Decay," *Florida Times-Union*, 18 December 1998 (Karrer); Josh Getlin, "The Truce Behind the Culture Wars," *Los Angeles Times*, 7 February 1999; Howard Kurtz, "Going Weak in the Knees for Clinton," *Washington Post*, 6 July 1998 (Burleigh).

50. Carey Goldberg et al., "Nation Through a Looking Glass . . . ," *New York Times*, 3 February 1998.

51. Woodward, *Shadow*, 475.

52. Goldberg et al., "Nation."

53. Ron Fournier, "Conservatives Losing Cultural War, Says One of Their Own," AP Wire, 16 February 1999; Ethan Bronner, "Left and Right Are Crossing Paths," *New York Times*, 11 July 1999.

54. "Interview with Bill Clinton."

55. Thomas B. Edsall, "Voter Values Determine Political Affiliation," *Washington Post*, 26 March 2001.

56. Walter J. Stone and Ronald B. Rapoport, "It's Perot Stupid! The Legacy of the 1992 Perot Movement in the Major-Party System, 1992–2000," *PS: Political Science and Politics* 34 (March 2001): 50.

57. Ronald Brownstein, "Election 2004: The National Fissure Remains Deep and Wide," *Los Angeles Times*, 3 November 2004; Paul Farhi and James V. Grimaldi, "GOP Won with Accent on Rural and Traditional," *Washington Post*, 4 November 2004; Jeff Brumley, "'Moral Values' Swayed Voters to Choose Bush," *Florida Times-Union*, 4 November 2004.

58. Brumley, "Moral Values."

59. Stuart Banner, *The Death Penalty: An American History* (Cambridge, Mass.: Harvard University Press, 2002), 277–278.

60. Earl Black, "The 2004 Presidential Election," lecture at the University of North Florida, 28 September 2004. See also Earl and Merle Black, *The Rise of the Southern Republicans* (Cambridge, Mass.: Harvard University Press, 2002).

61. David Brooks, *Bobos in Paradise: The New Upper Class and How They Got There* (New York: Touchstone, 2000).

62. Lilla, "A Tale of Two Reactions," 7.

63. Thomas Frank, *What's the Matter with Kansas?* (New York: Metropolitan Books, 2004).

64. James Gleick, *Faster: The Acceleration of Just About Everything* (New York: Putnam, 1999), 122 (20 percent), 167–172 (multitasking); A. Roger Ekirch, "Sleep We Have Lost: Pre-Industrial Slumber in the British Isles," *American Historical Review* 106 (April 2001): 384.

65. Thomas C. Reeves, *The Empty Church: The Suicide of Liberal Christianity* (New York: Free Press, 1996), 61 (most important reason); Putnam, *Bowling Alone*, 72, 454 note 32; Guy Noonan, personal communication.

66. Jean Bethke Elshtain, "Symposium on Humane Socialism and Traditional Conservatism," *New Oxford Review* 54 (October 1987): 16.

15. THE NEW ALCHEMY

Technology, Consumerism, and Environmental Advocacy

ANDREW KIRK

During the twentieth century, Americans struggled to reconcile their concerns for the environment with enthusiasm for technology-driven progress. In the first half of the century, both in times of scarcity and abundance, assumptions about technology shaped environmental activism. The postwar period added a new element to this long debate. Herbert Marcuse of Brandeis University argued in his book *One-Dimensional Man* that America had entered a condition of "post-scarcity," which he defined as a subversive trend whereby technology became an engine of mass consumption and false consciousness leading to a world of one-dimensional people who defined themselves through material consumption of technology. Marcuse's was only one of a growing number of critical views of science and technology controlled by government and big industry. While Marcuse was cynical about post-scarcity, others embraced this idea as a key to a new world-view where technology, science, and environmentalism could create a utopian society able to capitalize on the wealth of the nation while shepherding the environment into the future. Some of these technologically minded environmentalists called themselves the "new alchemists," enthusiastic about technological innovation and willing to think about the ways environmental concerns could move into the marketplace. Like the alchemists of ancient times, who sought to create gold out of ordinary materials, these environmentalists worked to bring science and nature together to create something new and better. A closer look at evolving ideas about the relationship between technology and the environment helps explain environmental activism in postwar America.

America's ability to ramp up industrial production rapidly and jumpstart new technologies proved a major factor in winning World War II. The war had ushered in a technological revolution that generated plastics and pesticides, atomic weapons and energy, revolutionary new drugs, and a whole universe of domestic consumer goods aimed at eliminating the drudgery of everyday life. The growth of these industries, and others that would inevitably follow in their wake, promised an unprecedented period of productivity, prosperity, and affluence. Proud of their technological achievements, most Americans celebrated the apparent victory of human technology and science over nature.

Haggard from fifteen years of thrift and privation enforced by grinding economic depression and wartime sacrifice, Americans in 1946 were ready to celebrate their emergence as the world's only economic superpower with an orgy of domestic consumption. In the years after the war, the mighty military industrial complex was converted into a machine for unprecedented peacetime affluence and consumption. The spectacular rise in birthrates between 1945 and 1964, an increase of fifty million, helped fuel the massive expansions in production of housing and consumer goods. Depression-era fears about the future of American progress and prosperity evaporated. Many Americans comfortably assumed that the twin engines of technological advancement and personal consumption were about to propel America into a future of boundless prosperity.

Always a future-oriented people, Americans had good reason for optimism. The speed and scope of technological advances in the postwar years appeared to promise a future free of many of the problems that had plagued humans for centuries. Not everyone, however, shared this faith in progress through technological advance and consumption. The horrors attending the destruction of Hiroshima and Nagasaki and the grim prospect of even more terrible atomic weapons cast a pall over technology and science. The unknown long-term effects on the environment of nuclear weapons and power plants caused a growing number of Americans to wonder if the costs of technology outweighed its benefits. In the decades following World War II, American conservationists and wilderness preservation advocates voiced concern that the growing American obsession with technology was obscuring our fundamental connections to the natural world.

CONSERVATIONISTS AND THE TECHNOLOGY OF ABUNDANCE

In 1947, prominent ornithologist William Vogt took time away from his studies of birds and penned a bleak book on the future of America and the human race.

The following year his *Road to Survival* sent a shock wave through the conservation community. Vogt's compelling narrative told a tale of misplaced faith in technology in the dawning atomic age and warned readers of the profound ecological consequences of the spread of industrial capitalism in the wake of World War II. Particularly concerned with the American obsession with progress, Vogt argued that "the rising living standard, as material progress is called, is universally assumed to be to the advantage of the human race. Yet . . . what is the effect of our allegedly rising living standard on the natural resources that are the basis of our survival?"[1] This cautionary tale reflected the central concerns of the dominant group of American conservationists of the 1940s and 1950s, such as the Audubon Society and the Sierra Club, and tapped into older Malthusian fears of resource depletion and scarcity. Conservationists predicated their environmental politics on the assumption that inefficiency, waste, and abuse of resources had created a potentially crippling scarcity.

Conservation-minded critics of technology often found themselves gainsaying widespread reverence toward science and industry. From 1945 through the 1950s, conservationists struggled to explain to the public why, during a period of apparent abundance, it was more important than ever to require limits on both production and consumption. Conservation advocates such as Vogt framed the debate in stark terms as a war between industrial technology and the environment.

The response of the conservationists was tempered by their inability to articulate a compelling and environmentally acceptable alternative to perpetual economic growth and technological mastery of nature. During the Progressive period and into the 1930s, conservationists had played a large role in shaping federal land management policies and influencing public opinion on important environmental issues. The movement was successful in raising environmental awareness and reversing some basic assumptions about the environment and the need for conservation and preservation. In spite of this success, by 1945 the authority of the conservationists was on the wane. Renewed resistance to conservation programs by western ranchers and the extractive industries forced conservationists on the defensive. General public interest in residential and business development, all linked by extensive highway systems, also posed a problem for advocates, who focused most of their attention on restriction of use and regulation of development in the name of conservation.

The major conservation organizations—the Sierra Club, the Izaak Walton League, and the Wilderness Society—tended to be upper-middle-class or upper-class, urban-based recreation groups. New issues and new leadership in the late 1940s began to shift the focus of the movement away from the simple ideal of efficient use of resources—for the greatest good over the longest period—toward a more focused effort to protect wildlands. The Sierra Club, guided by youthful board members such as David Brower, took the lead in establishing a new direction for the American conservation movement and began the subtle shifting of political and social consciousness that led to a move away from limited concerns about resource cultivation and protection and toward a more holistic ecological sensibility and ultimately the broad ecological sensibility known as environmentalism. Brower used his position as a board member and editor of the *Sierra Club Bulletin* to push the club to take a stand on controversial issues such as wilderness preservation, overpopulation, and pollution.

This shift from conservation to environmentalism required some significant changes in perspective from a new generation of environmentally aware Americans. From the late 1800s through World War II, most conservationists advocated a more efficient use of natural resources; like most Americans, conservationists were optimistic that American technological inventiveness could lead to a future of progress and conservation. One significant exception to this general trend was the Wilderness Society. Decades ahead of its time, the organization, founded in 1935 by an unusual collection of land planners, foresters, and wilderness enthusiasts, raised concerns about the relationship of consumer recreation technology and the health of the environment. Specifically, the Wilderness Society founders deplored the impact of auto recreation on the national parks and, more importantly, on forests that experienced radical increases in visitation with each expansion of auto tourism. Unlike their counterparts in the conservation movement, Wilderness Society members refused to embrace the technological enthusiasm of the Progressive conservationists.

Vogt's cautionary tale was followed by conservationist Aldo Leopold's influential book, *A Sand County Almanac* (1949). Leopold's beautifully written stories of life on a run-down farm and his efforts to restore the land provided a blueprint for a new land ethic and model of ecological thinking that inspired a generation of environmental advocates to broaden the scope of their activism. A sharp eye for subtle change enabled Leopold to give voice to those who recognized that the modern world was changing the environment in ways that few even noticed: "The sadness discernible in some marshes arises, perhaps, from their having once harbored cranes. Now they stand humbled, adrift in history." As the 1950s progressed, environmental advocacy moved away from the narrow concerns of the early conservationists and toward a nascent environmentalist embrace of a wide range of concerns from wildlife preservation to pollution and population control.

These new concerns sometimes created tensions between private environmental advocacy groups and federal agencies once closely allied with the conservation movement. At the same time, other federal bureaus, especially the water, soil, and wildlife agencies, led the way in raising the public awareness of the consequences of the postwar economic boom on the environment. Early on, the federal government sought to redress pollution as a blight on the environment and serious public health threat. In 1955, Congress made a cautious move toward environmental regulation with the passage of the first of a series of air pollution control acts that provided for research that would lead to the regulations on industrial emissions of the Clean Air Act of 1963. The first of many environmental laws aimed at placing restrictions on production, the first Air Pollution Control Act was important not for what it actually accomplished but for the environmental politics that supported it.

Clean air was of growing concern for many Americans in the late 1950s, and the rise of new concerns about persistent and growing problems such as air pollution highlighted two factors central to the emergence of modern environmentalism. Environmental advocates worried about changes in the postwar world of production and the long-term implications of those changes for the health of the environment. The chemical revolution, atomic science, reclamation, and increases in the scope of extractive industries created new and frightening environmental problems that galvanized a growing segment of the public behind the environmental movement. At the heart of the critique of production after 1945 was a growing fear of technology in general and the atom bomb in particular. These fears spawned a host of science fiction films and publications that depicted giant nuclear ants and other atomic mutants running through nightmare landscapes and polluted environments.

By the end of the 1940s the very real environmental consequences of unbridled technological enthusiasm were beginning to become clear to the American public. A defining moment came with the attempts, by the Bureau of Reclamation, to dam a large portion of the Grand Canyon and adjacent areas. The Colorado River Storage Project (CRSP) called for a chain of ten dams on the Colorado River. This project, while bold in scope, was not a departure for the bureau: it had been building dams to control flooding, provide irrigation, and supply hydroelectric power with broad support from Congress and the public.

Once uncritically hailed as technological wonders, dams by then had become a focal point for growing concern about the environmental consequences of rapid technological progress. The Bureau of Reclamation now found itself at odds with groups like the Sierra Club and a rapidly growing segment of the public that began to question the economic logic of the monumental dam projects. Controversy over dam building reached a head in 1950 with the announcement that the CRSP called for a dam to be built inside the boundaries of the Dinosaur National Monument at a spot known as Echo Park. Led by the Sierra Club and writers Bernard DeVoto and Arthur Carhart, conservationists built a coalition of organizations and individuals to thwart the Echo Park dam. In 1954, Congress, responding to intense public opposition, killed the project. Conservationists successfully defeated the Echo Park dam project by convincing enough politically active Americans that in the atomic age there needed to be limits on growth and that destruction of even remote areas such as Echo Park could affect quality of life. After Echo Park, many Americans came to view proposed technological solutions to human problems with a more critical eye. Most Americans only needed to look in their own backyards to see examples of technology-fueled growth affecting the environment in ways that threatened their own quality of life.

Environmental awareness shifted from the remote wilderness and scenic wonders that had inspired previous generations of environmental advocates and focused increasingly on lifestyle issues in the suburbs. Millions were drawn to suburbs precisely because they seemingly offered a more rural, more "natural" life than could be found in crowded cities. This heightened awareness of quality-of-life issues created a powerful new constituency as conservation groups moved toward a more encompassing critique of environmental policy. Suburban growth helped build a new power base for environmentalism. Perhaps more importantly, suburban growth, devouring an area the size of Rhode Island every year, proved that new technologies could completely reshape the natural world when harnessed to economic prosperity. Irving, Texas, saw its population rise from 2,621 in 1950 to over 45,000 in less than a decade, rendering the formerly rural countryside on the outskirts of Dallas unrecognizable; much the same happened to communities around the country. Suburbanites already living there watched through the picture window as forests, meadows, and even mountains were cleared to accommodate a flood of suburbanites. As suburbs encroached on wildlands previously used for recreation, more Americans began to support limits on growth and protection of at least some scenic lands even while they demanded more of the growth that caused the problems.

Of the new technologies of abundance, none shaped the environment more dramatically than assembly-line suburban housing. Tracts of mass-produced homes transformed enormous areas of rural landscape into seas of houses, shopping malls, and highways. Suburban pioneers such as William Levitt, builder of the prototypical modern tract suburb of Levittown in New York, were hailed as heroes in the years after the war, when serious housing shortages left some returning veterans living with parents or in converted chicken coops. Suburbs provided inexpensive housing for young families moving into the middle class, and the GI Bill offered low-cost mortgages for veterans. Suburbs filled an urgent housing need and promised a level of comfort and modernity unknown to city dwellers. Millions of people moved to suburbs that lined interstate highways spreading ever further into rural areas, often erasing all evidence of what existed before. The extent of suburban development was so dramatic and transformative during the 1950s and 1960s it prompted critics such as historian Godfrey Hodgson to write about a "suburban-industrial complex" comparable in influence to the military-industrial complex.² As suburbanites watched the lands around them being converted into concrete and strip malls, many of them also began to experience firsthand the unintended environmental consequences of other aspects of American postwar prosperity.

In the summer of 1962 marine biologist Rachael Carson released *Silent Spring*, an instant best-seller. The book was an indictment of pesticides, the general chemical assault on the environment, and the greed and irresponsibility of postwar America. Carson specifically focused on the shocking effects of DDT and other chemicals on bird populations. Carson advised readers to listen carefully to the "strange stillness" that had settled over the countryside as bird species poisoned by DDT vanished. The message was clear: if the extensive use of pesticides was not curbed, whole species would be wiped out. The decline of bird species was an indicator of the deep and long-term consequences of introducing chemicals into an ecosystem, including higher cancer rates among humans. Carson's book was a harsh and uncompromising attack on the American faith in progress through technological innovation. Millions of Americans who learned of Carson's compelling arguments reevaluated their views on human responsibility for their environmental future. Carson's death in 1964 from cancer, and a dawning realization that many human diseases were caused by the products designed to make life easier, only confirmed environmentalists' fears.

The same year that *Silent Spring* appeared, disturbing cases of birth defects began making their way into the popular media. Doctors, particularly in England, learned that the mothers of many babies who had been born with atrophied or missing arms and legs had during pregnancy taken Thalidomide, a drug to combat the effects of depression. The Thalidomide crisis presented another startling example of the long-term risks and unintended consequences of chemicals on nature.

While Thalidomide showed how modern medical technology could go terribly wrong, many environmental advocates were more concerned with the problems associated with medical technology that worked too well. After Vogt's alarming account of the consequences of the ever-expanding world population, many other writers published popular books and articles on the issue of overpopulation. The statistics about world population growth and future prospects were alarming. In 1948, ecologist Fairfield Osborn worried that with a growth rate of 1 percent per year the world population might top three billion by the year 2000. His popular book *Our Plundered Planet* was criticized for being alarmist. A decade later Osborn's predictions seemed conservative, as world population increased far more rapidly than even the most pessimistic environmentalists had predicted.

In the United States, the population growth was staggering. The baby boom between 1945 and 1964 created a massive demographic surge that strained resources and raised questions about the relationship between population and quality of life. By the mid-1960s the faith in progress through technological innovation was under fire from an increasingly diverse group of environmental advocates, informed by a growing ecological consciousness that far surpassed the cautious environmental protection of the conservation movement during the 1940s.

One consequence of the rejuvenated environmental movement was a resurgence of interest in the preservation of America's remaining wilderness regions. The affluence of the period and further expansion of highways made outdoor recreation more accessible to a greater number of Americans. Even those who did not travel to wilderness areas for recreation began to include wilderness as an important aspect of quality of life and to recognize the value of protecting large scenic and recreational areas from future development. Concerns about overdevelopment, pollution, overpopulation, and disappearing wildlife habitats led to a concerted grassroots effort in the early 1960s to pass wilderness legislation.

Although preservation organizations such as the Wilderness Society spearheaded this movement, the ultimate success of the legislation required wide support from middle-class Americans. In 1963, with public opinion running heavily in favor of wilderness legislation, lawmakers from both sides of the aisle passed the Wilderness Act; President Lyndon Johnson signed it into law the following year. The Wilderness Act protected millions of acres of public land from future development. Unlike forest reserves or national parks, wilderness areas could not be developed to accommodate visitors. Newly protected wilderness lands were to remain "untrammeled by man" and "roadless" in perpetuity. The passage of the Wilderness Act signaled a significant change in American environmental thinking. The new law was a major victory for conservationists and other advocates of wildland preservation. The act also reflected a shifting of American values and a growing willingness to accept limits to growth in return for greater quality of life.

TECHNOLOGY, ENVIRONMENT, AND SOCIAL CHANGE

As the 1960s progressed, new voices questioned the technology of abundance and environmentalism emerged as a major social movement. Appalled by the consequences of the period of prosperity engineered by their parents, many Americans born after World War II began envisioning a future for America where economy, culture, and politics took into account the health of the planet. Critics of the 1940s and 1950s world of mass production and consumption found evidence of their fears in the research of prominent academics like Barry Commoner, whose *The Closing Circle* provided persuasive evidence that the technological choices of the 1940s, such as DDT and atomic science, led directly to the environmental concerns of the 1960s. These concerns bridged the generation gap as a series of startling environmental catastrophes during the end of the 1960s cast a shadow on the accomplishments of the postwar period.

Despite the successes of the wilderness movement and some promising steps toward environmental regulation on the part of the federal government by the mid-1960s, environmentalism was still a movement on the fringes of mainstream American culture and politics. To win over average Americans, environmental advocates were obliged to refute longstanding assumptions about the limitless natural bounty of North America. Conservationists spent the better part of a century preaching restraint and regulation, but often to deaf ears. The prosperity of the postwar period contributed to a general apathy toward environmental issues. This began to change in the late 1960s when a series of events inspired general interest in the environment and forced Americans to think beyond regional issues.

One of these events sprang from the space program of the 1960s and early 1970s. Missions to orbit Earth and then land on the moon generated thousands of images of earth from space. In 1966, a young counterculture entrepreneur named Stewart Brand, who recognized the significance of these photos for the environmental movement, produced widely circulated buttons asking the simple question, "Why Haven't We Seen a Photograph of the Whole Earth Yet?" He realized that an image of Earth from space could generate awareness of environmental concerns shared by all who occupied "spaceship Earth." Both the photographs and the publication that grew from them helped transform the environmental movement and open the door to an alternative type of pragmatic environmental advocacy of great appeal to his generation.

In almost any used bookstore in America one may find, slumped in a corner, a pile of unwieldy *Whole Earth Catalogs*. Released in 1968, the *Whole Earth Catalog* was one of the most unlikely publishing success stories of the century. These oversize illustrated books juxtaposed a seeming hodgepodge of herbal health remedies, data on pollution, guides to communes and traditional folk arts, and celebrations of high-tech innovations straight out of the laboratories of MIT. It was a perfect representation of the "new alchemy" of environmental concern, technological enthusiasm, and business savvy that created an alternative strain of environmental politics in the 1970s. The catalog was particularly appealing to a generation of young environmentalists who found the whole scope of their varied and complex movement represented within its pages. This iconoclastic publication rose to prominence during a time of growing concern about the relationship between technological advancements, quality of life, and the health of the American environment.

The catalog reflected the tangled and shifting relationship among technology, consumerism, and environmentalism in postwar America. The makers and readers of the catalog did not always define themselves as environmentalists, and they did not fit the mold of the conservationists or preservationists who preceded them. Still, the universe of seemingly chaotic ideas in the catalog reveals the complex intertwining of social, economic, ecological, and political concerns that became known as environmentalism. The tension between the proponents and critics of technology within the environmental movement often divided organizations and split coalitions. Ultimately, though, this tension helped shape a compromise that dramatically broadened the public appeal of environmentalism. Environmental advocates gradually reconciled the American ideal of progress through technological innovation and the conquest of nature with America's growing concerns about the ecosystem of a fragile and overpopulated planet. Initially infatuated with technology, environmental advocates became wary of it, then accommodated to it before finally embracing environmentally sensitive technology as a means for solving environmental problems.

In the 1960s the debate over technology, prosperity, and scarcity accelerated. Increasingly convinced that nuclear power plants, giant reclamation projects, and other technological promises did more harm than good, a small but vocal segment of the environmental movement embraced an increasingly radical version of wilderness preservation or advocated a back-to-the-land ethic that demonized modern technology. This notion was anticipated by Helen and Scott Nearing, who in 1954 published a popular manifesto, *Living the Good Life*, for those who wanted to "live frugally and decently" by abandoning the status quo for a simpler preindustrial life in the countryside.

The Nearings' experiment in simple living inspired a significant back-to-the-land movement in the 1960s. Communes and collective farms sprang up all over the American West in rural communities like Taos, New Mexico. The technophobia of these back-to-the-land environmentalists sometimes created tensions between moderates and conservatives with the environmental movement. While these groups were a distinct minority in a culture that still embraced consumerism and technological progress, there was a general questioning of the Progressive faith in the ability to use technology to control the environment for perpetual economic growth. By the mid-1960s a growing number of environmental advocates found themselves somewhere between the old and new views.

Environmental advocates like twenty-nine-year-old Stewart Brand, for example, did not fit the mold of the either the Progressive conservationists or the back-to-the-landers. Instead he, along with many of his generation, looked at the relationship between a technology-driven consumer society at odds with a fragile and overpopulated planet. Brand wondered if maybe there was a practical middle ground between technological enthusiasm and environmentalism. Perhaps more importantly, Brand looked specifically at the ways environmentalism could positively influence consumerism. Like many in the counterculture movement of the 1960s, Brand resolved to protect the planet while saving the troubled souls of the American people. Brand was trained as a biologist at Stanford University, where he received his degree in 1960. At Stanford, Brand learned early that access to good data and tools was critical to accomplishing goals and producing productive results. After graduation Brand studied design in San Francisco, participated in legal LSD studies, researched and organized a multimedia event called "America Needs Indians," and spent two years on the road with Ken Kesey and his Merry Pranksters.

In March 1968, while flying over Nebraska, returning from the funeral of his father, Brand concocted an idea and scrawled it over the endpages of Barbara Ward's environmental book *Spaceship Earth*. Trying to think of a practical means to help preserve "spaceship Earth," Brand envisioned a blueprint for an information delivery system modeled on the L. L. Bean catalog, which he viewed as a priceless and practical "service to humanity." Brand's counterculture version would be a "catalog of goods that owed nothing to the suppliers and everything to the users."[3] He hoped to create a service that would blend the liberal social values of the counterculture and the environmental movement with the technological enthusiasm of his Stanford classmates and professors. He also wanted to provide a nexus of information on environmental solutions and commonsense economic advice on how to fund all of these areas. Brand backed up his lofty ideas with an impressive stock portfolio and real entrepreneurial genius. While he could talk counterculture philosophy with the best, Brand valued practical solutions, realistic schedules, and well-thought-out blueprints and business plans. He was a capitalist at heart with libertarian leanings and represented a new type of environmental advocate. The *Whole Earth Catalog* became his means to explore a counterculture business model. The book sold millions and won the National Book Award.

Brand's idea became a best-seller because he assemble a talented group of like-minded young veterans of the counterculture and first-rate supporters from the business community such as Richard Raymond of the education-oriented Portola Institute. With some financial backing and sound business advice coming from Raymond, Brand spent his time researching the business of publishing. He realized early on that to accomplish his goals he would need to break away from the traditional publication model and use a method that became commonplace in the 1990s: desktop publishing. Acquiring a then state-of-the-art IBM Selectric Composer, the first desktop typesetting machine, Brand was able to create the first *Whole Earth Catalog* out of his own shop. Once they were able to create the catalogs physically, they needed to forge partnerships with publishing houses to market their product. After much trial and error they were able to get their publication to market with such success that *Whole Earth* created a new model and market for self-published alternative books. The creative process and inventive thinking that went into the creation of the catalog rivaled the innovative content that it contained. *Whole Earth* brought a wide range of divergent counterculture and environmental trends under one roof and helped bring a new generation of young environmentalists into contact with the writings and philosophies of the environmental movement. Commune members, computer designers and hackers, psychedelic drug engineers, and environmentalists were but a few of those who could find something of interest in *Whole Earth*. While popular with counterculture commune dwellers the catalogs also became a manual for environmentally sensitive living in the cities and suburbs where younger Americans watched their environments change seemingly overnight. *The Whole Earth Catalog* and its successors extolled the virtues of steam-powered bicycles, windmills, solar collectors, and wood stoves alongside new "personal computers" and the latest telecommunications hardware.

All of these diverse products shared functional and political characteristics that fell under the broad term "appropriate technology." Brand and a growing number of environmentalists were convinced that access to innovative and potentially subversive information and energy technologies was a vital part of changing the cultural perceptions that contributed to environmental decay. Younger readers found the practical philosophy and focus on individual agency of appropriate technology particularly appealing. In addition to introducing millions to a broad selection of environmental ideas, *Whole Earth* provided a guilt free outlet for a new generation of socially aware consumers. While *Whole Earth's* readers learned about social, cultural, and technological alternatives to the old world of their parents, they also got an implicit and explicit lesson about green capitalism and green consumerism that significantly contributed to the broader acceptance of environmentalism in the following decades. While some critics argued that the growing emphasis on production and consumption represented a selling out of true counterculture values, the opposite was true. Brand and his cohort were very consistent in their enthusiasm for thoughtful consumption as a means of political empowerment. Hardly a thoughtless sellout who abandoned youthful idealism for profit, Brand was among an emerging class of counterculture business leaders who believed that "the consumer has more power for good or ill than the voter." Brand's publications helped popularize the ideas that the persistence of capitalism was inevitable and that reconciliation with this fact was critical to crafting a viable environmental ethic in the Western world.

Whole Earth represented the broad scope of evolving ideas about technology and environment. Individuals such as E. F. Schumacher, author of *Small Is Beautiful* (1973), and environmental organizations such as the New Alchemy Institute were actively working to research and promote new green technologies while explaining to the media and the public why existing technologies were inadequate and why corporations that claimed there were no alternatives were wrong. Small environmental companies and research groups like the Rocky Mountain Institute in Colorado often led the way in this area as they researched alternative technologies to solve specific regional problems such as waste water management, sustainable agriculture, and pollution control. Conservative industry groups lobbied strenuously against environmentalists during this time, working especially hard to discredit citizen activists and grassroots organizations promoting green technologies or alternatives in polluting industries. Industrial groups seemed to hold the cards in this confrontation, but often capitulated after the proposed alternatives were proven not only feasible but also profitable. The decade also saw a dramatic increase in research on appropriate technologies on university campuses and through newly formed research groups, with much of the impetus and funding coming directly from the federal government.

THE GROWTH OF APPROPRIATE TECHNOLOGY

By the 1970s, rejecting both the preservationists, who tended to view technology as the root of environmental problems, and the conservationists, who endorsed large-scale technological progress as the solution to environmental problems, the new environmentalists preferred to criticize the systems that developed and deployed technology in postwar America, not the technology itself. Bloated bureaucracies, massive corporations, and the military-industrial complex, they argued, caused the environmental crisis of the 1960s and 1970s. Proponents of appropriate technology insisted that decentralized technology built on a foundation of solid ecological principles and, once made accessible to average people and local communities, could provide solutions for even the most complex environmental problems.

In *Small Is Beautiful*, British economist Schumacher delineated a compelling model for decentralized humanistic economics "as if people mattered." Schumacher built on the structural critiques of modern industrial society that were coming out of the political movement known as the New Left, which emphasized that social and environmental problems in America stemmed not from a lack of resources but from a misguided waste of the technology of abundance. If Americans could be convinced to abandon their bourgeois quest for consumer goods, these critics argued, then valuable resources could be redirected from wasteful consumption toward establishing social equity and ecological harmony.

Unlike more pessimistic critics of the modern technocracy, Schumacher provided assurance that by striving to regain individual control of economics and environments, "our landscapes [could] become healthy and beautiful again and our people . . . regain the dignity of man, who knows himself as higher than the animal but never forgets that *noblesse oblige*."[4] Schumacher endorsed what he called "intermediate technologies," technical advances that stood "halfway between traditional and modern technology" as the solution to the dissonance between nature and technology in the modern world. These technologies could be as simple as using modern materials to construct better windmills or as advanced as more efficient portable water turbines for developing nations. The key to "intermediate technologies" was to apply advances in science to specific local communities and ecosystems. While New Left criticism was often discouragingly pessimistic or infuriatingly radical, a wide range of individuals and organizations, often with wildly different agendas. picked up and expanded upon Schumacher's concepts of appropriate technology. Those concerned with the plight of developing nations regarded Schumacher's ideas about intermediate technologies as a means of solving Third World poverty without extending industrialization and its attendant environmental and social problems. In America, appropriate technology quickly became a catchall for a wide spectrum of activities involving research into older technologies that had been lost after the industrial revolution, such as windmills, solar water heaters, and small-scale hydroelectric generators and the development of new high- and low-tech innovations such as geodesic domes and domestic photovoltaic systems. The most striking thing about appropriate technology, according to historian Samuel Hays, was "not so much the mechanical devices themselves as the kinds of knowledge and management they implied."[5] Alternative technology represented a move away from the Progressive faith in expertise and professionalization and toward an environmental philosophy predicated on self-education and individual experience. Appropriate technology also seemed to provide an avenue for Americans to work toward a more viable environmental future without giving up the consumerism that powered America's economy and underlay American notions of quality of life. But even as appropriate technology proponents were trying to accommodate technological innovation with environmental protection, a series of environmental catastrophes transformed the way Americans regarded the "environmental crisis."

THE FEDERAL GOVERNMENT RESPONDS

In January 1969, an oil well off the coast of Santa Barbara, California, caught fire and exploded, releasing 235,000 gallons of oil. Within several weeks, sticky oil tar covered thirty miles of Pacific beach. That same summer, the Cuyahoga

River in Cleveland, Ohio, into which tons of chemicals had been released by various industries, caught fire. For weeks, flames from the river shot high into the night sky above Cleveland. These spectacular environmental crises, vividly captured on the TV news, helped generate strong bipartisan political support for environmental regulation. Building on precedents set by the first clean air acts, Congress passed a series of sweeping environmental laws.

Of these, the National Environmental Policy Act (NEPA) of 1969 was most significant. Through the leadership of Senator Henry Jackson (D-Wash.) and the Senate Committee on Interior Affairs, NEPA created the first comprehensive legislation for dealing with broad environmental problems. Before the passage of NEPA, government environmental policy was criticized by slow and fragmented decision making on environmental issues and a consistent failure to reconcile federal environmental policy with contemporary environmental science. Jackson's committee worked to create a legislative package that would bring order and scientific thinking directly into environmental policy making. A central provision of NEPA was the requirement that all federally funded projects produce an Environmental Impact Statement (EIS), a detailed assessment of the ways that the project would affect the environment. The EIS became a very direct means of managing environmental impact according to contemporary scientific standards, and it forced all government projects to detail environmental consequences. Most significantly, NEPA created the massive Environmental Protection Agency (EPA), which quickly grew in both size and power to become one of the nation's most significant regulatory bodies. The passage of NEPA and the creation of the EPA permanently established the federal government as a caretaker not only of land and resources but also of environmental quality of life.

NEPA also required the EPA to set environmental regulations. During the 1970s it focused pollution-control efforts on water and air. The Clean Air Act of 1970 set tough new standards for airborne emissions and required factories to use new technologies like air scrubbers to remove the most dangerous pollutants from smokestack emissions. Scrubber mandates were met with strenuous resistance from industrialists such as the owners of coal-fueled power plants, who contended that the scrubbers were impractical, expensive, and ineffective and would preclude American industries from competing in world markets. In response, scrubber manufacturers improved the design and reliability of their scrubbers. EPA standards not only forced polluting industries to clean up production processes but also directly supported green technological innovation. The second Clean Water Act of 1972 set new technology standards for industries that emitted waste into water and required these industries to research technological alternatives for reducing emissions. The EPA's focus on technology standards helped move the public debate away from the rancorous 1960s dispute over culpability in the environmental crisis and toward practical solutions.

Throughout the 1970s, well-funded public agencies provided economic incentives for innovative technology research whose practical and economical solutions gained public support and helped silence critics of green technologies.

In addition to the EPA, several other federal and some state agencies and organizations promoted appropriate technology research. In 1972 Congress created the Office of Technology Assessment (OTA) to research technology and the environment. The OTA quietly contributed to significant advances in green technology. Throughout the 1970s public support for government-supported environmental research reached a high point. Public opinion polls revealed that a high percentage of Americans thought that the federal government should stimulate appropriate technologies to improve the environment. In the 1970s environmental policy and technology were linked in the minds of the public leading to a brief period of strong federal support for research in areas such as solar energy, wind and geothermal power, and a whole universe of alternative fixes to technologies of abundance that Americans had so enthusiastically embraced after World War II.

In 1973, public enthusiasm for appropriate technology research reached a new level of urgency. That year, after American assistance had helped Israel defeat an Egyptian-Syrian attack, the Arab-dominated Organization of Petroleum Exporting Countries (OPEC) embargoed oil exports to the West. Oil prices skyrocketed, filling stations ran out of gas, and panicked Americans waited for hours to fill their tanks. The OPEC embargo revived old resource-scarcity fears and reinvigorated the search or alternative sources of renewable energy. In California, where the energy crisis was particularly acute, appropriate technology research gained support from the state government. Governor Jerry Brown appointed appropriate technology researchers, including Stewart Brand, to key state posts and in 1976 created a state Office of Appropriate Technology in an effort to search for viable solutions to the reliance on foreign oil. President Jimmy Carter responded to the energy crisis by initiating federal energy conservation programs and by providing federal funding for appropriate technology research. In 1976 these programs came together under the umbrella of the National Center for Appropriate Technology, which consolidated various programs in an effort to foster cooperation and accelerate research. While the federal government took the lead during the 1970s in responding to growing public desire for research into viable alternatives to the status quo, private and grassroots organizations played an important role as well.

The celebration of the first Earth Day on April 22, 1970, dramatically demonstrated how far environmental awareness had come during the 1960s. Earth Day celebrations ranged from tree-planting festivals and litter cleanups to large-scale marches and rallies. An estimated twenty million people participated, making it the largest public demonstration in American history. While the conservation organizations of the 1950s and early 1960s were made up mainly of middle-aged or older professional men, most or the participants in Earth Day were schoolchildren and college-age adults. During these years, all of the major American environmental groups benefited from an infusion of new members, many of them young people. The National Wildlife Federation, for example, saw their membership double between 1966 and 1970. Invigorated by young, politically active new members, groups such as the Sierra Club and the Wilderness Society became increasingly more directly involved with political causes and lobbying efforts. Rising with the tide of popular concern and support for environmental legislation environmental groups became a significant force in American politics.

The federal environmental legislation of the 1970s and rise to prominence of environmental organizations represented a major advance for the environmental movement. There was, however, a serious downside to these gains for supporters of environmentalism. The power of the EPA and the uncompromising demands of some environmentalists precipitated a backlash among some industrialists, businessmen, farmers, and workers who felt that government regulation and environmental controls threatened their livelihood. Likewise, some critics worried that NEPA's checks on development and technology constituted a dangerous antimodernism that privileged nature over humans. The Endangered Species Act of 1973 became a focal point for advocates of this view.

The first significant application of the Endangered Species Act stopped construction of the Tellico Dam on the Little Tennessee River in 1977. Scientists discovered in the Little Tennessee River a tiny endangered fish called the snail darter and invoked the Endangered Species Act to halt the $116 million project. During the ensuing two-year legal battle, supporters of the dam and environmentalists fought an intense public-relations war. Ultimately the developers prevailed and the dam was built, destroying the snail darter habitat. For opponents of the Endangered Species Act, the defense of the snail darter was evidence that environmentalists were willing to sacrifice human quality of life to protect even obscure creatures. For environmentalists, the intense criticism and ridicule from their opponents provided disheartening evidence of how far they still had to go to demonstrate the connections between conditions for seemingly insignificant species with overall environmental health.

The presidency of Jimmy Carter (1977–81) marked the culmination of many environmental aspirations. Carter made environmental issues central to his domestic programs and won praise from environmentalists for his strong appeals for energy conservation and his support for other controversial environmental issues. He appointed environmentalists to key positions, such as Gus Speth, who headed the Council on Environmental Quality. Carter's secretary of state,

Edmund Muskie, worked to create the Global 2000 report and launched a campaign against costly reclamation projects that he felt wasted tax money and threatened America's landscape. The landmark Global 2000 study evaluated global trends in population and environmental quality and projected how long-term trends in the international economy might play out in the future. The Carter administration was particularly supportive of efforts to research and develop appropriate technologies. During the years between 1976 and Carter's departure in 1981 appropriate technology research expanded dramatically and achieved a much higher public profile. Ultimately, the rise of a conservative reaction against environmentalism and appropriate technology in general offset these gains.

Carter's support for environmental issues generated a backlash, especially as the economy slipped deeper into a recession. By the elections of 1980, many Americans, discouraged by a decade of bleak news, post-Watergate cynicism, and an extended economic slump, were looking for a change in both direction and perception. Republican presidential candidate Ronald Reagan and his conservative advisors assumed that environmental advocacy and the EPA had harmed business and threatened the economy. Particularly unsympathetic toward federal support for appropriate technology, Reagan made his feelings toward green technologies very clear when he ordered the removal of the White House solar panels installed by Carter, symbolically ending the era of appropriate technology.

Reagan also nominated a host of renowned anti-environmentalists to powerful positions within his administration. Most prominent among these was James Watt, director of the Mountain States Legal Foundation, a right-wing organization financed by big business to combat government environmental regulation. Mountain States had backing from conservative western businessmen such as brewer Joseph Coors. Reagan then named Anne Gorsuch to head the EPA. As a conservative Colorado state legislator, Gorsuch had consistently worked to undermine environmental legislation in the state.

Environmentalists steeled themselves for a prolonged fight against Reagan and his appointees; for many, the challenge invigorated the movement and strengthened their resolve. For supporters of appropriate technologies the appointment of right-wing politicians to key positions in federal environmental agencies meant the death of their dream. Without direct support of the federal government to fund expensive research and promote innovations, appropriate technology could not survive. In the first two years of the Reagan administration, the EPA lost almost 30 percent of its funding, the appropriate technology programs within the Department of Energy were slashed, and promising appropriate technology research programs such as the Solar Energy Research Division and other federally funded alternative energy efforts such as the Regional Energy/Environment Information Center were left completely without support.

In the long term, most of Reagan's appointees' plans to reduce the influence of environmentalists backfired and, ironically, did more to reenergize the environmental movement than did the pro-environment Carter administration. James Watt's attitude toward the environment and environmentalists quickly made him a liability to the administration. His controversial statements were a strong factor in the dramatic rise in membership in environmental organizations during the early 1980s. One environmentalist claimed that Watt "was the best organizer we ever had."[6] He was eventually forced to resign, as was Gorsuch, after an EPA accounting scandal left her disgraced and sent some of her deputies to jail. This wave of anti-environmental sentiment proved too extreme. Reagan and his advisors failed to understand the depth of pro-environmental sentiment among the general public. By the mid-1980s, the American environmental movement was deeply rooted in American society and culture. In the end, the Reagan administration's attacks on the environmental movement only served to demonstrate the extent to which environmentalism had become a fundamental aspect of American standards for quality of life. Even though some facets of environmentalism were widely accepted the quality of life environmentalism of the 1980s was very different from the structural changes hoped for by environmental advocates. While environmental groups continued to base their philosophy and politics on a structural critique of materialism and consumption Americans found environmentally conscious consumption one of the most appealing aspects environmental awareness. By the 1980s, environmental concerns played an important role in shaping consumer desires and demands.

While some environmentalists and advocacy groups derided this trend toward "green consumption" as a sellout, others embraced what they called "natural capitalism" as a realistic model for reconciling environmentalism and materialism toward a sustainable future. Alternative technology researchers were posed in the late 1970s to take advantage of technological advances and cultural trends to move their efforts into the mainstream of the American economy. Reagan's efforts to cut federal government programs and the cultural trends that supported these cuts put the brakes on the promising research of the 1970s.

For frustrated researchers and proponents of green technology, many of whose green solutions were viable and ready to be taken to the market, the sudden loss of federal funding during the Reagan years was devastating. Solar energy researchers in particular saw their promising and often money-saving solutions sent into the warehouse or to underfunded private organizations. Despite these setbacks environmentalism continued to be a force in American life. Strong gains were made in wilderness preservation, endangered species protection, and pollution control. America's air and water supply improved dramatically from the lows of the early 1970s. For example, the Great Lakes region, once a seemingly hopelessly polluted disaster, experienced dramatic improvements in water quality and wildlife regeneration as pollution controls and new technologies took affect. The relationship between quality environment and quality of life in the minds of the voting public ensured that politicians from both ends of the spectrum could not completely ignore environmental issues.

While the environment remained an important issue, environmental organizations faced significant challenges that transcended partisan politics. Coalitions carefully built during the 1960s and 1970s to fight for issues like wilderness protection dissolved as positions became more entrenched during the Reagan and Bush presidencies. Part of the reason for this shift rested with the decline of scarcity fears. As the energy crisis eased and the economy improved and then took off to stratospheric heights, Americans forgot about the efforts to craft a more environmentally friendly system of production and consumption. In the late 1980s, behemoth four-wheel-drive passenger cars, marketed as "sport utility vehicles" (SUVs), appeared in significant numbers on the nation's highways. They became more popular as they became larger. By 1996 the gas-guzzling SUVs constituted 15 percent of the total U.S. auto market. By the year 2000 that figure grew to almost 50 percent. While SUVs proliferated, alternative technology vehicles where shelved and solar power companies and other green industries went bankrupt all over the American West as demand and tax credits dried up in the flush 1980s.

But then, by the mid-1990s scarcity fears in the wake of the Gulf War and signs of a new energy crisis once again fueled a renewed interest in appropriate technology. The popular media prominently featured stories highlighting alternative green technologies. Hybrid gas-electric and fuel cell cars were touted as a solution to the proliferation of SUVs and dependence on foreign oil. What articles in the popular media often missed, however, was that the problem in the past had not been the creation of new environmentally friendly technology—innovative individuals and companies had been doing this for a century. The problem lay in convincing American producers and consumers that there was common ground between capitalism and environmentalism. The appropriate technology movement of the 1970s seemed to offer a solution to this persistent disjuncture. While the movement faded, the efforts to inject an environmental awareness into the American economy were very successful partly because by the late 1980s it was becoming clear to American businesses that they could profit from the public's desire for greater environmental quality of life.

Paul Hawken, Amory Lovins, and Hunter Lovins provided a captivatingly simple model for reconciling environmentalism and market economics in their influential book *Natural Capitalism* (1999). These optimistic authors built on

Hawken's earlier work in *The Ecology of Commerce* (1993) and *Growing a Business* (1987) to argue that an environmental ethic based on realistic use of existing appropriate technologies was the key not only to the health of the planet but also to the future of corporate success and profitability. These three books made a large splash in the media and were hailed by business leaders as "stunningly visionary." Of course what these contemporary authors proposed was not without precedent. In some ways their model hearkened to the wise use of natural resources as advocated by Teddy Roosevelt and the Progressive conservationists of the early twentieth century. More significantly, it built on the blueprint established by Stewart Brand and the *Whole Earth Catalog*.

Still in print through the 1990s, *Whole Earth* came to the fore of a new trend in American business. Brand and other entrepreneurs of the 1960s generation helped articulate and demonstrate a world of counterculture capitalism that moved rapidly from the fringes to the center of the American business world. Following *Whole Earth's* lead, a host of counterculture companies rose to prominence during the 1980s. For example, Ben & Jerry's, Apple Computers, Smith & Hawken, Williams-Sonoma, Virgin, and Patagonia used, in part, an environmental message to market their products and create a sense that shopping could be a form of political activism. Their stores became places where wealthy liberals who disdained the conspicuous consumption of their parents could, with a clear conscience, buy a $3,000 garden bench or $500 Everest-tested parka. The businessmen and women who founded these companies created powerful corporations by tapping into changing perceptions of technology, environment, and quality of life. They perfected cause-based selling, "liberation marketing," and other powerful concepts that would come to be taught at places like Harvard's Business School. For environmentalists who still worried about the long-term viability of a society that defined progress as a never-ending cycle of technological development, the "greening" of the American economy was a mixed blessing.

Environmentally savvy marketing on the part of companies like Patagonia, which sold expensive outdoor gear, and Ben & Jerry's, an upscale ice cream store, helped create a business model and environmental consumerism that inspired a new generation of business leaders. Ben & Jerry's sold flavors like "Rainforest Crunch," put environmental messages on its products, and publicly supported environmental groups. Likewise, Patagonia made environmentalism chic by marketing beautifully designed products, like brightly colored jackets manufactured from recycled plastic soda bottles and other waste that tapped into the outdoor enthusiasm and deep pockets of young professionals riding the wave of Reagan-era affluence. By uniting fashion and taste with environmental awareness, these two companies and many that followed created a powerful new avenue for supporting environmental protection while cashing in on emerging market trends.

Arguably, it is in the realm of business and economy where environmental advocates left perhaps their most lasting mark in the daily lives of ordinary Americans. The ideas and ideals brought together under the broad umbrella of appropriate technology provided a more viable model for reconciling ecological consciousness and technological enthusiasm than had cause-oriented environmental organizations. By demonstrating that there were possibilities for common ground between modern technology, consumerism, and environmental consciousness, the appropriate technology movement contributed substantially to the broad acceptance of environmentalism in mainstream American culture. Environmental consumerism in turn helped reenergize environmental advocates and reshape the environmental movement.

Environmental consumerism and the desire for environmentally friendly alternatives drove very successful national efforts to change American business practices without altering the fundamental economic system. One of the most successful of these was the 1987 grassroots "McToxics" campaign aimed at McDonald's restaurants' use of Styrofoam packaging. American consumers found it unacceptable that a corporation like McDonald's should dump 1.3 billion cubic feet of CFC laden Styrofoam into landfills each year. This effort soon went national with consumers engaging in boycotts and "send-it-back" efforts against McDonald's franchises that refused to switch to cardboard and paper packaging. McDonald's finally capitulated, and the foam was replaced with paper wrappers. The "McToxics" effort illustrated the degree to which environmentalism had successfully infiltrated consumer culture. It also demonstrated that while Americans were willing to use their economic power to advocate environmental issues, they were unwilling to challenge the basic economic system: they still wanted the hamburger, and they were willing to buy it from an enormous corporation, but they preferred that it not be wrapped in Styrofoam.

The promotion of renewable energy resources and energy conservation through technological invention provides another example of the success of environmental advocates efforts to transform consumer habits. Energy efficient houses, thermal windows, solar power, and high-efficiency heating and cooling have become widely accepted, perhaps even standard, features of American culture. Curbside recycling and the proliferation of waste recycling have also gained wide approval and become a part of daily life in cities across the nation. Many of these technologies and services, which seem so obvious and sensible that they go unnoticed today, resulted from the innovation of technologically enthusiastic environmentalists.

Between 1945 and the close of the twentieth century, American environmental advocates struggled to reconcile American ideals of progress through technological innovation and with growing concerns about a technology driven consumer society increasingly at odds with a fragile and overpopulated planet. In 1945, environmental advocates who questioned the dominant technological enthusiasm of the day were a distinct minority.

During the decades between 1945 and 2000, environmental advocacy evolved dramatically. Environmental advocates moved from technological infatuation toward wariness of technology, to technological accommodation, and finally back toward an embrace of green technology and wiser consumerism as a solution to environmental problems. The sometimes painful effort to deal with the persistence of American technological enthusiasm shaped debates within the environmental movement and reflected changing attitudes among the public about the balance between consumerism and environmental quality of life. Changing perceptions of technology fueled most of the big environmental debates of the second half of the twentieth century, from fears about dams and reclamation in the 1950s to widespread concern in the early 1960s about roads encroaching on once-remote wilderness areas to worries about pollution and energy in the 1970s. Environmental advocates lead the way in alerting the public to these concerns. Visionaries such as David Brower and Rachel Carson sounded the alarm. Growing economic prosperity led to new standards for quality of life and provided strong motivation for the broader public to take environmental issues as a serious concern. This broader concern placed pressure on the government and elected officials to enact a series of laws that provided unprecedented protection for the environment. Finally, the broad acceptance of environmentalism convinced American corporations, some from cynical self-interest and some from genuine concern about the consequences of their practices, to tailor their products to meet consumer's environmental demands. These trends raised some important questions for environmentalists at the end of the twentieth century.

Are environmentally minded technological innovators who wanted to bring their advances to the people through the market sellouts? Are consumers who wish for wiser environmental choices one-dimensional men who suffer from false consciousness? Is there a compromise between Americans' technological enthusiasm, consumer desires, and environmental concerns? Was the corporate cooptation of the environmental movement, the Ben & Jerry's phenomenon, its main significance? Obviously not. Environmentalists succeeded remarkably during the second half of the twentieth century in expanding the regulatory power of the federal government, preserving wide tracts of scenic and wild lands, protecting plants and animals, and creating a general awareness of environmental concern and ecological realism in a generation of Americans. These successes represented real, if always limited, changes in one of the fundamental ideals of American history; progress.

The accomplishments of the environmental movement are most easily recognizable in the vast tracts of wilderness preserved in perpetuity by the Wilderness

Act of 1964, the regeneration of species once thought lost, the revival of rivers and lakes that seemed hopelessly polluted. But it would be a mistake to leave the rise and remarkable growth of alternative technologies and green consumption off of this list of accomplishments. Green thinking has infiltrated consumerism to the extent that many consumers are aware of wide-ranging ecological issues. Even if the general level of environmental consciousness is negligible, small changes in the process of production and consumption can lead toward large returns for a country of close to three hundred million people. Further, while environmentalism may have been co-opted by marketers and corporations in search of new customers, much of the green production and consumption of the past three decades was carefully engineered by those within the movement who believed that the best contribution they could make to the health of the planet was to integrate their environmental sensibilities into their technological innovations and advocate for environmental responsibility in their business models.

At the turn of the twenty-first century, America was once again on the brink of a second energy crisis. Westerners, faced with 500 percent increases in power bills, scrambled for energy alternatives. Fears of foreign oil dependence in the wake of the terrorist attacks of September 11, 2001, breathed new life into the appropriate technology movement, dormant since the Reagan years. Soaring fuel prices and astronomical electric bills again raised the specter of scarcity and spawned new questions about green technologies and renewable energy solutions.

Future environmental advocates will need to capitalize on recurring patterns of scarcity to push the American public toward deeper changes in practices of production and consumption and develop new technologies that provide for quality of life without jeopardizing environmental health. The challenge for environmental advocates in the next century will be to move forward with the efforts of the past half-century and reconcile American notions of technological progress, consumerism, and economy with environmentalism to create a sustainable economics.

BIBLIOGRAPHIC NOTE

The literature of environmentalism is extensive. One of the best overviews of the postwar movement is Robert Gottlieb's *Forcing the Spring: The Transformation of the American Environmental Movement* (1993). Gottlieb analyzes environmentalism with a special emphasis on the social and cultural aspects of the movement. Likewise, Samuel P. Hays's *Beauty, Health, and Permanence: Environmental Politics in the United States, 1955–1985* (1987) supplies extensive coverage of all aspects of environmental politics. An excellent chapter on technology and environmental policy makes Hays's *A History of Environmental Politics Since 1945* (2000) an invaluable resource for those interested in technology and environment. In *The Bulldozer in the Countryside: Suburban Sprawl and the Rise of American Environmentalism* (2001), Adam Rome convincingly argues that suburbanization was a driving force in the creation of the modern environmental movement. Hal K. Rothman's *The Greening of a Nation? Environmentalism in the United States Since 1945* (1997) and Kirkpatrick Sales's *The Green Revolution: The American Environmental Movement, 1962–1992* (1993) provide concise thematic overviews of the evolution of environmentalism in the postwar decades.

Trends in appropriate technology are explored in Carroll Pursell's *The Machine in America: A Social History of Technology* (1995) and "The Rise and Fall of the Appropriate Technology Movement in the United States, 1965–1985," *Technology and Culture* 34 (1993): 629–637. For another view of appropriate technologies see, Thomas P. Hughes, *American Genesis: A Century of Invention and Technological Enthusiasm 1870–1970* (1989). Key alternative technology concepts were popularized by Ernest Callenbach's novel *Ecotopia* (1977). The relationship between environmentalism and technology is specifically explored in Jeffrey K. Stine and Joel A. Tarr, "At the Intersection of Histories: Technology and the Environment," *Technology and Culture* 39 (1998): 601–640. For two classic and influential perspectives on the subject, see Barry Commoner, *The Closing Circle: Nature, Man, and Technology* (1971), and E. F. Schumacher, *Small Is Beautiful: Economics as if People Mattered* (1973).

The Whole Earth Catalog had many incarnations. The most useful single issue is the "Thirtieth Anniversary Celebration" (1998). This edition of the catalog includes the entire first edition and a set of essays from early contributors and fellow travelers. The model of *Whole Earth* counterculture consumption is explored in depth in Sam Binkley, "The Seers of Menlo Park: The Discourse of Heroic Consumption in the Whole Earth Catalog," *Journal of Consumer Culture* 3, no. 3 (2003): 283–313. For more on green consumerism and the greening of American business, see Paul Hawken, Amory Lovins, and L. Hunter Lovins, *Natural Capitalism: Creating the Next Industrial Revolution* (1999), and David Brooks's scathingly humorous critique *Bobos in Paradise: The New Upper Class and How They Got There* (2000).

This essay greatly benefited from the thoughtful suggestions of David Wrobel, Mary Wammack, and Hal Rothman.

NOTES

1. William Vogt, *Road to Survival* (New York: William Sloan Associates, 1948), 37–38.

2. As quoted in Adam Rome, *The Bulldozer in the Countryside: Suburban Sprawl and the Rise of American Environmentalism* (Cambridge: Cambridge University Press, 2001), 43.

3. Stewart Brand, ed., *The Last Whole Earth Catalog* (New York: Random House, 1971), 439.

4. E. F. Schumacher, *Small Is Beautiful: Economics as if People Mattered* (New York: Harper & Row, 1973), 116–117.

5. Samuel P. Hays, *Beauty, Health, and Permanence: Environmental Politics in the United States, 1955–1985* (Cambridge: Cambridge University Press, 1987), 262.

6. Kirkpatrick Sale, *The Green Revolution: The American Environmental Movement, 1962–1992* (New York: Hill and Wang, 1993), 53.

16. CITIZENSHIP AND THE PROBLEM OF DESIRE IN THE POSTWAR LABOR AND CIVIL RIGHTS MOVEMENTS

THADDEUS RUSSELL

The 1963 March on Washington marked not only the achievement of national legitimacy for Martin Luther King Jr. and the civil rights movement, but also the convergence of the civil rights movement with a large portion of the American labor movement. The march, whose full title was the March on Washington for Jobs and Freedom, was the joint project of civil rights organizations and various labor unions, including the United Automobile Workers (UAW), arguably the most important and influential union in the United States. The UAW contributed a substantial portion of the money and organizers for the march and for civil rights work throughout the country.

The most prominent white speaker at the march was Walter Reuther, president of the UAW and vice president of the AFL-CIO, who since World War II had been recognized as the leading spokesman for the "social unionist" left wing of organized labor. Reuther had helped establish the UAW and the Congress of Industrial Organizations (CIO) in the 1930s, was elected president of the auto union in 1946, and served as the CIO president from 1952 until the merger with the American Federation of Labor (AFL) in 1955. Reuther was asked to speak at the March on Washington undoubtedly because of his union's support for the civil rights movement, but also because Reuther and King felt a great mutual affinity. In fact, many of the organizers of the march referred to the labor leader as "the white Martin Luther King."

Indeed, the two men were extraordinarily similar, both in their personal behavior and in their visions for America's working class. Reuther and King both sought to make their constituents into full citizens, granting them the protection of certain rights by the state but also requiring their participation in the economic, political, and mainstream cultural life of the United States. Their constituents enthusiastically greeted the rights Reuther and King championed. Masses of workers welcomed the protection of their right to organize unions, codified by the National Labor Relations Act of 1935, and African Americans overwhelmingly endorsed laws that protected them from violence and discrimination and granted them access to long-denied public space. But King and Reuther recognized that to create complete citizens out of African Americans and industrial workers—to make them full participants in American society— their cultures and even their psychologies would have to be changed. Both groups would have to merge their identities with their workplaces and the nation and take on the responsibilities of industrial and social management. The movement leaders well understood that this project required strict regulation of the desires of black and white working-class Americans for material wealth, for sensual pleasure, and for freedom from work.

King and Reuther displayed the self-denial necessary for full citizenship. Yet the problem they both faced, a problem that might have surpassed even their battles with southern racists and northern capitalists, was the resistance of the working class itself to the requisite sacrifices and responsibilities.

INDUSTRIAL DEMOCRACY, INDUSTRIAL DISCIPLINE, AND RESISTANCE

Reuther maintained a strikingly austere lifestyle. The UAW president never smoked, very rarely drank, and often berated colleagues who succumbed to such pleasures. He took home a salary that was the lowest of any major union president and refused to allow the UAW to pay for such things as business dinners and even laundry bills. All proceeds from Reuther's speeches and writings were turned over to his own nonprofit charity, and during his life he made only one financial investment—$1,000 in stock that earned him a net profit of $1.26 when he sold it eight years later. Reuther had virtually no life outside his career as a labor statesman. In *Who's Who in Labor*, he listed his hobbies as "wood & metal craft work [and] development of economic and production plans."

Historians have seldom recognized that Reuther's asceticism was a necessary component of his social philosophy. He and many of the leaders of the CIO argued that workers could not be considered full citizens until they were included in the management of the economy. The primary purpose of the labor movement, in the words of the CIO's cofounder and intellectual leader, Sidney Hillman, was to provide workers with "power to establish themselves as a full-fledged part of organized society." To accomplish this, according to Hillman advisor J. B. S. Hardman, labor would have to "assume responsibilities for production and ascend to active participation in the control of industry." This vision, which several historians have since labeled "corporatism," extended from the shop floor, where corporatists advocated worker participation in the management of day-to-day production, to every branch of the government, where labor representatives would work as partners with businessmen and politicians to create and maintain a well-ordered and efficient economic system. By accepting responsibility for industrial and social management, however, corporatist labor leaders also accepted the obligation to curtail their own desires and to police the desires of the workers they represented. Wages could not be driven too high or working hours too low to put employers out of business or to threaten national security; work discipline would have to be maintained in order to sustain production, and the leaders' own salaries and work ethic would provide the example of self-restraint and sacrifice for the social good. To be sure, corporatist leaders of the CIO negotiated contracts that dramatically increased wages in all the basic industries, but, as they often stated themselves, their intentions in doing so were to appease their rank and file and, more fundamentally, to eliminate the social disorder brought by poverty.[1]

The idea of "industrial democracy," central to both corporatism and Hillman and Reuther's original and related doctrine of socialism, served as recognition that workers would have to be voluntary participants in their own organization and management. As Reuther put it, "We want a disciplined organization. We believe that in a union, as in an army, discipline is of first rate importance." He instructed UAW shop stewards to behave like generals toward the members, but Reuther acknowledged that an army of conscripts could not win the war against capitalist autocracy and social disorder. His proposals for a fully regulated economic system were designed around what Reuther's leading biographer has called "counterplanning from the shop floor up." Workers managing their own industries would need skill and discipline, but because responsible self-management required maintaining high levels of worker output and upward limits on wages, workers also needed to embrace the principle of self-restraint in the service of a greater cause. Reuther told his members, "We must demonstrate that we are a disciplined, responsible organization, that we not only have power, but that we have power under control." Union generals would be necessary to lead the workers through the war for a share of control over their industries, but once victorious, the workers would police themselves. The unacknowledged irony of industrial democracy was that it required workers to internalize the discipline that had been invented to serve the interests of employers.[2]

The specter of working-class desire for material goods surfaced even before American entry into World War II. During negotiations with General Motors in 1941, Reuther explained to GM's bargaining team that he needed concessions from the company in order to maintain order on the shop floor. "I am a very practical young man and I happen to have a job seven days a week to handle the headaches and bellyaches of your employees," he said. "Why shouldn't I try to eliminate them in the future if I can by being practical at the moment?" Reuther repeatedly admonished members that the union should not be considered as a vehicle for material gain. In nearly every speech, he declared that the UAW was a "responsible" labor organization, not "another nickel-in-the-pay-envelope union." He said, "If the labor movement is not an instrument of social change, it is nothing. When [the labor movement] fails to be that kind of a creative, constructive instrument for social change and is just dealing with pressure group things—getting more—then I think it fails totally in its responsibilities." Yet masses of workers—in the UAW and in other unions as well—resisted Reuther's call to take on those responsibilities.

After the formal entry of the United States into the war, Reuther took the lead in disciplining workers for wartime production by attempting to tame their material desires. He strenuously enforced the no-strike pledge taken by the UAW and the CIO, but often to no avail, as more than six million workers walked off the job during the war. Defiance of the no-strike pledge was particularly fierce among workers in the vital automobile plants, which had been converted to defense production. In Reuther's industry, roughly half of the workforce participated in an unauthorized "wildcat" strike during the war. Significantly, many of these rebellious workers were African Americans, who entered the industrial workforce by the millions to replace whites serving in the military. Most damaging of all to the corporatist cause, the vast majority of wartime strikes were responses to attempts by employers and unions to impose speedups and enforce work discipline rules. Reuther often publicly complained that companies provoked the strikes, but he consistently defended the no-strike pledge and supported punishing leaders of the wildcats. Reuther faced similar resistance from workers over the issue of premium pay for overtime work. When several AFL unions refused to abandon bargaining demands for premium pay, Reuther coaxed a reluctant President Roosevelt into signing an executive order banning all premium pay for the duration of the war.[3]

Further challenging Reuther's vision of a centrally coordinated economy was the intense competition among labor unions for representation of the workers filling the newly created defense industry jobs. In the early 1940s, unions in Detroit and other centers of the defense industry fought one another as often as they fought employers. Reuther's corporatism depended upon the elimination of such conflict within the labor movement because it required that a monolithic union organization be created to organize and discipline the labor force and re-alize, as he put it, "our full productive potential." Despite repeated admonitions by Reuther and other leaders of the CIO that continued competition among la-bor organizations would diminish not only America's defense production but also labor's standing in the nation, legions of workers eagerly participated in this market for their patronage, shifting their membership to the union they believed would provide the most effective representation for the lowest dues. Union ri-valry, an instrument and expression of workers' materialist desires, undermined Reuther's notion of labor citizenship.

The problem of interunion competition persisted after the war. By the most conservative estimate, from the creation of the CIO in 1935 through the merger of the AFL and CIO in 1955, several million workers shifted their union affilia-tions in contests between rival unions. This vigorous market for labor represen-tation provided the rank and file with enormous leverage to achieve economic gains, as it forced union leaders to be accountable to their interests. In a com-petitive environment, a union leader who did not deliver the goods—higher wages, shorter hours, or better benefits—knew that he would lose out to a more responsive rival. As one labor leader ruefully remarked about a competitor's suc-cessful effort to lure away his members in 1908, "The methods employed emu-late those of the life insurance companies of our country, namely, they offer to pay greater financial benefits to seceders . . . than that which they were already guaranteed by the international union of their trade." [4]

Though most so-called new labor historians of the past three decades have avoided a serious examination of interunion competition, evidence of its mate-rial benefits for American workers abounds. Competition between the Interna-tional Longshoremen's and Warehousemen's Union (ILWU) of the CIO and the International Brotherhood of Teamsters (IBT) of the AFL led to the unionization and enrichment of most of the workers in the West Coast long-shore, warehousing, and trucking industries in the 1930s. In fact, competition from CIO unions was a principal determinant of the Teamsters' ascendancy from a small craft union of 146,000 members in 1935, when the CIO was cre-ated, to the largest labor organization in the United States, over one million strong in 1955, when the AFL and CIO merged. Because of its location in an in-dustry that was contiguous and interdependent with virtually every other sector of the economy, the Teamsters faced more jurisdictional competition than any other union in the United States and were continually forced to organize in new fields to counter the encroachments of their rivals. Most of the IBT's ex-pansion, especially its growth in industries other than trucking, was driven by competition from rival unions. In 1941, Teamster president Dan Tobin acknowl-edged that the tremendous growth of the IBT "was due to the fact that the CIO decided to spend their money in an endeavor to raid the International

Brotherhood of Teamsters." Moreover, the famed militancy of many Teamster leaders, most notably Jimmy Hoffa, who ascended to the IBT presidency in 1957 after two decades spent building the Teamsters' Midwestern unit into a massive organization, was often compelled by challenges from other unions. As one of Hoffa's colleagues noted about the character of the workers they hoped to lure away from a rival union, "these fellows are like a pendulum on a clock which swings back and forth—C.I.O.—A.F.L.—C.I.O.—A.F.L., depending entirely on who was the last group that talked to them . . . and what we have to do is get two or three good contracts behind us." [5]

Workers in many industries benefited from conflicts between unions for their allegiance. Overall, employees participating in representation elections conducted by the National Labor Relations Board have been far more likely to vote for union representation over "no union" in elections involving rival unions, and first-time union contracts with substantial wage increases, shorter hours, and improved working conditions were enjoyed by workers in the lumber, paper, textile, electrical, and retail industries as a result of unions' competing for representation rights. Rivalry also forced initiation fees and union dues downward. As historian Robert Zieger has noted, during the heyday of competition between the CIO and AFL, "workers shopped for union representation and found a buyer's market." [6]

No one was more keenly aware of the explosive potential of union rivalry than the owners of industry. When a battle erupted in 1939 between Reuther's UAW and an AFL affiliate for representation rights over autoworkers, the industry's own newsletter, *Ward's Automotive Reports*, noticed with great alarm that unions competing for the patronage of workers were compelled to not only undertake "all the usual interest-stimulating activities" such as strikes and picketing, but also, most dangerously, to push "new demands on the companies." Indeed, as the conflict between the warring unions escalated, so did their claims against the automakers, culminating in audacious announcements by both organizations that they would not settle for less than thirty-hour workweeks at forty hours of pay. One business leader nervously predicted in the *New York Times* that "regardless of the merits of the rival groups or the success they have in organization work, the average worker will be bound to benefit substantially from the rivalry built up." Noting the fears of automobile executives over the dynamism of union rivalry in their industry, the following year *Ward's Automotive Reports* wrote, "The general hope is that one side or the other acquires complete dominance and thereby is enabled to exercise control over the men." This wish was soon granted by the National Labor Relations Board, which, under the terms of Section 9 of the Wagner Act, designated the UAW as the exclusive representative of all production and skilled workers at General Motors. To the great misfortune of autoworkers, this put an end to union rivalry in their industry. Historians have generally agreed that the contract that followed, which was negotiated by Reuther, was a massive concession by the then-unchallenged union. It not only ignored the demand for shorter hours, but it also provided a wage increase of only one and a half cents per hour.[7]

Though interunion competition was beneficial to the rank and file, it severely disrupted the plans of union leaders seeking a disciplined and centrally organized labor force. The worker citizenship envisioned by Reuther and Hillman could not be realized if labor spoke with many and contradictory voices. During World War II, CIO leaders worked assiduously to quell rivalry, since, as Hillman explained, their "task was to make sure, as far as possible, that production proceeds without interruptions." After the war, numerous deals were worked out to establish union monopolies in basic industries while the national leaders of the CIO and AFL moved steadily toward merger and an end to jurisdictional competition.

The most significant result of the merger of the two federations in 1955 was the "No-Raid Pact" that all but eliminated competition among unions and took from the rank and file much of their power to force union leaders to be accountable to their interests. But from the point of view of Reuther and other proponents of labor citizenship, the end of rivalry and the establishment of a national union monopoly was a boon. It forced union members to register their dissent only through internal channels, converting them from consumers into subjects.

The principal architect of the no-raid agreement, United Steelworkers of America general counsel (and future secretary of labor and Supreme Court justice) Arthur Goldberg, defended it on the grounds that labor unions, like nation-states, depend on the allegiance and participation of their constituents. "To treat unions as outside agencies which, in return for the dues dollars, produce increases in wages, is to misunderstand the basic relationship between workers and their unions," he argued shortly after the merger. "In the ultimate sense only the workers themselves, by their willingness to go along with and support the decisions or recommendations of the leadership, can give the unions strength," he added. Workers should not be allowed to shop for representation, just as citizens should not be allowed to shop for a sovereign. According to Goldberg, the "concept of competition, if it has any application in union representation, has its appropriate expression within union organizations rather than in interunion raiding, just as the concept of competition in political representation has its appropriate expression in election contests rather than in secession." In short, the merger trapped union members within a single sovereignty and forced them to be its citizens. For this reason, along with the ironic fact that not a single major union in the United States allowed direct elections of its national officers until the 1990s, the merger very likely made great contributions to the stagnation, bureaucratization, and the decline in popularity of organized labor that followed.[8]

The consolidation of organized labor was achieved in conjunction with the lengthening of collective bargaining contracts, which further tied unions to the obligations of industrial citizenship. After winning the UAW presidency in 1946, Reuther negotiated a series of long-term agreements with the auto companies that locked wages to cost-of-living indices, allowed management to speed up production, and prohibited strikes. The crowning "Treaty of Detroit," a contract signed with General Motors in 1950 for an unprecedented term of five years, served as the template for all contracts in the industry. It effectively fulfilled Reuther's ambition to make the union into a joint manager of the labor force, as the UAW staff was made responsible for enforcing contract provisions by keeping the rank and file in line. The union even devised its own system of time-study techniques to enhance productivity. However, a series of wildcat strikes against the contracts demonstrated once again the resistance of much of the American working class to Reuther's project. Unauthorized strike activity increased sharply at all of the Big Three automakers during the life of the Treaty of Detroit, as workers fought incessantly against work rules, speed-ups, and limits on their wages that were enforced by the companies and the union.

In the 1950s, two massive rebellions within the UAW—one for greater material rewards, the other for freedom from work—threatened to subvert the ideal of a working-class citizenry. Skilled autoworkers, representing 15 percent of the union, staged a revolt against the egalitarian wage structures imposed by Reuther that kept their pay well below the levels of comparably skilled tradesmen in other professions. When the rank-and-file movement attracted thousands of members and resulted in the establishment of a rival union within the auto industry, Reuther joined the leaders of the auto companies in successfully pleading with the National Labor Relations Board to refuse to recognize the rival union, thereby trapping the skilled workers at a pay scale lower than they would have received at the market rate. And when a movement for a thirty-hour work-week at forty hours of pay gained enormous popularity among the UAW rank and file (again, significantly, in a local with a large black membership), Reuther attacked it as "irresponsible," a childish demand for a "Santa Claus," and a Communist attempt to "weaken the position of America in the total world picture at a time when that happens to be the most important objective." Only by deposing scores of its leaders was Reuther able to stop the shorter-hours movement in his union. Reuther did promote a Keynesian strategy of increased consumption, but only with increased work time and only as a means to improve production and national strength. He complained to Congress, "We are wasting 25 percent of the total industrial productive potential of the American economy. I wish that the Russian economy was operating at 25 percent below its industrial potential. Then the free world could relax." [9]

From 1957 through 1959, Reuther demonstrated his own commitment to labor citizenship during the U.S. Senate investigation of alleged corruption in unions. The work of the Select Committee on Improper Activities in the Labor and Management Field (known generally as the McClellan Committee), which gained great media attention, made Jimmy Hoffa and the Teamsters into the symbols of working-class decadence and irresponsibility and identified Reuther as their opposite. The UAW president was eager to cooperate with the Senate investigation even before it began. "American labor had better roll up its sleeves," Reuther declared when the investigation was first announced. "It had better get the stiffest broom and brush it can find, and the strongest disinfectant, and it had better take on the job of cleaning its own house from top to bottom and drive out every crook and gangster and racketeer we find." Reuther advocated complete submission to Congress, directing UAW locals to remove any officer who invoked the Fifth Amendment in refusing to testify before the committee.

During the investigation, the committee's young counsel, Robert F. Kennedy, discovered Reuther and his lieutenants in the UAW as the model from which to rebuild the house of labor. After a series of meetings with leaders of the auto union, Kennedy found them to match his idea of manly, ascetic citizenship. "I was impressed with the difference between these officials of the UAW and the men Jimmy Hoffa and Dave Beck surrounded themselves with in the Teamsters Union," Kennedy recalled. "It was a striking contrast—one I noted again and again as I came in contact with other UAW officials. These men wore simple clothes, not silk suits and hand-painted ties; sported no great globs of jewelry on their fingers or their shirts; there was no smell of the heavy perfume frequently wafted by the men around Hoffa."

When Kennedy and his brother, Senator John F. Kennedy, began drafting legislation to culminate the investigation, they found Reuther to be amenable to a wide array of regulatory measures, including government control of union funds and elections. The resulting Landrum-Griffin Act of 1959 further enmeshed the labor movement with the state by requiring unions to file comprehensive financial reports with the Labor Department and allowing the attorney general or the secretary of labor to correct what they considered to be union malfeasance. It also outlawed the secondary boycott, a principal means by which the Teamsters and other unions had competed against rival unions. The AFL-CIO Executive Council opposed the law, but it received a full endorsement from Reuther, the UAW, and most of the former CIO unions.[10]

Despite the efforts by Reuther and the federal government to normalize union members' behavior, during the 1960s and 1970s American workers put an end to the ideal of an industrial citizenry. At the most basic level, they more often demonstrated a desire to leave the workplace than to manage it. This was especially true in the automobile industry. A rank-and-file movement within the UAW for early retirement was ignored by Reuther until it gained enough strength to force him to register "30 and out" with a full pension as a union demand. In the 1960s, daily absenteeism in auto plants doubled, which Reuther found "shocking." Over the course of the decade the incidence of wildcats in all industries also doubled, reaching more than two thousand in 1969. In addition, during this period there was a marked increase of workplace sabotage, insubordination toward managers and union stewards, and other forms of industrial disobedience. As during World War II and the period of the Treaty of Detroit, many of these actions were rebellions against disciplinary apparatuses established by union contracts. And again, African American workers were in the vanguard of this rank-and-file rebellion as well, producing an enormous dissident movement within the UAW and other unions that gave Reuther the greatest challenge of his career.

There was perhaps no greater demonstration of working-class resistance to economic citizenship than the tax revolt of the late 1970s, which began in California in 1978 with the resounding victory of Proposition 13, a referendum that dramatically reduced property taxes. A massive antitax movement subsequently spread across the country, and by 1980, thirty-eight states had moved to reduce taxes. This was largely a movement of the working class, which, following the postwar economic boom, had for the first time attained a level of prosperity that made homeownership realizable. It was also a clear renunciation of the notion promulgated by Walter Reuther that the working class should surrender its material achievements to the interests of the community.[11]

WORKIN' MAN BLUES

Of course, while American workers overwhelmingly rejected the responsibilities of economic citizenship during this period, many celebrated their "Americanism." To gauge the depth of working-class cultural identification with the nation-state, one need not look any farther than popular reactions to American military ventures since Pearl Harbor. Even during the Vietnam War, hostility toward the antiwar movement was most intense in working-class quarters. The largest demonstrations in favor of the war were led by trade unions, and in the spring of 1970 construction workers in New York, St. Louis, and Tempe, Arizona, violently attacked antiwar protesters.

The rise of country music as a leading working-class cultural form amply demonstrated this commitment to the flag. During World War II, country music emerged as both a popular and a patriotic cultural form. By the end of the war at least sixty-five recording companies were putting out country records, and the popularity of country music continued to grow after the war, spreading well beyond its traditional roots in the South. In 1947, *Billboard* magazine noted that country stars were enormous box-office draws across the country, and that Pennsylvania, Ohio, and Michigan were among the largest markets for the music. Many country songs during World War II contained patriotic themes, including Roy Acuff's "Cowards Over Pearl Harbor," Bob Willis's "Stars and Stripes on Iwo Jima" and "White Cross on Okinawa," and Carson Robison's bluntly titled "We're Gonna Have to Slap the Dirty Little Jap (and Uncle Sam's the Guy Who Can Do It)." One of the most popular songs of any genre during the war was "There's a Star Spangled Banner Waving Some-where," recorded by the "hillbilly singer" Elton Britt, which tells the story of a crippled "mountain boy" who pleads with Uncle Sam to let him fight. "God gave me the right to be a free American," Britt sang, "and for that precious right I'd gladly die." In 1942, *Billboard* noted the pronounced patriotism in country music: "[The] popularity of fighting country tunes in the music boxes calls at-tention to the fact that [country music], far more than the pop field, has come through with war tunes of the type asked for by government officials . . . The output has continued . . . doing a fine morale job."

Country musicians' commitment to the nation continued into the Cold War, with such stridently anticommunist songs as Harry Choate's "Korea, Here We Come," Jimmie Osborne's "Thank God for Victory in Korea," Jimmie Dickens's "They Locked God Outside the Iron Curtain," and Elton Britt's "The Red We Want Is the Red We've Got (In That Old Red, White, and Blue)." Hank Williams said "No, No, Joe" to Stalin, and in "Advice to Joe" Roy Acuff warned the Soviet dictator of the day "when Moscow lies in ashes."

In the 1960s, despite the rise of the counterculture, country music contin-ued to be the music of much of the American working class. The number of ra-dio stations with an all-country format grew from 81 in 1961 to 328 in 1966, and by then the popularity of the music was clearly no longer just a "country" phe-nomenon. According to a market research study, by the mid-1960s the typical country listener was a skilled or semiskilled worker living in or near a metropol-itan area.

The content of country music became even more militantly patriotic during the Vietnam War, when country musicians led the attack against the antiwar movement. Scores of songs not only denounced the "hippies" and "doubters" who would "rather go to prison than heed their country's call," but also often threatened violence against them. Merle Haggard warned that antiwar protest-ers were walking on "The Fighting Side of Me." In Pat Boone's "Wish You Were Here, Buddy," the soldier-narrator promises his draft-dodging friend that at the end of the war, "I'll put away my rifle and uniform, and I'll come a-lookin' for you." And Victor Lundberg vowed in his "Open Letter To My Teenage Son" to disown his offspring if he were to burn his draft card.

Country music and the masses of working-class Americans who consumed it demonstrated other commitments to cultural citizenship as well. The nuclear, heterosexual family—the bedrock of the American nation—was honored and defended in country songs, especially songs sung and written by women. Tammy Wynette's "Stand by Your Man," the best-selling country record ever recorded by a woman, and "Don't Liberate Me, Love Me" became anthems of the profamily backlash against the women's movement. The other major women country stars of the period, Loretta Lynn and Dolly Parton, expressed more assertiveness in their songs than did Wynette, but they consistently upheld the virtues of the devoted, self-sacrificing housewife against those who "march for women's lib." Songs performed by women country singers of the 1960s and 1970s that promoted motherhood, chastity, monogamy, and childrearing outsold country songs about women expressing their sexuality, cheating on their mates, dancing at honky-tonks, or drinking. Several scholars have noted that in country lyrics, "satisfactory male-female relations are equated with good marriage."

On the great American work ethic, postwar country music expressed a deep and painful ambivalence. Songs such as Merle Travis's "Sixteen Tons," Johnny Paycheck's "Take This Job and Shove it," and Johnny Cash's "Oney" and "One Piece at a Time" told of small-scale rebellions against the dictates of the boss— similar to many of the wildcat strikes and other forms of individual workplace resistance discussed earlier—but did not challenge the moral obligation to work. Rather, country music lyrics simultaneously expressed a hatred of work and a pride in doing it. Merle Haggard, one of the biggest country stars of the late 1960s and early 1970s, best represented this contradiction. In the hit song "Workin' Man Blues," Haggard sings of the hardship of working with his "nose to the grindstone" to support "nine kids and a wife," which leads him to the tavern every night and a longing to "catch a train to another town." But family and the respectability of work keep him from leaving:

I go back working,
Gotta buy my kids a brand new pair of shoes . . .
I ain't never been on welfare
And that's one place I won't be
I'll be workin'
Long as my two hands are fit to use

This attachment to the work ethic was demonstrated in several songs scorning welfare. Loretta Lynn's argument that "They Don't Make 'Em Like My Daddy Anymore" is supported by her claims that her father was "one heck of a man that worked for what he got" and that he "never took a handout." Guy Drake was more explicit when he mocked the owner of a "Welfare Cadillac" who "never worked much" but who was able to purchase his luxury automobile with payments "from this here federal government." That these enormously popular songs represented the attitudes of broad sections of the American working class seems undeniable, and they suggest how wildcat strikes and the tax revolt could be the products of the same consciousness. But they may also point us to an explanation for the lack of a widespread or sustained shorter-hours movement in the twentieth-century United States (other than, ironically, the one in the UAW), as well as for the fact that by the end of the century, American employees worked on average from one hundred to three hundred hours more per year than did workers in Western Europe.

It was certainly no coincidence that country music became the soundtrack to the rise of the so-called New Right. George Wallace, who promised the "average citizen who works each day for a living" that he would bring tax relief, an end to welfare and foreign aid, a strengthened military, and a crackdown on antiwar protesters, made country music bands a central feature of his presidential campaign tours in 1964, 1968, and 1972, and received endorsements from several country performers. One of the most notable aspects of the Wallace campaigns was the enthusiastic support he received in the industrialized North, in particular, to the great dismay of Walter Reuther, among automobile workers. The "working man's candidate" won straw polls and union meeting endorsements at several major UAW locals in Michigan, Illinois, and New Jersey. The movement for Wallace within the union in 1968 was so great that Reuther mobilized six hundred full-time staff members and devoted half a million dollars of the union's money to stop it. Nonetheless, four years later, Wallace won the Democratic primary in Michigan, by most estimates taking the largest share of the union vote. Many of Wallace's working-class supporters were moved by his implicit attacks on African Americans in his references to welfare cheaters, crime, and busing, just as many country fans no doubt attached black faces to the loafers and urban predators mentioned in their favorite songs. But Wallace's explicit attacks were always directed at the "bureaucrats" and "theoreticians," who, like Walter Reuther, imposed their grand schemes of social management on the hard workers and taxpayers of the country.

Richard Nixon, who virtually repeated Wallace's pledges in his successful campaigns in 1968 and 1972, was endorsed by country stars Tex Ritter and Roy Acuff, and he invited Merle Haggard and Johnny Cash to perform at the White House. Likewise, Ronald Reagan found the winning formula in 1980 when he declared that "work and family are at the center of our lives; the foundation of our dignity as a free people," and vowed to protect that foundation with tax cuts and an aggressive military. The year of Reagan's victory over Jimmy Carter, more than two hundred radio stations switched to all-country formats, and between 1977 and 1983, the number of country stations doubled, from 1,140 to

2,266. Reagan, who as governor of California had pardoned Merle Haggard for his previous conviction on felony burglary charges, invited the "Okie from Muskogee" to the White House on several occasions.[12]

The New Right and its cultural expressions combined a rejection of economic responsibility (outside the family unit) with a fierce defense of other forms of obligation—to nation, family, and work—that comprised the responsibilities of American citizenship in the postwar period. However, it should be obvious to the most casual observer of American culture that this mass embrace of cultural citizenship was overwhelmingly white. As in earlier periods, citizenship and whiteness were constructed in tandem, with African Americans serving as the model of the noncitizen. Moreover, this dual investment in Americanness and whiteness was always presented as a self-regulating paternalism. The (normally male) individual would work hard to support his family without assistance from the state and would sacrifice himself to protect the family from its enemies, be they loose women, criminals, or Communists. The mission of the civil rights movement was to make African Americans, in reality and in the minds of whites, into American citizens.[13]

BLACK CITIZENS AND "BAD NIGGERS"

Since emancipation, many African Americans have struggled against the barriers to citizenship and the behaviors that set them apart from it. Members of the black middle class as well as what has sometimes been called the "respectable black working class" have understood what historians of the modern civil rights movement often have not, that the project of making black citizens required a radical reformation of African American culture. By 1954, the Supreme Court understood this as well.

Traditionally, the Court's decision in *Brown v. Board of Education* has been interpreted as a gift to African Americans, but in fact its principal justification was that educational integration would benefit employers and the state. The Court made explicit that nonnormative black behavior was at odds with the integration of African Americans into the body politic. In ruling segregation in education unconstitutional, the Court explained that by depriving blacks of full citizenship, the United States was also depriving itself of the opportunity to create a new class of disciplined and productive workers and soldiers. Writing for the unanimous justices, Earl Warren argued that the schools should be integrated in order to take advantage of this opportunity:

> Today, education is perhaps the most important function of state and local governments. Compulsory school attendance laws and the great expenditures for education

both demonstrate our recognition of the importance of education to our democratic society. It is required in the performance of our most basic public responsibilities, even service in the armed forces. It is the very foundation of good citizenship. Today it is a principal instrument in awakening the child to cultural values, in preparing him for later professional training, and in helping him to adjust normally to his environment.[14]

The civil rights movement that emerged shortly after *Brown*, when examined within the context of African American working-class culture, strikingly resembles the pattern of desire and repression evident in the postwar labor movement. For Martin Luther King Jr. and many of the leaders of the movement, the requirements of citizenship merged with a Christian asceticism that differed only in form from Walter Reuther's secular corporatism. In his sermons and writings, King called for African Americans to work hard, to shun immoral forms of sexuality, and to curb their materialism. They would no longer abdicate familial and social responsibilities and would undergo "a process of self-purification" to produce a "calm and loving dignity befitting good citizens."[15]

In advocating nonviolence, King asked African Americans to "present our very bodies" as living sacrifices to attain citizenship and respectability, and offered himself as a model of self-abnegation. After his house was bombed during the Montgomery Bus Boycott in 1956, King issued a statement to the press in which he sounded not only like the Apostle Paul but also like a citizen-soldier willing to die for his country. "The consequences for my personal life are not particularly important," King said. "It is the triumph of a cause that I am concerned about." In 1957 King cemented his position as national spokesman for civil rights with three interlocking projects: founding the Southern Christian Leadership Conference, launching a voting rights effort called the Campaign for Citizenship, and setting into motion an evangelical crusade to rid black people of un-Christian and un-American habits. The first two projects have been noted by historians as marking King's ascendancy to leadership of the civil rights movement. What is remarkable, however, is the almost complete silence among chroniclers of King's career on his crusade for moral reform among African Americans.[16]

In the summer of 1957, King delivered a series of sermons under the title, "Problems of Personality Integration." The sermons were clearly intended to prepare African Americans for entry into mainstream American culture. King encouraged "those who are giving their lives to a tragic life of pleasure and throwing away everything they have in riotous living" to "lose [their] ego in some great cause, some great purpose, some great ideal, some great loyalty." By doing so, King said, they would create in themselves what he called "the integrated personality."

In subsequent speeches, as well as in an advice column he began writing for *Ebony* in 1957 and in a book he published the following year, King endorsed Christian self-abnegation as a means to attain "first class citizenship." To become citizens, African Americans must "seek to gain the respect of others by improving on our shortcomings." King called for blacks to stop drinking and gambling and to curtail their desires for luxuries. On the issue of black crime, he blamed not only poverty and structural racism but also the lack of discipline and morality in the ghetto. "The church must extend its evangelistic program into all of the poverty-stricken and slum areas of the big cities, thereby touching the individuals who are more susceptible to criminal traits. By bringing them into the church and keeping them in touch with the great moral insights of religion, they will develop more inner stability and become more responsible citizens," King wrote.

Even poverty King attributed in large measure to what he considered the profligacy and laziness of African Americans. On these issues he approvingly paraphrased Booker T. Washington: "There is a great deal that the Negro can do to lift himself by his own bootstraps. Well has it been said by one that Negroes too often buy what they want and beg for what they need. Negroes must learn to practice systematic saving." King was particularly concerned that African Americans had rejected the white work ethic:

Don't set out to do a good Negro job. [We] must head out to do our jobs so well that nobody could do them better. No matter what this job is, you must decide to do it well. Do it so well that the living, the dead, or the unborn can't do it better. If it falls your lot to be a street sweeper, sweep streets like Raphael painted pictures; sweep streets like Michelangelo carved marble; sweep streets like Beethoven composed music; sweep streets like Shakespeare wrote poetry; sweep streets so well that all the host of heaven and earth will have to pause and say: "Here lived a great street sweeper, who swept his job well."[17]

King recognized that black sexuality posed a special threat to his assimilationist project. "We must walk the street every day, and let people know that as we walk the street, we aren't thinking about sex every time we turn around," he told one audience. In *Ebony* he impugned readers to avoid rock 'n' roll music, which "plunges men's minds into degrading and immoral depths." To one young reader who wrote in asking what he should do about his homosexuality, King replied that the boy should seek psychiatric help to get at the root of the problem. For many of the leaders of the civil rights movement, the heterosexual family was the most effective conveyance through which to create citizens (despite the well-known contradictions in their private behavior). King's belief in the primacy of social order over individual freedom was revealed in a column on childrearing:

It is quite true that many modern parents go too far in allowing their children to express themselves with hardly a modicum of discipline. Many parents justify this by arguing that the children must have freedom. But freedom can very easily run wild if not tempered with discipline and responsibility. . . . Somewhere along the way every child must be trained into the obligations of cooperative living. He must be made aware that he is a member of a group and that group life implies duties and restraints.[18]

The family was a central metaphor in civil rights discourse. Ella Baker, the intellectual founder of the Student Nonviolent Coordinating Committee, described in an interview the society she wished to create by reimagining the rural North Carolina hamlet in which she was raised. She told of a community in which people cared little for material possessions, were rooted in the soil, and governed themselves with an ethic of self-sacrifice, which she called "the Christian concept of sharing with others." She claimed that her parents lived on the same land her grandparents had worked as slaves, and that they, like all their neighbors, gave away their food, raised other people's children, cared for the sick, and volunteered to work on other people's farms. "Your relationship to human beings was more important than your relationship to the amount of money that you made," Baker recalled. Her reimagined village operated as a family, writ large. For Baker, this ideal black community was destroyed by the migration from communal obligation to individual desire:

> As people moved to towns and cities, the sense of community diminished. Whatever deep sense of community that may have been developed in that little place . . . didn't always carry over to the city when they migrated. They lost their roots . . . If people begin to place their values in terms of how high they can get in the political world, or how much worldly goods they can accumulate, or what kind of cars they have, or how much they have in the bank, that's where I begin to lose respect. To me, I'm part of the human family.[19]

One of the great untold stories of the civil rights movement is the flourishing and subsequent destruction of black ministers in the postwar period who were anathema to aspiring black citizens. It would not be an exaggeration to say that two of these ministers in particular, James Francis Jones, who was known as Prophet Jones, and Charles Manuel Grace, who operated under the moniker Sweet Daddy Grace, were the most popular religious figures among the black working class in the 1940s and 1950s, even more popular than the rising group of ministers who would lead the civil rights movement.

Prophet Jones headed the two largest Pentecostal congregations in Detroit during this period. He also broadcast a live weekly sermon over Canadian station CKLW, whose fifty-thousand-watt signal reached several Midwestern cities with sizable African American populations, and in 1955 began hosting a Sunday-night program on WXYZ-TV, making him the first African American preacher in Detroit to host a weekly television program. The radio and television shows were, according to several sources, the most popular programs among the city's African American population. With the help of sustained national mainstream media attention, including feature articles in *Life*, *Time*, *Newsweek*, and *The Saturday Evening Post*, by the mid-1950s Jones's admirers made up a substantial portion of the African American population as a whole. And he was almost certainly the most popular minister among Detroit's black working class. A researcher at Wayne State University who studied one of Jones's congregations wrote, "The devotees of the cult appear to constitute largely that class of persons who are near the bottom of the social and economic ladder." In 1955, the Detroit-area circulation for the *Saturday Evening Post* jumped 30 percent when the magazine ran an extensive and flattering profile of Jones.

Jones reveled in materialist self-aggrandizement. He spoke not from a pulpit but from a $5,000 throne. In public he often wore a full-length white mink coat draped over European suits, and at home he liked to relax in satin slippers and a flowing robe decorated with sequins and an Elizabethan collar. He was doused with cologne and festooned with enormous jeweled rings, and he drove a massive white Cadillac. But most impressive of all was his fifty-four-room mansion, called Dominion Residence, which included a perfume parlor, barbershop, ballroom, and shrine to his longtime companion, James Walton, who died in 1951. Jones had the mansion painted a different color each season of the year. Perhaps most astonishing, nearly all of his wealth came from gifts he received from his followers, whose devotion to Jones was never cooled by the press's constant exposure of his homosexuality.

Like Prophet Jones, Sweet Daddy Grace was a fount of self-love and an idol of the black working class. Beginning in Charlotte, North Carolina in the 1920s, then expanding into Washington, D.C., New York City, and finally New England, Grace built a Pentecostal empire up and down the East Coast that by the 1950s included at least half a million members in three hundred congregations in nearly seventy cities. Declared by *Ebony* to be "America's Richest Negro Minister," Grace made every effort to demonstrate the validity of the title. His shoulder-length hair splayed across the collar of his gold and purple cutaway coats, which often framed chartreuse vests and floral-print ties. More striking still were his five-inch-long fingernails, usually painted red, white, and blue. Grace, who immigrated from Cape Verde and worked as a dishwasher and migrant farm laborer before becoming a preacher, said the nails represented his rejection of work. It may be no coincidence that in the late twentieth century, this style of extraordinarily long and elaborately decorated fingernails became common among black, working-class women—many of whom worked at key-boards and cash registers but who refused to subordinate themselves to their jobs.

Grace rode in a custom-built Cadillac limousine, and he bought some of the most prestigious real estate in Manhattan, including the El Dorado on Central Park West, which was then the tallest apartment building in the world. By the mid-1950s, his total net worth was estimated at $25 million. Like Prophet Jones's fortune, most of it came from donations by Grace's working-class devotees. In many of his churches, the members constructed enormous, arklike containers covered with dollar bills, behind which sat Grace's throne. Grace's services were also sexually charged. They began with him slowly walking down the red-carpeted aisle as his followers pinned ten, twenty, fifty, and sometimes hundred-dollar bills onto his robe. While a rhythm and blues band played, the congregants danced ecstatically. Asked why he promoted such libidinous revelry, he replied, "Why should the devil have all the good times?" Grace gave himself the title "Boyfriend of the World," and his theme song featured the chorus, "Daddy, you feel so good."

In the mid-1950s, the period of *Brown v. Board of Education*, the Montgomery bus boycott, the integration of Little Rock High School, and the emergence of Martin Luther King as a national figure, the civil rights movement ended the careers of Prophet Jones and Sweet Daddy Grace. In January 1955, after years of neutral coverage of Jones, the *Michigan Chronicle*, Detroit's leading black newspaper, published a broadside attack against the preacher, calling him a "circus-type headline-seeker operating under the guise of religion." Three months later, after NBC scheduled an appearance by Jones on the *Today* program, the Detroit Urban League and the Detroit Council of Churches organized a successful protest to keep the prophet off the air. The most strident attacks came from C. L. Franklin, pastor of New Bethel Baptist Church and the emerging leader of the Detroit civil rights movement. Franklin had been friendly toward Jones for many years, but now he called the prophet "degrading not only to local religious circles but more significantly, a setback of hundreds of years to the integration of all races who are this time seeking democratic as well as Spiritual brotherhood."

Soon afterward, Jones was arrested for allegedly attempting to perform fellatio on an undercover police officer who had been assigned to investigate rumors that Jones ran a numbers-running operation. The local black press cheered the arrest. The *Michigan Chronicle* called it a victory for "an increasingly vociferous element in the community" who demanded that people like Jones, "who exist by the skillful intermixing of religion, fear, faith in God and outright fakery solely for personal aggrandizement be driven from their lofty perches." The *Detroit Tribune*, which in previous years had praised Jones, now denounced him for giving the impression to whites that the black race was "under the guidance of a sex-deviate." On the national level, *Ebony* devoted four punishing pages to Jones's trial, calling it a "day of reckoning." Yet despite his ostracism by the black leadership, Jones's followers remained as loyal as ever. They packed the courtroom every day of his trial, and when the jury declared him not guilty, hundreds of them raucously celebrated and shouted, "All is well!" Jones was subsequently shunned by the press and lost his visibility as a representative of the black working class, but his enduring popularity was confirmed by the crowd of more than two thousand people who attended his funeral in 1970, where his bronze casket was draped with his famous white mink coat.

Daddy Grace faced a similar fate. In 1957, Louvenia Royster, a retired Georgia schoolteacher, filed a lawsuit against Grace, claiming that he had been married to her in the 1920s but deserted her shortly after the birth of their child. Though the court quickly rejected the claim, the black press delivered a guilty verdict. *Jet's* headline read, "The Past That Haunts Daddy Grace—Dismissed Alimony Trial Reveals Secret of 1st Wife." The magazine called the preacher "America's richest cultist" and hopefully speculated that the trial would "shake [the] kingdom of Daddy Grace." Joining the attack, Martin Luther King pointed a damning finger at the profligacy and irresponsibility of preachers like Grace. He told his congregation in Montgomery, "Leaders are needed all over this South, in every community, all over this nation: intelligent, courageous, dedicated leadership. Not leaders in love with money, but in love with justice; not leaders in love with publicity, but in love with humanity."

The greatest threat posed by Grace and his followers was to the cause of integration. They were, according to King, too black:

> [If] we're going to get ready for integration, we can't spend all of our time trying to learn how to whoop and holler . . . We're talking about integrated churches . . . And we've got to have ministers who can stand up and preach the gospel of Jesus Christ. Not a Negro gospel; not a gospel merely to get people to shout and kick over benches, but a gospel that will make people think and live right and face the challenges of the Christian religion.[20]

The subjects of Grace's kingdom were unfazed. His supporters filled the courtroom to overflowing, and, eight months after the trial, tens of thousands attended his annual parade through downtown Charlotte. Yet by the time Grace died in 1960, the kingdoms of Sweet Daddy Grace and Prophet Jones had been conquered by a new generation of leaders.[21]

The civil rights leaders faced other competitors for the loyalty of African Americans, most famously black nationalists. But while the nationalists rejected integrationism and nonviolence, they shared with the civil rights leaders a contempt for the decadence of Jones and Grace as well as the ethic of sacrifice. Malcolm X and the Nation of Islam insisted on strict discipline, hard work, and the renunciation of drugs, tobacco, liquor, gluttony, laziness, emotional display, and promiscuity. They promised a new black nation "where we can reform ourselves, lift up our moral standards, and try to be godly." Whereas "the black man" in his current condition was "not fit for self," the "new black man" would relinquish his desires for "the good life" in service of the nation. According to Malcolm X, Islam taught black people "to reform ourselves of the vices and evils of this society, drunkenness, dope addiction, how to work and provide a living for our family, take care of our children and our wives." With a similar mission, the Black Panther Party, founded in 1966, organized itself into a semimilitary organization in which duty to the "community" took precedence over what they called "decadent and bourgeois" desires for wealth and pleasure. Black cultural nationalists such as Amiri Baraka, Ron Karenga, and Nikki Giovanni routinely denounced attachment to "materialistic fetishes" as "the white boys' snake medicine" and as the product of a "slave mentality." The Last Poets, an avant-garde musical group that grew out of the Black Arts movement, condemned "niggers" whose alligator shoes, Cadillacs, and preoccupation with sex made them "scared of revolution."[22]

Significantly, among the most ardent ascetics in the "black freedom movements" were whites. Applications for the Mississippi Freedom Summer Project in 1964 reveal that many of the white college students were attracted to the poverty and suffering of black southerners. In explaining his motivations for participating in Freedom Summer, one volunteer wrote, "This is not a struggle to be engaged in by the mere liberal, for the liberal can't be counted on to make the sacrifices required. . . . I have rejected my 'birthrights' and voluntarily identified with the suppressed classes." Another declared, "I am against much of what my family stands for. I realize that four families could live comfortably on what my father makes—[that is,] comfortably Mississippi Negro style." In one application, a graduate student wrote that he would end his career as an academic to join the movement. "I can simply no longer justify the pursuit of a PhD. When the folks in [Mississippi] have to struggle to comprehend the most elementary of materials on history and society and man's larger life, I feel ashamed to be greedily going after 'higher learning.' And when I reflect on the terrors and deprivations in daily lives here, I cannot return to the relative comforts and security of student life." Some of the volunteers could not contain their rage at those who chose to live in material comfort. In response to advice from white leaders of the National Council of Churches that the volunteers should project a respectable, middle-class image, one wrote: "We crap on the clean, antiseptic, decent middle-class image. It is that decency we want to change, to overcome. So crap on your middle class, on your decency, mister Church man. Get out of your god-damned new rented car. Get out of your pressed, proper clothes. Come join us who are sleeping on the floor. . . . Come with us and walk, not ride, the dusty streets of Gulfport."

The white volunteers devoted considerable energy to teaching black Mississippians the value of the ascetic life, thus suggesting that the people they actually encountered on the streets of Gulfport and elsewhere in the state did not share their calling. Many of the white volunteers helped establish "freedom schools" for poor black children and served as teachers. Staughton Lynd, a white radical who was then a professor at Spelman College, oversaw the freedom schools and developed their curriculum. A central purpose of the schools, as stated in the basic curriculum written by Lynd, was to inculcate values in black children that were antithetical to white middle-class life. One lesson was intended "to find out what the whites' so-called 'better life' is really like, and what it costs them." Another was "to help the students see clearly the conditions of the Negro in the North, and see that migration to the North is not a basic solution."

An entire unit of the Freedom School curriculum was devoted to explaining the differences between what were called "Material Things," which were associated with whites, and "Soul Things," which were associated with blacks. The purpose of this lesson was "to develop insights about the inadequacies of pure materialism." Among the "ideas to be developed" with the students were that "the possessions of men do not make them free" and that "Negroes will not be freed by: a. taking what the whites have; b. a movement directed at materialistic ends only." A list of questions designed to lead to these ideas included the following:

> Suppose you had a million dollars. You could buy a boat, a big car, a house, clothes, food, and many good things. But could you buy a friend? Could you buy a spring morning? Could you buy health? And how could we be happy without friends, health, and spring?
>
> This is a freedom movement: suppose this movement could get a good house and job for all Negroes. Suppose Negroes had everything that the middle class of America has . . . everything the rest of the country has . . . would it be enough? Why are there heart attacks and diseases and so much awful unhappiness in the middle class . . . which seems to be so free? Why the Bomb?

An exchange between a white Freedom Summer organizer and his black constituents indicates that they did not share the same aspirations. When black teenagers in Greenwood, Mississippi, demanded that violent tactics be used to gain access to a whites-only movie theater, Bob Zellner, the son of a white Methodist minister and a lead organizer of Freedom Summer, was brought in to change their minds. At a community forum, Zellner argued that rather than focus on the movie theater, the teenagers should focus on "more important" matters. "We feel that our concentration has to be on voter registration now," he told them. "Integrating all the movies in the South won't achieve anything basic." A sixteen-year-old girl then responded. "You say that we have to wait until we get the vote," she said. "But you know, by the time that happens the younger people are going to be too old to enjoy the bowling alley and the swimming pool." When the white volunteers arrived in Mississippi, they and the people they sought to emulate were often headed in opposite directions.[23]

While it is undeniably true that the civil rights and black nationalist organizations inspired great numbers of African Americans with visions of black uplift, movement leaders did not succeed in creating a mass commitment to the responsibilities and sacrifices necessary for revolution or for citizenship. The aversion to communal obligation was far greater among the black working class than among whites. As W. E. B. Du Bois, Langston Hughes, James Baldwin, and more recent scholars such as Robin D. G. Kelley, David Roediger, Saidiya Hartman, and Roderick Ferguson have suggested, the relatively liberated character of black American culture might very well have been the result of the fact that for most if not all of their history, African Americans have been to some degree excluded from citizenship and therefore far less likely to internalize its repression. It is certainly arguable that having created a culture of freedom out of slavery, segregation, and compulsory labor, when citizenship appeared attainable in the postwar period, the black working class demonstrated an unwillingness to relinquish the pleasures of that culture in exchange for their rights. As scholars have moved away from studies of black leaders and toward an examination of African American working-class culture, evidence of this resistance has mounted.

Draft evasion as well as insubordination against commanding officers in the military remained far greater among African Americans than among whites from the two world wars through the Korean and Vietnam wars. During World War I, the only black combat division in the American Expeditionary Force frequently ran away during battles, resulting in the removal of the entire division from the front. There is also substantial anecdotal evidence that during both world wars, large numbers of black men feigned illness or insanity to evade the draft. During World War II, despite exhortations by civil rights organizations that they should fight for the United States in order to demonstrate their patriotism and therefore their entitlement to citizenship, black men made up more than 18 percent of those imprisoned for draft evasion and 34 percent of delinquent draft registrants. Similarly, historian Gerald Gill has found that draft law delinquency during the Korean War was extraordinarily high in black urban neighborhoods. In the early months of the war it was estimated that 30 percent of eligible men in Harlem were delinquent in registering. At the national level, approximately 20 percent of those arrested for violating the Selective Service Act from 1951 through 1953 were African American. Black resistance to patriotic obligation peaked during the Vietnam War, when African Americans made up fully one-half of the eligible men who failed to register for the draft.

It is unlikely that this resistance to military service was chiefly motivated by pacifism. Indeed, evidence produced by several scholars has corroborated Timothy Tyson's claim that nonviolent integrationism, rather than combative and autonomous opposition to racism, "is the anomaly" in African American history, even during the civil rights era. This research has revealed mass uprisings against racist violence in Decatur, Mississippi; Monroe, North Carolina; and Columbia, Tennessee. It has also revealed countless examples of individual acts of violent self-defense throughout the South. In Birmingham, years of fighting in the streets against the racist police gave power to King's famous ultimatum to the city's white leadership. In his "Letter from Birmingham City Jail," King warned that "many streets of the South would be flowing with floods of blood" if black discontent were not "channelized through the creative outlet of nonviolent direct action." In northern cities, violent responses to poverty and police brutality were of course commonplace, and in the major uprisings in Watts (1965), Detroit (1967), and Newark (1967), they were coupled with militant demonstrations of material desires in the form of looting.[24]

Robin D. G. Kelley, Tera Hunter, and other historians have found a long tradition of resistance to labor discipline among black working men and women. According to Kelley, this most often involved "evasive, day-to-day strategies: from footdragging to sabotage, theft at the workplace to absenteeism, cursing and graffiti." Kelley criticizes scholars who, in attempting to counter racist stereotypes, "are often too quick to invert them, remaking the black proletariat into the hardest-working, thriftiest, most efficient labor force around." Rather, he says, "if we regard most work as alienating, especially work performed in a context of racist and sexist oppression, then we should expect black working people to minimize labor with as little economic loss as possible." It also should not be surprising that throughout the wartime and postwar periods, African Americans were in the vanguard of the wildcat strikes and resistance to industrial discipline that so bedeviled Walter Reuther.

African Americans escaped the obligations demanded of "good" citizens in other, often clandestine ways. Though many commentators have argued that the tax revolt of the 1970s was largely driven by resentful whites, African Americans were waging something of a tax revolt of their own, less visible and perhaps less consciously "political" than the white rebellion, but far broader. Studies of Internal Revenue Service records have shown that noncompliance to tax laws was significantly greater among African Americans in the 1960s and 1970s than among whites. Furthermore, these studies do not take into account the vast, untaxed underground economy, which economists have estimated produced between 8 and 14 percent of the total national income in the 1970s, and whose participants were disproportionately black. A study conducted by the Department of Labor in 1971 estimated that one of every five adult inhabitants of Harlem lived entirely on income derived from illegal enterprises.[25]

Perhaps most tellingly, the black popular culture that arose in the 1950s and 1960s—a phenomenon ignored by nearly all historians of the civil rights movement—showed a distinct lack of interest in King's project.

Despite civil rights leaders' admonishments to African Americans to forgo personal gratification for a higher purpose, the most popular black urban folk tales during the period continued the oral tradition of venerating "bad niggers" who rejected the "jive-ass jobs" assigned to them, defeated white opponents in athletic, sexual, and mental contests, and accumulated luxuries surpassing those of "Vanderbilt, Goldberg, and Henry Ford." Some of the most popular "party records" of the 1960s and 1970s were recordings of Rudy Ray Moore's stand-up comedy acts, in which he often recited X-rated versions of classic "bad nigger" tales such as "Dolemite," "Shine," "Pimpin' Sam," and "The Signifying Monkey." Similarly, Redd Foxx and Richard Pryor gained mass audiences with routines that unabashedly endorsed the sensuality of black culture. These performers established a dominant genre in African American comedy that proudly asserted black culture's embrace of pleasure and freedom over the repressive morality of whiteness. Moreover, these expressions of the superiority of African American "badness" were not exclusively masculine. No black comedian of the postwar period was more popular than Moms Mabley, whose orations on sex and soul food brought hundreds of thousands of black patrons to theaters across the country.

In film portrayals of African Americans, by the early 1970s, the sexless and self-sacrificing characters played by Sidney Poitier during the civil rights era had been replaced by hypersexual superheroes who had achieved spectacular wealth by means other than "working for the Man." The so-called blaxploitation genre was created not by Hollywood but by the independent black producers, writers, and directors of two films, *Sweet Sweetback's Baadasssss Song*, which was released in 1971, and *Superfly*, released in 1972. The hero of *Sweet Sweetback* is brought up in a brothel and becomes a pimp to pursue a life of fine clothes, fancy cars, and unlimited sex. After witnessing two white policemen savagely beating a young black man, Sweetback kills the cops and escapes across the Mexican border. *Ebony* called the film "trivial" and "tasteless," but the black working class voted with its feet. When the film opened at the Grand Circus Theater in Detroit, it broke the record for opening-night box-office receipts. *Sweet Sweetback*, which was made for $150,000, went on to gross more than $15 million. It was then the most successful independent film ever released.

Superfly was even more popular among black audiences, grossing more than $18 million, and it too was attacked by the civil rights leadership. The film portrayed a Harlem cocaine dealer who escapes the drug business and the ghetto by ripping off a white syndicate boss and overpowering corrupt cops. The hero rejects both his position of power and the work ethic, preferring a life of pleasure and freedom.

In popular music, the lyrics of African American songs in the era of civil rights and black power represented nearly all the desires those movements' leaders struggled to repress. Materialist aspirations were heralded by such enormously popular songs as "Money Honey," "The Payback," and "Money (That's What I Want)." Another staple of rhythm and blues lyrics was the rejection of compulsory labor. Fats Domino, Sam Cooke, and Smokey Robinson sang of hating "Blue Monday" and having to "Get a Job," but also of loving the liberation brought by the weekend. And, as if in response to King's plea for hard work and frugality, in "Rip It Up" Little Richard wailed,

> *Well, it's Saturday night and I just got paid*
> *Fool about my money, don't try to save*
> *My heart says Go! Go! Have a time*
> *'Cause it's Saturday night and I feel fine.*

Of course, R&B was also well stocked with paeans to sexual revelry, from The Clovers' "Good Lovin'" in the 1950s to James Brown's "Sex Machine" in the 1960s and Marvin Gaye's "Let's Get It On" in the 1970s.

Chuck Berry's songs perhaps best captured the black working-class evasion of citizenship. As in many earlier blues songs, movement was a common theme in Berry's lyrics. In songs such as "Maybellene," "No Particular Place To Go," "The Promised Land," and "You Can't Catch Me," Berry sang of riding in fast and luxurious cars toward the objects of his desire, from sex partners to "silk suits" to lavish meals. In these songs Berry is always on the move, never committing himself to a place. In "The Promised Land," he drives around, through, and away from Norfolk, Raleigh, Charlotte, Rock Hill, Atlanta, Birmingham, Mississippi, and New Orleans. In "You Can't Catch Me," he's up north, in New Jersey. But even there he refuses to stop. While cruising on the Turnpike, he encounters the state police. His car sprouts wings and takes off, into the sky and away from the law. "Bye bye, New Jersey," he says. "I'd be come and gone."

These sentiments were triumphant in the rise of disco, the most popular music of the 1970s. Having originated in gay black working-class nightclubs, by the middle of the decade disco dominated the airwaves, the Billboard Music Charts, and the dance floors. More generally, it was also at the center of the most sexually open era in American history. Disco culture celebrated the body, rejected work, and represented the antithesis of family values. Not surprisingly, some of its harshest critics came from the heirs of Martin Luther King. Virtually quoting King's condemnation of rock 'n' roll in the 1950s, Jesse Jackson attacked disco as "sex-rock" and as "garbage and pollution which is corrupting the minds and morals of our youth." Jackson threatened a boycott against stores that sold disco records, and his Operation PUSH held a series of conferences on the evils of the music. Disco did fade from the scene, but it gave birth to a cultural form that proved even more vexing to the remnants of the civil rights leadership. Since its arrival in the late 1970s, hip-hop has moved ever farther from King's vision. Today, the two dominant genres in the music and its visual accompaniments are the violently anti-integrationist "gangsta style," and "bling," a carnival of conspicuous consumption and sensual gratification.[26]

Significantly, the achievements and failures of the civil rights movement correspond with the desires and antipathies expressed in contemporary African American culture. Despite the insistence by Ella Baker and other movement leaders that the objectives of the sit-in movement were, as Baker said, "bigger than a hamburger" and "not limited to a drive for personal freedom," testimonies by sit-in participants indicate that many African Americans in the South welcomed the desegregation of public space as their entry into the consumer culture. After the lunch counter at the largest department store in Atlanta was desegregated, sit-in organizers were dismayed that the first black people to eat there honored the occasion by dressing in their finest clothes, including fur coats.

Other, broader accomplishments did not fulfill King's vision of a new black citizenry. Though the Voting Rights Act of 1965 created new opportunities to participate in American governance—what many movement historians hail as a "revolution" that opened the door to full citizenship for African Americans—black voter turnout actually began a steady decline shortly after the passage of the law. Meanwhile, however, trade unions made inclusive and nondiscriminatory by years of black rank-and-file struggle improved the material lives of hundreds of thousands of African Americans. This, coupled with the opportunities created by affirmative action policies, paved the way for a dramatic growth in the black middle class, which by some estimates more than tripled in size in the decade after King's death.[27]

THE GIFT

Despite the efforts by the civil rights movement to reform it, the black working class brought at least a degree of liberation to whites who rejected the obligations of citizenship and were attracted not to the suffering and deprivation of

African Americans but to the joys of their culture. A common theme in the writings of the most famous imitators of African Americans in the postwar period, the Beats, is the attempt to overcome their alienation as white middle-class youth through participation in black culture. In "Howl," Allen Ginsberg's "best minds" crashed through bourgeois barriers and into the Negro ghetto to revel in sex, drugs, and emotional catharsis. Jack Kerouac made this desire to be black and free explicit in *On the Road*. When the novel's hero arrives in Denver, he heads to the black neighborhood. "I walked . . . in the Denver colored section, wishing I were a Negro, feeling that the best the white world had offered was not enough ecstasy for me, not enough life, joy, kicks, darkness, music, not enough night." Like many white "race traitors," the Beats often reduced black culture to its most sensual aspects, but in doing so, they found a vehicle through which to escape the confines of whiteness and citizenship.

The Beats were only a very small part of what became a mass movement of white youth toward African American culture. In the 1950s, the revenue produced by black music grew from less than 5 percent of the total market to nearly 75 percent, and by the early 1960s, untold numbers of white Americans owned, listened to, and danced to R&B records. As was understood by white anti-integrationists who declared that "jungle rhythms" turned "white boys and girls" to "the level of the animal," the appeal of the sensual and emotional liberation represented by R&B threatened to subvert the social basis of their culture. This threat was manifested most powerfully by the masses of young white women who flocked to R&B concerts, where they were allowed to shed their sexual inhibitions and break racial taboos on the dance floor. Chuck Berry was candid about the meaning of black music for many white women. In songs such as "Brown-Eyed Handsome Man" and "Sweet Little Sixteen," Berry proclaimed that white sexual taboos were being violated, not by the black predations of the racist imagination, but by the desires of white women. Berry's boasts were essentially verified by the campaign conducted against him by law-enforcement agencies in the late 1950s. He was arrested twice for violation of the Mann Act, which prohibited the transportation of minors across state lines for immoral purposes. One of the cases was dropped after the alleged victim, a white woman, declared not only that her relationship with Berry was entirely consensual but also that she had initiated it. In the second case, Berry was found guilty and sentenced to three years in a federal penitentiary. And in 1959, Berry was arrested after a show in Meridian, Mississippi, when a white teenaged fan grabbed him by the neck and kissed him.

White men as well found black music enormously liberating and were often militant in defending their access to it. In the late 1950s and early 1960s, a black disk jockey named Shelley Stewart cultivated a large white following in the Birmingham area with his R&B shows on the local black radio station and by spinning records at a weekly, whites-only sock hop. In 1960, during one of the sock hops, eighty members of the local Ku Klux Klan surrounded the building and threatened to do bodily harm to Stewart for his alleged attempts to "dance with white girls." At that point, a large group of the young male dancers, estimated to be several hundred strong, attacked the Klan, allowing Stewart to escape.

By the late 1950s, the popularity of R&B among white youth had become so great that it paved the way for the integration of several southern universities. At Vanderbilt in 1958, editors of the student newspaper extended their love for R&B into a sustained critique of segregation in higher education. In a series of editorials, they compared white opposition to black music with violent repression of civil rights demonstrators and called for the immediate integration of their campus. At the University of Alabama in 1962, while the administration was refusing to admit the first black applicants in the school's history, the Cotillion Club conducted a poll among the all-white student body to determine which entertainers should be invited to perform on campus. Though no African Americans were listed among the performers on the poll, Ray Charles won by what the campus newspaper called "an overwhelming majority with a write-in vote." The president of the Cotillion Club duly invited the soul singer, but the university administration refused to allow him to perform on campus. Charles won the poll again in 1964 and was again barred by the administration. The following year, the chairman of the Southern Student Organizing Committee, a white civil rights group, reported a surprising degree of pro-integration sentiment at the university. And in 1966, facing a student revolt, the administration welcomed none other than James Brown to campus.[28]

The musicians who made rock 'n' roll the chief rival of country music on the popular music charts during the 1960s and early 1970s were deeply influenced by black working-class culture. As has been well documented, many white rock performers found their calling in black juke joints and nightclubs or by listening to R&B on the radio, and the music they created challenged all the tenets of American citizenship. It might be said that these refugees from citizenship and whiteness accepted what W. E. B. Du Bois described in his now-forgotten *The Gift of Black Folk*, an offering that most of the white working class has spurned. Rather than accept their place in American civilization, what Du Bois called "so pale and hard and thin a thing," these whites took the gift from the heirs of slaves who "brought into common labor certain new spiritual values not yet fully realized." Turning the morality of American citizenship on its head, Du Bois described the black worker as "a tropical product with a sensuous receptivity to the beauty of the world" who "was not as easily reduced to be the mechanical draft-horse which the northern European laborer became." Having refused to adopt the cruel rationalism of the master race, black folk "brought to modern manual labor a renewed valuation of life."

Among the small number of white working-class beneficiaries of the gift of black folk were the workers at the General Motors plant in Lordstown, Ohio, who in 1972 staged a walkout in rebellion against their employer and their union, the UAW. The national media noted that the strikers did not resemble the typical white workers of the time. Rather, they wore long hair and shaggy beards, indulged unreservedly in drugs and alcohol, opposed the war in Vietnam, and listened to rock every minute they could. Most stunning of all, they unashamedly rejected the work ethic. Many spoke publicly about committing acts of sabotage on the assembly line, spontaneous slowdowns and shutdowns, showing up late to work or not at all, general "goofing off," and "fucking up any time I can." While the immediate issue in the strike was a speedup imposed by GM, the workers quickly turned it into a rebellion against the UAW—"our union, Miss Goody Two Shoes"—which they accused of being more concerned with maintaining high production standards than with defending the freedom of the members. The rebels at Lordstown not only rejected Reuther's conception of industrial citizenship, but they also refused to abide by the cultural obligations of Americans.[29]

These alternative narratives of the modern labor and civil rights movements are intended to shake several conventional assumptions. First, they are constructed in such a way as to allow us to hear the desires of ordinary people, even when those desires do not correspond to the wishes of movement leaders or of the scholars who admire them. These stories also suggest that in addition to the struggles between classes, races, sexes, and nations, history is often driven by clashes between the guardians of community and community's discontents. Finally, they are an invitation to historians wishing to tell the story of American freedom to look not to movements seeking inclusion, control, and a share of sovereignty, or to moments like the March on Washington, but to moments like the Lordstown strike, to the subterranean desires and illicit behaviors of ordinary people, and to anyone who has carried forward the gift of the slaves.

BIBLIOGRAPHIC NOTE

Much of my interpretation of U.S. labor and African American history was inspired and made possible by the work of two extraordinary scholars. Jonathan Cutler's *Labor's Time: Shorter Hours, the UAW, and the Struggle for the American Unionism* (Temple University Press, 2004) presents the most thoroughgoing revision of American labor history in more than a generation. Robin D. G. Kelley, in particular in his essays on African American working-class culture in *Race Rebels: Culture, Politics, and the Black Working Class* (Free Press, 1994), has broken open the fields of labor and African American studies by showing how much is revealed by examining history from "way, way, below."

From the 1970s to the present, the study of the American working class has been dominated by what is known as the "new labor history." With very few exceptions, new labor historians who study unions in the twentieth century have focused exclusively on the CIO and its affiliates or their predecessors, even though the AFL was always much larger than the CIO. My book *Out of the Jungle: Jimmy Hoffa and the Remaking of the American Working Class* (Knopf, 2001), the basis of the section on labor in this essay, was an effort to bring the AFL unions back into the picture without idealizing them, to renew the discussion of interunion competition initiated in the "old" labor history, and to examine the corporatist leadership of the CIO in a critical light.

Much of my knowledge of the CIO and corporatism was gained from the work of scholars who share only some of my interpretations and none of my valuations, in particular Nelson Lichtenstein's *Labor's War at Home: The CIO in World War II* (Cambridge University Press, 1982) and *The Most Dangerous Man in Detroit: Walter Reuther and the Fate of American Labor* (Basic Books, 1995), and Steven Fraser, *Labor Will Rule: Sidney Hillman and the Rise of American Labor* (Cornell University Press, 1991), which is perhaps the best explication of the ideology of the CIO's corporatist leadership.

Like labor history, scholarship on the civil rights and black power movements is ripe for revision. Much of my thinking about the movements was built from work that does not address them directly but that offers interpretations of African American history that might lead to new directions in movement historiography. In addition to Kelley's *Race Rebels*, I am indebted to several works that are mentioned in the essay, including W. E. B. Du Bois, *The Gift of Black Folk: The Negroes in the Making of America* (Stratford, 1924); Langston Hughes, "The Negro and the Racial Mountain," *The Nation*, 23 June 1926; James Baldwin, "Freaks and the American Ideal of Manhood," in *Collected Essays* (Library of America, 1998), 814–829; Saidiya Hartman, *Scenes of Subjection: Terror, Slavery, and Self-Making in Nineteenth-Century America* (Oxford University Press, 1997); and Roderick A. Ferguson, "Specters of the Sexual: Race, Sociology, and the Conflict Over African-American Culture," Ph.D. diss., University of California, San Diego, 2000. My colleague Monica Miller's work on the black dandy figure in Anglo-American culture, soon to be published, also contributed to my thinking.

The theoretical basis of this essay was greatly influenced by several scholars working within what are now known as "whiteness studies" and "queer theory." In particular, my ideas about race and citizenship were shaped by David Roediger, *The Wages of Whiteness: Race and the Making of the American Working Class* (Verso, 1991) and *Towards the Abolition of Whiteness: Essays on Race, Politics, and Working Class History* (Verso, 1994); Michael Warner's introduction to his edited volume *Fear of a Queer Planet: Queer Politics and Social Theory*

(University of Minnesota Press, 1993); and Wendy Brown, *States of Injury: Power and Freedom in Late Modernity* (Princeton University Press, 1995).

NOTES

1. Nelson Lichtenstein, *The Most Dangerous Man in Detroit: Walter Reuther and the Fate of American Labor* (New York: Basic Books, 1995), 185, 355–356; Steven Fraser, *Labor Will Rule: Sidney Hillman and the Rise of American Labor* (Ithaca, N.Y.: Cornell University Press, 1991), 233; J. B. S. Hardman, "Postscripts to Ten Years of Labor Movement," in *American Labor Dynamics in the Light of Post-War Developments*, ed J. B. S. Hardman (New York: Harcourt Brace, 1928), 8.

2. *How to Win for the Union: A Discussion for UAW Stewards and Committeemen* (1941), excerpted in Nelson Lichtenstein and Eileen Boris, *Major Problems in the History of American Workers* (Lexington, Mass.: D. C. Heath, 1991), 369–372; Lichtenstein, *The Most Dangerous Man in Detroit*, 111, 162. For a useful discussion of the invention and elaboration of the idea of work discipline in the United States, see Daniel T. Rodgers, *The Work Ethic in Industrial America, 1850–1920* (Chicago: University of Chicago Press, 1978).

3. Lichtenstein, *Most Dangerous Man in Detroit*, 139–140, 196–198, 211–219; Frank Cormier and William Eaton, *Reuther* (New York: Prentice-Hall, 1970), 286, 396–397, 399. According to Joshua Freeman, "the massive influx of new workers into the industrial work force . . . who had never participated in the deeply transforming process of creating [the CIO] unions" meant that "much of the wartime activity of CIO workers had an undeveloped and at times even reactionary quality to it." See Joshua Freeman, "Delivering the Goods: Industrial Unionism During World War II," in *The Labor History Reader*, ed. Daniel J. Leab (Urbana: University of Illinois Press, 1985), 400–401. For accounts of the wartime strikes written by partisans of the strikers, see Martin Glaberman, *Wartime Strikes: The Struggle Against the No-Strike Pledge in the UAW During World War II* (Detroit: Bewick, 1980), and George Lipsitz, *Rainbow at Midnight: Labor and Culture in the 1940s* (Urbana: University of Illinois Press, 1994), 73–92.

4. Joseph Krislov, "The Extent and Trends of Raiding Among American Unions," *Quarterly Journal of Economics* 69, no. 1 (February 1955): 145–152; Gary N. Chaison, "The Frequency and Outcomes of Union Raids," *Industrial Relations* 15 (1976): 107–110; James B. Dworkin and James R. Fain, "Success in Multiple Union Elections: Exclusive Jurisdiction vs. Competition," *Journal of Labor Research* 10, no. 1 (Winter 1989): 91–101; quote from Robert A. Christie, *Empire in Wood: A History of the Carpenters' Union* (Ithaca, N.Y.: Cornell University Press, 1956), 112.

5. Thaddeus Russell, *Out of the Jungle: Jimmy Hoffa and the Remaking of the American Working Class* (New York: Knopf, 2001), 58–115, 128–146.

6. On the results of one-union elections versus multiple-union elections, see Joseph Krislov, "Organizational Rivalry Among American Unions," *Industrial and Labor Relations Review* 13, no. 2 (January 1960): 216–226; Michael Goldfield, *The*

Decline of Organized Labor in the United States (Chicago: University of Chicago Press, 1987), 204, 207; Gary N. Chaison, "The Outcomes of Multi-Union Representation Elections Involving Incumbents," *Public Personnel Management* 13 (1973): 435, 436–37; and Ronald L. Seeber, "Union Organizing in Manufacturing: 1973–1976," in *Advances in Industrial and Labor Relations* 1 (1983): 23, 26. On CIO-AFL rivalry in various industries, see Robert H. Zieger, *Rebuilding the Pulp and Paper Workers' Union, 1933–1941* (Knoxville: University of Tennessee Press, 1984), 144–221, quoted sentence on 177; Christie, *Empire in Wood*, 287–300; Russell, *Out of the Jungle*, 58–115, 128–146; Irving Bernstein, *The Turbulent Years: A History of the American Worker During the Great Depression* (New York: Houghton Mifflin, 1970); Walter Galenson, *The CIO Challenge to the AFL: A History of the American Labor Movement, 1935–1941* (Cambridge, Mass.: Harvard University Press, 1960), and *Rival Unionism in the United States* (New York: American Council on Public Affairs, 1940). See also George W. Brooks, *The Sources of Vitality in the American Labor Movement* (Ithaca, N.Y.: New York State School of Industrial and Labor Relations, 1964), 29–33; Jonathan C. Cutler, "A Slacker's Paradise: The Fight for 30 Hours Work at 40 Hours' Pay in the United Automobile Workers, 1941–1966," Ph.D. diss., City University of New York, 1998, chapter 13; Stewart J. Schwab, "Union Raids, Union Democracy, and the Market for Union Control," *University of Illinois Law Review* (1992): 367–416. On rivalry producing material gains for textile workers in the earlier part of the century, see David J. Goldberg, *A Tale of Three Cities: Labor Organization and Protest in Paterson, Passaic, and Lawrence, 1916–1921* (New Brunswick, N.J.: Rutgers University Press, 1989).

7. Jonathan Cutler, "'To Exercise Control Over the Men': Rival Unionism, Corporate Liberalism, and the Establishment of the United Automobile Workers," unpublished manuscript, 2003.

8. Gary N. Chaison, "A Note on Union Merger Trends, 1900–1978," *Industrial and Labor Relations Review* 34, no. 1 (October 1980): 114–120; Arthur Goldberg, *AFL-CIO: Labor United* (New York: McGraw-Hill, 1956), 167–169. Goldberg, like the leaders of the CIO generally, was not a great proponent of internal democracy: "If there is analogy to political government, the analogy is to a political government which may simultaneously face uncertainty as to its continued existence: i.e., a revolution, and which is periodically at war. The constraints which by common consent we accept temporarily in the political arena when such conditions exist may perhaps explain and justify the existence of similar, although permanent, restraints in the practice of union democracy." This echoed the sentiments of J. B. S. Hardman, arguably the intellectual progenitor of the CIO, in 1928: "It is dangerous to lay everything open to the members and through them before the employers. And how can one prevent demagoguery, or any kind of political opposition from taking advantage of easy opportunities to make it hot for the administration? Democracy is lovely, but not innocent." Arthur J. Goldberg, "Labor in a Free Society: A Trade Union Point of View," speech at Industrial Union Department Conference, May 3, 1958; Hardman, *American Labor Dynamics*, 167.

9. Lichtenstein, *Most Dangerous Man in Detroit*, 221–225, 289, 291, 414–417; Martin Glaberman, "Walter Reuther, 'Social Unionist,'" *Monthly Review* 48, no. 6

(November 1996): 52–57; Cutler, "A Slacker's Paradise," 88–106, 146–173, 386–388; Cormier and Eaton, *Reuther*, 396–397, 399.

10. Russell, *Out of the Jungle*, 178–185, 206–211.

11. Aaron Brenner, "Rank and File Rebellion, 1966–1975," Ph.D. diss., Columbia University, 1996; Lichtenstein, *The Most Dangerous Man in Detroit*, 399–400; Stanley Aronowitz, *False Promises: The Shaping of American Working Class Consciousness* (Durham, N.C.: Duke University Press, 1992), chapter 1; Kim Moody, *An Injury to All: The Decline of American Unionism* (London: Verso, 1988), 83–94; David Lowery and Lee Sigelman, "Understanding the Tax Revolt: Eight Explanations," *American Political Science Review* 75, no. 4 (December 1981): 963–974; Thomas Byrne Edsall with Mary D. Edsall, *Chain Reaction: The Impact of Race, Rights, and Taxes on American Politics* (New York: Norton, 1992), 116–136.

12. Joshua B. Freeman, "Hardhats: Construction Workers, Manliness, and the 1970 Pro-War Demonstrations," *Journal of Social History* (Summer 1993): 725–744; Bill C. Malone, *Country Music U.S.A.* (Washington, D.C.: American Folklore Society, 1968), 198–199, 210, 229; Eric Stein, "'Living Right and Being Free': Country Music and Modern American Conservatism," M.A. thesis, McGill University, 1998; Michael Kazin, *The Populist Persuasion: An American History* (New York: Basic Books, 1995), chapters 9–10; Lichtenstein, *The Most Dangerous Man in Detroit*, 427–428; Dan T. Carter, *The Politics of Rage: George Wallace, the Origins of the New Conservatism, and the Transformation of American Politics* (New York: Simon & Schuster, 1995), chapter 13.

13. There are clear similarities between these post-1945 cultural expressions and the ideologies of "whiteness" that have been identified by historians of the nineteenth century, but these continuities (and discontinuities) have yet to be traced by scholars of the twentieth-century United States. The finest articulation of the "whiteness" thesis can be found in the work of David Roediger, in particular *The Wages of Whiteness: Race and the Making of the American Working Class* (New York: Verso, 1991) and *Towards the Abolition of Whiteness: Essays on Race, Politics, and Working Class History* (New York: Verso, 1994).

14. Waldo E. Martin Jr., *Brown v. Board of Education: A Brief History with Documents* (Boston: Bedford/St. Martin's, 1998), 173.

15. Martin Luther King Jr., "Letter from Birmingham Jail," in *Why We Can't Wait* (New York: Penguin, 1964), 78–79.

16. For instance, David J. Garrow in *Bearing the Cross: Martin Luther King, Jr., and the Southern Christian Leadership Conference* (New York: Morrow, 1986), 97–102, mentions the founding conference of the Citizenship Crusade but not the emphasis on moral reform in the sermons King delivered over the rest of the year. King's statement is in Juan Williams, *Eyes on the Prize: America's Civil Rights Years* (New York: Viking, 1987).

17. "Some Things We Must Do," December 5, 1957, in *The Papers of Martin Luther King, Jr.*, vol. 4, http://www.stanford.edu/group/King/publications (accessed 28 January 2003).

18. "Conquering Self-Centeredness," August 11, 1957, ibid.; Martin Luther King Jr., *Stride Toward Freedom: The Montgomery Story* (New York: Harper & Row, 1958);

"Advice for Living" columns from *Ebony* also in *The Papers of Martin Luther King, Jr.,* *Vol. 4.* King developed these themes in earlier sermons. See "Rediscovering Lost Values," February 28, 1954 (vol. 2) and "Facing the Challenge of a New Age," December 3, 1956 (vol. 3).

19. "Ella Baker: Organizing for Civil Rights," in Ellen Cantarow, Susan O'Malley, and Sharon Hartman Strom, *Moving the Mountain: Women Working for Social Change* (New York: Feminist Press, 1980), 52–93; quoted sections on 60–61, 92–93.

20. King, "Some Things We Must Do."

21. Tim Retzloff, "'Seer or Queer?' Postwar Fascination with Detroit's Prophet Jones," *GLQ: A Journal of Lesbian and Gay Studies* 8, no. 3 (2002): 271–296; Richard Newman, "Grace, Charles Emmanuel," www.anb.org/articles/08/08–02030.html, *American National Biography Online,* February 2000 (accessed 18 January 2003); "America's Richest Negro Minister," *Ebony,* January 1952, 17–23; "Farewell to Daddy Grace," *Ebony,* April 1960, 25–34; Lenwood G. Davis, *Daddy Grace: An Annotated Bibliography* (Westport, Conn.: Greenwood Press, 1992); *Jet,* 30 January 1958, 20–25; 23 January 1958, 18–19; 9 January 1958, 18–19.

22. Malcolm X, "The Old Negro and the New Negro," in *The End of White World Supremacy: Four Speeches by Malcolm X,* ed. Imam Benjamin Karim (New York: Arcade, 1971), 83; "The Time Has Come" in Williams, *Eyes on the Prize;* William L. Van DeBurg, *New Day in Babylon: The Black Power Movement and American Culture, 1965–1975* (Chicago: University of Chicago Press, 1992), 177, 215, 261.

23. Doug McAdam, *Freedom Summer* (New York: Oxford University Press, 1988), 48, 135, 139; "Citizenship Curriculum," *Radical Teacher* 40 (Fall 1991): 9–18; Sally Belfrage, *Freedom Summer* (Charlottesville: University Press of Virginia, 1965), 174–175.

24. David M. Kennedy, *Over Here: The First World War and American Society* (New York: Oxford University Press, 1980), 199–200; Gerald Robert Gill, "Afro-American Opposition to the United States' Wars of the Twentieth Century: Dissent, Discontent and Disinterest," Ph.D. diss., Howard University, 1985, 185–231; Timothy B. Tyson, "Robert F. Williams, 'Black Power,' and the Roots of the African American Freedom Struggle," *Journal of American History* 85 (September 1998): 544; King, "Letter from Birmingham Jail," 87. See also Timothy B. Tyson, *Radio Free Dixie: Robert F. Williams, and the Roots of Black Power* (Chapel Hill: University of North Carolina Press, 1999); Gail Williams O'Brien, *The Color of the Law: Race, Violence, and Justice in the Post-World War II South* (Chapel Hill: University of North Carolina Press, 1999), 7–107; Robin D. G. Kelley, *Race Rebels: Culture, Politics, and the Black Working Class* (New York: Free Press, 1994), 55–100. Evidence of violent resistance to the Birmingham police force and to white civilians can be found in abundance in the James Morgan Papers and Bull Connor Papers, Birmingham Public Library Archives Division, in particular in the following sections: "Disturbances on Birmingham Transit Busses," "Racial Incidents," "Resisting Arrest," and "Injuries Received by Officers."

25. Kelley, *Race Rebels,* 7, 21–22; Tera Hunter, *To 'Joy My Freedom: Southern Black Women's Lives and Labors After the Civil War* (Cambridge, Mass.: Harvard University Press, 1997); Kurt J. Beron, Helen V. Tauchen, and Ann Dryden Witte, "The Effect of Audits and Socioeconomic Variables on Compliance," in *Why People Pay Taxes: Tax*

Compliance and Enforcement, ed. Joel Slemrod (Ann Arbor: University of Michigan Press, 1992), 81–82; Carl P. Simon and Ann D. Witte, *Beating the System: The Underground Economy* (Boston: Auburn House, 1982), 285–294.

26. Daryl Cumber Dance, *Shuckin' and Jivin': Folklore from Contemporary Black Americans* (Bloomington: Indiana University Press, 1978), 224–237; Van DeBurg, *New Day in Babylon*, 225–226. On the history of "bad man" or "bad nigger" narratives, see Lawrence W. Levine, *Black Culture and Black Consciousness: Afro-American Folk Thought from Slavery to Freedom* (New York: Oxford University Press, 1977), 407–420; John W. Roberts, *From Trickster to Badman: The Black Folk Hero in Slavery and Freedom* (Philadelphia: University of Pennsylvania Press, 1989), 171–215. On comedy, see Mel Watkins, *On the Real Side: Laughing, Lying, and Signifying: The Underground Tradition of African-American Humor* (New York: Simon & Schuster, 1994); Melvin van Peebles, dir., *Sweet Sweetback's Baadasssss Song* (Cinemation Industries, 1971); Donald Bogle, *Blacks in American Films and Television: An Illustrated Encyclopedia* (New York: Fireside, 1988), 210–212; Gerald Martinez, Diana Martinez, and Andres Chavez, *What It Is . . . What It Was! The Black Film Explosion of the '70s in Words and Pictures* (New York: Hyperion/Miramax, 1998), 37, 58; Gordon Parks Jr., dir., *Superfly* (Warner Bros., 1972); Rickey Vincent, *Funk: The Music, The People, and the Rhythm of the One* (New York: St. Martin's/Griffin, 1996), 207.

27. Howell Raines, *My Soul Is Rested: Movement Days in the Deep South Remembered* (New York: Putnam, 1977), 93; William Chafe, "The End of One Struggle, the Beginning of Another," and comment by J. Mills Thornton III, in *The Civil Rights Movement in America*, ed. Charles W. Eagles (Jackson: University Press of Mississippi, 1986).

28. Brian Ward, *Just My Soul Responding: Rhythm and Blues, Black Consciousness, and Race Relations* (Berkeley: University of California Press, 1998).

29. Stanley Aronowitz, *False Promises: The Shaping of American Working Class Consciousness* (New York: McGraw-Hill, 1973), chapter 1.

17. WHAT PRICE VICTORY?

American Intellectuals and the Problem of Cold War Democracy

MICHAEL E. LATHAM

In February 1941, Henry Luce, the influential publisher of *Time* and *Life* magazines, wrote a famous editorial defining a new vision of American internationalism. Boldly titling his essay "The American Century," Luce argued that even as the Nazis dominated Europe and Japan controlled the Pacific, the United States could reshape the political order of the world. Isolationism, he insisted, was a bankrupt philosophy grounded in self-deception. As long as Americans failed to recognize their interdependence with the rest of the world and denied the reality of their country's preeminent power, they would merely stand on the sidelines of history while the forces of dictatorship, oppression, and tyranny gathered force. The moment had arrived, Luce argued, for the United States to realize that "the sickness of the world is also our sickness" and to enter the war. Only then could Americans "accept wholeheartedly our duty and our opportunity as the most powerful and vital nation in the world" and "exert upon the world the full impact of our influence, for such purposes as we see fit and by such means as we see fit."

But what should those "purposes" be? On this point Luce was emphatic. The "American Century," he declared, would require "a sharing with all peoples of our Bill of Rights, our Declaration of Independence, our Constitution, our magnificent industrial products, our technical skills." America's "love of freedom, feeling for the equality of opportunity, [and] tradition of self-reliance and independence" made it a haven for democracy, a "sanctuary of the ideals of civilization." "It now becomes our time," he concluded, "to be the powerhouse from which the ideals spread throughout the world and do their mysterious work of lifting the life of mankind from the level of beasts to what the Psalmist called a little lower than the angels." Where nineteenth-century intellectuals had defined America's westward expansion as a "manifest destiny," Luce now articulated a messianic, global calling.

Luce's rhetoric of democratic mission might have seemed overblown and unrealistic in 1941, but by war's end it would appear prophetic. In the Atlantic Charter, signed only months after Luce's article appeared, Franklin Delano Roosevelt and Winston Churchill promised that the Allies would fight for self-determination for all, freedom of the seas, freedom from fear and want, and an open economic system that would ensure equal access to the world's wealth. By 1945, with fascism destroyed, Japan and Germany under occupation, and the United States standing at the summit of economic and geopolitical strength, it did indeed seem that America might begin the work of creating a liberal, capitalist world order. Escalating tensions with the Soviet Union over the shape of postwar Europe soon made that project more difficult and dangerous, but the start of the Cold War only hardened American determination to reengineer the world of nations. Trying to appease the Nazis, prominent policymakers and intellectuals warned, had resulted in disaster. Only if the United States resisted Communist aggression with a resolute, global commitment to democratic institutions would another such crisis be averted.

Lurking beneath the rhetoric of mission and resolve, however, was a profound cultural ambivalence about the costs of that struggle to democracy itself. What happened, after all, when a democracy went to war? In 1941 Luce himself had noted "the fearful forecast—that some form of dictatorship is required to fight a modern war." American democracy, of course, survived World War II, but the wartime restriction of civil liberties, a radical increase in centralized economic planning, and the creation of a staggeringly massive military machine raised profound, troubling questions about the costs of the conflict. Was it now possible that a much longer, much broader Cold War against communism might create even greater risks for America's democratic culture and institutions?

For American intellectuals, the ironic possibility that fighting a "war for freedom" might imperil American democracy remained a constant source of tension, debate, and conflict after 1945. Offering different definitions of "national security" and its requirements, intellectuals responded to the crises of the Cold War with strongly divergent arguments about the way that America's global mission affected the nation. From the Truman Doctrine to the collapse of the Berlin Wall, the pendulum of debate swung from center to left to right as the Cold War continued to raise new questions about the problem of reconciling democratic values with the costs of continual mobilization. Cold War liberals defined democracy as a resilient "fighting faith" in the late 1940s, but the bloody stalemate in Korea, the abuses of McCarthyism, concerns about the "military-industrial complex," and disaster in Vietnam all provoked radical challenges by the late 1960s. They also sowed the seeds for a pivotal neoconservative resurgence in the 1970s and 1980s that gave popular understandings of Cold War victory a nostalgic, moralistic cast that even today constrains serious inquiry into this vital problem. As the United States embarks on yet another global struggle in the wake of September 11, 2001, the dilemma of democracy and security remains unresolved.

WAR, DEMOCRACY, AND AMERICAN AMBIVALENCE

The problem of fighting the evils of tyranny and militarism abroad without creating them at home took on a new urgency in the mid-twentieth century. Since the Revolution, American intellectuals had expressed a distrust of large standing armies that might drain precious resources from other social goods, constrain economic growth, and dangerously concentrate extralegal power. Hoping to preserve their fragile republican experiment from the cycles of tyranny that plagued European history, early American political leaders maintained only a small military. Americans, they claimed, would be motivated for battle only by their ideals. Instead of compulsory drafts and taxes, Americans were expected to make voluntary contributions. Fears about the effects of war on democratic institutions were seemingly confirmed during the Civil War, when huge conscript armies exhausted the nation's human and economic resources and government subverted civil liberties.

American intellectuals were alarmed by the outbreak of war in Europe in 1914. The advent of poison gas, machine guns, trench warfare, and a global struggle that mobilized industry, science, education, food, and public opinion proved still more disconcerting. President Woodrow Wilson, himself an intellectual, argued that the war would make the world safe for democracy through a new order of collective security, free trade, and a League of Nations. Yet both the European powers and the U.S. Senate rejected that vision. Unable to claim a moral victory, Americans reflected uneasily on the fact that their wartime government centralized production, enforced new sedition and surveillance laws, repressed left-wing dissenters, and finally plunged into a "Red Scare" that resulted in thousands of arrests and deportations. Leaders who favored war suggested that the conflict would produce social benefits, new investments, technologies, medicines, and even new rights for women and black war workers. But many American intellectuals remained skeptical and pessimistic. As the critical essayist Randolph Bourne asked,

"If the war is too strong for you to prevent, how is it going to be weak enough for you to control and mould to your liberal purposes?"

World War II raised even more profound and disturbing questions. Throughout the 1930s most of the public and much of the Congress remained determined that the United States should avoid being drawn into yet another destructive, futile foreign conflict. Pearl Harbor swept away that commitment to neutrality, but liberals still worried about the effects of depression and war on American social life. Even in the United States, the Great Depression had given rise to demagogic figures such as Huey Long and Father Charles Coughlin. With their eyes on the German and Italian examples, many American intellectuals wondered if economic desperation and nationalistic appeals might also create a kind of homegrown fascism. The war against the Germans and the Japanese, commentators eventually agreed, was indeed necessary. But the problems of fighting against dictatorships without emulating their militarism and regimentation remained deeply perplexing.

The war also produced stunning domestic effects. Mobilization created seventeen million new American jobs and ultimately ended the lingering effects of the Depression, but the war also required a dramatic expansion of the state bureaucracy and a sharp limitation of personal freedoms. The federal budget rose from $9 billion in 1940 to $98 billion in 1945, and expenditures contributed strongly to a concentration of power among the largest industrial producers. A new War Production Board diverted supplies from civilian consumption to military markets, the Office of Price Administration enforced rationing and price controls, and a National War Labor Board mediated industrial disputes to create the most efficient war machine possible. By 1945 the American tax bill was nearly twenty times higher than it had been in 1940. Government censors opened and examined all overseas mail, instructed publishers and broadcasters to suppress information that might reveal war plans, and kept photos of American war dead out of newspapers until 1943. Women and blacks did find new work opportunities, but in many areas of American life the lines of racial and gender inequality hardened. African Americans, for example, were drafted into the army and fought in rigidly segregated units against the Nazi regime and its ideology of Aryan supremacy. Finally, and, most dramatically, 112,000 Japanese Americans, two-thirds of them native-born citizens, were removed from the West Coast and placed in internment camps for the duration of the war.

Roosevelt and his advisors, moreover, defined the war's significance in revolutionary terms. Shocked by Hitler's ability to intimidate the Allies and by his skillful use of propaganda, the president demanded a comprehensive response. "The world has grown so small and weapons of attack so swift," he argued, that "events of thunderous import have moved with lightning speed." From 1941 through the entire Cold War period, American policymakers would think less in terms of the static, quantifiable, material needs of "defense" and more in terms of the open-ended, ever-changing challenges of "security." Rejecting forever the idea that the United States might remain safe from foreign danger, insulated by massive oceans, they now envisioned a world of interdependence, expanded commitment, and heightened responsibility. Rather than attempting to preserve an order based on a balance of power, they began an ideological struggle over the direction of global civilization itself. How, they asked, could the United States create an international environment in which its values and institutions were most likely to spread and grow?

DEMOCRACY AS A "FIGHTING FAITH"

At the outset of the Cold War, therefore, Americans placed democracy at the heart of the matter. Containing the Soviets, Harry Truman declared in 1947, was not merely a question of military force. It was instead a liberal, democratic calling against a brutal, state-directed order. "At the present moment in world history," the president explained, "every nation must choose between alternative ways of life. . . . One way of life is based upon the will of the majority, and is distinguished by free institutions, representative government, free elections, guarantees of individual liberty, freedom of speech and religion, and freedom from political oppression. The second way of life is based upon the will of a minority forcibly imposed upon the majority. It relies upon terror and oppression, a controlled press and radio, fixed elections, and the suppression of personal freedoms." The Truman Doctrine cut the world in two and left no middle ground for nonalignment or indigenously defined revolution. It also gave the American definition of the Cold War a sharp moral clarity and unlimited scope. Final victory in a contest between two such mutually exclusive social orders, after all, would come only when one side abandoned its ideology altogether.

Cast in those terms, the Cold War became a kind of "long emergency," a crisis period in which the demands of an ever-expanding quest for "national security" clashed with traditional expectations about personal liberties and social freedoms. The previous world wars might be written off as aberrations, brief windows in time during which normal practices were temporarily suspended. The Cold War, however, opened a new set of problems for American intellectuals. If the peace that America had once enjoyed were now to be indefinitely deferred by a titanic struggle of uncertain duration and seemingly limitless range, what would become of America's own institutions? How would the costs of promoting democracy abroad be reconciled with the permanent damage war might do to democracy at home? In the early years of the Cold War, from 1947 to 1949, these questions would generate an intense debate between those seeking an alternative to the Cold War's course and those committed to its fundamental objectives. By 1950, however, the range of acceptable dissent would narrow to the point that even to question the costs of a war for democracy was to risk being considered naive at best and seditious or traitorous at worst.

Henry A. Wallace stands out among the early critics of the Cold War's logic. The son of an Iowa farm family long active in rural publishing and agricultural politics, Wallace served as Roosevelt's secretary of agriculture from 1933 to 1940 and as vice president from 1941 to 1945 before becoming the secretary of commerce under Truman. He was also a sharp, perceptive social thinker, essayist, and public speaker. Where Henry Luce had advocated the "American Century," Wallace used a 1942 speech to call for the "Century of the Common Man." Emphasizing a process in which America would assist the world but not attempt to stand above it, Wallace envisioned a kind of international New Deal in which modern technology would improve nutritional standards, promote industrial development, and enable poor nations to share in global prosperity.

He also became an outspoken dissenter against American Cold War policy. In the summer of 1946, troubled by the anti-Soviet hard line gaining momentum in the Truman White House, Wallace wrote a long letter to the president. Soviet policies that installed pro-Russian regimes in Eastern Europe, he argued, reflected less an aggressive determination to spread communism wherever possible than a response to fears and suspicions generated by the experience of invasion, thirty years of Western hostility, and the increasing American military budget. The American monopoly on the atomic bomb and the development of a ring of overseas bases around the USSR, he emphasized, only increased Soviet anxiety. In September 1946, Wallace made those views public at a massive political rally held at Madison Square Garden. Explicitly critical of both the American military buildup and the Soviet "suppression of basic liberties," Wallace rejected the view that Russian communism and American free enterprise could not coexist peacefully and insisted that a "get tough" policy toward the Soviets would only make peace impossible. Though Truman had reviewed the speech in advance, Wallace's dissent alienated other administration officials, and within days the president demanded his resignation.

Cast out of the government, Wallace began to give free rein to his progressive fears and quickly addressed the contradictions of a war to save democracy. Alarmed by the Truman Doctrine's stridency, Wallace worried that the administration was trying to frighten the American public into making the "down payment" on what would become an endless train of expenditures. In a climate of anticommunist panic, he thought, America might edge ever closer to the "garrison state" in which all public life was subordinated to security demands. Those concerns seemed validated when the administration created a Federal Employee Loyalty Program to investigate the political activity of all employees.

A state with such expanded powers, unlimited by any guidelines to determine the basis on which "loyalty" should be evaluated, Wallace thought, would certainly violate crucial civil liberties. Administration proposals for universal military service requirements, the creation of a new, centralized department of defense, and the resurrection of the draft all added to his fears that an ill-advised Cold War would quickly reduce American citizens to "gears in the war machine."

Wallace's dissent, however, was quickly marginalized by a new intellectual and political consensus, that of Cold War liberalism. Where Wallace stressed the dangers of an unlimited anti-Soviet struggle to American institutions, Cold War liberals such as Harvard historian Arthur M. Schlesinger Jr. and Protestant theologian Reinhold Niebuhr emphasized both the threatening nature of communism and the resilience of America's democratic heritage. Wallace, they argued, had failed to learn the "lessons of Munich." To seek an accommodation with the Russians, they insisted, was to repeat the mistake of appeasing the Nazis. The Truman Doctrine, Schlesinger claimed in *The Vital Center* (1949), was an essential "policy of locking doors against Soviet aggression," not a "blank check" for an unlimited U.S. government crusade. Because Wallace allowed Communist Party members to join his third-party Progressive campaign for the presidency in 1948, Schlesinger also attacked him as a dupe, a "well-intentioned, wooly minded, increasingly embittered man" who was "made to order for Communist exploitation" and supported by "all friends of Soviet totalitarianism." Men like Wallace, Cold War liberals declared, were guilty of a kind of blind utopianism that led them to underestimate the degree to which communism, like Nazism before it, threatened the world. In Niebuhr's more theological expression, they were the naive "children of light," thinkers whose "too consistent optimism in regard to man's ability and inclination to grant justice to his fellows obscures the perils of chaos" unleashed by the ruthless, self-interested "children of darkness."

The greatest danger to democracy, therefore, lay not in the costs of the Cold War but in a lack of resolution to fight it. Totalitarianism preyed on the anxious, alienated, and lonely masses of a free society. As Schlesinger warned, it subversively built on their "frustrations and cravings" to provide "a structure of belief, men to worship and men to hate and rites which guarantee salvation." The challenge for the United States, he insisted, was to preserve its liberties against totalitarianism of either the left or the right, to "make democracy a fighting faith." Looking back into American history, Cold War liberals emphasized the continuity of the country's democratic inheritance, the progressive role of voluntary associations, and a state that from the Jacksonian era through the New Deal had protected the security and welfare of its citizens. Where dissenters like Wallace considered the Cold War a new and troubling era in which previous restraints on state power might be cast aside to the detriment of democracy, Cold War liberals insisted that the anticommunist challenge itself could revitalize a sense of popular commitment and purpose. "Out of the effort, out of the struggle alone," Schlesinger averred, "can come the high courage and faith which will preserve freedom."

By the end of the 1940s, Cold War liberalism dominated American political culture. When Wallace ran for the presidency as a third-party Progressive candidate in 1948, he suffered a crushing defeat, receiving only slightly more than one million votes, a mere 2.4 percent of the national total. Arguments about the dangers of Communist aggression and America's moral responsibility to spread and defend liberal institutions around the world overwhelmed those of the critics. The United States, in this emerging consensus view, could have it all. It could wage the Cold War to fend off totalitarianism abroad while steadily extending the New Deal's economic and political reforms at home. Before long, however, Americans would discover that those two objectives were increasingly difficult to reconcile.

THE SHOOTING WAR AT HOME AND ABROAD

As the Cold War became hot and the anticommunist struggle collapsed the boundaries between the foreign and the domestic, fears about the dilemma of a democracy at war gained much greater weight. In 1949, detonation of a Soviet atomic bomb and the success of the Chinese Revolution raised popular anxiety and provided ammunition for Truman's Republican opponents. How was it, conservatives asked, that the Russians managed to catch up to the American technological lead so quickly? Why was it, they questioned, that the United States had "lost" the world's most populous country to the Communists? In Korea, Kim Il Sung's southward invasion provoked a strong American response in 1950. Here, too, victory proved elusive. While U.S. and United Nations troops managed to push the North Koreans back over the thirty-eighth parallel, Chinese entry into the war soon produced a bloody stalemate. To make matters worse, General Douglas MacArthur publicly challenged the president's leadership by rejecting the possibility of negotiations and ridiculing Truman's preference for a limited war. In the end, the Korean War cost 33,000 American lives and still left the two sides standing along virtually the same line of original division. It also contributed to a nearly fourfold increase in defense expenditures, from $13 billion in 1949 to $50 billion in 1952. By 1953, moreover, national security and military costs, including benefits for veterans and payments on the war-related national debt, accounted for more than 85 percent of the federal budget and nearly all the increases in government spending since the war started.

In that context, McCarthyism quickly effaced the lines drawn between the anticommunist crusade and the protection of domestic freedoms. In a Cold War defined fundamentally as a question of ideology and belief, it became all too easy for Senator Joseph McCarthy (R-Wis.) to lead a sensational search for subversive thought or conspiratorial action. While McCarthy and Richard Nixon, then a Republican congressman from California, attacked the State Department, accusing its personnel of disloyalty and treason, a much wider assault began as conservatives linked America's World War II alliance with the Soviets to the New Deal and liberalism itself. Support for labor unions, civil rights legislation, and federal regulation of the economy, they insisted, were "socialist" measures that cut against the grain of "American" support for free enterprise and individualism. Even Howard McGrath, Truman's attorney general, gave voice to the popular understanding that Communists in America were "everywhere—in factories, offices, butcher stores, on street corners, in private businesses. And each carries in himself the death of our society."

In that climate of fear a damaging American inquisition began to move through both formal, legal means as well as informal, unofficial channels. The House Un-American Activities Committee interrogated suspected subversives from Hollywood filmmakers to Ivy League academics, insisting that those subpoenaed testify about their own political histories as well as those of their associates. Those mechanisms of public exposure and the suspicions aroused by invoking the Fifth Amendment protection against self-incrimination damaged countless careers. Yet perhaps far more widespread were the less obvious yet still punishing informal means of blacklisting and private economic sanctions. In response to warnings from the Federal Bureau of Investigation and congressional staff, corporations, newspapers, and businesses across the country fired thousands of employees for their politics. The "chilling effect" of accusation and prosecution also fostered a rigorous self-censorship in university life and tightly restricted intellectual freedom. In 1949, Yale's president, Charles Seymour, declared, "there will be no witch hunts at Yale because there will be no witches."

Under intense scrutiny and political pressure, most of the country's liberal institutions and intellectuals produced only weak, ambivalent responses. Liberal members of Congress defended themselves by stressing their own anticommunism, and organizations such as the American Civil Liberties Union submitted "friend of the court briefs" but typically avoided direct engagement in highly publicized trials. The American Association of University Professors and other professional groups also remained largely silent. A few individuals dared to dissent against the wholesale firing of faculty with Communist Party affiliations. Harold Taylor, the president of Sarah Lawrence College, distinguished between disloyal actions and critical ideas, arguing that the first should be punished but the second protected. As he warned, "if we begin excluding Communists, we will end by excluding anyone who says anything provocative, unorthodox, or interesting." Through the mid-1950s, however, such voices were few.

Far more influential and widely accepted were the arguments made by intellectuals such as New York University political philosopher Sidney Hook. A critic of capitalism who had supported Communist political candidates in the early 1930s, Hook came to resent the party's rigid orthodoxy and in 1934 denounced Stalin's regime for creating a ruthless dictatorship over the working class. In 1950, with the American writer James T. Ferrell and European intellectuals Arthur Koestler, Michael Polanyi, and Raymond Aron, he also founded the Congress for Cultural Freedom, a Central Intelligence Agency (CIA)–supported group determined to convince the liberal left to abandon its pro-Russian sympathies. Because he considered the Cold War a struggle to defend freedom against repression, Hook was particularly appalled by those intellectuals who had attacked Nazism in the 1930s but now failed to condemn the brutality of Soviet totalitarianism.

In a series of articles first published in the *New York Times Magazine* and later in a book titled *Heresy, Yes, Conspiracy, No* (1952), Hook also set forth an argument explaining why liberals did not need to protect the civil liberties of Communists. Hook agreed with dissenters that the excesses of McCarthyism could damage democracy, but he was equally convinced that "our experience brings home to us the necessity of sacrificing some particular freedom" to preserve others. The "free market of ideas," he argued, was essential for democracy to function, but that belief itself was based on two essential "presuppositions": the intellectual "free market" might be controlled whenever its "likely effects constitute a clear and present danger to public peace or the security of the country" and "the competition will be honestly and openly conducted." The problem with the Communists was that their activities threatened to "make intelligent choice impossible." Liberals, Hook insisted, should therefore make a crucial distinction between "heresy," the open expression of unpopular and critical ideas, and "conspiracy," a "secret or underground movement which seeks to attain its ends not by normal political or educational process but by playing outside the rules of the game." Heretics expressed their views responsibly, claimed ownership of them, and accepted the price of social and political ostracism. Their function, moreover, was essential to productive debate. Conspirators, however, relied on "secrecy, anonymity, the use of false labels, and the calculated lie." They sought to "win by chicanery what cannot be fairly won in the process of free discussion." Dissenting ideas, even Communist ones, should be tolerated. But individuals who joined or supported a movement that had no respect for the institutions of freedom were not entitled to its protections. Liberals, therefore, had to be "realistic," not merely "ritualistic." They could not simply pass laws and expect

Communist Party members to abide by them. They also had to defend the free market of ideas by "cleaning their own house" and removing Communists from positions of authority in unions, schools, universities, and the government.

Arguments like Hook's sought to construct boundaries for the anticommunist campaign, to draw the line between urgent, vital investigation and dangerous, damaging excess. By the late 1950s, however, after McCarthy himself was discredited and the waves of repression began to recede, intellectuals confronted a broader and equally divisive set of questions. What had caused McCarthyism? What did that movement's powerful emergence reveal about the vitality of American democracy? Had American institutions weathered the dangers of reaction and radicalism well? Or did McCarthyism in fact signify that the costs of the Cold War were even higher than they appeared?

Though in some cases McCarthyism certainly was a right-wing political tactic, a tool Republicans used to assault the New Deal and discredit Democrats, intellectuals still faced the task of accounting for the high degree of popular support for the relentless anticommunist purge. One explanation, amplified by a broad cohort of American sociologists, historians, and political scientists, argued that McCarthyism was fundamentally a form of populist revolt, the expression of a sense of dispossession and "status anxiety" on the part of rural Americans. McCarthy's supporters, according to Daniel Bell, Edward Shils, Richard Hofstadter, and other intellectuals, were individuals trying to preserve their standing in a rapidly disappearing small-town America. They were citizens cast aside by a modernity they could not control, people alienated by the power of large collectives like labor unions, corporations, banking conglomerates, and the ever-expanding federal government. When McCarthy attacked Alger Hiss as a pinstriped, Harvard-trained, worldly representative of the Eastern corporate elite and emphasized the betrayal of honest, hardworking ordinary Americans by those born with every privilege, these scholars thought they recognized a much older strain in American public life. McCarthyism, they suggested, was not so much a reflection of the domestic dynamics of the Cold War as the resurgence of an irrational, emotional, paranoid style of politics that dated back to the Populists of the 1890s. Like other dissenters, these intellectuals observed, the McCarthyites had fallen prey to sweeping, moralistic appeals, resorted to elaborate conspiracy theories, and rejected the norms of bargaining, compromise, and "rational" discourse. According to this school of thought, the crucial lesson to be learned was not that an unlimited, ideologically framed war might destroy democratic values. The real danger lay in an excess of democracy itself, in a political system in which radical demagogues of the right or left might mobilize an irrational mass to jeopardize the essential consensus and stability required for educated, responsible elites to govern.

Other thinkers, more willing to believe that popular protest could produce meaningful and necessary reform, rejected that argument's conservative cast. Columbia University sociologist C. Wright Mills, for example, argued that American society suffered from an enervated and diminished democracy, not an excessive one. Interested in the way that capitalism had changed both labor patterns and class structures within the United States, Mills emerged as an important social critic and dissenter with *The Power Elite* (1956). An overlapping cohort drawn from the same educational and social circles, Mills argued, had increasingly centralized power in American life. Across corporate, military, and government sectors, a small elite made most crucial decisions virtually immune from public accountability or review. The Cold War, moreover, had intensified that concentration. "For the first time in American history," Mills observed, "men in authority are talking about an 'emergency' without a foreseeable end" and "war or a high state of war preparedness is felt to be the normal and seemingly permanent condition of the United States." From the Pentagon to Wall Street to the White House, Mills argued, an influential, interlocking directorate claimed expert authority, dominated channels of public communication, and presided over a mobilization of the entire society. Like the liberals he challenged, Mills believed that "the free ebb and flow of discussion" was crucial to the survival of democratic governance. Yet where Hook recommended a pragmatic distinction between heresy and conspiracy, while thinkers such as Bell and Hofstadter warned about the problem of demagoguery, Mills identified a deeper, structural flaw. The Cold War and the concentration of power it fostered, he argued, accelerated the decline of genuine public debate. In the absence of "autonomous organizations connecting the lower and middle levels of power with the top levels of decision," democracy became an empty form. In the United States, the ideal of a "public" in which individuals from a wide range of social classes participated in meaningful political discussion and planning had been lost. In its place stood a "mass," an "abstract collection of individuals" kept ignorant by the popular media and unable to find independent channels through which they might transform their opinions into action. Liberals committed to real democracy, Mills insisted, would have to do more than rhetorically celebrate American civil liberties; they would have to use those liberties to challenge the existing order, create new institutions, and reverse the postwar trend.

In the late 1950s, that pessimistic view of American democracy gained greater credence. Though they did not link their analyses directly to the Cold War's effects, David Riesman, William Whyte, and Paul Goodman, and other cultural critics made arguments that reinforced Mills's conclusions. American society, they agreed, had become increasingly dominated by a culture of conformity and aversion to risk. Once "inner-directed" by personal values, goals, and hopes, Americans had become "other-directed," vulnerable to the expectations of an abundant, affluent society that put a premium on wealth and security but denied genuine opportunities for self-realization and fulfillment. Americans "got ahead by getting along" and grew up as hollow, corporate "organization men," efficient and disciplined, yet lacking creativity, determination, and the capacity for free, independent thought. By early 1961, even Dwight David Eisenhower, the aged war hero and outgoing Republican president, delivered a televised farewell address that echoed Mills. Rather than elaborate on the evils of Soviet policy, Eisenhower warned Americans about the "economic, political, even spiritual" influence of a "military-industrial complex" that threatened to warp the formation of public policy and dominate the nation's culture. Just what kind of democracy was it, after all, that the United States promised to defend against Communist aggression and promote throughout the world?

GLOBAL REVOLUTION AND RADICAL CRITIQUE

John F. Kennedy's inaugural address betrayed none of the ambivalence of Eisenhower's farewell. While the elderly general sat behind him, wrapped in a heavy coat against the January chill, Kennedy stridently declared his country's resolve: "Let every nation know, whether it wishes us well or ill, that we shall pay any price, bear any burden, meet any hardship, support any friend, oppose any foe, to assure the survival and success of liberty." The United States, he vowed, would win the "long twilight struggle" at all costs. During the 1960s, however, the Cold War became an increasingly global affair as old European empires broke up, "new states" emerged, and revolutionary nationalism gained ground. In Cuba, the Dominican Republic, the Congo, Laos, and above all, Vietnam, the Kennedy and Johnson administrations suddenly faced the real limits of America's power to refashion the world. Obsessed with the preservation of American "credibility" and the demonstrations of fortitude deemed necessary to deter further Communist challenges, the U.S. government sought to derail "wars of national liberation" with a combination of military force and social engineering. American intellectuals also found themselves deeply divided over that project. While some held fast to the liberal faith and placed themselves directly in the service of the state, dissenters argued that the nation was neither spreading democracy abroad nor expanding it at home. To join the Cold War crusade and work within its boundaries, they charged, was to abandon one's critical sensitivity and intellectual responsibilities. Vietnam, like McCarthyism, once more tore down the walls dividing foreign war and domestic society. This time, however, the damage was so great that liberalism never fully recovered.

McGeorge Bundy, Kennedy's national security adviser, had little doubt about the normative role of intellectuals in the Cold War struggle. A professor of government who became dean of the faculty at Harvard before moving to the White House, Bundy welcomed the "high measure of interpenetration between universities and the intelligence-gathering agencies of the United States." Rejecting the model of the detached, independent scholar, he insisted that "it is wrong to suppose that the university is usefully disconnected from this society. I think rather that there is gain for both the political world and the academy from an intensified process of engagement and of choosing sides in the battle." Since World War II, American universities had increasingly aligned themselves in just the way Bundy advocated. While the country's academic leaders often collaborated with or at least refused to challenge McCarthyist inquiries, a massive flow of government funding pushed university research toward the demands of foreign policy. In addition to the resources that went into nuclear weapons research, the social science disciplines also received significant support for "policy relevant" projects. To control Communist expansion, policymakers and academics agreed, the United States would need to produce knowledge about Soviet strategy as well as the economies, political structures, and social systems of the "developing areas."

The result was a process of collaboration in which intellectuals and social scientists helped formulate an American program to channel the world's nationalist revolutions into liberal, capitalist, democratic directions. At Harvard, for example, the Carnegie Corporation and the CIA started the Russian Research Center, an institution staffed by economists, sociologists, and political scientists that sent its studies of the Soviet Union directly to the federal government well before they appeared in declassified, published form. Throughout the 1950s, the Ford Foundation also poured millions of dollars into behavioral science projects designed to identify ways that the United States could use the tools of social psychology and anthropology to foster democracy and promote stability abroad. After the Soviets launched the Sputnik satellite in 1957, the National Defense Education Act also increased federal government support for new area studies programs and language training. Committed to the Cold War, many intellectuals believed that collaboration with the state would allow knowledge and power to serve each other. Talcott Parsons, chair of Harvard's Department of Social Relations and one of the country's most prominent scholars, expected that the social sciences would ultimately create a "knowledge of human relations that can serve as the basis of a rational engineering control." Once that happened, he expected, the United States would be in a far better position to dictate the outcome of a global Cold War.

Impressed by their claims and eager to find new ways to combat the forces of revolution in decolonizing areas, the Kennedy and Johnson administrations recruited ambitious social scientists and placed them in positions of authority. Harvard economist Lincoln Gordon became an adviser on Latin

American affairs and the U.S. ambassador to Brazil. MIT political scientist Lucian Pye worked as a consultant for the U.S. Agency for International Development. Stanford University development expert Eugene Staley headed a mission to South Vietnam, and University of Michigan professor Samuel P. Hayes played an instrumental role in planning the Peace Corps. The most influential figure among that cohort, MIT economist Walt Rostow, became the chair of policy planning in Kennedy's state department and national security adviser in the Johnson White House.

Together those social scientists set about putting an abstract, intellectual theory of "modernization" into concrete political practice. Emphasizing the idea that all societies moved along a common, linear path from "tradition" to "modernity," they defined development as a universal process. Previously isolated, rural worlds governed by ancient, static cultures, these scholars argued, were suddenly destabilized and disoriented by contact with the technologies, affluence, and organizations of the more advanced world. Where values based in family, locality, and religion no longer provided security, people eagerly sought ways to become "modern," to catch up with the affluent, highly organized societies that they both feared and admired. The result was a "revolution of rising expectations" throughout Africa, Asia, and Latin America as newly independent peoples sought ways to overthrow colonial legacies and attain prosperity.

Fit into the context of the Cold War, modernization seemed to represent both danger and opportunity. Impatient, desperate populations, Kennedy and Johnson planners feared, might turn to Soviet models as a solution to their problems. Communist agents and advisers, they worried, might prey upon the anxieties and aspirations of the world's ambitious poor, providing them a vision of progress based on centralized planning and state control. Yet perhaps the United States might be able to compete more effectively on this plane. Foreign aid, development assistance, educational programs, and technical advising, Rostow and other intellectuals argued, could accelerate the passage of traditional societies through the "stages of growth." They could channel the revolutionary energy and expectations of those societies through a difficult transition toward a liberal, capitalist "takeoff" before the Communists could lead them astray. In that appealing vision, America was the world's most "modern" nation, the democratic, capitalist endpoint on the developmental scale. Its past, moreover, was a blueprint for the developing world's future. Widely disseminated throughout the Kennedy and Johnson administrations, the idea of modernization and its optimistic assessment about the possible results of American "nation building" efforts shaped many policy initiatives. Agricultural assistance to India, funding for Latin American development programs, and community planning agencies in Africa, for example, were all supported by concepts of modernization.

More than anywhere else, however, Vietnam loomed as the essential "test case" of America's ability to foster "democratic development" in opposition to radical nationalism. To allow communism to triumph in Vietnam, U.S. policy-makers feared, would do immeasurable damage to American credibility. It would embolden revolutionaries around the world, encourage Soviet aggression, and knock down the first in a long chain of revolutionary dominoes. Between 1955 and 1961, the United States poured more than $1 billion into economic and military aid for South Vietnam. American policymakers also constantly referred to Premier Ngo Dinh Diem's government as the best hope for a liberal, noncommunist solution. The challenge, they insisted, would be to win the "hearts and minds" of the Vietnamese people and demonstrate the potential for democratic, capitalist progress.

Throughout the 1960s, however, the gap between the rhetoric of democratic development and the realities of brutal, indiscriminate warfare became all too obvious. Though supporters of the war effort continued to refer to Diem as "the Winston Churchill of Southeast Asia," his regime's persecution of the Buddhists and ruthless suppression of all dissent raised troubling questions. American-sponsored counterinsurgency plans, moreover, linked the language of "nation building" to escalating violence. When they forced Vietnamese peasants to move from their ancestral lands into concentrated "strategic hamlets," Diem and his American supporters talked about providing medical care, education, and the chance to participate in democratic decision making at the local level. Yet it became all too clear that hamlet watchtowers faced in as well as out, and that the rings of bamboo stakes and barbed wire were designed to promote surveillance and social control as much as they were intended to protect peasants from Viet Cong violence. Intensified bombing also meant that the world outside the realm of rigid government control became a free-fire zone. When the Johnson administration decided to deploy American combat troops in 1965 and the American public began to watch the war on the nightly news, questions about the continued repression in South Vietnam and the ultimate purposes of the struggle quickly grew.

Among American intellectuals, the war's escalation triggered an especially intense debate about personal complicity and responsibility. Harvard political scientist Samuel Huntington, for one, had little doubt about the moral purpose of the war and its goals. In a 1968 article published in the journal *Foreign Affairs*, he insisted that the violence of the war itself might become a tool for essentially benevolent social engineering. "Societies," he explained, "are susceptible to revolution only at particular stages in their development." The effective response to the "war of national liberation" in Vietnam would be "forced-draft urbanization and modernization which rapidly brings the country in question out of the phase in which a rural revolutionary movement can hope to generate sufficient strength to come to power." Deploying combat troops and continually intensifying the war, Huntington argued, would do more than kill the enemy. It would also transform Vietnamese society. Driving refugees into government-controlled cities, it would expose them to the material advantages to be found in thriving, capitalist metropolitan centers and accelerate the development of modern values, loyalties, and ties between South Vietnam and its citizens. Where Air Force General Curtis LeMay had recommended that the United States bomb the Vietnamese "into the Stone Age," Huntington implied that America might bomb them into the future.

Members of the intellectual "New Left," however, launched a devastating attack on that logic. Interested in the way that power flowed through a wide range of institutions, they critically analyzed the way that the state exerted its control to manufacture public approval and constrain critical discourse. In addition to pointing out the absence of democratic reform in the dictatorial South Vietnamese government, they also challenged the way that liberals had framed intellectual responsibility itself. As historian Christopher Lasch argued in 1967, during the previous decade "American intellectuals, on a scale that is only now beginning to be understood, lent themselves . . . to purposes having nothing to do with the values they professed—purposes, indeed, that were diametrically opposed to them." Though claiming to act in the name of democracy, Cold War liberals wound up supporting and even designing government policies that only deepened violence and repression. MIT linguist Noam Chomsky, one of the most articulate critics of the war, went even further. Where Lasch described a failure of good intentions, Chomsky argued that by allowing themselves to become complicit with the power structure, intellectuals had willingly forfeited all ability to criticize it. Intellectuals, he explained, had a crucial function in society. Only they possessed the relative leisure, access to information, and training "to expose the lies of governments, to analyze actions according to their causes and motives and often hidden intentions." To conduct war-related research, to allow the dictates of the government to take precedence over the questions of one's own discipline and curiosity, Chomsky claimed, was to embrace a kind of moral blindness. Those who served the state at war in Vietnam abandoned a responsibility to "seek the truth hidden behind the veil of distortion and misrepresentation, ideology, and class interest through which the events of current history are presented to us."

Thousands of antiwar faculty and students agreed with those conclusions, and on campuses across America, dissenters identified the Vietnam War as a sign that the "garrison state" had indeed arrived. As early as their 1962 Port Huron Statement, Tom Hayden and his young colleagues in the Students for a Democratic Society (SDS) had lamented the "powerful congruence of interest and structure among military and business elites which affects so much of our development and destiny." In its place they proposed a broad-based "participatory democracy" that would mobilize public groups and bring citizens "out of isolation and into community." Inspired by the activism of the civil rights movement and appalled by the brutality of the war, they also began to discern a fundamental sickness at the core of American society itself. As SDS president Paul Potter asked in 1965, "What kind of a system is it that justifies the United States or any country seizing the destinies of the Vietnamese people and using them callously for its own purpose? What kind of a system is it that disenfranchises people in the South, leaves millions upon millions of people throughout the country impoverished . . . that consistently puts material values before human values—and still persists in calling itself free and still persists in finding itself fit to police the world?"

Where liberals had insisted that fighting a Cold War for democracy could proceed hand in hand with the expansion of progressive social reform at home, radical intellectuals, students, and activists now attacked that argument directly. The war in Vietnam had promoted brutally repressive regimes and drained millions of dollars from the "War on Poverty" that Lyndon Johnson had also promised to wage. Funding that could have been used to promote better schools, expanded health care, job training, and low-income housing poured into an increasingly bloody and seemingly endless struggle in Southeast Asia. Because of college and graduate school deferments, the draft also discriminated against black and working-class Americans, leading some of the country's most prominent liberal figures to reject the rationale of the Cold War consensus. "I could never again raise my voice against the violence of the oppressed in the ghetto," Martin Luther King declared in 1967, "without having first spoken out clearly to the greatest purveyor of violence in the world today—my own government. . . . This war is a blasphemy against all that America stands for."

By the end of the 1960s, the debate over Vietnam had helped to destroy the liberal "vital center." A decade earlier liberals had struggled to define their position on McCarthyism, to reconcile their anticommunist convictions with the obvious violation of democratic civil liberties. The war in Vietnam, however, presented a moral dilemma on which there was precious little middle ground. Attacked by an articulate left, liberals were forced to choose between holding fast to the Cold War's imperatives or, alternatively, recognizing the degree to which "paying any price" in the crusade against communism had become fundamentally irreconcilable with the promotion of democracy at home and abroad. As the American death toll mounted and demonstrations erupted across campuses and city centers, liberals became bitterly divided. Radical critiques succeeded in exposing the inherent contradictions between a limitless Cold

War, the values of self-determination abroad, and progressive reform at home. In sweeping away the established consensus, they also, ironically, contributed to a powerful neoconservative response.

NEOCONSERVATISM AND COLD WAR "VICTORY"

The crisis of the late 1960s forced liberal intellectuals to reassess their convictions and created a deep split within their ranks. Many of them found themselves turning against the war in Vietnam and calling for the United States to play a more collaborative, less dominant role in the world. Among them, Harvard professor Stanley Hoffman, for example, hoped that the United States might stabilize the international economy through multilateral institutions, promote regional peacekeeping, manage scarce resources, and address the pressing problem of global population growth. The world, these chastened liberals suggested, was becoming less bipolar as the vibrant economies of Eastern Asia and Western Europe gathered strength. It was time, they argued, for the United States to jettison its old Cold War assumptions, downplay the urgency of containment, and seek ways to build a new, cooperative order amid ideological diversity.

Others, however, rejected those prescriptions as hopelessly muddled and naively utopian. Troubled by the radicalism that erupted on campuses in the late 1960s, they resented what they considered the intolerant, self-righteous attitude of the left-wing critics and instead returned to the doctrines of Cold War liberalism first expressed in the late 1940s. For thinkers like Irving Kristol, Norman Podhoretz, and Nathan Glazer, the old verities still stood and ideology still mattered. According to them, America's mission in the world was a decidedly democratic one. Fulfilling it meant, above all, that the United States continue its campaign against the Communists abroad as well as the antiliberal, irrational demonstrators at home. Initially labeled the "new conservatives" by the liberals on their left, these defenders of the old "vital center" soon came to be known as "neoconservatives."

In journals like *Commentary* and the *Public Interest*, neoconservatives constantly emphasized the dangers of Soviet expansionism. The strategy of containment, they argued, was still fundamentally correct, and they criticized their liberal colleagues for suggesting that America might enjoy power without the burdens of responsibility. They also were also deeply embittered by the apparent collapse of America's international authority in the 1970s. The loss in Vietnam, the humiliating spectacle of the Iranian hostage crisis, the OPEC oil embargoes, and the seeming betrayal of purpose in attempts to achieve détente with the Soviets left the neoconservatives convinced that the United States had forgotten the crucial lessons of World War II and turned toward appeasement. The left-wing revolution in Nicaragua, the Soviet invasion of Afghanistan, and Cuban support for Communists in Angola also convinced the neoconservatives that the Soviets had little interest in mutual coexistence. While America failed to take a resolute stand, they warned, the USSR sought a clear Cold War victory.

Alienated by what they perceived as the Carter administration's lack of resolve, neoconservatives soon found a home in the ideology and rhetoric of Ronald Reagan. Yet in moving to the right they also sacrificed the original Cold War liberal ideal. As liberal anticommunists in the 1940s, Kristol and Glazer had identified the global promotion of democracy with a commitment to its expansion at home. Now, however, they aligned themselves with a resurgent Cold War crusade that promised an international moral victory but largely ignored questions of domestic progress. Like mainstream conservatives, they viewed the Great Society reforms of the 1960s as clear failures. Affirmative action, plans for expanded health insurance, and community development efforts, they suggested, had been based on flawed, simplistic theories. Far more interested in unrestricted markets than questions of social justice, they claimed to fight for democracy abroad but did little to assist America's own underclass. By attacking the Great Society as a misguided attempt to ensure equality of condition instead of equality of opportunity, they also provided the rationale for severe cuts in social welfare spending and a rapid expansion of the defense budget. Even as thinkers like Kristol blamed the economic stagnation of the 1970s on fiscal irresponsibility, they strongly supported legislation to "rearm" America and raise military spending by 40 percent between 1980 and 1984.

Neoconservatives also invoked the language of democracy to legitimate American support for decidedly undemocratic regimes. Jeane Kirkpatrick, a leading neoconservative theorist, argued that there was a fundamental difference between "authoritarian" and "totalitarian" regimes. As she put it in a 1979 essay, authoritarians suppressed the liberties of their citizens, but because their economies remained open to both American goods and ideas, they might gradually liberalize and slowly evolve in democratic directions. Totalitarians, however, shut their borders to foreign markets and ideas, sought to maintain a rigid, inflexible control, and would never reform. It was therefore a grave mistake, she concluded, for the United States to fail to support a dictatorial regime facing a leftist revolution. The cause of democracy, she insisted, demanded engagement in such cases, not a naïve, moralistic withdrawal. Impressed by that reasoning, Reagan appointed Kirkpatrick the U.S. ambassador to the United Nations in 1981. He also took her arguments to heart. As he declared in his 1985 State of the Union address, "we must stand by all our democratic allies" and "not break faith with those who are risking their lives—on every continent, from Afghanistan to Nicaragua—to defy Soviet-supported aggression and secure rights which have been ours from birth . . . Support for freedom fighters is self-defense."

It was difficult, however, to find much "freedom" in Reagan's Cold War policies. Covert operations supporting the government in El Salvador and the counterrevolutionary Nicaraguan "Contras" helped arm right-wing death squads that murdered thousands. The Iran-Contra affair, a plan to send the proceeds from Middle Eastern missile sales to the Contras in clear violation of a congressional ban on further support, also exposed the degree to which Reagan's Cold War against the Soviet "evil empire" challenged democratic principles at home.

During the 1980s, when the Berlin Wall finally fell and the Soviet Union collapsed, neoconservatives were quick to declare themselves vindicated. Though intellectuals like Norman Podhoretz were initially taken aback by Reagan's willingness to enter into arms-control agreements with Mikhail Gorbachev, they soon argued that "hanging tough" had paid off. The Soviet Union's implosion, they insisted, revealed the long-term success of containment and the wisdom of seeking peace only through strength. America's free market commitments and rapid military buildup, they declared, had driven the Russians into bankruptcy, exposed the fundamental contradictions of a totalitarian regime, and opened a new era of global freedom. Among all the triumphal statements, perhaps the most celebrated was Francis Fukuyama's essay "The End of History," published in the summer of 1989 in the *National Interest*. According to Fukuyama, the destruction of the Soviet system marked "an unabashed victory of economic and political liberalism." "What we may be witnessing," he declared, "is not just the end of the Cold War, or the passing of a particular period of postwar history, but the end of history as such: that is, the end point of mankind's ideological evolution and the universalization of Western liberal democracy as the final form of human government." Fascism and communism, the two great challenges to liberalism, had both collapsed, and although religion and nationalism might still lead societies astray, Fukuyama was confident that the future's evolutionary course was clear. America, the vanguard of human liberty and democratic values, had triumphed, and the Cold War's end marked the ultimate moral victory.

THE RECURRENT TENSION

Throughout the Cold War period, American intellectuals grappled with the problem of waging a war for democracy without jeopardizing their own democratic principles. How, they asked, would it be possible to defeat Soviet totalitarianism without taking steps that might restrict civil liberties, draw resources away from commitments to social reform, or destroy the very values Americans promised to defend? Cold War liberals expected that democracy would be a "fighting faith," that the war abroad could be managed in ways that would still ensure domestic freedom. The strains of the Korean War and McCarthyism challenged that view, and the deep divisions over Vietnam ultimately shattered the liberal consensus. Precisely because the Cold War was framed in ideological terms, as a struggle over the direction of world history, intellectuals thought and argued about the dilemma of democracy in absolute terms. Where radicals perceived the rise of a "power elite" and the arrival of a "garrison state," their opponents on the right warned that communism would never be defeated through compromise or peaceful coexistence. Only when the enemy surrendered its vision of the future would victory be complete. Neoconservatives believed that moment had finally arrived in 1989. When the Soviet system fell, they described a democratic triumph of universal significance. History itself, at least in terms of ideological conflict, would cease. American citizens would enjoy a well-deserved "peace dividend" in which the resources used to wage the long Cold War might once again return to benefit public life.

Yet since 1990 that vision has proven deeply flawed. Within only a few years of the Berlin Wall's collapse, the Gulf War and crises of ethnic conflict in Rwanda and the Balkans once again raised questions about the depth of the democratic triumph and the degree to which America might promote progressive "nation building." Continued violence in the Middle East and the terrorist attacks of September 11, 2001, moreover, thrust Americans back into the discourse of emergency once more. George W. Bush's arguments about a terrorist "axis of evil" strongly resonated with Reagan's calls to defeat a Soviet "evil empire," and American policymakers once again proclaimed national security as the ultimate objective and declared a war for democracy against a global enemy. That war does need to be fought. But to romanticize the Cold War as an unequivocal moral victory would be a mistake. Americans would do better to bear in mind the problems posed by an unlimited war for absolute ends. In a struggle against a decidedly undemocratic adversary, it will take more than mere statements of faith to preserve America's democratic values.

BIBLIOGRAPHIC NOTE

Michael Sherry, *In the Shadow of War: The United States Since the 1930s* (Yale University Press, 1995), provides an eloquent overview of the way global war affected America. On the creation of the consensus in the late 1940s, see Mark Kleinman, *A World of Hope, a World of Fear: Henry A. Wallace, Reinhold Niebuhr, and American Liberalism* (Ohio State University Press, 2000). Ellen Schrecker, *Many Are the Crimes: McCarthyism in America* (Little, Brown, 1998), explores the Red Scare's historical meaning; Michael Rogin, *The Intellectuals and McCarthy: The Radical Specter* (MIT Press, 1967), analyzes contemporary interpretations of it. On social scientists and the state, see Michael E. Latham, *Modernization as Ideology: American Social Science and "Nation Building" in the Kennedy Era* (University of North Carolina Press, 2000). For treatments of the New Left and its attacks on the Vietnam War, see James Miller, *Democracy Is in the Streets: From Port Huron to the Siege of Chicago* (Simon & Schuster, 1987), and Robert R. Tomes, *Apocalypse Then: American Intellectuals and the Vietnam War, 1954–1975* (New York University Press, 1998). James Ehrman, *The Rise of Neoconservatism: Intellectuals and Foreign Affairs, 1945–1994* (Yale University Press, 1995), is a particularly useful analysis of the neoconservative movement.

PART III

Government

18. MANAGERIAL CAPITALISM CONTESTED

Government Policy, Culture, and Corporate Investment

TONY A. FREYER

In the years following World War II, the liberal state imposed institutional and cultural constraints on the investment strategies of big business. Before the war, social and political disputes centered on progressivism's and then liberalism's response to industrialization, particularly increased social-class conflict associated with the growth of wage labor, greater dependence on what has been called "managerial capitalism," and the gradual development of state and federal governmental institutions to match the scale of corporate power. During the Depression, Franklin Roosevelt's New Deal reshaped progressivism's reform tradition to institute a liberal constitutional regime in which government for the first time was as big as business. After the war, policymakers and corporate managers grappled with how to maintain a dynamic consumer society and economic growth amidst persistent civil rights and civil liberties conflicts at home, the communist threat from abroad, and, following the end of the Cold War, new challenges identified with globalization.

At both the institutional and discourse levels there were two primary phases of change. During the initial postwar decades, government and corporate officials worked within a liberal consensus to adopt investment strategies to promote worldwide expansion of American managerial capitalism through a process of organizational and financial ordering—involving especially mergers— that enabled firms to diversify the production of goods demanded by the growing consumer economy. From the 1970s on, however, the chronic cycle of bust and boom reflected the dominance of entrepreneurially riskier investment and diversification strategies resting upon policies of government deregulation and a public discourse enshrining values of market fundamentalism and efficiency. Even so, central to the process of change was corporate restructuring through merger. Mergers involved the buying and selling of independent firms or divisions of firms on the stock market, giving the managing directors of the parent company direct control over the assets and earnings of subsidiaries, which usually were located in different states and nations. Managerial control facilitated a wide range of intercompany transactions, including the sale of assets of one subsidiary to another, the concealment of losses, the creative use of deficits to alter tax liability, or, as occurred in the burgeoning financial scandals after 2001, the manipulation of securities regulations to support the claim of nonexistent or grossly inflated profits. Ironically, the same governmental system that promoted American big business's organizational and investment flexibility also instituted constraints shaping management's search for capital to finance corporate expansion.

THE LIBERAL STATE AND CORPORATE DIVERSIFICATION, 1945–1970

During Harry Truman's presidency, the liberal administrative state and business organization attained a distinctive relationship. Truman said that the combination of economic opportunity and political democracy that constituted the postwar American way of life should spread throughout the world, but he also affirmed that the American people were weary of social or governmental experiments. Truman's assessment reflected a New Deal cultural and institutional settlement that accepted several principles:

- big business's oligopolistic domination of the leading manufacturing industries, including automobiles, chemicals, electronics, and steel; of the primary wholesalers such as Sears, Roebuck & Company; and of major service sector enterprises such as insurance;
- retention of competitive small business markets, including such enterprises as machine tools, venture capital firms, and most retail establishments;
- close government regulation of public utilities and telecommunications and supervision of capital and investment markets through the Securities and Exchange Commission and Federal Reserve;
- mitigation of labor unrest through a process of governmental dispute resolution;

- a guarantee of social welfare, especially social security, sufficient to undercut widespread social discontent and anticapitalist radicalism;
- financing the governmental regulatory apparatus and social welfare through deficit spending and a progressive tax on the nation's wealthiest individuals and corporations.

Elsewhere in the world, communist regimes or liberal democracies either owned industrial operations outright or exercised nearly complete control over them, setting prices subject to limited or no meaningful review by an independent judiciary. The American administrative state differed in the virtual absence of state ownership and the delegation of regulatory functions to governmental agencies possessing limited or no authority to set prices. What most distinguished the American regulatory state, nonetheless, was its ultimate accountability to the most constitutionally independent and powerful judicial establishment in the world. In a series of decisions during the 1930s and 1940s, the Supreme Court announced a constitutional presumption favoring individual rights, while leaving to the legislature and administrative agencies greater authority to regulate the economy. The Court formally declared this policy in footnote 4 of the *Carolene Products Co.* decision of 1938. Among constitutional lawyers, footnote 4 became famous for signaling that the Court would examine civil rights and liberties claims according to a standard of strict scrutiny; but where economic regulations were at issue, the Court would generally defer to the authority of the government. After the Second World War, the Supreme Court's historic promotion of this new rights consciousness, particularly under the leadership of Chief Justice Earl Warren, highlighted the irony that attaining greater democratic inclusiveness depended on an unelected federal judiciary. Even so, the federal judiciary generally sanctioned liberal trade and antitrust policies governing corporate investment strategies.

The liberal administrative state facilitated an organizational transformation within postwar American managerial capitalism. Before the Depression, two corporate organizational structures had emerged within American big business. The first was a "unitary" or "U" organizational form in which vice presidents for sales, production, purchasing and research and development (R&D), as well as staff officials such as those heading the legal department and publicity, reported directly to the president. Henry Ford's motor company was probably the most famous example of the "U" form. Ford not only pioneered assembly line production, but he also sought to avoid dependence on parts suppliers and raw materials producers by purchasing plants and mines, thereby establishing a vertically integrated corporate organization directly under his centralized control. The historic contraction of demand the Depression caused, however, revealed a fundamental weakness in the unitary organization and its underlying investment strategy: Ford's costly investment in fixed capital stock such as coal and iron ore mines or steel mills brought the company to the verge of bankruptcy.

DuPont and General Motors (GM) pioneered the second organizational structure. Managers in these firms realized that the U-form corporate organization inefficiently regulated the costs of producing the widely diversified products that were coming to dominate the growing consumer economy of the 1920s. At the start of that decade, DuPont purchased a controlling share in GM, delegating primary managerial authority to Alfred Sloan, formerly a ball-bearings manufacturer whose firm had merged with GM in 1916. Sloan's diverse experience equipped him to understand how the organizational restructuring of separate production and marketing operations through an investment strategy of diversification and merger could make GM more competitive than Ford. Sloan and his counterparts at DuPont developed, accordingly, the multidivisional organization known as the M-form, promoting an investment strategy of product diversification sustained by functionally independent divisions whose costs, prices, volume, and rate of return were monitored by a centralized administrative office. The M-form structure established within the firm an internal administrative balance between divisional chiefs possessing considerable initiative for independent action and the centralized assessment process that maintained organizational accountability. The circumscribed autonomy of each division was also particularly suited to a diversification investment strategy of acquiring through merger firms that had developed specialized products whose production and sale could be integrated in the dominant firm, just as GM had purchased Sloan's ball-bearings operation.

The multidivisional organization prevailed after 1945. This was so in part because it proved particularly adaptable to the postwar commercialization of technological innovation. Increasingly, the unusual American system of university, governmental defense, and industrial R&D took hold after the war, constituting an "institutionalization of research" whereby U.S. antitrust policies limited the right of firms to employ patent licenses to form cartel agreements like those that European governments often sanctioned in order to restrict the public use of technological innovation.[1] An important outcome of this antitrust policy was that the Truman administration's federal prosecution eventually compelled IBM to publicize its applications of computer technology the government had developed during the Second World War, creating competition in the computer-leasing business. Even so, while universities and the defense establishment provided much of the basic research vital to maintaining American capitalism's technological edge, the industrial laboratories of RCA, AT&T, IBM, DuPont, GM, Kodak, General Electric (GE), and other corporations—whose divisional specialization the M-form promoted—applied this research chiefly to product development. During the 1950s corporate America spent 78 percent of its research on product development and only 18 and 4 percent, respectively, for applied and basic research. At the same time, management's preoccupation with commercialization of technological innovation ensured returns to the corporation itself, rather than profits distributed to patent holders.

Thus, by the early 1950s the linkages between liberal state policies and corporate investment were firmly established. In the domestic American market, antitrust's patent and merger policies facilitated the adoption of the of M-form structure, especially to sell growing numbers of products developed through the commercialization of R&D. Liberals Adolf A. Berle and Gardiner C. Means, in their classic study *The Modern Corporation and Private Property* (1932), revealed a fundamental separation between corporate stock and securities owners and the decision-making managers who controlled the giant corporations dominating the nation's economy. During and shortly after the Second World War, Joseph A. Schumpeter predicted that this managerial capitalism was doomed primarily because the larger governmental bureaucracies and corporate organizations sustaining it would stifle ongoing technological innovation. Writing in 1954 following the liberal state's and managerial capitalism's impressive wartime and early Cold War performance, however, Berle argued that the separation between owners and managers constituted an enduring capitalist revolution making big business more socially benign. Berle also concluded that liberal antitrust and securities policies promoted the rise of large institutional investors such as pension trusts and mutual funds that eventually might dominate the investment strategies of the nation's leading corporations, further strengthening their societal accountability.

Berle's analysis suggested how profoundly liberal government polices shaped the early Cold War's corporate diversification process. During the Truman administration, Ford adopted the multidivisional form. Meanwhile, the managerial control the M-form instituted enabled DuPont, Westinghouse, Sears, Standard Oil, GM, and others to pursue successful investment strategies that enlarged domestic market penetration. Especially in the American South after the 1940s, as economic historian Gavin Wright has shown in *Old South, New South: Revolutions in the Southern Economy Since the Civil War* (1986), New Deal labor and agricultural policies—sustained in numerous Supreme Court decisions upholding the liberal state's restraint of the free market under the principles stated in *Carolene Products*—promoted the postwar movement of northern-based corporate subsidiaries southward, which in turn began to erode the economic incentives for maintaining the Jim Crow racial apartheid labor system. As a result, during the early 1950s in places such as Little Rock, Arkansas, whose 1957–58 school desegregation crises helped precipitate the civil rights movement, southern promoters competed to attract to their communities the employment and investment fostered by northern-headquartered corporate subsidiaries.

Yet the liberal state's promotion of corporate diversification also had unintended outcomes. Berle had argued that the increasing separation between managers and owners left stockholders only the right to collect dividends; by contrast, in early-nineteenth-century America and in postwar Europe, these shareholder owners possessed significant authority to control corporate investment strategies. Berle underestimated the significance of well-publicized proxy battles during the 1950s and later, which suggested the increasing clout of institutional investors. But he and other commentators were clearly correct that even as postwar Wall Street volumes reached new heights, American corporate management's general policy of fighting for market share, especially through advertising, rather than maximizing profits for investors, was the least risky strategy under oligopolistic competition. Moreover, commentators representing such diverse views of postwar corporate expansion as critic John Kenneth Galbraith and defender Peter Drucker acknowledged that profit maximization was secondary to the manager's personal motivations involved in winning power and creative influence resulting from running a bigger division or groups of divisions of the sort the M-form organization facilitated. However, the overriding goal driving management's early postwar investment strategy was its own well-being.

Yet, if the liberal state ensured managerial security, it also promoted challenges to that security. The period from the end of World War II to the end of the 1960s witnessed the most active antitrust enforcement to that point in U.S. history. Not only did federal antitrust authorities bring more cases than ever before, but during the 1960s private suits initiated by plaintiffs against corporate interests also increased sevenfold. Most government and private cases involved price fixing and other cartel practices, such as the enormous electrical equipment litigation that resulted in record civil damages and the imprisonment of corporate executives. The government and private litigants also initiated more cases challenging mergers, solidifying the more socially responsive managerial capitalism that Berle and other liberals condoned.

Increased activism against mergers also resulted in managers' pioneering a vigorous corporate takeover strategy. Clearly responding to the constraints liberal antitrust policy imposed, one such manager, Harold Geneen, instituted a new diversification investment strategy at International Telephone and Telegraph (ITT). In both the domestic and international market he diversified beyond ITT's telecommunications field to establish a conglomerate, the purchase through merger of functionally unrelated firms, including Avis Rent-a-Car, Levitt and Sons (construction), Sheraton (hotels), Rayonier (chemicals), Continental Baking, and Hartford Insurance. Geneen's adaptation of the M-form to incorporate such diverse companies made financial accounting the leading department within the conglomerate, facilitating growing managerial attention to cost efficiency and shareholder values.

The Truman administration's trade policies also had an unintended impact on international corporate expansion during the 1950s and 1960s. The Marshall Plan aided in the postwar recovery of Western European capitalist economies, while the U.S.-dominated Allied occupation ending in 1952 did the same for the Japanese economy. In addition, the United States promoted a postwar liberal trade order maintained under the General Agreement on Tariffs and Trade (GATT), the International Monetary Fund, and the World Bank. These liberal trade programs and policies stabilized international markets so that American firms expanded by adopting the M-form organization to the operation of the multinational corporation, much as they were doing with national operations in the domestic U.S. market. As the initial Cold War era unfolded, the success of this global corporate expansion was known abroad as the "American challenge." By the late 1950s, however, the culturally and institutionally distinctive European and Japanese capitalist economies—which sustained much higher levels of government-supported social welfare policies—had sufficiently recovered from the war's devastation that they too were increasingly enjoying impressive economic growth. Indeed, a few foreign firms even began employing direct investment in the domestic U.S. market. More generally, European and Japanese governments promoted the growth of their indigenous capitalist systems through favorable tariff, exchange rate, and pricing or cartel practices, as well as the formation of state-supported "national champion" enterprises, which increased competition among U.S., European, and Japanese firms within the liberal trade order.

By the 1960s, American managerial capitalism's international competitive advantage was eroding. European and Japanese firms steadily cut into American corporations' international market dominance: between the first and second half of the 1960s the annual average of the U.S. merchandise surplus was reduced from $5.4 billion to a $2.8 billion. Economic experts and trade-policy bureaucrats recognized, moreover, that U.S. steel companies did not invest in the cost-saving oxygen furnace, an Austrian invention, until foreign firms had employed it. Similarly, the U.S. textile industry lost market share to cheaper Japanese goods. This declining competitiveness undercut the market power of U.S. corporations abroad, which one commentator described as a confrontation "startlingly like that of a Middle East or South American oil company and the native inhabitants in the throes of colonial nationalism and the threats of withdrawal and shutdown on the one hand and expropriation on the other . . . In both cases the company is reduced to the threat of immigration."[2]

Thus, despite American managerial capitalism's impressive global reach, its international dominance was contested. In a significant *Foreign Affairs* article of 1968, Harvard professor Raymond Vernon argued that the multinational corporation's autonomy held national governments' "sovereignty at bay." At another level, however, the multinational corporation's multidivisional structure worked against

its own international competitiveness. American managers had to decide between U.S. or foreign capital markets to finance their foreign subsidiaries, which
by 1969 received approximately 20 percent of the manufactured products ex-
ported by U.S.-based firms. Nevertheless, the transnational diversification investment strategies the M-form structure fostered also brought American managers
up against the institutional and cultural reality that the operations of their firms'
foreign subsidiaries were tied to the local laws and trade policies of the sovereign
nation in which they did business. Moreover, the liberal trade order allowed nations to sanction a wide range of anticompetitive practices in which American
managers of foreign subsidiaries collaborated in order to implement their investment strategies. In response, despite opposition from American corporate executives, U.S. officials increasingly initiated and won extraterritorial antitrust
prosecutions challenging the transnational anticompetitive conduct of such firms
as Schlitz Brewing, Monsanto, Alcoa, 3M, GE, and Singer.

The U.S. government's trade policies in other ways indirectly weakened corporate America's international advantage. U.S. steel and textile firms, unable to
match foreign competition, lobbied for and received protectionist measures
from the government. As Schumpeter predicted, government protection undercut the competitive incentives for "creative destruction" through investment in
technological innovation. Similarly, in order to reduce the declining balance of
payments that the Vietnam War aggravated, the Johnson administration instituted from 1965 to 1968 the Foreign Direct Investment Program, which among
other things limited American multinational corporations' use of U.S. currency
to pursue direct investment abroad, including the acquisition of foreign firms.
Accordingly, many U.S. multinational firms increasingly relied on European
capital markets to finance foreign mergers and acquisitions. These mergers, in
turn, increased U.S. multinational corporations' dependence upon the local
laws and cultures of foreign nations, including incentives to engage in foreign
anticompetitive practices.

These conflicted governmental policies engendered a public discourse reimagining managerial capitalism's legitimacy within Cold War liberalism. Liberals like Berle argued that corporate management's apparent responsiveness to
diverse goals beyond mere profit making—including the maintenance of national
security, the promotion of philanthropy, and the abiding concern for its own
welfare—suggested the embrace of a new "social responsibility" and "corporate
conscience." The liberals' recognition of corporate America's social ethic was part
of what social theorist Talcott Parsons described as a displacement of the older
Progressive and New Deal discourse emphasizing economic conflict with one in
which social relations predominated. The Supreme Court's use of psychological
and sociological evidence as a basis for overturning the constitutional foundations
of racially segregated school systems in the *Brown* decision of 1954 was perhaps

the most conspicuous instance of this shift toward behaviorist concerns as a central criterion of policies establishing constitutional and legal accountability. Similarly, Galbraith, Berle, and others published influential books arguing that the New Deal settlement instituted a benign interest-group pluralism that held big business in check as it maintained the productive capacity and technological innovation necessary to promote the welfare and defense of American consumer society. Galbraith's image of big labor, large-scale mechanized agriculture, and big business jockeying against each other as "countervailing powers" efficiently sustaining the world's most "affluent society" epitomized the elite public discourse of the postwar pluralist administrative state at work.

This liberal pluralism was nonetheless contested. Conservative management theorist Peter Drucker argued in 1946 that profit making, social welfare, and personal freedom were compatible without excessive liberal state intervention because the organizational dynamics driving American management to adopt the multidivisional form undercut monopolistic tendencies. "All this is attainable only in a *decentralized* big business," Drucker affirmed. "Hence decentralization is the condition for the conversion of bigness from a social liability into a social asset." Even so, many conservatives condemned postwar liberal antitrust activism as unnecessary and even harmful because the targeting of many mergers undermined the manager's incentives to pursue single-mindedly the technological innovation essential to maintaining consumer welfare, international competitiveness, and even the defense of the anticommunist world. Radicals, by contrast, claimed that liberal pluralist policies ultimately ensured conservative outcomes. Contending that the liberal regulatory state had been captured by big business, leftist thinkers asserted that the "countless laws, such as the antitrust bills, pure food and drug acts, and the [antilabor] Taft-Hartley Law," as well as the "complex system of quasi-judicial regulatory agencies in the executive branch of government . . . systematically favor the interests of stronger against the weaker party in interest-group conflicts and tend to solidify the power of those who already hold it. The government, therefore, plays a conservative, rather than a neutral, role in the society."[3] Reflecting the contentiousness of this public discourse during the initial postwar era was increased antitrust activism.

ANTITRUST ACTIVISM AND CORPORATE INVESTMENT, 1945–1970

A professional culture of legal and economic experts employed antitrust policies and symbols to shape postwar managerial capitalism. Richard Hofstadter wrote in 1964 that earlier in the nation's history antitrust had been "largely an ideology," but since the Second World War it had become "like so many other things in our society, differentiated, specialized, and bureaucratized." According to Hofstadter, "the business of studying, attacking, defending, and evaluating oligopolistic behavior and its regulation has become one of our small industries," and it was the "almost exclusive concern of a technical elite of lawyers and economists." In particular, these expert professionals oversaw the bureaucracy that guided the "potentialities of antitrust action." The social and market conflict this bureaucratic order channeled, moreover, was part of an ongoing readjustment in the postwar public discourse about the legitimacy of both the liberal administrative state and big business. Even so, Hofstadter noted in accord with leftist criticism, big business understood that the antitrust process "can be considered an alternative to more obtrusive regulations as outright controls on prices," and in any case the "pieties at stake are too deep to risk touching." By contrast, liberal lawyers and economists, including vocal defenders of small business, advocated stronger antitrust enforcement because "they retained their old suspicion of business behavior." Conservatives and liberals nonetheless essentially agreed, Hofstadter asserted, that the "state of the public mind . . . accepts bigness but continues to distrust business morals."[4]

Antitrust lawyers in particular constituted their own professional culture. Since the late nineteenth century, big-city firms on Wall Street and elsewhere had served corporate giants as litigators, counselors, and lobbyists. After World War II such firms underwent further specialization. Former American Bar Association (ABA) president Bernard G. Segal argued that as a result of the Supreme Court's general sanction of more activist antitrust policies, postwar corporate managers had developed a new respect for and dependence upon the antitrust bar. The "revolving door" phenomenon, whereby after a number of years government lawyers took their expertise into the private sector, also became increasingly common; similarly, government lawyers left to join the growing numbers of public-interest law firms. In addition, the antitrust community was strengthened through the formation of the ABA's antitrust section, which maintained close and generally cordial ties with the FTC and the Antitrust Division. Washington, D.C., became the haven for firms possessing such connections. Numerous periodicals, including the section's *Antitrust Bulletin*, provided a steady flow of expert opinion and analysis.

Meanwhile, postwar economic theory diverged concerning the degree to which deductive mathematical assumptions underlying perfect price competition should incorporate more heterogeneous values. Most American economists built on the work of Schumpeter, Joan Robinson, and E. H. Chamberlin, incorporating into theories of technological innovation and imperfect oligopolistic competition a primary emphasis upon efficiency. One group applied efficiency assumptions to determine whether business scale and anticompetitive practices affected various social-welfare interests. Gradually, this group developed a theory of "workable competition" that attempted to strike a theoretical balance between efficiency and broader social values. According to Vanderbilt University economist George W. Stocking, workable competition assumed that "pure competition is not generally attainable and that pure monopoly rarely exists." The policy goal of experts was, accordingly, to analyze the structure of an individual industry in relation to the conduct and performance of the firms within it. "If an industry is dynamic, if business firms are efficient, if prices respond quickly to changes in the conditions of demand and supply, if entrepreneurs pass on to consumers promptly the cost reductions that follow technological innovation, and if profits are reasonable, an industry is workably competitive regardless of the number and size of the firms that comprise it." [5]

Another group of legal and economic experts, however, attacked these assumptions from a narrower standpoint of market efficiency. Many sources contributed to this academic, professional, and business criticism, but the most influential was the University of Chicago's economics department and its law school's law and economics program. Legal scholar Robert Bork was a prominent exponent of applying Chicago law and economics theories to antitrust. In *Fortune* articles written during the 1960s, Bork argued, "Too few people understand that it is the essential mechanism of competition and its prime virtue that more efficient firms take business away from the less efficient." Bork conceded that where "certain business behavior is likely to result in monopoly profits and misallocation of resources . . . [it] should be illegal." But he insisted that such behavior was exceptional. "All other behavior should be lawful so far as antitrust is concerned, since, in relation to consumer welfare, it is either neutral or motivated by considerations of efficiency. The market will penalize those that do not in fact create efficiency." [6]

Throughout the initial postwar era the proponents of workable competition were more influential among lawyers and judges. In the ALCOA decision of 1945 the federal court linked economically oriented efficiency concerns that emphasized corporate competition to the social benefits resulting from attacking bigness. Over the succeeding decades, the weight that the federal judiciary and the Supreme Court afforded social welfare versus narrower efficiency concerns varied from case to case; overall, the policy outcome reflected skepticism toward excessive market concentration and remained firmly opposed to anticompetitive patent and cartel practices. Princeton economist J. W. Markham explained why these policies promoted technological innovation. He wrote in 1969 that "firms obviously prefer above-competitive to competitive rates of return on capital, and will pursue whatever legal (occasionally even illegal) means as are available to attain such returns." Without procompetitive patent and antimonopoly policies, accordingly, "such activities as price-fixing, monopolization and cartel formation may compete with innovational effort (research and development) as means for attaining the higher rates of return." But when these practices were made illegal, the incentives for abandoning them improved. Thus as patent and antimonopoly policies "are administered more vigorously, as has been the case in the United States over the past two decades, business managers have very likely increased their respective firms' innovational effort (Rand D) outlays more than they otherwise would have."[7]

Merger and patent rules were reshaped, promoting corporate diversification but also engendering unintended consequences. While corporate combinations generally increased market concentration levels as measured by mathematical ratios, postwar antitrust prosecutions and federal court decisions curtailed horizontal mergers among firms in the same industry. Thus, as Chandler observed, while antitrust prevented monopoly, it also left the sectors identified with big business, such as automobiles, electronics, chemicals, steel, and large wholesalers, with only a few firms competing against each other as oligopolies. In addition, the Eisenhower administration won a noteworthy victory limiting vertical monopolistic restraints when the Supreme Court upheld a federal government order requiring DuPont to divest its share in GM. By contrast, the Eisenhower administration also decided that U.S. firms' participating in the international petroleum cartel did not violate the antitrust laws. In quiet cooperation with the Federal Trade Commission, the Justice Department also negotiated important consent decrees with RCA and other firms that placed valuable patent information in the public domain. U.S. multinational corporations and their subsidiaries were not the only ones to use this technology; foreign firms also had access to it, which increased competition with U.S. multinationals.

Even so, during the 1950s and the 1960s corporate lawyers recommended further corporate diversification, especially through conglomerate mergers. "In the post-war years, there have been some special pressures and temptations to diversify," reported *Fortune* magazine in 1954. "The trend of antitrust enforcement has made it difficult for many corporations to expand in their own industries." Similarly, a commentary on mergers in a December 1951 issue of *Business Week* noted, "Whatever happens, it won't be because all recent mergers were entered into blindly. There's plenty of evidence that they have been made only on careful advice of counsel. Most of the current deals do not look as though monopoly has been their goal. Rather, they seem aimed at some legitimate aims such as diversification." Commenting upon the appointment of Harvard law professor Donald Turner to head the Antitrust Division, *Business Week* reported on March 12, 1966, that he was trying "to channel the merger movement away from 'horizontals' . . . and, to a lesser extent, vertical mergers . . . into the conglomerate stream. Private lawyers are well aware of this attitude and advise corporate clients, 'If you're thinking about conglomerate mergers, do it now' . . . the [legal] climate . . . will never be better." As noted, ITT's Geneen and other managers followed this advice.

Antitrust activism also reshaped procompetition doctrines to promote the interests of private plaintiffs. By 1960 the number of private actions was the highest in history, at 228; yet over the next eighteen years the number rose to 1,611. Like the NAACP's use of social science evidence to win school desegregation suits, plaintiffs' lawyers employed economic theories to convince federal judges that corporate conduct hurting private litigants was anticompetitive or monopolistic. In 1950 Congress promoted such litigation, enacting the Celler-Kefauver Amendment, which closed the merger loophole, section 7a of the Clayton Antitrust Act of 1914. Economists such as Harvard's E. S. Mason and his law school colleague Turner melded law and economic theories into concepts that extended the grounds for applying the law in private and government actions challenging mergers. In addition, the massive electrical equipment litigation created new remedies and sanctions for antitrust violations, including the imprisonment of managers from GE and other companies and treble-damage verdicts totaling nearly $1 billion. Finally, the postwar corporate expansion resulted in a growing market for the services of antitrust lawyers who served a new class of private plaintiffs, including the nation's biggest investor-owned electric utilities, municipal, state, and foreign governments, and even leading industrial firms.

These antitrust policies shaped the conglomerate investment strategy of finance-oriented managers. The clear thrust of early postwar merger policy channeled financial management's diverse motivations regarding corporate takeovers. Harold Geneen summarized the experience of those managers who pioneered the takeover strategy. He understood that the "most important aspect" of antitrust policy was that the "concentration of markets within—I repeat—within industries" was of primary concern to government authorities and the courts, until "horizontal and vertical mergers" had "virtually ceased." Therefore, "only the so-called diversification or conglomerate mergers remain to business as a method of seeking more effective forms of management efficiency and growth, which could be translated into stockholder values without concentration of markets within an industry." [8] Private litigation, of course, generally involved restrictive practices rather than mergers, but given the clout of the large investors who were the plaintiffs in such suits, these cases indirectly facilitated financial management's attention to shareholder values, which in turn influenced its responsiveness to antitrust merger policy.

The changing international impact of antitrust further shaped corporate management's diversification strategy. During the initial postwar decades, the interplay between Cold War foreign policy and its reliance upon corporate investment—particularly in postcolonial and developing nations—made macroeconomic issues involving multilateral tariff reduction, exchange-rate equilibrium, and price stability the most conspicuous concerns confronting American trade bureaucrats and business interests alike. Still, corporate managers in chemicals, electronics, petroleum, and aluminum appealed to the White House, urging that strong antitrust enforcement at home—especially concerning mergers and patents—undercut American firms abroad because most national governments either tolerated or actively promoted widespread anticompetitive business cooperation. In addition, proliferating state-owned companies designated "national champions" were emerging as another source of vigorous competition. These pressures helped to defeat the implementation of the International Trade Organization (ITO) and subsequent United Nations efforts to revive the idea, including provisions for an international antitrust regime.

Antitrust policy was too well integrated into the postwar liberal state for international business interests to overturn. The ALCOA decision of 1945 fostered greater antitrust activism within U.S. borders by holding that monopolies could be prosecuted for the abuse of economic power, including threats to broader social welfare beyond mere market efficiency. In addition, the decision affirmed that violations under the Sherman Antitrust Act occurring in Canada were within U.S. jurisdiction if there were provable anticompetitive "effects" across the border. The decision reinforced the steady erosion of older precedents that had denied the Sherman Act's extraterritorial reach; by the 1950s numerous decisions virtually overturned earlier doctrine, giving antitrust litigation increased international force. Other nations, however, enacted "blocking" laws preventing the enforcement within their borders of U.S. extraterritorial antitrust actions.

The extraterritorial antitrust policy nonetheless imposed increased accountability upon management's transnational corporate diversification strategy. Harvard law professor Kingman Brewster's influential *Antitrust and American Business Abroad* (1958) eventually facilitated such accountability; encouraged by the New York City Bar Association, it was a pioneering study of international antitrust issues, arguing that the international competitiveness of American capitalism as well as national security required a more internationally encompassing antitrust policy. Similarly, economist Corwin Edwards published several studies of international cartel practices and the gradual adoption of antitrust regimes by other nations to address this problem. Periodically, Congress considered strengthening the government's unilateral power to address cartel practices of foreign nations. The prophetic insight of Brewster's and Edwards's works increasingly became apparent after the postwar era of growth.

MARKET FUNDAMENTALISM SINCE THE 1970S

The institutional imperatives and discourse shaping the legitimacy of managerial capitalism throughout the second phase of the postwar era triumphed during the 1970s. The shock of the 1973 oil embargo rippled through a nation adjusting to defeat in Vietnam, the emerging Watergate crisis, five years of mounting inflation, and nearly a decade of northern urban racial unrest and campus disorders. The combination of painful events—in conjunction with an unprecedented economic condition dubbed "stagflation"—repeatedly drove home how vulnerable America's consumer culture had become to forces beyond its control. Stagflation epitomized the nation's anxious condition. In the past Americans had experienced periods of inflationary price rises that eroded savings and the value of fixed assets but also resulted in higher cost-of-living salary increases; they had also encountered economic depression identified with high unemployment and collapsed productivity. These two conditions had generally not existed in the nation simultaneously. In the 1970s, however, both spiraling inflation and the highest unemployment since the Depression gripped the nation. Polls indicated that for the first time in twenty years growing numbers of Americans, including baby boomers who had known only relative prosperity and were beginning to enter the job market, doubted whether individually or as a nation future advancement was likely. During the long period of postwar growth, managerial capitalism generally received support because it had effectively adapted technological innovation and investment to promote America's consumer culture against the Cold War threat. Now that culture faced challenge, "searching for self-fulfillment in a world turned upside down." [9]

The declining share of U.S. international trade became a growing source of public anxiety during the 1970s. In 1950 the U.S. share was 16.6 percent of world exports; the share was 15.9 percent in 1960, and by 1973 it was only 12.2 percent. As long as postwar growth persisted, corporate America's declining international competitiveness was of concern primarily to trade-policy bureaucrats and other economic experts. On August 15, 1971, President Richard Nixon announced an end to the dollar's convertibility into gold. This action precipitated a crisis in the Bretton Woods monetary system, leading to new global arrangements during the 1970s. As a result, international monetary readjustment and stagflation converged, sharpening public perceptions of a dangerous interdependency between what big business did at home and abroad. Public apprehensiveness about trade exacerbated public resentment that the nations the U.S. had either defeated or saved from defeat during World War II and the Cold War were overcoming America's competitive advantage. Developing nations' assaults upon U.S. imperialism, expressed most powerfully through the Organization of Petroleum Exporting Countries (OPEC) oil embargo, further aroused American anger.

As the nation's competitiveness deteriorated during the 1970s, corporate management's investment strategy came under renewed attack. In 1972 the biggest 200 corporations held 60 percent of the nation's manufacturing assets, up from roughly 48 percent in 1948. In this same manufacturing sector, moreover, the concentration of profit shares was even greater than asset shares: in 1974, the 422 largest of more than 200,000 manufacturing corporations received 71 percent of the profits while the assets held were 68 percent. Massive layoffs and declining dividends prompted firms such as ITT to restructure. In 1968 the company had canceled several mergers because the Democratic Justice Department had begun to challenge the conglomerate investment strategy; anticipating a more sympathetic attitude after Republican Richard Nixon's election, however, ITT again began acquiring firms. Adhering to economic doctrines of workable competition, one group of legal economic experts urged Congress to enact legislation facilitating a broad attack on conglomerate mergers through extensive divestiture. Led by University of Chicago economist George Stigler, another group expressed doubt that conglomerate mergers possessed anticompetitive consequences, generally opposed divestiture, and therefore resisted the need for new legislation. After initial vacillation Nixon supported conglomerate mergers; when the conglomerate regulation bill was revived under the Carter administration, it was defeated amid the market uncertainty accompanying the second oil shock of 1979.

Although the conglomerate merger wave ended by 1974, it had a lasting impact. Contentiousness over the conglomerate investment strategy reflected a growing demand among corporate managers and investors alike for market efficiency. The persistent cycle of bust and boom after 1973 promoted an increasing reliance on market costs and gains as the primary measure of economic effectiveness. The U.S. Steel Company exemplified the adaptation of the diversification investment strategy to this new market environment. Since the Second World War, U.S. Steel's performance had steadily deteriorated, especially against mounting competition from Western Europe and Asia. By the 1970s, while steel production remained primary, U.S. Steel had separate divisions managing commercial real estate and coal properties, as well as divisions making cement, pails, and drums.

In 1979 the company hired David Roderick, a finance manager possessing no expertise in steel manufacturing. Roderick initiated an investment strategy aimed at reducing reliance on steel. He sold off the old divisions unrelated to the steel business itself in order to help finance the purchase of one of the world's major petrochemical firms, Marathon Oil; he then bought a leading oil and gas producer, Texas Oil and Gas, which controlled a large pipeline network. Within six years, the steel division generated only about 30 percent of the restructured company's revenues. Profits from the petrochemical and oil and gas divisions were needed to fund a $1.8 billion debt that the steel division also carried. The company had reimagined itself, replacing the venerable name of U.S. Steel with USX.

Such corporate restructuring required increased collaboration between financial experts and lawyers, transforming corporate governance. In the 1970s,

Kohlberg Kravis Roberts pioneered the market for legal and finance expertise. It specialized in the debt-financed leveraged buyout (LBO) of companies by re-molding antitrust/acquisitions and securities rules to pursue corporate take-overs on a scale never before seen; eventually these techniques reshaped the whole field of mergers and acquisitions. The goal of the LBO strategy was to make enormous profits by increasing long-term asset value. During the 1980s GE's Jack Welch employed the same techniques to restructure corporate gover-nance; by the succeeding decade, the executive boards of GM, IBM, American Express, and Kodak had followed suit. The whole process reflected a demand to drive up stock prices and hold management more accountable for performance. Thus, from the 1970s on, measures of managerial effectiveness increasingly be-came dependent on the short-term performance of the stock market, and profit maximization became the primary goal driving managerial capitalism's diversi-fication and takeover strategies.

The economic expert's newly ascendant "efficiency" discourse reshaped the public image of the regulatory state. In accordance with New Deal liberalism, the Nixon administration initially expanded regulatory control, establishing the Environmental Protection Agency and the Occupational Health and Safety Administration. The dislocation of the business cycle beginning in the 1970s was too disruptive, however, for the reliance upon liberal regulatory policymak-ing to persist unchallenged. As a result, leaders in and out of government seized upon market-oriented efficiency theories supporting deregulation. Notwith-standing a general rhetorical condemnation of government control, this reform effort to bring laws and regulations more in line with market efficiencies actu-ally substituted one regulatory regime for another.

Indeed, the substance of deregulation policies varied among nations de-pending on culture and history. In the United States, direct bureaucratic inter-vention declined in leading market sectors, including telecommunications, trucking and railroads, financial services, oil and gas, electrical power, and avia-tion; the role of civil litigation as a regulatory device grew apace. Even so, the complexities of stagflation enlarged the role of economists who were equipped to apply new cost theories to rate making. Initially, Alfred Kahn's original syn-thesis of earlier economic ideas into a marginal-cost theory dominated the pub-lic discourse on deregulation. Employing a dramatic public relations style, he used a position on the New York Public Service Commission and then the chairmanship of the federal Civil Aeronautics Board during Jimmy Carter's ad-ministration to popularize his approach to deregulation.

After the second oil shock of 1979 and Ronald Reagan's election the following year, however, the Chicago school's promarket theories gained greater influence. On the defensive in the 1960s against such theories as "workable competition," Chicago market fundamentalism thrived during the following decade, as suggested by Nixon's acceptance of Stigler's advice favoring conglomerate mergers. Reagan's reliance on Chicago economic efficiency theories, in turn, dominated the deregulation movement during the 1980s. A leading example of the triumph of the Chicago school's more narrowly focused market fundamentalism was that under Reagan, antitrust cases against mergers declined to the lowest point since the Second World War. William Baxter, the assistant attorney general in charge of the Antitrust Division, did break up AT&T on the grounds that it was a monopoly; but the Reagan administration's approach to market concentration allowed most mergers. Meanwhile, the Reagan antitrust authorities dramatically increased the prosecution of price-fixing agreements in the domestic market but displayed little concern about cartel practices involving U.S. multinational corporations.

The dominance of this market-efficiency discourse coincided with a revived distrust of big business. During the postwar era of growth, management's domestic and global corporate diversification and merger strategy was driven less by profit maximization than by other institutional and psychological factors. As a result, liberal-pluralist discourse affirmed that a more socially responsive corporate consciousness prevailed. During the 1970s, however, there was a reversion to anti–big business popular discourse reminiscent of earlier periods of American history. Thus, an associate of consumer advocate Ralph Nader dismissed the "corporate social responsibility" to which liberals tendered their respect; it was merely a hollow myth hiding the corporate "shell game." A conspicuous voice for liberal reform, Nader publicized the dangers corporate power posed to America. Moreover, he and other liberals won impressive legal victories improving consumer, environmental, and other regulatory protections. Nevertheless, the policy remedies embodied such conflicted ideological tensions that they proved vulnerable to the rising popular distrust of liberal big government and faith in the more efficient "free market." Nader himself suggested the contrariness of liberal reform policy prescriptions in 1972: "Some look to the courts, others dismiss the judiciary; some value regulation, others disdain it; some value 'corporate democracy,' others disparage it; some opt for public enterprise, others for competitive capitalism." [10]

New Left radical discourse was still more diffuse. Social theorist Talcott Parsons had argued that underlying the mid-twentieth-century American liberal consensus was a broad shift from a cultural discourse focusing on economic conflict to one emphasizing social relations. New Left advocates accepted the fundamental logic of social relations, but they rejected liberalism's Vietnam foreign policy, racial desegregation efforts, and compromising affirmation of gender equality. Liberalism was inadequate because it co-opted popular feeling and masked the domination of conservative forces. The radicals enlarged the social relational imperatives to embrace more meaningful forms of self-identity and community solidarity favoring absolute racial and gender equality, while their critique of capitalism dismissed America's preoccupation with consumerism as contrary to these more authentic social relationships. Still, the radical discourse did little to explain the cultural malaise and pervasive sense of impotence accompanying the onslaught of stagflation during the seventies. The recession of 1981–82, the worst since the Depression, and the success of the Federal Reserve's subsequent use of high interest rates to reduce inflation facilitated a growing public acceptance of the need for market efficiency. The vacillating economic conditions persisting into the early 1990s, and then the long boom that followed, further undermined whatever broader cultural appeal the New left radical critique may have had.

The public discourse concerning the multidivisional corporation's impact on domestic and global markets also changed. In 1971 Raymond Vernon pointed out that, not unlike the transfer of industrial corporate divisions and plants from the northern states to the south in the U.S. domestic market, the international divisions of GE, Ford, the oil companies, and IBM brought technological innovation that increased a foreign nation's exports and employment. But from the mid-1970s on a more critical view gained influence, stressing the harm corporate autonomy did to American and foreign local communities. Within the U.S. market, this criticism condemned the environmental degradation that corporate diversification caused, the racial and gender discrimination that corporate managers practiced, and, above all, the threat to local employment that corporate mobility posed. Domestically, the empty steel mills and automobile plants in Indiana or Ohio and their removal to the Sun Belt sustained the force of this critical discourse. The international critique was similar in its condemnation of environmental destruction and the ease with which corporate management shifted jobs from American communities abroad; it also drew attention to the readiness of multinational corporations to engage in anticompetitive conduct and cartels to the detriment of the economic opportunity and social welfare of both the home and foreign state. The conflicted discourse accompanying athletic shoe and apparel manufacturer Nike's diversification into Thailand was representative.

In these terms, managerial capitalism was contested during the second phase of the postwar era. The market-centered discourse dominated public perceptions of and policy prescriptions for the chaotic business cycle of recession and boom prevailing from the mid-1970s to the millennium. Within the nation's political culture, as the Cold War dissipated and suddenly ended, trade policy increasingly symbolized the insecurities Americans felt stemming from what they believed were "unfair" foreign competitive advantages. In the 1990s these doubts and fears fostered widespread ambivalence toward globalization and its symbols: the World Trade Organization, the International Monetary

Fund, and the World Bank. Even so, American capitalism—more than ever identified with multinational corporations and an expansive materialistic consumer culture—was praised or condemned for technological and organizational innovation in the face of international market dislocation. Lauding the efficiency gains that greater managerial accountability fostered, financial and legal experts aggressively pursued the corporate takeover investment strategy, exploiting the ever-rising stock market. Business groups, liberal labor and consumer interests, and representatives of state and local governments argued, however, that the takeover and merger mania sacrificed American capitalism and the nation's sovereignty to greedy financial speculators and allied foreign governments and corporations. Meanwhile, diverse radicals mounted an international campaign against the joint "evils" of globalization and capitalism.

THE GLOBALIZATION OF ANTITRUST
SINCE THE 1970S

Within this contested discourse of global and economic insecurity, the practice and symbol of antitrust gradually acquired international significance. In 1968 Donald Turner had instituted merger guidelines intended to draw a clearer line between legal and illegal conduct in all types of mergers, including anticompetitive effects resulting from conglomerates. Antitrust policy was nonetheless changing to facilitate diversification investment strategies favoring corporate takeovers. Initially, the Nixon administration supported aggressive antitrust prosecutions against ITT and other conglomerates as a way of preserving "Mom and Pop" stores and other independent enterprises. Soon, however, Nixon switched course in favor of Robert Bork's vigorous condemnation of the conglomerate prosecutions. Still, throughout the rest of Nixon's troubled presidency, ITT and other conglomerates settled cases, agreeing to modest divestiture rather than risk defeat in the Supreme Court. In any case, the conglomerate merger wave had run its course by the mid-1970s. Under the Ford administration, congressional opponents defeated stronger antimerger legislation, such as the "no-fault" Monopolization Bill, the Industrial Reorganization Act, and the Monopolization Reform Act. During the same period, U.S. officials grappled with international opposition to their extraterritorial antitrust prosecution of multinational corporations the Turner guidelines had also sanctioned.

Still, Gerald Ford signed the Hart-Scott-Rodino Antitrust Improvement Act of 1976 (HSR). Reflecting the growing community and state agitation over corporate diversification resulting in the loss of local jobs, taxes, and other resources, the law included the *parens patriae* provision authorizing federal funds for state attorneys general to prosecute antitrust actions, including certain corporate takeovers. But the law also made merger decisions more transparent and thus open to takeover strategies. HSR required firms to inform the Justice Department and the FTC before going ahead with mergers that exceeded the size limits the Turner guidelines had established; it imposed, too, a mandatory waiting period before certain acquisitions and tender offers could proceed. The Justice Department and the FTC also maintained a lenient policy toward mergers. The Supreme Court's *GTE Sylvania* decision underlined the shift: in 1979, it applied the rule of reason to allow a territorial vertical restraint on the basis of economic efficiency. The decision reversed a Warren Court precedent that held that such restraints were illegal. While the Carter administration vacillated on the matter of mergers, Antitrust Division head Donald I. Baker rejected a $10 million congressional appropriation to strengthen antitrust prosecutions by state attorneys general. The refusal corresponded with the Supreme Court's *Illinois Brick* decision, which imposed limitations on state actions.

By the mid-1970s, Chicago efficiency theories achieved growing power over the thinking of legal and economic experts. These theories clearly dominated the influential Airlie House Conferences; the lawyers, economists, and other policymakers attending the conferences systematically repudiated the pluralist economic theories associated with "workable competition" and Turner's effort to institute rules governing conglomerate mergers. In 1974, University of Chicago law professor Philip Neal and others published a collection of essays, *Industrial Concentration: The New Learning*, a comprehensive statement of the Chicago law and economics program's teachings.

In 1978 Bork published what became an even more influential statement of the Chicago school's antitrust vision, *The Antitrust Paradox*. Dismissing antitrust theories possessing pluralistic policy goals as merely "a jumble of half-digested notions and mythologies," Bork affirmed that antitrust policy had one legitimate purpose: "consumer welfare maximization." For courts, legislatures, and legal-economic professionals the "important point" was that the "ultimate goal of consumer welfare provides a common denominator by which gains in destruction of monopoly power can be estimated against losses in efficiency, and economic theory provides the means of assessing the probable sizes of the gains and losses." He asserted, moreover, a "high probability, amounting in fact to a virtual certainty, that dissolving any oligopolistic firm that grew to its present size would inflict a serious welfare loss." Nevertheless, Bork attested, contradictory court decisions sustained an antitrust policy "at war with itself." Although Bork protested "ideological" antitrust values, he recognized that antitrust symbols shaped policymaking, including corporate takeover rules. Antitrust law, Bork wrote, had a "unique symbolic and educative influence over public attitudes toward free markets and capitalism." Accordingly, he condemned the Nixon administration's prosecutions of conglomerate mergers because they enforced a policy undercutting the manager's freedom to choose an "efficient" corporate diversification investment strategy.[11]

Indeed, applied across the whole field of antitrust, tax and securities law, market efficiency theories gave broad symbolic and instrumental legitimacy to corporate takeovers. A case in point was the diversification of Stern Metals during the 1970s. Originally a small dental and gold refining supply company, Kohlberg Kravis Roberts used the LBO finance techniques to acquire a diverse investment portfolio including Thompson Wire, Boren Clay Products, Barrows Industries (a jewelry manufacturer), and Eagle Motors. During the 1980s and 1990s, GE's Walsh and his counterparts throughout corporate America employed this entrepreneurial manipulation of mergers-and-acquisitions and securities law to pursue more complex mergers and sell-offs; moreover, in the boom of the 1990s the same techniques were used to reconstitute many of the firms that had been sold off because of low profit performance.

The efficiency discourse legitimating the corporate takeover movement was nonetheless contested. Within the nation's consumer culture, broad public opposition arose against corporate takeovers. A Harris poll showed that 58 percent of those surveyed believed that hostile takeovers did "more harm than good," while nearly the exact same percentage of stockholders and corporate employees stated the same opinion. Moreover, 78 percent of the respondents endorsed the assertion that "most hostile takeovers are engineered by groups of big investors who are trying to drive up the price of the stock just to make a profit for themselves."[12] Business defenders such as Peter Drucker, Lee Iacocca, the Business Round Table, and the National Association of Manufacturers, as well as liberals such as John Kenneth Galbraith and the consumer organization Stockholders of America Foundation, united in opposing takeover investment strategies. Business interests and liberals were too divided among themselves, however, to stem the corporate takeover tide.

The 1987 stock market crash, financial scandals, and recurring recessions, popularized how insecure corporate investment had become. The 500-point drop in October 1987 was the worst stock market collapse since 1929; it demonstrated the profound risk underlying the post-1970s global equities market. The savings and loan crises of the late 1980s revealed, moreover, the unintended opportunities for corruption following financial deregulation. With American taxpayers footing the bill for a $300 billion bailout, the first Bush administration supported congressional legislation reestablishing some meaningful regulation of financial intermediaries. Even so, despite the recession of 1990–91, the increased managerial responsibility implicit in the efficiency discourse seemed vindicated by the long boom that followed.

But as Federal Reserve Chairman Alan Greenspan noted, the tightened linkages between a firm's asset base and the stock market imposed upon corporate executives an overriding demand for short-term profitability. Accordingly, amid the collapse of the technology securities market and the mild turn-of-the-century recession, Enron became the world's largest bankrupt firm. Belatedly, Enron managers conceded that they had fraudulently shifted debts to corporate divisions to claim enormous profits. Similarly, in 2002 it was reported that at the time of its takeover of MCI in 1999–2000, WorldCom claimed a grossly inflated rate of profits; this announcement followed earlier reports that the company had fraudulently declared $3.8 billion in profits in other large acquisitions during the 1990s. Such revelations prompted increased securities regulation and criminal prosecution of corporate executives.

Globalization exacerbated the American consumer culture's conflicted acceptance of market efficiency. The direct investment resulting from the diversification of foreign-based corporations within the United States went from $50 billion in 1979 to over $200 billion in 1986; it was an increase of historic proportions, and the growth accelerated during the 1990s. As consumers, Americans readily embraced the international merchandise market that globalization represented; as citizens and workers, however, they shared a sense of national and personal vulnerability for which globalization was to blame. In 1988, less than six months after the 1987 stock market crash, "more than 75% of U.S. adults surveyed in a poll conducted . . . for a group of Japanese firms agreed that foreign acquisitions have boosted U.S. economic growth, employment, and competitiveness. Nevertheless, nearly 75% viewed the increased foreign presence as undesirable." As suggested by Tennessee, the South was a leading recipient of foreign direct investment: in 1994, manufacturing, sales, and distribution for 113 Japanese firms accounted for 26,840 jobs as a result of a $4.8 billion state-wide investment. According to Tennessee Governor Lamar Alexander, the "English, the Germans, and the Dutch each own about as much of us as the Japanese do. Altogether, foreign investment in Tennessee is about the same as GM's investment in the new Saturn Plant . . . only about five per cent of our manufacturing base." [13]

Trade policymakers reflected these tensions as they sought to balance global corporate accountability and market demands. During the 1980s, in order to address America's return to debtor-nation status for the first time since World War I, trade bureaucrats and politicians shifted between Japan-bashing stereotypes and bilateral power diplomacy, culminating in the yen-centered international currency stabilization of the Plaza Accords of 1985. Thus, Japan and other nations agreed to a historic 50 percent devaluation of the dollar's value in order to lower the cost of American multinational corporations' exports and the accompanying huge U.S. trade deficit. As the October 1987 stock market crash suggested, the agreement ultimately did little to solve the trade-deficit problem; the underlying reason for the failure was nonetheless that the Reagan administration's tax cuts and increased defense spending had imposed upon America an intractable national debt.

Meanwhile, Japan's postwar economic "miracle" ended in 1989 and was followed by a long-lingering recession. The nation's travails resulted in trade disputes that exacerbated international concerns that currency exchange, tariff, and pricing policies were no longer sufficient to preserve the postwar liberal trade order. Accordingly, Raymond Vernon observed in 1989, U.S. trade policymakers should understand that multinational corporations were increasingly involved in anticompetitive practices that in order to be remedied demanded international antitrust action. Since 1947 successive GATT rounds lowered macroeconomic trade barriers throughout the world, facilitating the integration of domestic economies into a global business order based on internationally deregulated capital markets, which nonetheless remained rooted in the multinational corporation's host state. A measure of this market globalization was that in 1995 the world GNP was $25,223 billion, with two hundred multinational corporations turning over $7,850 billion. Thus, multinational corporations' anticompetitive practices were an unintended consequence of effective trade liberalization that macroeconomic trade policies left unregulated; even so, these very same cartel and monopoly practices were broadly within the jurisdiction of antitrust laws.

The search for corporate accountability engendered a new international antitrust activism. With the U.S.-Japan Structural Impediments Initiative of the early 1990s, antitrust officials in both nations cooperated to address anticompetitive conduct in the Japanese market. In the member states of the European Union antitrust was more significant than ever, in part because the end of the Cold War opened Eastern European nations to future EU membership, but only if the former Communist states met strict accession standards that included adopting effective antitrust regimes. Similarly, in Japan the long recession facilitated the most effective antitrust enforcement by Japanese authorities in their own right since the Allied occupation forces departed in 1952. Meanwhile, in the *Boeing/McDonnell Douglas* case European and U.S. antitrust authorities arrived at contrary outcomes concerning the proper balance between efficiency and larger social welfare benefits in the global market for large commercial airplanes. In a case concerning Microsoft's European operations, however, U.S. and European Union antitrust officials cooperated to impose a procompetitive remedy. Even so, Bill Clinton's administration initiated a better-known prosecution of Microsoft in the U.S. market. The company attempted to rebut clear evidence of predatory conduct by arguing that its investment strategy of internal growth had led to extraordinary technological innovation. Economic and legal experts disagreed as to whether the anticompetitive behavior should outweigh the efficiency gains. Federal trial and appellate courts decided against Microsoft on the merits, though the latter court ordered a remedy that apparently excluded the company's breakup.

The Clinton administration also applied antitrust policy against proliferating international cartels. In cooperation with antitrust authorities in several

European nations, Japan, and Korea, U.S. antitrust officials won a record $1.1 billion worth of fines in the *Archer Daniels Midland* and related vitamins price-fixing cases ending in 1999. As international cooperation among antitrust regimes increased as never before, demands arose for some sort of global antitrust authority that would address the full scope of competition policy. Although the future of such an organization remained problematic at the turn of the new century, antitrust policy's traditional concern with curbing economic power—and not solely with the maintenance of narrowly defined market efficiency—had achieved global importance.

The process of globalization thus altered the discourse within which managerial capitalism's legitimacy was contested. American trade policy experts argued that international cooperation among antitrust authorities threatened U.S. sovereignty. Especially after the European Union's antitrust office refused to approve Honeywell's takeover of another U.S. company despite approval from U.S. antitrust officials, the critics urged American reliance upon unilateral trade policies. In that vein, the George W. Bush administration moved to protect American steel companies and agricultural producers from foreign competition.

Meanwhile, starting with the 1999 Seattle meeting of the World Trade Organization, antiglobalization groups became increasingly active. Condemning international capitalism identified with multinational corporations and international governmental organizations, the protestors represented a loose alliance, including nongovernmental organizations such as Oxfam, radical environmentalist such as Greenpeace, advocates of consumers and workers throughout developed and underdeveloped nations, assorted right- and left-wing defenders of traditional society, and nihilists urging the violent destruction of the entire capitalist system. While the antiglobalization and anticapitalist discourse condemned the relentless proliferation of American consumerism with an internationalist rhetoric, it was reminiscent of the New Left's yearning for more authentic, humane, and equitable social relations. Also joining the visionary chorus were members of the international establishment such as Nobel Prize–winning economist Joseph Stiglitz, whose book *Globalization and Its Discontents* (2002) argued that the International Monetary Fund was destroying the poor nations it was established to assist.

While postwar American managerial capitalism presented a formidable image, its power and legitimacy were continuously challenged. Before the early 1970s, corporate managers, motivated by diverse organizational and cultural imperatives, adapted the multidivisional structure to expanding domestic and international markets. Exploiting the weak control exercised by stock and securities holders, managers employed investment strategies that increasingly achieved growth through diversification and conglomerate mergers. Management's strategy reflected a conflicted acceptance of the dominant liberal and pluralist public discourse that conditioned legitimacy on the pursuit of social-welfare goals as well as profit making. The liberal regulatory state—especially antitrust, securities, and trade policies enforced by legal and economic experts possessing their own professional culture—channeled and maintained the legitimacy of corporate management's decision making in accordance with this wider public discourse. Radicals and conservatives exposed the tensions within liberal and pluralist policies.

Not until the 1970s, however, did national insecurity arising from international and domestic economic dislocation and political crisis converge to promote an institutional and cultural discourse centered on market efficiency. This market fundamentalism transformed both the rules and image of accountability embodied in the deregulation movement; government's implementation of deregulation, in turn, facilitated a shift of power away from managers toward investors and corporate takeover experts. American consumer society's response to competition from European and Asian capitalist systems unleashed additional cultural and institutional tensions. The resulting international cooperation among antitrust regimes and trade bureaucrats, amid radical antiglobalization assaults, further reshaped the standards of accountability that define managerial capitalism's legitimacy and its limits.

BIBLIOGRAPHIC NOTE

Alfred D. Chandler's defining study of managerial capitalism, *The Visible Hand: The Managerial Revolution in American Business* (1977), is qualified by the antitrust focus of Neil Fligstein, *The Transformation of Corporate Control* (1990), and the international approach of Thomas K. McCraw, ed., *Creating Modern Capitalism: How Entrepreneurs, Companies and Countries Triumphed in Three Industrial Revolutions* (2000), comparing the distinctive capitalist systems of America, Japan, and Germany.

The postwar liberal state and the limitations the deregulation movement instituted from the 1970s on are explored in Louis Galambos, "The U.S. Corporate Economy in the Twentieth Century," and Richard H. K. Vietor, "Government Regulation of Business," in *The Cambridge Economic History of the United States,* ed. Stanley L. Engerman and Robert E. Gallman (2000), 3:927–968, 3:969–1012; and Joseph Stanislaw, *The Commanding Heights: The Battle Between Government and the Market That Is Remaking the Modern World* (1998).

For the rise of liberal pluralism, see the contemporary critique of Berle, Galbraith, Drucker, Schumpeter, and others in William Lee Baldwin, *Antitrust and the Changing Corporation* (1961). Oliver Zunz, *Why the American Century?* (1998), and Reuel E. Schiller, "Enlarging the Administrative Polity: Administrative Law and the Changing Definition of Pluralism, 1945–1970," *Vanderbilt Law Review* 53, no. 5 (October 2000): 1389–1453, place this liberal pluralist discourse in a wider cultural and institutional context. For the shift from "economics" to "social relations," see Howard Brick, "Talcott Parsons's 'Shift Away from Economics,' 1937–1946," *Journal of American History* 87, no. 2 (September 2000): 490–514. For the emergence of the market-efficiency discourse, see the examination of Alfred Kahn in Thomas K. McCraw, *Prophets of Regulation: Charles Francis Adams, Louis D. Brandeis, James M. Landis, Alfred Kahn* (1984), 222–299; for the role of legal-financial experts in fostering the triumph of the market-centered discourse, see George P. Baker and George David Smith, *The New Financial Capitalists: Kohlberg Kravis Roberts and the Creation of Corporate Value* (1999). I borrow from Joseph Stiglitz, *Globalization and Its Discontents* (2002), the term "market fundamentalism" to describe the public discourse of legal economic experts that triumphed during the 1980s.

Two studies locating antitrust in the U.S. and international context are my *Regulating Big Business, Antitrust in Great Britain and America, 1880–1990* (1992), and "Antitrust and Bilateralism: The U.S., Japanese, and E.U. Comparative and Historical Relationships," in *Competition Policy in the Global Trading System Perspectives from the EU, Japan, and the USA*, ed. Clifford Jones and Mitsuo Matsushita (2002), 3–52. The antiglobalization critique is suggested by Jerry Mander and Edward Goldsmith's *The Case Against the Global Economy and for a Turn Toward the Local* (1996). Japan's leading role in the international financial structure is considered in R. Taggart Murphy, *The Weight of the Yen* (1997), and Chalmers Johnson, "Japanese 'Capitalism' Revisited," *JPRI Occasional Paper No. 22* (August 2001), 1–11.

ACKNOWLEDGMENT

For support, I thank Dean Kenneth C. Randall of the University of Alabama School of Law, the Law School Foundation, and the Edward Brett Randolph Fund. I am grateful as well to the Abe Fellowship from the Center for Global Partnership and the Social Science Research Council for supporting my research in Japan in 1995–96.

NOTES

1. David Mowery and Nathan Rosenberg, "Twentieth-Century Technological Change," in *Cambridge Economic History of the United States: The Twentieth Century*, ed. Stanley L. Engerman and Robert E. Gallman (Cambridge: Cambridge University Press, 2000), 3:908–909.

2. Norton E. Long, "The Corporation, Its Satellites, and the Local Community," in *The Corporation In Modern Society*, ed. Edward S. Mason (Cambridge, Mass.: Harvard University Press, 1960), 215.

3. Peter Drucker, *The Concept of the Corporation* (New York, 1946), 228, italics in original; Robert Paul Wolff, "Beyond Tolerance," in *A Critique of Pure Tolerance*, ed. Robert Paul Wolff, Barrington Moore Jr., and Herbert Marcuse (Boston: Beacon Press, 1969), 46.

4. Richard Hofstadter, "What Happened to the Antitrust Movement? Notes on the Evolution of an American Creed," in *The Business Establishment*, ed. Earl Frank Cheit (New York: Wiley, 1964), 150, 151.

5. George W. Stocking, *Workable Competition and Antitrust Policy* (Nashville: Vanderbilt University Press, 1961), 190.

6. *Fortune*, September 1963, 200–201; *Fortune*, September 1969, 104.

7. J. W. Markham, "The Constraints Imposed by Anti-Trust," in *International Conference on Monopolies, Mergers, and Restrictive Practices, Cambridge, England, 1969*, ed. J. B. Heath (London: Her Majesty's Stationery Office, 1971), 97–98.

8. Harold Geneen, *Vital Speeches of the Day, October 23, 1969* (Southold, N.Y.: City News, 1969), 149.

9. Daniel Yankelovich, *New Rules: Searching for Self-Fulfillment in a World Turned Upside Down* (New York: Random House, 1981).

10. Ralph Nader, "Preface," and Joel F. Henning, "Corporate Social Responsibility: Shell Game for the Seventies?" in *Corporate Power in America*, ed. Ralph Nader and Mark J. Green (New York: Grossman, 1973), vii, 151–170.

11. Robert Bork, *The Antitrust Paradox: A Policy at War with Itself* (New York: Basic Books, 1978), 3, 7, 54, 79, 196.

12. Margaret Cox Sullivan, *The Hostile Corporate Takeover Phenomenon of the 1980's* (Washington, D.C.: Stockholders of America Foundation, 1997), 237.

13. Choong Soon Kim, *Japanese Industry in the American South* (New York: Routledge, 1995), 136, 138, 139–140.

19. FEDERAL EDUCATION POLICY

AND POLITICS

MARIS A. VINOVSKIS

Since World War II, education has become an increasingly important facet of American life. For example, today almost all children complete high school, and more than half will receive at least some college education. At the same time, the federal government has become increasingly more involved in the provision of financial aid and the issuing of regulations. With growing politicization since the 1970s, education has emerged as an important national domestic political issue between Republicans and Democrats.

Americans have traditionally relied on education to transmit cultural values, alleviate serious social problems, and enhance citizenship. Indeed, they often have exaggerated the ability of education by itself to address national crises and maintained unrealistic and unfair expectations of the influence of schools. While the rationales in support of education have always been diverse, there have been some general shifts in societal and personal motivations for increased schooling.

In colonial America, Puritans believed that everyone should be able to read the Bible; therefore, rudimentary education was necessary for the entire white population. In the early nineteenth century, when almost all white males were granted the right to vote, earlier religious imperatives for literacy were coupled with the need for an educated electorate. Because nineteenth-century mothers were seen as primary educators for young children, the schooling of white women was also encouraged. Thanks to the efforts of Horace Mann in the mid-nineteenth century, education was widely acknowledged as a stimulus for economic productivity. In the twentieth century, the idea that everyone, including African Americans and Hispanics, deserved the same educational opportunities gradually became commonplace.

As rationales for educating Americans changed, so did the views about who should provide and control it. In early America, parents had the primary responsibility to educate and catechize their own children as well as other members of their household (although local communities sometimes intervened if parents did not carry out their educational responsibilities). In the eighteenth and early nineteenth centuries, local schools became increasingly important, and funding shifted from a combination of public and private to mainly public support.

In the decades before the Civil War—and increasingly thereafter—state governments played a larger role in the control and financing of local common school education. The growing involvement of the state coincided with the movement toward centralization as smaller school districts were consolidated into larger ones. The arguments over local versus state control of education anticipated many of the same concerns evoked after World War II about the growing federal involvement in education.

Responsibility for education, then, shifted from home to school, and broad education policymaking migrated somewhat from the states to the federal level. Many Americans remain uncomfortable with the changes, for, more than in other areas of social service delivery, the conviction persists that ultimate control of education should rest with parents and local communities—especially as the power of school bureaucracies, the involvement of state governments, and the proliferation of federal regulations and mandates increased. Moreover, colonial and early-nineteenth-century education often rested upon a loose and imprecisely defined combination of public and private (usually religious) support and control of schooling; but many Americans and policymakers today believe that any sharing of responsibilities and resources for educating children with private K-12 institutions fundamentally betrays our heritage of public schooling in the early republic.

THE DEMOGRAPHIC
AND STATISTICAL CONTEXT

The changing composition of American society in the twentieth century transformed the context in which education developments occurred. The population of the United States grew from 132 million in 1940 to 282 million by 2000. Over time, moreover, Americans have become more diverse ethnically and more likely to live in urban communities. In 2000, three-fourths of Americans identified themselves as white-only, one-eighth as black-only, and 3.6 percent as Asian-only, with another 2.7 percent stating that they were of more than one race. People of Hispanic origin of any race made up one-eighth of the U.S. population. About three-fourths of Americans now lived in urban rather than rural areas, and more than four out of ten individuals resided in cities larger than 100,000 people.

In addition to being more numerous and urban, postwar Americans were generally more affluent. The proportion of persons living below the poverty level declined dramatically from 22.2 percent in 1960 to 12.6 percent in 1970; thereafter it rose to 13.8 percent in 1995 before dropping again to 11.3 percent in 2000.

Yet considerable differences in the median family income by race and ethnic origin persisted. While fewer than one out of ten whites lived below the poverty level in 2000, more than one out of five blacks or Hispanics were below that level. Moreover, the number of poor who live in high-poverty areas declined by nearly one-quarter from 1990 to 2000. This was a promising development because high concentrations of poor correlate with lower student achievement scores in local school districts.

The relative number of children in the population also declined. As the birthrate decreased in the twentieth century, the share of school-age children in the population dropped. At the same time, the proportion of families without a school-age child present increased. The relative diminution in the number of children in the population helped to hold down the aggregate costs of schooling, but it also reduced the parental constituency that traditionally has supported public school funding.

Yet even though there were relatively fewer youngsters in American society, children were more likely to attend school and to remain enrolled at a later age. The total annual number of children educated at all levels of schooling grew substantially after 1940. Large fluctuations in the birth rates, however, led to periodic crises as school boards struggled to find adequate classroom space and qualified teachers for the baby boomers and their children.

The number of students in grades K-8 rose from 20.3 million in 1940 to 35.5 million in 1965; by 1990 it had dropped to 33.2 million; ten years later it again rose to 36.8 million. Secondary school attendance also rose from 7.1 million in 1940 to 16.5 million in 1965; by 1990 it had decreased to 12.8 million; a decade later it reached 14.9 million. While not all high school graduates attended institutions of higher learning, college enrollments increased faster than either elementary or secondary attendance. The 1.5 million undergraduate and graduate students in 1940 grew rapidly to 5.9 million in 1965. College enrollment continued to soar with 13.6 million attending in 1990. Ten years later, college enrollment reached 15.3 million.

There were considerable variations in school attendance by the age of the child. Almost all children ages 6–17 were enrolled in elementary or secondary schools. This is not surprising, because states mandated schooling for this general age group. But prekindergarten and kindergarten participation tripled from almost 600,000 in 1940 to nearly 2 million in 1960 (including attendance in nursery schools). With the creation of the Head Start program in the mid-1960s, opportunities for early education expanded even further. An estimated 37.5 percent of children ages 3–5 were enrolled in prekindergarten and kindergarten programs in 1970; and that figure rose to 64.5 percent in 1998.

Access to early education still varies by family income and race/ethnicity. About half of the young children in households below the poverty rate in 1999 received early education, while even more children (62.1 percent) from more prosperous homes attended early education programs. Almost three-quarters of African American children were enrolled in prekindergarten or kindergarten programs, but only 44.2 percent of Hispanic children participated; six out of ten white children attended.

As early school attendance increased, high school enrollments also grew. High school graduates as a percentage of seventeen-year-olds increased rapidly from 50.8 percent in 1940 to 69.3 percent in 1999. As a result, the percentage of Americans aged 25–29 who completed high school rose from 38.1 percent in 1940 to 60.7 percent in 1960. Twenty years later, 85.4 percent had completed at least high school, a proportion that remained basically unchanged for the next two decades.

Despite the increasing value of a high school diploma after World War II, substantial numbers of teenagers and young adults did not graduate. One useful measure of high school dropouts is the status dropout rate—the percentage of youth ages 16–24 who are not enrolled in school and who have not earned a high school credential, that is, a diploma or an alternative such as a General Educational Development (GED) certificate. The status dropout rates dropped from 14.6 percent in 1972 to 10.7 percent in 2001. The high school graduation gap between white and black students has almost disappeared, but Hispanic students continue to trail both black and white youths in high school completion.

Increasingly, completion of high school was not the last exposure to formal schooling, as larger numbers of young men and women entered institutions of higher education. The proportion of the 25–29 cohort that has completed at least some college rose steadily in recent years. In 1971, 43.6 percent of that age group had at least some college training; in 1980, slightly more than half of this age group had completed at least some college; and by the end of 2000 that figure had risen to two-thirds.

American spending on education grew substantially. Total expenditures on public and private education, in constant 1999–2000 dollars, went from $63.7

billion in 1949–50 to $306.8 billion in 1969–70. During the next three decades it more than doubled, to $646.8 billion. And the proportion of all education dollars spent on colleges and universities increased from 29.9 percent in 1949–50 to 39.5 percent. To pay for these increased expenditures, the share of the gross domestic product devoted to education rose from 3.3 percent in 1949–50 to 6.9 percent in 1969–70. It remained at around 6–7 percent during the next thirty years.

Americans have spent more to educate each student. The current expenditures per pupil attending a public elementary or secondary school, in constant 1997–98 dollars, rose from $1,020 in 1939–40 to $4,733 in 1979–80, and to $6,662 in 1997–98. Costs per student were considerably higher in higher education institutions. Current fund expenditures per student in higher education, in constant 1995–96 dollars, rose from $14,281 in 1970–71 to $18,383 in 1995–96.

The salaries for public elementary and secondary school teachers have generally improved during the past four decades, in constant 1998–99 dollars, from $27,972 in 1959–60 to a temporary high of $38,806 in 1970–71. In 1980–81, salaries declined precipitously to $33,514 before recovering and reaching $40,582 in 1998–99. The number of female teachers continued upward, so that nearly three-fourths of public school teachers in 1996 were women; the proportion of male or female teachers who were single declined, while those who were married reached three-quarters (and another eighth were widowed, divorced, or separated). Today, almost all teachers have at least a bachelor's degree, and the proportion of those with a master's, a specialized degree, or a doctoral degree doubled from 23.5 percent in 1961 to 56.2 percent in 1996.

The sources of public school funding shifted from municipalities, townships, and counties to the states; the federal government provided only modest support. In 1940, the principal sources of funding for public elementary and secondary schools were local (68 percent), with some state assistance (30 percent) and almost no federal help (less than 2 percent). Twenty years later, local authorities were still the major source (57 percent), but the states now provided a substantial amount (39 percent); the federal government still made only a small contribution (4 percent). By 1980, the federal (10 percent) and state (47 percent) shares had risen substantially while the local assistance had dropped (43 percent). In 1997, the relative federal contribution had dropped (7 percent), state assistance remained roughly the same (48 percent), but local aid grew (45 percent).

Moreover, while the relative federal support for K-12 education today is modest, federal regulations and guidelines accompanying those funds frequently expanded the impact of Washington policies on state and local education policies well beyond the actual federal monetary contributions—leading critics to complain about unfunded and counterproductive federal mandates. For example, as the language of fundamental rights has become increasingly incorporated in our education legislation since the mid-1960s, individuals and groups now make demands on the state for assistance, regardless of costs or other societal priorities, and look to the courts for the enforcement of those rights. Thus, the broad rights now acknowledged in federal legislation for the handicapped are often used to force local communities and the states to provide equal access to education opportunities for everyone—even though the federal government has never come close to fully funding that national mandate.

THE FEDERAL ROLE IN K-12 EDUCATION

As the federal government expanded its role in domestic affairs during the twentieth century, it received periodic calls for increased elementary and secondary education assistance. Those who in principle opposed more federal intrusion into schooling, as well as those who feared that increased federal involvement might challenge segregated schools in the South or provide aid to parochial schools ignored these pleas. The 1944 GI Bill of Rights, which provided World War II veterans with substantial educational support, as well as other types of assistance, was a temporary exception to the continued federal reluctance to provide more assistance for schooling. Additional federal funding for K-12 education, however, was slow in coming.

In the 1950s, the White House and Congress were reluctant to expand the role of the federal government in education, but the judiciary played a key role in increasing federal intervention in public schooling—especially in the area of school desegregation. For example, in the landmark 1954 decision *Brown v. Board of Education of Topeka*, the Supreme Court declared segregated schools inherently unequal and unconstitutional; the Supreme Court outlawed separate black and white public school systems and mandated equal educational opportunities for all children. Although the South managed to stall desegregating most of its schools for more than a decade, the Supreme Court finally mandated immediate compliance in the 1968 *Green* decision and the 1969 *Alexander* decision. When policymakers later moved to desegregate schools in the North, which usually entailed busing black inner-city students to white schools in the suburbs, the economic benefits of integration no longer seemed as evident and the political costs increased. Congress responded in the 1970s by restricting the ability of local communities to use federal funds to pay for school busing.

In the 1970s and 1980s, state and federal courts actively intervened in other educational matters such as bilingual education, school financing, and special education. Indeed, courts now were willing to assume supervisory control of entire school systems, including the administration of day-to-day activities. As a result, states and local school districts soon found themselves forced to change their policies in order to comply with judicial directives. While court injunctions often failed, in practice, to achieve their objectives, the judicial system increased state and federal intervention into the education process; at the same time, however, the court interventions often provoked considerable local opposition—especially as many of the court-ordered practices such as school busing, bilingual education, and more equitable financing of local education were not popular among significant segments of the population.

Concerns about the nation's vulnerability during the Cold War led to increased federal defense and science spending as well as to some additional support for higher education. Shocked by the unexpected Soviet launch of Sputnik, the first artificial satellite, in October 1957, President Dwight D. Eisenhower, a Republican, outlined a modest program of federal education aid. The Democrats proposed a more ambitious measure, and Congress passed the National Defense Education Act (NDEA) in October 1958. The legislation created a student loan fund for college students (those who entered the teaching profession would be forgiven one-half of their federal loans); graduate fellowships for national defense–related areas; matching federal funds for public and private schools to purchase science, math, and foreign language teaching equipment; and monies for a small cooperative research program in the U.S. Office of Education.

Compared to the substantial increase in defense and space expenditures, the funds allocated to NDEA were small. Nevertheless, NDEA reinforced the idea that the federal government could provide categorical educational assistance, and the Sputnik crisis encouraged national and local critics of the current educational system to continue calls for long-overdue reforms. Opponents of the post–World War II emphasis on teaching life-adjustment practices, for example, welcomed the focus on improving cognitive skills and fostering academic excellence (though mainly in science, math, and foreign languages rather than in the humanities or social sciences).

Yet the pressure to improve American schools to meet Soviet challenges was insufficient to persuade Congress to pass major federal legislation to provide financial assistance for K-12 education. President John F. Kennedy tried to pass education legislation from 1961 to 1963. But opponents in Congress stalled or defeated most of his elementary and secondary education bills. The Kennedy administration's legislative education agenda in 1963, for example, called for expanded funding in both K-12 schools and higher education but did not directly address the issues of poverty and economic disadvantage. While the vocational education and higher education bills were enacted, proposals for general funding of K-12 schooling did not pass.

EDUCATION AND THE
DISCOVERY OF POVERTY

Following Kennedy's assassination, former Vice President Lyndon B. Johnson won a landslide 1964 presidential victory over Barry Goldwater, the Republican candidate, and helped to elect an unusually high number of Democrats to Congress. Johnson, a former schoolteacher, saw himself as an "education president." The White House and the 89th Congress passed a series of bills as part of the Johnson administration's War on Poverty that considerably expanded federal involvement in education. Especially important was the landmark Elementary and Secondary Education Act (ESEA) of 1965, which targeted federal funds for at-risk children. Moreover, Project Head Start, based in the Office of Economic Opportunity (OEO), was also created in 1965 to provide preschool education, medical, and social services for disadvantaged youngsters. With the enactment of these and other initiatives, the federal government became more centrally involved in state and local education. Although federal funds were still only a small proportion of overall K-12 school budgets, many Americans and educators increasingly looked to Washington for both additional resources and leadership.

Continued political opposition to federal funding of general K-12 education had led to the targeting of these monies through categorical assistance programs such as Title I of ESEA. Rather than assign the Title I monies to individual economically disadvantaged children to take with them to any public or private schools they attended (as the federal government later did for college students via the Pell grant program), the 1965 bill specified that the Title I funds go to poorer school districts and schools; then the funds would be used to help individual children (who were not necessarily always poor, but at least educationally disadvantaged). Moreover, the legislation stated that the federal government could not "exercise any direction, supervision, or control over" the curriculum, the administration of the program, or the instructional materials utilized.

These administrative and legislative decisions in the mid-1960s were an attempt to circumvent the strong political opposition to federal aid for private schools. They set important precedents for how federal education assistance was organized and distributed. When additional legislation was later enacted to expand assistance for disadvantaged students, such as children of migrant workers, the principle of categorical aid to states or schools was maintained—as opposed to providing direct assistance to individual pupils. Moreover, while the original 1965 ESEA contained only five titles and a dozen programs, by the 1978 reauthorization it had expanded to thirteen titles and more than a hundred programs.

At the same time, passage of ESEA and other federal legislation contributed to the creation of powerful lobby groups, which usually sided with the existing educational bureaucracies and often endorsed more traditional educational interventions. ESEA, for example, provided funds to state departments of education, permitting expansion of their staffs and operations. The additional funds also wedded state departments to federal programs as Washington financed the salaries and expenses of many state education professionals. Similarly, after the creation of regional educational laboratories and research and development (R&D) centers in the mid-1960s, these institutions dominated the field of federal educational research by using political allies in Congress to earmark ample funding for their institutions—often neglecting better alternatives for research and development.

Finally, the methods of federal aid distribution to disadvantaged students affected—albeit unintentionally—the quality of the services provided. Congressional insistence that Title I funds be distributed to almost every county in the United States meant that schools with children in the most disadvantaged circumstances received only modest assistance. However, widespread geographic distribution of funds meant that almost all senators and representatives, even those from relatively affluent districts, had at least some constituents who received Title I monies.

Fears in the civil rights community that these funds were not adequately focused on poor children led to the creation of separate school programs to help disadvantaged children (despite the general pedagogical ineffectiveness of these special initiatives). Often local Title I programs hired low-paid—but not well-trained—teacher aides who did not provide at-risk children with high-quality instruction.

CRISES IN EDUCATION AND THE ECONOMY

The high hopes and often exaggerated claims of Johnson-era Great Society programs—including the education initiatives—were frequently not achieved in practice. Various national, state, and local evaluations of Title I and Head Start in the late 1960s and 1970s suggested that while these interventions might provide some temporary help for at-risk children, the programs alone were insufficient to close the large, long-term achievement gaps between economically disadvantaged students and their more fortunate counterparts. As Marshall Smith and Carl Kaestle concluded in the early 1980s, "after almost two decades of interventions the Title I program stands primarily as a symbol of national concern for the poor rather than as a viable response to their needs."

Rather than blame state and local school boards for continuing deficiencies in education, many politicians and citizens began to pinpoint shortcomings in the new federal elementary and secondary compensatory education programs. Others, especially strong proponents of the new federal education programs, tried to ignore or minimize the critical evaluations and insisted that Title I and Head Start were effective in helping disadvantaged students. The limited benefits of the federal aid to education were more easily tolerated during the prosperous 1960s, when many observers still believed that the programs were working as had been promised; but the subsequent economic downturn spotlighted both the cost of federal aid and its failure to train young Americans for the changing workplace.

The Organization of Petroleum Exporting Countries (OPEC) oil embargo of the 1970s contributed to rising inflation and a growing unemployment rate. Economic challenges from abroad, especially from Japan, worried Americans that their economy was no longer able to keep pace with foreign competitors. The stagnating standard of living during the 1970s and 1980s persuaded policymakers that American schools were not producing a highly skilled, technologically literate workforce necessary for survival in the new global economy. These fears were reinforced by the widespread media perception that the quality of American schools had declined, as evidenced by such crude and controversial indicators such as declines in SAT scores: verbal scores dropped from 543 in 1967 to 500 in 1990; math scores decreased from 516 to 501 in the same period.

In reality, America's difficulty in competing economically and its uneven education quality were much more complex than the popular media pictured. Policymakers and the public, however, responded to the crisis in characteristically simplistic fashion. Southern governors, whose states trailed economically during the postwar period, championed state and local educational improvements as essential for improving the well-being of their states and citizens. Governors such as Lamar Alexander (R-Tenn.), Bill Clinton (D-Ark.), and Richard Riley (D-S.C.) led the fight to improve schools in their states and later played key roles in designing and implementing federal education policies. As governors, they also helped to develop and popularize many reform strategies; their emphasis on student achievement became hallmarks of education reforms in the 1980s and 1990s.

The governors played a crucial role in initiating and sustaining education reforms. They mobilized public and political opinion on behalf of school reforms and provided an opportunity for states to experiment with different school reform approaches. Key gubernatorial organizations, such as the Southern Regional Education Board and the National Governors' Association, provided invaluable forums and staff assistance to develop comprehensive and coordinated state education initiatives. Moreover, many governors carried their commitment and enthusiasm for education reform with them to Washington. Their earlier experiences and continued rapport with fellow governors smoothed the way for the expansion of federal education involvement during the last two decades of the twentieth century. The governors' enhanced role in state and national education reforms during the 1970s and 1980s also reflected the broader societal changes mentioned earlier. State financing of schooling increased considerably during the twentieth century; federal education programs such as ESEA provided monies for expanding state education agencies. These agencies not only dealt with the central government but also played a larger role in regulating local schooling.

Many late-twentieth-century federal education-reform programs were premised on enhancing the state role in education. Republicans, who remained suspicious of increased federal involvement, were often willing to provide federal monies directly to states and allow them to decide how to allocate those funds. When, as president, Bill Clinton embraced systemic—or standards-based—education reform in the 1990s, he focused on state-level alignment of academic standards, curriculum, and assessments. Although some federal monies and guidelines were aimed directly at local school districts, states and governors enjoyed an expanded, political role in school reform during these years.

As many governors helped to draft and implement new federal initiatives, they drew upon their own extensive experiences in shaping education reform. While this real-world experience improved education policies in many ways, it may also have contributed to unanticipated shortcomings. Federal policies often gave considerable attention to state initiatives but did not adequately appreciate the difficulty of implementing policy at the school district and classroom levels. This was not a new problem; the White House and Congress frequently passed legislation without properly appreciating the difficulty of local implementation. Most education and policy professionals recognized this problem in principle but found it difficult to overcome in practice: formulating broader policies is easier than thinking through the complex implementation issues or supplying the necessary resources to sustain new programs.

THE REAGAN REVOLUTION AND EDUCATION

As Democratic and Republican governors mobilized to improve local schools, conservatives blamed federal education programs for contributing to the decline of American education. These critics denounced President Jimmy Carter's creation of the Department of Education in 1979 and sought to eliminate—or at least reduce—federal intrusion in state and local education. The election of President Ronald Reagan and a Republican-dominated Senate in November 1980 seemed to provide momentum to reduce the federal role in education. Yet moderate congressional Republicans, such as Senate Majority Leader Howard Baker (R-Tenn.), joined their liberal Democratic colleagues to protect many existing federal education initiatives. Although Reagan failed to abolish the

Department of Education, his administration terminated or limited monies for some current federal education programs. However, both Democrats and Republicans spared a few popular (and seemingly effective) education programs, such as Head Start.

Ironically, the Reagan administration frequently used the Department of Education effectively as a convenient platform from which to publicize its views of American education shortfalls. The Department of Education created the National Commission on Excellence in Education—a panel whose influential 1983 report, A *Nation at Risk*, warned Americans about the mediocre state of K-12 education: "If an unfriendly foreign power had attempted to impose on America the mediocre educational performance that exists today, we might well have viewed it as an act of war. As it stands, we have allowed this to happen to ourselves. We have even squandered the gains in student achievement made in the wake of the Sputnik challenge. Moreover, we have dismantled essential support systems that helped make those gains possible. We have in effect, been committing an act of unthinking, unilateral educational disarmament."

The following year, Secretary of Education Terrel Bell began releasing the highly publicized annual "wall charts," which used controversial indicators such as SAT scores to rank-order the states according to student educational achievement. His successor, Bill Bennett, used his post as secretary to denounce ineffective school practices and rally public opinion behind more state- and local-oriented school reforms. Bennett labeled public schools in many places as "a futile enterprise" and unsuccessfully urged the use of vouchers to distribute federal education funds, which would enable "parents to choose the educational program that best meets the needs of their children."

Although the Reagan administration failed to eliminate most of the existing federal education programs, it did publicize their shortcomings and advocate higher academic standards and requirements in public elementary and secondary schools.

NATIONAL EDUCATION GOALS
AND AMERICA 2000

During the 1988 presidential campaign, George H. W. Bush did not threaten to eliminate the Department of Education or reduce federal involvement in schooling; rather, he pledged to be the "education president." Although it was not initially clear what this promise might entail, it was the catalyst for gathering the nation's governors at the Charlottesville Education Summit in September 1989 and announcing six national education goals four months later.

The historic summit and follow-up activities committed the governors and the White House to a bipartisan effort for attaining the ambitious national education goals by 2000. Members of Congress were not invited, but the important role of states in developing and overseeing education reforms was acknowledged. The summit reaffirmed the country's commitment to education reforms and offered new assurances that the nation would make substantial education progress by the year 2000.

By agreeing to a limited number of national education goals that focused on improving student academic outcomes, the White House and the nation's governors challenged Americans to improve local schools and to hold political leaders accountable for reform results. They also created a bipartisan group, the National Education Goals Panel (NEGP), to oversee implementation of the national education goals and monitor progress toward reaching those objectives. After the divisive 1980s partisan bickering over education improvements, it appeared that the White House and Democratic and Republican governors might be able to set aside political differences and forge an education-reform partnership between the federal government and the states.

Continued partisan differences between congressional Democrats and the Bush White House, however, threatened to undermine school reform efforts. Most Democratic legislators, and even some of the more moderate congressional Republicans, argued that the 1988 reauthorized ESEA Title I program worked well and required only additional federal funds. Many other Republicans, however, questioned the ability of current programs to help at-risk children, and these legislators called for new approaches (including such controversial initiatives as allowing disadvantaged children to use federal monies to attend private schools).

At first the Bush administration, under the direction of Secretary of Education Lauro Cavazos, crafted a modest but unsuccessful addition to ESEA (the proposed Educational Excellence Act of 1989). Widespread disappointment with Cavazos's overall performance led to his forced resignation. Lamar Alexander, the former Tennessee governor who replaced him, developed the ambitious and creative America 2000 program, which used the six national education goals as its framework. America 2000 urged development of "break-the-mold" New American Schools and formation of partnerships with America 2000 communities. It called for increased flexibility and accountability in using federal, state, and local education monies and emphasized the need to focus on student academic outcomes rather than merely on resources put into the schools. The Republicans' insistence on the controversial school choice programs, however, aroused strong Democratic opposition and contributed to the legislative defeat of America 2000 in the 102nd Congress.

The America 2000 program was an important departure from the Reagan administration's efforts to dismantle the Department of Education and eliminate federal involvement in state and local school affairs. President Bush and Secretary Alexander persuaded key GOP policymakers to reconsider their former opposition to the federal role in education and even endorse the development of voluntary national education standards and tests. Indeed, many Republicans now accepted a more intrusive federal education role—a position some of them would abandon after the GOP lost control of the White House.

The 1991 and 1992 partisan battles over America 2000 yielded important short-term results and had several major long-term consequences. First, Republicans and Democrats agreed upon the centrality of the national education goals, although they differed on how to reach them. Debates over the need for a new American 2000 initiative also highlighted the shortcomings of current ESEA programs. In addition, while many congressional Democrats remained satisfied with current federal programs, they recognized the political value of presenting an alternative to the GOP package—lest voters in the 1994 elections conclude that the Republican approach to education reform was more innovative and more comprehensive. Thus in 1991, Senator Edward Kennedy (D-Mass.) and the Democrats adopted ideas about systemic reform in order to draft their Strengthening Education for American Families Act. Although the Democratic version failed, it provided some of the intellectual framework and stimulation for subsequent Democratic initiatives.

Another consequence of the 1991–92 GOP debates regarding America 2000—and the Democratic alternatives to the GOP position—was that both parties recognized the need to provide new, comprehensive strategies for disadvantaged students. Many Democrats gradually acknowledged that earlier ESEA legislation had proven inadequate for such children. The Bush administration drafted ambitious and politically plausible alternatives to earlier Democratic education programs. Republican members of Congress, who had previously urged abolition of the Department of Education, now sided with the Republican White House and accepted the need for a strong, if revised, federal presence in education. As American voters became more accustomed to weighing the relative merits of GOP and Democratic education initiatives, they were less likely simply to endorse current programs.

At the same time, the bitter partisan differences regarding federal education policy within the 101st and 102nd Congresses heightened tensions between GOP and Democratic members and set the stage for renewed fighting following the 1992 elections. This occurred even though both parties agreed on key facets of education reform such as the value of the national education goals and the need to establish rigorous academic standards for all students.

THE CLINTON ADMINISTRATION AND GOALS 2000

In some respects, Bill Clinton followed the path of Bush's America 2000 initiatives. Like Bush, Clinton wanted to be remembered as the "education president," and he brought extensive gubernatorial education experiences to the White House. Rather than accept conventional Democratic wisdom that ESEA and other federal education programs worked effectively, Clinton also called for a major restructuring of federal education programs. His administration joined the growing chorus of ESEA critics and advocated standards-based reform.

Instead of dismissing America 2000 altogether, the Clinton administration incorporated key components of the GOP plan. It retained the America 2000 communities, renaming them Goals 2000 communities. The six national education goals, which Clinton had helped to draft while governor, were expanded and codified in the Goals 2000 legislation. And the administration endorsed the New American Schools, although the schools never played the central role envisioned by Bush policymakers.

At the same time, observers noticed explicit and implicit differences between the Bush and Clinton approaches to school reform. Although the Clinton administration supported the Goals 2000 communities, it placed more emphasis than had the GOP on the state role in education reform—especially in developing and aligning state academic standards, related curricula, and student performance assessments. Unlike the Bush administration, the Democrats opposed private-school vouchers.

While Clinton endorsed rigorous academic standards, liberal Democratic House allies, such as George Miller (D-Calif.), also forced him to accept mandatory opportunity-to-learn standards, which were meant to ensure that children in the poorer school districts had sufficient resources and opportunities to learn the higher content standards for which they now would be held accountable. Republican congressional education leaders, such as Representative Bill Goodling (R-Pa.), attacked the opportunity-to-learn standards as a dangerous threat to state and local control of educational resources. The heated partisan debates regarding the need for opportunity-to-learn standards and the newly created National Education Standards and Improvement Council (NESIC) further divided the Democrats and Republicans, even threatening passage of Goals 2000 and ESEA.

Goals 2000 shifted emphasis from primarily categorical programs geared toward disadvantaged children to an approach encouraging success for all students by funding state development of standards-based plans and implementations. Undersecretary Marshall Smith, a key intellectual architect of the Clinton education initiatives, noted, "Never before has the federal government enacted legislation designed to help states and school districts to upgrade the quality of the core academic program for *all* students." The Clinton administration combined attempts to redirect more Title I funds to the poorest districts with initiatives to reform entire schools, thus moving away from the more traditional, categorical approaches of federal compensatory education programs—which historically selected individual disadvantaged students for special assistance within those schools.

In April 1994, Congress passed Goals 2000, and in October 1994, the revised ESEA legislation, now called the Improving America's Schools Act (IASA). Under continued pressure from congressional Republicans and several influential Washington-based education organizations, the final version of the legislation retained the systemic framework but considerably weakened the opportunity-to-learn provisions. Despite the improvements in the legislation, conservative Republicans continued to oppose Goals 2000 because they feared that in the near future liberal Democrats—whether in Congress or the White House—would amend the legislation or use administrative regulations to impose more federal control over state and local education.

Just as Goals 2000 and ESEA were slated to be implemented, the GOP stunned the nation by capturing both the House and Senate in the November 1994 midterm elections. Led by Newt Gingrich (R-Ga.) and a conservative House, the 104th Congress tried to reverse the liberal agenda of the previous congresses—including abolishing the Department of Education and repealing Goals 2000. Following two contentious federal government shutdowns, conservative Republicans were forced to jettison much of their education agenda. The Clinton administration, however, acknowledged GOP control of Congress and its concerns about the upcoming 1996 presidential and congressional elections; thus, the White House abandoned efforts to coerce states to adopt particular standards or assessments. Democrats and Republicans agreed to eliminate NESIC, and the administration quietly dropped support for additional projects to develop national English or economics standards.

The Clinton White House continued to defend Goals 2000 funding, but the program in practice simply became a block grant to help states develop strategic plans and implement standards and assessments. Over time, the administration downplayed the Goals 2000 initiative and chose not to attempt reauthorization in the late 1990s. Republicans, many of whom had questioned the value of Goals 2000, were content to let the program expire.

As the Goals 2000 program was gradually abandoned, the national education goals and the goals oversight panel (NEGP) were relegated to secondary status. The 103rd Congress had added goals on teacher professionalization and parental participation as well as increased the number of academic subjects covered under goal three. As a result, the goals became even more ambitious and diffused, but there was no realistic prospect for achieving them within the next six years. A largely unpublicized shift occurred in the mid-1990s as federal and citizen attention moved to a compressed academic agenda that emphasized reading, writing, math, and science. For example, history and geography—integral parts of the original national education goal—now received minimal attention and funding from the federal government.

Faced initially with the prospect of a difficult 1996 reelection, Clinton proposed a series of relatively small, but specific, education initiatives. He advocated hiring 100,000 new teachers, reducing class size, and promoting school uniforms. Rather than continue with a focus on comprehensive reforms and allowing states more flexibility in how to spend federal education dollars, as originally envisioned in the Goals 2000 and ESEA programs, the Clinton administration now opted for targeted and mandated education initiatives. As a result, the relative share of Title I monies allocated for federal compensatory education programs decreased and those for Goals 2000 disappeared entirely.

By the time Clinton left office, the federal education budget had increased substantially. Much of this growth occurred during his second term as Republicans and Democrats competed to persuade voters that their respective parties were the more committed to improving education. While the Clinton administration and its supporters insisted that systemic reform worked and was raising the academic achievements of at-risk children, others contested that optimistic claim. Critics pointed to continued disappointing NAEP achievement scores and even questioned whether the Clinton administration was being entirely forthright in interpreting and promptly releasing federally funded evaluations that might have challenged White House claims.

GEORGE W. BUSH'S "NO CHILD LEFT BEHIND" INITIATIVE

As the GOP readied itself for the 2000 elections, it faced an uphill fight for the presidency. Clinton had soundly defeated Senator Bob Dole (R-Kan.) in 1996, and the strong domestic economy suggested that Vice President Al Gore would be able to retain Democratic control of the White House. The Republicans therefore turned to a candidate who seemed able to attract both conservatives and moderates—Texas Governor George W. Bush, son of the former president. Bush's landslide 1998 gubernatorial reelection revealed his popularity among Hispanic voters and made him a formidable GOP candidate.

While Bush retained his core conservative supporters via a pro-life stance on abortion and a promise to reduce taxes, he also wanted to be seen as a "compassionate conservative." The education issue provided him with this opportunity. Having demonstrated commitment to public school reform in Texas, Bush abandoned mid-1990s GOP calls to abolish the Department of Education or reduce federal education involvement. Stressing the need to improve early reading instruction, Bush called for a revised Title I program that would "leave no child behind." Although he provided lukewarm support for public and private school vouchers, Bush stressed the need to give states greater flexibility in allocating federal education dollars. But he insisted that all children from the third through the eighth grades take annual reading and math tests and that states and schools be accountable for improving student academic achievement.

Lest the Democrats once again outflank the GOP on the education issue, candidate Bush and Republicans in the 106th Congress matched Democrats by supporting a large federal education budget increase for fiscal year 2000— although they opposed Clinton administration efforts to target those increases to specific, categorical education programs such as hiring more teachers, reducing class size, and increasing after-school programs. As a net result of this stance, Republicans neutralized much of the Democrats' normal electoral advantage on the education issue; to do this, however, they had to jettison some conservative policies previously advocated by GOP House members.

During protracted negotiations regarding Bush's "No Child Left Behind" initiative, Bush was forced to abandon traditional GOP issues such as private school vouchers and state conversion of ESEA funds into block grants in exchange for negotiated performance agreements. Moreover, Bush had to accept a higher federal education budget. The budget grew by $6.7 billion to $48.9 billion—about $4.4 billion more than the White House had requested. Whether the compromises that yielded bipartisan ESEA reauthorization will leave no child behind remains to be seen. But it is clear that many Republicans, under pressure from the White House, accepted an expanded federal role in education. Nevertheless, considerable unease remained among conservative Republicans regarding increased federal involvement in state and local education.

ONGOING DEBATES

The period from 1940 to 2000 saw major changes in American society and education. While almost all youngsters completed their elementary education and most received at least some high school training in 1940, the number of years of education acquired by students increased significantly. The overall costs of educating Americans in the past six decades have risen substantially—partly to accommodate the much larger number of children in the population; partly to pay for the additional years of schooling expected of most Americans; and partly to finance better-paid teachers, smaller class sizes, and improved school buildings. The overall cost of American education in constant 1999–2000 dollars skyrocketed tenfold from $63.7 billion in 1949–50 to nearly $650 billion at the end of the century (with an increasing proportion of those expenditures devoted to higher education).

Schooling is becoming increasingly necessary for occupational success in the United States, especially as the real income of many individuals has diminished since the 1970s. Young adults ages 25–34 who have completed a bachelor's degree earn more than those with only some college education, a high school diploma (or its equivalent), or less than a high school degree. Between 1980 and 1999, the earnings of young adults with a bachelor's degree have improved relative to those with less than a high school diploma or its equivalent. Large differences in income earned persist by gender.

Considerable controversy exists over whether elementary and secondary students have improved their academic achievements in post–World War II America. Some critics point to the long-term decline in SAT scores as evidence of declining skills, while others emphasize the increasing numbers and diversity of students now taking those examinations.

Since the early 1970s, student test results from the National Assessment of Education Progress (NAEP) have produced a mixed picture. Reading scores for nine- and thirteen-year-olds in 1999 were higher than in 1971, but scores for seventeen-year-olds remained the same. In math, nine-, thirteen-, and seventeen-year-olds showed improvement from 1973 to 1999; science scores were slightly higher for thirteen-year-olds, but lower for seventeen-year-olds.

There was a large achievement gap between white and black students according to NAEP scores. While the gap generally narrowed between 1971 and 1988, trends toward equality usually were reversed in the late 1980s and 1990s. Moreover, when American student performance was measured against predetermined standards of achievement, most students performed at or above the basic level, but failed to reach the level of proficiency.

Debates also continue over the effectiveness of federal education interventions such as Head Start and Title I in helping disadvantaged students close their academic achievement gap with their more fortunate counterparts. Most of the major evaluations of federal compensatory education programs suggest only limited, if any, consistent and lasting benefits of those interventions for the most disadvantaged students (often with better results for those less disadvantaged). Much of the existing education evaluations and research, however, continue to suffer from weak designs and limited statistical analyses, and therefore the conclusions are often just suggestive.

President George H. W. Bush and the nation's governors pledged in 1990 that by the year 2000, U.S. students would be "the first in the world in mathematics and science achievement" and that "all students will leave grades 4, 8, and 12 having demonstrated competency over challenging subject matter." American students had failed to live up to those high expectations by the year 2000 and had made only modest, if any, progress toward those objectives. Because most analysts and educators are no longer content with just replicating past educational achievements, there is a greater pressure to find better ways for boosting student academic performance—especially for children living in the most disadvantaged households and neighborhoods.

Popular perception of the quality of American public schools has not changed dramatically since the 1970s. Most individuals assign a grade of C to the nation's public schools, but view their own community schools more favorably (somewhere between a C+ and a B–). Not surprisingly, public school parents rate their local public schools higher than parents who send their children to private schools; and individuals without any children in school tend to grade their local public schools somewhere between the ratings of parents whose children attend those schools and the ratings of the other parents who placed their children in private schools.

Both Republican and Democratic presidents have pledged to improve substantially the educational skills of all children within the next ten to twelve years, but their record of accomplishment to date has been disappointing. This should not be surprising, since any education reforms are likely to be incremental at best—especially those initiatives emanating from the federal government, which still provides only a small share of the overall K-12 public school financing. Moreover, the almost total lack of scientifically rigorous evaluations of education strategies and programs means that while there are innumerable theories and speculations about how to educate at-risk children, we have very few service-delivery models that are known to be effective in different settings. Indeed, one might wonder just how long the American public will continue to accept the exaggerated pledges of our national political leaders about education in light of their inability to fulfill earlier promises.

BIBLIOGRAPHIC NOTE

The statistics presented in this chapter are from U.S. Bureau of the Census, *Historical Statistics of the United States, Colonial Times to 1970, Bicentennial Edition*, Part 1 (1975); U.S. Bureau of the Census, *Statistical Abstract of the United States: 2002* (2002); U.S. Department of Education, *The Condition of Education, 2003* (2003); U.S. Department of Education, National Center for Education Statistics, *Digest of Education Statistics, 2000* (2001); and U.S. Department, Education, National Center for Education Statistics, *120 Years of American Education: A Statistical Portrait* (1993), all published by the U.S. Government Printing Office.

For general overviews of American education during the twentieth century, see Lawrence A. Cremin, *American Education: The Metropolitan Experience, 1876–1980* (Harper & Row, 1988), and Gerald L. Gutek, *American Education, 1945–2000* (Waveland Press, 2000).

On the early involvement of the federal government in education, see Maurice R. Berube, *American Presidents and Education* (Greenwood Press, 1991); Donald

R. Warren, *To Enforce Education: A History of the Founding Years of the United States Office of Education* (Wayne State University Press, 1974); and Roger L. Williams, *The Origins of Federal Support for Higher Education: George W. Atherton and the Land-Grant College Movement* (Pennsylvania State University Press, 1991).

On the changing federal role in education, see Hugh Graham Davis, *The Uncertain Triumph: Federal Education Policy in the Kennedy and Johnson Years* (University of North Carolina Press, 1984); Carl F. Kaestle and Marshall S. Smith, "The Federal Role in Elementary and Secondary Education, 1940–1980," *Harvard Educational Review* 52 (November 1982): 384–408; and Marci Kanstoroom and Chester E. Finn Jr., eds., *New Directions: Federal Education Policy in the Twenty-First Century* (Thomas B. Fordham Foundation, 1999).

There are almost no studies of the history of education reforms in local communities or states in postwar America. One notable exception is Jeffrey Mirel, *The Rise and Fall of an Urban School System, 1907–81* (University of Michigan Press, 1999).

On the GI Bill of Rights, see Michael J. Bennett, *When Dreams Came True: The GI Bill and the Making of Modern America* (Brassey's, 1996). On the impact of Sputnik and the National Defense Act on American education, see Peter B. Dow, *Schoolhouse Politics: Lessons from the Sputnik Era* (Harvard University Press, 1991), and Sidney C. Safrin, *Administering the National Defense Education Act* (Syracuse University Press, 1963).

Analyses of the impact of *Brown v. Board of Education* and the problems of desegregation can be found in Ellen Condliffe Lagemann and Lamar P. Miller, eds., *Brown v. Board of Education: The Challenge for Today's Schools* (Teachers College Press, 1996); Gary Orfield, *The Reconstruction of Southern Education: The Schools and the 1964 Civil Rights Act* (Wiley, 1969); and Beryl A. Radin, *Implementation, Change, and the Federal Bureaucracy: School Desegregation in H.E.W., 1964–1968* (Teachers College Press, 1977).

On the Title I program, consult Stephen K. Bailey and Edith K. Mosher, *ESEA: The Office of Education Administers a Law* (Syracuse University Press, 1965); Eugene Eidenberg and Roy Morey, *An Act of Congress: The Legislative Process and the Making of Education Policy* (Norton, 1969); and Julie Ray Jeffrey, *Education for the Children of the Poor: A Study of the Origins and Implementation of the Elementary and Secondary Education Act of 1965* (Ohio State University Press, 1978).

Studies of early childhood education can be found in Barbara Beatty, *Preschool Education in America: The Culture of Young Children from the Colonial Period to the Present* (Yale University Press, 1995); Edward Zigler and Susan Muenchow, *Head Start: The Inside Story of America's Most Successful Educational Experiment* (Basic Books, 1992); and Maris A. Vinovskis, *The Birth of*

Head Start: Preschool Education Policies in the Kennedy and Johnson Administrations (University of Chicago Press, 2005).

Analysis of postwar secondary schools can be found in David L. Angus and Jeffrey E. Mirel, *The Failed Promise of the American High School, 1890–1995* (Teachers College Press, 1999); Sherman Dorn, *Creating the Dropout: An Institutional and Social History of School Failure* (Praeger, 1996); Jurgen Herbst, *The Once and Future School: Three Hundred and Fifty Years of American Secondary Education* (Routledge, 1996); and David F. Labaree, *How to Succeed in School Without Really Learning: The Credentials Race in American Education* (Yale University Press, 1997).

For introductions to the history of the standards movement, see John F. Jennings, *Why National Standards and Tests? Politics and the Quest for Better Schools* (Sage, 1998), and Diane Ravitch, *National Standards in American Education: A Citizen's Guide* (Brookings Institution, 1995).

Historical perspectives on recent education policies can be found in David T. Gordon, ed., *A Nation Reformed? American Education 20 Years After A Nation at Risk* (Harvard Education Press, 2003); Paul Peterson, ed., *Our Schools and Our Future . . . Are We Still at Risk?* (Hoover Institution Press, 2003); Diane Ravitch, *The Troubled Crusade: American Education, 1945–1980* (Basic Books, 1983), and *Left Back: A Century of Failed School Reforms* (Simon & Schuster, 2000); Diane Ravitch and Maris A. Vinovskis, eds., *Learning from the Past: What History Teaches Us About School Reform* (Johns Hopkins University Press, 1995); David Tyack and Larry Cuban, *Tinkering toward Utopia: A Century of Public School Reform* (Harvard University Press, 1995); and Maris A. Vinovskis, *History and Educational Policymaking* (Yale University Press, 1999).

CONTRIBUTORS

Mark C. Carnes, Ann Whitney Olin Professor of History, Barnard College, is general editor of the *American National Biography*. Other edited works include *Meanings for Manhood* (1991), *Past Imperfect: History According to the Movies* (1995), *Novel History* (2001), and *Invisible Giants* (2002). His books include *American Destiny* (2003), *Mapping America's Past* (1996), *The American Nation* (2005), and *Secret Ritual and Manhood in Victorian America* (1989).

Ken Cmiel was professor of history at the University of Iowa and director of its Center for Human Rights until his death in 2006. He wrote, among other works, *Democratic Eloquence: The Fight Over Popular Speech in Nineteenth Century America* (1990) and *A Home of Another Kind: One Chicago Orphanage and the Tangle of Child Welfare* (1995).

Tom Collins is a freelance writer and graduate student in the American Culture Studies program at Washington University in St. Louis. He has written for many publications, including *The American National Biography* (1999), for which he served as a writing fellow. He also contributed to *One Day in History: December 7, 1941* (2002) and *The Encyclopedia of American Material Culture*.

George Cotkin is professor of history at California Polytechnic State University in San Luis Obispo. He is author of *Existential America* (2003), *Reluctant Modernism: American Thought and Culture, 1880–1900*, and *William James, Public Philosopher*. He is now at work on a book on how Americans have since 1945 thought about and represented inhumanity.

David T. Courtwright is the John A. Delaney Presidential Professor at the University of North Florida. He is the author of *Violent Land: Single Men and Social Disorder from the Frontier to the Inner City* (1996) and *Forces of Habit: Drugs and the Making of the Modern World* (2001). He is currently writing a history of the culture war.

Paula S. Fass, Margaret Byrne Professor of History at the University of California at Berkeley, is the author, most recently, of *Kidnapped: Child Abduction in America* (1997). She is also editor-in-chief of *The Encyclopedia of Children and Childhood in History and Society* (2004). Her other books include *The Damned and the Beautiful: American Youth in the 1920s* (1977) and *Outside In: Minorities and the Transformation of American Education* (1989).

Tony A. Freyer is University Research Professor of History and Law, University of Alabama. His books include *Hugo L. Black and the Dilemma of American Liberalism* (1990), *Producers Versus Capitalists* (1994), and *Regulating Big Business* (1992).

Susan Hartmann is professor of history at Ohio State University. Her two most recent books are *The Other Feminists: Activists in the Liberal Establishment* (1998) and *The American Promise: A History of the United States* (2004). She is currently writing a book on gender and the political realignment.

Andrew Kirk is associate professor of history and director of the public history program at the University of Nevada—Las Vegas. He is the author of *Collecting Nature: The American Environmental Movement and the Conservation Library* (2001) and is currently finishing a brief history of the *Whole Earth Catalog* and counterculture environmentalism.

Michael E. Latham is associate professor of history at Fordham University. He is the author of *Modernization as Ideology: American Social Science and "Nation Building" in the Kennedy Era* (2000) and coeditor of *Staging Growth: Modernization, Development, and the Global Cold War* (2003). His work centers on the intellectual and cultural history of U.S. foreign relations.

Richard Lingeman is a senior editor of *The Nation*. His books include *Small Town America: A Narrative History* (1980); *Don't You Know There's a War On? The American Home Front, 1941–1945* (1970); *An American Journey: Theodore Dreiser* (1986–90); and *Sinclair Lewis: Rebel from Main Street* (2002).

Donald J. Mrozek, professor of history at Kansas State University, is author of *Air Power and the Ground War in Vietnam* (1989), *Sport and American Mentality* (1983), and *The U.S. Air Force After Vietnam* (1990), among other works. He is also coeditor of *A Guide to the Sources of U.S. Military History* (1975–86) and of *Sports Periodicals* (1977).

Sandra Opdycke is associate director of the Institute for Innovation in Social Policy at Vassar College. She is the author of *The Routledge Historical Atlas of Women in America* (2000); *Placing a Human Face on the Uninsured: 50 New Yorkers Tell Their Stories* (2000); and *No One Was Turned Away: The Role of Public Hospitals in New York City Since 1900* (1999).

Thaddeus Russell teaches history at The New School University and is author of *Out of the Jungle: Jimmy Hoffa and the Remaking of the American Working Class* (2000). He is at work on a study of the relationship between African American working-class culture and the civil rights movement.

Rick Shenkman, associate professor of history at George Mason University, is the editor of the History News Network (http://hnn.us). He is the author of *Presidential Ambition: Gaining Power at Any Cost* (1999).

Michael Sherry is Richard W. Leopold Professor of History at Northwestern University and the author of, among other works, *In the Shadow of War: The United States Since the 1930s* (1995), for which he plans a sequel.

Maris A. Vinovskis is Bentley Professor of History, Research Professor at the Institute for Social Research, and professor of public policy at the Gerald R. Ford School of Public Policy at the University of Michigan. He is the author of many books, including *The Birth of Head Start: Preschool Education Policies in the Kennedy and Johnson Administrations* (2005).

Julian E. Zelizer is professor of history at Boston University. He is the author of *Taxing America: Wilbur D. Mills, Congress, and the State, 1945–1975* (1998) and *On Capitol Hill: The Struggle to Reform Congress and Its Consequences, 1948–2000* (2004), editor of *New Directions in American Political History and The American Congress: The Building of Democracy* (2004), and coeditor of *The Democratic Experiment: New Directions in American Political History* (2003).